Date Due

MEMOIRS OF THE LIFE

OF

SIR WALTER SCOTT

BY

JOHN GIBSON LOCKHART

IN FIVE VOLUMES

VOLUME III

The Riverside Press

BOSTON AND NEW YORK
HOUGHTON MIFFLIN COMPANY
The Riverside Press Cambridge

SIR WALTER SCOTT

CHAPTER XXXIV

PROGRESS OF THE LORD OF THE ISLES. — CORRESPOND-
ENCE WITH MR. JOSEPH TRAIN. — RAPID COMPLETION
OF THE LORD OF THE ISLES. — " REFRESHING THE
MACHINE." — "SIX WEEKS AT A CHRISTMAS." — PUBLI-
CATION OF THE POEM, — AND OF GUY MANNERING. —
LETTERS TO MORRITT, TERRY, AND JOHN BALLANTYNE.
— ANECDOTES BY JAMES BALLANTYNE. — VISIT TO
LONDON. — MEETING WITH LORD BYRON. — DINNERS
AT CARLTON HOUSE

1814–1815

By the 11th of November, then, The Lord of the Isles
had made great progress, and Scott had also authorized
Ballantyne to negotiate among the booksellers for the
publication of a second novel. But before I go further
into these transactions, I must introduce the circumstances of Scott's first connection with an able and amiable man, whose services were of high importance to him,
at this time and ever after, in the prosecution of his
literary labors. Calling at Ballantyne's printing-office
while Waverley was in the press, he happened to take
up a proof sheet of a volume entitled "Poems, with notes
illustrative of traditions in Galloway and Ayrshire, by
Joseph Train, Supervisor of Excise at Newton-Stewart."
The sheet contained a ballad on an Ayrshire tradition,
about a certain "Witch of Carrick," whose skill in the
black art was, it seems, instrumental in the destruction

of one of the scattered vessels of the Spanish Armada.
The ballad begins: —

> "Why gallops the palfrey with Lady Dunore ?
> Who drives away Turnberry's kine from the shore ?
> Go tell it in Carrick, and tell it in Kyle —
> Although the proud Dons are now passing the Moil,[1]
>   On this magic clew,
>   That in fairyland grew,
> Old Elcine de Aggart has taken in hand
> To wind up their lives ere they win to our strand."

Scott immediately wrote to the author, begging to be
included in his list of subscribers for a dozen copies, and
suggesting at the same time a verbal alteration in one
of the stanzas of this ballad. Mr. Train acknowledged
his letter with gratitude, and the little book reached him
just as he was about to embark in the lighthouse yacht.
He took it with him on his voyage, and, on returning
home again, wrote to Mr. Train, expressing the gratification he had received from several of his metrical pieces,
but still more from his notes, and requesting him, as he
seemed to be enthusiastic about traditions and legends,
to communicate any matters of that order connected with
Galloway which he might not himself think of turning
to account; "for," said Scott, "nothing interests me so
much as local anecdotes; and, as the applications for
charity usually conclude, the smallest donation will be
thankfully accepted."

Mr. Train, in a little narrative with which he has
favored me, says, that for some years before this time
he had been engaged, in alliance with a friend of his,
Mr. Denniston, in collecting materials for a History of
Galloway; they had circulated lists of queries among the
clergy and parish schoolmasters, and had thus, and by
their own personal researches, accumulated "a great
variety of the most excellent materials for that purpose;"
but that, from the hour of his correspondence with Walter Scott, he "renounced every idea of authorship for

[1] The Mull of Cantyre.

himself," resolving, "that thenceforth his chief pursuit should be collecting whatever he thought would be most interesting to *him;*" and that Mr. Denniston was easily persuaded to acquiesce in the abandonment of their original design. "Upon receiving Mr. Scott's letter," says Mr. Train, "I became still more zealous in the pursuit of ancient lore, and being the first person who had attempted to collect old stories in that quarter with any view to publication, I became so noted, that even beggars, in the hope of reward, came frequently from afar to Newton-Stewart, to recite old ballads and relate old stories to me." Erelong, Mr. Train visited Scott both at Edinburgh and at Abbotsford; a true affection continued ever afterwards to be maintained between them; and this generous ally was, as the prefaces to the Waverley Novels signify, one of the earliest confidants of that series of works, and certainly the most efficient of all the author's friends in furnishing him with materials for their composition. Nor did he confine himself to literary services: whatever portable object of antiquarian curiosity met his eye, this good man secured and treasured up with the same destination; and if ever a catalogue of the museum at Abbotsford shall appear, no single contributor, most assuredly, will fill so large a space in it as Mr. Train.[1]

---

[1] [Joseph Train was born in 1779, at Gilminscroft, Sorn, Ayrshire, where his father was grieve and land-steward. The boy was apprenticed at an early age to a weaver in Ayr, but, notwithstanding the narrowness of his circumstances, and a very imperfect education, he even then showed a love of learning and a passion for antiquarian lore. From 1799 to 1802 he served in the Ayrshire militia. While the regiment was stationed at Inverness, he became a subscriber to Currie's edition of Burns, and his colonel, Sir David Hunter-Blair, seeing the volumes at the bookseller's, was surprised to learn that they had been ordered by one of his men. Greatly pleased thereat, Sir David had the books handsomely bound and sent to Train, free of charge; and later obtained for him an appointment in the Excise in the Ayr district. He was a faithful and efficient officer, but owing to the then prevalent custom of giving the higher places in the Excise to Englishmen, all Scott's efforts for the advancement of his friend were unavailing; he remained supervisor till he went on the retired list

His first considerable communication, after he had formed the unselfish determination above mentioned, consisted of a collection of anecdotes concerning the Galloway gypsies, and "a local story of an astrologer, who calling at a farmhouse at the moment when the goodwife was in travail, had, it was said, predicted the future fortune of the child, almost in the words placed in the mouth of John MacKinlay, in the Introduction to Guy Mannering." Scott told him, in reply, that the story of the astrologer reminded him of "one he had heard in his youth;" that is to say, as the Introduction explains, from this MacKinlay; but Mr. Train has, since his friend's death, recovered a rude *Durham* ballad, which in fact contains a great deal more of the main fable of Guy Mannering than either his own written, or MacKinlay's oral edition of the *Gallovidian* anecdote had conveyed; and — possessing, as I do, numberless evidences of the haste with which Scott drew up his beautiful Prefaces and Introductions of 1829, 1830, and 1831 — I am strongly inclined to think that he must in his boyhood have read the Durham Broadside or Chapbook itself — as well as heard the old serving-man's Scottish version of it.

However this may have been, Scott's answer to Mr. Train proceeded in these words: —

I am now to solicit a favor, which I think your inter-

in 1836. In 1829 Train was admitted a member of the Scottish Society of Antiquaries. Though the death of Scott made a sad blank in his life, his interest in his favorite studies continued to the end. The latter part of his life was spent in a cottage at Castle Douglas, where he was visited shortly before his death by James Hannay, who found him in a little parlor, crowded with antiquities of interest and value, — the antiquary, "a tall old man, with an autumnal red in his face, hale looking, and of simple, quaint manners." (See *Household Words*, July 10, 1853.) Train's last extended works were an *Historical and Statistical Account of the Isle of Man, with a view of its peculiar customs and popular superstitions* (1845) ; and a study of a local religious sect in *The Buchanites from First to Last* (1846) ; but he was an occasional contributor to various periodicals. He died December 1, 1852.]

est in Scottish antiquities will induce you readily to comply with. I am very desirous to have some account of the present state of *Turnberry Castle* — whether any vestiges of it remain — what is the appearance of the ground — the names of the neighboring places — and, above all, what are the traditions of the place (if any) concerning its memorable surprise by Bruce, upon his return from the coast of Ireland, in the commencement of the brilliant part of his career. The purpose of this is to furnish some hints for notes to a work in which I am now engaged, and I need not say I will have great pleasure in mentioning the source from which I derive my information. I have only to add, with the modest importunity of a lazy correspondent, that the sooner you oblige me with an answer (if you can assist me on the subject), the greater will the obligation be on me, who am already your obliged humble servant,

W. Scott.

The recurrence of the word *Turnberry*, in the ballad of Elcine de Aggart, had of course suggested this application, which was dated on the 7th of November. "I had often," says Mr. Train, "when a boy, climbed the brown hills, and traversed the shores of Carrick, but I could not sufficiently remember the exact places and distances as to which Mr. Scott inquired; so, immediately on receipt of his letter, I made a journey into Ayrshire to collect all the information I possibly could, and forwarded it to him on the 18th of the same month." Among the particulars thus communicated, was the local superstition, that on the anniversary of the night when Bruce landed at Turnberry from Arran, the same meteoric gleam which had attended his voyage reappeared, unfailingly, in the same quarter of the heavens. With this circumstance Scott was much struck. "Your information," he writes on the 22d November, "was particularly interesting and acceptable, especially that which relates to the supposed preternatural appearance of the fire, etc., which I hope to make some use of." What use he did make of it, if any reader has forgotten, will be seen by reference to stanzas 7–17 of the 5th Canto of the Poem; and the notes to the same Canto embody, with due acknowledgment, the more authentic results of Mr. Train's pilgrimage to Carrick.

I shall recur presently to this communication from Mr. Train; but must pause for a moment to introduce two letters, both written in the same week with Scott's request as to the localities of Turnberry. They both give us amusing sketches of his buoyant spirits at this period of gigantic exertion; — and the first of them, which relates chiefly to Maturin's Tragedy of Bertram, shows how he could still contrive to steal time for attention to the affairs of brother authors less energetic than himself.

TO DANIEL TERRY, ESQ.

ABBOTSFORD, November 10, 1814.

MY DEAR TERRY, — I should have long since answered your kind letter by our friend Young, but he would tell you of my departure with our trusty and well-beloved Erskine, on a sort of a voyage to Nova Zembla. Since my return, I have fallen under the tyrannical dominion of a certain Lord of the Isles. Those Lords were famous for oppression in the days of yore, and if I can judge by the posthumous despotism exercised over me, they have not improved by their demise. The *peine forte et dure* is, you know, nothing in comparison to being obliged to grind verses; and so devilish repulsive is my disposition, that I can never put my wheel into constant and regular motion, till Ballantyne's devil claps in his proofs, like the hot cinder which you Bath folks used to clap in beside an unexperienced turnspit, as a hint to be expeditious in his duty. O long life to the old hermit of Prague, who never saw pen and ink! — much happier in that negative circumstance than in his alliance with the niece of King Gorboduc.

To talk upon a blither subject, I wish you saw Abbotsford, which begins this season to look the whimsical, gay, odd cabin, that we had chalked out. I have been obliged to relinquish Stark's plan, which was greatly too expensive. So I have made the old farmhouse my *corps de logis*, with some outlying places for kitchen, laundry, and two spare bedrooms, which run along the east wall of the farm-court, not without some picturesque effect. A perforated cross, the spoils of the old kirk of Galashiels, decorates an advanced door, and looks very well. This little sly bit of sacrilege has given our spare rooms the name of *the chapel*. I earnestly invite you to a *pew* there, which you will find as commodious for the purpose of a nap as you have ever experienced when, under the guidance of old Mrs. Smollett, you were led to St. George's, Edinburgh.

I have been recommending to John Kemble (I dare say without any chance of success) to peruse a MS. Tragedy of Maturin's author of Montorio: it is one of those things which will either succeed greatly or be damned gloriously, for its merits are marked, deep, and striking, and its faults of a nature obnoxious to ridicule. He had our old friend Satan (none of your sneaking St. John Street devils, but the arch-fiend himself) brought on the stage bodily. I believe I have exorcised the foul fiend — for, though in reading he was a most terrible fellow, I feared for his reception in public. The last act is ill contrived. He piddles (so to speak) through a cullender, and divides the whole horrors of the catastrophe (though God wot there are enough of them) into a kind of drippity-droppity of four or five scenes, instead of inundating the audience with them at once in the finale, with a grand "*gardez l'eau*." With all this, which I should say had I written the thing myself, it is grand and powerful; the language most animated and poetical; and the characters

sketched with a masterly enthusiasm. Many thanks for
Captain Richard Falconer.[1] To your kindness I owe
the two books in the world I most longed to see, not so
much for their intrinsic merits, as because they bring
back with vivid associations the sentiments of my childhood — I might almost say infancy. Nothing ever disturbed my feelings more than when, sitting by the old
oak table, my aunt, Lady Raeburn, used to read the
lamentable catastrophe of the ship's departing without
Captain Falconer, in consequence of the whole party
making free with lime-punch on the eve of its being
launched. This and Captain Bingfield,[2] I much wished

[1] " *The Voyages, Dangerous Adventures, and Imminent Escapes of Capt.
Rich. Falconer.* Containing the Laws, Customs, and Manners of the Indi-
ans in America; his shipwrecks; his marrying an Indian wife; his narrow
escape from the Island of Dominico, etc. Intermixed with the Voyages
and Adventures of Thomas Randal, of Cork, Pilot; with his Shipwreck
in the Baltick, being the only man that escap'd. His being taken by the
Indians of Virginia, etc. And an Account of his Death. The Fourth
Edition. London. Printed for J. Marshall, at the Bible in Gracechurch
Street. 1734."
On the fly-leaf is the following note, in Scott's handwriting: " This
book I read in early youth. I am ignorant whether it is altogether fictitious and written upon De Foe's plan, which it greatly resembles, or
whether it is only an exaggerated account of the adventures of a real person. It is very scarce, for, endeavoring to add it to the other favorites of
my infancy, I think I looked for it ten years to no purpose, and at last
owed it to the active kindness of Mr. Terry. Yet Richard Falconer's adventures seem to have passed through several editions."
[2] " *The Travels and Adventures of William Bingfield, Esq.,* containing,
as surprizing a Fluctuation of Circumstances, both by Sea and Land, as
ever befel one man. With an Accurate Account of the Shape, Nature,
and Properties of that most furious, and amazing Animal, the Dog-
Bird. Printed from his own Manuscript. With a beautiful Frontispiece.
2 vols. 12mo. London: Printed for E. Withers, at the Seven Stars, in
Fleet Street. 1753." On the fly-leaf of the first volume Scott has written
as follows: " I read this scarce little *Voyage Imaginaire* when I was about
ten years old, and long after sought for a copy without being able to find
a person who would so much as acknowledge having heard of William
Bingfield or his Dog-birds, until the indefatigable kindness of my friend
Mr. Terry, of the Haymarket, made me master of this copy. I am therefore induced to think the book is of very rare occurrence." [In consequence of these Notes, both Falconer and Bingfield have been recently
reprinted in London. — (1839.)]

to read once more, and I owe the possession of both to your kindness. Everybody that I see talks highly of your steady interest with the public, wherewith, as I never doubted of it, I am pleased but not surprised. We are just now leaving this for the winter: the children went yesterday. Tom Purdie, Finella, and the greyhounds, all in excellent health; the latter have not been hunted this season! ! ! Can add nothing more to excite your admiration. Mrs. Scott sends her kind compliments. W. SCOTT.

The following, dated a day after, refers to some lines which Mr. Morritt had sent him from Worthing.

TO J. B. S. MORRITT, ESQ., M. P., WORTHING.

ABBOTSFORD, November 11, 1814.

MY DEAR MORRITT, — I had your kind letter with the beautiful verses. May the Muse meet you often on the verge of the sea or among your own woods of Rokeby! May you have spirits to profit by her visits (and that implies all good wishes for the continuance of Mrs. M.'s convalescence), and may I often, by the fruits of your inspiration, have my share of pleasure! My Muse is a Tyranness, and not a Christian queen, and compels me to attend to longs and shorts, and I know not what, when, God wot, I had rather be planting evergreens by my new old fountain. You must know that, like the complaint of a fine young boy who was complimented by a stranger on his being a smart fellow, "I am sair halded down by *the bubbly jock*." In other words, the turkey cock, at the head of a family of some forty or fifty infidels, lays waste all my shrubs. In vain I remonstrate with Charlotte upon these occasions; she is in league with the hen-wife, the natural protectress of these pirates; and I have only the inhuman consolation that I may one day, like a cannibal, eat up my enemies. This is but dull fun, but what else have I to tell you about? It

would be worse if, like Justice Shallow's Davy, I should
consult you upon sowing down the headland with wheat.
My literary tormentor is a certain Lord of the Isles,
famed for his tyranny of yore, and not unjustly. I am
bothering some tale of him I have had long by me into
a sort of romance. I think you will like it: it is Scotti-
fied up to the teeth, and somehow I feel myself like the
liberated chiefs of the Rolliad, "who boast their native
philabeg restored." I believe the frolics one can cut in
this loose garb are all set down by you Sassenachs to the
real agility of the wearer, and not the brave, free, and
independent character of his clothing. It is, in a word,
the real Highland fling, and no one is supposed able to
dance it but a native. I always thought that epithet of
Gallia *Braccata* implied subjugation, and was never
surprised at Cæsar's easy conquests, considering that his
Labienus and all his merry men wore, as we say, bottom-
less breeks.

Ever yours,   W. S.

Well might he describe himself as being hard at work
with his Lord of the Isles. The date of Ballantyne's
letter to Miss Edgeworth (November 11), in which he
mentions the third Canto as completed; that of the communication from Mr. Train (November 18), on which
so much of Canto Fifth was grounded; and that of a note
from Scott to Ballantyne (December 16, 1814), announcing that he had sent the last stanza of the poem: these
dates, taken together, afford conclusive evidence of the
fiery rapidity with which the three last Cantos of The
Lord of the Isles were composed.

He writes, on the 25th December, to Constable that
he "had corrected the last proofs, and was setting out
for Abbotsford to refresh the machine." And in what
did his refreshment of the machine consist? Besides
having written within this year the greater part (almost,
I believe, the whole) of the Life of Swift — Waverley

— and The Lord of the Isles — he had given two essays to the Encyclopædia Supplement, and published, with an Introduction and notes, one of the most curious pieces of family history ever produced to the world, on which he labored with more than usual zeal and diligence, from his warm affection for the noble representative of its author. This inimitable Memorie of the Somervilles came out in October; and it was speedily followed by an annotated reprint of the strange old treatise, entitled "Rowland's letting off the humours of the blood in the head vein, 1611." He had also kept up his private correspondence on a scale which I believe never to have been exemplified in the case of any other person who wrote continually for the press — except, perhaps, Voltaire; and, to say nothing of strictly professional duties, he had, as a vast heap of documents now before me proves, superintended from day to day, except during his Hebridean voyage, the still perplexed concerns of the Ballantynes, with a watchful assiduity that might have done credit to the most diligent of tradesmen. The "machine" might truly require "refreshment."

It was, as has been seen, on the 7th of November that Scott acknowledged the receipt of that communication from Mr. Train which included the story of the Galloway astrologer. There can be no doubt that this story recalled to his mind, if not the Durham ballad, the similar but more detailed corruption of it which he had heard told by his father's servant, John MacKinlay, in the days of George's Square and Green-breeks, and which he has preserved in the introduction to Guy Mannering, as the groundwork of that tale. It has been shown that the three last Cantos of The Lord of the Isles were written between the 11th of November and the 25th of December; and it is therefore scarcely to be supposed that any part of this novel had been penned before he thus talked of "refreshing the machine." It is quite certain that when James Ballantyne wrote to Miss Edgeworth on the

11th November, he could not have seen one page of Guy Mannering, since he in that letter announces that the new novel of his nameless friend would depict manners *more ancient* than those of 1745. And yet it is equally certain, that before The Lord of the Isles was *published*, which took place on the 18th of January, 1815, two volumes of Guy Mannering had been not only written and copied by an amanuensis, but printed.

Scott thus writes to Morritt, in sending him his copy of The Lord of the Isles: —

TO J. B. S. MORRITT, ESQ., M. P., WORTHING.

EDINBURGH, 19th January, 1815.

My DEAR MORRITT, — I have been very foolishly putting off my writing until I should have time for a good long epistle; and it is astonishing what a number of trifles have interfered to prevent my commencing on a great scale. The last of these has been rather of an extraordinary kind, for your little friend Walter has chose to make himself the town talk, by taking what seemed to be the small-pox, despite of vaccination in infancy, and inoculation with the variolous matter thereafter, which last I resorted to by way of making assurance double sure. The medical gentleman who attended him is of opinion that he *has* had the real small-pox, but it shall never be averred by me — for the catastrophe of Tom Thumb is enough to deter any thinking person from entering into a feud with the cows. Walter is quite well again, which was the principal matter I was interested in. We had very nearly been in a bad scrape, for I had fixed the Monday on which he sickened, to take him with me for the Christmas vacation to Abbotsford. It is probable that he would not have pleaded headache when there was such a party in view, especially as we were to shoot wild ducks one day together at Cauldshiels Loch; and what the consequence of such a journey might have been, God alone knows.

I am clear of The Lord of the Isles, and I trust you have your copy. It closes my poetic labors upon an extended scale: but I dare say I shall always be dabbling in rhyme until the *solve senescentem*. I have directed the copy to be sent to Portland Place. I want to shake myself free of Waverley, and accordingly have made a considerable exertion to finish an odd little tale within such time as will mystify the public, I trust — unless they suppose me to be Briareus. Two volumes are already printed, and the only persons in my confidence, W. Erskine and Ballantyne, are of opinion that it is much more interesting than Waverley. It is a tale of private life, and only varied by the perilous exploits of smugglers and excisemen. The success of Waverley has given me a spare hundred or two, which I have resolved to spend in London this spring, bringing up Charlotte and Sophia with me. I do not forget my English friends — but I fear they will forget me, unless I show face now and then. My correspondence gradually drops, as must happen when people do not meet; and I long to see Ellis, Heber, Gifford, and one or two more. I do not include Mrs. Morritt and you, because we are much nearer neighbors, and within a whoop and a holla in comparison. I think we should come up by sea, if I were not a little afraid of Charlotte being startled by the March winds — for our vacation begins 12th March.

You will have heard of poor Caberfae's death? What a pity it is he should have outlived his promising young representative. His state was truly pitiable — all his fine faculties lost in paralytic imbecility, and yet not so entirely so but that he perceived his deprivation as in a glass darkly. Sometimes he was fretful and anxious because he did not see his son; sometimes he expostulated and complained that his boy had been allowed to die without his seeing him; and sometimes, in a less clouded state of intellect, he was sensible of, and lamented his loss in its full extent. These, indeed, are the "fears of the brave, and follies of the wise,"[1] which sadden and humiliate the lingering hours of prolonged existence. Our friend Lady Hood will now be Caberfae herself. She has the spirit of a chieftainess in every drop of her blood, but there are few situations in which the cleverest women are so apt to be imposed upon as in the management of landed property, more especially of an Highland estate. I do fear the accomplishment of the prophecy, that when there should be a deaf Caberfae, the house was to fall.[2]

I am delighted to find Mrs. Morritt is recovering health and strength — better walking on the beach at Worthing than on the *plainstanes* of Prince's Street, for the weather is very severe here indeed. I trust Mrs. M. will, in her milder climate, lay in such a stock of health and strength as may enable you to face the north in Autumn. I have got the nicest crib for you possible, just about twelve feet square, and in the harmonious vicinity of a piggery. You never saw so minute an es-

---

[1] Johnson's *Vanity of Human Wishes*.

[2] Francis, Lord Seaforth, died 11th January, 1815, in his 60th year, having outlived four sons, all of high promise. His title died with him, and he was succeeded in his estates by his daughter, Lady Hood, now the Hon. Mrs. Stewart-Mackenzie of Seaforth. — See some verses on Lord Seaforth's death, in Scott's *Poetical Works*, vol. viii. p 392 [Cambridge Ed. p. 419]. The Celtic designation of the chief of the clan MacKenzie, *Caberfae*, means *Staghead*, the bearing of the family. The prophecy which Scott alludes to in this letter is also mentioned by Sir Humphry Davy in one of his Journals (see his *Life*, by Dr. Davy, vol. ii. p. 72), — and it was, if the account be correct, a most extraordinary one, for it connected the fall of the house of Seaforth not only with the appearance of a deaf *Caberfae*, but with the contemporaneous appearance of various different physical misfortunes in several of the other great Highland chiefs ; all of which are said — and were certainly believed both by Scott and Davy — to have actually occurred within the memory of the generation that has not yet passed away. Mr. Morritt can testify thus far — that he " heard the prophecy quoted in the Highlands at a time when Lord Seaforth had two sons both alive and in good health — so that it certainly was not made *après coup*." [Mrs. Stewart-Mackenzie died at Brahan Castle in 1862, in her 79th year. " Her funeral was one of the largest ever witnessed in the North." The Seaforth estates passed to the eldest of her three sons.]

tablishment, — but it has all that we wish for, and all our friends will care about; and we long to see you there. Charlotte sends the kindest remembrances to Mrs. Morritt.

As for politics, I have thought little about them lately; the high and exciting interest is so completely subsided, that the wine is upon the lees. As for America, we have so managed as to give her the appearance of triumph, and what is worse, encouragement to resume the war upon a more favorable opportunity. It was our business to have given them a fearful memento that the babe unborn should have remembered; but, having missed this opportunity, I believe that this country would submit with great reluctance to continue a war, for which there is really no specific object. As for the Continental monarchs, there is no guessing what the folly of Kings and Ministers may do; but God knows! would any of them look at home, enough is to be done which might strengthen and improve their dominions in a different manner than by mere extension. I trust Ministers will go out rather than be engaged in war again, upon any account. If France is wise (I have no fear that any superfluous feeling of humanity will stand in the way), she will send 10,000 of her most refractory troops to fight with Christophe and the yellow fever in the Island of St. Domingo, and then I presume they may sit down in quiet at home.

But my sheet grows to an end, and so does the pleading of the learned counsel, who is thumping the poor bar as I write. He hems twice. Forward, sweet Orator Higgins! — at least till I sign myself, dear Morritt,

Yours most truly,

WALTER SCOTT.

Guy Mannering was published on the 24th of February — that is, exactly two months after The Lord of the Isles was dismissed from the author's desk; and — making but a narrow allowance for the operations of the transcriber, printer, bookseller, etc., I think the dates I have gathered together confirm the accuracy of what I have often heard Scott say, that his second novel " was the work of six weeks at a Christmas." Such was his recipe "for refreshing the machine."

I am sorry to have to add, that this severity of labor, like the repetition of it which had such deplorable effects at a later period of his life, was the result of his anxiety to acquit himself of obligations arising out of his connection with the commercial speculations of the Ballantynes. The approach of Christmas, 1814, brought with it the prospect of such a recurrence of difficulties about the discount of John's bills, as to render it absolutely necessary that Scott should either apply again for assistance to his private friends, or task his literary powers with some such extravagant effort as has now been recorded. The great object, which was still to get rid of the heavy stock that had been accumulated before the storm of May, 1813, at length determined the chief partner to break up, as soon as possible, the concern which his own sanguine rashness, and the gross irregularities of his mercurial lieutenant, had so lamentably perplexed; but Constable, having already enabled the firm to avoid public exposure more than once, was not now, any more than when he made his contract for The Lord of the Isles, disposed to burden himself with an additional load of Weber's Beaumont and Fletcher, and other almost as unsalable books. While they were still in hopes of overcoming his scruples, it happened that a worthy friend of Scott's, the late Mr. Charles Erskine, his sheriff-substitute in Selkirkshire, had immediate occasion for a sum of money which he had some time before advanced, at Scott's personal request, to the firm of John Ballantyne and Company; and on receiving his application, Scott wrote as follows: —

TO MR. JOHN BALLANTYNE, BOOKSELLER, EDINBURGH

ABBOTSFORD, October 14, 1814.

DEAR JOHN, — Charles Erskine wishes his money, as he has made a purchase of land. This is a new perplexity — for paid he must be forthwith — as his advance was friendly and confidential. I do not at this moment see how it is to be raised, but believe I shall find means. In the mean while, it will be necessary to propitiate the Leviathans of Paternoster Row. My idea is, that you or James should write to them to the following effect: That a novel is offered you by the Author of Waverley; that the author is desirous it should be out before Mr. Scott's poem, or as soon thereafter as possible; and that having resolved, as they are aware, to relinquish publishing, you only wish to avail yourselves of this offer to the extent of helping off some of your stock. I leave it to you to consider whether you should condescend on any particular work to offer them as bread to their butter — or on any particular amount — as £500. One thing must be provided, that Constable shares to the extent of the Scottish sale — they, however, managing. My reason for letting them have this scent of roast meat is, in case it should be necessary for us to apply to them to renew bills in December. Yours,   W. S.

Upon receiving this letter, John Ballantyne suggested to Scott that he should be allowed to offer, not only the new novel, but the next edition of Waverley, to Longman, Murray, or Blackwood — in the hope that the prospect of being let in to the profits of the already established favorite, would overcome effectually the hesitation of one or other of these houses about venturing on the encumbrance which Constable seemed to shrink from with such pertinacity; but upon this ingenious proposition Scott at once set his *veto*. He writes (October 17, 1814): —

DEAR JOHN, — Your expedients are all wretched, as
far as regards me. I never will give Constable, or any
one, room to say I have broken my word with him in the
slightest degree. If I lose everything else, I will at least
keep my honor unblemished; and I do hold myself bound
in honor to offer him a Waverley, while he shall continue
to comply with the conditions annexed. I intend the
new novel to operate as something more permanent than
a mere accommodation; and if I can but be permitted to
do so, I will print it before it is sold to any one, and then
propose, first to Constable and Longman — second, to
Murray and Blackwood — to take the whole at such a
rate as will give them one half of the fair profits; granting acceptances which, upon an edition of 3000, which
we shall be quite authorized to print, will amount to an
immediate command of £1500; and to this we may
couple the condition, that they must take £500 or £600
of the old stock. I own I am not solicitous to deal with
Constable alone, nor am I at all bound to offer him the
new novel on any terms; but he, knowing of the intention, may expect to be treated with, at least, although it
is possible we may not deal. However, if Murray and
Blackwood were to come forward with any handsome
proposal as to the stock, I should certainly have no objection to James's giving the pledge of the Author of W.
for his next work. You are like the crane in the fable,
when you boast of not having got anything from the
business; you may thank God that it did not bite your
head off. Would to God I were at let-a-be for let-a-be;
— but you have done your best, and so must I.

Yours truly,   W. S.

Both Mr. Murray, and Longman's partner, Mr. Rees,
were in Scotland about this time; and the former at least
paid Scott a visit at Abbotsford. Of course, however,
whatever propositions they may have made were received
by one or other of the Ballantynes. The result was,

that the house of Longman undertook Guy Mannering on the terms dictated by Scott — namely, granting bills for £1500, and relieving John Ballantyne and Company of stock to the extent of £500 more; and Constable's first information of the transaction was from Messrs. Longman themselves, when they, in compliance with Scott's wish, as signified in the letter last quoted, offered him a share in the edition which they had purchased. With one or two exceptions, originating in circumstances nearly similar, the house of Constable published all the subsequent series of the Waverley Novels.

I must not, however, forget that The Lord of the Isles was published a month before Guy Mannering. The poem was received with an interest much heightened by the recent and growing success of the mysterious Waverley. Its appearance, so rapidly following that novel, and accompanied with the announcement of another prose tale, just about to be published, by the same hand, puzzled and confounded the mob of dulness.[1] The more sagacious few said to themselves — Scott is making one serious effort more in his old line, and by this it will be determined whether he does or does not altogether renounce that for his new one.

The Edinburgh Review on The Lord of the Isles begins with, —

" Here is another genuine Lay of the Great Minstrel, with all his characteristic faults, beauties, and irregularities. The same glow of coloring — the same energy of narration — the same amplitude of description are conspicuous — with the same still more characteristic disdain of puny graces and small originalities — the true poetical hardihood, in the strength of which he urges on his Pegasus fearlessly through dense and rare, and aiming gallantly at the great ends of truth and effect,

---

[1] John Ballantyne put forth the following paragraph in the *Scots Magazine* of December, 1814 : —

" Mr. Scott's poem of *The Lord of the Isles* will appear early in January. The Author of *Waverley* is about to amuse the public with a new novel, in three volumes, entitled *Guy Mannering*."

stoops but rarely to study the means by which they are to be
attained; avails himself without scruple of common sentiments
and common images wherever they seem fitted for his purpose;
and is original by the very boldness of his borrowing, and impressive by his disregard of epigram and emphasis."

The conclusion of the contemporaneous article in the
Quarterly Review is as follows:—

"The many beautiful passages which we have extracted
from the poem, combined with the brief remarks subjoined to
each canto, will sufficiently show, that although The Lord of the
Isles is not likely to add very much to the reputation of Mr.
Scott, yet this must be imputed rather to the greatness of his
previous reputation, than to the absolute inferiority of the poem
itself. Unfortunately, its merits are merely incidental, while
its defects are mixed up with the very elements of the poem.
But it is not in the power of Mr. Scott to write with tameness;
be the subject what it will (and he could not easily have chosen
one more impracticable), he impresses upon whatever scenes he
describes so much movement and activity, — he infuses into
his narrative such a flow of life, and, if we may so express ourselves, of animal spirits, that without satisfying the judgment,
or moving the feelings, or elevating the mind, or even very
greatly interesting the curiosity, he is able to seize upon, and,
as it were, exhilarate the imagination of his readers, in a manner which is often truly unaccountable. This quality Mr.
Scott possesses in an admirable degree; and supposing that he
had no other object in view than to convince the world of the
great poetical powers with which he is gifted, the poem before
us would be quite sufficient for his purpose. But this is of
very inferior importance to the public; what they want is a
good poem, and, as experience has shown, this can only be constructed upon a solid foundation of taste, and judgment, and
meditation."

These passages appear to me to condense the result of
deliberate and candid reflection, and I have therefore
quoted them. The most important remarks of either
Essayist on the details of the plot and execution are annexed to the last edition of the poem; and show such an

exact coincidence of judgment in two masters of their calling, as had not hitherto been exemplified in the professional criticism of his metrical romances. The defects which both point out are, I presume, but too completely explained by the preceding statement of the rapidity with which this, the last of those great performances, had been thrown off; nor do I see that either Reviewer has failed to do sufficient justice to the beauties which redeem the imperfections of The Lord of the Isles — except as regards the whole character of Bruce, its real hero, and the picture of the battle of Bannockburn, which, now that one can compare these works from something like the same point of view, does not appear to me in the slightest particular inferior to the Flodden of Marmion.

This poem is now, I believe, about as popular as Rokeby; but it has never reached the same station in general favor with the Lay, Marmion, or The Lady of the Lake. The first edition of 1800 copies in quarto was, however, rapidly disposed of, and the separate editions in 8vo, which ensued before his poetical works were collected, amounted together to 12,250 copies. This, in the case of almost any other author, would have been splendid success ; but as compared with what he had previously experienced, even in his Rokeby, and still more so as compared with the enormous circulation at once attained by Lord Byron's early tales, which were then following each other in almost breathless succession, the falling off was decided. One evening, some days after the poem had been published, Scott requested James Ballantyne to call on him, and the printer found him alone in his library, working at the third volume of Guy Mannering. I give what follows from Ballantyne's Memoranda : —

" ' Well, James,' he said, ' I have given you a week — what are people saying about The Lord of the Isles ? ' I hesitated a little, after the fashion of Gil Blas, but he speedily brought the matter to a point. ' Come,' he said, ' speak out, my good

fellow ; what has put it into your head to be on so much ceremony *with me* all of a sudden ? But, I see how it is, the result is given in one word — *Disappointment.*' My silence admitted his inference to the fullest extent. His countenance
certainly did look rather blank for a few seconds ; in truth, he
had been wholly unprepared for the event; for it is a singular
fact, that before the public, or rather the booksellers, had given
their decision, he no more knew whether he had written well
or ill, than whether a die thrown out of a box was to turn up a
size or an ace. However, he instantly resumed his spirits, and
expressed his wonder rather that his poetical popularity should
have lasted so long, than that it should have now at last given
way. At length he said, with perfect cheerfulness, 'Well,
well, James, so be it — but you know we must not droop, for
we can't afford to give over. Since one line has failed, we
must just stick to something else : ' — and so he dismissed me
and resumed his novel."

Ballantyne concludes the anecdote in these words : —

"He spoke thus, probably unaware of the undiscovered wonders then slumbering in his mind. Yet still he could not but
have felt that the production of a few poems was nothing in
comparison of what must be in reserve for him, for he was at
this time scarcely more than forty.[1] An evening or two after,
I called again on him, and found on the table a copy of The
Giaour, which he seemed to have been reading. Having an
enthusiastic young lady in my house, I asked him if I might
carry the book home with me, but chancing to glance on the
autograph blazon, ' *To the Monarch of Parnassus from one of
his subjects,*' instantly retracted my request, and said I had
not observed Lord Byron's inscription before. ' What inscription ? ' said he ; ' oh yes, I had forgot, but inscription or no inscription, you are equally welcome.' I again took it up, and
he continued, ' James, Byron hits the mark where I don't
even pretend to fledge my arrow.' At this time he had never
seen Byron, but I knew he meant soon to be in London, when,
no doubt, the mighty consummation of the meeting of the two
bards would be accomplished ; and I ventured to say that he
must be looking forward to it with some interest. His coun-

[1] He was not forty-four till August, 1815.

tenance became fixed, and he answered impressively, 'Oh, of course.' In a minute or two afterwards he rose from his chair, paced the room at a very rapid rate, which was his practice in certain moods of mind, then made a dead halt, and bursting into an extravaganza of laughter, 'James,' cried he, 'I'll tell you what Byron should say to me when we are about to accost each other, —

> " Art thou the man whom men famed Grizzle call ? "

And then how germane would be my answer, —

> " Art thou the still more famed Tom Thumb the small ? " '

This," says the printer, " is a specimen of his peculiar humor; it kept him full of mirth for the rest of the evening."

The whole of the scene strikes me as equally and delightfully characteristic; I may add, hardly more so of Scott than of his printer; for Ballantyne, with all his profound worship of his friend and benefactor, was in truth, even more than he, an undoubting acquiescer in "the decision of the public, or rather of the booksellers;" and among the many absurdities into which his reverence for the popedom of Paternoster Row led him, I never could but consider with special astonishment, the facility with which he seemed to have adopted the notion that the Byron of 1814 was really entitled to supplant Scott as a popular poet. Appreciating, as a man of his talents could hardly fail to do, the splendidly original glow and depth of Childe Harold, he always appeared to me quite blind to the fact, that in The Giaour, in The Bride of Abydos, in Parisina, and indeed in all his early serious narratives, Byron owed at least half his success to clever, though perhaps unconscious imitation of Scott, and no trivial share of the rest to the lavish use of materials which Scott never employed, only because his genius was, from the beginning to the end of his career, under the guidance of high and chivalrous feelings of moral rectitude. All this Lord Byron himself seems to have felt most completely — as witness the whole sequence of

sketches of scenery; the rapid, ever heightening interest of the narrative; the unaffected kindliness of feeling, the manly purity of thought, everywhere mingled with a gentle humor and a homely sagacity; but, above all, the rich variety and skilful contrast of characters and manners, at once fresh in fiction, and stamped with the unforgeable seal of truth and nature: these were charms that spoke to every heart and mind; and the few murmurs of pedantic criticism were lost in the voice of general delight, which never fails to welcome the invention that introduces to the sympathy of imagination a new group of immortal realities.

The earlier chapters of the present narrative have anticipated much of what I might, perhaps with better judgment, have reserved for this page. Taken together with the author's Introduction and Notes, those anecdotes of his days of youthful wandering must, however, have enabled the reader to trace almost as minutely as he could wish, the sources from which the novelist drew his materials, both of scenery and character; and the Durham Garland, which I print in the Appendix to this volume, exhausts my information concerning the humble groundwork on which fancy reared this delicious romance.[1]

The first edition was, like that of Waverley, in three little volumes, with a humility of paper and printing which the meanest novelist would now disdain to imitate;

---

[1] I leave my text as it stood in the former editions; but since the last of these appeared, a writer in The Gentleman's Magazine (July, 1840) has pointed out some very remarkable coincidences between the narrative of Guy Mannering and the very singular history of James Annesley, claimant in 1743 of the honors and estates of the Earls of Anglesey, in Ireland. That Sir Walter must have read the records of this celebrated trial, as well as Smollett's edition of the story in Peregrine Pickle, there can be no doubt. How the circumstance had not recurred to his memory when writing the explanatory Introduction to his Novel, I can offer no conjecture. Very possibly the Garland itself may have been framed after the Annesley trial took place. — (1841.) [The paper in The Gentleman's Magazine, referred to above, will be found in the Appendix to this volume.]

the price a guinea. The 2000 copies of which it consisted were sold the day after the publication; and within three months came a second and a third impression, making together 5000 copies more. The sale, before those novels began to be collected, had reached nearly 10,000; and since then (to say nothing of foreign reprints of the text, and myriads of translations into every tongue of Europe) the domestic sale has amounted to 50,000.

On the rising of the Court of Session in March, Mr. and Mrs. Scott went by sea to London with their eldest girl, whom, being yet too young for general society, they again deposited with Joanna Baillie at Hampstead, while they themselves resumed, for two months, their usual quarters at kind Miss Dumergue's in Piccadilly. Six years had elapsed since Scott last appeared in the metropolis; and brilliant as his reception had then been, it was still more so on the present occasion. Scotland had been visited in the interim, chiefly from the interest excited by his writings, by crowds of the English nobility, most of whom had found introduction to his personal acquaintance — not a few had partaken of his hospitality at Ashestiel or Abbotsford. The generation among whom, I presume, a genius of this order feels his own influence with the proudest and sweetest confidence — on whose fresh minds and ears he has himself made the first indelible impressions — the generation with whose earliest romance of the heart and fancy his idea had been blended, was now grown to the full stature; the success of these recent novels, seen on every table, the subject of every conversation, had, with those who did not doubt their parentage, far more than counterweighed his declination, dubious after all, in the poetical balance; while the mystery that hung over them quickened the curiosity of the hesitating and conjecturing many — and the name on which ever and anon some new circumstance accumulated stronger suspicion, loomed larger through the haze in which he had thought fit to envelop it. More-over, this was a period of high national pride and excitement.

> " O who that shared them ever shall forget
> The emotions of the spirit-rousing time,
> When breathless in the mart the couriers met,
> Early and late, at evening and at prime;
> When the loud cannon and the merry chime
> Hail'd news on news, as field on field was won,
> When Hope, long doubtful, soared at length sublime,
> And our glad eyes, awake as day begun,
> Watch'd Joy's broad banner rise, to meet the rising sun?

> " O these were hours, when thrilling joy repaid
> A long, long course of darkness, doubts, and fears!
> The heart-sick faintness of the hope delayed,
> The waste, the woe, the bloodshed, and the tears
> That tracked with terror twenty rolling years —
> All was forgot in that blithe jubilee.
> Her downcast eye even pale Affliction rears,
> To sigh a thankful prayer amid the glee
> That hailed the Despot's fall, and peace and liberty!"[1]

At such a time, Prince and people were well prepared to hail him who, more perhaps than any other master of the pen, had contributed to sustain the spirit of England throughout the struggle, which was as yet supposed to have been terminated on the field of Toulouse. "Thank Heaven you are coming at last!" Joanna Baillie had written a month or two before. "Make up your mind to be stared at only a little less than the Czar of Muscovy, or old Blücher."

And now took place James Ballantyne's "mighty consummation of the meeting of the two bards." Scott's own account of it, in a letter to Mr. Moore, must have been seen by most of my readers; yet I think it ought also to find a place here. He says: —

" It was in the spring of 1815, that, chancing to be in London, I had the advantage of a personal introduction

[1] *Lord of the Isles*, Canto vi.

to Lord Byron. Report had prepared me to meet a man of peculiar habits and a quick temper, and I had some doubts whether we were likely to suit each other in society. I was most agreeably disappointed in this respect. I found Lord Byron in the highest degree courteous, and even kind. We met for an hour or two almost daily, in Mr. Murray's drawing-room, and found a great deal to say to each other.[1] We also met frequently in parties and evening society, so that for about two months I had the advantage of a considerable intimacy with this distinguished individual. Our sentiments agreed a good deal, except upon the subjects of religion and politics, upon neither of which I was inclined to believe that Lord Byron entertained very fixed opinions. I remember saying to him, that I really thought that if he lived a few years he would alter his sentiments. He answered, rather sharply, ' I suppose you are one of those who prophesy I shall turn Methodist.' I replied: ' No, I don't expect your conversion to be of such an ordinary kind. I would rather look to see you retreat upon the Catholic faith, and distinguish yourself by the austerity of your penances. The species of religion to which you must, or may, one day attach yourself, must exercise a strong power on the imagination.' He smiled gravely, and seemed to allow I might be right.

" On politics, he used sometimes to express a high strain of what is now called Liberalism; but it appeared to me that the pleasure it afforded him, as a vehicle for displaying his wit and satire against individuals in office, was at the bottom of this habit of thinking, rather than any real conviction of the political principles on which he talked. He was certainly proud of his rank and ancient family, and, in that respect, as much an aristocrat

---

[1] [John Murray — the third of the name — gives some interesting notes of his recollections of these meetings in Albemarle Street, in the *Memoirs* of his father (vol. i. p. 267).]

as was consistent with good sense and good breeding. Some disgusts, how adopted I know not, seemed to me to have given this peculiar and (as it appeared to me) contradictory cast of mind; but, at heart, I would have termed Byron a patrician on principle.

" Lord Byron's reading did not seem to me to have been very extensive, either in poetry or history. Having the advantage of him in that respect, and possessing a good competent share of such reading as is little read, I was sometimes able to put under his eye objects which had for him the interest of novelty. I remember particularly repeating to him the fine poem of Hardyknute, an imitation of the old Scottish ballad, with which he was so much affected, that some one who was in the same apartment asked me what I could possibly have been telling Byron by which he was so much agitated.

" I saw Byron for the last time in 1815, after I returned from France. He dined, or lunched, with me at Long's, in Bond Street. I never saw him so full of gayety and good-humor, to which the presence of Mr. Mathews, the comedian, added not a little. Poor Terry was also present. After one of the gayest parties I ever was present at, my fellow-traveller, Mr. Scott of Gala, and I set off for Scotland, and I never saw Lord Byron again. Several letters passed between us — one perhaps every half-year. Like the old heroes in Homer, we exchanged gifts. I gave Byron a beautiful dagger mounted with gold, which had been the property of the redoubted Elfi Bey. But I was to play the part of Diomed in the Iliad, for Byron sent me, some time after, a large sepulchral vase of silver. It was full of dead men's bones, and had inscriptions on two sides of the base. One ran thus: 'The bones contained in this urn were found in certain ancient sepulchres within the long walls of Athens, in the month of February, 1811.' The other face bears the lines of Juvenal: '*Expende — quot libras in duce summo invenies? — Mors sola fatetur quantula sint hominum corpuscula.'*

"To these I have added a third inscription, in these words, ' The gift of Lord Byron to Walter Scott.' [1] There was a letter with this vase, more valuable to me than the gift itself, from the kindness with which the donor expressed himself towards me. I left it naturally in the urn with the bones; but it is now missing. As the theft was not of a nature to be practised by a mere domestic, I am compelled to suspect the inhospitality of some individual of higher station, most gratuitously exercised certainly, since, after what I have here said, no one will probably choose to boast of possessing this literary curiosity.

"We had a good deal of laughing, I remember, on what the public might be supposed to think, or say, concerning the gloomy and ominous nature of our mutual gifts.

"I think I can add little more to my recollections of Byron. He was often melancholy — almost gloomy. When I observed him in this humor, I used either to wait till it went off of its own accord, or till some natural and easy mode occurred of leading him into conversation, when the shadows almost always left his countenance, like the mist rising from a landscape. In conversation he was very animated.

"I met with him very frequently in society; our mutual acquaintances doing me the honor to think that he liked to meet with me. Some very agreeable parties I can recollect — particularly one at Sir George Beaumont's — where the amiable landlord had assembled some persons

[1] Mr. Murray had, at the time of giving the vase, suggested to Lord Byron, that it would increase the value of the gift to add some such inscription ; but the noble poet answered modestly, —

"April 9, 1815. DEAR MURRAY, — I have a great objection to your proposition about inscribing the vase — which is, that it would appear *ostentatious* on my part ; and of course I must send it as it is, without any alteration. Yours ever, BYRON."

distinguished for talent. Of these I need only mention the late Sir Humphry Davy, whose talents for literature were as remarkable as his empire over science. Mr. Richard Sharpe and Mr. Rogers were also present.

"I think I also remarked in Byron's temper starts of suspicion, when he seemed to pause and consider whether there had not been a secret, and perhaps offensive, meaning in something casually said to him. In this case, I also judged it best to let his mind, like a troubled spring, work itself clear, which it did in a minute or two. I was considerably older, you will recollect, than my noble friend, and had no reason to fear his misconstruing my sentiments towards him, nor had I ever the slightest reason to doubt that they were kindly returned on his part. If I had occasion to be mortified by the display of genius which threw into the shade such pretensions as I was then supposed to possess, I might console myself that, in my own case, the materials of mental happiness had been mingled in a greater proportion.

"I rummage my brains in vain for what often rushes into my head unbidden — little traits and sayings which recall his looks, manner, tone, and gestures; and I have always continued to think that a crisis of life was arrived, in which a new career of fame was opened to him, and that had he been permitted to start upon it, he would have obliterated the memory of such parts of his life as friends would wish to forget."

I have nothing to add to this interesting passage, except that Joanna Baillie's tragedy of The Family Legend being performed at one of the theatres during Scott's stay in town, Lord Byron accompanied the authoress and Mr. and Mrs. Scott to witness the representation; and that the vase with the Attic bones appears to have been sent to Scott very soon after his arrival in London, not, as Mr. Moore had gathered from the hasty diction of his Reminiscences, at some "subsequent period of their acquaintance." This is sufficiently proved by the following note: —

TO THE RIGHT HONORABLE LORD BYRON, ETC., ETC.

PICCADILLY, Monday.

MY DEAR LORD, — I am not a little ashamed of the value of the shrine in which your Lordship has enclosed the Attic relics; but were it yet more costly, the circumstance could not add value to it in my estimation, when considered as a pledge of your Lordship's regard and friendship. The principal pleasure which I have derived from my connection with literature has been the access which it has given me to those who are distinguished by talents and accomplishments; and, standing so high as your Lordship justly does in that rank, my satisfaction in making your acquaintance has been proportionally great. It is one of those wishes which, after having been long and earnestly entertained, I have found completely gratified upon becoming personally known to you; and I trust you will permit me to profit by it frequently, during my stay in town. I am, my dear Lord, your truly obliged and faithful

WALTER SCOTT.

It was also in the spring of 1815 that Scott had, for the first time, the honor of being presented to the Prince Regent. His Royal Highness had (as has been seen from a letter to Joanna Baillie, already quoted) signified, more than a year before this time, his wish that the poet should revisit London — and, on reading his Edinburgh Address in particular, he said to Mr. Dundas, that "Walter Scott's charming behavior about the laureateship had made him doubly desirous of seeing him at Carlton House." More lately, on receiving a copy of The Lord of the Isles, his Royal Highness's librarian had been commanded to write to him in these terms: —

CARLTON HOUSE, January 19, 1815.

MY DEAR SIR, — You are deservedly so great a favorite
with the Prince Regent, that his librarian is not only directed
to return you the thanks of his Royal Highness for your valuable present, but to inform you that the Prince Regent particularly wishes to see you whenever you come to London ;
and desires you will always, when you are there, come into his
library whenever you please.   Believe me always, with sincerity, one of your warmest admirers, and most obliged friends,

J. S. CLARKE.

On hearing from Mr. Croker (then Secretary to the
Admiralty) that Scott was to be in town by the middle
of March, the Prince said, "Let me know when he
comes, and I 'll get up a snug little dinner that will suit
him; " and, after he had been presented and graciously
received at the levee, he was invited to dinner accordingly, through his excellent friend Mr. Adam (now Lord
Chief Commissioner of the Jury Court in Scotland),[1]
who at that time held a confidential office in the royal
household.   The Regent had consulted with Mr. Adam
also as to the composition of the party.   "Let us have,"
said he, "just a few friends of his own — and the more
Scotch the better; " and both the Chief Commissioner
and Mr. Croker assure me that the party was the most
interesting and agreeable one in their recollection.   It
comprised, I believe, the Duke of York — the late Duke
of Gordon (then Marquis of Huntly) — the Marquis of
Hertford (then Lord Yarmouth) — the Earl of Fife —

---

[1] This most amiable and venerable gentleman, my dear and kind friend,
died at Edinburgh on the 17th February, 1839, in the 89th year of his
age.   He retained his strong mental faculties in their perfect vigor to the
last days of this long life, and with them all the warmth of social feelings
which had endeared him to all who were so happy as to have any opportunity of knowing him.   The reader will find an affectionate tribute to
his worth, from Sir Walter Scott's Diary, in a subsequent volume of these
Memoirs. — (March, 1839.)

and Scott's early friend Lord Melville. "The Prince and Scott," says Mr. Croker, "were the two most brilliant story-tellers in their several ways, that I have ever happened to meet; they were both aware of their *forte*, and both exerted themselves that evening with delightful effect. On going home, I really could not decide which of them had shone the most. The Regent was enchanted with Scott, as Scott with him; and on all his subsequent visits to London, he was a frequent guest at the royal table." The Lord Chief Commissioner remembers that the Prince was particularly delighted with the poet's anecdotes of the old Scotch judges and lawyers, which his Royal Highness sometimes *capped* by ludicrous traits of certain ermined sages of his own acquaintance. Scott told, among others, a story, which he was fond of telling; and the commentary of his Royal Highness on hearing it amused Scott, who often mentioned it afterwards. The anecdote is this: A certain Judge, whenever he went on a particular circuit, was in the habit of visiting a gentleman of good fortune in the neighborhood of one of the assize towns, and staying at least one night, which, being both of them ardent chess-players, they usually concluded with their favorite game. One Spring circuit the battle was not decided at daybreak, so the Judge said, "Weel, Donald, I must e'en come back this gate in the harvest, and let the game lie ower for the present;" and back he came in October, but not to his old friend's hospitable house; for that gentleman had, in the interim, been apprehended on a capital charge (of forgery), and his name stood on the *Porteous Roll*, or list of those who were about to be tried under his former guest's auspices. The laird was indicted and tried accordingly, and the jury returned a verdict of *guilty*. The Judge forthwith put on his cocked hat (which answers to the black cap in England), and pronounced the sentence of the law in the usual terms: "To be hanged by the neck until you be dead; and may the Lord have

mercy upon your unhappy soul!" Having concluded
this awful formula in his most sonorous cadence, the
Judge, dismounting his formidable beaver, gave a familiar nod to his unfortunate acquaintance, and said to him
in a sort of chuckling whisper, "And now, Donald, my
man, I think I've checkmated you for ance." The Regent laughed heartily at this specimen of judicial humor;
and "I' faith, Walter," said he, "this old big-wig seems
to have taken things as coolly as my tyrannical self.
Don't you remember Tom Moore's description of me at
breakfast, —

> ' The table spread with tea and toast,
> Death-warrants and the Morning Post?' "

Towards midnight, the Prince called for "a bumper,
with all the honors, to the Author of Waverley," and
looked significantly, as he was charging his own glass,
to Scott. Scott seemed somewhat puzzled for a moment,
but instantly recovering himself, and filling his glass to
the brim, said, "Your Royal Highness looks as if you
thought I had some claim to the honors of this toast. I
have no such pretensions, but shall take good care that
the real Simon Pure hears of the high compliment that
has now been paid him." He then drank off his claret,
and joined in the cheering, which the Prince himself
timed. But before the company could resume their seats,
his Royal Highness exclaimed, "Another of the same,
if you please, to the Author of Marmion — and now,
Walter, my man, I have checkmated you for *ance*."
The second bumper was followed by cheers still more
prolonged: and Scott then rose and returned thanks in a
short address, which struck the Lord Chief Commissioner
as "alike grave and graceful." This story has been circulated in a very perverted shape. I now give it on the
authority of my venerated friend. He adds, that having
occasion, the day after, to call on the Duke of York, his
Royal Highness said to him: "Upon my word, Adam,
my brother went rather too near the wind about Waver-

ley — but nobody could have turned the thing more prettily than Walter Scott did — and upon the whole I never had better fun." [1]

The Regent, as was his custom with those he most delighted to honor, uniformly addressed the poet, even at their first dinner, by his Christian name, "Walter."

Before he left town, he again dined at Carlton House, when the party was a still smaller one than before, and the merriment, if possible, still more free. That nothing might be wanting, the Prince sung several capital songs in the course of that evening — as witness the lines in Sultan Serendib: [2] —

> " I love a Prince will bid the bottle pass,
>   Exchanging with his subjects glance and glass,
>   In fitting time can, gayest of the gay,
>   Keep up the jest and mingle in the lay.
>   Such Monarchs best our freeborn humor suit,
>   But despots must be stately, stern, and mute." [3]

Before he returned to Edinburgh, on the 22d of May, the Regent sent him a gold snuff-box, set in brilliants, with a medallion of his Royal Highness's head on the lid, "as a testimony" (writes Mr. Adam, in transmitting it) "of the high opinion his Royal Highness entertains of your genius and merit."

I transcribe what follows from James Ballantyne's *Memoranda :* —

" After Mr. Scott's first interview with his Sovereign, one or two intimate friends took the liberty of inquiring, what judgment he had formed of the Regent's talents? He declined

---

[1] Since this narrative was first published, I have been told by two gentlemen who were at this dinner, that, according to their recollection, the Prince *did not* on that occasion run so " near the wind " as my text represents ; and I am inclined to believe that a scene at Dalkeith, in 1822, may have been unconsciously blended with a gentler rehearsal of Carlton House, 1815. The Chief Commissioner had promised to revise my sheets for the present edition; but alas, he never did so — and I must now leave the matter as it stands. — (1839.)

[2] [*The Search after Happiness*]

[3] Scott's *Poetical Works*, vol. xi. p. 353 [Cambridge Ed. p. 431].

giving any definite answer — but repeated that ' he was the first gentleman he had seen — certainly the first *English* gentleman of his day ; — there was something about him which, independently of the *prestige,* the "divinity, which hedges a King," marked him as standing entirely by himself ; but as to his abilities, spoken of as distinct from his charming manners, how could any one form a fair judgment of that man who introduced whatever subject he chose, discussed it just as long as he chose, and dismissed it when he chose ? ' "

Ballantyne adds : —

"What I have now to say is more important, not only in itself, but as it will enable you to give a final contradiction to an injurious report which has been in circulation ; namely, that the Regent asked him as to the authorship of Waverley, and received a distinct and solemn denial. I took the bold freedom of requesting to know *from him* whether his Royal Highness had questioned him on that subject, and what had been his answer. He glanced at me with a look of mild surprise, and said, ' What answer I might have made to such a question, put to me by my Sovereign, perhaps I do not, or rather perhaps I do know ; but I was never put to the test. He is far too well-bred a man ever to put so ill-bred a question.' "

The account I have already given of the convivial scene alluded to would probably have been sufficient; but it can do no harm to place Ballantyne's, or rather Scott's own testimony, also on record.

I ought not to have omitted, that during Scott's residence in London, in April, 1815, he lost one of the English friends, to a meeting with whom he had looked forward with the highest pleasure. Mr. George Ellis died on the 15th of that month, at his seat of Sunning Hill. This threw a cloud over what would otherwise have been a period of unmixed enjoyment. Mr. Canning penned the epitaph for that dearest of his friends, but he submitted it to Scott's consideration before it was engraved.

CHAPTER XXXV

1815

GOETHE expressed, I fancy, a very general sentiment,
when he said, that to him the great charm and value of
my friend's Life of Buonaparte seemed quite independent of the question of its accuracy as to small details;
that he turned eagerly to the book, not to find dates
sifted, and countermarches analyzed, but to contemplate
what could not but be a true record of the broad impressions made on the mind of Scott by the marvellous revo-
lutions of his own time in their progress. Feeling how
justly in the main that work has preserved those impressions, though gracefully softened and sobered in the retrospect of peaceful and more advanced years, I the less
regret that I have it not in my power to quote any letters
of his touching the reappearance of Napoleon on the soil
of France — the immortal march from Cannes — the
reign of the Hundred Days, and the preparations for
another struggle, which fixed the gaze of Europe in May,
1815.

That he should have been among the first civilians

who hurried over to see the field of Waterloo, and hear
English bugles sound about the walls of Paris, could
have surprised none who knew the lively concern he had
always taken in the military efforts of his countrymen,
and the career of the illustrious captain, who had taught
them to reëstablish the renown of Agincourt and Blen-
heim, —

> " Victor of Assaye's Eastern plain,
> Victor of all the fields of Spain."

I had often heard him say, however, that his determination was, if not fixed, much quickened by a letter of an
old acquaintance of his, who had, on the arrival of the
news of the 18th of June, instantly repaired to Brussels,
to tender his professional skill in aid of the overburdened
medical staff of the conqueror's army. When, therefore,
I found the letter in question preserved among Scott's
papers, I perused it with a peculiar interest; and I now
venture, with the writer's permission, to present it to
the reader. It was addressed by Sir Charles Bell to his
brother, an eminent barrister in Edinburgh, who transmitted it to Scott. "When I read it," said he, "it set
me on fire." The marriage of Miss Maclean Clephane
of Torloisk with the Earl Compton (now Marquis of
Northampton), which took place on the 24th of July,
was in fact the only cause why he did not leave Scotland
instantly; for that dear young friend had chosen Scott
for her guardian, and on him accordingly devolved the
chief care of the arrangements on this occasion. The
extract sent to him by Mr. George Joseph Bell is as
follows: —

> " Brussels, 2d July, 1815.

" This country, the finest in the world, has been of late quite
out of our minds. I did not, in any degree, anticipate the
pleasure I should enjoy, the admiration forced from me, on
coming into one of these antique towns, or in journeying
through the rich garden. Can you recollect the time when
there were gentlemen meeting at the Cross of Edinburgh, or
those whom we thought such? They are all collected here

You see the very men, with their scraggy necks sticking out of the collars of their old-fashioned square-skirted coats — their canes — their cocked-hats ; and, when they meet, the formal bow, the hat off to the ground, and the powder flying in the wind. I could divert you with the odd resemblances of the Scottish faces among the peasants, too — but I noted *them* at the time with my pencil, and I write to you only of things that you won't find in my pocket-book.

"I have just returned from seeing the French wounded received in their hospital ; and could you see them laid out naked, or almost so — 100 in a row of low beds on the ground — though wounded, exhausted, beaten, you would still conclude with me that these were men capable of marching unopposed from the west of Europe to the east of Asia. Strong, thickset, hardy veterans, brave spirits and unsubdued, as they cast their wild glance upon you, — their black eyes and brown cheeks finely contrasted with the fresh sheets, — you would much admire their capacity of adaptation. These fellows are brought from the field after lying many days on the ground ; many dying — many in the agony — many miserably racked with pain and spasms ; and the next mimics his fellow, and gives it a tune, — *Aha, vous chantez bien !* How they are wounded you will see in my notes. But I must not have you to lose the present impression on me of the formidable nature of these fellows as exemplars of the breed in France. It is a forced praise ; for from all I have seen, and all I have heard of their fierceness, cruelty, and bloodthirstiness, I cannot convey to you my detestation of this race of trained banditti. By what means they are to be kept in subjection until other habits come upon them, I know not ; but I am convinced that these men cannot be left to the bent of their propensities.

" This superb city is now ornamented with the finest groups of armed men that the most romantic fancy could dream of. I was struck with the words of a friend — E. ' I saw,' said he, ' *that* man returning from the field on the 16th.' (This was a Brunswicker, of the Black or Death Hussars.) ' He was wounded, and had had his arm amputated on the field. He was among the first that came in. He rode straight and stark upon his horse — the bloody clouts about his stump — pale as death, but upright, with a stern, fixed expression of feature, as if loath to lose his revenge.' These troops are very remarkable in their fine military appearance; their dark and ominous dress sets off to advantage their strong, manly, northern features and white mustachios; and there is something more than commonly impressive about the whole effect.

"This is the second Sunday after the battle, and many are not yet dressed. There are 20,000 wounded in this town, besides those in the hospitals, and the many in the other towns; — only 3000 prisoners; 80,000, they say, killed and wounded on both sides."

I think it not wonderful that this extract should have set Scott's imagination effectually on fire; that he should have grasped at the idea of seeing probably the last shadows of real warfare that his own age would afford; or that some parts of the great surgeon's simple phraseology are reproduced, almost verbatim, in the first of Paul's Letters to his Kinsfolk. No sooner was Scott's purpose known, than some of his young neighbors in the country proposed to join his excursion; and, in company with three of them, namely, his kinsman, John Scott of Gala, Alexander Pringle, the younger, of Whytbank (now M. P. for Selkirkshire), and Robert Bruce, advocate (now Sheriff of Argyle), he left Edinburgh for the south, at 5 A. M. on the 27th of July.

They travelled by the stage-coach, and took the route of Hull and Lincoln to Cambridge; for Gala and Whytbank, being both members of that university, were anxious to seize this opportunity of revisiting it themselves, and showing its beautiful architecture to their friend. After this wish had been gratified, they proceeded to Harwich, and thence, on the 3d of August, took ship for Helvoetsluys.

"The weather was beautiful," says Gala, "so we all went outside the coach from Cambridge to Harwich. At starting, there was a general complaint of thirst, the consequence of some experiments overnight on the celebrated *bishop* of my *Alma Mater;* our friend, however, was in great glee, and never was a merrier *basket* than he made it all the morning. He had cautioned us, on leaving Edinburgh, never to *name names* in such situations, and our adherence to this rule was rewarded by some amusing incidents. For example, as we entered the town where we were to dine, a heavy-looking man, who was to stop there, took occasion to thank Scott for the pleasure his anecdotes had afforded him : ' You have a good memory, sir,' said he ; ' mayhap, now, you sometimes write down what you hear or be a-reading about ? ' He answered, very gravely, that he did occasionally put down a *few* notes, if anything struck him particularly. In the afternoon, it happened that he sat on the box, while the rest of us were behind him. Here, by degrees, he became quite absorbed in his own reflections. He frequently repeated to himself, or *composed* perhaps, for a good while, and often smiled or raised his hand, seeming completely occupied and amused. His neighbor, a vastly scientific and rather grave professor, in a smooth drab Benjamin and broad-brimmed beaver, cast many a curious sidelong glance at him, evidently suspecting that all was not right with the upper story, but preserved perfect politeness. The poet was, however, discovered by the captain of the vessel in which we crossed the Channel ; — and a perilous passage it was, chiefly in consequence of the unceasing tumblers in which this worthy kept drinking his health."

Before leaving Edinburgh, Scott had settled in his mind the plan of Paul's Letters; for on that same day, his agent, John Ballantyne, addressed the following letter, from his marine villa near Newhaven : —

TO MESSRS. CONSTABLE & CO.

TRINITY, 27th July, 1815.

DEAR SIRS, — Mr. Scott left town to-day for the Continent. He proposes writing from thence a series of letters on a peculiar plan, varied in matter and style, and to different supposititious correspondents.

The work is to form a demy 8vo volume of twenty-two sheets, to sell at 12s. It is to be begun immediately on his arrival in France, and to be published, if possible, the second week of September, when he proposes to return.

We print 3000 of this, and I am empowered to offer you one third of the edition, Messrs. Longman & Co. and Mr. Murray having each the same share: the terms, twelve months' acceptance for paper and print, and half profits at six months, granted now as under. The over copies will pay the charge for advertising. I am, etc., JOHN BALLANTYNE.

Charge —

22 sheets printing, — £3 15 0		£82 10 0
145 reams demy, — 1 10 0		217 10 0
		£300 0 0

3000 at 8s. £1200 0 0
Cost, 300 0 0

£900 0 0 profit — One half is £450.

Before Scott reached Harwich, he knew that this offer had been accepted without hesitation; and thenceforth, accordingly, he threw his daily letters to his wife into the form of communications meant for an imaginary group, consisting of a spinster sister, a statistical laird, a rural clergyman of the Presbyterian Kirk, and a brother, a veteran officer on half-pay. The rank of this last personage corresponded, however, exactly with that of his own elder brother, John Scott, who also, like the Major of the book, had served in the Duke of York's unfortunate campaign of 1797; the sister is only a slender disguise for his aunt Christian Rutherford, already often mentioned; Lord Somerville, long President of the Board of Agriculture, was Paul's laird; and the shrewd and unbigoted Dr. Douglas of Galashiels was his "minister of the gospel." These epistles, after having been devoured by the little circle at Abbotsford, were transmitted to Major John Scott, his mother, and Miss Rutherford, in Edinburgh; from their hands they passed to those of James Ballantyne and Mr. Erskine, both of whom assured me that the copy ultimately sent to the press consisted, in great part, of the identical sheets that had successively reached Melrose through the post. The rest had of course been, as Ballantyne expresses it, "somewhat cobbled;" but, on the whole, Paul's Letters are to be considered as a true and faithful journal of this expedition; insomuch, that I might perhaps content myself, in this place, with a simple reference to that delightful volume. He found time, however, to write letters during his absence from Britain, to some others of his friends; and a specimen or two of these may interest the reader. I have also gathered, from the companions of the journey, a few more particulars, which Scott's modesty withheld him from recording; and some trivial circumstances which occur to me, from recollection of his own conversation, may also be acceptable.

But I hope that, if the reader has not perused Paul's Letters recently, he will refresh his memory, before he proceeds further, by bestowing an hour on that genuine fragment of the author's autobiography. He is now, unless he had the advantage of Scott's personal familiarity, much better acquainted with the man than he could have been before he took up this compilation of his private correspondence — and especially before he perused the full diary of the lighthouse yacht in 1814; and a thousand little turns and circumstances which may have, when he originally read the book, passed lightly before his eye, will now, I venture to say, possess a warm and vivid interest, as inimitably characteristic of a departed friend. The kindest of husbands and fathers never portrayed himself with more unaffected truth than in this vain effort, if such he really fancied he was making, to sustain the character of "a cross old bachelor." The whole man, just as he was, breathes in every line, with all his compassionate and benevolent sympathy of heart, all his sharpness of observation, and sober shrewdness of reflection; all his enthusiasm for nature, for country life, for simple manners and simple pleasures, mixed up with an equally glowing enthusiasm, at which many may smile, for the tiniest relics of feudal antiquity — and last, not least, a pulse of physical rapture for the "circumstance of war," which bears witness to the blood of *Bolt-foot* and *Fire-the-Braes*.

At Brussels, Scott found the small English garrison left there in command of Major-General Sir Frederick Adam, the son of his highly valued friend, the Lord Chief Commissioner. Sir Frederick had been wounded at Waterloo, and could not as yet mount on horseback; but one of his aides-de-camp, Captain Campbell, escorted Scott and his party to the field of battle, on which occasion they were also accompanied by another old acquaintance of his, Major Pryse Gordon, who being then on half-pay, happened to be domesticated with his family at Brussels. Major Gordon has since published two lively volumes of Personal Memoirs; and Gala bears witness to the fidelity of certain reminiscences of Scott at Brussels and Waterloo, which occupy one of the chapters of this work. I shall, therefore, extract the passage: —

"Sir Walter Scott accepted my services to conduct him to Waterloo: the General's aide-de-camp was also of the party. He made no secret of his having undertaken to write something on the battle ; and perhaps he took the greater interest on this account in everything that he saw. Besides, he had never seen the field of such a conflict; and never having been before on the Continent, it was all new to his comprehensive mind. The day was beautiful ; and I had the precaution to send out a couple of saddle-horses, that he might not be fatigued in walking over the fields, which had been recently ploughed up. In our rounds we fell in with Monsieur de Costar, with whom he got into conversation. This man had attracted so much notice by his pretended story of being about the person of Napoleon, that he was of too much importance to be passed by : I did not, indeed, know as much of this fellow's charlatanism at that time as afterwards, when I saw him confronted with a blacksmith of La Belle Alliance, who had been his companion in a hiding-place ten miles from the field during the whole day ; a fact which he could not deny. But he had got up a tale so plausible and so profitable, that he could afford to bestow hush-money on the companion of his flight, so that the imposition was but little known ; and strangers continued to be gulled. He had picked up a good deal of information about the positions and details of the battle ; and, being naturally a sagacious Walloon, and speaking French pretty fluently, he became the favorite cicerone, and every lie he told was taken for gospel. Year after year, until his death in 1824, he continued his popularity, and raised the price of his rounds from a couple of francs to five ; besides as much for the hire of a horse, his own property ; for he pretended that the fatigue of walking so many hours was beyond his powers. It has been said that in this way he realized every summer a couple of hundred Napoleons.

"When Sir Walter had examined every point of defence and attack, we adjourned to the ' Original Duke of Wellington ' at Waterloo, to lunch after the fatigues of the ride. Here he had a crowded levee of peasants, and collected a great many trophies, from cuirasses down to buttons and bullets. He picked up himself many little relics, and was fortunate in purchasing a grand cross of the Legion of Honor. But the most precious memorial was presented to him by my wife — a French soldier's book, well stained with blood, and containing some songs popular in the French army, which he found so interesting that he introduced versions of them in his Paul's Letters ; of which he did me the honor to send me a copy, with a letter, saying, ' that he considered my wife's gift as the most valuable of all his Waterloo relics.'

"On our return from the field, he kindly passed the evening with us, and a few friends whom we invited to meet him. He charmed us with his delightful conversation, and was in great spirits from the agreeable day he had passed ; and with great good-humor promised to write a stanza in my wife's album. On the following morning he fulfilled his promise by contributing some beautiful verses on Hougomont. I put him into my little library to prevent interruption, as a great many persons had paraded in the *Parc* opposite my window to get a peep of the celebrated man, many having dogged him from his hotel.

"Brussels affords but little worthy of the notice of such a traveller as the Author of Waverley; but he greatly admired the splendid tower of the Maison de Ville, and the ancient sculpture and style of architecture of the buildings which surround the Grand Place.

"He told us, with great humor, a laughable incident which had occurred to him at Antwerp. The morning after his arrival at that city from Holland, he started at an early hour to visit the tomb of Rubens in the church of St. Jacques, before his party were up. After wandering about for some time, without finding the object he had in view, he determined to make inquiry, and observing a person stalking about, he addressed him in his best French; but the stranger, pulling off his hat, very respectfully replied in the pure Highland accent, 'I'm vary sorry, sir, but I canna speak onything besides English.' — 'This is very unlucky indeed, Donald,' said Sir Walter, 'but we must help one another; for, to tell you the truth, I'm not good at any other tongue but the English, or rather, the Scotch.' — 'Oh, sir, maybe,' replied the Highlander, 'you are a countryman, and ken my maister Captain Cameron of the 79th, and could tell me whare he lodges. I'm just cum in, sir, frae a place they ca' *Machlin*,[1] and ha' forgotten the name of the captain's quarters; it was something like the *Laaborer*.' — 'I can, I think, help you with this, my friend,' rejoined Sir Walter. 'There is an inn just opposite to you' (pointing to the *Hôtel du Grand Laboureur*): 'I dare say that will be the captain's quarters;' and it was so. I cannot do justice to the humor with which Sir Walter recounted this dialogue."[2]

The following is the letter which Scott addressed to the Duke of Buccleuch immediately after seeing the field of Waterloo; and it may amuse the reader to compare it with Major Gordon's chapter, and with the writer's own fuller, and, of course, "cobbled" detail, in the pages of Paul: —

[1] Mechlin — the Highlander gave it the familiar pronunciation of a Scotch village. Mauchline, celebrated in many of Burns's poems.

[2] See Major Gordon's *Personal Memoirs* (1830), vol. ii. pp. 325-338.

MY DEAR LORD DUKE, — I promised to let you hear of my wanderings, however unimportant; and have now the pleasure of informing your Grace that I am at this present time an inhabitant of the Premier Hotel de Cambrai, after having been about a week upon the Continent. We landed at Helvoet, and proceeded to Brussels, by Bergen-op-Zoom and Antwerp, both of which are very strongly fortified. The ravages of war are little remarked in a country so rich by nature; but everything seems at present stationary, or rather retrograde, where capital is required. The châteaux are deserted, and going to decay; no new houses are built, and those of older date are passing rapidly into the possession of a class inferior to those for whom we must suppose them to have been built. Even the old gentlewoman of Babylon has lost much of her splendor, and her robes and pomp are of a description far subordinate to the costume of her more magnificent days. The dresses of the priests were worn and shabby, both at Antwerp and Brussels, and reminded me of the decayed wardrobe of a bankrupt theatre: yet, though the gentry and priesthood have suffered, the eternal bounty of nature has protected the lower ranks against much distress. The unexampled fertility of the soil gives them all, and more than they want; and could they but sell the grain which they raise in the Netherlands, nothing else would be wanting to render them the richest people (common people, that is to say) in the world.

On Wednesday last, I rode over the field of Waterloo, now forever consecrated to immortality. The more ghastly tokens of the carnage are now removed, the bodies both of men and horses being either burned or buried; but all the ground is still torn with the shot and shells, and covered with cartridges, old hats, and shoes, and various relics of the fray which the peasants have not

thought worth removing. Besides, at Waterloo and all
the hamlets in the vicinage, there is a mart established
for cuirasses; for the eagles worn by the imperial guard
on their caps; for casques, swords, carabines, and similar
articles. 1 have bought two handsome cuirasses, and
intend them, one for Bowhill, and one for Abbotsford,
if I can get them safe over, which Major Pryse Gordon
has promised to manage for me. I have also, for your
Grace, one of the little memorandum-books, which I
picked up on the field, in which every French soldier was
obliged to enter his receipts and expenditure, his services,
and even his punishments. The field was covered with
fragments of these records. I also got a good MS.
collection of French songs, probably the work of some
young officer, and a croix of the Legion of Honor. I
enclose, under another cover, a sketch of the battle, made
at Brussels. It is not, I understand, strictly accurate;
but sufficiently so to give a good notion of what took
place. In fact, it would require twenty separate plans
to give an idea of the battle at its various stages. The
front, upon which the armies engaged, does not exceed a
long mile. Our line, indeed, originally extended half
a mile farther towards the village of Brain-la-Leude; but
as the French indicated no disposition to attack in that
direction, the troops which occupied this space were
gradually concentrated by Lord Wellington, and made
to advance till they had reached Hougomont — a sort of
château, with a garden and wood attached to it, which
was powerfully and effectually maintained by the Guards
during the action. This place was particularly interesting. It was a quiet-looking gentleman's house, which
had been burnt by the French shells. The defenders,
burnt out of the house itself, betook themselves to the
little garden, where, breaking loopholes through the brick
walls, they kept up a most destructive fire on the assail-
ants, who had possessed themselves of a little wood which
surrounds the villa on one side. In this spot vast num-

bers had fallen; and, being hastily buried, the smell is most offensive at this moment. Indeed, I felt the same annoyance in many parts of the field; and, did I live near the spot, I should be anxious about the diseases which this steaming carnage might occasion. The rest of the ground, excepting this château, and a farmhouse called La Hay Sainte, early taken, and long held, by the French, because it was too close under the brow of the descent on which our artillery was placed to admit of the pieces being depressed so as to play into it, — the rest of the ground, I say, is quite open, and lies between two ridges, one of which (Mont St. Jean) was constantly occupied by the English; the other, upon which is the farm of La Belle Alliance, was the position of the French. The slopes between are gentle and varied; the ground everywhere practicable for cavalry, as was well experienced on that memorable day. The cuirassiers, despite their arms of proof, were quite inferior to our heavy dragoons. The meeting of the two bodies occasioned a noise, not unaptly compared to the tinkering and hammering of a smith's shop. Generally the cuirassiers came on stooping their heads very low, and giving point; the British frequently struck away their casques while they were in this position, and then laid at the bare head. Officers and soldiers all fought hand to hand without distinction; and many of the former owed their life to dexterity at their weapon, and personal strength of body. Shaw, the milling Life-Guardsman, whom your Grace may remember among the champions of The Fancy, maintained the honor of the fist, and killed or disabled upwards of twenty Frenchmen with his single arm, until he was killed by the assault of numbers.[1] At one place, where there is a precipitous sand or gravel pit, the heavy English cavalry drove many of the cuirassiers over pell-mell, and followed over themselves, like fox-hunters. The conduct of the infantry and artillery was equally,

[1] The skull of Shaw is now in the Museum at Abbotsford.

or, if possible, more distinguished, and it was all fully
necessary; for, besides that our army was much outnum-
bered, a great part of the sum-total were foreigners. Of
these, the Brunswickers and Hanoverians behaved very
well; the Belgians but sorrily enough. On one occasion,
when a Belgic regiment fairly ran off, Lord Wellington
rode up to them, and said, "My lads, you must be a
little blown; come, do take your breath for a moment,
and then we'll go back, and try if we can do a little
better;" and he actually carried them back to the charge.
He was, indeed, upon that day, everywhere, and the soul
of everything; nor could less than his personal endeavors
have supported the spirits of the men through a contest
so long, so desperate, and so unequal. At his last attack, Buonaparte brought up 15,000 of his Guard, who
had never drawn trigger during the day. It was upon
their failure that his hopes abandoned him.

I spoke long with a shrewd Flemish peasant, called
John de Costar, whom he had seized upon as his guide,
and who remained beside him the whole day, and afterwards accompanied him in his flight as far as Charleroi.
Your Grace may be sure that I interrogated Mynheer
very closely about what he heard and saw. He guided
me to the spot where Buonaparte remained during the
latter part of the action. It was in the highway from
Brussels to Charleroi, where it runs between two high
banks, on each of which was a French battery. He was
pretty well sheltered from the English fire; and, though
many bullets flew over his head, neither he nor any of
his suite were touched. His other stations, during that
day, were still more remote from all danger. The story
of his having an observatory erected for him is a mistake.
There is such a thing, and he repaired to it during the
action; but it was built or erected some months before,
for the purpose of a trigonometrical survey of the country, by the King of the Netherlands. Bony's last position was nearly fronting a tree where the Duke of Wel-

lington was stationed; there was not more than a quarter of a mile between them; but Bony was well sheltered, and the Duke so much exposed, that the tree is barked in several places by the cannon-balls levelled at him. As for Bony, De Costar says he was very cool during the whole day, and even gay. As the cannon-balls flew over them, De Costar ducked; at which the Emperor laughed, and told him they would hit him all the same. At length, about the time he made his grand and last effort, the fire of the Prussian artillery was heard upon his right, and the heads of their columns became visible pressing out of the woods. Aide-de-camp after aide-de-camp came with the tidings of their advance, to which Bony only replied, *Attendez, attendez un instant*, until he saw his troops, *fantassins et cavaliers*, return in disorder from the attack. He then observed hastily to a general beside him, *Je crois qu'ils sont mêlés*. The person to whom he spoke hastily raised the spyglass to his eye; but Bony, whom the first glance had satisfied of their total discomfiture, bent his face to the ground, and shook his head twice, his complexion being then as pale as death. The general then said something, to which Buonaparte answered, *C'est trop tard — sauvons nous*. Just at that moment, the allied troops, cavalry and infantry, appeared in full advance on all hands; and the Prussians, operating upon the right flank of the French, were rapidly gaining their rear. Bony, therefore, was compelled to abandon the high-road, which, besides, was choked with dead, with baggage, and with cannon; and, gaining the open country, kept at full gallop, until he gained, like Johnnie Cope, the van of the flying army. The marshals followed his example; and it was the most complete *sauve qui peut* that can well be imagined. Nevertheless, the prisoners who were brought into Brussels maintained their national impudence, and boldly avowed their intention of sacking the city with every sort of severity. At the same time they had friends there.

One man of rank and wealth went over to Bony during the action, and I saw his hotel converted into an hospital for wounded soldiers. It occupied one half of one of the sides of the Place Royale, a noble square, which your Grace has probably seen. But, in general, the inhabitants of Brussels were very differently disposed; and their benevolence to our poor wounded fellows was unbounded. The difficulty was to prevent them from killing their guests with kindness, by giving them butcher's meat and wine during their fever. As I cannot put my letter into post until we get to Paris, I shall continue it as we get along.

12th August, Roye, in Picardy. — I imagine your Grace about this time to be tolerably well fagged with a hard day on the moors. If the weather has been as propitious as with us, it must be delightful. The country through which we have travelled is most uncommonly fertile, and skirted with beautiful woods; but its present political situation is so very uncommon, that I would give the world your Grace had come over for a fortnight. France may be considered as neither at peace nor war. Valenciennes, for example, is in a state of blockade; we passed through the posts of the allies, all in the utmost state of vigilance, with patrols of cavalry and vedettes of infantry, up to the very gates, and two or three batteries were manned and mounted. The French troops were equally vigilant at the gates, yet made no objections to our passing through the town. Most of them had the white cockade, but looked very sulky, and were in obvious disorder and confusion. They had not yet made their terms with the King, nor accepted a commander appointed by him; but as they obviously feel their party desperate, the soldiers are running from the officers, and the officers from the soldiers. In fact, the multiplied hosts which pour into this country, exhibiting all the various dresses and forms of war which can be imagined, must necessarily render resistance impracticable. Yet, like Satan, these fellows retain the unconquered propensity to defiance, even in the midst of defeat and despair. This morning we passed a great number of the disbanded garrison of Condé, and they were the most horrid-looking cut-throats I ever saw, extremely disposed to be very insolent, and only repressed by the consciousness that all the villages and towns around are occupied by the allies. They began by crying to us in an ironical tone, *Vive le Roi;* then followed, *sotto voce*, *Sacre B——*, *Mille diables*, and other graces of French eloquence. I felt very well pleased that we were armed, and four in number; and still more so that it was daylight, for they seemed most mischievous ruffians. As for the appearance of the country, it is notwithstanding a fine harvest, most melancholy. The windows of all the detached houses on the road are uniformly shut up; and you see few people, excepting the peasants who are employed in driving the contributions to maintain the armies. The towns are little better, having for the most part been partially injured by shells or by storm, as was the case both of Cambrai and Peronne. The men look very sulky; and if you speak three words to a woman, she is sure to fall a-crying. In short, the *politesse* and good-humor of this people have fled with the annihilation of their self-conceit; and they look on you as if they thought you were laughing at them, or come to enjoy the triumph of our arms over theirs. Postmasters and landlords are all the same, and hardly to be propitiated even by English money, although they charge us about three times as much as they durst do to their countryfolks. As for the Prussians, a party of cavalry dined at our hotel at Mons, eat and drank of the best the poor devils had left to give, called for their horses, and laughed in the face of the landlord when he offered his bill, telling him they should pay as they came back. The English, they say, have always paid honorably, and upon these they indemnify themselves. It is impossible to *marchander*, for if you object, the poor landlady begins to cry, and tells you she will accept whatever *your lordship* pleases, but that she is almost ruined and bankrupt, etc., etc., etc.

This is a long stupid letter, but I will endeavor to send a better from Paris. Ever your Grace's truly obliged,

WALTER SCOTT.

The only letter which Scott addressed to Joanna Baillie, while in Paris, goes over partly the same ground: I transcribe the rest.

PARIS, 6th September, 1815.

MY DEAR FRIEND, — I owe you a long letter, but my late travels and the date of this epistle will be a tolerable plea for your indulgence. The truth is, I became very restless after the battle of Waterloo, and was only detained by the necessity of attending a friend's marriage, from setting off instantly for the Continent. At length, however, I got away to Brussels, and was on the memorable field of battle about five weeks after it had been fought. . . .

If our army had been all British, the day would have been soon decided; but the Duke, or, as they call him here, from his detestation of all manner of foppery, the *Beau*, had not above 35,000 British. All this was to be supplied by treble exertion on the part of our troops. The Duke was everywhere during the battle; and it was the mercy of Heaven that protected him, when all his staff had been killed or wounded round him. I asked him, among many other questions, if he had seen Buonaparte; he said, "No; but at one time, from the repeated shouts of *Vive l' Empereur*, I thought he must be near." This was when John de Costar placed him in the hollow way. I think, so near as I can judge, there may at that time have been a quarter of a mile between these two great generals.

The fate of the French, after this day of decisive appeal, has been severe enough. There were never people more mortified, more subdued, and apparently more broken in spirit. They submit with sad civility to the extortions of the Prussians and the Russians, and avenge themselves at the expense of the English, whom they charge three prices for everything, because they are the only people who pay at all. They are in the right, however, to enforce discipline and good order, which not only maintains the national character in the mean time, but will prevent the army from suffering by habits of indulgence. I question if the Prussians will soon regain their discipline and habits of hardihood. At present their powers of eating and drinking, which are really something preternatural, are exerted to the very utmost. A thin Prussian boy, whom I sometimes see, eats in one day as much as three English ploughmen. At daybreak he roars for chocolate and eggs; about nine he breakfasts more solemnly, à la fourchette, when, besides all the usual apparatus of an English déjeuner, he eats a world of cutlets, oysters, fruit, etc., and drinks a glass of brandy and a bottle of champagne. His dinner might serve Garagantua, at which he gets himself about three parts drunk — a circumstance which does not prevent the charge upon cold meat, with tea and chocolate, about six o'clock; and concluding the whole with an immense supper. Positively the appetite of this lad reminds one of the Eastern tale of a man taken out of the sea by a ship's crew, who, in return, ate up all the provisions of the vessel. He was, I think, flown away with by a roc; but from what quarter of the heavens the French are to look for deliverance from these devourers, I cannot presume to guess.

The needless wreck and ruin which they make in the houses adds much to the inconvenience of their presence. Most of the châteaux, where the Prussians are quartered, are what is technically called *rumped*, that is to say, plundered out and out. In the fine château of Montmorency, for instance, the most splendid apartments,

highly ornamented with gilding and carving, were converted into barracks for the dirtiest and most savage-
looking hussars I have yet seen. Imagine the work these
fellows make with velvet hangings and embroidery. I
saw one hag boiling her camp-kettle with part of a picture frame; the picture itself has probably gone to Prussia. With all this greediness and love of mischief, the
Prussians are not bloodthirsty; and their utmost violence seldom exceeds a blow or two with the flat of the
sabre. They are also very civil to the women, and in
both respects behave much better than the French did
in their country; but they follow the bad example quite
close enough for the sake of humanity and of discipline.
As for our people, they live in a most orderly and regular manner. All the young men pique themselves on
imitating the Duke of Wellington in *nonchalance* and
coolness of manner; so they wander about everywhere,
with their hands in the pockets of their long waistcoats,
or cantering upon Cossack ponies, staring and whistling,
and trotting to and fro, as if all Paris was theirs. The
French hate them sufficiently for the *hauteur* of their
manner and pretensions, but the grounds of dislike
against us are drowned in the actual detestation afforded
by the other powers.

This morning I saw a grand military spectacle — about
20,000 Russians pass in review before all the Kings and
Dominations who are now resident at Paris. The Emperor, King of Prussia, Duke of Wellington, with their
numerous and brilliant attendance of generals, staff-offi-
cers, etc., were in the centre of what is called the Place
Louis Quinze, almost on the very spot where Louis XVI.
was beheaded. A very long avenue, which faces the
station where they were placed, was like a glowing furnace,
so fiercely were the sunbeams reflected from the arms of
the host by which it was filled. A body of Cossacks
kept the ground with their pikes, and, by their wild appearance, added to the singularity of the scene. On one

hand was the extended line of the Tuileries, seen through the gardens and the rows of orange-trees; on the other, the long column of troops advancing to the music. Behind was a long colonnade, forming the front to the palace, where the Chamber of Representatives are to hold their sittings; and in front of the monarchs was a superb row of buildings, on which you distinguish the bronze pillar erected by Napoleon to commemorate his victories over Russia, Prussia, and Austria, whose princes were now reviewing their victorious armies in what was so lately his capital. Your fancy, my dear friend, will anticipate, better than I can express, the thousand sentiments which arose in my mind from witnessing such a splendid scene, in a spot connected with such various associations. It may give you some idea of the feelings of the French — once so fond of *spectacles* — to know that, I think, there were not a hundred of that nation looking on. Yet this country will soon recover the actual losses she has sustained, for never was there a soil so blessed by nature, or so rich in corn, wine, and oil, and in the animated industry of its inhabitants. France is at present the fabled giant, struggling, or rather lying supine, under the load of mountains which have been precipitated on her; but she is not, and cannot be crushed. Remove the incumbent weight of 600,000 or 700,000 foreigners, and she will soon stand upright — happy, if experience shall have taught her to be contented to exert her natural strength only for her own protection, and not for the annoyance of her neighbors. I am cut short in my lucubrations by an opportunity to send this letter with Lord Castlereagh's despatches, which is of less consequence, as I will endeavor to see you in passing through London. I leave this city for Dieppe on Saturday, but I intend to go round by Harfleur, if possible.

Ever your truly obliged and affectionate

WALTER SCOTT.

"Paul" modestly acknowledges, in his last letter, the personal attentions which he received, while in Paris, from Lords Cathcart, Aberdeen, and Castlereagh; and hints that, through their intervention, he had witnessed several of the splendid *fêtes* given by the Duke of Wellington, where he saw half the crowned heads of Europe grouped among the gallant soldiers who had cut a way for them to the guilty capital of France. Scott's reception, however, had been distinguished to a degree of which Paul's language gives no notion. The Noble Lords above named welcomed him with cordial satisfaction; and the Duke of Wellington, to whom he was first presented by Sir John Malcolm, treated him then, and ever afterwards, with a kindness and confidence, which, I have often heard him say, he considered as "the highest distinction of his life." He used to tell, with great effect, the circumstances of his introduction to the Emperor Alexander, at a dinner given by the Earl of Cathcart. Scott appeared, on that occasion, in the blue and red dress of the Selkirkshire Lieutenancy; and the Czar's first question, glancing at his lameness, was, "In what affair were you wounded?" Scott signified that he suffered from a natural infirmity; upon which the Emperor said, "I thought Lord Cathcart mentioned that you had served." Scott observed that the Earl looked a little embarrassed at this, and promptly answered, "Oh yes; in a certain sense I have served — that is, in the yeomanry cavalry; a home force resembling the Landwehr, or Landsturm." — "Under what commander?" — "Sous M. le Chevalier Rae." — "Were you ever engaged?" — "In some slight actions — such as the battle of the Cross Causeway and the affair of Moredun-Mill." — "This," says Mr. Pringle of Whytbank, "was, as he saw in Lord Cathcart's face, quite sufficient, so he managed to turn the conversation to some other subject." It was at the same dinner that he first met Platoff,[1] who

---

[1] Scott acknowledges, in a note to *St. Ronan's Well* (chap. xv.), that he

seemed to take a great fancy to him, though, adds my friend, "I really don't think they had any common language to converse in." Next day, however, when Pringle and Scott were walking together in the Rue de la Paix, the Hetman happened to come up, cantering with some of his Cossacks; as soon as he saw Scott, he jumped off his horse, leaving it to the Pulk, and, running up to him, kissed him on each side of the cheek with extraordinary demonstrations of affection — and then made him understand, through an aide-de-camp, that he wished him to join his staff at the next great review, when he would take care to mount him on the gentlest of his Ukraine horses.

It will seem less surprising that Scott should have been honored with much attention by the leading soldiers and statesmen of Germany then in Paris. The fame of his poetry had already been established for some years in that country. Yet it may be doubted whether Blücher had heard of Marmion any more than Platoff; and old Blücher struck Scott's fellow-travellers as taking more interest in him than any foreign general, except only the Hetman.

A striking passage in Paul's 10th letter indicates the high notion which Scott had formed of the personal qualities of the Prince of Orange. After depicting, with almost prophetic accuracy, the dangers to which the then recent union of Holland and Belgium must be exposed, he concludes with expressing his hope that the firmness and sagacity of the King of the Netherlands, and the admiration which his heir's character and bearing had already excited among all, even Belgian observers, might

took from Platoff this portrait of Mr. Touchwood: "His face, which at the distance of a yard or two seemed hale and smooth, appeared, when closely examined, to be seamed with a million of wrinkles, crossing each other in every direction possible, but as fine as if drawn by the point of a very small needle." Thus did every little peculiarity remain treasured in his memory, to be used in due time for giving the air of minute reality to some imaginary personage.

ultimately prove effective in redeeming this difficult experiment from the usual failure of "*arrondissements*, in-
demnities, and all the other terms of modern date, under
sanction of which cities and districts, and even kingdoms,
have been passed from one government to another, as
the property of lands or stock is transferred by a bargain
between private parties."

It is not less curious to compare, with the subsequent
course of affairs in France, the following brief hint in
Paul's 16th letter: "The general rallying point of the
Libéralistes is an avowed dislike to the present monarch
and his immediate connections. They will sacrifice, they
pretend, so much to the general inclinations of Europe,
as to select a king from the Bourbon race; but he must
be one of their own choosing, and the Duke of Orleans
is most familiar in their mouths." Thus, in its very
bud, had his eye detected the *conjuration de quinze ans!*

Among the gay parties of this festive period, Scott
mentioned with special pleasure one fine day given to an
excursion to Ermenonville, under the auspices of Lady
Castlereagh. The company was a large one, including
most of the distinguished personages whom I have been
naming, and they dined *al fresco* among the scenes of
Rousseau's retirement, but in a fashion less accordant
with the spirit of his *rêveries d'un promeneur solitaire*,
than with the song which commemorates some earlier
tenants of that delicious valley, —

> " La belle Gabrielle
>   Etoit dans ces lieux —
>   Et le souvenir d'elle
>   Nous rend heureux," etc.

At some stage of this merry day's proceedings, the
ladies got tired of walking, and one of Lord Castlereagh's
young diplomatists was despatched into a village in quest
of donkeys for their accommodation. The *attaché* returned by and by with a face of disappointment, complaining that the charge the people made was so extrava-

gant, he could not think of yielding to the extortion.
"*Marshal Forwards*" said nothing, but nodded to an
aide-de-camp. They had passed a Prussian picket a little
while before; — three times the requisite number of donkeys appeared presently, driven before half-a-dozen hussars, who were followed by the screaming population of
the refractory hamlet; and "an angry man was Blücher,"
said Scott, "when Lord Castlereagh condescended to go
among them, all smiles, and sent them back with more
Napoleons than perhaps the fee-simple of the whole stud
was worth."

Another evening of more peaceful enjoyment has left
a better record. But I need not quote here the lines on
Saint Cloud.[1] They were sent, on the 16th of August,
to the late Lady Alvanley, with whom and her daughters
he spent much of his time while in Paris.

As yet, the literary reputation of Scott had made but
little way among the French nation; but some few of
their eminent men vied even with the enthusiastic Ger-
mans in their courteous and unwearied attentions to him.
The venerable *Chevalier*, in particular, seemed anxious
to embrace every opportunity of acting as his cicerone;
and many mornings were spent in exploring, under his
guidance, the most remarkable scenes and objects of
historical and antiquarian interest both in Paris and its
neighborhood. He several times also entertained Scott
and his young companions at dinner; but the last of
those dinners was thoroughly poisoned by a preliminary
circumstance. The poet, on entering the saloon, was
presented to a stranger, whose physiognomy struck him
as the most hideous he had ever seen; nor was his disgust lessened, when he found, a few minutes afterwards,
that he had undergone the *accolade* of David "of the
blood-stained brush."

From Paris, Mr. Bruce and Mr. Pringle went on to

[1] See *Poetical Works* (Edin. Ed.), vol. xi. p. 295 [Cambridge Ed.
p. 420].

Switzerland, leaving the poet and Gala to return home together, which they did by way of Dieppe, Brighton, and London. It was here, on the 14th of September, that Scott had that last meeting with Lord Byron, alluded to in his communication to Mr. Moore, already quoted. He carried his young friend in the morning to call on Lord Byron, who agreed to dine with them at their hotel, where he met also Charles Mathews and Daniel Terry. The only survivor of the party [1] has recorded it in his note-book as the most interesting day he ever spent. "How I did stare," he says, "at Byron's beautiful pale face, like a spirit's — good or evil. But he was *bitter* — what a contrast to Scott! Among other anecdotes of British prowess and spirit, Scott mentioned that a young gentleman —— —— —— had been awfully shot in the head while conveying an order from the Duke, and yet staggered on, and delivered his message when at the point of death. ' Ha! ' said Byron, ' I dare say he could do as well as most people without his head — it was never of much use to him.' Waterloo did not delight him, probably — and Scott could talk or think of scarcely anything else."

Mathews accompanied them as far as Warwick and Kenilworth, both of which castles the poet had seen before, but now reëxamined with particular curiosity. They spent a night at Sheffield; and early next morning Scott sallied forth to provide himself with a planter's knife of the most complex contrivance and finished workmanship. Having secured one to his mind, and which for many years after was his constant pocket-companion, he wrote his name on a card, "Walter Scott, Abbotsford," and directed it to be engraved on the handle. On his mentioning this acquisition at breakfast, young Gala expressed his desire to equip himself in like fashion, and was directed to the shop accordingly. When he had

---

[1] John Scott, Esq., of Gala, died at Edinburgh, 19th April, 1840. — (1842.)

purchased a similar knife, and produced his name in turn
for the engraver, the master cutler eyed the signature
for a moment, and exclaimed, "John Scott of Gala!
Well, I hope your ticket may serve me in as good stead
as another Mr. Scott's has just done. Upon my word,
one of my best men, an honest fellow from the North,
went out of his senses when he saw it — he offered me
a week's work if I would let him keep it to himself —
and I took *Saunders* at his word." Scott used to talk
of this as one of the most gratifying compliments he ever
received in his literary capacity.

Their next halt was at Rokeby; but since Scott had
heard from thence, Mrs. Morritt's illness had made such
alarming progress, that the travellers regretted having
obtruded themselves on the scene of affliction, and resumed their journey early next morning.

Reaching Abbotsford, Scott found with his family his
old friend Mr. Skene of Rubislaw, who had expected
him to come home sooner, and James Ballantyne, who
had arrived with a copious budget of bills, calendars,
booksellers' letters, and proof sheets. From each of
these visitors' *memoranda* I now extract an anecdote.
Mr. Skene's is of a small enough matter, but still it
places the man so completely before myself, that I am
glad he thought it worth setting down.

"During Scott's absence," says his friend, "his wife had
had the tiny drawing-room of the cottage fitted up with new
chintz furniture, — everything had been set out in the best style,
— and she and her girls had been looking forward to the pleasure which they supposed the little surprise of the arrangements
would give him. He was received in the spruce fresh room,
set himself comfortably down in the chair prepared for him,
and remained in the full enjoyment of his own fireside, and
a return to his family circle, without the least consciousness
that any change had taken place — until, at length, Mrs. Scott's
patience could hold out no longer, and his attention was expressly called to it. The vexation he showed at having caused

such a disappointment, struck me as amiably characteristic —
and in the course of the evening he every now and then threw
out some word of admiration to reconsole *mamma*."

Ballantyne's note of their next morning's conference is
in these terms : —

"He had just been reviewing a pageant of emperors and
kings, which seemed, like another Field of the Cloth of Gold,
to have been got up to realize before his eyes some of his own
splendid descriptions. I begged him to tell me what was the
general impression left on his mind. He answered, that he
might now say he had seen and conversed with all classes of
society, from the palace to the cottage, and including every
conceivable shade of science and ignorance — but that he had
never felt awed or abashed except in the presence of one man
— the Duke of Wellington. I expressed some surprise. He
said I ought not, for that the Duke of Wellington possessed
every one mighty quality of the mind in a higher degree than
any other man did, or had ever done. He said he beheld in
him a great soldier and a great statesman — the greatest of
each. When it was suggested that the Duke, on his part, saw
before him a great poet and novelist, he smiled, and said,
'What would the Duke of Wellington think of a few *bits of
novels*, which perhaps he had never read, and for which the
strong probability is that he would not care a sixpence if he
had?' You are not" (adds Ballantyne) "to suppose that he
looked either sheepish or embarrassed in the presence of the
Duke — indeed you well know that he did not, and could not
do so ; but the feeling, qualified and modified as I have described it, unquestionably did exist to a certain extent. Its
origin forms a curious moral problem ; and may probably be
traced to a secret consciousness, which he might not himself
advert to, that the Duke, however great as a soldier and statesman, was so defective in imagination as to be incapable of
appreciating that which had formed the charm of his own life,
as well as of his works."

It is proper to add to Mr. Ballantyne's solution of his
"curious moral problem," that he was in his latter days
a strenuous opponent of the Duke of Wellington's poli-

tics; to which circumstance he ascribes, in these same
memoranda, the only coolness that ever occurred between
him and Scott. I need hardly repeat, what has been
already distinctly stated more than once, that Scott never
considered any amount of literary distinction as entitled
to be spoken of in the same breath with mastery in the
higher departments of practical life — least of all, with
the glory of a first-rate captain. To have done things
worthy to be written was in his eyes a dignity to which
no man made any approach, who had only written things
worthy to be read. He on two occasions, which I can
never forget, betrayed painful uneasiness when his works
were alluded to as reflecting honor on the age that had
produced Watt's improvement of the steam-engine, and
the safety-lamp of Sir Humphry Davy. Such was his
modest creed — but from all I ever saw or heard of his
intercourse with the Duke of Wellington, I am not disposed to believe that he partook it with the only man in
whose presence he ever felt awe and abashment.[1]

A charming page in Mr. Washington Irving's Abbotsford and Newstead affords us another anecdote connected
with this return from Paris. Two years after this time,
when the amiable American visited Scott, he walked
with him to a quarry, where his people were at work.

" The face of the humblest dependent," he says, " brightened
at his approach — all paused from their labor to have a plea-

---

[1] I think it very probable that Scott had his own first interview with
the Duke of Wellington in his mind when he described the introduction of
Roland Græme to the Regent Murray, in the novel of *The Abbot*, chap.
xviii. : — " Such was the personage before whom Roland Græme now presented himself with a feeling of breathless awe. very different from the
usual boldness and vivacity of his temper. In fact, he was, from education and nature, . . . much more easily controlled by the moral superiority
arising from the elevated talents and renown of those with whom he conversed, than by pretensions founded only on rank or external show. He
might have braved with indifference the presence of an Earl merely distinguished by his belt and coronet; but he felt overawed in that of the
eminent soldier and statesman, the wielder of a nation's power, and the
leader of her armies."

sant 'crack wi' the laird.' Among the rest was a tall straight old fellow, with a healthful complexion and silver hairs, and a small round-crowned white hat. He had been about to shoulder a hod, but paused, and stood looking at Scott with a slight sparkling of his blue eye as if waiting his turn ; for the old fellow knew he was a favorite. Scott accosted him in an affable tone, and asked for a pinch of snuff. The old man drew forth a horn snuff-box. ' Hoot man,' said Scott, ' not that old mull. Where 's the bonnie French one that I brought you from Paris ? ' — ' Troth, your honor,' replied the old fellow, ' sic a mull as that is nae for week-days.' On leaving the quarry, Scott informed me, that, when absent at Paris, he had purchased several trifling articles as presents for his dependents, and, among others, the gay snuff-box in question, which was so carefully reserved for Sundays by the veteran. ' It was not so much the value of the gifts,' said he, ' that pleased them, as the idea that the laird should think of them when so far away.' "

One more incident of this return — it was told to me by himself, some years afterwards, with gravity, and even sadness. "The last of my chargers," he said, "was a high-spirited and very handsome one, by name Daisy, all over white, without a speck, and with such a mane as Rubens delighted to paint. He had, among other good qualities, one always particularly valuable in my case, that of standing like a rock to be mounted. When he was brought to the door, after I came home from the Continent, instead of signifying, by the usual tokens, that he was pleased to see his master, he looked askant at me like a devil; and when I put my foot in the stirrup, he reared bolt upright, and I fell to the ground rather awkwardly. The experiment was repeated twice or thrice, always with the same result. It occurred to me that he might have taken some capricious dislike to my dress; and Tom Purdie, who always falls heir to the white hat and green jacket, and so forth, when Mrs. Scott has made me discard a set of garments, was sent for, to try whether these habiliments would produce him a similar reception from his old friend Daisy: but Daisy allowed Tom to back him with all manner of gentleness. The thing was inexplicable — but he had certainly taken some part of my conduct in high dudgeon and disgust; and after trying him again, at the interval of a week, I was obliged to part with Daisy — and wars and rumors of wars being over, I resolved thenceforth to have done with such dainty blood. I now stick to a good sober cob." ·Somebody suggested that Daisy might have considered himself as ill-used, by being left at home when *the laird* went on his journey. "Ay," said he, "these creatures have many thoughts of their own, no doubt, that we can never penetrate." Then, laughing, "Troth," said he, "maybe some bird had whispered Daisy that I had been to see the grand reviews at Paris on a little scrag of a Cossack, while my own gallant trooper was left behind bearing Peter and the post-bag to Melrose."

A few letters, written shortly after this return to Abbotsford, will, among other things, show with what zeal he at once resumed his literary industry, if indeed that can be said to have been at all interrupted by a journey, in the course of which a great part of Paul's narrative, and also of the poem of The Field of Waterloo, must have been composed.

TO J. B. S. MORRITT, ESQ., M. P., ROKEBY PARK.

ABBOTSFORD, 2d October, 1815.

MY DEAR MORRITT, — Few things could have given me more real pain, than to see Mrs. Morritt under such severe suffering, and the misery you sustain in witnessing it. Yet let us trust in the goodness of Providence, which restored the health so deservedly dear to you, from as great a state of depression upon a former occasion. Our visit was indeed a melancholy one, and, I fear, added to your distress, when, God knows, it required no addition. — The contrast of this quiet bird's-nest of a place, with the late scene of confusion and military splendor which I have witnessed, is something of a stun-

ning nature — and, for the first five or six days, I have
been content to fold my hands, and saunter up and down
in a sort of indolent and stupefied tranquillity, my only
attempt at occupation having gone no farther than prun-
ing a young tree now and then. Yesterday, however,
and to-day, I began, from necessity, to prune verses, and
have been correcting proofs of my little attempt at a
poem on Waterloo. It will be out this week, and you
shall have a copy by the Carlisle coach, which pray judge
favorably, and remember it is not always the grandest
actions which are best adapted for the arts of poetry and
painting. I believe I shall give offence to my old friends
the Whigs, by not condoling with Buonaparte. Since
his sentence of transportation, he has begun to look wonderfully comely in their eyes. I would they had hanged
him, that he might have died a perfect Adonis. Every
reasonable creature must think the Ministers would have
deserved the cord themselves, if they had left him in a
condition again to cost us the loss of 10,000 of our best
and bravest, besides thirty millions of good money. The
very threats and frights which he has given the well-
meaning people of this realm (myself included), deserved
no less a punishment than banishment, since the "putting
in bodily fear " makes so material a part of every criminal indictment. But, no doubt, we shall see Ministers
attacked for their want of generosity to a fallen enemy,
by the same party who last year, with better grounds,
assailed them for having left him in a situation again to
disturb the tranquillity of Europe. — My young friend
Gala has left me, after a short visit to Abbotsford. He
is my nearest (conversible) neighbor, and I promise myself much comfort in him, as he has a turn both for the
sciences and for the arts, rather uncommon among our
young Scotch lairds. He was delighted with Rokeby and
its lord, though he saw both at so melancholy a period,
and endured, not only with good-humor but with sympathy, the stupidity of his fellow-traveller, who was not by

any means *dans son brillant* for some time after leaving
you.

We visited Corby Castle on our return to Scotland,
which remains, in point of situation, as beautiful as when
its walks were celebrated by David Hume, in the only
rhymes he was ever known to be guilty of. Here they
are, from a pane of glass in an inn at Carlisle: —

> " Here chicks in eggs for breakfast sprawl,
> Here godless boys God's glories squall,
> Here Scotchmen's heads do guard the wall,
> But Corby's walks atone for all."

Would it not be a good quiz to advertise *The Poetical
Works of David Hume*, with notes, critical, historical,
and so forth — with an historical inquiry into the use of
eggs for breakfast, a physical discussion on the causes
of their being addled; a history of the English Church
music, and of the choir of Carlisle in particular; a full
account of the affair of 1745, with the trials, last
speeches, and so forth, of the poor *plaids* who were
strapped up at Carlisle; and, lastly, a full and particular
description of Corby, with the genealogy of every family
who ever possessed it? I think, even without more than
the usual waste of margin, the Poems of David would
make a decent twelve-shilling touch. I shall think about
it when I have exhausted mine own *century of inven-
tions*.

I do not know whether it is perverseness of state, or
old associations, but an excellent and very handsome modern house, which Mr. Howard has lately built at Corby,
does not, in my mind, assimilate so well with the scenery
as the old irregular monastic hall, with its weather-beaten
and antique appearance, which I remember there some
years ago.

Out of my Field of Waterloo has sprung an odd wild
sort of thing, which I intend to finish separately, and
call it The Dance of Death.[1] These matters take up my

---

[1] This was published in the *Edinburgh Annual Register* in 1815. — See
Poetical Works (Ed. 1834), vol. xi. p. 297 [Cambridge Ed. p. 421].

time so much, that I must bid you adieu for the present.
Besides, I am summoned to attend a grand *chasse*, and
I see the children are all mounted upon the ponies. By
the way, Walter promises to be a gallant horseman. Ever
most truly yours,   WALTER SCOTT.

I shall close this chapter with a transcript of some
Notes on the proof sheets of The Field of Waterloo.
John Ballantyne being at Abbotsford on the 3d of October, his brother the printer addressed the packet containing the sheets to him. John appears to have considered
James's observations on the margin before Scott saw
them; and the record of the style in which the Poet repelled, or yielded to, his critics, will at all events illustrate his habitual good-nature.

John Ballantyne writes on the fly-leaf of the proofs,
to his confidential clerk: "Mr. Hodgson, I beg these
sheets and all the MS. may be carefully preserved just
as they stand, and put in my father's desk. J. B."

James prefaces his animadversions with this quotation:—

> " Cut deep and spare not. — *Penruddock*."

The *Notes* are these:—

STANZA I. — " Fair Brussels, thou art far behind."

James Ballantyne. — I do not like this line. It is tame, and the phrase
" far behind," has, to my feeling, some associated vulgarity.
Scott. — Stet.

STANZA II. — " Let not *the* stranger with disdain
                  The architecture view."

James. — These two words are cacophonous. Would not *its* do ?
Scott. — Th. is a bad sound. Ts. a much worse. Read *their*.

STANZA IV. — " A stranger might reply."

James. — My objection to this is probably fantastical, and I state it only
because, from the first moment to the last, it has always made me boggle.
I don't like *a stranger* — Query, " The questioned " — The " spectator "
— " gazer," etc.
Scott. — *Stranger* is appropriate — it means stranger to the circumstances.

STANZA VI. — *James.* — You had changed "garner-house profound," which I think quite admirable, to "garner under ground," which I think quite otherways. I have presumed not to make the change — must I ?

Scott. — I acquiesce, but with doubts ; *profound* sounds affected.

STANZA VIII. — " The deadly tug of war at length
　　　　　　Must limits find in human strength,
　　　　　　And *cease* when these are passed.
　　　　　　Vain hope ! " etc.

James. — I must needs repeat, that the deadly tug *did* cease in the case supposed. It lasted long — very long ; but, when the limits of resistance, of human strength, were past — that is, after they had fought for ten hours, then the deadly tug *did* cease. Therefore the " hope " was not " vain."

Scott. — I answer, it did *not*, — because the observation relates to the strength of those actually engaged, and when *their* strength was exhausted, other squadrons were brought up. Suppose you saw two lawyers scolding at the bar, you might say this must have an end — human lungs cannot hold out — but, if the debate were continued by the senior counsel, your well-grounded expectations would be disappointed — " Cousin, thou wert not wont to be so dull ! " —

IBID. — " Nor ceased the *intermitted* shot."

James. — Mr. Erskine contends that " intermitted " is redundant.
Scott. — " Nor ceased the *storm of shell and shot.*"

STANZA X. — " —— Never shall our country say
　　　　　　We gave one inch of ground away,
　　　　　　When battling for her right."

James. — *In conflict ?*
John B. — *Warring ?* I am afraid *battling* must stand.
Scott. — All worse than the text.

STANZA XI. — " Peal'd wildly the imperial name."

James. — I submit with diffidence whether this be not a somewhat tame conclusion to so very animated a stanza ? And, at any rate, you will observe, that as it stands, you have no rhyme whatever to " The Cohort eagles *fly.*" — You have no rhyme to *fly*. *Flew* and *fly*, also, are perhaps too near, considering that each word closes a line of the same sort. I don't well like " *Thus* in a torrent," either. If it were, " In one broad torrent," etc., it strikes me that it would be more spirited.

Scott. — Granted as to most of these observations — Read, " in one *dark* torrent broad and strong," etc. — The " imperial name " is *true*, therefore must stand.

STANZA XII. — " Nor was one forward footstep *stopped.*"

James. — This staggering word was intended, I presume, but I don't like it.

Scott. — Granted. Read *staid*, etc.

IBID. — " Down were the eagle banners sent,
Down, down the horse and horsemen went."

James. — This is very spirited and very fine ; but it is unquestionably liable to the charge of being very nearly a direct repetition of yourself. See *Lord of the Isles*, Canto vi. Stanza 24 : —

" *Down! down!* in headlong overthrow,
Horseman and horse, the foremost go," etc.

This passage is at once so striking and so recent, that its close similarity to the present, if not indeed its identity, must strike every reader ; and really, to borrow from one's self is hardly much better than to borrow from one's neighbors. And yet again, a few lines lower —

" As hammers on the *anvils* reel,
Against the cuirass *clangs* the steel."

See *Lady of the Lake*, Canto vi. Stanza 18 : —

" I heard the broadswords' deadly *clang*,
As if an hundred *anvils* rang."

Here is precisely the same image, in very nearly the same words.

Scott. — I have altered the expression, but made a note, which, I think, will vindicate my retaining the simile.

STANZA XIII. — " As their own Ocean-rocks hold *stance*."

John. — I do not know such an English word as *stance*.
Scott. — Then we 'll make it one for the *nance*.

IBID. — " And *newer* standards fly."

James. — I don't like *newer*.
Scott. — " And *other* standards fly."

IBID. — " Or can thy memory fail to *quote*,
Heard to thy cost the vengeful note."

James. — Would to God you would alter this *quote* !
John. — Would to God *I* could ! — I certainly should. —
Scott. — " Or can thy memory fail to know,
Heard oft before in hour of woe."
Or —

" Or dwells not in thy memory still,
Heard frequent in thine hour of ill."

STANZA XV. — " Wrung forth by pride, *regret*, and shame."

James. — I have ventured to submit to your choice —

" Wrung forth by pride, *and rage*, and shame."

Regret appearing a faint epithet amidst such a combination of bitter feelings.
Scott. — Granted.

IBID. — " So mingle banner, wain, and gun,
  Where in one tide of horror run
  The warriors," etc.

James. — In the first place, warriors *running* in a tide is a clashing metaphor; in the second, the warriors *running* at all is a little homely. It is true, no doubt; but really running is little better than scampering. For these causes, one or both, I think the lines should be altered.

Scott. — You are wrong in one respect. A tide is always said to *run*, — but I thought of the tide without attending to the equivoque, which must be altered. Read, —

  " Where the tumultuous flight rolls on."

STANZA XVI. — " —— found *gallant* grave."

James. — This is surely a singular epithet to a grave. I think the whole of this stanza eminently fine ; and, in particular, the conclusion.
Scott. — " —— found *soldier's* grave." ——

STANZA XXI. — " *Redoubted* Picton's soul of fire."

James. — From long association, this epithet strikes me as conveying a semi-ludicrous idea.
Scott. — It is here appropriate, and your objection seems merely personal to your own association.

  IBID. — " Through his friends' heart to *wound* his own."

James. — Quære — *Pierce*, or rather *stab* — *wound* is faint.
Scott. — " *Pierce.*"

STANZA XXII. — " Forgive, *brave fallen*. the imperfect lay."

James. — Don't like " brave fallen " at all ; nor " appropriate praise," three lines after. The latter in particular is prosaic.
Scott. — " Forgive, *brave dead.*"
  —— " *The dear-earned praise.*"

CHAPTER XXXVI

FIELD OF WATERLOO PUBLISHED. — REVISION OF PAUL'S LETTERS, ETC. — QUARREL AND RECONCILIATION WITH HOGG. — FOOTBALL MATCH AT CARTERHAUGH. — SONGS ON THE BANNER OF BUCCLEUCH. — DINNER AT BOWHILL. — DESIGN FOR A PIECE OF PLATE TO THE SUTORS OF SELKIRK. — LETTERS TO THE DUKE OF BUCCLEUCH, JOANNA BAILLIE, AND MR. MORRITT

1815

THE poem of The Field of Waterloo was published before the end of October; the profits of the first edition being the author's contribution to the fund raised for the relief of the widows and children of the soldiers slain in the battle. This piece appears to have disappointed those most disposed to sympathize with the author's views and feelings. The descent is indeed heavy from his Bannockburn to his Waterloo: the presence, or all but visible reality of what his dreams cherished, seems to have overawed his imagination, and tamed it into a weak pomposity of movement. The burst of pure native enthusiasm upon the *Scottish* heroes that fell around the Duke of Wellington's person bears, however, the broadest marks of the "Mighty Minstrel:" —

> " Saw gallant Miller's fading eye
> Still bent where Albyn's standards fly,
> And Cameron, in the shock of steel,
> Die like the offspring of Lochiel," etc.; —

and this is far from being the only redeeming passage. There is one, indeed, in which he illustrates what he then thought Buonaparte's poorness of spirit in adver-

sity, which always struck me as preëminently characteristic of Scott's manner of interweaving, both in prose
and verse, the moral energies with analogous natural
description, and combining thought with imagery, —

> " Or is thy soul like mountain tide,
> That, swelled by winter storm and shower,
> Rolls down in turbulence of power,
>   A torrent fierce and wide ;
> Reft of these aids, a rill obscure,
> Shrinking unnoticed, mean and poor,
>   Whose channel shows displayed
> The wrecks of its impetuous course,
> But not one symptom of the force
>   By which these wrecks were made ! "

The poem was the first upon a subject likely to be sufficiently hackneyed; and, having the advantage of coming
out in a small cheap form — (prudently imitated from
Murray's innovation with the tales of Byron, which was
the death-blow to the system of verse in quarto) — it
attained rapidly a measure of circulation above what had
been reached either by Rokeby or The Lord of the Isles.

Meanwhile the revision of Paul's Letters was proceeding; and Scott had almost immediately on his return to
Abbotsford concluded his bargain for the first edition of
a third novel — The Antiquary — to be published also in
the approaching winter. Harold the Dauntless, too, was
from time to time taken up as the amusement of *horæ
subsecivæ*. As for Scott's out-of-doors occupations of
that autumn, sufficient light will be thrown on them by
the following letter; from which it is seen that he had
now completed a rather tedious negotiation with another
bonnet-laird, and definitively added the lands of *Kaeside*
to the original estate of Abbotsford.

TO MISS JOANNA BAILLIE, HAMPSTEAD.

ABBOTSFORD, November 12, 1815.

I have been long in acknowledging your letter, my
dear friend. and yet you have not only been frequent in
my thoughts, as must always be the case, but your name

has been of late familiar in my mouth as a household word. You must know that the pinasters you had the goodness to send me some time since, which are now fit to be set out of the nursery, have occupied my mind as to the mode of disposing of them. Now, mark the event: there is in the middle of what will soon be a bank of fine young wood, a certain old gravel-pit, which is the present scene of my operations. I have caused it to be covered with better earth, and gently altered with the spade, so as, if possible, to give it the air of one of those accidental hollows which the surface of a hill frequently presents. Having arranged my ground, I intend to plant it all round with the pinasters, and other varieties of the pine species, and in the interior I will have a rustic seat, surrounded by all kinds of evergreen shrubs (laurels in particular), and all varieties of the holly and cedar, and so forth, and this is to be called and entitled *Joanna's Bower*. We are determined in the choice of our ornaments by necessity, for our ground fronts (in poetic phrase) the rising sun, or, in common language, looks to the east; and being also on the north side of the hill — (don't you shiver at the thought?) — why, to say truth, George Wynnos and I are both of opinion that nothing but evergreens will flourish there; but I trust I shall convert a present deformity into a very pretty little hobby-horsical sort of thing. It will not bear looking at for years, and that is a pity; but it will so far resemble the person from whom it takes name, that it is planted, as she has written, for the benefit as well of posterity as for the passing generation. Time and I, says the Spaniard, against any two; and fully confiding in the proverb, I have just undertaken another grand task. You must know, I have purchased a large lump of wild land, lying adjoining to this little property, which greatly more than doubles my domains. The land is said to be reasonably bought, and I am almost certain I can turn it to advantage by a little judicious expenditure; for this place is already allowed to be worth twice what it cost me; and our people here think so little of planting, and do it so carelessly, that they stare with astonishment at the alteration which well-planted woods make on the face of a country. There is, besides, a very great temptation, from the land running to within a quarter of a mile of a very sweet wild sheet of water, of which (that is, one side of it) I have every chance to become proprietor: this is a poetical circumstance not to be lost sight of, and accordingly I keep it full in my view. Amid these various avocations, past, present, and to come, I have not thought much about Waterloo, only that I am truly glad you like it. I might, no doubt, have added many curious anecdotes, but I think the pamphlet long enough as it stands, and never had any design of writing copious notes.

I do most devoutly hope Lord Byron will succeed in his proposal of bringing out one of your dramas; that he is your sincere admirer is only synonymous with his being a man of genius; and he has, I am convinced, both the power and inclination to serve the public, by availing himself of the treasures you have laid before them. Yet I long for "some yet untasted spring," and heartily wish you would take Lord B. into your counsels, and adjust, from your yet unpublished materials, some drama for the public. In such a case, I would, in your place, conceal my name till the issue of the adventure. It is a sickening thing to think how many angry and evil passions the mere name of admitted excellence brings into full activity. I wish you would consider this hint, and I am sure the result would be great gratification to the public, and to yourself that sort of satisfaction which arises from receiving proofs of having attained the mark at which you aimed. Of this last, indeed, you cannot doubt, if you consult only the voices of the intelligent and the accomplished; but the object of the dramatist is professedly to delight the public at large, and therefore I think you should make the experiment fairly.

Little Sophia is much obliged by your kind and continued recollection: she is an excellent good child, sufficiently sensible, very affectionate, not without perception of character; but the gods have not made her poetical, and I hope she will never attempt to act a part which nature has not called her to. I am myself a poet, writing to a poetess, and therefore cannot be suspected of a wish to degrade a talent, to which, in whatever degree I may have possessed it, I am indebted for much happiness: but this depends only on the rare coincidence of some talent falling in with a novelty in style and diction and conduct of story, which suited the popular taste; and were my children to be better poets than me, they would not be such in general estimation, simply because the second cannot be the first, and the first (I mean in point of date) is everything, while others are nothing, even with more intrinsic merit. I am therefore particularly anxious to store the heads of my young damsels with something better than the tags of rhymes; and I hope Sophia is old enough (young though she be) to view her little incidents of celebrity, such as they are, in the right point of view. Mrs. Scott and she are at present in Edinburgh; the rest of the children are with me in this place; my eldest boy is already a-bold horseman and a fine shot, though only about fourteen years old. I assure you I was prouder of the first black-cock he killed, than I have been of anything whatever since I first killed one myself, and that is twenty years ago. This is all stupid gossip; but, as Master Corporal Nym says, "things must be as they may:" you cannot expect grapes from thorns, or much amusement from a brain bewildered with thorn hedges at Kaeside, for such is the sonorous title of my new possession, in virtue of which I subscribe myself,

ABBOTSFORD & KAESIDE.

There is now to be mentioned a little pageant of

December, 1815, which perhaps interested *Abbotsford
and Kaeside* not very much less than the "Field of the
Cloth of Gold," as James Ballantyne calls it, of the preceding autumn. This was no other than a football match,
got up under the auspices of the Duke of Buccleuch, between the men of the Vale of Yarrow and the Burghers
of Selkirk, the particulars of which will be sufficiently
explained by an extract from Ballantyne's newspaper,
written, I can have no doubt, by the Sheriff of the Forest.
But the part taken in this solemnity by the Ettrick Shepherd reminds me of an extraordinary epistle which Scott
had received from him some months before this time,
and of the account given by Hogg himself, in one of his
autobiographies, of the manner in which Scott's kindness
terminated the alienation it refers to.

The Shepherd, being as usual in pecuniary straits,
had projected a work, to be called The Poetic Mirror, in
which should appear some piece by each popular poet of
the time, the whole to be edited by himself, and published for his benefit; and he addressed, accordingly, to
his brother bards a circular petition for their best assistance. Scott — like Byron and most of the other persons
thus applied to — declined the proposition. The letter
in which he signified his refusal has not been preserved;
— indeed it is sufficiently remarkable, that of all the
many letters which Hogg must have received from his
distinguished contemporaries, he appears to have kept
not one; but Scott's decided aversion to joint-stock adventures in authorship must have been well known ere
now to Hogg — and, at all events, nobody can suspect
that his note of refusal was meant to be an unfriendly
communication. The Shepherd, however, took some
phrase in high dudgeon, and penned an answer viru-
lently insolent in spirit and in language, accusing him of
base jealousy of his own superior natural genius. I am
not sure whether it was on this or another occasion of
the like sort, that James varied the usual formulas of

epistolary composition, by beginning with "Damned Sir," and ending, "Believe me, Sir, yours with disgust, etc.;" but certainly the performance was such that no intercourse took place between the parties for some weeks, or perhaps months, afterwards. The letter in which Hogg at length solicits a renewal of kindliness says nothing, it may be observed, of the circumstance which, according to his autobiography, confirmed by the recollection of two friends, whom he names in the letter itself (Mr. John Grieve and Mr. William Laidlaw), had really caused him to repent of his suspicions, and their outrageous expression. The fact was, that hearing, shortly after the receipt of the offensive epistle, that Hogg was confined to his lodgings, in an obscure alley of Edinburgh, called Gabriel's Road, by a dangerous illness, Scott called on Mr. Grieve to make inquiries about him, and to offer to take on himself the expenses of the best medical attendance. He had, however, cautioned the worthy hatter that no hint of this offer must reach Hogg; and, in consequence, it might perhaps be the Shepherd's feeling at the time that he should not, in addressing his lifelong benefactor, betray any acquaintance with this recent interference on his behalf. There can be no doubt, however, that he obeyed the genuine dictates of his better nature when he penned this apologetic effusion: —

TO WALTER SCOTT, ESQ., CASTLE STREET.

GABRIEL'S ROAD, February 28, 1815.

MR. SCOTT, — I think it is great nonsense for two men who are friends at heart, and who ever must be so, — indeed it is not in the nature of things that they can be otherwise, — should be professed enemies.

Mr. Grieve and Mr. Laidlaw, who were very severe on me, and to whom I was obliged to show your letter, have long ago convinced me that I mistook part of it, and that it was not me you held in such contempt, but the opinion of the public. The

idea that you might mean that (though I still think the reading
will bear either construction) has given me much pain ; for I
know I answered yours intemperately, and in a mortal rage.
I meant to have enclosed yours, and begged of you to return
mine, but I cannot find it, and am sure that some one to whom
I have been induced to show it, has taken it away. However,
as my troubles on that subject were never like to wear to an
end, I could no longer resist telling you that I am extremely
vexed about it. I desire not a renewal of our former intimacy,
for haply, after what I have written, your family would not
suffer it; but I wish it to be understood that, when we meet
by chance, we might shake hands, and speak to one another as
old acquaintances, and likewise that we may exchange a letter
occasionally, for I find there are many things which I yearn to
communicate to you, and the tears rush to my eyes when I consider that I may not.

If you allow of this, pray let me know, and if you do not,
let me know. Indeed, I am anxious to hear from you, for " as
the day of trouble is with me, so shall my strength be." To be
friends *from the teeth forwards* is common enough; but it
strikes me that there is something still more ludicrous in the
reverse of the picture, and so to be enemies — and why should
I be, *from the teeth forwards*, yours sincerely,

JAMES HOGG ?

Scott's reply was, as Hogg says, "a brief note, telling
him to think no more of the business, and come to breakfast next morning." The misunderstanding being thus
closed, they appear to have counselled and coöperated
together in the most cordial fashion, in disciplining their
rural allies for the muster of Carterhaugh — the Duke of
Buccleuch's brother-in-law, the Earl of Home, having
appointed the Shepherd his Lieutenant over the Yarrow
Band, while the Sheriff took under his special cognizance
the *Sutors*, i. e., *shoemakers*, of Selkirk — for so the bur-
gesses of that town have for ages styled themselves, and
under that denomination their warlike prowess in days
of yore has been celebrated in many an old ballad, besides the well-known one which begins with

" 'T is up wi' the Sutors o' Selkirk,
    And 't is down wi' the Earl of Home ! "

In order to understand all the allusions in the newspaper
record of this important day, one must be familiar with
the notes to the Minstrelsy of the Scottish Border; but
I shall not burden it with further comment here.

FOOTBALL MATCH.

"On Monday, 4th December, there was played, upon the
extensive plain of Carterhaugh, near the junction of the Ettrick
and Yarrow, the greatest match at the ball which has taken
place for many years. It was held by the people of the Dale
of Yarrow, against those of the parish of Selkirk ; the former
being brought to the field by the Right Hon. the Earl of Home,
and the Gallant Sutors by their Chief Magistrate, Ebenezer
Clarkson, Esq. Both sides were joined by many volunteers
from other parishes ; and the appearance of the various parties
marching from their different glens to the place of rendezvous,
with pipes playing and loud acclamations, carried back the
coldest imagination to the old times when the Foresters assembled with the less peaceable purpose of invading the English
territory, or defending their own. The romantic character of
the scenery aided the illusion, as well as the performance of a
feudal ceremony previous to commencing the games.

" His Grace the Duke of Buccleuch and Queensberry came
upon the ground about eleven o'clock, attended by his sons, the
young Earl of Dalkeith and Lord John Scott; the Countess of
Home ; the Ladies Anne, Charlotte, and Isabella Scott; Lord
and Lady Montagu and family ; the Hon. General Sir Edward Stopford, K. B. ; Sir John Riddell of Riddell ; Sir Alexander Don of Newton ; Mr. Elliot Lockhart, member for the
county ; Mr. Pringle of Whytbank, younger ; Mr. Pringle of
Torwoodlee ; Captain Pringle, Royal Navy ; Mr. Boyd of
Broadmeadows and family ; Mr. Chisholm of Chisholm ; Major
Pott of Todrig ; Mr. Walter Scott, Sheriff of Selkirkshire, and
family, — and many other gentlemen and ladies. — The ancient
banner of the Buccleuch family, a curious and venerable relique,
emblazoned with armorial bearings, and with the word ' Bellen-
daine,' the ancient war-cry of the clan of Scott, was then dis-

played, as on former occasions when the Chief took the field in person, whether for the purpose of war or sport. The banner was delivered by Lady Anne Scott to Master Walter Scott, younger of Abbotsford, who attended suitably mounted and armed, and riding over the field displayed it to the sound of the war-pipes, and amid the acclamations of the assembled spectators, who could not be fewer than 2000 in number. That this singular renewal of an ancient military custom might not want poetical celebrity, verses were distributed among the spectators, composed for the occasion by Mr. Walter Scott and the Ettrick Shepherd. — Mr. James Hogg acted as aide-de-camp to the Earl of Home in the command of the Yarrow men, and Mr. Robert Henderson of Selkirk to Mr. Clarkson, both of whom contributed not a little to the good order of the day.

"The ball was thrown up between the parties by the Duke of Buccleuch, and the first game was gained, after a severe conflict of an hour and a half duration, by the Selkirk men. The second game was still more severely contested, and after a close and stubborn struggle of more than three hours, with various fortune, and much display of strength and agility on both sides, was at length carried by the Yarrow men. The ball should then have been thrown up a third time, but considerable difficulty occurred in arranging the voluntary auxiliaries from other parishes, so as to make the match equal ; and, as the day began to close, it was found impossible to bring the strife to an issue, by playing a decisive game.

"Both parties, therefore, parted with equal honors, but, before they left the ground, the Sheriff threw up his hat, and in Lord Dalkeith's name and his own, challenged the Yarrow men, on the part of the Sutors, to a match to be played upon the first convenient opportunity, with 100 picked men only on each side. The challenge was mutually accepted by Lord Home, on his own part, and for Lord John Scott, and was received with acclamation by the players on both sides. The principal gentlemen present took part with one side or other, except the Duke of Buccleuch, who remains neutral. Great play is expected, and all bets are to be paid by the losers to the poor of the winning parish. We cannot dismiss the subject without giving our highest commendation to the Earl of Home, and to Mr. Clarkson, for the attention which they showed in promoting the spirit and good order of the day. For the players themselves, it was impossible to see a finer set of active and athletic young fellows than appeared on the field. But what we chiefly admired in their conduct was, that though several hundreds in number, exceedingly keen for their respective parties, and engaged in so rough and animated a contest, they maintained the most perfect good-humor, and showed how unnecessary it is to discourage manly and athletic exercises among the common people, under pretext of maintaining subordination and good order. We have only to regret that the great concourse of spectators rendered it difficult to mention the names of the several players who distinguished themselves by feats of strength or agility; but we must not omit to record that the first ball was *hailed* by Robert Hall, mason in *Selkirk*, and the second by George Brodie, from *Greatlaws*, upon *Aillwater*.

" The Selkirk party wore slips of fir as their mark of distinction — the Yarrow men, sprigs of heath.

" Refreshments were distributed to the players by the Duke of Buccleuch's domestics, in a booth erected for the purpose; and no persons were allowed to sell ale or spirits on the field.

" In the evening there was a dance at the Duke's hunting-seat at Bowhill, attended by the nobility and gentry who had witnessed the sport of the day; and the fascination of Gow's violin and band detained them in the dancing-room till the dawn of the winter morning."

The newspaper then gives the songs above alluded to — namely, Scott's Lifting of the Banner: —

" From the brown crest of Newark its summons extending,
    Our signal is waving in smoke and in flame,
And each Forester blithe, from his mountain descending,
    Bounds light o'er the heather to join in the game;
Then up with the Banner! let forest winds fan her!
She has blazed over Ettrick eight ages and more;
In sport we 'll attend her, in battle defend her,
    With heart and with hand, like our Fathers before," etc.[1]

— and that excellent ditty by Hogg, entitled The Ettrick

[1] See *Poetical Works* (Ed. 1834), vol. xi. p. 312 [Cambridge Ed. p. 424].

Garland, to the Ancient Banner of the House of Buccleuch: —

> " And hast thou here, like hermit gray,
> Thy mystic characters unroll'd,
> O'er peaceful revellers to play,
> Thou emblem of the days of old ?
> All hail ! memorial of the brave,
> The liegeman's pride, the Border's awe !
> May thy gray pennon never wave
> On sterner field than Carterhaugh ! " etc.

I have no doubt the Sheriff of the Forest was a prouder
man, when he saw his boy ride about Carterhaugh with
the pennon of Bellenden, than when Platoff mounted
himself for the imperial review of the *Champ de Mars*.
It is a pity that I should have occasion to allude, before
I quit a scene so characteristic of Scott, to another outbreak of Hogg's jealous humor.　His Autobiography informs us, that when the more distinguished part of the
company assembled on the conclusion of the sport to dine
at Bowhill, he was proceeding to place himself at a particular table — but the Sheriff seized his arm, told him
that was reserved for the nobility, and seated him at an
inferior board — "between himself and the Laird of
Harden " — the first gentleman of the clan Scott.　"The
fact is," says Hogg, "I am convinced he was sore afraid
of my getting to be too great a favorite among the young
ladies of Buccleuch!"　Who can read this, and not be
reminded of Sancho Panza and the Duchess?　And,
after all, he quite mistook what Scott had said to him;
for certainly there was, neither on this, nor on any similar occasion at Bowhill, any *high table for the nobility*,
though there was a *side-table for the children*, at which,
when the Shepherd of Ettrick was about to seat himself,
his friend probably whispered that it was reserved for
the "*little* lords and ladies, and their playmates." This
blunder may seem undeserving of any explanation; but
it is often in small matters that the strongest feelings are
most strikingly betrayed — and this story is, in exact

proportion to its silliness, indicative of the jealous feeling which mars and distorts so many of Hogg's representations of Scott's conduct and demeanor.

It appears from the account of this football match in the Edinburgh Journal, that Scott took a lead in proposing a renewal of the contest. This, however, never occurred; and that it ought not to do so had probably occurred from the first to the Duke of Buccleuch, who is mentioned as having alone abstained from laying any bets on the final issue.

When Mr. Washington Irving visited Scott two years afterwards at Abbotsford, he told his American friend that "the old feuds and local interests, and rivalries and animosities of the Scotch, still slept in their ashes, and might easily be roused; their hereditary feeling for names was still great; it was not always safe to have even the game of football between villages; — the old clannish spirit was too apt to break out."[1]

The good Duke of Buccleuch's solitary exemption from these heats of Carterhaugh might read a significant lesson to minor politicians of all parties on more important scenes. In pursuance of the same peace-making spirit, he appears to have been desirous of doing something gratifying to the men of the town of Selkirk, who had on this occasion taken the field against his Yarrow tenantry. His Grace consulted Scott about the design of a piece of plate to be presented to their community; and his letter on this weighty subject must not be omitted in the memoirs of a Sheriff of Selkirk: —

TO HIS GRACE THE DUKE OF BUCCLEUCH, ETC., BOWHILL.

EDINBURGH, Thursday.

MY DEAR LORD, — I have proceeded in my commission about the cup. It will be a very handsome one. But I am still puzzled to dispose of the birse[2] in a

---

[1] Irving's *Abbotsford and Newstead*, 1835, p. 40.
[2] A *birse*, or bunch of hog's *bristles*, forms the cognizance of the Sutors.

becoming manner. It is a most unmanageable decoration.
I tried it upright on the top of the cup; it looked like
a shaving-brush, and the goblet might be intended to
make the lather. Then I thought I had a brilliant idea.
The arms of Selkirk are a female seated on a sarcoph-
agus, decorated with the arms of Scotland, which will
make a beautiful top to the cup. So I thought of putting the birse into the lady's other hand; but, alas, it
looked so precisely like the rod of chastisement uplifted
over the poor child, that I laughed at the drawing for
half an hour. Next I tried to take off the castigatory
appearance, by inserting the bristles in a kind of handle;
but then it looked as if the poor woman had been engaged in the capacities of housemaid and child-keeper
at once, and, fatigued with her double duty, had sat
down on the wine-cooler, with the broom in one hand,
and the bairn in the other. At length, after some conference with Charles Sharpe, I have hit on a plan, which,
I think, will look very well, if tolerably executed, —
namely, to have the lady seated in due form on the top
of the lid (which will look handsome, and will be well
taken), and to have a thistle wreathed around the sar-
cophagus and rising above her head, and from the top
of the thistle shall proceed the birse. I will bring a
drawing with me, and they shall get the cup ready in the
mean time. I hope to be at Abbotsford on Monday
night, to stay for a week. My cat has eat two or three
birds, while regaling on the crumbs that were thrown for
them. This was a breach of hospitality; but *oportet
vivere* — and *micat inter omnes* — with which stolen pun,
and my respectful compliments to Lord Montagu and the
ladies, I am, very truly, your Grace's most faithful and
obliged servant,   WALTER SCOTT.

When a new burgess is admitted into their community, *the birse* passes
round with the cup of welcome, and every elder brother dips it into the
wine, and draws it through his mouth, before it reaches the happy neo-
phyte, who of course pays it similar respect.

P. S. — Under another cover, which I have just received, I send the two drawings of the front and reverse of the lid of the proposed cup. Your Grace will be so good as understand that the thistle — the top of which is garnished with the bristle — is entirely detached, in working, from the figure, and slips into a socket. The following lines are humbly suggested for a motto, being taken from an ancient Scottish canzonetta, — unless the Yarrow committee can find any better: —

> " The sutor ga'e the sow a kiss :
> Grumph ! quo' the sow, it 's a' for my birss."

Some weeks before the year 1815 closed, Mr. Morritt sustained the heaviest of domestic afflictions; and several letters on that sad subject had passed between Rokeby and Abbotsford,[1] before the date of the following : —

TO J. B. S. MORRITT, ESQ., M. P., ROKEBY PARK.

EDINBURGH, 22d December, 1815.

MY DEAR MORRITT, — While you know what satisfaction it would have given me to have seen you here, I am very sensible of the more weighty reasons which you urge for preferring to stay at Rokeby for some time. I only hope you will remember that Scotland has claims on you, whenever you shall find your own mind so far at ease as to permit you to look abroad for consolation; and if it should happen that you thought of being here about our time of vacation, I have my time then entirely at my own command, and I need not say, that as much of it as could in any manner of way contribute to your amusement, is most heartily at yours. I have myself at present the melancholy task of watching the declining health of my elder brother, Major Scott, whom, I think, you have seen.

---

[1] [A touching letter from Morritt, written shortly before his wife's death, and one of Scott's, written after that event, will be found in *Familiar Letters*, vol. i. pp. 352–354.]

My literary occupation is getting through the press the Letters of Paul, of whose lucubrations I trust soon to send you a copy. As the observations of a bystander, perhaps you will find some amusement in them, especially as I had some channels of information not accessible to every one. The recess of our courts, which takes place to-morrow, for three weeks, will give me ample time to complete this job, and also the second volume of Triermain, which is nearly finished, — a strange rude story, founded partly on the ancient northern traditions respecting the Berserkers, whose peculiar habits and fits of martial frenzy make such a figure in the Sagas. I shall then set myself seriously to The Antiquary, of which I have only a very general sketch at present; but when once I get my pen to the paper it will walk fast enough. I am sometimes tempted to leave it alone, and try whether it will not write as well without the assistance of my head as with it. A hopeful prospect for the reader. In the mean while, the snow, which is now falling so fast as to make it dubious when this letter may reach Rokeby, is likely to forward these important avocations, by keeping me a constant resident in Edinburgh, in lieu of my plan of going to Abbotsford, where I had a number of schemes in hand, in the way of planting and improving. I believe I told you I have made a considerable addition to my little farm, and extended my domains towards a wild lake, which I have a good prospect of acquiring also. It has a sort of legendary fame; for the persuasion of the solitary shepherds who approach its banks is, that it is tenanted by a very large amphibious animal called by them a water-bull, and which several of them pretend to have seen. As his dimensions greatly exceed those of an otter, I am tempted to think with Trinculo, "This is the devil, and no monster." But, after all, is it not strange, that as to almost all the lakes in Scotland, both Lowland and Highland, such a belief should prevail? and that the description popularly given uniformly corresponds with that of the hippopotamus? Is it possible, that at some remote period, that remarkable animal, like some others which have now disappeared, may have been an inhabitant of our large lakes? Certainly the vanishing of the mammoth and other animals from the face of the creation renders such a conjecture less wild than I would otherwise esteem it. It is certain we have lost the beaver, whose bones have been more than once found in our Selkirkshire bogs and marlmosses. The remains of the wild bull are very frequently found; and I have more than one skull with horns of most formidable dimensions.

About a fortnight ago we had a great football match in Selkirkshire, when the Duke of Buccleuch raised his banner (a very curious and ancient pennon) in great form. Your friend Walter was banner-bearer, dressed, like a forester of old, in green, with a green bonnet, and an eagle feather in it; and, as he was well mounted, and rode handsomely over the field, he was much admired by all his clansmen.

I have thrown these trifles together, without much hope that they will afford you amusement; but I know you will wish to know what I am about, and I have but trifles to send to those friends who interest themselves about a trifler. My present employment is watching, from time to time, the progress of a stupid cause, in order to be ready to reduce the sentence into writing, when the Court shall have decided whether Gordon of Kenmore or MacMichan of Meikleforthhead be the superior of the lands of Tarschrechan and Dalbrattie, and entitled to the feudal casualties payable forth thereof, which may amount to twopence sterling, once in half a dozen of years. Marry, sir, they make part of a freehold qualification, and the decision may wing a voter. I did not send the book you received by the Selkirk coach. I wish I could have had sense enough to send anything which could afford you consolation. I think our friend

Lady Louisa was likely to have had this attention; she has, God knows, been herself tried with affliction, and is well acquainted with the sources from which comfort can be drawn. My wife joins in kindest remembrances, as do Sophia and Walter. Ever yours affectionately,

WALTER SCOTT.

This letter is dated the 22d of December. On the 26th, John Ballantyne, being then at Abbotsford, writes to Messrs. Constable: "Paul is *all* in hand;" and an envelope, addressed to James Ballantyne on the 29th, has preserved another little fragment of Scott's playful doggerel: —

" Dear James — I 'm done, thank God, with the long yarns
  Of the most prosy of Apostles — Paul ;
  And now advance, sweet Heathen of Monkbarns,
  Step out, old quizz, as fast as I can scrawl."

CHAPTER XXXVII

PUBLICATION OF PAUL'S LETTERS TO HIS KINSFOLK. —
GUY MANNERING "TERRY-FIED." — DEATH OF MAJOR
JOHN SCOTT. — LETTERS TO THOMAS SCOTT. — PUB-
LICATION OF THE ANTIQUARY. — HISTORY OF 1814
FOR THE EDINBURGH ANNUAL REGISTER. — LETTERS
ON THE HISTORY OF SCOTLAND PROJECTED. — PUB-
LICATION OF THE FIRST TALES OF MY LANDLORD BY
MURRAY AND BLACKWOOD. — ANECDOTES BY MR.
TRAIN. — QUARTERLY REVIEW ON THE TALES. —
BUILDING AT ABBOTSFORD BEGUN. — LETTERS TO
MORRITT, TERRY, MURRAY, AND THE BALLANTYNES

1816

THE year 1815 may be considered as, for Scott's
peaceful tenor of life, an eventful one. That which followed has left almost its only traces in the successive
appearance of nine volumes, which attest the prodigal
genius, and hardly less astonishing industry of the man.
Early in January were published Paul's Letters to his
Kinsfolk, of which I need not now say more than that
they were received with lively curiosity, and general,
though not vociferous applause. The first edition was
an octavo, of 6000 copies; and it was followed, in the
course of the next two or three years, by a second and
a third, amounting together to 3000 more. The popularity of the novelist was at its height; and this admitted,
if not avowed, specimen of Scott's prose must have been
perceived, by all who had any share of discrimination, to
flow from the same pen.

Mr. Terry produced, in the spring of 1816, a dramatic

piece, entitled Guy Mannering, which met with great success on the London boards, and still continues to be a favorite with the theatrical public. What share the novelist himself had in this first specimen of what he used to call "the art of *Terryfying*," I cannot exactly say; but his correspondence shows that the pretty song of the Lullaby [1] was not his only contribution to it; and I infer that he had taken the trouble to modify the plot, and rearrange, for stage purposes, a considerable part of the original dialogue. The casual risk of discovery, through the introduction of the song which had, in the mean time, been communicated to one of his humble friends, the late Mr. Alexander Campbell,[2] editor of Albyn's Anthology — (commonly known at Abbotsford as, by way of excellence, *The Dunniewassal*,) — and Scott's suggestions on that difficulty will amuse the reader of the following letter: —

TO D. TERRY, ESQ., ALFRED PLACE, BLOOMSBURY, LONDON.

ABBOTSFORD, 18th April, 1816.

MY DEAR TERRY, — I give you joy of your promotion to the dignity of an householder, and heartily wish you all the success you so well deserve, to answer the approaching enlargement of your domestic establishment. You will find a house a very devouring monster, and that the purveying for it requires a little exertion, and a great

[1] See Scott's *Poetical Works* (Ed. 1834), vol. xi. p. 317 [Cambridge Ed. p. 425].

[2] This Mr. Campbell was the same whom the poet's mother employed to teach her boys to sing, as recorded in the Autobiographical Fragment — *ante*, vol. i. p. 44. I believe he was also the "litigious Highlander" of a story told in Irving's *Abbotsford and Newstead*, p. 57.

[In the November of this year, Scott writes to Lady Abercorn : "The only thing I have been doing of late is to write two or three songs for a poor man called Campbell. . . . He has made an immense collection of Highland airs. and I have given him words for some of them. One of them is the only good song I ever wrote — it is a fine Highland Gathering tune called *Pibroch an Donuil Dhu*, that is, the Pibroch of Donald the Black." — *Familiar Letters*, vol. i. p. 374.]

deal of self-denial and arrangement. But when there is domestic peace and contentment, all that would otherwise be disagreeable, as restraining our taste and occupying our time, becomes easy. I trust Mrs. Terry will get her business easily over, and that you will soon "dandle Dickie on your knee." — I have been at the spring circuit, which made me late in receiving your letter, and there I was introduced to a man whom I never saw in my life before, namely, the proprietor of all the Pepper and Mustard family, — in other words, the genuine Dandie Dinmont. Dandie is himself modest, and says, "he b'lives it's only the dougs that is in the buik, and no himsel'." As the surveyor of taxes was going his ominous rounds past Hyndlea, which is the abode of Dandie, his whole pack rushed out upon the man of execution, and Dandie followed them (conscious that their number greatly exceeded his return), exclaiming, "The tae hauf o' them is but whalps, man." In truth, I knew nothing of the man, except his odd humor of having only two names for twenty dogs. But there are lines of general resemblance among all these hill-men, which there is no missing; and Jamie Davidson of Hyndlea certainly looks Dandie Dinmont remarkably well. He is much flattered with the compliment, and goes uniformly by the name among his comrades, but has never read the book. Ailie used to read it to him, but it set him to sleep. All this you will think funny enough. I am afraid I am in a scrape about the song, and that of my own making; for as it never occurred to me that there was anything odd in my writing two or three verses for you, which have no connection with the novel, I was at no pains to disown them; and Campbell is just that sort of crazy creature, with whom there is no confidence, not from want of honor and disposition to oblige, but from his flighty temper. The music of *Cadil gŭ lo* is already printed in his publication, and nothing can be done with him, for fear of setting his tongue a-going. Erskine and you may consider whether you should barely acknowledge an obligation to an unknown friend, or pass the matter altogether in silence. In my opinion, my *first* idea was preferable to both, because I cannot see what earthly connection there is between the song and the novel, or how acknowledging the one is fathering the other. On the contrary, it seems to me that acknowledgment tends to exclude the idea of farther obligation than to the extent specified. I forgot also that I had given a copy of the lines to Mrs. Macleod of Macleod, from whom I had the air. But I remit the matter entirely to you and Erskine, for there must be many points in it which I cannot be supposed a good judge of. At any rate, don't let it delay your publication, and believe I shall be quite satisfied with what you think proper.

I have got from my friend Glengarry the noblest dog ever seen on the Border since Johnnie Armstrong's time. He is between the wolf and deer greyhound, about six feet long from the tip of the nose to the tail, and high and strong in proportion: he is quite gentle, and a great favorite: tell Will Erskine he will eat off his plate without being at the trouble to put a paw on the table or chair.[1] I showed him to Mathews, who dined one day in Castle Street before I came here, where, except for Mrs. S., I am like unto

---

[1] [In the letter accompanying his gift, Glengarry says: "His name is Maida, out of respect for that action in which my brother had the honor to lead the 78th Highlanders to victory." Writing to Joanna Baillie, April 12, Scott describes his new friend as "the finest dog of the kind in Scotland. . . . He is between the deer greyhound and mastiff, with a shaggy mane like a lion; he always sits beside me at dinner, his head as high as the back of my chair; yet it will gratify you to know that a favorite cat keeps him in the greatest possible order, and insists upon all rights of precedence, and scratches with impunity the nose of an animal who would make no bones of a wolf, and pulls down a red deer without fear or difficulty. I heard my friend set up some most piteous howls, and I assure you the noise was no joke, all occasioned by his fear of passing puss, who had stationed himself on the stairs." — *Familiar Letters*, vol. i. p. 358.]

"The spirit who bideth by himself,
In the land of mist and snow " — [1]

for it is snowing and hailing eternally, and will kill all the lambs to a certainty, unless it changes in a few hours. At any rate, it will cure us of the embarrassments arising from plenty and low markets. Much good luck to your dramatic exertions: when I can be of use, command me. Mrs. Scott joins me in regards to Mrs. Terry, and considers the house as the greatest possible bargain: the situation is all you can wish. Adieu! yours truly,

WALTER SCOTT.

P. S. — On consideration, and comparing difficulties, I think I will settle with Campbell to take my name from the verses, as they stand in his collection. The verses themselves I cannot take away without imprudent explanations; and as they go to other music, and stand without any name, they will probably not be noticed, so you need give yourself no farther trouble on the score. I should like to see my copy: pray send it to the post-office, under cover to Mr. Freeling, whose unlimited privilege is at my service on all occasions.

Early in May appeared the novel of The Antiquary, which seems to have been begun a little before the close of 1815. It came out at a moment of domestic distress.

Throughout the year 1815, Major John Scott had been drooping. He died on the 8th of May, 1816; and I extract the letter in which this event was announced to Mr. Thomas Scott by his only surviving brother.

TO THOMAS SCOTT, ESQ., PAYMASTER OF THE 70TH REGIMENT, CANADA.

EDINBURGH, 15th May, 1816.

MY DEAR TOM, — This brings you the melancholy news of our brother John's concluding his long and lingering illness by death, upon Thursday last. We had

[1] Coleridge — *Ancient Mariner.*

thought it impossible he should survive the winter, but, as the weather became milder, he gathered strength, and went out several times. In the beginning of the week he became worse, and on Wednesday kept his bed. On Thursday, about two o'clock, they sent me an express to Abbotsford — the man reached me at nine. I immediately set out, and travelled all night — but had not the satisfaction to see my brother alive. He had died about four o'clock, without much pain, being completely exhausted. You will naturally feel most anxious about my mother's state of health and spirits. I am happy to say she has borne this severe shock with great firmness and resignation, is perfectly well in her health, and as strong in her mind as ever you knew her. She feels her loss, but is also sensible that protracted existence, with a constitution so irretrievably broken up, could have been no blessing. Indeed I must say, that, in many respects, her situation will be more comfortable on account of this removal, when the first shock is over; for to watch an invalid, and to undergo all the changes of a temper fretted by suffering, suited ill with her age and habits. The funeral, which took place yesterday, was decent and private, becoming our father's eldest son, and the head of a quiet family. After it, I asked Hay Donaldson and Mr. Macculloch[1] to look over his papers, in case there should be any testamentary provision, but none such was found; nor do I think he had any intention of altering the destination which divides his effects between his surviving brothers. — Your affectionate   W. S.

A few days afterwards, he hands to Mr. Thomas Scott a formal statement of pecuniary affairs; the result of which was, that the Major had left something not much under £6000. Major Scott, from all I have heard, was

---

[1] The late Mr. Hay Donaldson, W. S., — an intimate friend of both Thomas and Walter Scott, — and Mr. Macculloch of Ardwell, the brother of Mrs. Thomas Scott.

a sober, sedate bachelor, of dull mind and frugal tastes, who, after his retirement from the army, divided his time between his mother's primitive fireside, and the society of a few whist-playing brother officers, that met for an evening rubber at Fortune's tavern. But, making every allowance for his retired and thrifty habits, I infer that the payments made to each of the three brothers out of their father's estate must have, prior to 1816, amounted to £5000. From the letter conveying this statement (29th May), I extract a few sentences: —

DEAR TOM, — . . . Should the possession of this sum, and the certainty that you must, according to the course of nature, in a short space of years succeed to a similar sum of £3000 belonging to our mother, induce you to turn your thoughts to Scotland, I shall be most happy to forward your views with any influence I may possess; and I have little doubt that, sooner or later, something may be done. But, unfortunately, every avenue is now choked with applicants, whose claims are very strong; for the number of disbanded officers, and public servants dismissed in consequence of Parliament turning restive and refusing the income-tax, is great and increasing. Economy is the order of the day, and I assure you they are shaving properly close. It would, no doubt, be comparatively easy to get you a better situation where you are, but then it is bidding farewell to your country, at least for a long time, and separating your children from all knowledge of those with whom they are naturally connected. I shall anxiously expect to hear from you on your views and wishes. I think, at all events, you ought to get rid of the drudgery of the paymastership — but not without trying to exchange it for something else. I do not know how it is with you — but I do not feel myself quite so *young* as I was when we met last, and I should like well to see my only brother return to his own country and settle, without thoughts of leaving it, till it is exchanged for one that is dark and distant. . . . I left all Jack's personal trifles at my mother's disposal. There was nothing of the slightest value, excepting his gold watch, which was my sister's, and a good one. My mother says he had wished my son Walter should have it, as his male representative — which I can only accept on condition *your* little Walter will accept a similar token of regard from his remaining uncle. — Yours affectionately, **W. S.**

The letter in which Scott communicated his brother's death to Mr. Morritt gives us his own original opinion of The Antiquary. It has also some remarks on the separation of Lord and Lady Byron — and the "domestic verses" of the noble poet.

TO J. B. S. MORRITT, ESQ., M. P., LONDON.

EDINBURGH, May 16, 1816.

MY DEAR MORRITT, — I have been occupied of late with scenes of domestic distress, my poor brother, Major John Scott, having last week closed a life which wasting disease had long rendered burthensome. His death, under all the circumstances, cannot be termed a subject of deep affliction; and though we were always on fraternal terms of mutual kindness and good-will, yet our habits of life, our taste for society and circles of friends, were so totally different, that there was less frequent intercourse between us than our connection and real liking to each other might have occasioned. Yet it is a heavy consideration to have lost the last but one who was interested in our early domestic life, our habits of boyhood, and our first friends and connections. It makes one look about and see how the scene has changed around him, and how he himself has been changed with it. My only remaining brother is in Canada, and seems to have an intention of remaining there; so that my mother, now upwards of eighty, has now only one child left to her

out of thirteen whom she has borne. She is a most excellent woman, possessed, even at her advanced age, of
all the force of mind and sense of duty which have carried her through so many domestic griefs, as the successive deaths of eleven children, some of them come to
men and women's estate, naturally infers. She is the
principal subject of my attention at present, and is, I
am glad to say, perfectly well in body and composed in
mind.

Nothing can give me more pleasure than the prospect
of seeing you in September, which will suit our motions
perfectly well. I trust I shall have an opportunity to
introduce you to some of our glens which you have not
yet seen. But I hope we shall have some mild weather
before that time, for we are now in the seventh month
of winter, which almost leads me to suppose that we shall
see no summer this season. As for spring, that is past
praying for. In the month of November last, people
were skating in the neighborhood of Edinburgh; and
now, in the middle of May, the snow is lying white on
Arthur's Seat, and on the range of the Pentlands. It
is really fearful, and the sheep are perishing by scores.
Jam satis terræ nivis, etc., may well be taken up as the
song of eighteen hundred and sixteen.

So Lord Byron's romance seems to be concluded for
one while — and it is surely time, after he has announced,
or rather they themselves have announced, half-a-dozen
blackguard newspaper editors, to have been his confidants
on the occasion. Surely it is a strange thirst of public
fame that seeks such a road to it. But Lord Byron,
with high genius and many points of a noble and generous feeling, has Childe Harolded himself, and outlawed
himself, into too great a resemblance with the pictures
of his imagination. He has one excuse, however, and it
is a sad one. I have been reckoned to make a good hit
enough at a pirate, or an outlaw, or a smuggling bandit;
but I cannot say I was ever so much enchanted with my

work as to think of carrying off a *drift* of my neighbor's sheep, or half a dozen of his milk cows. Only I remember, in the rough times, having a scheme with the Duke of Buccleuch, that when the worst came to the worst, we should repair Hermitage Castle, and live, like Robin Hood and his merry men, at the expense of all round us. But this presupposed a grand *bouleversement* of society. In the mean while, I think my noble friend is something like my old peacock, who chooses to bivouac apart from his lady, and sit below my bedroom window, to keep me awake with his screeching lamentation. Only I own he is not equal in melody to Lord Byron, for *Fare-thee-well — and if for ever*, etc., is a very sweet dirge indeed. After all, *C'est génie mal logé*, and that's all that can be said about it.

I am quite reconciled to your opinions on the income-tax, and am not at all in despair at the prospect of keeping £200 a year in my pocket, since the ministers can fadge without it. But their throwing the helve after the hatchet, and giving up the malt-duty because they had lost the other, was droll enough. After all, our fat friend[1] must learn to live within compass, and fire off no more crackers in the Park, for John Bull is getting dreadfully sore on all sides when money is concerned.

I sent you, some time since, The Antiquary. It is not so interesting as its predecessors — the period did not

---

[1] Shortly after Beau Brummell (immortalized in *Don Juan*) fell into disgrace with the Prince Regent, and was dismissed from the society of Carlton House, he was riding with another gentleman in the Park, when the Prince met them. His Royal Highness stopt to speak to Brummell's companion — the Beau continued to jog on — and when the other dandy rejoined him, asked with an air of sovereign indifference, "Who is your fat friend?" Such, at least, was the story that went the round of the newspapers at the time, and highly tickled Scott's fancy. I have heard that nobody enjoyed so much as the Prince of Wales himself an earlier specimen of the Beau's assurance. Taking offence at some part of His Royal Highness's conduct or demeanor, "Upon my word," observed Mr. Brummell, "if this kind of thing goes on, I shall be obliged to cut Wales and bring the old King into fashion."

admit of so much romantic situation. But it has been more fortunate than any of them in the sale, for 6000 went off in the first six days, and it is now at press again; which is very flattering to the unknown author. Another incognito proposes immediately to resume the second volume of Triermain, which is at present in the state of the Bear and Fiddle.[1] Adieu, dear Morritt.

Ever yours,   WALTER SCOTT.

Speaking of his third novel in a letter of the same date to Terry, Scott says : "It wants the romance of Waverley and the adventure of Guy Mannering; and yet there is some salvation about it, for if a man will paint from nature, he will be likely to amuse those who are daily looking at it."

After a little pause of hesitation, The Antiquary attained popularity not inferior to Guy Mannering; and though the author appears for a moment to have shared the doubts which he read in the countenance of James Ballantyne, it certainly was, in the sequel, his chief favorite among all his novels. Nor is it difficult to account for this preference, without laying any stress on the fact, that, during a few short weeks, it was pretty commonly talked of as a falling off from its immediate predecessors — and that some minor critics reëchoed this stupid whisper in print. In that view, there were many of its successors that had much stronger claims on the parental instinct of protection. But the truth is, that although Scott's Introduction of 1830 represents him as pleased with fancying that, in the principal personage, he had embalmed a worthy friend of his boyish days, his own antiquarian propensities, originating perhaps in the kind attentions of George Constable of Wallace-Craigie, and fostered not a little, at about as ductile a period, by those of old Clerk of Eldin, and John Ramsay of Ochter-tyre, had by degrees so developed themselves, that he

[1] See *Hudibras*.

could hardly, even when The Antiquary was published, have scrupled about recognizing a quaint caricature of the founder of Abbotsford Museum, in the inimitable portraiture of the Laird of Monkbarns. The Descriptive Catalogue of that collection, which he began towards the close of his life, but, alas, never finished, is entitled "Reliquiæ Trottcosianæ — or the Gabions of the late Jonathan Oldbuck, Esq."

But laying this, which might have been little more than a good-humored pleasantry, out of the question, there is assuredly no one of all his works on which more of his own early associations have left their image. Of those early associations, as his full-grown tastes were all the progeny, so his genius, in all its happiest efforts, was the "Recording Angel;" and when George Constable first expounded his "Gabions" to the child that was to immortalize his name, they were either wandering hand in hand over the field where the grass still grew rank upon the grave of *Balmawhapple*, or sauntering on the beach where the *Mucklebackets* of Prestonpans dried their nets, singing, —

> " Weel may the boatie row, and better may she speed,
> O weel may the boatie row that wins the bairns' bread " —

or telling wild stories about cliff-escapes and the funerals of shipwrecked fishermen.

Considered by itself, without reference to these sources of personal interest, this novel seems to me to possess, almost throughout, in common with its two predecessors, a kind of simple unsought charm, which the subsequent works of the series hardly reached, save in occasional snatches: like them it is, in all its humbler and softer scenes, the transcript of actual Scottish life, as observed by the man himself. And I think it must also be allowed that he has nowhere displayed his highest art, that of skilful contrast, in greater perfection. Even the tragic romance of Waverley does not set off its Macwheebles and Callum Begs better than the oddities of

Jonathan Oldbuck and his circle are relieved, on the one
hand, by the stately gloom of the Glenallans, on the other,
by the stern affliction of the poor fisherman, who, when
discovered repairing the "auld black bitch o' a boat" in
which his boy had been lost, and congratulated by his
visitor on being capable of the exertion, makes answer,
— "And what would you have me to do, unless I wanted
to see four children starve, because one is drowned?
*It 's weel wi' you gentles, that can sit in the house wi'
handkerchers at your een, when ye lose a friend; but the
like o' us maun to our wark again, if our hearts were
beating as hard as my hammer.*"

It may be worth noting, that it was in correcting the
proof sheets of this novel that Scott first took to equip-
ping his chapters with mottoes of his own fabrication.
On one occasion he happened to ask John Ballantyne,
who was sitting by him, to hunt for a particular passage
in Beaumont and Fletcher. John did as he was bid, but
did not succeed in discovering the lines. "Hang it,
Johnnie," cried Scott, "I believe I can make a motto
sooner than you will find one." He did so accordingly;
and from that hour, whenever memory failed to suggest
an appropriate epigraph, he had recourse to the inexhaust-
ible mines of "*old play*" or "*old ballad*," to which we
owe some of the most exquisite verses that ever flowed
from his pen.

Unlike, I believe, most men, whenever Scott neared
the end of one composition, his spirits seem to have
caught a new spring of buoyancy, and before the last
sheet was sent from his desk, he had crowded his brain
with the imagination of another fiction. The Antiquary
was published, as we have seen, in May, but by the
beginning of April he had already opened to the Ballantynes the plan of the first Tales of my Landlord; and —
to say nothing of Harold the Dauntless, which he began
shortly after The Bridal of Triermain was finished, and
which he seems to have kept before him for two years

as a congenial plaything, to be taken up whenever the coach brought no proof sheets to jog him as to serious matters — he had also, before this time, undertaken to write the historical department of the Register for 1814. Mr. Southey had, for reasons upon which I do not enter, discontinued his services to that work: and it was now doubly necessary, after trying for one year a less eminent hand, that if the work were not to be dropped altogether, some strenuous exertion should be made to sustain its character. Scott had not yet collected the materials requisite for his historical sketch of a year distinguished for the importance and complexity of its events; but these, he doubted not, would soon reach him, and he felt no hesitation about pledging himself to complete, not only that sketch, but four new volumes of prose romances — and his Harold the Dauntless also, if Ballantyne could make any suitable arrangement on that score — between the April and the Christmas of 1816.

The Antiquary had been published by Constable, but I presume that, in addition to the usual stipulations, he had been again, on that occasion, solicited to relieve John Ballantyne and Co.'s stock to an extent which he did not find quite convenient; and at all events he had of late shown a considerable reluctance to employ James Ballantyne and Co. as printers. One or other of these impediments is alluded to in a note of Scott's, which, though undated, has been pasted into John Ballantyne's private letter-book among the documents of the period in question. It is in these words: —

DEAR JOHN, — I have seen the great swab, who is supple as a glove, and will do ALL, which some interpret NOTHING. However, we shall do well enough.

W. S.

Constable had been admitted, almost from the beginning, into the *secret* of the Novels — and for that, among

other reasons, it would have been desirable for the Novelist to have him continue the publisher without interruption; but Scott was led to suspect, that if he were called
upon to conclude a bargain for a fourth novel before the
third had made its appearance, his scruples as to the
matter of *printing* might at least protract the treaty;
and why Scott should have been urgently desirous of
seeing the transaction settled before the expiration of
the half-yearly term of Whitsunday is sufficiently explained by the fact, that though so much of the old unfortunate stock of John Ballantyne and Co. still remained
on hand — and with it some occasional recurrence of
commercial difficulty as to floating bills was to be expected — while James Ballantyne's management of the
pecuniary affairs of the printing-house had continued to
be highly negligent and irregular [1] — nevertheless, the
sanguine author had gone on purchasing one patch of
land after another, until his estate at Abbotsford had
already grown from 150 to nearly 1000 acres.   The property all about his original farm had been in the hands
of various small holders (Scotticè *cock-lairds;*) these
persons were sharp enough to understand, erelong, that
their neighbor could with difficulty resist any temptation
that might present itself in the shape of an offer of more
acres; and thus he proceeded buying up lot after lot of
unimproved ground, at extravagant prices, — his "appetite increasing by what it fed on," while the ejected yeomen set themselves down elsewhere, to fatten at their
leisure upon the profits — most commonly the anticipated
profits — of "The Scotch Novels."

He was ever and anon pulled up with a momentary
misgiving, — and resolved that the latest acquisition
should be the last, until he could get rid entirely of
"John Ballantyne and Co."   But John Ballantyne was,

---

[1] In February, 1816, when James Ballantyne married, it is clearly proved
by letters in his handwriting, that he owed to Scott more than £3000 of
personal debt. — (1839.)

from the utter lightness of his mind, his incapacity to look a day before him, and his eager impatience to enjoy the passing hour, the very last man in the world who could, under such circumstances, have been a serviceable agent. Moreover, John, too, had his professional ambition: he was naturally proud of his connection, however secondary, with the publication of these works — and this connection, though subordinate, was still very profitable; he must have suspected, that should his name disappear altogether from the list of booksellers, it would be a very difficult matter for him to retain any concern in them; and I cannot, on the whole, but consider it as certain that, the first and more serious embarrassments being overcome, he was far from continuing to hold by his patron's anxiety for the total abolition of their unhappy copartnership. He, at all events, unless when some sudden emergency arose, flattered Scott's own gay imagination, by uniformly representing everything in the most smiling colors; and though Scott, in his replies, seldom failed to introduce some passing hint of caution — such as "*Nullum numen abest si sit prudentia*" — he more and more took home to himself the agreeable cast of his *Rigdum's* anticipations, and wrote to him in a vein as merry as his own — *e. g.* — "As for our stock,

> " 'T will be wearing awa', John,
> Like snaw-wreaths when it 's thaw, John," etc., etc., etc.

I am very sorry, in a word, to confess my conviction that John Ballantyne, however volatile and light-headed, acted at this period with cunning selfishness, both by Scott and by Constable. He well knew that it was to Constable alone that his firm had more than once owed its escape from utter ruin and dishonor; and he must also have known, that had a fair straightforward effort been made for that purpose, after the triumphant career of the Waverley series had once commenced, nothing could have been more easy than to bring all the affairs of his "back-stock," etc., to a complete close, by entering

into a distinct and candid treaty on that subject, in connection with the future works of the great Novelist,
either with Constable or with any other first-rate house
in the trade. But John, foreseeing that, were that unhappy concern quite out of the field, he must himself
subside into a mere clerk of the printing company, seems
to have parried the blow by the only arts of any consequence in which he ever was an adept. He appears to
have systematically disguised from Scott the extent to
which the whole Ballantyne concern had been sustained
by Constable — especially during his Hebridean tour of
1814, and his Continental one of 1815 — and prompted
and enforced the idea of trying other booksellers from
time to time, instead of adhering to Constable, merely
for the selfish purposes, — first, of facilitating the immediate discount of bills; — secondly, of further perplexing
Scott's affairs, the entire disentanglement of which would
have been, as he fancied, prejudicial to his own personal
importance.

It was resolved, accordingly, to offer the risk and half
profits of the first edition of another new novel — or
rather collection of novels — not to Messrs. Constable,
but to Mr. Murray of Albemarle Street, and Mr. Blackwood, who was then Murray's agent in Scotland; but it
was at the same time resolved, partly because Scott
wished to try another experiment on the public sagacity,
but partly also, no question, from the wish to spare Constable's feelings, that the title-page of the Tales of my
Landlord should not bear the magical words "By the
Author of Waverley." The facility with which both
Murray and Blackwood embraced such a proposal, as no
untried novelist, being sane, could have dreamt of hazard-
ing, shows that neither of them had any doubt as to the
identity of the author. They both considered the with-
holding of the avowal on the forthcoming title-page as
likely to check very much the first success of the book;
but they were both eager to prevent Constable's acquir-

ing a sort of prescriptive right to publish for the unrivalled novelist, and willing to disturb his tenure at this
additional, and, as they thought it, wholly unnecessary
risk.

How sharply the unseen parent watched this first negotiation of his *Jedediah Cleishbotham* will appear from
one of his letters: —

TO MR. JOHN BALLANTYNE, HANOVER STREET, EDINBURGH.

ABBOTSFORD, April 29, 1816.

DEAR JOHN, — James has made one or two important
mistakes in the bargain with Murray and Blackwood.
Briefly as follows: —

1stly, Having only authority from me to promise 6000
copies, he proposes they shall have the copyright *forever*.
I will see their noses cheese first.

2dly, He proposes I shall have twelve months' bills —
I have always got six. However, I would not stand on
that.

3dly, He talks of volumes being put into the publisher's hands to consider and decide on. No such thing;
a bare perusal at St. John Street [1] only.

Then for omissions — It is NOT stipulated that we
supply the paper and print of successive editions. This
must be nailed, and not left to understanding. — Secondly, I will have London bills as well as Blackwood's.

If they agree to these conditions, good and well. If
they demur, Constable must be instantly tried; giving
half to the Longmans, and *we* drawing on *them* for that
moiety, or Constable lodging their bill in our hands.
You will understand it is a four-volume touch — a work
totally different in style and structure from the others;
a new cast, in short, of the net which has hitherto made
miraculous draughts. I do not limit you to terms, because I think you will make them better than I can do.

[1] James Ballantyne's dwelling-house was then in this street, adjoining
the Canongate of Edinburgh.

But he must do more than others, since he will not or cannot print with us. For every point but that, I would rather deal with Constable than any one; he has always shown himself spirited, judicious, and liberal. Blackwood must be brought to the point *instantly*; and *whenever* he demurs, Constable must be treated with; for there is no use in suffering the thing to be blown on. At the same time, you need not conceal from him that there were some proposals elsewhere, but you may add, with truth, I would rather close with him. Yours truly,

W. S.

P. S. — I think Constable should jump at this affair; for I believe the work will be very popular.

Messrs. Murray and Blackwood agreed to all the author's conditions here expressed. They also relieved John Ballantyne and Co. of stock to the value of £500; and at least Mr. Murray must, moreover, have subsequently consented to anticipate the period of his payments. At all events, I find, in a letter of Scott's, dated in the subsequent August, this new echo of the old advice: —

TO MR. JOHN BALLANTYNE.

DEAR JOHN, — I have the pleasure to enclose Murray's acceptances. I earnestly recommend to you to push, realizing as much as you can.

> " Consider weel, gude man,
>   We hae but borrowed gear ;
>   The horse that I ride on,
>   It is John Murray's mear."

Yours truly,   W. SCOTT.

I know not how much of the tale of The Black Dwarf had been seen by Blackwood, in St. John Street, before he concluded this bargain for himself and his friend Murray; but when the closing sheets of that novel

reached him, he considered them as by no means sustain-
ing the delightful promise of the opening ones. He was
a man of strong talents, and, though without anything
that could be called learning, of very respectable information — greatly superior to what has, in this age, been
common in his profession; acute, earnest, eminently zealous in whatever he put his hand to; upright, honest, sincere, and courageous. But as Constable owed his first
introduction to the upper world of literature and of society in general to his Edinburgh Review, so did Blackwood his to the Magazine, which has now made his name
familiar to the world — and at the period of which I
write, that miscellany was unborn; he was known only
as a diligent antiquarian bookseller of the old town of
Edinburgh, and the Scotch agent of the great London
publisher, Murray. The abilities, in short, which he
lived to develop, were as yet unsuspected — unless, perhaps, among a small circle; and the knowledge of the
world, which so few men gather from anything but painful collision with various conflicting orders of their fel-
low-men, was not his. He was to the last plain and
blunt; at this time I can easily believe him to have been
so to a degree which Scott might look upon as "ungra-
cious" — I take the epithet from one of his letters to
James Ballantyne. Mr. Blackwood, therefore, upon
reading what seemed to him the lame and impotent conclusion of a well-begun story, did not search about for
any glossy periphrase, but at once requested James Ballantyne to inform the unknown author that such was his
opinion. This might possibly have been endured; but
Blackwood, feeling, I have no doubt, a genuine enthusiasm for the author's fame, as well as a just tradesman's
anxiety as to his own adventure, proceeded to suggest
the outline of what would, in his judgment, be a better
upwinding of the plot of The Black Dwarf, and concluded
with announcing his willingness, in case the proposed
alteration were agreed to, that the whole expense of can-

celling and reprinting a certain number of sheets should
be charged to his own account. He appears to have
further indicated that he had taken counsel with some
literary person, on whose taste he placed great reliance,
and who, if he had not originated, at least approved of
the proposed process of recasting. Had Scott never possessed any such system of inter-agency as the Ballantynes
supplied, he would, among other and perhaps greater
inconveniences, have escaped that of the want of personal
familiarity with several persons, with whose confidence,
— and why should I not add? — with the innocent gratification of whose little vanities — his own pecuniary interests were often deeply connected. A very little personal contact would have introduced such a character
as Blackwood's to the respect, nay, to the affectionate
respect, of Scott, who, above all others, was ready to
sympathize cordially with honest and able men, in whatever condition of life he discovered them. He did both
know and appreciate Blackwood better in after-times;
but in 1816, when this communication reached him, the
name was little more than a name, and his answer to
the most solemn of go-betweens was in these terms, which
I sincerely wish I could tell how Signior Aldiborontiphos-
cophornio translated into any dialect submissible to
Blackwood's apprehension: —

DEAR JAMES, — I have received Blackwood's impudent proposal. G— d— his soul! Tell him and his
coadjutor that I belong to the Black Hussars of Literature, who neither give nor receive criticism. I 'll be
cursed but this is the most impudent proposal that ever
was made.   W. S.[1]

[1] *May*, 1839. Since this book was first published, I have received
from the representatives of Mr. Blackwood several documents which throw
light on the transaction here mentioned. It will be apparent from one of
those I am about to quote, that Blackwood, before he sent his message to
Jedediah Cleishbotham, had ascertained that no less a person than Mr. Gifford concurred in his opinion — nay, that James Ballantyne himself took

While these volumes were in progress, Scott found
time to make an excursion into Perthshire and Dumbar-

the same view of the matter. But the reader will be not less amused in
comparing the "Black Hussar's" missive in the text, with the edition of
it which actually reached Blackwood — and which certainly justifies the
conjecture I had ventured to express.

TO WILLIAM BLACKWOOD, ESQ.

EDINBURGH, 4th October, 1816.

MY DEAR SIR, — Our application to the author of *Tales of my Landlord*
has been anything but successful; and in order to explain to you the reason
why I must decline to address him in this way in future, I shall copy his
answer *verbatim:* —

"My respects to our friends the Booksellers. I belong to the Death-
head Hussars of Literature, who neither *take* nor *give* criticism. I am extremely sorry they showed my work to Gifford, nor would I cancel a leaf
to please all the critics of Edinburgh and London; and so let that be as it
is: They are mistaken if they think I don't know when I am writing ill,
as well as Gifford can tell me. I beg there may be no more communications with critics."

Observe — that I shall at all times be ready to convey anything from
you to the author in a written form, but I do not feel warranted to interfere farther. Yours very truly,   J. BALLANTYNE.

TO JAMES BALLANTYNE, ESQ.

EDINBURGH, 5th October, 1816.

MY DEAR SIR, — I am not a little vexed at having ventured to suggest anything to the author of the *Tales of my Landlord*, since I find he
considers it in the light of *sutor ultra crepidam*. I never had for one moment the vanity to think, that from any poor remark of mine, or indeed of
any human being, he would be induced to blot one line or alter a single
incident, unless the same idea occurred to his own powerful mind. On
stating to you what struck me, and finding that your opinion coincided
with mine, I was induced to request of you to state it to the author, in
order that he might be aware that the expense of cancelling the sheets was
no object to me. I was the more anxious to do this, in case the author
should have given you the MS. of this portion of the work sooner than he
intended, in order to satisfy the clamoring for it which I teased you with.
I trust the author will do me the justice to believe that it is quite impossible for any one to have a higher admiration of his most extraordinary talents; and speaking merely as a bookseller, it would be quite unnecessary
to be at the expense of altering even one line, although the author himself
(who alone can be the proper judge) should wish it, as the success of the
work must be rapid, great, and certain.

With regard to the first volume having been shown to Mr. Gifford, I
must state in justification of Mr. Murray, that Mr. G. is the only friend
whom he consults on all occasions, and to whom his most secret transac-

tonshire, for the sake of showing the scenery, made
famous in The Lady of the Lake and Waverley, to his

tions are laid open. He gave him the work, not for the purpose of criticism, but that as a friend he might partake of the enjoyment he had in
such an extraordinary performance. No language could be stronger than
Mr. Gifford's, as I mentioned to you; and as the same thing had occurred
to Mr. G. as to you and me, you thought there would be no harm in stating this to the author.

I have only again to express my regret at what has taken place, and
to beg you will communicate this to the author in any way you may think
proper. Yours, etc.,   W. BLACKWOOD.

[A much fuller and more accurate knowledge of this whole transaction, than that possessed by Lockhart, can be gathered from the annals of
the two great publishing houses concerned in it; — Smiles's *Memoir of John
Murray* (vol. i chap. xviii.), and Mrs. Oliphant's *William Blackwood and
his Sons* (vol. i. pp. 56–92), especially from the latter work, in which the
whole incident is set in its proper light. Notwithstanding the heavy
preliminary tax for unsalable books from the Ballantynes' "wretched
stock," neither publisher seems to have had a moment's doubt as to the
acceptance of the offer of the ostensibly anonymous Work of Fiction,
though they were much fretted by the delays, uncertainties, and mysteries
attending the matter. "One in business must submit to many things, and
swallow many a bitter pill, when such a man as Walter Scott is the object
in view," writes Blackwood to Murray, — the bitterness being largely the
dealing with James Ballantyne. "John I always considered as no better
than a swindler, but James I put some trust and confidence in. You
judged him more accurately." . . . And on another occasion, — "Except
my wife, there is not a friend whom I dare advise with. I have not ventured to mention the business to my brother on account of the cursed mysteries and injunctions of secrecy connected with it. I know he would
blame me for engaging in it, for he has a very small opinion of the Ballantynes." Apart from the vexations attending their office as intermedia-
ries, for which the Ballantynes were only partially responsible, this shrewd,
if irritated, observer appears to have formed opinions of the brothers as
business men, in some respects not differing greatly from those held by
Lockhart in later days.

The delight of the two publishers in at last receiving the MS. of *The
Black Dwarf* and the manner in which it passed into the hands of Constable, even before the stipulated 6000 copies were disposed of, — it must
be owned he treated his rivals somewhat unhandsomely, finally severing
them from Scott's literary career, — are fully set forth by the historian of
the House of Blackwood. With her "one cannot but feel that this was
one of those tragically insignificant circumstances which so often shape
life apart from any consciousness of ours. Probably ruin would never
have overtaken Sir Walter had he been in the steady and careful hands
of Murray and Blackwood, for it is unlikely that even the glamour of the
great Magician would have turned heads so reasonable and sober."]

wife's old friends, Miss Dumergue and Mrs. Sarah Nicolson,[1] who had never before been in Scotland. The account which he gives of these ladies' visit at Abbotsford, and this little tour, in a letter to Mr. Morritt, shows the "Black Hussar of Literature" in his gentler and more habitual mood.

TO J. B. S. MORRITT, ESQ., M. P., ROKEBY PARK.

ABBOTSFORD, 21st August, 1816.

MY DEAR MORRITT, — I have not had a moment's kindly leisure to answer your kind letter, and to tell how delighted I shall be to see you in this least of all possible dwellings, but where we, nevertheless, can contrive a pilgrim's quarters and the warmest welcome for you and any friend of your journey; — if young Stanley, so much the better. Now, as to the important business with the which I have been occupied: You are to know we have had our kind hostesses of Piccadilly upon a two months' visit to us. We owed them so much hospitality, that we were particularly anxious to make Scotland agreeable to the good girls. But, alas, the wind has blown, and the rain has fallen, in a style which beats all that ever I remembered. We accomplished, with some difficulty, a visit to Loch Katrine and Loch Lomond, and, by dint of the hospitality of Cambusmore and the Ross, we defied bad weather, wet roads, and long walks. But the weather settled into regular tempest, when we settled at Abbotsford; and, though the natives, accustomed to bad weather (though not at such a time of year), contrived to brave the extremities of the season, it only served to increase the dismay of our unlucky visitors, who, accustomed only to Paris and London, expected *fiacres* at the Milestane Cross, and a pair of oars at the Deadman's Haugh. Add to this a strong disposition to *commérage*, when there was no possibility of gratifying it, and a

[1] The sister of Miss Jane Nicolson. — See *ante*, vol. i. pp. 248, 346.

total indisposition to scenery or rural amusements, which were all we had to offer — and you will pity both hosts and guests. I have the gratification to think I fully supported the hospitality of my country. I walked them to death, I talked them to death, I showed them landscapes which the driving rain hardly permitted them to see, and told them of feuds about which they cared as little as I do about their next-door news in Piccadilly. Yea, I even played at cards, and as I had Charlotte for a partner, so ran no risk of being scolded, I got on pretty well. Still the weather was so execrable, that, as the old drunken landlord used to say at Arroquhar, "I was perfectly ashamed of it;" and, to this moment, I wonder how my two friends fought it out so patiently as they did. But the young people and the cottages formed considerable resources. Yesterday they left us, deeply impressed with the conviction, which I can hardly blame, that the sun never shone in Scotland, — which that noble luminary seems disposed to confirm, by making this the first fair day we have seen this month — so that his beams will greet them at Longtown, as if he were determined to put Scotland to utter shame.

In you I expect a guest of a different calibre; and I think (barring downright rain) I can promise you some sport of one kind or other. We have a good deal of game about us; and Walter, to whom I have resigned my gun and license, will be an excellent attendant. He brought in six brace of moor-fowl on the 12th, which had (*si fas est diceri*) its own effect in softening the minds of our guests towards this unhappy climate. In other respects things look melancholy enough here. Corn is, however, rising, and the poor have plenty of work, and wages which, though greatly inferior to what they had when hands were scarce, assort perfectly well with the present state of the markets. Most folks try to live as much on their own produce as they can, by way of fighting off distress; and though speculating farmers and landlords must suffer, I think the temporary ague-fit will, on the whole, be advantageous to the country. It will check that inordinate and unbecoming spirit of expense, or rather extravagance, which was poisoning all classes, and bring us back to the sober virtues of our ancestors. It will also have the effect of teaching the landed interest, that their connection with their farmers should be of a nature more intimate than that of mere payment and receipt of rent, and that the largest offerer for a lease is often the person least entitled to be preferred as a tenant. Above all, it will complete the destruction of those execrable quacks, terming themselves land-doctors, who professed, from a two days' scamper over your estate, to tell you its constitution, — in other words its value, — acre by acre. These men, paid according to the golden hopes they held out, afforded by their reports one principal means of deceiving both landlord and tenant, by setting an ideal and extravagant value upon land, which seemed to entitle the one to expect, and the other to offer, rent far beyond what any expectation formed by either, upon their own acquaintance with the property, could rationally have warranted. More than one landed gentleman has cursed, in my presence, the day he ever consulted one of those empirics, whose prognostications induced him to reject the offers of substantial men, practically acquainted with the *locale.*

Ever, my dear Morritt, most truly yours,

WALTER SCOTT.

In October, 1816, appeared the Edinburgh Annual Register, containing Scott's historical sketch of the year 1814 — a composition which would occupy at least four such volumes as the reader has now in his hand.[1] Though executed with extraordinary rapidity, the sketch is as clear as spirited; but I need say no more of it here, as the author travels mostly over the same ground again in his Life of Napoleon.

[1] [Referring to the edition of 1839, in ten volumes.]

Scott's correspondence proves, that during this autumn he had received many English guests besides the good spinsters of Piccadilly and Mr. Morritt. I regret to add, it also proves that he had continued all the while to be annoyed with calls for money from John Ballantyne; yet before the 12th of November called him to Edinburgh, he appears to have nearly finished the first Tales of my Landlord. He had, moreover, concluded a negotiation with Constable and Longman for a series of Letters on the History of Scotland: of which, however, if he ever wrote any part, the MS. has not been discovered. It is probable that he may have worked some detached fragments into his long-subsequent Tales of a Grandfather.[1] The following letter shows likewise that he was now busy with plans of building at Abbotsford, and deep in consultation on that subject with an artist eminent for his skill in Gothic architecture, — Mr. Edward Blore: —

TO DANIEL TERRY, ESQ.

November 12, 1816.

My dear Terry, — I have been shockingly negligent in acknowledging your repeated favors; but it so happened, that I have had very little to *say*, with a great

---

[1] [Scott says in a letter to John Murray, written October 20, 1814: "In casting about how I might show you some mark of my sense of former kindness, a certain MS. History of Scotland in *Letters to my Children* has occurred to me, which I consider as a desideratum; it is upon the plan of *Lord Lyttelton's Letters*, as they are called." Nearly a year later he returns to the subject, and says: "I intend to revise my letters on Scottish History for you, but I will not get to press till November, for the country affords no facilities for consulting the necessary authorities. I hope it may turn out a thing of some interest, though I rather intend to keep to its original purpose as a book of instruction to children." These references seem to show that the work may have been further advanced than Lockhart supposed. The announcement of the proposed book by Constable and Longman naturally excited the indignation of Blackwood and Murray, as is shown in a vigorous letter from the Edinburgh to the London publisher, blaming equally the Ballantynes and Constable. — See *Memoirs of John Murray*, vol. i. pp. 245, 246, 462.]

deal to *do;* so that I trusted to your kindness to forgive
my apparent want of kindness, and indisputable lack of
punctuality. You will readily suppose that I have heard
with great satisfaction of the prosperity of your household, particularly of the good health of my little namesake and his mother. Godmothers of yore used to be
fairies; and though only a godfather, I think of sending
you, one day, a *fairy* gift — a little drama, namely,
which, if the audience be indulgent, may be of use to
him. Of course, you will stand godfather to it yourself:
it is yet only in embryo — a sort of poetical Hans in
Kelder — nor am I sure when I ean bring him forth;
not for this season, at any rate. You will receive, in
the course of a few days, my late *whereabouts* in four
volumes: there are two tales — the last of which I really
prefer to any fictitious narrative I have yet been able to
produce — the first is wish-washy enough. The subject
of the second tale lies among the old Scottish Camero-
nians — nay, I 'll tickle ye off a Covenanter as readily as
old Jack could do a young Prince; and a rare fellow he
is, when brought forth in his true colors. Were it not
for the necessity of using Scriptural language, which is
essential to the character, but improper for the stage, it
would be very dramatic. But of all this you will judge
by and by. To give the go-by to the public, I have
doubled and leaped into my form, like a hare in snow:
that is, I have changed my publisher, and come forth
like a maiden knight's white shield (there is a conceit!)
without any adhesion to fame gained in former adventures (another!) or, in other words, with a virgin title-
page (another!) — I should not be so light-hearted about
all this, but that it is very nearly finished and out, which
is always a blithe moment for Mr. Author. And now
to other matters. The books came safe, and were un-
packed two days since, on our coming to town — most
ingeniously were they stowed in the legs of the very
handsome stand for Lord Byron's vase, with which our

friend George Bullock has equipped me. I was made
very happy to receive him at Abbotsford, though only
for a start; and no less so to see Mr. Blore, from whom
I received your last letter. He is a very fine young
man, modest, simple, and unaffected in his manners, as
well as a most capital artist. I have had the assistance
of both these gentlemen in arranging an addition to the
cottage at Abbotsford, intended to connect the present
farmhouse with the line of low buildings to the right of
it. Mr. Bullock will show you the plan, which I think
is very ingenious. He has promised to give it his consideration with respect to the interior; and Mr. Blore
has drawn me a very handsome elevation, both to the
road and to the river. I expect to get some decorations
from the old Tolbooth of Edinburgh, particularly the
cope-stones of the doorway, or lintels, as we call them,
and a *niche* or two — one very handsome indeed! Better
get a niche *from* the Tolbooth than a niche *in* it, to
which such building operations are apt to bring the pro-
jectors. This addition will give me: first, a handsome
boudoir, in which I intend to place Mr. Bullock's Shakespeare,[1] with his superb cabinet, which serves as a
pedestal. This opens into the little drawing-room, to
which it serves as a chapel of ease; and on the other
side, to a handsome dining-parlor of 27 feet by 18, with
three windows to the north, and one to the south, — the
last to be Gothic, and filled with stained glass. Besides
these commodities, there is a small conservatory or greenhouse; and a study for myself, which we design to fit
up with ornaments from Melrose Abbey. Bullock made
several casts with his own hands — masks, and so forth,
delightful for cornices, etc.

Do not let Mrs. Terry think of the windows till little

---

[1] A cast from the monumental effigy at Stratford-upon-Avon — now in
the library at Abbotsford — was the gift of Mr. George Bullock, long distinguished in London as a collector of curiosities. This ingenious man was,
as the reader will see in the sequel, a great favorite with Scott.

Wat is duly cared after.[1] I am informed by Mr. Blore that he is a fine thriving fellow, very like papa. About my armorial bearings: I will send you a correct drawing of them as soon as I can get hold of Blore; namely — of the scutcheons of my grandsires on each side, and my own. I could detail them in the jargon of heraldry, but it is better to speak to your eyes by translating them into colored drawings, as the sublime science of armory has fallen into some neglect of late years, with all its mascles, buckles, crescents, and boars of the first, second, third, and fourth.

I was very sorry I had no opportunity of showing attention to your friend Mr. Abbot, not being in town at the time. I grieve to say that neither the genius of Kean nor the charms of Miss O'Neill could bring me from the hillside and the sweet society of Tom Purdie. All our family are very well — Walter as tall nearly as I am, fishing salmon and shooting moor-fowl and black-cock, in good style; the girls growing up, and, as yet, not losing their simplicity of character; little Charles excellent at play, and not deficient at learning, when the young dog will take pains. Abbotsford is looking pretty at last, and the planting is making some show. I have now several hundred acres thereof, running out as far as beyond the lake. We observe with great pleasure the steady rise which you make in public opinion, and expect, one day, to hail you stage-manager. Believe me, my dear Terry, always very much yours,

W. SCOTT.

P. S. — The Counsellor and both the Ballantynes are well and hearty.

On the first of December, the first series of the Tales of my Landlord appeared, and notwithstanding the silence of the title-page, and the change of publishers, and

---

[1] Mrs. Terry had offered the services of her elegant pencil in designing some windows of painted glass for Scott's armory, etc.

the attempt which had certainly been made to vary the style both of delineation and of language, all doubts whether they were or were not from the same hand with Waverley had worn themselves out before the lapse of a week. — The enthusiasm of their reception among the highest literary circles of London may be gathered from the following letter: —

TO WALTER SCOTT, ESQ., EDINBURGH.

ALBEMARLE STREET, 14th December, 1816.

DEAR SIR, — Although I dare not address you as the author of certain "Tales" (which, however, must be written either by Walter Scott or the Devil), yet nothing can restrain me from thinking it is to your influence with the author that I am indebted for the essential honor of being one of their publishers, and I must intrude upon you to offer my most hearty thanks — not divided, but doubled — alike for my worldly gain therein, and for the great acquisition of professional reputation which their publication has already procured me. I believe I might, under any oath that could be proposed, swear that I never experienced such unmixed pleasure as the reading of this exquisite work has afforded me ; and if you could see me, as the author's literary chamberlain, receiving the unanimous and vehement praises of every one who has read it, and the curses of those whose needs my scanty supply could not satisfy, you might judge of the sincerity with which I now entreat you to assure him of the most complete success. Lord Holland said, when I asked his opinion — "Opinion ! We did not one of us go to bed last night — nothing slept but my gout." Frere, Hallam, Boswell,[1] Lord Glenbervie, William Lamb,[2] all agree that it surpasses all the other novels. Gifford's estimate is increased at every reperusal. Heber says there are only two men in the world — Walter Scott and Lord Byron. Between you, you have given existence to a THIRD — Ever your faithful servant,

JOHN MURRAY.

To this cordial effusion Scott returned the following answer. It was necessary, since he had fairly resolved

---

[1] The late James Boswell, Esq., of the Temple — second son of Bozzy.
[2] The Honorable William Lamb — now Lord Melbourne.

against compromising his incognito, that he should be prepared not only to repel the impertinent curiosity of strangers, but to evade the proffered congratulations of overflowing kindness. He contrived, however, to do so, on this and all similar occasions, in a style of equivoque which could never be seriously misunderstood:[1] —

TO JOHN MURRAY, ESQ., ALBEMARLE STREET, LONDON.

EDINBURGH, 18th December, 1816.

MY DEAR SIR, — I give you heartily joy of the success of the Tales, although I do not claim that paternal interest in them which my friends do me the credit to assign me. I assure you I have never read a volume of them until they were printed, and can only join with the rest of the world in applauding the true and striking portraits which they present of old Scottish manners. I do not expect implicit reliance to be placed on my disavowal, because I know very well that he who is disposed not to own a work must necessarily deny it, and that otherwise

---

[1] [Even such keen observers as Murray and Blackwood had their intervals of doubt regarding the authorship of the Novels. In June, 1816, Blackwood writes: "There have been various rumors with regard to Greenfield being the author, but I never paid much attention to it; the thing appeared to me so very improbable. . . . But from what I have heard lately, and from what you state, I now begin to think that Greenfield may probably be the author." And only a month after the date of his letter to Scott, here given, Murray writes to Blackwood : —

"I can assure you, but *in the greatest confidence*, that I have discovered the author of all these Novels to be Thomas Scott, Walter Scott's brother. He is now in Canada. I have no doubt but that Mr. Walter Scott did a great deal to the first Waverley Novel, because of his anxiety to save his brother, and his doubt about the success of the work. This accounts for the many stories about it. Many persons had previously heard from Mr. Scott, but you may rely upon the certainty of what I have told you." By this time Blackwood is firm in the faith of Scott's authorship; but Bernard Barton writes to Murray that he has heard that James Hogg is the author of *Tales of my Landlord*, and that he has had intimation from himself to that effect; while Lady Mackintosh is informed on excellent authority that the writer is Mrs. Thomas Scott. Writing to Blackwood in February, 1817, Murray avers. — "I will believe, till within an inch of my life, that the author of *Tales of my Landlord* is Thomas Scott." — See Smiles's *Memoir of John Murray*, vol. i. pp. 461, 473, 474.]

his secret would be at the mercy of all who choose to ask the question, since silence in such a case must always pass for consent, or rather assent. But I have a mode of convincing you that I am perfectly serious in my denial — pretty similar to that by which Solomon distinguished the fictitious from the real mother — and that is, by reviewing the work, which I take to be an operation equal to that of quartering the child. But this is only on condition I can have Mr. Erskine's assistance, who admires the work greatly more than I do, though I think the painting of the second Tale both true and powerful. I knew Old Mortality very well; his name was Paterson, but few knew him otherwise than by his nickname. The first Tale is not very original in its concoction, and lame and impotent in its conclusion. My love to Gifford. I have been over head and ears in work this summer, or I would have sent the Gypsies; indeed I was partly stopped by finding it impossible to procure a few words of their language.

Constable wrote to me about two months since, desirous of having a new edition of Paul; but not hearing from you, I conclude you are still on hand. Longman's people had then only sixty copies.

Kind compliments to Heber, whom I expected at Abbotsford this summer; also to Mr. Croker and all your four o'clock visitors. I am just going to Abbotsford to make a small addition to my premises there. I have now about 700 acres, thanks to the booksellers and the discerning public. Yours truly,

WALTER SCOTT.

P. S. — I have much to ask about Lord Byron if I had time. The third canto of the Childe is inimitable. Of the last poems, there are one or two which indicate rather an irregular play of imagination.[1] What a pity that a man of such exquisite genius will not be contented

---

[1] *Parisina — The Dream —* and the " Domestic Pieces," had been recently published.

to be happy on the ordinary terms![1] I declare my heart bleeds when I think of him, self-banished from the country to which he is an honor.[2]

[1] [On November 27 Scott had written to Joanna Baillie, who had just returned from a tour on the Continent : —

"All I ever longed for on the Continent was their light wines, which you do not care about, and their fine climate, which we should both value equally ; and to say truth, I never saw scene or palace which shook my allegiance to Tweedside and Abbotsford, though so inferior in every respect, and though the hills, or rather braes, are just high enough ' to lift us to the storm ' when the storms are not so condescending as to sweep both crest and base, which, to do them justice, is seldom the case. What have I got to send you ? . . . Alas, nothing but the history of petty employments and a calendar of increasing bad weather. The latter was much mitigated by enjoying for a good portion of the summer the society of John Morritt, of Rokeby, who has so much of that which is delightful, both in his grave and gay moods, that he can make us forget the hillside while sitting by the fireside. His late loss has cast a general shade of melancholy over him, which renders him yet dearer to his friends, by the gentle and unaffected manner in which his natural gayety of temper gleams through it and renders it still more interesting. . . .

"A far different object of interest, yet still of interest, checkered with pity and disapprobation, is Lord Byron, whose present situation seems to rival all that ever has been said and sung of the misfortunes of a too irritable imagination. The last part of *Childe Harold* intimates a terrible state of mind, and with all the power and genius which characterized his former productions, the present seems to indicate a more serious and desperate degree of misanthropy. I own I was not much moved by the scorn of the world which his first poems implied, because I know it is a humor of mind which those whom fortune has spoilt by indulgence, or irritated by reverses, are apt to assume, because it looks melancholy and gentlemanlike, and becomes a bard as well as being desperately in love, or very fond of the sunrise, though he lies in bed till noon, or anxious in recommending to others to catch cold by visiting old abbeys by moonlight, which he never happened to see under the chaste moonbeam himself ; but this strange poem goes much deeper, and either the Demon of Misanthropy is in full possession of him, or he has already invited ten guests, equally desperate, to the swept and garnished mansion of Harold's understanding." — *Familiar Letters*, vol. i. p. 369.]

[2] [This is probably the " expression of kindness " which encouraged Murray to beg Scott to review in the *Quarterly* Byron's recently published volumes, *Childe Harold, Canto III.,* and *The Prisoner of Chillon, a Dream, and Other Poems*. The request was promptly complied with, and the article appeared in the next number issued (*dated* October, 1816). — a review full of generous, and also judicious, appreciation. For some reason, hard now to discover, unless it were the kindliness of the writer's tone towards the younger poet, some of Lady Byron's friends, among whom was Joanna

Mr. Murray, gladly embracing this offer of an article for his journal on the Tales of my Landlord, begged Scott to take a wider scope, and dropping all respect for the idea of a divided parentage, to place together any materials he might have for the illustration of the Waverley Novels in general; he suggested in particular, that, instead of drawing up a long-promised disquisition on the Gypsies in a separate shape, whatever he had to say concerning that picturesque generation might be introduced by way of comment on the character of Meg Merrilies. What Scott's original conception had been I know not; he certainly gave his reviewal all the breadth which Murray could have wished, and, *inter alia*, diversified it with a few anecdotes of the Scottish Gypsies. But the late excellent biographer of John Knox, Dr. Thomas M'Crie, had, in the mean time, considered the representation of the Covenanters, in the story of Old Mortality, as so unfair as to demand at his

Baillie, seem to have taken strong exception to the paper, and Miss Baillie wrote to Scott at some length on the matter, even animadverting upon the purely literary criticism of the reviewer. Much of the correspondence which ensued, including a characteristic letter from Lady Byron, can be found in the *Familiar Letters* (vol. i. pp. 413–422).

Of the review, Byron writes to Murray (March 3, 1817) : —

. . . "It seems to me (as far as the subject of it may be permitted to judge) to be *very well* written as a composition, and . . . even those who may condemn its partiality, must praise its generosity. The temptations to take another and less favorable view of the question have been so great and numerous, that, what with public opinion, politics, etc., he must be a gallant as well as a good man, who has ventured in that place and at this time to write such an article even anonymously. Such things, however, are their own reward ; and I even flatter myself that the writer, whoever he may be (and I have no guess), will not regret that the perusal of this has given me as much gratification as any composition of that nature could give, and more than any other has ever given, — and I have had a good many in my time of one kind or the other. It is not the mere praise, but there is a tact and a delicacy throughout, not only with regard to me, but to others, which, as it has not been observed elsewhere, I had till now doubted, whether it could be observed anywhere." He writes a few weeks later, on learning that Scott wrote the article : . . . "It cannot add to my good opinion of him, but it adds to that of myself." — *Letters and Journals of Lord Byron* (1900), vol. iv. pp. 63, 85.]

hands a very serious rebuke. The Doctor forthwith published, in a magazine called the Edinburgh Christian Instructor, a set of papers, in which the historical foundations of that tale were attacked with indignant warmth; and though Scott, when he first heard of these invectives, expressed his resolution never even to read them, he found the impression they were producing so strong, that he soon changed his purpose, and finally devoted a very large part of his article for the Quarterly Review to an elaborate defence of his own picture of the Covenanters.[1]

Before the first Tales of my Landlord were six weeks old, two editions of 2000 copies disappeared, and a third of 2000 was put to press; but notwithstanding this rapid success, which was still further continued, and the friendly relations which always subsisted between the

[1] Since I have mentioned this reviewal, I may as well, to avoid recurrence to it, express here my conviction, that Erskine, not Scott, was the author of the critical estimate of the Waverley Novels which it embraces — although, for the purpose of mystification, Scott had taken the trouble to transcribe the paragraphs in which that estimate is contained. At the same time I cannot but add that, had Scott really been the sole author of this reviewal, he need not have incurred the severe censure which has been applied to his supposed conduct in the matter. After all, his judgment of his own works must have been allowed to be not above, but very far under the mark; and the whole affair would, I think, have been considered by every candid person exactly as the letter about Solomon and the rival mothers was by Murray, Gifford, and the "four o'clock visitors" of Albemarle Street — as a good joke. A better joke, certainly, than the allusion to the report of Thomas Scott being the real author of Waverley, at the close of the article, was never penned; and I think it includes a confession over which a misanthrope might have chuckled: "We intended here to conclude this long article, when a strong report reached us of certain Transatlantic confessions, which, if genuine (though of this we know nothing), assign a different author to these volumes than the party suspected by our Scottish correspondents. Yet a critic may be excused seizing upon the nearest suspicious person, on the principle happily expressed by Claverhouse, in a letter to the Earl of Linlithgow. He had been, it seems, in search of a gifted weaver, who used to hold forth at conventicles: 'I sent for the webster (weaver), they brought in his *brother* for him : though he, maybe, cannot preach like his brother, I doubt not but he is as well-principled as he, wherefore I thought it would be no great fault to give him the trouble to go to jail with the rest!'" — *Miscellaneous Prose Works*, vol. xix. pp. 85, 86.

author and Mr. Murray, circumstances erelong occurred
which carried the publication of the work into the hands
of Messrs. Constable.

The author's answer to Dr. M'Crie, and his Introduction of 1830, have exhausted the historical materials on
which he constructed his Old Mortality; and the origin
of The Black Dwarf — as to the conclusion of which story
he appears on reflection to have completely adopted the
opinion of honest Blackwood — has already been sufficiently illustrated by an anecdote of his early wanderings
in Tweeddale. The latter tale, however imperfect, and
unworthy as a work of art to be placed high in the catalogue of his productions, derives a singular interest from
its delineation of the dark feelings so often connected
with physical deformity; feelings which appear to have
diffused their shadow over the whole genius of Byron —
and which, but for this single picture, we should hardly
have conceived ever to have passed through Scott's happier mind.[1] All the bitter blasphemy of spirit which,
from infancy to the tomb, swelled up in Byron against
the unkindness of nature; which sometimes perverted
even his filial love into a sentiment of diabolical malig-
nity; all this black and desolate train of reflections must
have been encountered and deliberately subdued by the
manly parent of The Black Dwarf. Old Mortality, on
the other hand, is remarkable as the *novelist's* first attempt to repeople the past by the power of imagination
working on materials furnished by books. In Waverley
he revived the fervid dreams of his boyhood, and drew,
not from printed records, but from the artless oral narratives of his *Invernahyles*. In Guy Mannering and The
Antiquary he embodied characters and manners familiar

---

[1] [On reading *The Black Dwarf*, Mrs. Leigh believed her brother to be
the author, and wrote to him to that effect. Byron had not yet seen the
book, and says in his reply : " I am not P. P. [Peter Pattieson], I assure you
on my honor, and do not understand to what book you allude, so that all
your compliments are quite thrown away." — Byron's *Letters and Journals*
(1900), vol. iv. p. 56.]

to his own wandering youth. But whenever his letters mention Old Mortality in its progress, they represent him as strong in the confidence that the industry with which he had pored over a library of forgotten tracts would enable him to identify himself with the time in which they had birth, as completely as if he had listened with his own ears to the dismal sermons of Peden, ridden with Claverhouse and Dalzell in the rout of Bothwell, and been an advocate at the bar of the Privy Council, when Lauderdale catechised and tortured the assassins of Archbishop Sharp. To reproduce a departed age with such minute and lifelike accuracy as this tale exhibits, demanded a far more energetic sympathy of imagination than had been called for in any effort of his serious verse. It is indeed most curiously instructive for any student of art to compare the Roundheads of Rokeby with the Bluebonnets of Old Mortality. For the rest — the story is framed with a deeper skill than any of the preceding novels: the canvas is a broader one; the characters are contrasted and projected with a power and felicity which neither he nor any other master ever surpassed; and, notwithstanding all that has been urged against him as a disparager of the Covenanters, it is to me very doubtful whether the inspiration of romantic chivalry ever prompted him to nobler emotions than he has lavished on the re-animation of their stern and solemn enthusiasm. This work has always appeared to me the Marmion of his novels.[1]

---

[1] [Lady Louisa Stuart, whose approbation Scott writes he values " beyond a whole wilderness of critics," says in a letter of December 5, 1816:

" [Old Mortality] is super-excellent in all its points; it breaks up fresh ground, and has all the raciness of originality. I cannot help thinking it will bear down the world before it triumphantly. As usual it makes its personages our intimate acquaintance, and its scenes so present to the eye, that, last night, after sitting up unreasonably late over it, I got no sleep, from a kind of fever of mind it had occasioned. It seemed as if I had been an eye and ear witness of all the passages, and I could not lull the agitation into calmness. Mause and Cuddie hurried my spirits in another way; they forced me to laugh out aloud, which one seldom does alone. On a

I have disclaimed the power of farther illustrating its
historical groundworks, but I am enabled by Mr. Train's
kindness to give some interesting additions to Scott's
own account of this novel as a composition. The generous Supervisor visited him in Edinburgh in May, 1816,
a few days after the publication of The Antiquary, carrying with him several relics which he wished to present to
his collection; among others a purse that had belonged

second slower reading I expect to be still better pleased, and then also I
suppose I shall find out the faults. At present it has, in the Scotch phrase,
'taken me off my feet,' and I do not criticise, though I think you will believe me when I say I do not and will not flatter. One thing I regret, that
like the author of The Antiquary, Jedediah did not add a glossary ; because
even I, a mongrel, occasionally paying long visits to Scotland, and hearing
Girsy at Bothwell gate and Peggy Macgowan hold forth in the village, —
even I, thus qualified, have found a great many words absolute Hebrew to
me, and I fear the altogether English will find many more beyond their
comprehension or conjecture. But this may be remedied in another edition.
I have as yet only one great attack to make, and that upon a single word ;
but such a word ! such an anachronism ! Claverhouse says he has no time
to hear *sentimental* speeches. My dear sir ! tell Jedediah that Claverhouse
never heard the sound of those four syllables in his life. We are used to
them ; but *sentiment* and *sentimental* were, I believe, first introduced into
the language by Sterne, and are hardly as old as I am. Let alone the
Covenanters' days, I am persuaded you would look in vain for them in the
works of Richardson and Fielding. Nay, the French, from whom they
were borrowed, did not talk of *le sentiment* in that sense till long after
Louis XIV.'s reign. No such thing is to be found in Madame de Sévigné,
la Bruyère, etc., etc., etc. At home or abroad I defy Lord Dundee ever
to have met with the expression. Mr. Peter Pattieson had been reading
the *Man of Feeling*, and it was a slip of his tongue, which I am less inclined to excuse than Mause's abstruse Scotch, which I duly reverence, as
she did Kettledrummle's sermons, because I do not understand it. Once
more I shall be much disappointed if this work does not quickly acquire a
very great reputation. I fancy Mr. Morritt is in the secret ; yet, as I am
not certain, I will keep on the secure side and not mention it when I write
to him, however one may long to *intercommune* on such subjects with those
likely to hold the same faith."

At the close of his reply, Scott says : "I must not forget to thank
your Ladyship for your acute and indisputable criticism on the application
of the word *sentimental*. How it escaped my pen I know not, unless that
the word owed me a grudge for the ill will I have uniformly borne it, and
was resolved to slip itself in for the express purpose of disgracing me. I
will certainly turn it out the first opportunity." This was done in the
second edition. — *Familiar Letters*, vol. i. pp. 394, 400.]

to Rob Roy, and also a fresh heap of traditionary glean-
ings, which he had gathered among the tale-tellers of his
district. One of these last was in the shape of a letter
to Mr. Train from a Mr. Broadfoot, "schoolmaster at
the clachan of Penningham, and author of the *celebrated
song* of the Hills of Galloway" — with which I confess
myself unacquainted. Broadfoot had facetiously signed
his communication *Clashbottom*, — "a professional appellation derived," says Mr. Train, "from the use of the
birch, and by which he was usually addressed among his
companions, — who assembled, not at the Wallace Inn
of Gandercleuch, but at the sign of the Shoulder of Mutton in Newton-Stewart." Scott received these gifts with
benignity, and invited the friendly donor to breakfast
next morning. He found him at work in his library,
and surveyed with enthusiastic curiosity the furniture of
the room, especially its only picture, a portrait of Graham of Claverhouse. Train expressed the surprise with
which every one, who had known Dundee only in the
pages of the Presbyterian Annalists, must see for the
first time that beautiful and melancholy visage, worthy
of the most pathetic dreams of romance. Scott replied,
"that no character had been so foully traduced as the
Viscount of Dundee; that, thanks to Wodrow, Cruick-
shanks, and such chroniclers, he, who was every inch a
soldier and a gentleman, still passed among the Scottish
vulgar for a ruffian desperado, who rode a goblin horse,
was proof against shot, and in league with the Devil."
"Might he not," said Mr. Train, "be made, in good
hands, the hero of a national romance as interesting as
any about either Wallace or Prince Charlie?" "He
might," said Scott, "but your western zealots would require to be faithfully portrayed in order to bring him
out with the right effect." [1] "And what," resumed

---

[1] [Scott's old friend, John Richardson, who was from the first in the
secret of the Waverley Novels, was a stanch Whig, as beseemed the descendant of an old Covenanting family. Some of his ancestral traditions

Train, "if the story were to be delivered as if from the mouth of *Old Mortality?* Would *he* not do as well as *the Minstrel* did in the Lay?" "Old Mortality!" said Scott — "who was he?" Mr. Train then told what he could remember of old Paterson, and seeing how much his story interested the hearer, offered to inquire farther about that enthusiast on his return to Galloway. "Do so by all means," said Scott; "I assure you I shall look with anxiety for your communication." He said nothing at this time of his own meeting with Old Mortality in the churchyard of Dunnottar — and I think there can be no doubt that that meeting was thus recalled to his recollection; or that to this intercourse with Mr. Train we owe the whole machinery of the Tales of my Landlord, as well as the adoption of Claverhouse's period for the scene of one of its first fictions. I think it highly probable that we owe a further obligation to the worthy Supervisor's presentation of Rob Roy's *spleuchan*.

The original design for the First Series of Jedediah Cleishbotham was, as Scott told me, to include four separate tales illustrative of four districts of the country, in the like number of volumes; but, his imagination once kindled upon any theme, he could not but pour himself out freely — so that notion was soon abandoned.

suggested certain passages in *Old Mortality*, and he has recorded that during a visit to Abbotsford Scott gave him the proof sheets of the first volume to read, and how he lost a night's sleep in doing it. Twelve years later, in writing to Scott regarding *The Tales of a Grandfather*, he says that in this work, — "You have paid a debt which you owed to the manes of the Covenanters for the flattering picture which you drew of Claverhouse in *Old Mortality*."

Scott says in his reply (December, 1828): "As to Covenanters and Malignants, they were both a set of cruel and bloody bigots, and had, notwithstanding, those virtues with which bigotry is sometimes allied. Their characters were of a kind much more picturesque than beautiful; neither had the least idea either of toleration or humanity, so that it happens that, so far as they can be distinguished from each other, one is tempted to hate most the party which chances to be uppermost for the time." — See *Journal*, note, vol. ii. p. 404.]

CHAPTER XXXVIII

1817

WITHIN less than a month, The Black Dwarf and Old
Mortality were followed by "Harold the Dauntless, by
the author of The Bridal of Triermain." This poem had
been, it appears, begun several years back; nay, part of
it had been actually printed before the appearance of
Childe Harold, though that circumstance had escaped
the author's remembrance when he penned, in 1830, his
Introduction to The Lord of the Isles; for he there says,
"I am still astonished at my having committed the gross
error of selecting the very name which Lord Byron had
made so famous." The volume was published by Messrs.
Constable, and had, in those booksellers' phrase, "considerable success." It has never, however, been placed
on a level with Triermain; and though it contains many
vigorous pictures, and splendid verses, and here and
there some happy humor, the confusion and harsh transi-

tions of the fable, and the dim rudeness of character and manners, seem sufficient to account for this inferiority in public favor. It is not surprising that the author should have redoubled his aversion to the notion of any more serious performances in verse. He had seized on an instrument of wider compass, and which, handled with whatever rapidity, seemed to reveal at every touch treasures that had hitherto slept unconsciously within him. He had thrown off his fetters, and might well go forth rejoicing in the native elasticity of his strength.

It is at least a curious coincidence in literary history, that, as Cervantes, driven from the stage of Madrid by the success of Lope de Vega, threw himself into prose romance, and produced, at the moment when the world considered him as silenced forever, the Don Quixote which has outlived Lope's two thousand triumphant dramas — so Scott, abandoning verse to Byron, should have rebounded from his fall by the only prose romances, which seem to be classed with the masterpiece of Spanish genius, by the general judgment of Europe.

I shall insert two letters, in which he announces the publication of Harold the Dauntless. In the first of them he also mentions the light and humorous little piece entitled The Sultan of Serendib, or the Search after Happiness, originally published in a weekly paper, after the fashion of the old Essayists, which about this time issued from John Ballantyne's premises, under the appropriate name of "The SALE-ROOM." The paper had slender success; and though Scott wrote several things for it, none of them, except this metrical essay, attracted any notice. The Sale-Room was, in fact, a dull and hopeless concern; and I should scarcely have thought it worth mentioning, but for the confirmation it lends to my suspicion that Mr. John Ballantyne was very unwilling, after all his warnings, to retire completely from the field of publishing.

EDINBURGH, January 30, 1817.

MY DEAR MORRITT, — I hope to send you in a couple of days Harold the Dauntless, which has not turned out so good as I thought it would have done. I begin to get too old and stupid, I think, for poetry, and will certainly never again adventure on a grand scale. For amusement, and to help a little publication that is going on here, I have spun a doggerel tale called The Search after Happiness, of which I shall send you a copy by post, if it is of a frankable size; if not, I can put it up with the Dauntless. Among other misfortunes of Harold is his name, but the thing was partly printed before Childe Harold was in question.

My great and good news at present is, that the bog (that perpetual hobby-horse) has produced a commodity of most excellent marle, and promises to be of the very last consequence to my wild ground in the neighborhood; for nothing can equal the effect of marle as a top-dressing. Methinks (in my mind's eye, Horatio) I see all the blue-bank, the hinny-lee, and the other provinces of my poor kingdom, waving with deep rye-grass and clover, like the meadows at Rokeby. In honest truth, it will do me yeoman's service.

My next good tidings are, that Jedediah carries the world before him. Six thousand have been disposed of, and three thousand more are pressing onward, which will be worth £2500 to the worthy pedagogue of Gander-cleuch. Some of the Scotch Whigs, of the right old fanatical leaven, have waxed wroth with Jedediah, —

> " But shall we go mourn for that, my dear ?
> The cold moon shines by night,
> And when we wander here and there,
> We then do go most right." [1]

After all, these honest gentlemen are like Queen Eliza-

[1] Joanna Baillie's *Orra*.

beth in their ideas of portrait-painting. They require
the pictures of their predecessors to be likenesses, and at
the same time demand that they shall be painted without
shade, being probably of opinion, with the virgin majesty
of England, that there is no such thing in nature.

I presume you will be going almost immediately to
London — at least all our Scotch members are requested
to be at their posts, the meaning of which I cannot pretend
to guess. The finances are the only ticklish matter, but
there is, after all, plenty of money in the country, now
that our fever-fit is a little over. In Britain, when there
is the least damp upon the spirits of the public, they are
exactly like people in a crowd, who take the alarm, and
shoulder each other to and fro till some dozen or two of
the weakest are borne down and trodden to death;
whereas, if they would but have patience and remain
quiet, there would be a safe and speedy end to their embarrassment. How we want Billie Pitt now to get up
and give the tone to our feelings and opinions!

As I take up this letter to finish the same, I hear the
Prince Regent has been attacked and fired at. Since he
was not hurt (for I should be sincerely sorry for my fat
friend), I see nothing but good luck to result from this
assault. It will make him a good manageable boy, and,
I think, secure you a quiet session of Parliament. —
Adieu, my dear Morritt, God bless you. Let me know
if the gimcracks come safe — I mean the book, etc.

Ever yours,   WALTER SCOTT.

TO THE LADY LOUISA STUART, GLOUCESTER PLACE, LONDON.

EDINBURGH, January 31, 1817.

MY DEAR LADY LOUISA, — This accompanies Harold
the Dauntless. I thought once I should have made it
something clever, but it turned vapid upon my imagination; and I finished it at last with hurry and impatience.
Nobody knows, that has not tried the feverish trade of
poetry, how much it depends upon mood and whim. I

don't wonder, that, in dismissing all the other deities of Paganism, the Muse should have been retained by common consent; for, in sober reality, writing good verses seems to depend upon something separate from the volition of the author. I sometimes think my fingers set up for themselves, independent of my head; for twenty times I have begun a thing on a certain plan, and never in my life adhered to it (in a work of imagination, that is) for half an hour together. I would hardly write this sort of egotistical trash to any one but yourself, yet it is very true for all that. What my kind correspondent had anticipated on account of Jedediah's effusions has actually taken place; and the author of a very good Life of Knox has, I understand, made a most energetic attack, upon the score that the old Covenanters are not treated with decorum. I have not read it, and certainly never shall. I really think there is nothing in the book that is not very fair and legitimate subject of raillery; and I own I have my suspicions of that very susceptible devotion which so readily takes offence: such men should not read books of amusement; but do they suppose, because they are virtuous, and choose to be thought outrageously so, "there shall be no cakes and ale"? — "Ay, by our lady, and ginger shall be hot in the mouth too."[1] As for the consequences to the author, they can only affect his fortune or his temper — the former, such as it is, has been long fixed beyond shot of these sort of fowlers; and for my temper, I considered always, that by subjecting myself to the irritability which much greater authors have felt on occasions of literary dispute, I should be laying in a plentiful stock of unhappiness for the rest of my life. I therefore make it a rule never to read the attacks made upon me. I remember being capable of something like this sort of self-denial at a very early period of life, for I could not be six years old. I had been put into my bed in the nursery, and two servant

[1] *Twelfth Night*, Act II. Scene 3.

girls sat down by the embers of the fire, to have their
own quiet chat, and the one began to tell a most dismal
ghost story, of which I remember the commencement
distinctly at this moment; but perceiving which way the
tale was tending, and though necessarily curious, being
at the same time conscious that, if I listened on, I should
be frightened out of my wits for the rest of the night,
I had the force to cover up my head in the bed-clothes,
so that I could not hear another word that was said.
The only inconvenience attending a similar prudential
line of conduct in the present case is, that it may seem
like a deficiency of spirit; but I am not much afraid of
that being laid to my charge — my fault in early life (I
hope long since corrected) having lain rather the other
way. And so I say, with mine honest Prior, —

> " Sleep, Philo, untouch'd, on my peaceable shelf,
>   Nor take it amiss that so little I heed thee ;
> I 've no malice at thee, and some love for myself —
>   Then why should I answer, since first I must read thee ? "

So you are getting finely on in London. I own I am
very glad of it. I am glad the banditti act like banditti,
because it will make men of property look round them
in time. This country is very like the toys which folks
buy for children, and which, tumble them about in any
way the urchins will, are always brought to their feet
again, by the lead deposited in their extremities. The
mass of property has the same effect on our Constitution,
and is a sort of ballast which will always *right* the vessel, to use a sailor's phrase, and bring it to its due equi-
poise.

Ministers have acted most sillily in breaking up the
burgher volunteers in large towns. On the contrary,
the service should have been made coercive. Such men
have a moral effect upon the minds of the populace, besides their actual force, and are so much interested in
keeping good order, that you may always rely on them,
especially as a corps in which there is necessarily a com-

mon spirit of union and confidence. But all this is nonsense again, quoth my Uncle Toby to himself. Adieu,
my dear Lady Louisa; my sincere good wishes always
attend you.   W. S.

Not to disturb the narrative of his literary proceedings, I have deferred until now the mention of an attempt
which Scott made during the winter of 1816–1817, to
exchange his seat at the Clerk's table for one on the
Bench of the Scotch Court of Exchequer. It had often
occurred to me, in the most prosperous years of his life,
that such a situation would have suited him better in
every respect than that which he held, and that his never
attaining a promotion, which the Scottish public would
have considered so naturally due to his character and
services, reflected little honor on his political allies.
But at the period when I was entitled to hint this to
him, he appeared to have made up his mind that the
rank of Clerk of Session was more compatible than that
of a Supreme Judge with the habits of a literary man,
who was perpetually publishing, and whose writings were
generally of the imaginative order. I had also witnessed
the zeal with which he seconded the views of more than
one of his own friends, when their ambition was directed
to the Exchequer Bench. I remained, in short, ignorant
that he ever had seriously thought of it for himself, until
the ruin of his worldly fortunes in 1826; nor had I any
information that his wish to obtain it had ever been distinctly stated, until certain letters, one of which I shall
introduce, were placed in my hands after his death, by
the present Duke of Buccleuch. The late Duke's answers to these letters are also before me; but of them it
is sufficient to say, that while they show the warmest
anxiety to serve Scott, they refer to private matters,
which rendered it inconsistent with his Grace's feelings
to interfere at the time in question with the distribution
of Crown patronage. I incline to think, on the whole,

that the death of this nobleman, which soon after left the influence of his house in abeyance, must have, far more than any other circumstance, determined Scott to renounce all notions of altering his professional position.

TO THE DUKE OF BUCCLEUCH, ETC., ETC.

EDINBURGH, 11th December, 1816.

My DEAR LORD DUKE, — Your Grace has been so much my constant and kind friend and patron through the course of my life, that I trust I need no apology for thrusting upon your consideration some ulterior views, which have been suggested to me by my friends, and which I will either endeavor to prosecute, time and place serving, or lay aside all thoughts of, as they appear to your Grace feasible, and likely to be forwarded by your patronage. It has been suggested to me, in a word, that there would be no impropriety in my being put in nomination as a candidate for the situation of a Baron of Exchequer, when a vacancy shall take place. The difference of the emolument between that situation and those which I now hold, is just £400 a year, so that, in that point of view, it is not a very great object. But there is a difference in the rank, and also in the leisure afforded by a Baron's situation; and a man may, without condemnation, endeavor, at my period of life, to obtain as much honor and ease as he can handsomely come by. My pretensions to such an honor (next to your Grace's countenancing my wishes) would rest very much on the circumstance that my nomination would vacate two good offices (Clerk of Session and Sheriff of Selkirkshire) to the amount of £1000 and £300 a year; and, besides, would extinguish a pension of £300 which I have for life, over and above my salary as Clerk of Session, as having been in office at the time when the Judicature Act deprived us of a part of our vested fees and emoluments. The extinction of this pension would be just so much saved to the public. I am pretty confident also that I should

be personally acceptable to our friend the Chief Baron.[1]
But whether all or any of these circumstances will weigh
much in my favor, must solely and entirely rest with
your Grace, without whose countenance it would be folly
in me to give the matter a second thought. *With* your
patronage, both my situation and habits of society may
place my hopes as far as any who are likely to apply;
and your interest would be strengthened by the opportunity of placing some good friend in Selkirkshire, besides
converting the Minstrel of the Clan into a Baron, — a
transmutation worthy of so powerful and kind a chief.
But if your Grace thinks I ought to drop thoughts of
this preferment, I am bound to say, that I think myself
as well provided for by my friends and the public as I
have the least title to expect, and that I am perfectly
contented and grateful for what I have received. Ever
your Grace's faithful and truly obliged servant,

WALTER SCOTT.

The following letter, to the same noble friend, contains
a slight allusion to this affair of the Barony; but I insert
it for a better reason. The Duke had, it seems, been
much annoyed by some depredations on his game in the
district of Ettrick Water; and more so by the ill use
which some boys from Selkirk made of his liberality in
allowing the people of that town free access to his beautiful walks on the banks of the Yarrow, adjoining Newark and Bowhill. The Duke's forester, by name Thomas
Hudson, had recommended rigorous measures with reference to both these classes of offenders, and the Sheriff
was of course called into council: —

TO HIS GRACE THE DUKE OF BUCCLEUCH, ETC., ETC., ETC.

ABBOTSFORD, January 11, 1817.

MY DEAR LORD DUKE, — I have been thinking anxiously about the disagreeable affair of Tom Hudson,

---

[1] The late Right Honorable Robert Dundas of Arniston, Chief Baron
of the Scotch Exchequer; one of Scott's earliest and kindest friends in
that distinguished family.

and the impudent ingratitude of the Selkirk rising generation, and I will take the usual liberty your friendship
permits me, of saying what occurs to me on each subject.
Respecting the shooting, the crime is highly punishable,
and we will omit no inquiries to discover the individuals
guilty. Charles Erskine, who is a good police-officer,
will be sufficiently active. I know my friend and kinsman, Mr. Scott of Harden, feels very anxious to oblige
your Grace, and I have little doubt that if you will have
the goodness to mention to him this unpleasant circumstance, he would be anxious to put his game under such
regulations as should be agreeable to you. But I believe
the pride and pleasure he would feel in obliging your
Grace, as heading one of the most ancient and most respectable branches of your name (if I may be pardoned
for saying so much in our favor), would be certainly
much more gratified by a compliance with your personal
request, than if it came through any other channel.
Your Grace knows there are many instances in life in
which the most effectual way of conferring a favor is
condescending to accept one. I have known Harden
long and most intimately — a more respectable man,
either for feeling, or talent, or knowledge of human life,
is rarely to be met with. But he is rather indecisive —
requiring some instant stimulus in order to make him
resolve to do, not only what he knows to be right, but
what he really wishes to do, and means to do one time
or other. He is exactly Prior's Earl of Oxford: —

> " Let that be done which Mat doth say."
> " Yea," quoth the Earl, " *but not to-day.*"

And so exit Harden, and enter Selkirk.

I know hardly anything more exasperating than the
conduct of the little blackguards, and it will be easy to
discover and make an example of the biggest and most
insolent. In the mean while, my dear Lord, pardon my
requesting you will take no general or sweeping resolution as to the Selkirk folks. Your Grace lives near

them — your residence, both from your direct benefi-
cence, and the indirect advantages which they derive from
that residence, is of the utmost consequence; and they
must be made sensible that all these advantages are endangered by the very violent and brutal conduct of their
children. But I think your Grace will be inclined to
follow this up only for the purpose of correction, not for
that of requital. They are so much beneath you, and
so much in your power, that this would be unworthy of
you — especially as all the inhabitants of the little country town must necessarily be included in the punishment.
Were your Grace really angry with them, and acting
accordingly, you might ultimately feel the regret of my
old schoolmaster, who, when he had knocked me down,
apologized by saying he did not know his own strength.
After all, those who look for anything better than ingratitude from the uneducated and unreflecting mass of
a corrupted population, must always be deceived; and
the better the heart is that has been expanded towards
them, their wants and their wishes, the deeper is the
natural feeling of disappointment. But it is our duty to
fight on, doing what good we can (and surely the disposition and the means were never more happily united than
in your Grace), and trusting to God Almighty, whose
grace ripens the seeds we commit to the earth, that our
benefactions shall bear fruit. And now, my Lord, asking your pardon for this discharge of my conscience, and
assuring your Grace I have no wish to exchange my
worsted gown, or the remote *Pisgah* exchange of a silk
one, for the cloak of a Presbyterian parson, even with
the certainty of succeeding to the first of your numerous
Kirk-presentations, I take the liberty to add my own
opinion. The elder boys must be looked out and pun-
ished, and the parents severely reprimanded, and the
whole respectable part of the town made sensible of the
loss they must necessarily sustain by the discontinuance
of your patronage. And at, or about the same time, I

should think it proper if your Grace were to distinguish
by any little notice such Selkirk people working with
you as have their families under good order.

I am taking leave of Abbotsford *multum gemens*,
and have been just giving directions for planting upon
Turn-again. When shall we eat a cold luncheon there,
and look at the view, and root up the monster in his
abyss? I assure you none of your numerous vassals can
show a finer succession of *distant* prospects. For the
home-view — ahem! — We must wait till the trees grow.

Ever your Grace's truly faithful   W. Scott.

While the abortive negotiation as to the exchequer
was still pending, Scott was visited, for the first time
since his childish years, with a painful illness, which
proved the harbinger of a series of attacks, all nearly of
the same kind, continued at short intervals during more
than two years. Various letters, already introduced,
have indicated how widely his habits of life when in
Edinburgh differed from those of Abbotsford. They at
all times did so to a great extent; but he had pushed his
liberties with a most robust constitution to a perilous
extreme while the affairs of the Ballantynes were laboring, and he was now to pay the penalty.

This first serious alarm occurred towards the close of
a merry dinner-party in Castle Street (on the 5th of
March), when Scott suddenly sustained such exquisite
torture from cramp in the stomach, that his masculine
powers of endurance gave way, and he retired from the
room with a scream of agony which electrified his guests.
This scene was often repeated, as we shall see presently.
His friends in Edinburgh continued all that spring in
great anxiety on his account. Scarcely, however, had the
first symptoms yielded to severe medical treatment, than
he is found to have beguiled the intervals of his suffering
by planning a dramatic piece on a story supplied to him
by one of Train's communications, which he desired to

present to Terry, on behalf of the actor's first-born son, who had been christened by the name of Walter Scott.[1] Such was the origin of the Fortunes of Devorgoil — a piece which, though completed soon afterwards, and submitted by Terry to many manipulations with a view to the stage, was never received by any manager, and was first published, towards the close of the author's life, under the title, slightly altered for an obvious reason, of The Doom of Devorgoil. The sketch of the story which he gives in the following letter will probably be considered by many besides myself as well worth the drama. It appears that the actor had mentioned to Scott his intention of *Terryfying* The Black Dwarf.

TO DANIEL TERRY, ESQ., LONDON.

EDINBURGH, 12th March, 1817.

DEAR TERRY, — I am now able to write to you on your own affairs, though still as weak as water from the operations of the medical faculty, who, I think, treated me as a recusant to their authority, and having me once at advantage, were determined I should not have strength to rebel again in a hurry. After all, I believe it was touch and go; and considering how much I have to do for my own family and others, my elegy might have been that of the Auld Man's Mare, —

> "The peats and turf are all to lead,
> What ail'd the beast to die ? "

You don't mention the nature of your undertaking in your last, and in your former you spoke both of the Black Dwarf and of Triermain. I have some doubts whether the town will endure a second time the following up a well-known tale with a dramatic representation — and there is no *vis comica* to redeem the Black Dwarf, as in the case of Dominie Sampson. I have thought of

---

[1] This young gentleman is now an officer in the East India Company's army. — (1837.)   Mr. W. S. Terry lived to distinguish himself as a soldier, and fell in action against the Afghans. — (1848.)

two subjects for you, if, like the Archbishop's homilies, they do not smell of the apoplexy. The first is a noble and very dramatic tradition preserved in Galloway, which runs briefly thus: The Barons of Plenton (the family name, I think, was —— by Jupiter, forgot!) boasted of great antiquity, and formerly of extensive power and wealth, to which the ruins of their huge castle, situated on an inland loch, still bear witness. In the middle of the seventeenth century, it is said, these ruins were still inhabited by the lineal descendant of this powerful family. But the ruinous halls and towers of his ancestors were all that had descended to him, and he cultivated the garden of the castle, and sold its fruits for a subsistence. He married in a line suitable rather to his present situation than the dignity of his descent, and was quite sunk into the rank of peasantry, excepting that he was still called — more in mockery, or at least in familiarity, than in respect — the Baron of Plenton. A causeway connected the castle with the mainland; it was cut in the middle, and the moat only passable by a drawbridge which yet subsisted, and which the poor old couple contrived to raise every night by their joint efforts, the country being very unsettled at the time. It must be observed that the old man and his wife occupied only one apartment in the extensive ruins, a small one adjoining to the drawbridge; the rest was waste and dilapidated.

As they were about to retire one night to rest, they were deterred by a sudden storm which, rising in the wildest manner possible, threatened to bury them under the ruins of the castle. While they listened in terror to the complicated sounds of thunder, wind, and rain, they were astonished to hear the clang of hoofs on the causeway, and the voices of people clamoring for admittance. This was a request not rashly to be granted. The couple looked out, and dimly discerned through the storm that the causeway was crowded with riders. "How many of

you are there?" demanded John. — "Not more than the
hall will hold," was the answer; "but open the gate,
lower the bridge, and do not keep the *ladies* in the rain."
— John's heart was melted for the *ladies*, and, against
his wife's advice, he undid the bolts, sunk the drawbridge, and bade them enter in the name of God. Having done so, he instantly retired into his *sanctum sanc-
torum* to await the event, for there was something in the
voices and language of his guests that sounded mysterious
and awful. They rushed into the castle, and appeared
to know their way through all its recesses. Grooms
were heard hurrying their horses to the stables — senti-
nels were heard mounting guard — a thousand lights
gleamed from place to place through the ruins, till at
length they seemed all concentrated in the baronial hall,
whose range of broad windows threw a resplendent illumination on the moss-grown court below.

After a short time, a domestic, clad in a rich but very
antique dress, appeared before the old couple, and commanded them to attend his lord and lady in the great
hall. They went with tottering steps, and to their great
terror found themselves in the midst of a most brilliant
and joyous company; but the fearful part of it was, that
most of the guests resembled the ancestors of John's
family, and were known to him by their resemblance to
pictures which mouldered in the castle, or by traditionary
description. At the head, the founder of the race,
dressed like some mighty baron, or rather some Galwe-
gian prince, sat with his lady. There was a difference
of opinion between these ghostly personages concerning
our honest John. The chief was inclined to receive him
graciously; the lady considered him, from his mean marriage, as utterly unworthy of their name and board. The
upshot is, that the chief discovers to his descendant the
means of finding a huge treasure concealed in the castle;
the lady assures him that the discovery shall never avail
him. — In the morning no trace can be discovered of

the singular personages who had occupied the hall. But John sought for and discovered the vault where the spoils of the Southrons were concealed, rolled away the covering stone, and feasted his eyes on a range of massy chests of iron, filled doubtless with treasure. As he deliberated on the best means of bringing them up, and descending into the vault, he observed it began slowly to fill with water. Bailing and pumping were resorted to, and when he had exhausted his own and his wife's strength, they summoned the assistance of the neighborhood. But the vengeance of the visionary lady was perfect; the waters of the lake had forced their way into the vault, and John, after a year or two spent in draining and so forth, died broken-hearted, the last Baron of Plenton.

Such is the tale, of which the incidents seem new, and the interest capable of being rendered striking; the story admits of the highest degree of decoration, both by poetry, music, and scenery, and I propose (in behalf of my godson) to take some pains in dramatizing it. As thus; — you shall play John, as you can speak a little Scotch; I will make him what the Baron of Bradwardine would have been in his circumstances, and he shall be alternately ridiculous from his family pride and prejudices, contrasted with his poverty, and respectable from his just and independent tone of feeling and character. I think Scotland is entitled to have something on the stage to balance Macklin's two worthies.[1] You understand the dialect will be only tinged with the national dialect — not that the baron is to speak broad Scotch, while all the others talk English. His wife and he shall have one child, a daughter, suitored unto by the conceited young parson or schoolmaster of the village, whose addresses are countenanced by her mother, — and by Halbert the hunter, a youth of unknown descent. Now this youth shall be the rightful heir and representative of the English owners of the treasure, of which they had been

Sir Archy Mac-Sarcasm and Sir Pertinax Mac-Sycophant.

robbed by the baron's ancestors, for which unjust act, their spirits still walked the earth. These, with a substantial character or two, and the ghostly personages, shall mingle as they may — and the discovery of the youth's birth shall break the spell of the treasure-chamber. I will make the ghosts talk as never ghosts talked in the body or out of it; and the music may be as unearthly as you can get it. The rush of the shadows into the castle shall be seen through the window of the baron's apartment in the flat scene. The ghosts' banquet, and many other circumstances, may give great exercise to the scene-painter and dresser. If you like this plan, you had better suspend any other for the present. In my opinion it has the infinite merit of being perfectly new in plot and structure, and I will set about the sketch as soon as my strength is restored in some measure by air and exercise. I am sure I can finish it in a fortnight then. Ever yours truly,   W. SCOTT.

About the time when this letter was written, a newspaper paragraph having excited the apprehension of two — or I should say three — of his dearest friends, that his life was in actual danger, Scott wrote to them as follows: —

TO J. B. S. MORRITT, ESQ., M. P., PORTLAND PLACE, LONDON.

EDINBURGH, 20th March, 1817.

MY DEAR MORRITT, — I hasten to acquaint you that I am in the land of life, and thriving, though I have had a slight shake, and still feel the consequences of medical treatment. I had been plagued all through this winter with cramps in my stomach, which I endured as a man of mould might, and endeavored to combat them by drinking scalding water, and so forth. As they grew rather unpleasantly frequent, I had reluctant recourse to Baillie. But before his answer arrived on the 5th, I had a most violent attack, which broke up a small party at

my house, and sent me to bed roaring like a bull-calf.
All sorts of remedies were applied, as in the case of Gil
Blas's pretended colic, but such was the pain of the real
disorder, that it outdevilled the Doctor hollow. Even
heated salt, which was applied in such a state that it
burned my shirt to rags, I hardly felt when clapped to
my stomach. At length the symptoms became inflammatory, and dangerously so, the seat being the diaphragm.
They only gave way to very profuse bleeding and blistering, which under higher assistance saved my life. My
recovery was slow and tedious from the state of exhaustion. I could neither stir for weakness and giddiness,
nor read for dazzling in my eyes, nor listen for a whiz-
zing sound in my ears, nor even think for lack of the
power of arranging my ideas. So I had a comfortless
time of it for about a week. Even yet I by no means
feel, as the copy-book hath it,

> " The lion bold, which the lamb doth hold — "

on the contrary, I am as weak as water. They tell me
(of course) I must renounce every creature comfort, as
my friend Jedediah calls it. As for dinner and so forth,
I care little about it — but toast and water, and three
glasses of wine, sound like hard laws to me. However,
to parody the lamentation of Hassan, the camel-driver,

> " The lily health outvies the grape's bright ray,
>   And life is dearer than the usquebæ — "

so I shall be amenable to discipline. But in my own
secret mind I suspect the state of my bowels more than
anything else. I take enough of exercise and enough
of rest; but unluckily they are like a Lapland year, divided as one night and one day. In the vacation I never
sit down; in the session-time I seldom rise up. But all
this must be better arranged in future; and I trust I
shall live to weary out all your kindness.

I am obliged to break off hastily. I trust I shall be
able to get over the Fell in the end of summer, which

will rejoice me much, for the sound of the woods of Rokeby is lovely in mine ear. Ever yours,

WALTER SCOTT.

TO MRS. MACLEAN CLEPHANE, OF TORLOISK, MULL.

EDINBURGH, 23d March, 1817.

MY DEAR MRS. AND MISS CLEPHANE, — Here comes to let you know you had nearly seen the last sight of me, unless I had come to visit you on my red beam like one of Fingal's heroes, which, Ossianic as you are, I trow you would readily dispense with. The cause was a cramp in my stomach, which, after various painful visits, as if it had been sent by Prospero, and had mistaken me for Caliban, at length chose to conclude by setting fire to its lodging, like the Frenchmen as they retreated through Russia, and placed me in as proper a state of inflammation as if I had had the whole Spafields committee in my unfortunate stomach. Then bleeding and blistering was the word; and they bled and blistered till they left me neither skin nor blood. However, they beat off the foul fiend, and I am bound to praise the bridge which carried me over. I am still very totterish, and very giddy, kept to panada, or rather to porridge, for I spurned at all foreign slops, and adhered to our ancient oatmeal manufacture.[1] But I have no apprehension of any return of the serious part of the malady, and I am now recovering my strength, though looking somewhat cadaverous upon the occasion.

I much approve of your going to Italy by sea; indeed it is the only way you ought to think of it. I am only

[1] [On the 17th of March, Scott had written to Joanna Baillie: "Two *remarkables* struck me in my illness: the first was, that my great wolf-dog clamored wildly and fearfully about my bed when I was very ill, and would hardly be got out of the room; the other, that when I was recovering, all acquired and factitious tastes seemed to leave me, and I could eat nothing but porridge, and listen to no better reading than a stupid Scottish diary which would have made a whole man sick." — *Familiar Letters*, vol. i. p. 421.]

sorry you are going to leave us for a while; but indeed the isle of Mull might be Florence to me in respect of separation, and cannot be quite Florence to you, since Lady Compton is not there. I lately heard her mentioned in a company where my interest in her was not known, as one of the very few English ladies now in Italy whom their acquirements, conduct, and mode of managing time, induce that part of foreign society, whose approbation is valuable, to consider with high respect and esteem. This I think is very likely; for, whatever folks say of foreigners, those of good education and high rank among them, must have a supreme contempt for the frivolous, dissatisfied, empty, gad-about manners of many of our modern belles. And we may say among ourselves, that there are few upon whom high accomplishments and information sit more gracefully.

John Kemble is here to take leave, acting over all his great characters, and with all the spirit of his best years. He played Coriolanus last night (the first time I have ventured out) fully as well as I ever saw him; and you know what a complete model he is of the Roman. He has made a great reformation in his habits; given up wine, which he used to swallow by pailfuls, — and renewed his youth like the eagles. He seems to me always to play best those characters in which there is a predominating tinge of some overmastering passion, or acquired habit of acting and speaking, coloring the whole man. The patrician pride of Coriolanus, the stoicism of Brutus and Cato, the rapid and hurried vehemence of Hotspur, mark the class of characters I mean. But he fails where a ready and pliable yielding to the. events and passions of life makes what may be termed a more natural personage. Accordingly I think his Macbeth, Lear, and especially his Richard, inferior in spirit and truth. In Hamlet, the natural fixed melancholy of the prince places him within Kemble's range; — yet many delicate and sudden turns of passion slip through his fingers. He is

a lordly vessel, goodly and magnificent when going large
before the wind, but wanting the facility to go "*ready
about*," so that he is sometimes among the breakers before he can wear ship. Yet we lose in him a most excellent critic, an accomplished scholar, and one who graced
our forlorn drama with what little it has left of good
sense and gentlemanlike feeling. And so exit he. He
made me write some lines to speak when he withdraws,
and he has been here criticising and correcting till he
got them quite to his mind, which has rather tired me.

Most truly yours while

WALTER SCOTT.

On the 29th of March, 1817, John Philip Kemble,
after going through the round of his chief parts, to the
delight of the Edinburgh audience, took his final leave
of them as Macbeth, and in the costume of that character
delivered a farewell address, penned for him by Scott.[1]
No one who witnessed that scene, and heard the lines as
then recited, can ever expect to be again interested to
the same extent by anything occurring within the walls

---

[1] See *Poetical Works*, vol. xi. p. 348 [Cambridge Ed. p. 436]. Scott's
farewell for Kemble first appeared in *The Sale-Room* for April 5, 1817;
and in the introductory note James Ballantyne says: "The character fixed
upon, with happy propriety, for Kemble's closing scene, was Macbeth. He
had labored under a severe cold for a few days before, but on the memorable night the physical annoyance yielded to the energy of his mind. 'He
was,' he said in the Green-room, immediately before the curtain rose, 'determined to leave behind him the most perfect specimen of his art which
he had ever shown;' and his success was complete. At the moment of the
tyrant's death, the curtain fell by the universal acclamation of the audience. The applauses were vehement and prolonged; they ceased — were
resumed — rose again -- were reiterated — and again were hushed. In a
few minutes the curtain ascended, and Mr. Kemble came forward, in the
dress of Macbeth (the audience by a consentaneous movement rising to
receive him), to deliver his *farewell*." . . . "Mr. Kemble delivered the
lines with exquisite beauty, and with an effect that was evidenced by the
tears and sobs of many of the audience. His own emotions were very conspicuous. When his farewell was closed, he lingered long on the stage,
as if unable to retire. The house again stood up, and cheered him with
the waving of hats and long shouts of applause."

of a theatre; nor was I ever present at any public dinner in all its circumstances more impressive than was that which occurred a few days afterwards, when Kemble's Scotch friends and admirers assembled around him — Francis Jeffrey being chairman, Walter Scott and John Wilson the croupiers.

Shortly before this time, Mr. William Laidlaw had met with misfortunes, which rendered it necessary for him to give up the lease of a farm, on which he had been for some years settled, in Mid-Lothian. He was now anxiously looking about him for some new establishment, and it occurred to Scott that it might be mutually advantageous, as well as agreeable, if his excellent friend would consent to come and occupy a house on his property, and endeavor, under his guidance, to make such literary exertions as might raise his income to an amount adequate for his comfort. The prospect of obtaining such a neighbor was, no doubt, the more welcome to "Abbotsford and Kaeside," from its opening at this period of fluctuating health; and Laidlaw, who had for twenty years loved and revered him, considered the proposal with far greater delight than the most lucrative appointment on any noble domain in the island could have afforded him. Though possessed of a lively and searching sagacity as to things in general, he had always been as to his own worldly interests simple as a child. His tastes and habits were all modest; and when he looked forward to spending the remainder of what had not hitherto been a successful life, under the shadow of the genius that he had worshipped almost from boyhood, his gentle heart was all happiness. He surveyed with glistening eyes the humble cottage in which his friend proposed to lodge him, his wife, and his little ones, and said to himself that he should write no more sad songs on *Forest Flittings*.[1]

[1] Mr. Laidlaw has not published many verses; but his song of *Lucy's Flitting* — a simple and pathetic picture of a poor Ettrick maiden's

Scott's notes to him at this time afford a truly charming picture of thoughtful and respectful delicacy on both
sides. Mr. Laidlaw, for example, appears to have
hinted that he feared his friend, in making the proposal
as to the house at Kaeside, might have perhaps in some
degree overlooked the feelings of "Laird Moss," who,
having sold his land several months before, had as yet
continued to occupy his old homestead. Scott answers:—

TO MR. W. LAIDLAW.

EDINBURGH, April 5, 1817.

MY DEAR SIR, — Nothing can give me more pleasure
than the prospect of your making yourself comfortable
at Kaeside till some good thing casts up. I have not
put Mr. Moss to any inconvenience, for I only requested
an answer, giving him leave to sit if he had a mind —
and of free will he leaves my premises void and redd at
Whitsunday. I suspect the house is not in good order,
but we shall get it brushed up a little. Without affectation I consider myself the obliged party in this matter —
or at any rate it is a mutual benefit, and you shall have
grass for a cow, and so forth — whatever you want. I
am sure when you are so near I shall find some literary
labor for you that will make ends meet. Yours, in
haste,   W. SCOTT.

He had before this time made considerable progress in
another historical sketch (that of the year 1815) for the
Edinburgh Annual Register; and the first literary labor
which he provided for Laidlaw appears to have been
arranging for the same volume a set of newspaper articles, usually printed under the head of *Chronicle*, to
which were appended some little extracts of new books
of travels, and the like miscellanies. The Edinburgh

feelings in leaving a service where she had been happy — has long been,
and must ever be, a favorite with all who understand the delicacies of the
Scottish dialect, and the manners of the district in which the scene is laid.

Monthly Magazine, subsequently known by the name
of its projector, Blackwood, commenced in April of this
year; and one of its editors, Mr. Thomas Pringle, being
a Teviotdale man and an old acquaintance of Laidlaw's,
offered to the latter the care of its *Chronicle department*
also, — not perhaps without calculating that, in case
Laidlaw's connection with the new journal should become
at all a strict one, Scott would be induced to give it
occasionally the benefit of his own literary assistance.
He accordingly did not write — being unwell at the time
— but *dictated* to Pringle a collection of anecdotes concerning Scottish gypsies, which attracted a good deal of
notice;[1] and, I believe, he also assisted Laidlaw in drawing up one or more articles on the subject of Scottish
superstitions.   But the bookseller and Pringle soon quar-
relled, and the Magazine assuming, on the retirement
of the latter, a high Tory character, Laidlaw's Whig
feelings induced him to renounce its alliance; while
Scott, having no kindness for Blackwood personally, and
disapproving (though he chuckled over it) the reckless
extravagance of juvenile satire which, by and by, distinguished his journal, appears to have easily acquiesced in
the propriety of Laidlaw's determination.   I insert
meantime a few notes, which will show with what care
and kindness he watched over Laidlaw's operations for
the Annual Register.

TO MR. LAIDLAW, AT KAESIDE.

EDINBURGH, June 16, 1817.

DEAR SIR, — I enclose you "rare guerdon," better
than remuneration, — namely, a cheque for £25, for the
Chronicle part of the Register.   The incidents selected
should have some reference to amusement as well as information, and may be occasionally abridged in the narration; but, after all, paste and scissors form your prin-

[1] These anecdotes were subsequently inserted in the Introduction to
Guy Mannering.

cipal materials. You must look out for two or three good original articles; and, if you would read and take pains to abridge one or two curious books of travels, I would send out the volumes. Could I once get the head of the concern fairly round before the wind again, I am sure I could make it £100 a year to you. In the present instance it will be at least £50.

Yours truly, W. S.

TO THE SAME.

EDINBURGH, July 3, 1817.

MY DEAR SIR, — I send you Adam's and Riley's Travels. You will observe I don't want a review of the books, or a detail of these persons' adventures, but merely a short article expressing the light, direct or doubtful, which they have thrown on the interior of Africa. "Recent Discoveries in Africa" will be a proper title. I hope to find you materially amended, or rather quite stout, when I come out on Saturday. I am quite well this morning. Yours, in haste,

W. S.

P. S. — I add Mariner's Tonga Islands, and Campbell's Voyage. Pray take great care of them, as I am a coxcomb about my books, and hate specks or spots. Take care of yourself, and want for nothing that Abbotsford can furnish.

These notes have carried us down to the middle of the year. But I must now turn to some others, which show that before Whitsuntide, when Laidlaw settled at Kaeside, negotiations were on foot respecting another novel.

TO MR. JOHN BALLANTYNE, HANOVER STREET, EDINBURGH.

ABBOTSFORD, Monday. [April, 1817.]

DEAR JOHN, — I have a good subject for a work of fiction *in petto*. What do you think Constable would give for a smell of it? You ran away without taking leave the other morning, or I wished to have spoken to you about it. I don't mean a continuation of Jedediah, because there might be some delicacy in putting that by the original publishers. You may write if anything occurs to you on this subject. It will not interrupt my History. By the way, I have a great lot of the Register ready for delivery, and no man asks for it. I shall want to pay up some cash at Whitsunday, which will make me draw on my brains. Yours truly,

W. SCOTT.

TO THE SAME.

ABBOTSFORD, Saturday, May 3, 1817.

DEAR JOHN, — I shall be much obliged to you to come here with Constable on Monday, as he proposes a visit, and it will save time. By the way, you must attend that the usual quantity of stock is included in the arrangement — that is £600 for 6000 copies. My sum is £1700, payable in May — a round advance, by'r Lady, but I think I am entitled to it, considering what I have twined off hitherto on such occasions.

I make a point on your coming with Constable, health allowing. Yours truly,   W. S.

The result of this meeting is indicated in a note, scribbled by John Ballantyne at the bottom of the foregoing letter, before it was seen by his brother the printer: —

Half-past 3 o'clock, Tuesday.

DEAR JAMES, — I am at this moment returned from Abbotsford, with entire and full success. Wish me joy. I shall gain above £600 — Constable taking my share of stock also. This title is *Rob Roy — by the Author of Waverley ! ! !* Keep this letter for me.   J. B.

On the same page there is written, in fresher ink, which marks, no doubt, the time when John pasted it into his collection of private papers now before me, —

N. B. — I did gain above £1200. — J. B.

The title of this novel was suggested by Constable, and he told me years afterwards the difficulty he had to get it adopted by the author. "What!" said he, "Mr. Accoucheur, must you be setting up for Mr. Sponsor too? — but let's hear it." Constable said the name of the real hero would be the best possible name for the book. "Nay," answered Scott, "never let me have to write up to a name. You well know I have generally adopted a title that told nothing." — The bookseller, however, persevered; and after the trio had dined, these scruples gave way.

On rising from table, according to Constable, they sallied out to the green before the door of the cottage, and all in the highest spirits enjoyed the fine May evening. John Ballantyne, hopping up and down in his glee, exclaimed, "Is Rob's gun here, Mr. Scott; would you object to my trying the auld barrel with a *few de joy*?" — "Nay, Mr. Puff," said Scott, "it would burst, and blow you to the devil before your time." — "Johnny, my man," said Constable, "what the mischief puts drawing at sight into *your* head?" Scott laughed heartily at this innuendo; and then observing that the little man felt somewhat sore, called attention to the notes of a bird in the adjoining shrubbery. "And by the bye," said he, as they continued listening, "'t is a long time, Johnny, since we have had the Cobbler of Kelso." Mr. Puff forthwith jumped up on a mass of stone, and seating himself in the proper attitude of one working with his awl, began a favorite interlude, mimicking a certain son of Crispin, at whose stall Scott and he had often lingered when they were schoolboys, and a blackbird, the only companion of his cell, that used to sing to him, while he talked and whistled to it all day long. With this performance Scott was always delighted: nothing could be richer than the contrast of the bird's wild sweet notes, some of which he imitated with wonderful skill, and the accompaniment of the Cobbler's hoarse cracked voice, uttering all manner of endearing epithets, which Johnny multiplied and varied in a style worthy of the Old Women in Rabelais at the birth of Pantagruel. I often wondered that Mathews, who borrowed so many good things from John Ballantyne, allowed this Cobbler, which was certainly the masterpiece, to escape him.

Scott himself had probably exceeded that evening the three glasses of wine sanctioned by his Sangrados. "I never," said Constable, "had found him so disposed to be communicative about what he meant to do. Though he had had a return of his illness but the day before, he continued for an hour or more to walk backwards and forwards on the green, talking and laughing — he told us he was sure he should make a hit in a Glasgow weaver, whom he would *ravel up with Rob ;* and fairly outshone the Cobbler, in an extempore dialogue between the bailie and the cateran — something not unlike what the book gives us as passing in the Glasgow tolbooth."

Mr. Puff might well exult in the "full and entire success" of this trip to Abbotsford. His friend had made it a *sine qua non* with Constable that he should have a third share in the bookseller's moiety of the bargain — and though Johnny had no more trouble about the publishing or selling of Rob Roy than his own Cobbler of Kelso, this stipulation had secured him a *bonus* of £1200, before two years passed. Moreover, one must admire his adroitness in persuading Constable, during their journey back to Edinburgh, to relieve him of that fraction of his own old stock, with which his unhazardous share in the new transaction was burdened. Scott's kindness continued, as long as John Ballantyne lived, to provide for him a constant succession of similar advantages at the same easy rate; and Constable, from deference to Scott's wishes, and from his own liking for the humorous auctioneer, appears to have submitted with hardly a momentary grudge to this heavy tax on his most important ventures.

The same week Scott received Southey's celebrated letter to Mr. William Smith, M. P. for Norwich. The poet of Keswick had also forwarded to him somewhat earlier his Pilgrimage to Waterloo, which piece contains a touching allusion to the affliction the author had recently sustained in the death of a fine boy. Scott's letter on this occasion was as follows: —

TO ROBERT SOUTHEY, ESQ., KESWICK.

SELKIRK, May 9, 1817.

MY DEAR SOUTHEY, — I have been a strangely negligent correspondent for some months past, more especially as I have had you rarely out of my thoughts, for I think you will hardly doubt of my sincere sympathy in events which have happened since I have written. I shed sincere tears over the Pilgrimage to Waterloo. But in the crucible of human life, the purest gold is tried by the strongest heat, and I can only hope for the continuance of your present family blessings to one so well formed to enjoy the pure happiness they afford. My health has, of late, been very indifferent. I was very nearly succumbing under a violent inflammatory attack, and still feel the effects of the necessary treatment. I believe they took one third of the blood of my system, and blistered in proportion: so that both my flesh and my blood have been in a woefully reduced state. I got out here some weeks since, where, by dint of the insensible exercise which one takes in the country, I feel myself gathering strength daily, but am still obliged to observe a severe regimen. It was not to croak about myself, however, that I took up the pen, but to wish you joy of your triumphant answer to that coarse-minded William Smith. He deserved all he has got, and, to say the truth, you do not spare him, and have no cause. His attack seems to have proceeded from the vulgar insolence of a low mind desirous of attacking genius at disadvantage. It is the ancient and eternal strife of which the witch speaks in

Thalaba. Such a man as he, feels he has no alliance with such as you, and his evil instincts lead him to treat as hostile whatever he cannot comprehend. I met Smith once during his stay in Edinburgh,[1] and had, what I seldom have with any one in society, a high quarrel with him. His mode of travelling had been from one gentleman's seat to another, abusing the well-known hospitality of the Highland lairds, by taking possession of their houses, even during their absence, domineering in them when they were present, and not only eating the dinner of to-day, but requiring that the dinner of to-morrow should also be made ready and carried forward with him, to save the expense of inns. All this was no business of mine, but when, in the middle of a company consisting of those to whom he had owed this hospitality, he abused the country, of which he knew little — the language, of which he knew nothing — and the people, who have their faults, but are a much more harmless, moral, and at the same time high-spirited population, than, I venture to say, he ever lived amongst — I thought it was really too bad, and so e'en took up the debate, and gave it him over the knuckles as smartly as I could. Your pamphlet, therefore, fed fat my ancient grudge against him as well as the modern one, for you cannot doubt that my blood boiled at reading the report of his speech. Enough of this gentleman, who, I think, will not walk out of the round in a hurry again, to slander the conduct of individuals.

I am at present writing at our head-court of freeholders — a set of quiet, unpretending, but sound-judging country gentlemen, and whose opinions may be very well taken a fair specimen of those men of sense and honor, who are not likely to be dazzled by literary talent, which

---

[1] Scott's meeting with this Mr. Smith occurred at the table of his friend and colleague, Hector Macdonald Buchanan. The company, except Scott and Smith, were all, like their hospitable landlord, Highlanders.

lies out of their beat, and who, therefore, cannot be of partial counsel in the cause; and I never heard an opinion more generally, and even warmly expressed, than that your triumphant vindication brands Smith as a slanderer in all time coming. I think you may not be displeased to know this, because what men of keen feelings and literary pursuits must have felt, cannot be unknown to you, and you may not have the same access to know the impression made upon the general class of society.

I have to thank you for the continuation of the History of Brazil — one of your gigantic labors; the fruit of a mind so active, yet so patient of labor. I am not yet far advanced in the second volume, reserving it usually for my hour's amusement in the evening, as children keep their dainties for *bonne bouche:* but as far as I have come, it possesses all the interest of the commencement, though a more faithless and worthless set than both Dutch and Portuguese I have never read of; and it requires your knowledge of the springs of human action, and your lively description of "hair - breadth 'scapes," to make one care whether the hog bites the dog, or the dog bites the hog. Both nations were in rapid declension from their short-lived age of heroism, and in the act of experiencing all those retrograde movements which are the natural consequence of selfishness on the one hand, and bigotry on the other.

I am glad to see you are turning your mind to the state of the poor. Should you enter into details on the subject of the best mode of assisting them, I would be happy to tell you the few observations I have made — not on a very small scale neither, considering my fortune, for I have kept about thirty of the laborers in my neighborhood in constant employment this winter. This I do not call charity, because they executed some extensive plantations and other works, which I could never have got done so cheaply, and which I always intended one day to do. But neither was it altogether selfish on my part, because I was putting myself to inconvenience in incurring the expense of several years at once, and certainly would not have done so, but to serve mine honest neighbors, who were likely to want work but for such exertion. From my observation, I am inclined greatly to doubt the salutary effect of the scheme generally adopted in Edinburgh and elsewhere for relieving the poor. At Edinburgh, they are employed on public works at so much a day — tenpence, I believe, or one shilling, with an advance to those who have families. This rate is fixed below that of ordinary wages, in order that no person may be employed but those who really cannot find work elsewhere. But it is attended with this bad effect, that the people regard it partly as charity, which is humiliating — and partly as an imposition, in taking their labor below its usual salable value; to which many add a third view of the subject — namely, that this sort of half-pay is not given them for the purpose of working, but to prevent their rising in rebellion. None of these misconceptions are favorable to hard labor, and the consequence is, that I never have seen such a set of idle *fainéants* as those employed on this system in the public works, and I am sure that, notwithstanding the very laudable intention of those who subscribed to form the fund, and the yet more praiseworthy, because more difficult, exertions of those who superintend it, the issue of the scheme will occasion full as much mischief as good to the people engaged in it. Private gentlemen, acting on something like a similar system, may make it answer better, because they have not the lazy dross of a metropolis to contend with — because they have fewer hands to manage — and, above all, because an individual always manages his own concerns better than those of the country can be managed. Yet all who have employed those who were distressed for want of work at under wages, have had, less or more, similar complaints to make. I think I have avoided this in my own case, by inviting the country people to do piece-work by the contract. Two things only are necessary — one is, that the nature of the work should be such as will admit of its being ascertained, when finished, to have been substantially executed. All sort of spade-work and hoe-work, with many other kinds of country labor, fall under this description, and the employer can hardly be cheated in the execution if he keeps a reasonable lookout. The other point is, to take care that the undertakers, in their anxiety for employment, do not take the job too cheap. A little acquaintance with country labor will enable one to regulate this; but it is an essential point, for if you do not keep them to their bargain, it is making a jest of the thing, and forfeiting the very advantage you have in view — that, namely, of inducing the laborer to bring his heart and spirit to his work. But this he will do where he has a fair bargain, which is to prove a good or bad one according to his own exertions. In this case you make the poor man his own friend, for the profits of his good conduct are all his own. It is astonishing how partial the people are to this species of contract, and how diligently they labor, acquiring or maintaining all the while those habits which render them honorable and useful members of society. I mention this to you, because the rich, much to their honor, do not, in general, require to be so much stimulated to benevolence, as to be directed in the most useful way to exert it.

I have still a word to say about the poor of our own parish of Parnassus. I have been applied to by a very worthy friend, Mr. Scott of Sinton, in behalf of an unfortunate Mr. Gilmour, who, it seems, has expended a little fortune in printing, upon his own account, poems which, from the sample I saw, seem exactly to answer the description of Dean Swift's country house: —

> " Too bad for a blessing, too good for a curse,
> I wish from my soul they were better or worse."

But you are the dean of our corporation, and, I am informed, take some interest in this poor gentleman. If you can point out any way in which I can serve him, I am sure my inclination is not wanting, but it looks like a very hopeless case. I beg my kindest respects to Mrs. Southey, and am always sincerely and affectionately yours,

WALTER SCOTT.

About this time Hogg took possession of Altrive Lake, and some of his friends in Edinburgh set on foot a subscription edition of his Queen's Wake (at a guinea each copy), in the hope of thus raising a sum adequate to the stocking of the little farm. The following letter alludes to this affair; and also to the death of Frances, Lady Douglas, sister to Duke Henry of Buccleuch, whose early kindness to Scott has been more than once mentioned.

TO THE RIGHT HON. LORD MONTAGU.

ABBOTSFORD, June 8, 1817.

MY DEAR LORD, — I am honored with your letter, and will not fail to take care that the Shepherd profits by your kind intentions, and those of Lady Montagu. This is a scheme which I did not devise, for I fear it will end in disappointment, but for which I have done, and will do, all I possibly can. There is an old saying of the seamen's, "Every man is not born to be a boatswain," and I think I have heard of men born under a sixpenny planet, and doomed never to be worth a groat. I fear something of this vile sixpenny influence had gleamed in at the cottage window when poor Hogg first came squeaking into the world. All that he made by his original book he ventured on a flock of sheep to drive into the Highlands to a farm he had taken there, but of which he could not get possession, so that all the stock was ruined and sold to disadvantage. Then he tried another farm, which proved too dear, so that he fairly broke upon it. Then put forth divers publications, which had little sale — and brought him accordingly few pence, though some praise. Then came this Queen's Wake, by which he might and ought to have made from £100 to £200 — for there were, I think, three editions — when lo! his bookseller turned bankrupt, and paid him never a penny. The Duke has now, with his wonted generosity, given him a cosie bield, and the object of the present attack upon the public is to get if possible as much cash together as will stock it. But no one has loose guineas now to give poor poets, and I greatly doubt the scheme succeeding, unless it is more strongly patronized than can almost be expected. In bookselling matters, an author must either be the conjurer, who commands the devil, or the witch who serves him — and few are they whose situation is sufficiently independent to enable them to assume the higher character — and this is injurious to the indigent author in every respect, for not only is he obliged to turn his pen to every various kind of composition, and so to injure himself with the public by writing hastily, and on subjects unfitted for his genius; but, moreover, those honest gentlemen, the booksellers, from a natural association, consider the books as of least value, which they find they can get at least expense of copy-money, and therefore are proportionally careless in pushing the sale of the work. Whereas a good round sum out of their purse, like a moderate rise of rent on a farm, raises the work thus acquired in their own eyes, and serves as a spur to make them clear away every channel, by which they can discharge their quires upon the public. So much for bookselling, the most ticklish and unsafe and hazardous of all professions, scarcely with the exception of horse-jockeyship.

You cannot doubt the sincere interest I take in Lady Montagu's health. I was very glad to learn from the Duke, that the late melancholy event had produced no permanent effect on her constitution, as I know how much her heart must have suffered.[1] I saw our regretted friend for the last time at the Theatre, and made many schemes to be at Bothwell this next July. But thus the world glides from us, and those we most love and honor are withdrawn from the stage before us. I know not why it was that among the few for whom I had so much respectful regard, I never had associated the idea of early deprivation with Lady Douglas. Her excellent sense, deep information, and the wit which she wielded with so much good-humor, were allied apparently to a healthy constitution, which might have permitted us to enjoy, and be instructed by her society for many years. *Dis aliter visum*, and the recollection dwelling on all the delight which she afforded to society, and the good which she did in private life, is what now remains to us of her wit, wisdom, and benevolence. The Duke keeps his usual health, with always just so much of the gout, however, as would make me wish that he had more — a kind wish, for which I do not observe that he is sufficiently grateful. I hope to spend a few days at Drumlanrig Castle, when that ancient mansion shall have so far limited its courtesy as to stand covered in the presence of the wind and rain, which I believe is not yet the case. I am no friend to ceremony, and like a house as well when it does not carry its roof *en chapeau bras*. I heartily wish your Lordship joy of the new mansion at Ditton, and hope my good stars will permit me to pay my respects there one day. The discovery of the niches certainly bodes good luck to the house of Montagu, and as there are three of them, I presume it is to come threefold. From the care with which they were concealed, I presume they had been closed in the days of Cromwell, or a little before, and that the artist employed (like the

---

[1] Lady Montagu was the daughter of the late Lord Douglas by his first marriage with Lady Lucy Graham, daughter of the second Duke of Montrose.

General, who told his soldiers to fight bravely against the Pope, since they were Venetians before they were Christians) had more professional than religious zeal, and did not even, according to the practice of the time, think it necessary to sweep away Popery with the besom of destruction.[1] I am here on a stolen visit of two days, and find my mansion gradually enlarging. Thanks to Mr. Atkinson (who found out a practical use for our romantic theory), it promises to make a comfortable station for offering your Lordship and Lady Montagu a pilgrim's meal, when you next visit Melrose Abbey, and that without any risk of your valet (who I recollect is a substantial person) sticking between the wall of the parlor and the backs of the chairs placed round the table. This literally befell Sir Harry Macdougal's fat butler, who looked like a ship of the line in the loch at Bowhill, altogether unlike his master, who could glide wherever a weasel might make his way. Mr. Atkinson has indeed been more attentive than I can express, when I consider how valuable his time must be.[2] We are attempting no castellated conundrums to rival those Lord Napier used to have executed in sugar, when he was Commissioner, and no cottage neither, but an irregular somewhat — like an old English hall, in which your squire of £500 a year used to drink his ale in days of yore.

I am making considerable plantations (that is, considering), being greatly encouraged by the progress of those I formerly laid out. Read the veracious Gulliver's account of the Windsor Forest of Lilliput, and you will

---

[1] Lord Montagu's house at Ditton Park, near Windsor, had recently been destroyed by fire — and the ruins revealed some niches with antique candlesticks, etc., belonging to a domestic chapel that had been converted to other purposes from the time, I believe, of Henry VIII.

[2] Mr. Atkinson, of St. John's Wood, was the architect of Lord Montagu's new mansion at Ditton, as well as the artist ultimately employed in arranging Scott's interior at Abbotsford.

have some idea of the solemn gloom of my Druid shades.
Your Lordship's truly faithful

WALTER SCOTT.

This is the 8th of June, and not an ash-tree in leaf
yet. The country cruelly backward, and whole fields
destroyed by the grub. I dread this next season.

CHAPTER XXXIX

EXCURSION TO THE LENNOX, GLASGOW, AND DRUMLAN-
RIG. — PURCHASE OF TOFTFIELD. — ESTABLISHMENT
OF THE FERGUSON FAMILY AT HUNTLY BURN. —
LINES WRITTEN IN ILLNESS. — VISITS OF WASHING-
TON IRVING, LADY BYRON, AND SIR DAVID WILKIE.
— PROGRESS OF THE BUILDING AT ABBOTSFORD. —
LETTERS TO MORRITT, TERRY, ETC. — CONCLUSION OF
ROB ROY

1817

DURING the summer term of 1817, Scott seems to have
labored chiefly on his History of 1815 for the Register,
which was published in August; but he also found time
to draw up the Introduction for a richly embellished
quarto, entitled Border Antiquities, which came out a
month later.   This valuable essay, containing large additions to the information previously embodied in the Minstrelsy, has been included in the late collection of his
Miscellaneous Prose, and has thus obtained a circulation
not to be expected for it in the original costly form.

Upon the rising of the Court in July, he made an excursion to the Lennox, chiefly that he might visit a cave
at the head of Loch Lomond, said to have been a favorite
retreat of his hero, Rob Roy.   He was accompanied to
the seat of his friend, Mr. Macdonald Buchanan, by
Captain Adam Ferguson — the *long Linton* of the days
of his apprenticeship; and thence to Glasgow, where,
under the auspices of a kind and intelligent acquaintance,
Mr. John Smith, bookseller, he refreshed his recollection of the noble cathedral, and other localities of the
birthplace of Bailie Jarvie.   Mr. Smith took care also

to show the tourists the most remarkable novelties in the great manufacturing establishments of his flourishing city; and he remembers particularly the delight which Scott expressed on seeing the process of *singeing* muslin — that is, of divesting the finished web of all superficial knots and irregularities, by passing it, with the rapidity of lightning, over a bar of red-hot iron. "The man that imagined this," said Scott, "was *the Shakespeare* of *the Wabsters*, —

> ' Things out of hope are compass'd oft with vent'ring.' " [1]

The following note indicates the next stages of his progress : —

TO HIS GRACE THE DUKE OF BUCCLEUCH, DRUMLANRIG CASTLE.

SANQUHAR, 2 o'clock, July 30,[2] 1817.

From Ross, where the clouds on Benlomond are sleeping —
From Greenock, where Clyde to the Ocean is sweeping —
From Largs, where the Scotch gave the Northmen a drilling —
From Ardrossan, whose harbor cost many a shilling —
From Old Cumnock, where beds are as hard as a plank, sir —
From a chop and green pease, and a chicken in Sanquhar,
This eve, please the Fates, at Drumlanrig we anchor.

W. S.

The Poet and Captain Ferguson remained a week at Drumlanrig, and thence repaired together to Abbotsford. By this time, the foundations of that part of the existing house, which extends from the hall westwards to the original courtyard, had been laid; and Scott now found a new source of constant occupation in watching the proceedings of his masons. He had, moreover, no lack of employment further a-field, — for he was now negotiating with another neighboring landowner for the purchase of an addition, of more consequence than any he had hith-

---

[1] Shakespeare's Poems —*Venus and Adonis.*
[2] [A misprint of some earlier date, possibly the *16th.* See the more detailed account of Scott's movements at this time, to be found in *Familiar Letters,* vol. i. pp. 432–436.]

erto made, to his estate. In the course of the autumn he concluded this matter, and became, for the price of £10,000, proprietor of the lands of *Toftfield*,[1] on which there had recently been erected a substantial mansion-house, fitted, in all points, for the accommodation of a genteel family. This circumstance offered a temptation which much quickened Scott's zeal for completing his arrangement. The venerable Professor Ferguson had died a year before; Captain Adam Ferguson was at home on half-pay; and Scott now saw the means of se-curing for himself, henceforth, the immediate neighbor-hood of the companion of his youth, and his amiable sisters. Ferguson, who had written, from the lines of Torres Vedras, his hopes of finding, when the war should be over, some sheltering cottage upon the Tweed, within a walk of Abbotsford, was delighted to see his dreams realized; and the family took up their residence next spring at the new house of Toftfield, on which Scott then bestowed, at the ladies' request, the name of Huntly Burn: this more harmonious designation being taken from the mountain brook which passes through its grounds and garden, — the same famous in tradition as the scene of Thomas the Rhymer's interviews with the Queen of Fairy. The upper part of the *Rhymer's Glen*, through which this brook finds its way from the Cauldshiels Loch to Toftfield, had been included in a previous pur-chase. He was now master of all these haunts of "True Thomas," and of the whole ground of the battle of Mel-rose, from *Skirmish-field* to *Turn-again*. His enjoy-ment of the new territories was, however, interrupted by various returns of his cramp, and the depression of spirit which always attended, in his case, the use of opium,

---

[1] On completing this purchase, Scott writes to John Ballantyne : — " Dear John, — I have closed with Usher for his beautiful patrimony, which makes me a great laird. I am afraid the people will take me up for coining. Indeed, these novels, while their attractions last, are some-thing like it. I am very glad of *your* good prospects. Still I cry, *Prudence! Prudence !* — Yours truly,   W. S."

the only medicine that seemed to have power over the disease.[1]

It was while struggling with such languor, on one lovely evening of this autumn, that he composed the following beautiful verses. They mark the very spot of their birth, — namely, the then naked height overhanging the northern side of the Cauldshiels Loch, from which Melrose Abbey to the eastward, and the hills of Ettrick and Yarrow to the west, are now visible over a wide range of rich woodland, — all the work of the poet's hand: —

---

[1] [On August 1, 1817, Jeffrey writes to Scott, asking if he could not be induced to write a notice of Mr. C. K. Sharpe's edition of Kirkton's *Secret and True History of the Church of Scotland*, for the *Edinburgh Review*, to which Scott replies, August 5 : —

"I flatter myself it will not require many protestations to assure you with what pleasure I would undertake any book that can give you pleasure ; but in the present case I am hampered by two circumstances : one, that I promised Gifford a review of this very Kirkton for the *Quarterly*; the other that I shall certainly be unable to keep my word with him. I am obliged to take exercise three or four hours in the forenoon and two after dinner, to keep off the infernal spasms which since last winter have attacked me with such violence, as if all the imps that used to plague poor Caliban were washing, wringing, and ironing the unshapely but useful bag which Sir John Sinclair treats with such distinction — my stomach, in short. Now, as I have much to do of my own, I fear I can hardly be of use to you in the present case, which I am very sorry for, as I like the subject, and would be pleased to give my own opinion respecting the Jacobitism of the editor, which, like my own, has a good spice of affectation in it, mingled with some not unnatural feelings of respect for a cause which, though indefensible in common sense and ordinary policy, has a great deal of high-spirited Quixotry about it.

"Can you not borrow from your briefs and criticism a couple of days to look about you here ? I dare not ask Mrs. Jeffrey till next year, when my hand will be out of the mortar-tub ; and at present my only spare bed was till of late but accessible by the feudal accommodation of a drawbridge made of two deals, and still requires the clue of Ariadne. . . . I am like one of Miss Edgeworth's heroines, master of all things in miniature — a little hill, and a little glen, and a little horse-pond of a loch, and a little river, I was going to call it, — the Tweed ; but I remember the minister was mobbed by his parishioners for terming it, in his statistical report, an inconsiderable stream. So pray do come and see me, and if I can stead you, or pleasure you, in the course of the winter, you shall command me." — Cockburn's *Life of Jeffrey*, vol. i. p. 417.]

" The sun upon the Weirdlaw Hill,
  In Ettrick's vale, is sinking sweet ;
The westland wind is hush and still —
  The lake lies sleeping at my feet.
Yet not the landscape to mine eye
  Bears those bright hues that once it bore ;
Though evening, with her richest dye,
  Flames o'er the hills of Ettrick's shore.

" With listless look along the plain
  I see Tweed's silver current glide,
And coldly mark the holy fane
  Of Melrose rise in ruin'd pride.
The quiet lake, the balmy air,
  The hill, the stream, the tower, the tree, —
Are they still such as once they were,
  Or is the dreary change in me ?

" Alas ! the warp'd and broken board,
  How can it bear the painter's dye !
The harp of strain'd and tuneless chord,
  How to the minstrel's skill reply !
To aching eyes each landscape lowers,
  To feverish pulse each gale blows chill ;
And Araby's or Eden's bowers
  Were barren as this moorland hill."

He again alludes to his illness in a letter to Mr. Morritt: —

TO J. B. S. MORRITT, ESQ., M. P., ROKEBY.

ABBOTSFORD, August 11, 1817.

MY DEAR MORRITT, — I am arrived from a little tour in the west of Scotland, and had hoped, in compliance with your kind wish, to have indulged myself with a skip over the Border as far as Rokeby, about the end of this month. But my fate denies me this pleasure; for, in consequence of one or two blunders, during my absence, in executing my new premises, I perceive the necessity of remaining at the helm while they are going on. Our masons, though excellent workmen, are too little accustomed to the gimcracks of their art, to be trusted with the execution of a *bravura* plan, without constant inspection. Besides, the said laborers lay me under the neces-

sity of laboring a little myself; and I find I can no longer
with impunity undertake to make one week's hard work
supply the omissions of a fortnight's idleness. Like you,
I have abridged my creature-comforts, — as Old Mortality would call them, — renouncing beer and ale on all
ordinary occasions; also pastry, fruit, etc., and all that
tends to acidity. These are awkward warnings; but *sat
est vixisse*. To have lived respected and regarded by
some of the best men in our age is enough for an individual like me; the rest must be as God wills, and when
He wills.

The poor-laws, into which you have ventured for the
love of the country, form a sad quagmire. They are like
John Bunyan's Slough of Despond, into which, as he ob-
serves, millions of cart-loads of good resolutions have been
thrown, without perceptibly mending the way. From
what you say, and from what I have heard from others,
there is a very natural desire to trust to one or two em-
pirical remedies, such as general systems of education,
and so forth. But a man with a broken constitution
might as well put faith in Spilsbury or Godbold. It is
not the knowledge, but the use which is made of it, that
is productive of real benefit. To say that the Scottish
peasant is less likely than the Englishman to become
an incumbrance on his parish, is saying, in other words,
that this country is less populous, — that there are fewer
villages and towns, — that the agricultural classes, from
the landed proprietor down to the cottager, are individ-
ually more knit and cemented together; — above all,
that the Scotch peasant has harder habits of life, and can
endure from his infancy a worse fare and lodging than
your parish almshouses offer. — There is a terrible evil
in England to which we are strangers, — the number, to
wit, of tippling-houses, where the laborer, as a matter
of course, spends the overplus of his earnings. In Scotland there are few; and the Justices are commendably
inexorable in rejecting all application for licenses where

there appears no public necessity for granting them. A man, therefore, cannot easily spend much money in liquor, since he must walk three or four miles to the place of suction and back again, which infers a sort of *malice prepense* of which few are capable; and the habitual opportunity of indulgence not being at hand, the habits of intemperance, and of waste connected with it, are not acquired. If financiers would admit a general limitation of the ale-houses over England to one fourth of the number, I am convinced you would find the money spent in that manner would remain with the peasant, as a source of self-support and independence.

All this applies chiefly to the country; — in towns, and in the manufacturing districts, the evil could hardly be diminished by such regulations. There would, perhaps, be no means so effectual as that (which will never be listened to) of taxing the manufacturers according to the number of hands which they employ on an average, and applying the produce in maintaining the manufacturing poor. If it should be alleged that this would injure the manufacturers, I would boldly reply, — "And why not injure, or rather limit, speculations, the excessive stretch of which has been productive of so much damage to the principles of the country, and to the population, whom it has, in so many respects, degraded and demoralized?" For a great many years, manufactures, taken in a general point of view, have not partaken of the character of a regular profession, in which all who engaged with honest industry and a sufficient capital might reasonably expect returns proportional to their advances and labor — but have, on the contrary, rather resembled a lottery, in which the great majority of the adventurers are sure to be losers, although some may draw considerable advantage. Men continued for a great many years to exert themselves, and to pay extravagant wages, not in hopes that there could be a reasonable prospect of an orderly and regular demand for the goods they wrought

up, but in order that they might be the first to take advantage of some casual opening which might consume
their cargo, let others shift as they could. Hence extravagant wages on some occasions; for these adventurers
who thus played at hit or miss, stood on no scruples
while the chance of success remained open. Hence, also,
the stoppage of work, and the discharge of the workmen,
when the speculators failed of their object. All this
while the country was the sufferer; — for whoever gained,
the result, being upon the whole a loss, fell on the
nation, together with the task of maintaining a poor,
rendered effeminate and vicious by over-wages and
over-living, and necessarily cast loose upon society. I
cannot but think that the necessity of making some
fund beforehand, for the provision of those whom they
debauch, and render only fit for the almshouse, in prosecution of their own adventures, though it operated as
a check on the increase of manufactures, would be a
measure just in itself, and beneficial to the community.
But it would never be listened to; — the weaver's beam,
and the sons of Zeruiah, would be too many for the pro-
posers.

This is the eleventh of August: Walter, happier than
he will ever be again, perhaps, is preparing for the
moors. He has a better dog than Trout, and rather less
active. Mrs. Scott and all our family send kind love.

Yours ever,   W. S.

Two or three days after this letter was written, Scott
first saw Washington Irving, who has recorded his visit
in a delightful Essay, which, however, having been
penned nearly twenty years afterwards, betrays a good
many slips of memory as to names and dates. Mr. Irving says he arrived at Abbotsford on the 27th of August, 1816; but he describes the walls of the new house
as already overtopping the old cottage; and this is far
from being the only circumstance he mentions which

proves that he should have written 1817.[1] The picture
which my amiable friend has drawn of his reception
shows to all who remember the Scott and the Abbotsford
of those days, how consistent accuracy as to essentials
may be with forgetfulness of trifles.

Scott had received The History of New York by
Knickerbocker, shortly after its appearance in 1812,
from an accomplished American traveller, Mr. Brevoort;
and the admirable humor of this early work had led him
to anticipate the brilliant career which its author has
since run.   Mr. Thomas Campbell, being no stranger to
Scott's high estimation of Irving's genius, gave him a
letter of introduction, which, halting his chaise on the
high-road above Abbotsford, he modestly sent down to
the house, "with a card, on which he had written, that
he was on his way to the ruins of Melrose, and wished
to know whether it would be agreeable to Mr. Scott to
receive a visit from him in the course of the morning."
Scott's family well remember the delight with which
he received this announcement: — he was at breakfast,
and sallied forth instantly, dogs and children after him
as usual, to greet the guest, and conduct him in person
from the highway to the door.

"The noise of my chaise," says Irving, "had disturbed the
quiet of the establishment.   Out sallied the warder of the
castle, a black greyhound, and leaping on one of the blocks of
stone, began a furious barking.   This alarm brought out the
whole garrison of dogs, all open-mouthed and vociferous.   In
a little while, the lord of the castle himself made his appearance.   I knew him at once, by the likenesses that had been

---

[1] I have before me two letters of Mr. Irving's to Scott, both written in
September, 1817, from Edinburgh, and referring to his visit (which certainly was his only one at Abbotsford) as immediately preceding.   There
is also in my hands a letter from Scott to his friend John Richardson, of
Fludyer Street, dated 22d September, 1817, in which he says, "When you
see Tom Campbell, tell him, with my best love, that I have to thank him
for making me known to Mr. Washington Irving, who is one of the best
and pleasantest acquaintances I have made this many a day."

published of him. He came limping up the gravel walk, aiding himself by a stout walking staff, but moving rapidly and with vigor. By his side jogged along a large iron-gray staghound, of most grave demeanor, who took no part in the clamor of the canine rabble, but seemed to consider himself bound, for the dignity of the house, to give me a courteous reception.

"Before Scott reached the gate, he called out in a hearty tone, welcoming me to Abbotsford, and asking news of Campbell. Arrived at the door of the chaise, he grasped me warmly by the hand : 'Come, drive down, drive down to the house,' said he ; 'ye 're just in time for breakfast, and afterwards ye shall see all the wonders of the Abbey.'

"I would have excused myself on the plea of having already made my breakfast. 'Hut, man,' cried he, 'a ride in the morning in the keen air of the Scotch hills is warrant enough for a second breakfast.'

"I was accordingly whirled to the portal of the cottage, and in a few moments found myself seated at the breakfast-table. There was no one present but the family, which consisted of Mrs. Scott; her eldest daughter, Sophia, then a fine girl about seventeen; Miss Anne Scott, two or three years younger; Walter, a well-grown stripling; and Charles, a lively boy, eleven or twelve years of age.

"I soon felt myself quite at home, and my heart in a glow, with the cordial welcome I experienced. I had thought to make a mere morning visit, but found I was not to be let off so lightly. 'You must not think our neighborhood is to be read in a morning like a newspaper,' said Scott; 'it takes several days of study for an observant traveller, that has a relish for auld-world trumpery. After breakfast you shall make your visit to Melrose Abbey ; I shall not be able to accompany you, as I have some household affairs to attend to; but I will put you in charge of my son Charles, who is very learned in all things touching the old ruin and the neighborhood it stands in ; and he and my friend Johnnie Bower will tell you the whole truth about it, with a great deal more that you are not called upon to believe, unless you be a true and nothing-doubting antiquary. When you come back, I 'll take you out on a ramble about the neighborhood. To-morrow we will take a look at the Yarrow, and the next day we will drive over to Dryburgh Abbey, which is a fine old ruin, well worth your seeing.' — In a word, before Scott had got through with his plan, I found myself committed for a visit of several days, and it seemed as if a little realm of romance was suddenly open before me."

After breakfast, while Scott, no doubt, wrote a chapter of Rob Roy, Mr. Irving, under young Charles's guidance, saw Melrose Abbey, and Johnnie Bower the elder, whose son long since inherited his office as showman of the ruins, and all his enthusiasm about them and their poet. The senior on this occasion was loud in his praises of the affability of Scott. "He'll come here sometimes," said he, "with great folks in his company, and the first I'll know of it is hearing his voice calling out Johnnie! — Johnnie Bower! — and when I go out I'm sure to be greeted with a joke or a pleasant word. He'll stand and crack, an' laugh wi' me just like an auld wife, — and *to think that of a man that has such an awfu' knowledge o' history!*"[1]

---

[1] [From the journal of three English ladies, travellers in Scotland in the summer of 1817, we get another glimpse of Johnnie Bower, and a pleasant sketch of Sophia Scott: —

"In the chancel Miss Scott, a very charming, lively girl of seventeen, pointed out to us 'The Wizard's Grave,' and then the black stone in the form of a coffin, to which the allusion is made in the poem,' A Scottish monarch sleeps below,' — said to be the tomb of Alexander II. 'But I will tell you a secret,' she half whispered ; ' only don't you tell Johnnie Bower. There is no Scottish monarch there at all, nor anybody else, for papa had the stone taken up, not long ago, and no coffin nor anything was to be found. And then Johnnie came and begged me not to tell people so. "For what wull I do, Miss Scott, when I show the ruins, if I canna point to this bit, and say, 'A Scottish monarch sleeps below' ? "' As, however, he had the pleasure of saying this to us the evening before, Miss Scott thought we might fairly have her secret. . . .

"We now set out for Dryburgh, about five miles. Mr. Scott placed his daughter in our carriage, that she might point out the different places as we passed them. We could not have had a better director, nor a more lively, entertaining companion. Every spot was known to her, and in this fairyland her quick imagination seemed to delight in all the legendary lore she had heard, and could so promptly apply. . . . At the view of some distant mountains, Miss Scott suddenly exclaimed, ' Look, there are

On his return from the Abbey, Irving found Scott ready for a ramble. I cannot refuse myself the pleasure of extracting some parts of his description of it.

"As we sallied forth, every dog in the establishment turned out to attend us. There was the old staghound, Maida, that I have already mentioned, a noble animal, and Hamlet, the black greyhound, a wild thoughtless youngster, not yet arrived at the years of discretion; and Finette, a beautiful setter, with soft, silken hair, long pendent ears, and a mild eye, the parlor favorite. When in front of the house, we were joined by a superannuated greyhound, who came from the kitchen wagging his tail; and was cheered by Scott as an old friend and comrade. In our walks, he would frequently pause in conversation, to notice his dogs, and speak to them as if rational companions; and, indeed, there appears to be a vast deal of rationality in these faithful attendants on man, derived from their close intimacy with him. Maida deported himself with a gravity becoming his age and size, and seemed to consider himself called upon to preserve a great degree of dignity and decorum in our society. As he jogged along a little distance ahead of us, the young dogs would gambol about him, leap on his neck, worry at his ears, and endeavor to tease him into a gambol. The old dog would keep on for a long time with imperturbable solemnity, now and then seeming to rebuke the wantonness of his young companions. At length he would make a sudden turn, seize one of them, and tumble him in the dust, then giving a

the Cheviots; are you not glad to see England again?' We assured her we were, though we should quit Scotland with so much regret. 'Well,' she said, 'I should not have liked you if you were not glad to return home.' Her father had taken her to London the year before, and she was delighted to get back again, and to hail the Cheviots on her return. It was plain to see she was her father's darling, and she talked of him with enthusiasm. She has a very natural, unaffected character, with a strong tincture of romantic feeling, which seemed judiciously kept in check by him, as she said he did not allow her to read much poetry, nor had she even read all his own poems, which were never to be found *in the way*, at their house. She spoke of her sister and her brothers, with a warmth of affection very pleasing. On asking what was become of Camp, she shook her head, and said he was dead. 'You must never come to Abbotsford when any of the dogs die, for there is a sad weeping amongst us all.'" — Lang's *Life of Lockhart*, vol. i. pp. 232-234.]

glance at us, as much as to say, 'You see, gentlemen, I can't help giving way to this nonsense,' would resume his gravity, and jog on as before. Scott amused himself with these peculiarities. 'I make no doubt,' said he, 'when Maida is alone with these young dogs, he throws gravity aside, and plays the boy as much as any of them ; but he is ashamed to do so in our company, and seems to say — Ha' done with your nonsense, youngsters : what will the laird and that other gentleman think of me if I give way to such foolery ? '

"Scott amused himself with the peculiarities of another of his dogs, a little shamefaced terrier, with large glassy eyes, one of the most sensitive little bodies to insult and indignity in the world. 'If ever he whipped him,' he said, 'the little fellow would sneak off and hide himself from the light of day in a lumber garret, from whence there was no drawing him forth but by the sound of the chopping-knife, as if chopping up his victuals, when he would steal forth with humiliated and downcast look, but would skulk away again if any one regarded him.'

"While we were discussing the humors and peculiarities of our canine companions, some object provoked their spleen, and produced a sharp and petulant barking from the smaller fry ; but it was some time before Maida was sufficiently roused to ramp forward two or three bounds, and join the chorus with a deep-mouthed *bow wow*. It was but a transient outbreak, and he returned instantly, wagging his tail, and looking up dubiously in his master's face, uncertain whether he would receive censure or applause. 'Ay, ay, old boy ! ' cried Scott, ' you have done wonders ; you have shaken the Eildon hills with your roaring : you may now lay by your artillery for the rest of the day. Maida,' continued he, ' is like the great gun at Constantinople ; it takes so long to get it ready, that the smaller guns can fire off a dozen times first : but when it does go off, it plays the very devil.'

"These simple anecdotes may serve to show the delightful play of Scott's humors and feelings in private life. His domestic animals were his friends. Everything about him seemed to rejoice in the light of his countenance.

"Our ramble took us on the hills commanding an extensive prospect. 'Now,' said Scott, ' I have brought you, like the pilgrim in the Pilgrim's Progress, to the top of the Delectable

Mountains, that I may show you all the goodly regions here-abouts. Yonder is Lammermuir, and Smailholm; and there you have Galashiels, and Torwoodlee, and Gala Water; and in that direction you see Teviotdale and the Braes of Yarrow, and Ettrick stream winding along like a silver thread, to throw itself into the Tweed.' He went on thus to call over names celebrated in Scottish song, and most of which had recently received a romantic interest from his own pen. In fact, I saw a great part of the Border country spread out before me, and could trace the scenes of those poems and romances which had in a manner bewitched the world.

"I gazed about me for a time with mute surprise, I may almost say with disappointment. I beheld a mere succession of gray waving hills, line beyond line, as far as my eye could reach, monotonous in their aspect, and so destitute of trees, that one could almost see a stout fly walking along their profile; and the far-famed Tweed appeared a naked stream, flowing between bare hills, without a tree or thicket on its banks; and yet such had been the magic web of poetry and romance thrown over the whole, that it had a greater charm for me than the richest scenery I had beheld in England. I could not help giving utterance to my thoughts. Scott hummed for a moment to himself, and looked grave; he had no idea of having his Muse complimented at the expense of his native hills. 'It may be pertinacity,' said he at length; 'but to my eye, these gray hills, and all this wild Border country, have beauties peculiar to themselves. I like the very nakedness of the land; it has something bold, and stern, and solitary about it. When I have been for some time in the rich scenery about Edinburgh, which is like ornamented garden land, I begin to wish myself back again among my own honest gray hills; and if I did not see the heather, at least once a year. *I think I should die!*' The last words were said with an honest warmth, accompanied by a thump on the ground with his staff, by way of emphasis, that showed his heart was in his speech. He vindicated the Tweed, too, as a beautiful stream in itself; and observed that he did not dislike it for being bare of trees, probably from having been much of an angler in his time; and an angler does not like to have a stream overhung by trees, which embarrass him in the exercise of his rod and line.

"I took occasion to plead, in like manner, the associations of early life for my disappointment in respect to the surrounding scenery. I had been so accustomed to see hills crowned with forests, and streams breaking their way through a wilderness of trees, that all my ideas of romantic landscape were apt to be well wooded. 'Ay, and that's the great charm of your country,' cried Scott. 'You love the forest as I do the heather; but I would not have you think I do not feel the glory of a great woodland prospect. There is nothing I should like more than to be in the midst of one of your grand wild original forests, with the idea of hundreds of miles of untrodden forest around me. I once saw at Leith an immense stick of timber, just landed from America. It must have been an enormous tree when it stood in its native soil, at its full height, and with all its branches. I gazed at it with admiration; it seemed like one of the gigantic obelisks which are now and then brought from Egypt to shame the pigmy monuments of Europe; and, in fact, these vast aboriginal trees, that have sheltered the Indians before the intrusion of the white men, are the monuments and antiquities of your country.'

"The conversation here turned upon Campbell's poem of Gertrude of Wyoming, as illustrative of the poetic materials furnished by American scenery. Scott cited several passages of it with great delight. 'What a pity it is,' said he, 'that Campbell does not write more, and oftener, and give full sweep to his genius! He has wings that would bear him to the skies; and he does, now and then, spread them grandly, but folds them up again, and resumes his perch, as if he was afraid to launch away. What a grand idea is that,' said he, 'about prophetic boding, or, in common parlance, second sight —

"Coming events cast their shadows before!" —

The fact is,' added he, ' Campbell is, in a manner, a bugbear to himself. The brightness of his early success is a detriment to all his further efforts. *He is afraid of the shadow that his own fame casts before him.*'

"We had not walked much farther, before we saw the two Miss Scotts advancing along the hillside to meet us. The morning's studies being over, they had set off to take a ramble on the hills, and gather heather blossoms with which to decorate

their hair for dinner. As they came bounding lightly like
young fawns, and their dresses fluttering in the pure summer
breeze, I was reminded of Scott's own description of his children, in his introduction to one of the cantos of Marmion : —

> ' My imps, though hardy, bold, and wild,
>   As best befits the mountain child,' etc.

As they approached, the dogs all sprang forward, and gambolled
around them. They joined us with countenances full of health
and glee. Sophia, the eldest, was the most lively and joyous,
having much of her father's varied spirit in conversation, and
seeming to catch excitement from his words and looks ; Anne
was of a quieter mood, rather silent, owing, in some measure,
no doubt, to her being some years younger." [1]

Having often, many years afterwards, heard Irving
speak warmly of William Laidlaw, I must not omit the
following passage : —

"One of my pleasantest rambles with Scott about the neighborhood of Abbotsford was taken in company with Mr. William Laidlaw, the steward of his estate. This was a gentleman for whom Scott entertained a particular value. He had
been born to a competency, had been well educated, his mind
was richly stored with varied information, and he was a man
of sterling moral worth. Having been reduced by misfortune,
Scott had got him to take charge of his estate. He lived at a
small farm, on the hillside above Abbotsford, and was treated

---

[1] [" His daughter Sophia and his son Charles were those of his family
who seemed most to feel and understand his humors, and to take delight
in his conversation. Mrs. Scott did not always pay the same attention,
and would now and then make a casual remark which would operate a
little like a damper. Thus, one morning at breakfast, when Dominie
Thomson the tutor was present, Scott was going on with great glee to
relate an anecdote of the laird of Macnab, ' who, poor fellow ! ' premised
he, ' is dead and gone.' ' Why, Mr. Scott,' exclaimed the good lady, ' Macnab 's not dead, is he ? ' ' Faith, my dear,' replied Scott, with humorous
gravity, ' if he 's not dead, they 've done him a great injustice, — for
they 've buried him.'

"The joke passed harmless and unnoticed by Mrs. Scott, but hit the poor
Dominie just as he had raised a cup of tea to his lips . . . sending half its
contents about the table." — Irving's *Abbotsford*.]

by Scott as a cherished and confidential friend, rather than a dependant.

"That day at dinner we had Mr. Laidlaw and his wife, and a female friend who accompanied them. The latter was a very intelligent respectable person, about the middle age, and was treated with particular attention and courtesy by Scott. Our dinner was a most agreeable one, for the guests were evidently cherished visitors to the house, and felt that they were appreciated. When they were gone, Scott spoke of them in the most cordial manner. ' I wished to show you,' said he, ' some of our really excellent, plain Scotch people : not fine gentlemen and ladies, for such you can meet everywhere, and they are everywhere the same. The character of a nation is not to be learnt from its fine folks.' He then went on with a particular eulogium on the lady who had accompanied the Laidlaws. She was the daughter, he said, of a poor country clergyman, who had died in debt, and left her an orphan and destitute. Having had a good plain education, she immediately set up a child's school, and had soon a numerous flock under her care, by which she earned a decent maintenance. That, however, was not her main object. Her first care was to pay off her father's debts, that no ill word or ill will might rest upon his memory. This, by dint of Scotch economy, backed by filial reverence and pride, she accomplished, though in the effort she subjected herself to every privation. Not content with this, she in certain instances refused to take pay for the tuition of the children of some of her neighbors, who had befriended her father in his need, and had since fallen into poverty. ' In a word,' added Scott, ' she 's a fine old Scotch girl, and I delight in her more than in many a fine lady I have known, and I have known many of the finest.'

"The evening passed away delightfully in a quaint-looking apartment, half study, half drawing-room. Scott read several passages from the old Romance of Arthur, with a fine deep sonorous voice, and a gravity of tone that seemed to suit the antiquated black-letter volume. It was a rich treat to hear such a work read by such a person, and in such a place ; and his appearance, as he sat reading, in a large armchair, with his favorite hound Maida at his feet, and surrounded by books and reliques and Border trophies, would have formed

an admirable and most characteristic picture. When I retired
for the night, I found it almost impossible to sleep : the idea of
being under the roof of Scott ; of being on the Borders on the
Tweed ; in the very centre of that region which had, for some
time past, been the favorite scene of romantic fiction ; and,
above all, the recollections of the ramble I had taken, the company in which I had taken it, and the conversation which had
passed, all fermented in my mind, and nearly drove sleep from
my pillow.

" On the following morning the sun darted his beams from
over the hills through the low lattice of my window. I rose at
an early hour, and looked out between the branches of eglantine
which overhung the casement. To my surprise, Scott was already up, and forth, seated on a fragment of stone, and chatting
with the workmen employed in the new building. I had supposed, after the time he had wasted upon me yesterday, he
would be closely occupied this morning : but he appeared like
a man of leisure, who had nothing to do but bask in the sunshine, and amuse himself. I soon dressed myself and joined
him. He talked about his proposed plans of Abbotsford :
happy would it have been for him could he have contented himself with his delightful little vine-covered cottage, and the simple, yet hearty and hospitable, style in which he lived at the
time of my visit." [1]

Among other visitors who succeeded the distinguished
American that autumn, were Lady Byron, the wife of the
poet, and the great artist, Mr., now Sir David Wilkie,
who then executed for Captain Ferguson that pleasing
little picture, in which Scott and his family are represented as a group of peasants, while the gallant soldier

---

[1] [That this visit remained a vivid and delightful memory to the end of
Irving's life is shown in some words spoken not long before his death :
" Oh ! Scott was a master spirit — as glorious in his conversation as in his
writings. Jeffrey was delightful, and had *eloquent runs* in conversation ;
but there was a consciousness of talent with it. Scott had nothing of that.
He spoke from the fulness of his mind, pouring out an incessant flow of
anecdote, story, with dashes of humor, and then never monopolizing, but
always ready to listen to and appreciate what came from others. I never
felt such a consciousness of happiness as when under his roof." — *Washington Irving's Life and Letters*, vol. iv. p. 260.]

himself figures by them in the character of a gamekeeper, or perhaps poacher. Mr. Irving has given, in
the little work from which I have quoted so liberally,
an amusing account of the delicate scruples of Wilkie
about soliciting Scott to devote a morning to the requisite sitting, until, after lingering for several days, he at
length became satisfied that, by whatever magic his host
might contrive to keep Ballantyne's presses in full play,
he had always abundance of leisure for matters less important than Ferguson's destined heirloom. I shall now,
however, return to his correspondence; and begin with
a letter to Joanna Baillie on Lady Byron's visit.

TO MISS JOANNA BAILLIE, HAMPSTEAD.

ABBOTSFORD, September 26, 1817.

MY DEAR MISS BAILLIE, — A series of little trinketty
sort of business, and occupation, and idleness, have succeeded to each other so closely, that I have been scarce
able, for some three weeks past, to call my time my own
for half an hour together; but enough of apologies —
they are vile things, and I know you will impute my
negligence to anything rather than forgetting or under-
valuing your friendship. You know, by this time, that
we have had a visit from Lady Byron, delightful both
on its own account, and because it was accompanied with
good news and a letter from you. I regret we could not
keep her longer than a day with us, which was spent on
the banks of the Yarrow, and I hope and believe she was
pleased with us, because I am sure she will be so with
everything that is intended to please her: meantime her
visit gave me a most lawyer-like fit of the bile. I have
lived too long to be surprised at any instance of human
caprice, but still it vexes me. Now, one would suppose
Lady Byron, young, beautiful, with birth, and rank, and
fortune, and taste, and high accomplishments, and admirable good sense, qualified to have made happy one whose
talents are so high as Lord Byron's, and whose marked

propensity it is to like those who are qualified to admire
and understand his talents; and yet it has proved otherwise. I can safely say my heart ached for her all the
time we were together; there was so much patience and
decent resignation to a situation which must have pressed
on her thoughts, that she was to me one of the most
interesting creatures I had seen for a score of years. I
am sure I should not have felt such strong kindness
towards her had she been at the height of her fortune,
and in the full enjoyment of all the brilliant prospects
to which she seemed destined. — You will wish to hear
of my complaint. I think, thank God, that it is leaving
me — not suddenly, however, for I have had some repetitions, but they have become fainter and fainter, and I
have not been disturbed by one for these three weeks. I
trust, by care and attention, my stomach will return to
its usual tone, and I am as careful as I can. I have
taken hard exercise with good effect, and am often six
hours on foot without stopping or sitting down, to which
my plantations and enclosures contribute not a little. I
have, however, given up the gun this season, finding
myself unable to walk up to the dogs; but Walter has
taken it in hand, and promises to be a first-rate shot; he
brought us in about seven or eight brace of birds the
evening Lady Byron came to us, which papa was of
course a little proud of. The blackcocks are getting
very plenty on our moor-ground at Abbotsford, but I
associate them so much with your beautiful poem,[1] that
I have not the pleasure I used to have in knocking them
down. I wish I knew how to send you a brace. I get
on with my labors here; my house is about to be roofed
in, and a comical concern it is.

Yours truly,   W. S.

---

[1] " Good-morrow to thy sable beak,
    And glossy plumage dark and sleek,
    Thy crimson moon, and azure eye,
    Cock of the heath, so wildly shy ! " etc.

The next letter refers to the Duke of Buccleuch's preparations for a cattle-show at Bowhill, which was followed by an entertainment on a large scale to his Grace's Selkirkshire neighbors and tenantry, and next day by a fox-hunt, after Dandie Dinmont's fashion, among the rocks of the Yarrow. The Sheriff attended *with his tail on;* and Wilkie, too, went with him. It was there that Sir David first saw Hogg, and the Shepherd's greeting was graceful. He eyed the great painter for a moment in silence, and then stretching out his hand, said: "Thank God for it. I did not know that you were so young a man!"

TO THE DUKE OF BUCCLEUCH, ETC., ETC., ETC., DRUMLANRIG CASTLE.

My dear Lord Duke, — I am just honored with your Grace's of the 27th. The posts, which are as cross as pie-crust, have occasioned some delay. Depend on our attending at Bowhill on the 20th, and staying over the show. I have written to Adam Ferguson, who will come with a whoop and a hollo. So will the Ballantynes — flageolet[1] and all — for the festival, and they shall be housed at Abbotsford. I have an inimitably good songster in the person of Terence Magrath, who teaches my girls. He beats almost all whom I have ever heard attempt Moore's songs, and I can easily cajole him also out to Abbotsford for a day or two. In jest or earnest, I never heard a better singer in a room, though his voice is not quite full enough for a concert; and for an after-supper song, he almost equals Irish Johnstone.[2]

Trade of every kind is recovering, and not a loom idle

[1] The *flageolet* alludes to Mr. Alexander Ballantyne, the third of the brothers — a fine musician, and a most amiable and modest man, never connected with Scott in any business matters, but always much his favorite in private.

[2] Mr. Magrath has now been long established in his native city of Dublin. His musical excellence was by no means the only merit that attached Scott to his society while he remained in Edinburgh.

in Glasgow. The most faithful respects of this family
attend the Ladies and all at Drumlanrig. I ever am
your Grace's truly obliged and grateful

WALTER SCOTT.

Given from my Castle of Grawacky,
this second day of the month called
October, One Thousand Eight Hundred and Seventeen Years.

There is a date nearly as long as the letter.

I hope we shall attack the foxes at Bowhill. I will
hazard Maida.

We have some allusions to this Bowhill party in another letter; the first of several which I shall now insert
according to their dates, leaving them, with a few mar-
ginal notes, to tell out the story of 1817 : —

TO DANIEL TERRY, ESQ., LONDON.

ABBOTSFORD, October 24, 1817.

DEAR TERRY, — Bullock has not gone to Skye, and
I am very glad he has not, for to me who knew the
Hebrides well, the attempt seemed very perilous at this
season. I have considerably enlarged my domains since
I wrote to you, by the purchase of a beautiful farm adja-
cent. The farmhouse, which is new and excellent, I
have let to Adam Ferguson and his sisters. We will
be within a pleasant walk of each other, and hope to end
our lives, as they began, in each other's society. There
is a beautiful brook, with remnants of natural wood,
which would make Toftfield rival Abbotsford, but for
the majestic Tweed. I am in treaty for a field or two
more; one of which contains the only specimen of a Peelhouse, or defensive residence of a small proprietor, which
remains in this neighborhood. It is an orchard, in the
hamlet of Darnick, to which it gives a most picturesque
effect. Blore admires it very much. We are all well
here, but crowded with company. I have been junket-

ing this week past at Bowhill. Mr. Magrath has been with us these two or three days, and has seen his ward, Hamlet, behave most *princelike* on Newark Hill and elsewhere. He promises to be a real treasure.[1] Notwithstanding, Mr. Magrath went to Bowhill with me one day, where his vocal talents gave great pleasure, and I hope will procure him the notice and protection of the Buccleuch family. The Duke says my building engrosses, as a common centre, the thoughts of Mr. Atkinson and Mr. Bullock, and wishes he could make them equally anxious in his own behalf. You may believe this flatters me not a little.

P. S. — I agree with you that the tower will look rather rich for the rest of the building; yet you may be assured, that with diagonal chimneys and notched gables, it will have a very fine effect, and is in Scotch architecture by no means incompatible. My house has been like a *cried fair*, and extreme the inconvenience of having no corner sacred to my own use, and free from intrusion.

Ever truly yours,   W. S.

TO THE SAME.

ABBOTSFORD, 29th October, 1817.

MY DEAR TERRY, — I enclose a full sketch of the lower story, with accurate measurements of rooms, casements, doorways, chimneys, etc., that Mr. Atkinson's good will may not want means to work upon. I will speak to the subjects of your letters separately, that I may omit none of them. 1*st*, I cannot possibly surrender the window to the west in the library,[2] although I subscribe to all you urge about it. Still it is essential in point of light to my old eyes, and the single northern

---

[1] This fine greyhound, a gift from Terry, had been sent to Scotland under the care of Mr. Magrath. Terry had called the dog *Marmion*, but Scott rechristened him *Hamlet*, in honor of his " inky coat."

[2] Before the second and larger part of the present house of Abbotsford was built, the small room, subsequently known as the breakfast parlor, was during several years Scott's *sanctum*.

aspect would not serve me. Above all, it looks into the
yard, and enables me to summon Tom Purdie without
the intervention of a third party. Indeed, as I can have
but a few books about me, it is of the less consequence.
2*dly*, I resign the idea of *coving* the library to your better judgment, and I think the Stirling Heads[1] will be
admirably disposed in the glass of the armory window.
I have changed my mind as to having doors on the book-
presses, which is, after all, a great bore. No person
will be admitted into my sanctum, and I can have the
door locked during my absence. 3*dly*, I expect Mr.
Bullock here every day, and should be glad to have the
drawings for the dining-room wainscot, as he could explain them to the artists who are to work them. This
(always if quite convenient) would be the more desirable,
as I must leave this place in a fortnight at farthest, — the
more 's the pity, — and, consequently, the risk of blunders will be considerably increased. I should like if the
panelling of the wainscot could admit of a press on each
side of the sideboard. I don't mean a formal press with
a high door, but some crypt, or, to speak vulgarly, *cup-
board*, to put away bottles of wine, etc. You know I
am my own butler, and such accommodation is very convenient. We begin roofing to-morrow. Wilkie admires
the whole as a composition, and that is high authority.
I agree that the fountain shall be out of doors in front of
the greenhouse; there may be an enclosure for it with
some ornamented mason work, as in old gardens, and it
will occupy an angle, which I should be puzzled what to
do with, for turf and gravel would be rather meagre, and
flowers not easily kept. I have the old fountain belonging to the Cross of Edinburgh, which flowed with wine
at the coronation of our kings and on other occasions of

---

[1] This alludes to certain pieces of painted glass, representing the heads
of some of the old Scotch kings, copied from the carved ceiling of the
presence-chamber in Stirling Castle. There are engravings of them in a
work called *Lacunar Strevelinense*. Edinb. 4to, 1817.

public rejoicing. I send a sketch of this venerable relic, connected as it is with a thousand associations. It is handsome in its forms and proportions — a freestone basin about three feet in diameter, and five inches and a half in depth, very handsomely hollowed. A piece has been broken off one edge, but as we have the fragment, it can easily be restored with cement. There are four openings for pipes in the circumference — each had been covered with a Gothic masque, now broken off and defaced, but which may be easily restored. Through these the wine had fallen into a larger and lower reservoir. I intend this for the centre of my fountain. I do not believe I should save £100 by retaining Mrs. Redford, by the time she was raised, altered, and beautified, for, like the Highlandman's gun, she wants stock, lock, and barrel, to put her into repair. In the mean time, "the cabin is convenient." Yours ever,   W. S.

TO MR. WILLIAM LAIDLAW, KAESIDE.

EDINBURGH, November 15, 1817.

DEAR WILLIE, — I have no intention to let the White-haugh without your express approbation, and I wish you to act as my adviser and representative in these matters. I would hardly have ventured to purchase so much land without the certainty of your counsel and coöperation. . . . On the other side you will find a small order on the banker at Galashiels, to be renewed half yearly; not by way of recompensing your friendship "with a load of barren money," but merely to ease my conscience in some degree for the time which I must necessarily withdraw from the labor which is to maintain your family. Believe me, dear Willie, yours truly,

W. SCOTT.

TO THE SAME.

EDINBURGH, 19th November, 1817.

DEAR WILLIE, — I hope you will not quarrel with my last. Believe me that, to a sound-judging, and philo-

sophical mind, this same account of Dr. and Cr., which
fills up so much time in the world, is comparatively of
very small value.   When you get rich, unless I thrive
in the same proportion, I will request your assistance for
less, for little, or for nothing, as the case may require;
but while I wear my seven-leagued boots to stride in
triumph over moss and muir, it would be very silly in
either of us to let a cheque twice a year of £25 make a
difference between us.   But all this we will talk over
when we meet.   I meditate one day a *coup-de-maître*,
which will make my friend's advice and exertion essential — indeed worthy of much better remuneration.
When you come, I hope you will bring us information
of all my rural proceedings.   Though so lately come to
town, I still remember, at my waking hours, that I can
neither see Tom Purdie nor Adam Paterson,[1] and rise
with the more unwillingness.   I was unwell on Monday
and Tuesday, but am quite recovered.

Yours truly,   W. S.

TO THOMAS SCOTT, ESQ., PAYMASTER, 70TH REGIMENT,
KINGSTON, CANADA.

EDINBURGH, 13th December, 1817.

My DEAR TOM, — I should be happy to attend to your
commission about a dominie for your boy, but I think
there will be much risk in yoking yourself with one for
three or four years.   You know what sort of black cattle
these are, and how difficult it is to discern their real
character, though one may give a guess at their attainments.   When they get good provender in their guts,
they are apt to turn out very different animals from what
they were in their original low condition, and get frisky
and troublesome.   I have made several inquiries, however, and request to know what salary you would think
reasonable, and also what acquisitions he ought to pos-

---

[1] Adam Paterson was the intelligent foreman of the company of masons
then employed at Abbotsford.

sess. There is no combating the feelings which you express for the society of your son, otherwise I really think that a Scottish education would be highly desirable; and should you at any time revert to this plan, you may rely on my bestowing the same attention upon him as upon my own boys.

I agree entirely with you on the necessity of your remaining in the regiment while it is stationary, and retiring on half-pay when it marches; but I cannot so easily acquiesce in your plan of settling in Canada. On the latter event taking place, on the contrary, I think it would be highly advisable that you should return to your native country. In the course of nature you must soon be possessed of considerable property, now life-rented by our mother, and I should think that even your present income would secure you comfort and independence here. Should you remain in Canada, you must consider your family as settlers in that state, and as I cannot believe that it will remain very long separated from America, I should almost think this equal to depriving them of the advantages of British subjects — at least of those which they might derive from their respectable connections in this country. With respect to your son, in particular, I have little doubt that I could be of considerable service to him in almost any line of life he might chance to adopt here, but could of course have less influence on his fortunes were he to remain on the Niagara. I certainly feel anxious on this subject, because the settlement of your residence in America would be saying, in other words, that we two, the last remains of a family once so numerous, are never more to meet upon this side of time. My own health is very much broken up by the periodical recurrence of violent cramps in the stomach, which neither seem disposed to yield to medicine nor to abstinence. The complaint, the doctors say, is not dangerous in itself, but I cannot look forward to its continued recurrence, without being certain that it is to break my health, and anticipate old age in cutting me short. Be it so, my dear Tom — *Sat est vixisse* — and I am too much of a philosopher to be anxious about protracted life, which, with all its infirmities and deprivations, I have never considered as a blessing. In the years which may be before me, it would be a lively satisfaction to me to have the pleasure of seeing you in this country, with the prospect of a comfortable settlement. I have but an imperfect account to render of my doings here. I have amused myself with making an addition to my cottage in the country. One little apartment is to be fitted up as an armory for my old relics and curiosities. On the wicket I intend to mount your *deer's foot* [1] — as an appropriate knocker. I hope the young ladies liked their watches, and that all your books, stationery, etc., came safe to hand. I am told you have several kinds of the oak peculiar to America. If you can send me a few good acorns, with the names of the kinds they belong to, I will have them reared with great care and attention. The heaviest and smoothest acorns should be selected, as one would wish them, sent from such a distance, to succeed, which rarely happens unless they are particularly well ripened. I shall be as much obliged to you as Sancho was to the Duchess, or, to speak more correctly, the Duchess to Sancho, for a similar favor. Our mother keeps her health surprisingly well now, nor do I think there is any difference, unless that her deafness is rather increased. My eldest boy is upwards of six feet high; therefore born, as Sergeant Kite says, to be a great man. I should not like such a rapid growth, but that he carries strength along with it; my youngest boy is a very sharp little fellow — and the girls give us great satisfaction. Ever affectionately yours,   WALTER SCOTT.

---

[1] Thomas Scott had sent his brother the horns and feet of a gigantic stag, shot by him in Canada. The feet were ultimately suspended to bell-cords in the armory at Abbotsford; and the horns mounted as drinking-cups.

The following note is without date. It accompanied, no doubt, the last proof sheet of Rob Roy, and was therefore in all probability written about ten days before the 31st of December, 1817 — on which day the novel was published.

TO MR. JAMES BALLANTYNE, ST. JOHN STREET.

DEAR JAMES, —

> With great joy
> I send you Roy.
> 'T was a tough job,
> But we 're done with Rob.

I forget if I mentioned Terry in my list of Friends. Pray send me two or three copies as soon as you can. It were pity to make the Grinder[1] pay carriage.

Yours ever,   W. S.

The novel had indeed been "a tough job" — for lightly and airily as it reads, the author had struggled almost throughout with the pains of cramp or the lassitude of opium. Calling on him one day to dun him for copy, James Ballantyne found him with a clean pen and a blank sheet before him, and uttered some rather solemn exclamation of surprise. "Ay, ay, Jemmy," said he, "'t is easy for you to bid me get on, but how the deuce can I make Rob Roy's wife speak, with such a *curmurring* in my guts?"

[1] They called Daniel Terry among themselves "The Grinder," in double allusion to the song of *Terry the Grinder*, and to some harsh under-notes of their friend's voice.

CHAPTER XL

ROB ROY PUBLISHED. — NEGOTIATION CONCERNING THE
SECOND SERIES OF TALES OF MY LANDLORD. — COM-
MISSION TO SEARCH FOR THE SCOTTISH REGALIA. —
LETTERS TO THE DUKE OF BUCCLEUCH, MR. CROKER,
MR. MORRITT, MR. MURRAY, MR. MATURIN, ETC. —
CORRESPONDENCE ON RURAL AFFAIRS WITH MR. LAID-
LAW, AND ON THE BUILDINGS AT ABBOTSFORD WITH
MR. TERRY. — DEATH OF MRS. MURRAY KEITH AND
MR. GEORGE BULLOCK

1818

ROB ROY and his wife, Bailie Nicol Jarvie and his
housekeeper, Die Vernon and Rashleigh Osbaldistone —
these boldly drawn and happily contrasted personages —
were welcomed as warmly as the most fortunate of their
predecessors.[1] Constable's resolution to begin with an

---

[1] [On the 16th of February, Lady Louisa Stuart wrote : —

"I have read *Rob Roy* twice. . . . The scale with me would be *Waverley*,
Old Mortality, *Guy Mannering* — so far I am sure. I am not sure which
of the others I could positively prefer ; there are striking beauties in each.
In *Rob Roy* the painting of character is as vivid as in anything the author
ever wrote. Rob himself, Die Vernon, Nicol Jarvie, Andrew Fairservice,
not to speak of the Tory baronet and his cubs, or the Jesuit Rashleigh.
The beginning and end, I am afraid, I quarrel with ; . . . but beginnings
signify little ; ends signify more. Now, I fear the end of this is huddled,
as if the author were tired and wanted to get rid of his personages as fast
as he could, knocking them on the head without mercy. Die Vernon has
what a Lord Bellamont (famous in my day and before it for profligacy
and affectation) used to call such ' a catastrophical countenance ' that one
cannot reconcile oneself to her being married and settled like her sober
neighbors. It is almost as bad as if Flora MacIvor had married the Colonel's nephew. . . . You see I give my opinion (let it be worth something or nothing) as if I were writing to a person not supposed to be in any

edition of 10,000 proved to have been as sagacious as
brave; for within a fortnight a second impression of 3000
was called for; and the subsequent sale of this novel has
considerably exceeded 40,000 more.

Scott, however, had not waited for this new burst of
applause. As soon as he came within view of the completion of Rob Roy, he desired John Ballantyne to propose to Constable and Co. a second series of the Tales of
my Landlord, to be comprised, like the first, in four
volumes, and ready for publication by "the King's birthday;" that is, the 4th of June, 1818. "I have hungered
and thirsted," he wrote, "to see the end of those shabby
borrowings among friends; they have all been wiped out
except the good Duke's £4000 — and I will not suffer
either new offers of land or anything else to come in the
way of that clearance. I expect that you will be able
to arrange this resurrection of Jedediah, so that £5000
shall be at my order."

Mr. Rigdum used to glory in recounting that he acquitted himself on this occasion with a species of dexterity not contemplated in his commission. He well knew
how sorely Constable had been wounded by seeing the
first Tales of Jedediah published by Murray and Blackwood — and that the utmost success of Rob Roy would
only double his anxiety to keep them out of the field,
when the hint should be dropt that a second MS. from
Gandercleuch might shortly be looked for. John therefore took a convenient opportunity to mention the new
scheme as if casually — so as to give Constable the im-

way sib to the mysterious Unknown; but it is because I believe you have
too distinguishing a taste to relish all sugar and treacle. Goldsmith's
metaphor was bad when he said, ' Who peppers the highest is surest to
please,' for flattery resembles neither pepper nor salt. Apropos of the
mystery, those who see far into a millstone are now sure that the *Tales of
my Landlord* were written by a different person, and parts of them by different hands. When they give their reasons with a complacent delight in
their own sagacity, I think to myself, how often must I have talked as
much wise nonsense upon subjects which I knew nothing about." — *Familiar Letters*, vol. ii. p. 11.]

pression that the author's purpose was to divide the second series also between his old rival in Albemarle Street, of whom his jealousy was always sensitive, and his neighbor Blackwood, whom, if there had been no other grudge, the recent conduct and rapidly increasing sale of his Magazine would have been sufficient to make Constable hate with a perfect hatred. To see not only his old "Scots Magazine" eclipsed, but the authority of the Edinburgh Review itself bearded on its own soil by this juvenile upstart, was to him gall and wormwood; and, moreover, he himself had come in for his share in some of those grotesque *jeux d'esprit* by which, at this period, Blackwood's young Tory wags delighted to assail their elders and betters of the Whig persuasion. To prevent the proprietor of this new journal from acquiring anything like a hold on the author of Waverley, and thus competing with himself not only in periodical literature, but in the highest of the time, was an object for which, as John Ballantyne shrewdly guessed, Constable would have made at that moment almost any sacrifice. When, therefore, the haughty but trembling bookseller — "The Lord High Constable" (as he had been dubbed by these jesters) — signified his earnest hope that the second Tales of my Landlord were destined to come out under the same auspices with Rob Roy, the plenipotentiary answered with an air of deep regret, that he feared it would be impossible for the author to dispose of the work — unless to publishers who should agree to take with it *the whole* of the remaining stock of "John Ballantyne and Co.;" and Constable, pertinaciously as he had stood out against many more modest propositions of this nature, was so worked upon by his jealous feelings, that his resolution at once gave way. He agreed on the instant to do all that John seemed to shrink from asking — and at one sweep cleared the Augean stable in Hanover Street of unsalable rubbish to the amount of £5270! I am assured by his surviving partner, that when he had finally redisposed of the stock, he found himself a loser by fully two thirds of this sum.

Burthened with this heavy condition, the agreement for the sale of 10,000 copies of the embryo series was signed before the end of November, 1817; and on the 7th January, 1818, Scott wrote as follows to his noble friend: —

TO THE DUKE OF BUCCLEUCH, ETC., ETC.

My DEAR LORD DUKE, — I have the great pleasure of enclosing the discharged bond which your Grace stood engaged in for me, and on my account. The accommodation was of the greatest consequence to me, as it enabled me to retain possession of some valuable literary property, which I must otherwise have suffered to be sold at a time when the booksellers had no money to buy it. My dear Lord, to wish that all your numerous and extensive acts of kindness may be attended with similar advantages to the persons whom you oblige, is wishing you what to your mind will be the best recompense; and to wish that they may be felt by all as gratefully as by me, though you may be careless to hear about that part of the story, is only wishing what is creditable to human nature. I have this moment your more than kind letter, and congratulate your Grace that, in one sense of the word, you can be what you never will be in any other, *ambidexter*. But I am sorry you took so much trouble, and I fear *pains* besides, to display your new talent.

Ever your Grace's truly faithful,

WALTER SCOTT.

The closing sentence of this letter refers to a fit of the gout which had disabled the Duke's right hand, but not cooled his zeal on a subject which, throughout January, 1818, occupied, I firmly believe, much more of his correspondent's thoughts by day and dreams by night, than any one, or perhaps than all others, besides. The time now approached when a Commission to examine the Crown-room in the Castle of Edinburgh, which had sprung from one of Scott's conversations with the Prince Regent in 1815, was at length to be acted upon. The minstrel of the "Rough Clan" had taken care that the name of his chief should stand at the head of the document; but the Duke's now precarious health ultimately prevented him from being present at the discovery of the long buried and almost forgotten Regalia of Scotland. The two following letters on this subject are of the same date — Edinburgh, 14th January, 1818.

TO THE DUKE OF BUCCLEUCH, ETC., ETC., BOWHILL.

MY DEAR LORD, — You will hear from the Advocate that the Commission for opening the Regalia is arrived, and that the Commissioners held their first meeting yesterday. They have named next Wednesday (in case your Grace can attend) for opening the mysterious chest. So this question will be put to rest forever.

I remember among the rebel company which debauched my youth, there was a drunken old Tory, who used to sing a ballad made about these same Regalia at the time of the Union, in which they were all destined to the basest uses; the crown, for example,

> " To make a can for Brandy Nan
>   To puke in when she 's tipsy."

The rest of the song is in a tone of equally pure humor; the chorus ran : —

> " Farewell, thou ancient kingdom —
>   Farewell, thou ancient kingdom.
>   Who sold thyself for English pelf —
>   Was ever such a thing done ? "

I hope your Grace feels yourself sufficiently interested in the recovery of these ancient symbols of national independence, so long worn by your forefathers, and which were never profaned by the touch of a monarch of a for-

eign dynasty. Here is fine planting weather. I trust it
is as good in the Forest and on Tweedside.

Ever your Grace's truly faithful

WALTER SCOTT.

TO J. B. S. MORRITT, ESQ., M. P., ROKEBY.

DEAR MORRITT, — Our fat friend has remembered a
petition which I put up to him, and has granted a Commission to the Officers of State and others (my unworthy
self included) — which trusty and well-beloved persons
are to institute a search after the Regalia of Scotland.
There has an odd mystery hung about the fate of these
royal symbols of national independence. The spirit of
the Scotch at the Union clung fondly to these emblems;
and to soothe their jealousy it was specially provided
by an article of the Union, that the Regalia should never
be removed, under any pretext, from the kingdom of
Scotland. Accordingly they were deposited, with much
ceremony, as an authentic instrument bears, in a strong
chest, secured by many locks, and the chest itself placed
in a strong room, which again was carefully bolted up
and secured, leaving to national pride the satisfaction of
pointing to the barred window, with the consciousness
that there lay the Regalia of Scotland. But this gratification was strangely qualified by a surmise, which somehow became generally averred, stating, that the Regalia
had been sent to London; and you may remember that
we saw at the Jewel Office a crown, *said to be* the ancient Crown of Scotland. If this transfer (by the way,
highly illegal) was ever made, it must have been under
some secret warrant; for no authority can be traced for
such a proceeding in the records of the Secretary of
State's Office. Fifteen or twenty years ago, the Crown-
room, as it is called, was opened by certain Commissioners, under authority of a sign-manual. They saw the
fatal chest, strewed with the dust of an hundred years,
about six inches thick: a coating of like thickness lay on

the floor; and I have heard the late President Blair say, that the uniform and level appearance of the dust warranted them to believe that the chest, if opened at all after 1707, must have been violated within a short time of that date, since, had it been opened at a later period, the dust accumulated on the lid, and displaced at opening it, must have been lying around the chest. But the Commissioners did not think their warrant entitled them to force this chest, for which no keys could be found; especially as their warrant only entitled them to search for *records* — not for crowns and sceptres.

The mystery, therefore, remained unpenetrated; and public curiosity was left to console itself with the nursery rhyme: —

> " On Tintock tap there is a mist,
> And in the mist there is a kist."

Our fat friend's curiosity, however, goes to the point at once, authorizing and enjoining an express search for the Regalia. Our friend of Buccleuch is at the head of the Commission, and will, I think, be as keen as I or any one, to see the issue.

I trust you have read Rob by this time. I think he smells of the cramp. Above all, I had too much flax on my distaff; and as it did not consist with my patience or my plan to make a fourth volume, I was obliged at last to draw a rough, coarse, and hasty thread. But the book is well liked here, and has reeled off in great style. I have two stories on the anvil, far superior to Rob Roy in point of interest. Ever yours,

WALTER SCOTT.

The Commissioners, who finally assembled on the 4th of February, were, according to the record, "the Right Hon. Charles Hope, Lord President of the Court of Session; the Right Hon. David Boyle, Lord Justice-Clerk; the Right Hon. William Adam, Lord Chief Commissioner of the Ju.y Court; Major-General John Hope

(Commanding the Forces in Scotland); the Solicitor-General (James Wedderburn, Esq.); the Lord Provost of Edinburgh (Kincaid Mackenzie, Esq.); William Clerk, Esq., Principal Clerk of the Jury Court; Henry Jardine, Esq., Deputy Remembrancer in the Exchequer; Thomas Thomson, Esq., Deputy Clerk-Register of Scotland; and Walter Scott, Esq., one of the Principal Clerks of Session."

Of the proceedings of this day, the reader has a full and particular account in an Essay which Scott penned shortly afterwards, and which is included in his Prose Miscellanies (vol. vii.). But I must not omit the contemporaneous letters in which he announced the success of the quest to his friend the Secretary of the Admiralty, and through him to the Regent: —

TO J. W. CROKER, ESQ., M. P., ETC., ETC., ADMIRALTY,
LONDON.

EDINBURGH, 4th February, 1818.

MY DEAR CROKER, — I have the pleasure to assure you the Regalia of Scotland were this day found in perfect preservation. The Sword of State and Sceptre showed marks of hard usage at some former period; but in all respects agree with the description in Thomson's work.[1] I will send you a complete account of the opening to-morrow, as the official account will take some time to draw up. In the mean time, I hope you will remain as obstinate in your unbelief as St. Thomas, because then you will come down to satisfy yourself. I know nobody entitled to earlier information, save ONE, to whom you can perhaps find the means of communicating the result of our researches. The post is just going off.

Ever yours truly,

WALTER SCOTT.

[1] *Collection of Inventories and other Records of the Royal Wardrobe and Jewel-House, etc.* Edin. 1815, 4to.

EDINBURGH, 5th February, 1818.

MY DEAR CROKER, — I promised I would add something to my report of yesterday, and yet I find I have but little to say. The extreme solemnity of opening sealed doors of oak and iron, and finally breaking open a chest which had been shut since 7th March, 1707, about a hundred and eleven years, gave a sort of interest to our researches, which I can hardly express to you, and it would be very difficult to describe the intense eagerness with which we watched the rising of the lid of the chest, and the progress of the workmen in breaking it open, which was neither an easy nor a speedy task. It sounded very hollow when they worked on it with their tools, and I began to lean to your faction of the Little Faiths. However, I never could assign any probable or feasible reason for withdrawing these memorials of ancient independence; and my doubts rather arose from the conviction that many absurd things are done in public as well as in private life, merely out of a hasty impression of passion or resentment. For it was evident the removal of the Regalia might have greatly irritated people's minds here, and offered a fair pretext of breaking the Union, which for thirty years was the predominant wish of the Scottish nation.

The discovery of the Regalia has interested people's minds much more strongly than I expected, and is certainly calculated to make a pleasant and favorable impression upon them in respect to the kingly part of the constitution. It would be of the utmost consequence that they should be occasionally shown to them, under proper regulations, and for a small fee. The Sword of State is a most beautiful piece of workmanship, a present from Pope Julius II. to James IV. The scabbard is richly decorated with filigree work of silver, double gilded, representing oak leaves and acorns, executed in

a taste worthy that classical age in which the arts revived. A draughtsman has been employed to make
sketches of these articles, in order to be laid before his
Royal Highness. The fate of these Regalia, which his
Royal Highness's goodness has thus restored to light and
honor, has on one or two occasions been singular enough.
They were, in 1652, lodged in the Castle of Dunnottar,
the seat of the Earl Marischal, by whom, according to
his ancient privilege, they were kept. The castle was
defended by George Ogilvie of Barra, who, apprehensive
of the progress which the English made in reducing the
strong places in Scotland, became anxious for the safety
of these valuable memorials. The ingenuity of his lady
had them conveyed out of the castle in a bag on a woman's back, among some *hards*, as they are called, of
lint. They were carried to the Kirk of Kinneff, and
entrusted to the care of the clergyman, named Grainger,
and his wife, and buried under the pulpit. The Castle
of Dunnottar, though very strong and faithfully defended, was at length under necessity of surrendering,
being the last strong place in Britain on which the royal
flag floated in those calamitous times. Ogilvie and his
lady were threatened with the utmost extremities by the
Republican General Morgan, unless they should produce
the Regalia. The governor stuck to it that he knew
nothing of them, as in fact they had been carried away
without his knowledge. The lady maintained she had
given them to John Keith, second son of the Earl Marischal, by whom, she said, they had been carried to
France. They suffered a long imprisonment, and much
ill usage. On the Restoration, the old Countess Marischal, founding upon the story Mrs. Ogilvie had told to
screen her husband, obtained for her own son, John
Keith, the earldom of Kintore, and the post of Knight
Marischal, with £400 a year, as if he had been in truth
the preserver of the Regalia. It soon proved that this
reward had been too hastily given, for Ogilvie of Barra

produced the Regalia, the honest clergyman refusing to deliver them to any one but those from whom he received them. Ogilvie was made a Knight Baronet, however, and got a new charter of the lands, acknowledging the good service. Thus it happened oddly enough, that Keith, who was abroad during the transaction, and had nothing to do with it, got the earldom, pension, etc., Ogilvie only inferior honors, and the poor clergyman nothing whatever, or, as we say, *the hare's foot to lick.* As for Ogilvie's lady, she died before the Restoration, her health being ruined by the hardships she endured from the Cromwellian satellites. She was a Douglas, with all the high spirit of that proud family. On her deathbed, and not till then, she told her husband where the honors were concealed, charging him to suffer death rather than betray them. Popular tradition says, not very probably, that Grainger and his wife were *booted* (that is, tortured with the engine called the boots). I think that the Knight Marischal's office rested in the Kintore family until 1715, when it was resumed on account of the bearded Earl's accession to the Insurrection of that year. He escaped well, for they might have taken his estate and his earldom. I must save post, however, and conclude abruptly. Yours ever,

WALTER SCOTT.

On the 5th, after the foregoing letter had been written at the Clerk's table, Scott and several of his brother Commissioners revisited the Castle, accompanied by some of the ladies of their families. His daughter tells me that her father's conversation had worked her feelings up to such a pitch, that when the lid was again removed, she nearly fainted, and drew back from the circle. As she was retiring, she was startled by his voice exclaiming, in a tone of the deepest emotion, "something between anger and despair," as she expresses it, — "By G—, No!" One of the Commissioners, not quite enter-

ing into the solemnity with which Scott regarded this
business, had, it seems, made a sort of motion as if he
meant to put the crown on the head of one of the young
ladies near him, but the voice and aspect of the Poet
were more than sufficient to make the worthy gentleman
understand his error; and, respecting the enthusiasm
with which he had not been taught to sympathize, he laid
down the ancient diadem with an air of painful embarrassment. Scott whispered, "Pray, forgive me;" and
turning round at the moment, observed his daughter
deadly pale, and leaning by the door. He immediately
drew her out of the room, and when the air had somewhat recovered her, walked with her across the Mound
to Castle Street. "He never spoke all the way home,"
she says, "but every now and then I felt his arm trem-
ble; and from that time I fancied he began to treat me
more like a woman than a child. I thought he liked me
better, too, than he had ever done before."

These little incidents may give some notion of the profound seriousness with which his imagination had invested this matter. I am obliged to add, that in the
society of Edinburgh at the time, even in the highest
Tory circles, it did not seem to awaken much even of
curiosity — to say nothing of any deeper feeling. There
was, however, a great excitement among the common
people of the town, and a still greater among the peasantry, not only in the neighborhood, but all over Scotland; and the Crown-room, becoming thenceforth one
of the established *lions* of a city much resorted to, moreover, by stranger tourists, was likely, on the most moderate scale of admission-fee, to supply a revenue sufficient
for remunerating responsible and respectable guardian-
ship. This post would, as Scott thought, be a very suitable one for his friend, Captain Adam Ferguson; and
he exerted all his zeal for that purpose. The Captain
was appointed: his nomination, however, did not take
place for some months after; and the postscript of a

letter to the Duke of Buccleuch, dated May 14, 1818, plainly indicates the interest on which Scott mainly relied for its completion: "If you happen," he writes, "to see Lord Melville, pray give him a jog about Ferguson's affair; but between ourselves, I depend chiefly on the kind offices of Willie Adam, who is an auld sneck-drawer." The Lord Chief-Commissioner, at all times ready to lend Scott his influence with the Royal Family, had, on the present occasion, the additional motive of warm and hereditary personal regard for Ferguson.

I have placed together such letters as referred principally to the episode of the Regalia; but shall now give, in the order of time, a few which will sufficiently illustrate the usual course of his existence, while The Heart of Mid-Lothian was in progress. It appears that he resumed, in the beginning of this year, his drama of Devorgoil. His letters to Terry are of course full of that subject, but they contain, at the same time, many curious indications of his views and feelings as to theatrical affairs in general — and mixed up with these a most characteristic record of the earnestness with which he now watched the interior fitting up, as he had in the season before the outward architecture, of the new edifice at Abbotsford. Meanwhile it will be seen that he found leisure hours for various contributions to periodical works, — among others, an article on Kirkton's Church History, and another on (of all subjects in the world) *military bridges*, for the Quarterly Review; a spirited version of the old German ballad on the Battle of Sempach, and a generous criticism on Mrs. Shelley's romance of Frankenstein, for Blackwood's Magazine. This being the first winter and spring of Laidlaw's establishment at Kaeside, communications as to the affairs of the farm were exchanged weekly whenever Scott was in Edinburgh, and they afford delightful evidence of that paternal solicitude for the well-being of his rural dependents, which all along kept pace with Scott's zeal as to the economical improvement, and the picturesque adornment of his territories.

EDINBURGH, 23d January, 1818.

My DEAR TERRY, — You have by this time the continuation of the drama, down to the commencement of the third act, as I have your letter on the subject of the first. You will understand that I only mean them as sketches; for the first and second acts are too short, and both want much to combine them with the third. I can easily add music to Miss Devorgoil's part. As to Braham, he is a beast of an actor, though an angel of a singer, and truly I do not see what he could personify. Let me know, however, your thoughts and wishes, and all shall be moulded to the best of my power to meet them: the point is to make it *take* if we can; the rest is all leather and prunella. A great many things must occur to you technically better, in the way of alteration and improvement, and you know well that, though too indolent to amend things on my own conviction, I am always ready to make them meet my friends' wishes if possible. We shall both wish it better than I can make it, but there is no reason why we should not do for it all that we can. I advise you to take some sapient friend into your counsels, and let me know the result, returning the MS. at the same time.

I am now anxious to complete Abbotsford. I think I told you I mean to do nothing whatever to the present house, but to take it away altogether at some future time, so that I finish the upper story without any communication with Mrs. Redford's *ci-devant* mansion, and shall place the opening in the lower story, wherever it will be most suitable for the new house, without regard to defacing the temporary drawing-room. I am quite feverish about the armory. I have two pretty complete suits of armor — one Indian one, and a cuirassier's, with

boots, casque, etc.; many helmets, corselets, and steel
caps, swords and poniards without end, and about a
dozen of guns, ancient and modern. I have besides two
or three battle-axes and maces, pikes and targets, a
Highlander's accoutrement complete, a great variety of
branches of horns, pikes, bows and arrows, and the clubs
and creases of Indian tribes. Mr. Bullock promised to
give some hint about the fashion of disposing all these
matters; and now our spring is approaching, and I want
but my plans to get on. I have reason to be proud of
the finishing of my castle, for even of the tower, for
which I trembled, not a stone has been shaken by the
late terrific gale, which blew a roof clear off in the neighborhood. It was lying in the road like a saddle, as Tom
Purdie expressed it. Neither has a slate been lifted,
though about two yards of slating were stripped from the
stables in the haugh, which you know were comparatively
less exposed.

I am glad to hear of Mrs. Terry's improved health
and good prospects. As for young Master Mumblecrust,
I have no doubt he will be a credit to us all.

Yours ever truly,   W. SCOTT.

As the letters to Mr. Laidlaw did not travel by post,
but in the basket which had come laden with farm-pro-
duce for the use of the family in Edinburgh, they have
rarely any date but the day of the week. This is, however, of no consequence.

TO MR. LAIDLAW, KAESIDE.

Wednesday. [January, 1818.]

DEAR WILLIE, — Should the weather be rough, and
you nevertheless obliged to come to town, do not think
of riding, but take the Blucher.[1] Remember, your
health is of consequence to your family. Pray talk generally with the notables of Darnick — I mean Ruther-

---

[1] A stage-coach, so called, which ran betwixt Edinburgh and Jedburgh.

ford, and so forth — concerning the best ordering of the road to the marle; and also of the foot-road. It appears to me some route might be found more convenient than the present, but that which is most agreeable to those interested shall also be most agreeable for me. As a patriotic member of the community of Darnick, I consider their rights equally important as my own.

I told you I should like to convert the present steading at Beechland into a little hamlet of laborers, which we will name Abbotstown. The art of making people happy is to leave them much to their own guidance, but some little regulation is necessary. In the first place, I should like to have active and decent people there; then it is to be considered on what footing they should be. I conceive the best possible is, that they should pay for their cottages, and cow-grass, and potato ground, and be paid for their labor at the ordinary rate. I would give them some advantages sufficient to balance the following conditions, which, after all, are conditions in my favor: 1*st*, That they shall keep their cottages and little gardens, and doors, tolerably neat; and 2*d*, That the men shall on no account shoot, or the boys break timber or take birds' nests, or go among the planting. I do not know any other restrictions, and these are easy. I should think we might settle a few families very happily here, which is an object I have much at heart, for I have no notion of the proprietor who is only ambitious to be lord of the "beast and the brute," and chases the human face from his vicinity. By the bye, could we not manage to have a piper among the colonists?

We are delighted to hear that your little folks like the dells. Pray, in your walks try to ascertain the locality of St. John's Well, which cures the botts, and which John Moss claims for Kaeside; also the true history of the Carline's Hole. Ever most truly yours,

W. Scott.

I hope Mrs. Laidlaw does not want for anything that she can get from the garden or elsewhere.

TO DANIEL TERRY, ESQ.

8th February, 1818.

MY DEAR TERRY, — Yours arrived, unluckily, just half an hour after my packet was in the post-office, so this will cost you 9*d.*, for which I grieve.   To answer your principal question first, — the drama is

" Yours, Terry, yours in every thought."

I should never have dreamed of making such an attempt in my own proper person; and if I had such a vision, I should have been anxious to have made it something of a legitimate drama, such as a literary man, uncalled upon by any circumstance to connect himself with the stage, might have been expected to produce.   Now this is just what any gentleman in your situation might run off, to give a little novelty to the entertainment of the year, and as such will meet a mitigated degree of criticism, and have a better chance of that *productive* success, which is my principal object in my godson's behalf.   If any time should come when you might wish to disclose the secret, it will be in your power, and our correspondence will always serve to show that it was only at my earnest request, annexed as the condition of bringing the play forward, that you gave it your name — a circumstance which, with all the attending particulars, will prove plainly that there was no assumption on your part.

A beautiful drama might be made on the concealment of the Scotch Regalia during the troubles.   But it would interfere with the democratic spirit of the times, and would probably

—— " By party rage,
Or right or wrong, be hooted from the stage." [1]

[1] Slightly altered from Dr. Johnson's Prologue to the comedy of *A Word to the Wise.*

I will never forgive you if you let any false idea of my authorial feelings prevent your acting in this affair as if you were the real parent, not the godfather of the piece. Our facetious friend J. B. knows nought of such a matter being *en train*, and never will know. I am delighted to hear my windows are finished. Yours very truly,

WALTER SCOTT.

TO MR. LAIDLAW, KAESIDE.

Wednesday. [February, 1818.]

DEAR WILLIE, — I am not desirous to buy more land at present, unless I were to deal with Mr. Rutherford or Heiton, and I would rather deal with them next year than this, when I would have all my payments made for what I am now buying. Three or four such years as the last would enable me with prudence and propriety to ask Nicol[1] himself to flit and remove.

I like the idea of the birch-hedge much, and if intermixed with holly and thorns, I think it might make an impenetrable thicket, having all the advantages of a hedge without the formality. I fancy you will also need a great number of (black) Italian poplars — which are among the most useful and best growers, as well as most beautiful of plants which love a wet soil.

I am glad the saws are going.[2] We may begin by and by with wrights, but I cannot but think that a handy laborer might be taught to work at them. I shall insist on Tom learning the process perfectly himself.

As to the darkness of the garrets, they are intended for the accommodation of travelling geniuses, poets, painters, and so forth, and a little obscurity will refresh their shattered brains. I dare say Lauchie[3] will *shave*

---

[1] Mr. Nicol Milne of Faldonside. This gentleman's property is a valuable and extensive one, situated immediately to the westward of Abbotsford; and Scott continued, year after year, to dream of adding it also to his own.

[2] A sawmill had just been erected at Toftfield.

[3] A cocklaird adjoining Abbotsford at the eastern side. His farm is

his knoll, if it is required — it may to the barber's with
the Laird's hebdomadal beard — and Packwood would
have thought it the easier job of the two.

I saw Blackwood yesterday, and Hogg the day before,
and I understand from them you think of resigning the
Chronicle department of the Magazine. Blackwood told
me that if you did not like that part of the duty, he
would consider himself accountable for the same sum he
had specified to you for any other articles you might
communicate from time to time. He proposes that Hogg
should do the Chronicle: He will not do it so well as
you, for he wants judgment and caution, and likes to
have the appearance of eccentricity where eccentricity
is least graceful; that, however, is Blackwood's affair.
If you really do not like the Chronicle, there can be no
harm in your giving it up. What strikes me is, that
there is a something certain in having such a department
to conduct, whereas you may sometimes find yourself at
a loss when you have to cast about for a subject every
month. Blackwood *is* rather in a bad pickle just now —
sent to Coventry by the trade, as the booksellers call
themselves, and all about the parody of the two beasts.[1]

properly *Lochbreist;* but in the neighborhood he was generally known
as *Laird Lauchie* — or *Lauchie Langlegs.* Washington Irving describes
him in his *Abbotsford,* with high gusto. He was a most absurd original.

[1] An article in one of the early numbers of *Blackwood's Magazine,* entitled *The Chaldee MS.,* in which the literati and booksellers of Edinburgh
were quizzed *en masse* — Scott himself among the rest. It was in this
lampoon that Constable first saw himself designated in print by the *sobriquet* of " The Crafty," long before bestowed on him by one of his own most
eminent Whig supporters; but nothing nettled him so much as the passages in which he and Blackwood are represented entreating the support
of Scott for their respective Magazines, and waved off by " the Great Magician " in the same identical phrases of contemptuous indifference. The
description of Constable's visit to Abbotsford may be worth transcribing —
for Sir David Wilkie, who was present when Scott read it, says he was
almost choked with laughter, and he afterwards confessed that the Chal-
dean author had given a sufficiently accurate version of what really passed
on the occasion : —
" 26. But when the Spirits were gone, he (The Crafty) said unto himself,

Surely these gentlemen think themselves rather formed of porcelain clay than of common potter's ware. Dealing in satire against all others, their own dignity suffers so cruelly from an ill-imagined joke! If B. had good books to sell, he might set them all at defiance. His Magazine does well, and beats Constable's: but we will talk of this when we meet.[1]

As for Whiggery in general, I can only say, that as no man can be said to be utterly overset until his rump has been higher than his head, so I cannot read in history of any free state which has been brought to slavery until the rascal and uninstructed populace had had their short hour of anarchical government, which naturally

I will arise and go unto a magician, which is of my friends: of a surety he will devise some remedy, and free me out of all my distresses.

" 27. So he arose and came unto that great magician which hath his dwelling in the old fastness, hard by the River Jordan, which is by the Border.

" 28. And the magician opened his mouth and said, Lo! my heart wisheth thy good, and let the thing prosper which is in thy hands to do it.

" 29. But thou seest that my hands are full of working, and my labor is great. For, lo, I have to feed all the people of my land, and none knoweth whence his food cometh; but each man openeth his mouth, and my hand filleth it with pleasant things.

" 30. Moreover, thine adversary also is of my familiars.

" 31. The land is before thee : draw thou up thine hosts for the battle on the mount of Proclamation, and defy boldly thine enemy, which hath his camp in the place of Princes ; quit ye as men, and let favor be shown unto him which is most valiant.

" 32. Yet be thou silent ; peradventure will I help thee some little.

" 33. But the man which is Crafty saw that the magician loved him not. For he knew him of old, and they had had many dealings ; and he perceived that he would not assist him in the day of his adversity.

" 34. So he turned about, and went out of his fastness. And he shook the dust from his feet, and said, Behold I have given this magician much money, yet see now, he hath utterly deserted me. Verily, my fine gold hath perished." — Chap. iii.

[1] [The story of the composition of *The Chaldee Manuscript*, its publication in the first number of the magazine, destined to so long and brilliant a career, and the extraordinary commotion caused thereby, is admirably told in the *Annals of a Publishing House*, which also gives the details regarding Laidlaw's brief connection with the new periodical, and the correspondence of Scott and Blackwood during its early months. — See Mrs. Oliphant's *William Blackwood and His Sons*, vol. i. chap. iii.]

leads to the stern repose of military despotism. Property, morals, education, are the proper qualifications for those who should hold political rights, and extending them very widely greatly lessens the chance of these qualifications being found in electors. Look at the sort of persons chosen at elections where the franchise is very general, and you will find either fools who are content to flatter the passions of the mob for a little transient popularity, or knaves who pander to their follies, that they may make their necks a footstool for their own promotion. With these convictions, I am very jealous of Whiggery, under all modifications; and I must say, my acquaintance with the total want of principle in some of its warmest professors does not tend to recommend it. Somewhat too much of this. My compliments to the goodwife. Yours truly,

WALTER SCOTT.

TO THE SAME.

Wednesday. [February, 1818.]

DEAR WILLIE, — I have no idea Usher [1] will take the sheepland again, nor would I press it on him. As my circumstances stand, immediate revenue is much less my object than the real improvement of this property, which amuses me besides; our wants are amply supplied by my £1600 a year official income: nor have we a wish or a motive to extend our expenses beyond that of the decencies and hospitality of our station in life; so that my other resources remain for buying land in future, or improving what we have. No doubt Abbotsford, in maintaining our establishment during the summer, may be reckoned £150 or £200 saved on what we must otherwise buy; and if we could arrange to have mutton and beef

---

[1] John Usher, the ex-proprietor of Toftfield, was eventually Scott's tenant on part of those lands for many years. He was a man of far superior rank and intelligence to the rest of the displaced lairds — and came presently to be one of Scott's trusty rural friends, and a frequent companion of his sports.

occasionally from the farm in winter, it would be a still greater saving. All this you will consider: for Tom, thoroughly honest and very clever in his way, has no kind of generalizing, and would often like to save sixpence in his own department at the expense of my paying five shillings in another. This is his fault, and when you join to it a Scotch slovenliness which leads him to see things half-finished without pain or anxiety, I do not know any other he has — but such as they are, these must be guarded against. For our housemaid (for housekeeper we must not call her), I should like much a hawk of a nest so good as that you mention: but would not such a place be rather beneath her views? Her duty would be to look to scrupulous cleanliness within doors, and employ her leisure in spinning, or plain-work, as wanted. When we came out for a blink, she would be expected to cook a little in a plain way, and play maid of all work; when we were stationary, she would assist the housemaid and superintend the laundry. Probably your aunt's granddaughter will have pretensions to something better than this; but as we are to be out on the 12th March, we will talk it over. Assuredly a well-connected steady person would be of the greatest consequence to us. I like your plan of pitting much; and to compromise betwixt you and Tom, do one half with superior attention, and slit in the others for mere nurses. But I am no friend to that same slitting.

I adhere to trying a patch or two of larches, of a quarter of an acre each, upon the Athole plan, by way of experiment. We can plant them up if they do not thrive. On the whole, three-and-a-half feet is, I think, the right distance. I have no fear of the ground being impoverished. Trees are not like arable crops, which necessarily derive their sustenance from the superficial earth — the roots of trees go far and wide, and, if incommoded by a neighbor, they send out suckers to procure nourishment elsewhere. They never hurt each other till their tops interfere, which may be easily prevented by timely weeding.

I rejoice in the sawmill. Have you settled with Harper? — and how do Og and Bashan [1] come on? I cannot tell you how delighted I am with the account Hogg gives me of Mr. Grieve. The great Cameron was chaplain in the house of my great something grandfather, and so I hope Mr. Grieve will be mine. If, as the King of Prussia said to Rousseau, "a little persecution is necessary to make his home entirely to his mind," he shall have it; and what persecutors seldom promise, I will stop whenever he is tired of it. I have a pair of thumbikins also much at his service, if he requires their assistance to glorify God and the Covenant. Sincerely, I like enthusiasm of every kind so well, especially when united with worth of character, that I shall be delighted with this old gentleman. Ever yours,

W. SCOTT.

The last paragraph of this letter refers to an uncle of Laidlaw's (the father of Hogg's friend, John Grieve), who at this time thought of occupying a cottage on Scott's estate. He was a preacher of the Cameronian sect, and had long ministered to a very small remnant of "the hill-folk" scattered among the wilds of Ettrick. He was a very good man, and had a most venerable and apostolical benignity of aspect; but his prejudices were as extravagant as those of Cameron, his patriarch, himself could have been. The project of his removal to Tweedside was never realized.

The following admirable letter was written at the request of Messrs. Constable, who had, on Scott's recommendation, undertaken the publication of Mr. Maturin's novel, Women, or *Pour et Contre*. The reverend author's Bertram had, it may be remembered, undergone some rather rough usage in Coleridge's Biographia Lite-

---

[1] A yoke of oxen.

raria; and he was now desirous to revenge himself by a
preface of the polemical sort: —

26th February, 1818.

DEAR SIR, — I am going to claim the utmost and best
privilege of sincere friendship and good-will, that of
offering a few words of well-meant advice; and you may
be sure that the occasion seems important to induce me
to venture so far upon your tolerance. It respects the
preface to your work, which Constable and Co. have
sent to me. It is as well written as that sort of thing
can be; but will you forgive me if I say — it is too much
in the tone of the offence which gave rise to it, to be
agreeable either to good taste or to general feeling.
Coleridge's work has been little read or heard of, and
has made no general impression whatever — certainly no
impression unfavorable to you or your play. In the
opinion, therefore, of many, you will be resenting an
injury of which they are unacquainted with the existence.
If I see a man beating another unmercifully, I am apt
to condemn him upon the first blush of the business, and
hardly excuse him though I may afterwards learn he had
ample provocation. Besides, your diatribe is not *hujus
loci*. We take up a novel for amusement, and this current of controversy breaks out upon us like a stream of
lava out of the side of a beautiful green hill; men will
say you should have reserved your disputes for reviews
or periodical publications, and they will sympathize less
with your anger, because they will not think the time
proper for expressing it. We are bad judges, bad physicians, and bad divines in our own case; but, above all,
we are seldom able, when injured or insulted, to judge
of the degree of sympathy which the world will bear in
our resentment and our retaliation. The instant, however, that such degree of sympathy is exceeded, we hurt
ourselves, and not our adversary. I am so convinced

of this, and so deeply fixed in the opinion, that besides the uncomfortable feelings which are generated in the course of literary debate, a man lowers his estimation in the public eye by engaging in such controversy, that, since I have been dipped in ink, I have suffered no personal attacks (and I have been honored with them of all descriptions) to provoke me to reply. A man will certainly be vexed on such occasions, and I have wished to have the knaves *where the muircock was the bailie* — or, as *you* would say, *upon the sod* — but I never let the thing cling to my mind, and always adhered to my resolution, that if my writings and tenor of life did not confute such attacks, my words never should. Let me entreat you to view Coleridge's violence as a thing to be contemned, not retaliated — the opinion of a British public may surely be set in honest opposition to that of one disappointed and wayward man. You should also consider, *en bon Chrétien*, that Coleridge has had some room to be spited at the world, and you are, I trust, to continue to be a favorite with the public — so that you should totally neglect and despise criticism, however virulent, which arises out of his bad fortune and your good.

I have only to add that Messrs. Constable and Co. are seriously alarmed for the effects of the preface upon the public mind as unfavorable to the work. In this they must be tolerable judges, for their experience as to popular feeling is very great; and as they have met your wishes, in all the course of the transaction, perhaps you will be disposed to give some weight to their opinion upon a point like this. Upon my own part I can only say that I have no habits of friendship, and scarce those of acquaintance with Coleridge — I have not even read his Autobiography — but I consider him as a man of genius, struggling with bad habits and difficult circumstances. It is, however, entirely upon your account that I take the liberty of stating an opinion on a subject of such delicacy. I should wish you to give your excellent talents fair play, and to ride this race without carrying any superfluous weight; and I am so well acquainted with my old friend the public, that I could bet a thousand pounds to a shilling, that the preface (if that controversial part of it is not cancelled) will greatly prejudice your novel.

I will not ask your forgiveness for the freedom I have used, for I am sure you will not suspect me of any motives but those which arise from regard to your talents and person; but I shall be glad to hear (whether you follow my advice or no) that you are not angry with me for having volunteered to offer it.

My health is, I think, greatly improved; I have had some returns of my spasmodic affection, but tolerable in degree, and yielding to medicine. I hope gentle exercise and the air of my hills will set me up this summer. I trust you will soon be out now. I have delayed reading the sheets in progress after Vol. I., that I might enjoy them when collected. Ever yours, etc.,

WALTER SCOTT.

TO MR. LAIDLAW.

EDINBURGH, Wednesday. [March, 1818.]

DEAR WILLIE, — I am delighted to hear the plantings get on so well. The weather here has been cruelly changeable — fresh one day — frost the next — snow the third. This morning the snow lay three inches thick, and before noon it was gone, and blowing a tempest. Many of the better ranks are ill of the typhus fever, and some deaths. How do your poor folks come on? Let Tom advance you money when it is wanted. I do not propose, like the heroine of a novel, to convert the hovels of want into the abodes of elegant plenty, but we have enough to spare to relieve actual distress, and do not wish to economize where we can find out (which is difficult) where the assistance is instantly useful.

Don't let Tom forget hedgerow trees, which he is very

unwilling to remember; and also to plant birches, oaks, elms, and such like round-headed trees along the verges of the Kaeside plantations; they make a beautiful outline, and also a sort of fence, and were not planted last year because the earth at the sunk fences was too newly travelled. This should be mixed with various bushes, as hollies, thorns, so as to make a wild hedge, or thickety obstruction to the inroads of cattle. A few sweetbriers, alders, honeysuckles, laburnums, etc., should be thrown in. A verdant screen may be made in this way, of the wildest and most beautiful description, which should never be clipt, only pruned, allowing the loose branches to drop over those that are taken away. Tom is very costive about trees, and talks only of 300 poplars. I shall send at least double that number; also some hagberries, etc. He thinks he is saving me money when he is starving my projects; but he is a pearl of honesty and good intention, and I like him the better for needing driving where expense is likely. Ever yours,

W. SCOTT.

TO JOHN MURRAY, ESQ., ALBEMARLE STREET, LONDON.

ABBOTSFORD, 23d March, 1818.

DEAR MURRAY, —

"Grieve not for me, my dearest dear,
 I am not dead but sleepeth here." —

I have little to plead for myself, but the old and vile apologies of laziness and indisposition. I think I have been so unlucky of late as to have always the will to work when sitting at the desk hurts me, and the irresistible propensity to be lazy, when I might, like the man whom Hogarth introduces into Bridewell with his hands strapped up against the wall, "better work than stand thus." I laid Kirkton[1] aside half finished, from a desire

---

[1] Scott's article on Kirkton's *History of the Church of Scotland*, edited by Mr. C. K. Sharpe, appeared in the 36th number of the *Quarterly Review*. — See *Miscellaneous Prose Works*, vol. xix. p. 213.

to get the original edition of the lives of Cameron, etc.,
by Patrick Walker, which I had not seen since a boy,
and now I have got it, and find, as I suspected, that
some curious *morceaux* have been cut out by subsequent
editors.[1]   I will, without loss of time, finish the article,
which I think you will like.   Blackwood kidnapped an
article for his Magazine on the Frankenstein story,[2]
which I intended for you.   A very old friend and school
companion of mine, and a gallant soldier, if ever there
was one, Sir Howard Douglas, has asked me to review
his work on Military Bridges.   I must get a friend's
assistance for the scientific part, and add some balaam
of mine own (as printers' devils say) to make up four or
five pages.   I have no objection to attempt Lord Orford
if I have time, and find I can do it with ease.   Though
far from admiring his character, I have always had a
high opinion of his talents, and am well acquainted with
his works.   The letters you have published are, I think,
his very best — lively, entertaining, and unaffected.[3]   I
am greatly obliged to you for these and other literary
treasures which I owe to your goodness from time to
time.   Although not thankfully acknowledged as they
should be in course, these things are never thanklessly
received.

I could have sworn that Beppo was founded on Whis-
tlecraft, as both were on Anthony Hall,[4] who, like
Beppo, had more wit than grace.

---

[1] Scott expressed great satisfaction on seeing the *Lives of the Covenanters* — Cameron, Peden, Semple, Wellwood, Cargill, Smith, Renwick, etc.
— reprinted without mutilation in the *Biographia Presbyteriana*.   Edin.
1827.   The publisher of this collection was the late Mr. John Stevenson,
long chief clerk to John Ballantyne, and usually styled by Scott "True
Jock," in opposition to one of his old master's many *aliases* — namely,
"Leein' Johnnie."

[2] See Scott's *Prose Miscellanies*, vol. xviii. p. 250.

[3] The Letters of Horace Walpole to George Montagu.

[4] *Anthony Hall* is only known as Editor of one of Leland's works.   I
have no doubt Scott was thinking of *John Hall Stevenson*, author of *Crazy
Tales ;* the friend, and (it is said) the *Eugenius* of Sterne.

I am not, however, in spirits at present for treating
either these worthies, or my friend Rose,[1] though few
have warmer wishes to any of the trio. But this confounded changeable weather has twice within this fortnight brought back my cramp in the stomach. Adieu.
My next shall be with a packet. — Yours truly,

W. SCOTT.

In the next letter we have Scott's lamentation over the
death of Mrs. Murray Keith — the Mrs. Bethune Baliol
of his Chronicles of the Canongate. The person alluded
to under the designation of "Prince of the Black Marble
Islands" was Mr. George Bullock, already often mentioned as, with Terry and Mr. Atkinson, consulted about
all the arrangements of the rising house at Abbotsford.
Scott gave him this title from the Arabian Nights, on
occasion of his becoming the lessee of some marble quar-
ries in the Isle of Anglesea.

TO D. TERRY, ESQ., LONDON.

April 30, 1818 — SELKIRK.

MY DEAR TERRY, — Your packet arrived this morning. I was much disappointed not to find the Prince of
the Black Islands' plan in it, nor have I heard a word
from him since anent it, or anent the still more essential
articles of doors and windows. I heard from Hector
Macdonald Buchanan, that the said doors and windows
were packing a fortnight since, but there are no news of
them. Surely our friend's heart has grown as hard as
his materials; or the spell of the enchantress, which confined itself to the extremities of his predecessor, has
extended over his whole person. Mr. Atkinson has kept
tryst charmingly, and the ceiling of the dining-room will
be superb. I have got I know not how many casts, from
Melrose and other places, of pure Gothic antiquity. I

---

[1] I believe Mr. Rose's *Court and Parliament of Beasts* is here alluded
to.

must leave this on the 12th, and I could bet a trifle the doors, etc., will arrive the very day I set out, and be all put up *à la bonne aventure*. Meantime I am keeping open house, not much to my convenience, and I am afraid I shall be stopped in my plastering by the want of these matters. The exposed state of my house has led to a mysterious disturbance. The night before last we were awaked by a violent noise, like drawing heavy boards along the new part of the house. I fancied something had fallen, and thought no more about it. This was about *two* in the morning. Last night, at the same witching hour, the very same noise occurred. Mrs. S., as you know, is rather *timbersome*, so up got I, with Beardie's broadsword under my arm,

> "So bolt upright,
> And ready to fight."

But nothing was out of order, neither can I discover what occasioned the disturbance. However, I went to bed, grumbling against Tenterden Street,[1] and all its works. If there was no entrance but the keyhole, I should warrant myself against the ghosts. We have a set of idle fellows called workmen about us, which is a better way of accounting for nocturnal noises than any that is to be found in Baxter or Glanville.

When you see Mr. Atkinson, will you ask him how far he is satisfied with the arch between the armory and the ante-room, and whether it pleases him as it now stands? I have a brave old oaken cabinet, as black as ebony, 300 years old at least, which will occupy one side of the ante-room for the present. It is seven feet and a half long, about eighteen inches deep, and upwards of six feet high — a fine stand for china, etc.

You will be sorry to hear that we have lost our excellent old friend, Mrs. Murray Keith. She enjoyed all her spirits and excellent faculties till within two days of her death, when she was seized with a feverish complaint,

---

[1] Bullock's manufactory was in this street.

which eighty-two years were not calculated to resist.
Much tradition, and of the very best kind, has died with
this excellent old lady; one of the few persons whose
spirits and cleanliness, and freshness of mind and body,
made old age lovely and desirable. In the general case,
it seems scarce endurable.

It seems odd to me that Rob Roy [1] should have made
good fortune; pray let me know something of its history.
There is in Jedediah's present work a thing capable of
being woven out a *bourgeoise* tragedy. I think of con-
triving that it shall be in your hands some time before
the public see it, that you may try to operate upon it
yourself. This would not be difficult, as vol. 4, and part
of 3d, contain a different story. *Avowedly* I will never
write for the stage; if I do, "call me *horse*." And indeed I feel severely the want of knowledge of theatrical
business and effect: however, something we will do. I
am writing in the noise and babble of a head-court of
freeholders; therefore my letter is incoherent, and therefore it is written also on long paper; but therefore, moreover, it will move by frank, as the member is here, and
stands upon his popularity. Kind compliments to Mrs.
Terry and Walter.

Yours very truly,

WALTER SCOTT.

On the morning that Mr. Terry received the foregoing
letter in London, Mr. William Erskine was breakfasting
with him; and the chief subject of their conversation
was the sudden death of George Bullock, which had occurred on the same night, and, as nearly as they could
ascertain, at the very hour when Scott was roused from
his sleep by the "mysterious disturbance" here described,
and sallied from his chamber with old Beardie's Killiecrankie claymore in his hand. This coincidence, when

---

[1] A drama founded on the novel of *Rob Roy* had been produced, with
great success, on the London stage.

Scott received Erskine's minute detail of what had happened in Tenterden Street, made a much stronger impression on his mind than might be gathered from the tone of an ensuing communication.

TO D. TERRY, ESQ., LONDON.

ABBOTSFORD, 4th May, 1818.

DEAR TERRY, — I received with the greatest surprise, and the most sincere distress, the news of poor George Bullock's death. In the full career of honorable industry, — distinguished by his uncommon taste and talent, — esteemed by all who transacted business with him, — and loved by those who had the pleasure of his more intimate acquaintance, — I can scarce conceive a more melancholy summons. It comes as a particular shock to me, because I had, particularly of late, so much associated his idea with the improvements here, in which his kind and enthusiastic temper led him to take such interest; and in looking at every unfinished or projected circumstance, I feel an impression of melancholy which will for some time take away the pleasure I have found in them. I liked George Bullock because he had no trumpery selfishness about his heart, taste, or feelings. Pray let me know about the circumstances of his family, etc. I feel most sincerely interested in all that concerns him. It must have been a dreadful surprise to Mr. Atkinson and you who lived with him so much. I need not, I am sure, beg you to be in no hurry about my things. The confusion must be cruelly great, without any friend adding to it; and in fact, at this moment, I am very indifferent on the subject. The poor kind fellow! He took so much notice of little Charles, and was so domesticated with us all, that I really looked with a schoolboy's anxiety for his being here in the season, to take his own quiet pleasures, and to forward mine. But God's will be done. All that surviving friends can do upon such a loss is, if possible, to love each other still better. — I beg to be kindly remembered to Mrs. Terry and Monsieur Walter. Ever most truly yours,

WALTER SCOTT.

TO THE SAME.

EDINBURGH, 16th May, 1818.

MY DEAR TERRY, — Mr. Nasmyth [1] has obligingly given me an opportunity of writing to you a few lines, as he is setting out for London. I cannot tell you how much I continue to be grieved for our kind-hearted and enthusiastic friend Bullock. I trust he has left his family comfortably settled, though, with so many plans which required his active and intelligent mind to carry them through, one has natural apprehensions upon that score. When you can with propriety make inquiry how my matters stand, I should be glad to know. Hector Macdonald tells me that my doors and windows were ready packed, in which case, perhaps, the sooner they are embarked the better, not only for safety, but because they can only be in the way, and the money will now be the more acceptable. Poor Bullock had also the measures for my chimney-pieces, for grates of different kinds, and orders for beds, dining-room tables and chairs. But how far these are in progress of being executed, or whether they can now be executed, I must leave to your judgment and inquiry. Your good sense and delicacy will understand the *façon de faire* better than I can point it out. I shall never have the pleasure in these things that I expected.

I have just left Abbotsford to attend the summer session — left it when the leaves were coming out — the most delightful season for a worshipper of the country like me. The Home-bank, which we saw at first green with turnips, will now hide a man somewhat taller than Johnny Ballantyne in its shades. In fact, the trees

[1] Mr. Alexander Nasmyth, an eminent landscape painter of Edinburgh — the father of Mrs. Terry.

cover the ground, and have a very pretty bosky effect; from six years to ten or twelve, I think wood is as beautiful as ever it is afterwards until it figures as aged and magnificent. Your hobbledehoy tree of twenty-five years' standing is neither so beautiful as in its infancy, nor so respectable as in its age.

Counsellor Erskine is returned, much pleased with your hospitality, and giving an excellent account of you. Were you not struck with the fantastical coincidence of our nocturnal disturbances at Abbotsford with the melancholy event that followed? I protest to you the noise resembled half-a-dozen men hard at work putting up boards and furniture, and nothing can be more certain than that there was nobody on the premises at the time. With a few additional touches, the story would figure in Glanville or Aubrey's Collection. In the mean time you may set it down with poor Dubisson's warnings,[1] as a remarkable coincidence coming under your own observation. I trust we shall see you this season. I think we could hammer a neat *comédie bourgeoise* out of The Heart of Mid-Lothian. Mrs. Scott and family join in kind compliments to Mrs. Terry; and I am ever yours truly,

WALTER SCOTT.

It appears from one of these letters to Terry, that, so late as the 30th of April, Scott still designed to include two separate stories in the second series of the Tales of my Landlord. But he must have changed his plan soon after that date; since the four volumes, entirely occupied with The Heart of Mid-Lothian, were before the public in the course of June. The story thus deferred, in consequence of the extent to which that of Jeanie Deans grew on his hands, was The Bride of Lammermoor.

[1] See *ante*, vol. ii. p. 220.

CHAPTER XLI

1818

ON the 12th of May, as we have seen, Scott left Abbotsford, for the summer session in Edinburgh.

At this moment, his position, take it for all in all,
was, I am inclined to believe, what no other man had
ever won for himself by the pen alone. His works were
the daily food, not only of his countrymen, but of all
educated Europe. His society was courted by whatever
England could show of eminence. Station, power,
wealth, beauty, and genius, strove with each other in
every demonstration of respect and worship, and — a few
political fanatics and envious poetasters apart — wherever he appeared in town or in country, whoever had
Scotch blood in him, "gentle or simple," felt it move
more rapidly through his veins when he was in the presence of Scott. To descend to what many looked on as
higher things, he considered himself, and was considered
by all about him, as rapidly consolidating a large fortune: the annual profits of his novels alone had, for
several years, been not less than £10,000: his domains

were daily increased — his castle was rising — and perhaps few doubted that erelong he might receive from
the just favor of his Prince some distinction in the way
of external rank, such as had seldom before been dreamt
of as the possible consequence of a mere literary celebrity. It was about this time that the compiler of these
pages first had the opportunity of observing the plain
easy modesty which had survived the many temptations
of such a career; and the kindness of heart pervading,
in all circumstances, his gentle deportment, which made
him the rare, perhaps the solitary, example of a man
signally elevated from humble beginnings, and loved
more and more by his earliest friends and connections,
in proportion as he had fixed on himself the homage of
the great, and the wonder of the world.

It was during the sitting of the General Assembly of
the Kirk in May, 1818, that I first had the honor of
meeting him in private society: the party was not a large
one, at the house of a much-valued common friend —
Mr. Home Drummond of Blair Drummond, the grandson
of Lord Kames. Mr. Scott, ever apt to consider too
favorably the literary efforts of others, and more especially of very young persons, received me, when I was
presented to him, with a cordiality which I had not been
prepared to expect from one filling a station so exalted.
This, however, is the same story that every individual,
who ever met him under similar circumstances, has had
to tell. When the ladies retired from the dinner-table,
I happened to sit next him; and he, having heard that
I had lately returned from a tour in Germany, made
that country and its recent literature the subject of some
conversation. In the course of it, I told him that when,
on reaching the inn at Weimar, I asked the waiter
whether Goethe was then in the town, the man stared as
if he had not heard the name before; and that on my
repeating the question, adding *Goethe der grosse dichter*
(the great poet), he shook his head as doubtfully as

before — until the landlady solved our difficulties, by suggesting that perhaps the traveller might mean "the *Herr Geheimer-Rath* (Privy Counsellor) *Von Goethe*." Scott seemed amused with this, and said, "I hope you will come one of these days and see me at Abbotsford; and when you reach Selkirk or Melrose, be sure you ask even the landlady for nobody but *the Sheriff*." He appeared particularly interested when I described Goethe as I first saw him, alighting from a carriage, crammed with wild plants and herbs which he had picked up in the course of his morning's botanizing among the hills above Jena. "I am glad," said he, "that my old master has pursuits somewhat akin to my own. I am no botanist, properly speaking; and though a dweller on the banks of the Tweed, shall never be knowing about Flora's beauties; [1] but how I should like to have a talk with him about trees!" I mentioned how much any one must be struck with the majestic beauty of Goethe's countenance (the noblest certainly by far that I have ever yet seen): "Well," said he, "the grandest demigod I ever saw was Dr. Carlyle, minister of Musselburgh, commonly called *Jupiter Carlyle*, from having sat more than once for the king of gods and men to Gavin Hamilton — and a shrewd, clever old carle was he, no doubt, but no more a poet than his precentor. As for poets, I have seen, I believe, all the best of our own time and country — and, though Burns had the most glorious eyes imaginable, I never thought any of them would come up to an artist's notion of the character, except Byron." A reverend gentleman present (I think, Principal Nicoll of St. Andrews) expressed his regret that he had never seen Lord Byron. "And the prints," resumed Scott, "give one no impression of him — the lustre is there, Doctor, but it is not lighted up. Byron's countenance is *a thing to dream of*. A certain fair lady, whose name has been too often

---

[1] " What beauties does Flora disclose,
How sweet are her smiles upon Tweed," etc. — *Crawford*.

mentioned in connection with his, told a friend of mine,
that when she first saw Byron, it was in a crowded room,
and she did not know who it was, but her eyes were instantly nailed, and she said to herself, *that pale face is
my fate.* And, poor soul, if a godlike face and godlike
powers could have made any excuse for devilry, to be
sure she had one." In the course of this talk, an old
friend and schoolfellow of Scott's [1] asked him across the
table if he had any faith in the antique busts of Homer.
"No, truly," he answered, smiling, "for if there had
been either limners or stuccoyers worth their salt in those
days, the owner of such a headpiece would never have
had to trail the poke. They would have alimented the
honest man decently among them for a lay-figure."

A few days after this, I received a communication
from the Messrs. Ballantyne, to the effect that Mr.
Scott's various avocations had prevented him from ful-
filling his agreement with them as to the historical department of the Edinburgh Annual Register for 1816,
and that it would be acceptable to him as well as them,
if I could undertake to supply it in the course of the
autumn. This proposal was agreed to on my part, and I
had consequently occasion to meet him pretty often during that summer session. He told me, that if the war
had gone on, he should have liked to do the historical
summary as before; but that the prospect of having no
events to record but radical riots, and the passing or rejecting of corn bills and poor bills, sickened him; that
his health was no longer what it had been; and that
though he did not mean to give over writing altogether
— (here he smiled significantly, and glanced his eye
towards a pile of MS. on the desk by him) — he thought
himself now entitled to write nothing but what would
rather be an amusement than a fatigue to him — "*Juni-
ores ad labores.*"

[1] The late Sir Patrick Murray of Ochtertyre, Bart. — one of the Scotch
Barons of Exchequer.

He at this time occupied as his *den* a square small room, behind the dining parlor in Castle Street. It had but a single Venetian window, opening on a patch of turf not much larger than itself, and the aspect of the place was on the whole sombrous. The walls were entirely clothed with books; most of them folios and quartos, and all in that complete state of repair which at a glance reveals a tinge of bibliomania. A dozen volumes or so, needful for immediate purposes of reference, were placed close by him on a small movable frame — something like a dumb-waiter. All the rest were in their proper niches, and wherever a volume had been lent, its room was occupied by a wooden block of the same size, having a card with the name of the borrower and date of the loan, tacked on its front. The old bindings had obviously been retouched and regilt in the most approved manner; the new, when the books were of any mark, were rich, but never gaudy — a large proportion of blue morocco — all stamped with his *device* of the portcullis, and its motto, *clausus tutus ero* — being an anagram of his name in Latin. Every case and shelf was accurately lettered, and the works arranged systematically; history and biography on one side — poetry and the drama on another — law books and dictionaries behind his own chair. The only table was a massive piece of furniture which he had had constructed on the model of one at Rokeby, with a desk and all its appurtenances on either side, that an amanuensis might work opposite to him when he chose; and with small tiers of drawers, reaching all round to the floor. The top displayed a goodly array of session papers, and on the desk below were, besides the MS. at which he was working, sundry parcels of letters, proof sheets, and so forth, all neatly done up with red tape. His own writing apparatus was a very handsome old box, richly carved, lined with crimson velvet, and containing ink-bottles, taper-stand, etc., in silver — the whole in such order that it might have come from the silversmith's

window half an hour before. Besides his own huge
elbow-chair, there were but two others in the room, and
one of these seemed, from its position, to be reserved
exclusively for the amanuensis. I observed, during the
first evening I spent with him in this *sanctum*, that while
he talked, his hands were hardly ever idle — sometimes
he folded letter-covers — sometimes he twisted paper into
matches, performing both tasks with great mechanical
expertness and nicety; and when there was no loose
paper fit to be so dealt with, he snapped his fingers, and
the noble Maida aroused himself from his lair on the
hearth-rug, and laid his head across his master's knees,
to be caressed and fondled. The room had no space for
pictures except one, an original portrait of Claverhouse,
which hung over the chimney-piece, with a Highland
target on either side, and broadswords and dirks (each
having its own story), disposed star-fashion round
them. A few green tin-boxes, such as solicitors keep
title-deeds in, were piled over each other on one side of
the window; and on the top of these lay a fox's tail,
mounted on an antique silver handle, wherewith, as often
as he had occasion to take down a book, he gently
brushed the dust off the upper leaves before opening it.
I think I have mentioned all the furniture of the room
except a sort of ladder, low, broad, well carpeted, and
strongly guarded with oaken rails, by which he helped
himself to books from his higher shelves. On the top
step of this convenience, Hinse of Hinsfeldt, (so called
from one of the German *Kinder-märchen*,) a venerable
tom-cat, fat and sleek, and no longer very locomotive,
usually lay watching the proceedings of his master and
Maida with an air of dignified equanimity; but when
Maida chose to leave the party, he signified his inclinations by thumping the door with his huge paw, as vio-
lently as ever a fashionable footman handled a knocker
in Grosvenor Square; the Sheriff rose and opened it for
him with courteous alacrity, — and then Hinse came

down purring from his perch, and mounted guard by the
footstool, *vice* Maida absent upon furlough.[1] Whatever
discourse might be passing, was broken every now and
then by some affectionate apostrophe to these four-footed
friends. He said they understood everything he said to
them — and I believe they did understand a great deal of
it. But at all events, dogs and cats, like children, have
some infallible tact for discovering at once who is and
who is not really fond of their company; and I venture
to say, Scott was never five minutes in any room before
the little pets of the family, whether dumb or lisping,
had found out his kindness for all their generation.

I never thought it lawful to keep a journal of what
passes in private society, so that no one need expect from
the sequel of this narrative any detailed record of Scott's
familiar talk. What fragments of it have happened to
adhere to a tolerably retentive memory, and may be put
into black and white without wounding any feelings
which my friend, were he alive, would have wished to
spare, I shall introduce as the occasion suggests or
serves. But I disclaim on the threshold anything more
than this; and I also wish to enter a protest once for
all against the general fidelity of several literary gentlemen who have kindly forwarded to me private lucubra-

---

[1] [Of Hinse, Washington Irving writes in his *Abbotsford* : —

"Among the other important and privileged members of the household
who figured in attendance at dinner, was a large gray cat, who, I observed,
was regaled from time to time with titbits from the table. This sage
grimalkin was a favorite of both master and mistress, and slept at night in
their room, and Scott laughingly observed, that one of the least wise parts
of their establishment was that the window was left open at night for puss
to go in and out. The cat assumed a kind of ascendency among the quadrupeds — sitting in state in Scott's armchair, and occasionally stationing
himself on a chair beside the door, as if to review his subjects as they
passed, giving each dog a cuff beside the ears as he went by. This clap-
per-clawing was always taken in good part; it appeared to be, in fact, a
mere act of sovereignty on the part of grimalkin to remind the others of
their vassalage; which they acknowledged by the most perfect acquiescence. A general harmony prevailed between sovereign and subjects, and
they would all sleep together in the sunshine."]

tions of theirs, designed to *Boswellize* Scott, and which they may probably publish hereafter. To report conversations fairly, it is a necessary prerequisite that we should be completely familiar with all the interlocutors, and understand thoroughly all their minutest relations, and points of common knowledge and common feeling with each other. He who does not, must be perpetually in danger of misinterpreting sportive allusion into serious statement; and the man who was only recalling, by some jocular phrase or half-phrase, to an old companion, some trivial reminiscence of their boyhood or youth, may be represented as expressing, upon some person or incident casually tabled, an opinion which he had never framed, or if he had, would never have given words to in any mixed assemblage — not even among what the world calls *friends* at his own board. In proportion as a man is witty and humorous, there will always be about him and his a widening maze and wilderness of cues and catchwords, which the uninitiated will, if they are bold enough to try interpretation, construe, ever and anon, egregiously amiss — not seldom into arrant falsity. For this one reason, to say nothing of many others, I consider no man justified in journalizing what he sees and hears in a domestic circle where he is not thoroughly at home; and I think there are still higher and better reasons why he should not do so where he is.

Before I ever met Scott in private, I had, of course, heard many people describe and discuss his style of conversation. Everybody seemed to agree that it overflowed with hearty good-humor, as well as plain unaffected good sense and sagacity; but I had heard not a few persons of undoubted ability and accomplishment maintain that the genius of the great poet and novelist rarely, if ever, revealed itself in his talk. It is needless to say, that the persons I allude to were all his own countrymen, and themselves imbued, more or less, with the conversational habits derived from a system of education in which the

study of metaphysics occupies a very large share of attention. The best table-talk of Edinburgh was, and probably still is, in a very great measure made up of brilliant
disquisition — such as might be transferred without alteration to a professor's note-book, or the pages of a critical Review — and of sharp word-catchings, ingenious
thrusting and parrying of dialectics, and all the quips
and quibblets of bar pleading. It was the talk of a
society to which lawyers and lecturers had, for at least
a hundred years, given the tone. From the date of the
Union, Edinburgh ceased to be the headquarters of the
Scotch nobility — and long before the time of which I
speak, they had all but entirely abandoned it as a place
of residence. I think I never knew above two or three
of the Peerage to have houses there at the same time —
and these were usually among the poorest and most insignificant of their order. The wealthier gentry had
followed their example. Very few of that class ever
spent any considerable part of the year in Edinburgh,
except for the purposes of educating their children, or
superintending the progress of a lawsuit; and these were
not more likely than a score or two of comatose and
lethargic old Indians, to make head against the established influences of academical and forensic celebrity.
Now Scott's tastes and resources had not much in common with those who had inherited and preserved the chief
authority in this provincial hierarchy of rhetoric. He
was highly amused with watching their dexterous logom-
achies — but his delight in such displays arose mainly,
I cannot doubt, from the fact of their being, both as to
subject-matter and style and method, remote *a Scævolæ
studiis*. He sat by, as he would have done at a stage-
play or a fencing-match, enjoying and applauding the
skill exhibited, but without feeling much ambition to
parade himself as a rival either of the foil or the buskin.
I can easily believe, therefore, that in the earlier part of
his life — before the blaze of universal fame had over-

awed local prejudice, and a new generation, accustomed
to hear of that fame from their infancy, had grown up —
it may have been the commonly adopted creed in Edinburgh, that Scott, however distinguished otherwise, was
not to be named as a table-companion in the same day
with this or that master of luminous dissertation or quick
rejoinder, who now sleeps as forgotten as his grandmother.
It was natural enough that persons brought up in the same
circle with him, who remembered all his beginnings, and
had but slowly learned to acquiesce in the justice of his
claim to unrivalled honor in literature, should have clung
all the closer for that late acquiescence to their original
estimate of him as inferior to themselves in other titles to
admiration. It was also natural that their prejudice on
that score should be readily taken up by the young aspirants who breathed, as it were, the atmosphere of their
professional renown. Perhaps, too, Scott's steady Toryism, and the effect of his genius and example in modify-
ing the intellectual sway of the long dominant Whigs in
the north, may have had some share in this matter. However all that may have been, the substance of what I had
been accustomed to hear certainly was, that Scott had a
marvellous stock of queer stories, which he often told with
happy effect, but that, bating these drafts on a portentous
memory, set off with a simple old-fashioned *naïveté* of
humor and pleasantry, his strain of talk was remarkable
neither for depth of remark nor felicity of illustration;
that his views and opinions on the most important topics
of practical interest were hopelessly perverted by his blind
enthusiasm for the dreams of bygone ages; and that, but
for the grotesque phenomenon presented by a great writer
of the nineteenth century gravely uttering sentiments
worthy of his own Dundees and Invernahyles, the main
texture of his discourse would be pronounced, by any en-
lightened member of modern society, rather bald and
poor than otherwise. I think the epithet most in vogue
was *commonplace*.

It will easily be believed that, in companies such as I have been alluding to, made up of, or habitually domineered over, by voluble Whigs and political economists, Scott was often tempted to put forth his Tory doctrines and antiquarian prejudices in an exaggerated shape — in colors, to say the truth, altogether different from what they assumed under other circumstances, or which had any real influence upon his mind and conduct on occasions of practical moment. But I fancy it will seem equally credible, that the most sharp-sighted of these social critics may not always have been capable of tracing, and doing justice to, the powers which Scott brought to bear upon the topics which they, not he, had chosen for discussion. In passing from a gas-lit hall into a room with wax candles, the guests sometimes complain that they have left splendor for gloom; but let them try by what sort of light it is most satisfactory to read, write, or embroider, or consider at leisure under which of the two, either men or women look their best.

The strongest, purest, and least observed of all lights, is, however, daylight; and his talk was commonplace, just as sunshine is, which gilds the most indifferent objects, and adds brilliancy to the brightest. As for the old-world anecdotes which these clever persons were condescending enough to laugh at as pleasant extravagances, serving merely to relieve and set off the main stream of debate, they were often enough, it may be guessed, connected with the theme in hand by links not the less apt that they might be too subtle to catch their bedazzled and self-satisfied optics. There might be keener knowledge of human nature than was "dreamt of in their philosophy" — which passed with them for *commonplace*, only because it was clothed in plain familiar household words, not dressed up in some pedantic masquerade of antithesis. "There are people," says Landor, "who think they write and speak finely, merely because they have forgotten the language in which their fathers and mothers used to talk to them;" and surely there are a thousand homely old proverbs, which many a dainty modern would think it beneath his dignity to quote either in speech or writing, any one of which condenses more wit (take that word in any of its senses) than could be extracted from all that was ever said or written by the *doctrinaires* of the Edinburgh school. Many of those gentlemen held Scott's conversation to be commonplace exactly for the same reason that a child thinks a perfectly limpid stream, though perhaps deep enough to drown it three times over, must needs be shallow. But it will be easily believed that the best and highest of their own idols had better means and skill of measurement: I can never forget the pregnant expression of one of the ablest of that school and party — Lord Cockburn — who, when some glib youth chanced to echo in his hearing the consolatory tenet of local mediocrity, answered quietly: "I have the misfortune to think differently from you — in my humble opinion, Walter Scott's *sense* is a still more wonderful thing than his *genius*."

Indeed I have no sort of doubt that, long before 1818, full justice was done to Scott, even in these minor things, by all those of his Edinburgh acquaintance, whether Whig or Tory, on whose personal opinion he could have been supposed to set much value. With few exceptions, the really able lawyers of his own or nearly similar standing had ere that time attained stations of judicial dignity, or were in the springtide of practice; and in either case they were likely to consider general society much in his own fashion, as the joyous relaxation of life, rather than the theatre of exertion and display. Their tables were elegantly, some of them sumptuously spread; and they lived in a pretty constant interchange of entertainments upon a large scale, in every circumstance of which, conversation included, it was their ambition to imitate those voluptuous metropolitan circles, wherein most of them had from time to time mingled, and several of them with distinguished success. Among such prosperous gentlemen, like himself past the *mezzo cammin*, Scott's picturesque anecdotes, rich easy humor, and gay involuntary glances of mother-wit, were, it is not difficult to suppose, appreciated above contributions of a more ambitious stamp; and no doubt his London *réputation de salon* (which had by degrees risen to a high pitch, although he cared nothing for it) was not without its effect in Edinburgh. But still the old prejudice lingered on in the general opinion of the place, especially among the smart praters of *the Outer-House*, whose glimpses of the social habits of their superiors were likely to be rare, and their gall-bladders to be more distended than their purses.

In truth, it was impossible to listen to Scott's oral narrations, whether gay or serious, or to the felicitous fun with which he parried absurdities of all sorts, without discovering better qualities in his talk than *wit* — and of a higher order; I mean especially a power of *vivid painting* — the true and primary sense of what is called *Imagination*. He was like Jaques — though not a "Melancholy Jaques;" and "moralized" a common topic "into a thousand similitudes." Shakespeare and the banished Duke would have found him "full of matter." He disliked mere disquisitions in Edinburgh, and prepared *impromptus* in London; and puzzled the promoters of such things sometimes by placid silence, sometimes by broad merriment. To such men he seemed *commonplace* — not so to the most dexterous masters in what was to some of them almost a science; not so to Rose, Hallam, Moore, or Rogers, — to Ellis, Mackintosh, Croker, or Canning.

Scott managed to give and receive such great dinners as I have been alluding to, at least as often as any other private gentleman in Edinburgh; but he very rarely accompanied his wife and daughters to the evening assemblies, which commonly ensued under other roofs —

for *early to rise*, unless in the case of spare-fed ancho-
rites, takes for granted *early to bed*. When he had no
dinner engagement, he frequently gave a few hours to
the theatre; but still more frequently, when the weather
was fine, and still more, I believe, to his own satisfaction, he drove out with some of his family, or a single
friend, in an open carriage; the favorite rides being
either to the Blackford Hills, or to Ravelston, and so
home by Corstorphine; or to the beach of Portobello,
where Peter was always instructed to keep his horses as
near as possible to the sea. More than once, even in
the first summer of my acquaintance with him, I had the
pleasure of accompanying him on these evening excursions; and never did he seem to enjoy himself more fully
than when placidly surveying, at such sunset or moonlight hours, either the massive outlines of his "own romantic town," or the tranquil expanse of its noble estu-
ary. He delighted, too, in passing, when he could,
through some of the quaint windings of the ancient city
itself, now deserted, except at mid-day, by the upper
world. How often have I seen him go a long way round
about, rather than miss the opportunity of halting for
a few minutes on the vacant esplanade of Holyrood, or
under the darkest shadows of the Castle rock, where it
overhangs the Grassmarket, and the huge slab that still
marks where the gibbet of Porteous and the Covenanters
had its station. His coachman knew him too well to
move at a Jehu's pace amidst such scenes as these. No
funeral hearse crept more leisurely than did his landau
up the Canongate or the Cowgate; and not a queer tottering gable but recalled to him some long-buried memory of splendor or bloodshed, which, by a few words, he
set before the hearer in the reality of life. His image is
so associated in my mind with the antiquities of his native place, that I cannot now revisit them without feeling
as if I were treading on his gravestone.

Whatever might happen on the other evenings of the

week, he always dined at home on Sunday, and usually
some few friends were then with him, but never any
person with whom he stood on ceremony. These were,
it may be readily supposed, the most agreeable of his
entertainments. He came into the room rubbing his
hands, his face bright and gleesome, like a boy arriving
at home for the holidays, his Peppers and Mustards gam-
bolling about his heels, and even the stately Maida grinning and wagging his tail in sympathy. Among the
most regular guests on these happy evenings were, in my
time, as had long before been the case, Mrs. Maclean
Clephane of Torloisk (with whom he agreed cordially on
all subjects except the authenticity of Ossian), and her
daughters, whose guardian he had become, at their own
choice. The eldest of them had been for some years
married to the Earl Compton (now Marquis of Northampton), and was of course seldom in the north; but the
others had much of the same tastes and accomplishments
which so highly distinguished the late Lady Northampton; and Scott delighted especially in their proficiency
in the poetry and music of their native isles. Mr. and
Mrs. Skene of Rubislaw were frequent attendants — and
so were the Macdonald-Buchanans of Drumakiln, whose
eldest daughter, Isabella, was his chief favorite among
all his *nieces* of the Clerk's table — as was, among the
nephews, my own dear friend and companion, Joseph
Hume, a singularly graceful young man, rich in the
promise of hereditary genius, but, alas, cut off in the
early bloom of his days. The well-beloved Erskine was
seldom absent; and very often Terry or James Ballantyne came with him — sometimes, though less frequently,
Constable. Among other persons who now and then
appeared at these "dinners without the silver dishes," as
Scott called them, I may mention — to say nothing of
such old cronies as Mr. Clerk, Mr. Thomson, and Mr.
Kirkpatrick Sharpe — Sir Alexander Boswell of Auchinleck, who had all his father *Bozzy's* cleverness, good-

humor, and joviality, without one touch of his meaner
qualities, — wrote Jenny dang the Weaver, and some
other popular songs, which he sang capitally — and was
moreover a thorough bibliomaniac; the late Sir Alexander Don of Newton, in all courteous and elegant accomplishments the model of a cavalier; and last, not least,
William Allan, R. A., who had shortly before this time
returned to Scotland from several years of travel in Russia and Turkey. At one of these plain hearty dinners,
however, the company rarely exceeded three or four, besides the as yet undivided family.

Scott had a story of a topping goldsmith on the Bridge,
who prided himself on being the mirror of Amphitryons,
and accounted for his success by stating that it was his
invariable custom to set his own stomach at ease, by a
beefsteak and a pint of port in his back-shop, half an
hour before the arrival of his guests. But the host of
Castle Street had no occasion to imitate this prudent
arrangement, for his appetite at dinner was neither keen
nor nice. Breakfast was his chief meal. Before that
came, he had gone through the severest part of his day's
work, and he then set to with the zeal of Crabbe's Squire
Tovell —

> "And laid at once a pound upon his plate."

No fox-hunter ever prepared himself for the field by
more substantial appliances. His table was always provided, in addition to the usually plentiful delicacies of
a Scotch breakfast, with some solid article, on which he
did most lusty execution — a round of beef — a pasty,
such as made Gil Blas's eyes water — or, most welcome
of all, a cold sheep's head, the charms of which primitive
dainty he has so gallantly defended against the dispar-
aging sneers of Dr. Johnson and his bear-leader.[1] A
huge brown loaf flanked his elbow, and it was placed
upon a broad wooden trencher, that he might cut and
come again with the bolder knife. Often did the *Clerks'*

[1] See Croker's *Boswell* (edit. 1831), vol. iii. p. 38.

coach, commonly called among themselves *the Lively* —
which trundled round every morning to pick up the brotherhood, and then deposited them at the proper minute
in the Parliament Close — often did this lumbering hackney arrive at his door before he had fully appeased what
Homer calls "the sacred rage of hunger;" and vociferous
was the merriment of the learned *uncles*, when the surprised poet swung forth to join them, with an extemporized sandwich, that looked like a ploughman's luncheon,
in his hand.   But this robust supply would have served
him in fact for the day.   He never tasted anything more
before dinner, and at dinner he ate almost as sparingly
as Squire Tovell's niece from the boarding-school, —

> —— " Who cut the sanguine flesh in frustums fine,
> And marvelled much to see the creatures dine."

The only dishes he was at all fond of were the old-
fashioned ones to which he had been accustomed in the
days of Saunders Fairford; and which really are excellent dishes, — such, in truth, as Scotland borrowed from
France before Catherine de' Medici brought in her Italian *virtuosi* to revolutionize the kitchen like the court.
Of most of these, I believe, he has in the course of his
novels found some opportunity to record his esteem.
But, above all, who can forget that his King Jamie,
amidst the splendors of Whitehall, thinks himself an ill-
used monarch unless his first course includes *cocky-leeky ?*

It is a fact, which some philosophers may think worth
setting down, that Scott's organization, as to more than
one of the senses, was the reverse of exquisite.   He had
very little of what musicians call an ear; his smell was
hardly more delicate.   I have seen him stare about, quite
unconscious of the cause, when his whole company betrayed their uneasiness at the approach of an overkept
haunch of venison; and neither by the nose nor the palate could he distinguish corked wine from sound.   He
could never tell Madeira from sherry, — nay, an Oriental friend having sent him a butt of *sheeraz*, when he

remembered the circumstance some time afterwards, and called for a bottle to have Sir John Malcolm's opinion of its quality, it turned out that his butler, mistaking the label, had already served up half the bin as *sherry*. Port he considered as physic: he never willingly swallowed more than one glass of it, and was sure to anathematize a second, if offered, by repeating John Home's epigram: —

> " Bold and erect the Caledonian stood,
>   Old was his mutton, and his claret good ;
>   Let him drink port, the English statesman cried —
>   He drank the poison, and his spirit died."

In truth, he liked no wines except sparkling champagne and claret; but even as to this last he was no connoisseur; and sincerely preferred a tumbler of whiskey-toddy to the most precious "liquid ruby" that ever flowed in the cup of a prince. He rarely took any other potation when quite alone with his family; but at the Sunday board he circulated the champagne briskly during dinner, and considered a pint of claret each man's fair share afterwards. I should not omit, however, that his Bordeaux was uniformly preceded by a small libation of the genuine *mountain dew*, which he poured with his own hand, *more majorum*, for each guest — making use for the purpose of such a multifarious collection of ancient Highland *quaighs* (little cups of curiously dovetailed wood, inlaid with silver) as no Lowland sideboard but his was ever equipped with — but commonly reserving for himself one that was peculiarly precious in his eyes, as having travelled from Edinburgh to Derby in the canteen of Prince Charlie. This relic had been presented to "the wandering Ascanius" by some very careful follower, for its bottom is of glass, that he who quaffed might keep his eye the while upon the dirk hand of his companion.

The sound of music (even, I suspect, of any sacred music but psalm-singing) would be considered indeco-

rous in the streets of Edinburgh on a Sunday night; so,
upon the occasions I am speaking of, the harp was silent,
and Otterburne and The Bonnie House of Airlie must
needs be dispensed with. To make amends, after tea
in the drawing-room, Scott usually read some favorite
author for the amusement of his little circle; or Erskine,
Ballantyne, or Terry, did so, at his request. He himself read aloud high poetry with far greater simplicity,
depth, and effect, than any other man I ever heard; and
in Macbeth or Julius Cæsar, or the like, I doubt if Kemble could have been more impressive. Yet the changes
of intonation were so gently managed, that he contrived
to set the different interlocutors clearly before us, without the least approach to theatrical artifice. Not so the
others I have mentioned; they all read cleverly and
agreeably, but with the decided trickery of stage recitation. To them he usually gave the book when it was a
comedy, or, indeed, any other drama than Shakespeare's
or Joanna Baillie's. Dryden's Fables, Johnson's two
Satires, and certain detached scenes of Beaumont and
Fletcher, especially that in The Lover's Progress, where
the ghost of the musical innkeeper makes his appearance,
were frequently selected. Of the poets, his contemporaries, however, there was not one that did not come in for
his part. In Wordsworth, his pet pieces were, I think,
the Song for Brougham Castle, the Laodamia, and some
of the early sonnets; in Southey, Queen Orraca, Fer-
nando Ramirez, the Lines on the Holly Tree — and, of
his larger poems, the Thalaba. Crabbe was perhaps,
next to Shakespeare, the standing resource; but in those
days Byron was pouring out his spirit fresh and full:
and, if a new piece from his hand had appeared, it was
sure to be read by Scott the Sunday evening afterwards,
and that with such delighted emphasis as showed how
completely the elder bard had kept all his enthusiasm for
poetry at the pitch of youth, all his admiration of genius,
free, pure, and unstained by the least drop of literary

jealousy. Rare and beautiful example of a happily constituted and virtuously disciplined mind and character!

Very often something read aloud by himself or his friends suggested an old story of greater compass than would have suited a dinner-table — and he told it, whether serious or comical, or, as more frequently happened, part of both, exactly in every respect in the tone and style of the notes and illustrations to his novels. A great number of his best oral narratives have, indeed, been preserved in those parting lucubrations; and not a few in his letters. Yet very many there were of which his pen has left no record — so many, that, were I to task my memory, I could, I believe, recall the outlines at least of more than would be sufficient to occupy a couple of these volumes. Possibly, though well aware how little justice I could do to such things, rather than think of their perishing forever, and leaving not even a shadow behind, I may at some future day hazard the attempt.

Let me turn, meanwhile, to some dinner-tables very different from his own, at which, from this time forward, I often met Scott. It is very true of the societies I am about to describe, that he was "among them, not of them;" and it is also most true that this fact was apparent in all the demeanor of his bibliopolical and typographical allies towards him whenever he visited them under their roofs — not a bit less so than when they were received at his own board; but still, considering how closely his most important worldly affairs were connected with the personal character of the Ballantynes, I think it a part, though neither a proud nor a very pleasing part, of my duty as his biographer, to record my reminiscences of them and their doings in some detail.

James Ballantyne then lived in St. John Street, a row of good, old-fashioned, and spacious houses, adjoining the Canongate and Holyrood, and at no great distance from his printing establishment. He had married a few years before the daughter of a wealthy farmer in Berwickshire — a quiet, amiable woman, of simple manners, and perfectly domestic habits: a group of fine young children were growing up about him; and he usually, if not constantly, had under his roof his aged mother, his and his wife's tender care of whom it was most pleasing to witness. As far as a stranger might judge, there could not be a more exemplary household, or a happier one; and I have occasionally met the poet in St. John Street when there were no other guests but Erskine, Terry, George Hogarth,[1] and another intimate friend or two, and when James Ballantyne was content to appear in his own true and best colors, the kind head of his family, the respectful but honest schoolfellow of Scott, the easy landlord of a plain, comfortable table. But when any great event was about to take place in the business, especially on the eve of a new novel, there were doings of a higher strain in St. John Street; and to be present at one of those scenes was truly a rich treat, even — if not especially — for persons who, like myself, had no more *knowledge* than the rest of the world as to the authorship of Waverley. Then were congregated about the printer all his own literary allies, of whom a considerable number were by no means personally familiar with "THE GREAT UNKNOWN:" — who, by the way, owed to him that widely adopted title; — and He appeared among the rest with his usual open aspect of buoyant good-humor — although it was not difficult to trace, in the occasional play of his features, the diversion it afforded him to watch all the procedure of his swelling confidant, and the curious neophytes that surrounded the well-spread board.

The feast was, to use one of James's own favorite epi-

---

[1] George Hogarth, Esq., W. S., brother of Mrs. James Ballantyne. This gentleman is now well known in the literary world; especially by a History of Music, of which all who understand that science speak highly. [He was the father-in-law of Charles Dickens, and for many years a musical and dramatic critic in London.]

thets, *gorgeous;* an aldermanic display of turtle and venison, with the suitable accompaniments of iced punch, potent ale, and generous Madeira. When the cloth was drawn, the burly preses arose, with all he could muster of the port of John Kemble, and spouted with a sonorous voice the formula of Macbeth: —

> " Fill full!
> I drink to the general joy of the whole table! "

This was followed by "The King, God bless him!" and second came — "Gentlemen, there is another toast which never has been nor shall be omitted in this house of mine — I give you the health of Mr. Walter Scott with three times three!" All honor having been done to this health, and Scott having briefly thanked the company with some expressions of warm affection to their host, Mrs. Ballantyne retired; the bottles passed round twice or thrice in the usual way; and then James rose once more, every vein on his brow distended, his eyes solemnly fixed upon vacancy, to propose, not as before in his stentorian key, but with "'bated breath," in the sort of whisper by which a stage conspirator thrills the gallery, — "*Gentlemen, a bumper to the immortal Author of Waverley!*" The uproar of cheering, in which Scott made a fashion of joining, was succeeded by deep silence, and then Ballantyne proceeded —

> " In his Lord Burleigh look, serene and serious,
> A something of imposing and mysterious " —

to lament the obscurity in which his illustrious but too modest correspondent still chose to conceal himself from the plaudits of the world, to thank the company for the manner in which the *nominis umbra* had been received, and to assure them that the Author of Waverley would, when informed of the circumstance, feel highly delighted — "the proudest hour of his life," etc., etc. The cool, demure fun of Scott's features during all this mummery was perfect; and Erskine's attempt at a gay *nonchalance* was still more ludicrously meritorious. Aldiborontiphos-

sophornio, however, bursting as he was, knew too well
to allow the new novel to be made the subject of discussion. Its name was announced, and success to it crowned
another cup; but after that, no more of Jedediah. To
cut the thread, he rolled out unbidden some one of his
many theatrical songs, in a style that would have done
no dishonor to almost any orchestra — The Maid of Lodi
— or perhaps, The Bay of Biscay, O! — or The Sweet
Little Cherub that Sits up Aloft. Other toasts followed,
interspersed with ditties from other performers; — old
George Thomson, the friend of Burns, was ready, for
one, with The Moorland Wedding, or Willie Brew'd a
Peck o' Maut; — and so it went on, until Scott and Erskine, with any clerical or very staid personage that had
chanced to be admitted, saw fit to withdraw. Then the
scene was changed. The claret and olives made way for
broiled bones and a mighty bowl of punch; and when a
few glasses of the hot beverage had restored his powers,
James opened *ore rotundo* on the merits of the forthcoming romance. "One chapter, one chapter only," was the
cry. After "*Nay, by'r Lady, nay!*" and a few more
coy shifts, the proof sheets were at length produced, and
James, with many a prefatory hem, read aloud what he
considered as the most striking dialogue they contained.

The first I heard so read was the interview between
Jeanie Deans, the Duke of Argyle, and Queen Caroline,
in Richmond Park; and notwithstanding some spice of
the pompous tricks to which he was addicted, I must say
he did the inimitable scene great justice. At all events,
the effect it produced was deep and memorable, and no
wonder that the exulting typographer's *one bumper more
to Jedediah Cleishbotham* preceded his parting stave,
which was uniformly The Last Words of Marmion, executed certainly with no contemptible rivalry of Braham.

What a different affair was a dinner, although probably including many of the same guests, at the junior
partner's! He in those days retained, I think, no pri-

vate apartments attached to his auction-rooms in Hanover Street, over the door of which he still kept emblazoned "John Ballantyne and Company, Booksellers." At any rate, such of his entertainments as I ever saw Scott partake of, were given at his villa near to the Frith of Forth, by Trinity; — a retreat which the little man had named "Harmony Hall," and invested with an air of dainty voluptuous finery, contrasting strikingly enough with the substantial citizen-like snugness of his elder brother's domestic appointments. His house was surrounded by gardens so contrived as to seem of considerable extent, having many a shady tuft, trellised alley, and mysterious alcove, interspersed among their bright parterres. It was a fairy-like labyrinth, and there was no want of pretty Armidas, such as they might be, to glide half-seen among its mazes. The sitting-rooms opened upon gay and perfumed conservatories, and John's professional excursions to Paris and Brussels in quest of objects of *virtu*, had supplied both the temptation and the means to set forth the interior in a fashion that might have satisfied the most fastidious *petite maîtresse* of Norwood or St. Denis. John, too, was a married man: he had, however, erected for himself a private wing, the accesses to which, whether from the main building or the *bosquet*, were so narrow that it was physically impossible for the handsome and portly lady who bore his name to force her person through any one of them. His dinners were in all respects Parisian, for his wasted palate disdained such John Bull luxuries as were all in all with James. The piquant pasty of Strasburg or Perigord was never to seek; and even the *pièce de résistance* was probably a boar's head from Coblentz, or a turkey ready stuffed with truffles from the Palais Royal. The pictures scattered among John's innumerable mirrors were chiefly of theatrical subjects — many of them portraits of beautiful actresses — the same Peg Woffingtons, Bellamys, Kitty Clives, and so forth, that found their way in the sequel to Charles Mathews's gallery at Highgate. Here that exquisite comedian's own mimicries and parodies were the life and soul of many a festival, and here, too, he gathered from his facetious host not a few of the richest materials for his *at homes* and *monopolylogues*. But, indeed, whatever actor or singer of eminence visited Edinburgh, of the evenings when he did not perform several were sure to be reserved for Trinity. Here Braham quavered, and here Liston drolled his best — here Johnstone, and Murray, and Yates mixed jest and stave — here Kean revelled and rioted — and here the Roman Kemble often played the Greek from sunset to dawn. Nor did the popular *cantatrice* or *danseuse* of the time disdain to freshen her roses, after a laborious week, amidst these Paphian arbors of Harmony Hall.

Johnny had other tastes that were equally expensive. He had a well-furnished stable, and followed the fox-hounds whenever the cover was within an easy distance. His horses were all called after heroes in Scott's poems or novels; and at this time he usually rode up to his auction on a tall milk-white hunter, yclept *Old Mortality*, attended by a leash or two of greyhounds, — Die Vernon, Jenny Dennison, and so forth, by name. The featherweight himself appeared uniformly, hammer-in-hand, in the half-dress of some sporting club — a light gray frock, with emblems of the chase on its silver buttons, white cord breeches, and jockey-boots in Meltonian order. Yet he affected in the pulpit rather a grave address; and was really one of the most plausible and imposing of the Puff tribe. Probably Scott's presence overawed his ludicrous propensities; for the poet was, when sales were going on, almost a daily attendant in Hanover Street, and himself not the least energetic of the numerous competitors for Johnny's uncut *fifteeners*, Venetian lamps, Milanese cuirasses, and old Dutch cabinets. Maida, by the way, was so well aware of his master's habits, that about the time when the Court of Session was likely to break up for the day, he might usually be seen couched in expectation among Johnny's own *tail* of greyhounds at the threshold of the mart.

It was at one of those Trinity dinners this summer that I first saw Constable. Being struck with his appearance, I asked Scott who he was, and he told me — expressing some surprise that anybody should have lived a winter or two in Edinburgh without knowing, by sight at least, a citizen whose name was so familiar to the world. I happened to say that I had not been prepared to find the great bookseller a man of such gentlemanlike and even distinguished bearing. Scott smiled, and answered, "Ay, Constable is indeed a grand-looking chield. He puts me in mind of Fielding's apology for Lady Booby — to wit, that Joseph Andrews had an air which, to those who had not seen many noblemen, would give an idea of nobility." I had not in those days been much initiated in the private jokes of what is called, by way of excellence, *the trade*, and was puzzled when Scott, in the course of the dinner, said to Constable, "Will your Czarish Majesty do me the honor to take a glass of champagne?" I asked the master of the feast for an explanation. "Oh!" said he, "are you so green as not to know that Constable long since dubbed himself *The Czar of Muscovy*, John Murray, *The Emperor of the West*, and Longman and his string of partners *The Divan?*" "And what title," I asked, "has Mr. John Ballantyne himself found in this new *almanach imperial?*" — "Let that flee stick to the wa'," quoth Johnny: "When I set up for a bookseller, The Crafty christened me *The Dey of Alljeers* — but he now considers me as next thing to dethroned." He added, "His Majesty the autocrat is too fond of these nicknames. One day a partner of the house of Longman was dining with him in the country, to settle an important piece of business, about which there occurred a good deal of difficulty. 'What fine

swans you have in your pond there! ' said the Londoner,
by way of parenthesis. — ' Swans! ' cried Constable;
' they are only geese, man.   There are just five of them,
if you please to observe, and their names are Longman,
Hurst, Rees, Orme, and Brown.'   This skit cost The
Crafty a good bargain."

It always appeared to me that James Ballantyne felt
his genius rebuked in the presence of Constable: his
manner was constrained, his smile servile, his hilarity
elaborate.   Not so with Johnny: the little fellow never
seemed more airily frolicsome than when he capered for
the amusement of the Czar.[1]   I never, however, saw
those two together, where, I am told, the humors of them
both were exhibited to the richest advantage — I mean at
the dinners with which Constable regaled, among others,
his own circle of literary serfs, and when "Jocund
Johnny" was very commonly his croupier.   There are
stories enough of practical jokes upon such occasions,
some of them near akin to those which the author of
Humphrey Clinker has thought fit to record of his own
suburban villa, in the most diverting of young Melford's
letters to Sir Watkin Philips.   I have heard, for example, a luculent description of poor *Allister Campbell*,
and another drudge of the same class, running a race
after dinner for a new pair of breeches, which Mr. David
Bridges, tailor in ordinary to this northern potentate, —
himself a wit, a virtuoso, and the croupier on that day in
lieu of Rigdum, — had been instructed to bring with him,
and display before the threadbare rivals.   But I had
these pictures from John Ballantyne, and I dare say they
might be overcharged.   That Constable was a most
bountiful and generous patron to the ragged tenants of
Grub Street, there can, however, be no doubt: and as

---

[1] " Now, John," cried Constable, one evening after he had told one of
his best stories, " now, John, is that true ? "   His object evidently was, in
Iago's phrase, *to let down the pegs;* but Rigdum answered gayly, " True,
indeed !   Not 'one word of it ! — any blockhead may stick to truth, my
hearty — but 't is a sad hamperer of genius."

little that John himself acted on all occasions by them in the same spirit, and this to an extent greatly beyond what prudence (if he had ever consulted that guide in anything) would have dictated.

When I visited Constable, as I often did at a period somewhat later than that of which I now speak, and for the most part in company with Scott, I found the book-seller established in a respectable country gentleman's seat, some six or seven miles out of Edinburgh, and doing the honors of it with all the ease that might have been looked for had he been the long-descended owner of the place; there was no foppery, no show, no idle luxury, but to all appearance the plain abundance and simple enjoyment of hereditary wealth. His conversation was manly and vigorous, abounding in Scotch anecdotes of the old time, which he told with a degree of spirit and humor only second to his great author's. No man could more effectually control, when he had a mind, either the extravagant vanity which, on too many occasions, made him ridiculous, or the despotic temper, which habitually held in fear and trembling all such as were in any sort dependent on his Czarish Majesty's pleasure. In him I never saw (at this period) anything but the unobtrusive sense and the calm courtesy of a well-bred gentleman. His very equipage kept up the series of contrasts between him and the two Ballantynes. Constable went back and forward between the town and Polton in a deep-hung and capacious green barouche, without any pretence at he-raldic blazonry, drawn by a pair of sleek, black, long-tailed horses, and conducted by a grave old coachman in plain blue livery. The Printer of the Canongate drove himself and his wife about the streets and suburbs in a snug machine, which did not overburthen one powerful and steady cob; while the gay auctioneer, whenever he left the saddle for the box, mounted a bright blue dog-cart, and rattled down the Newhaven road with two high-mettled steeds, prancing *tandem* before him, and

most probably — especially if he was on his way to the
races at Musselburgh — with some "sweet singer of
Israel" flaming, with all her feathers, beside him. On
such occasions, by the bye, Johnny sometimes had a
French horn with him, and he played on it with good
skill, and with an energy by no means prudent in the
state of his lungs.

The Sheriff told with peculiar unction the following
anecdote of this spark. The first time he went over to
pick up curiosities at Paris, it happened that he met, in
the course of his traffickings, a certain brother bookseller
of Edinburgh, as unlike him as one man could well be to
another — a grave, dry Presbyterian, rigid in all his
notions as the buckle of his wig. This precise worthy
having ascertained John's address, went to call on him,
a day or two afterwards, with the news of some richly
illuminated missal, which he might possibly be glad to
make prize of. On asking for his friend, a smiling
laquais de place informed him that *Monsieur* had gone
out, but that *Madame* was at home. Not doubting that
Mrs. Ballantyne had accompanied her husband on his
trip, he desired to pay his respects to *Madame*, and was
ushered in accordingly. "But oh, Mr. Scott!" said,
or rather groaned, the austere elder, on his return from
this modern Babylon, "oh, Mr. Scott, there was nae
Mrs. John yonder, but a painted Jezebel sittin' up in
her bed, wi' a wheen impudent French limmers like her-
sel', and twa or three whiskered blackguards, takin' their
collation o' knickknacks and champagne wine! I ran out
o' the house as if I had been shot. What judgment will
this wicked warld come to! The Lord pity us!" Scott
was a severe enough censor in the general of such levi-
ties, but somehow, in the case of Rigdumfunnidos, he
seemed to regard them with much the same toleration
as the naughty tricks of a monkey in the "Jardin des
Plantes."

Why did Scott persist in mixing up all his most important concerns with such people as I have been describing? I asked himself that question too unceremoniously at a long subsequent period, and in due time the reader shall see the answer I received; but it left the main question, to my apprehension, as much in the dark as ever. I shall return to the sad subject hereafter more seriously; but in the mean time let it suffice to say, that he was the most patient, long-suffering, affectionate, and charitable of mankind; that in the case of both the Ballantynes he could count, after all, on a sincerely, nay, a passionately devoted attachment to his person; that, with the greatest of human beings, use is in all but unconquerable power; and that he who so loftily tossed aside the seemingly most dangerous assaults of flattery, the blandishment of dames, the condescension of princes, the enthusiasm of crowds — had still his weak point, upon which two or three humble besiegers, and one unwearied, though most frivolous underminer, well knew how to direct their approaches. It was a favorite saw of his own, that the wisest of our race often reserve the average stock of folly to be all expended upon some one flagrant absurdity.

CHAPTER XLII

1818

HOPING to be forgiven for a long digression, the biographer willingly returns to the thread of Scott's story.
The Heart of Mid-Lothian appeared, as has been mentioned, before the close of June, 1818, and among the
letters which he received soon afterwards from the friends
by this time in the secret, there is one which (though I
do not venture to name the writer) I am tempted to take
the liberty of quoting: [1] —

"Now for it, dear Mr. Scott. I can speak to the purpose,
as I have not only read it myself, but am in a house where
everybody is tearing it out of each other's hands, and talking
of nothing else. So much for its success — the more flattering,
because it overcomes a prejudice. People were beginning to
say the author would wear himself out; it was going on too

[1] [This letter was written August 11, by Lady Louisa Stuart, and it appears in its original and complete form in *Familiar Letters*, vol. ii. p. 18.
To the end of her long life, the writer was somewhat influenced by the
feeling prevailing in her youth as to the loss of caste suffered by women
of good social position who appeared in print. Writing to Mrs. Lockhart after her father's death, and enclosing some of his letters, Lady Louisa
says: "If Mr. Lockhart wishes to insert any of these, I will beg not to
be named. It is not that I am not proud enough of having been honored
with *his* regard, but I never yet saw my name in print, and hope I never
shall." Mr. Lockhart evidently in part overcame this objection.]

long in the same key, and no striking notes could possibly be produced. On the contrary, I think the interest is stronger here than in any of the former ones — (always excepting my first-love Waverley) — and one may congratulate you upon having effected what many have tried to do, and nobody yet succeeded in, making the perfectly good character the most interesting. Of late days, especially since it has been the fashion to write moral and even religious novels, one might almost say of some of the wise good heroines, what a lively girl once said to [me] of her well-meaning aunt — 'Upon my word she is enough to make anybody wicked.' And though beauty and talents are heaped on the right side, the writer, in spite of himself, is sure to put agreeableness on the wrong ; the person from whose errors he means you should take warning, runs away with your secret partiality in the mean time. Had this very story been conducted by a common hand, Effie would have attracted all our concern and sympathy — Jeanie only cold approbation. Whereas Jeanie, without youth, beauty, genius, warm passions, or any other novel-perfection, is here our object from beginning to end. This is 'inlisting the affections in the cause of virtue' ten times more than ever Richardson did ; for whose male and female pedants, all-excelling as they are, I never could care half so much as I found myself inclined to do for Jeanie before I finished the first volume. . . .

"You know I tell you my opinion just as I should do to a third person, and I trust the freedom is not unwelcome. I was a little tired of your Edinburgh lawyers in the introduction ; English people in general will be more so as well as impatient of the passages alluding to Scotch law throughout. Mr. Saddletree will not entertain them. The latter part of the fourth volume unavoidably flags to a certain degree ; after Jeanie is happily settled at Roseneath, we have no more to wish for. But the chief fault I have to find relates to the reappearance and shocking fate of the boy. I hear on all sides, 'Oh, I do not like that !' I cannot say what I would have had instead ; but I do not like it either ; it is a lame, huddled conclusion. I know you so well in it, by the bye ! — you grow tired yourself, want to get rid of the story, and hardly care how. Sir George Staunton finishes his career very fitly ; he ought not to die in his bed, and for Jeanie's sake one would not have him hanged.

It is unnatural, though, that he should ever have gone within twenty miles of the Tolbooth, or shown his face in the streets of Edinburgh, or dined at a public meeting, if the Lord Commissioner had been his brother. Here ends my *per contra* account. The opposite page would make my letter too long if I entered equally into particulars. Carlisle and Corby Castles in Waverley did not affect me more deeply than the prison and trial scenes. The end of poor Madge Wildfire is also most pathetic. The meeting at Muschat's Cairn tremendous. Dumbiedikes and Rory Bean are delightful. And I shall own that my prejudices were secretly gratified by the light in which you place [Uncle] John of Argyle, whom Mr. Coxe so ran down to please Lord Orford. You have drawn him to the very life. I heard so much of him in my youth, so many anecdotes, so often ' as the Duke of Argyle used to say ' — that I really believe I am almost as good a judge as if I had seen and lived with him. . . . [My beloved mother] has told me, that when she married, [in 1737, the very time], he was still remarkably handsome ; with manners more graceful and engaging than she ever saw in any one else ; the most agreeable person in conversation, the best teller of a story. When fifty-seven thus captivates eighteen, the natural powers of pleasing must be extraordinary. You have likewise colored Queen Caroline exactly right — but I was bred up in another creed about Lady Suffolk, of whom, as a very old deaf woman, I have some faint recollection. [My mother] knew her intimately, and never would allow she had been the King's mistress, though she owned it was currently believed. She said he had just enough liking for her to make the Queen very civil to her, and very jealous and spiteful ; the rest remained always uncertain at most, like a similar scandal in our days, where I, for one, imagine love of seeming influence on one side, and love of lounging, of an easy house and a good dinner on the other, to be all the criminal passions concerned. However, I confess, [my mother] had that in herself which made her not ready to think the worst of her fellow-women.

" Did you ever hear the history of John, Duke of Argyle's marriage, and constant attachment, before and after, to a woman not handsomer or much more elegant than Jeanie Deans, though very unlike her in understanding ? I can give it you, if you wish it, for it is at my fingers' ends. [I was so much the youngest of a numerous family that I had no playfellow, and for that reason listened with all my ears to the grown people's conversation, most especially when my mother and the friends of her youth got upon old stories ; nor did I lose my taste for them when I grew old enough to converse with her on equal terms, and enquire into particulars.] Now I am [an] ancient [tabby] myself, I should be a great treasure of anecdote to anybody who had the same humor, — but I meet with few who have. They read vulgar tales in books, Wraxall, and so forth, what the footmen and maids only gave credit to at the moment, but they desire no farther information. I dare swear many of your readers never heard of the Duke of Argyle before. ' Pray, who was Sir Robert Walpole,' they ask me, ' and when did he live ? ' — or perhaps — ' Was not the great Lord Chatham in Queen Anne's days ? ' [1]

" [Amongst the persons most pleased here is Lady Charlotte Lindsay. She has the true North humor, and love of humor, and she does enjoy it heartily. They] have, to help [them], an exempl'fication on two legs in [their] country apothecary, whom you have painted over and over without the honor of knowing him ; an old, dry, arguing, prosing, obstinate Scotchman, very shrewd, rather sarcastic, a sturdy Whig and Presbyterian, *tirant un peu sur le démocrat*. Your books are birdlime to him, however ; he hovers about the house to obtain a volume when others have done with it. I long to ask him whether Douce Davie was any way *sib* to him. He acknowledges he would not *now* go to Muschat's Cairn at night for any money — he had such a horror of it ' sixty years ago ' when a laddie. But I am come to the end of my fourth page, and will not tire you with any more scribbling. . . .

" P. S. — If I had known nothing, and the whole world had told me the contrary, I should have found you out in that one parenthesis, — ' for the man was mortal, and had been a school-master.' "

---

[1] [In 1827, Lady Louisa wrote for Caroline, Lady Scott, a great-grand-daughter of the duke, *Some Account of John, Duke of Argyle, and his Family*. This delightful memoir was first printed (privately) in 1863. It was published in 1899, in *Selections from the Manuscripts of Lady Louisa Stuart*.]

This letter was addressed from a great country house in the south;[1] and may, I presume, be accepted as a fair index of the instantaneous English popularity of Jeanie Deans. From the choice of localities, and the splendid blazoning of tragical circumstances that had left the strongest impression on the memory and imagination of every inhabitant, the reception of this tale in Edinburgh was a scene of all-engrossing enthusiasm, such as I never witnessed there on the appearance of any other literary novelty. But the admiration and delight were the same all over Scotland. Never before had he seized such really noble features of the national character as were canonized in the person of his homely heroine: no art had ever devised a happier running contrast than that of her and her sister, or interwoven a portraiture of lowly manners and simple virtues, with more graceful delineations of polished life, or with bolder shadows of terror, guilt, crime, remorse, madness, and all the agony of the passions.

In the introduction and notes to The Heart of Mid-Lothian, drawn up in 1830, we are presented with details concerning the suggestion of the main plot, and the chief historical incidents made use of, to which I can add nothing of any moment.

The 12th of July restored the author as usual to the supervision of his trees and carpenters; but he had already told the Ballantynes that the story which he had found it impossible to include in the recent series of Jedediah should be forthwith taken up as the opening one of a third; and instructed John to embrace the first favorable opportunity of offering Constable the publication of this, on the footing of 10,000 copies again forming the first edition; but now at length without any more stipulations connected with the unfortunate "old stock" of the Hanover Street Company.

[1] [Sheffield Place, the seat of Lord Sheffield, the friend and editor of Gibbon.]

Before he settled himself to his work, however, he made a little tour of the favorite description with his wife and children — halting for a few days at Drumlanrig, thence crossing the Border to Carlisle and Rokeby, and returning by way of Alnwick. On the 17th August he writes thus to John Ballantyne from Drumlanrig: "This is heavenly weather, and I am making the most of it, as I shall have a laborious autumn before me. I may say of my head and fingers as the farmer of his mare, when he indulged her with an extra feed, —

> 'Ye ken that Maggie winna sleep
> For that or Simmer.'

We have taken our own horses with us, and I have my pony, and ride when I find it convenient."

The following seems to have been among the first letters he wrote after his return: —

TO J. B. S. MORRITT, ESQ., M. P., ROKEBY.

ABBOTSFORD, 10th September, 1818.

MY DEAR MORRITT, — We have been cruising to and fro since we left your land of woods and streams. Lord Melville wished me to come and stay two days with him at Melville Castle, which has broken in upon my time a little, and interrupted my purpose of telling you as how we arrived safe at Abbotsford, without a drop of rain, thus completing a tour of three weeks in the same fine weather in which we commenced it — a thing which never fell to my lot before. Captain Ferguson is inducted into the office of Keeper of the Regalia, to the great joy, I think, of all Edinburgh. He has entered upon a farm (of eleven acres) in consequence of this advancement, for you know it is a general rule, that whenever a Scotsman gets his head *above water*, he immediately turns it *to land*. As he has already taken all the advice of all the *notables* in and about the good village of Darnick, we expect to see his farm look like a tailor's

book of patterns, a snip of every several opinion which
he has received occupying its appropriate corner. He
is truly what the French call *un drôle de corps*.

I wish you would allow your coachman to look out for
me among your neighbors a couple of young colts (rising
three would be the best age) that would match for a carriage some two years hence. I have plenty of grass for
them in the mean while, and should never know the expense of their keep at Abbotsford. He seemed to think
he could pick them up at from £25 to £30, which would
make an immense saving hereafter. Peter Matheson
and he had arranged some sort of plan of this kind. For
a pair of very ordinary carriage-horses in Edinburgh they
ask £140 or more; so it is worth while to be a little pro-
vident. Even then you only get one good horse, the
other being usually a brute. Pray you excuse all this
palaver, —

> "These little things are great to little men."

Our harvest is almost all in, but as farmers always
grumble about something, they are now growling about
the lightness of the crop. All the young part of our
household are wrapt up in uncertainty concerning the
Queen's illness — for — if her Majesty parts cable, there
will be no Forest Ball, and that is a terrible prospect.
On Wednesday (when no post arrives from London)
Lord Melville chanced to receive a letter with a black
seal by express, and as it was of course argued to contain
the expected intelligence of poor Charlotte, it sold a good
many ells of black cloth and stuffs before it was ascertained to contain no such information. Surely this came
within the line of high treason, being an imagining of
the Queen's death.

Ever yours truly,

WALTER SCOTT.

P. S. — Once more *anent* the colts. I am indifferent
about color; but, *cœteris paribus*, would prefer black
or brown, to bright bay or gray. I mention two off —

as the age at which they can be best judged of by the buyer.

Of the same date I find written in pencil, on what must have been the envelope of some sheriff's-process, this note, addressed to Mr. Charles Erskine, the Sheriff-Substitute of Selkirkshire: —

September 10, 1818.

DEAR CHARLES, — I have read these papers with all attention this morning — but think you will agree with me that there must be an Eke to the Condescendence. Order the Eke against next day. — Tom leaves with this packet a blackcock, and (more's the pity) a gray hen. Yours,   W. S.

And again he thus writes by post to James Ballantyne:

ABBOTSFORD, September 10, 1818.

DEAR JAMES, — I am quite satisfied with what has been done as to the London bills. I am glad the presses move. I have been interrupted sadly since my return by tourist gazers. This day a confounded pair of Cambridge boys have robbed me of two good hours, and you of a sheet of copy — though whether a good sheet or no, deponent saith not. The story is a dismal one, and I doubt sometimes whether it will bear working out to much length after all. Query, if I shall make it so effective in two volumes as my mother does in her quarter of an hour's crack by the fireside? But *nil desperandum*. You shall have a bunch to-morrow or next day — and when the proofs come in, my pen must and shall step out. By the bye, I want a supply of pens — and ditto of ink. Adieu for the present, for I must go over to Toftfield, to give orders *anent* the dam and the footpath, and see *item* as to what should be done *anent* steps at the Rhymer's Waterfall, which I think may be made to turn out a decent bit of a linn, as would set True Thomas his worth and dignity. Ever yours,   W. S.

It must, I think, be allowed that these careless scraps, when combined, give a curious picture of the man who was brooding over the first chapters of The Bride of Lammermoor. One of his visitors of that month was Mr. R. Cadell, who was of course in all the secrets of the house of Constable; and observing how his host was harassed with lion-hunters, and what a number of hours he spent daily in the company of his work-people, he expressed, during one of their walks, his wonder that Scott should ever be able to write books at all while in the country. "I know," he said, "that you contrive to get a few hours in your own room, and that may do for the mere pen-work; but when is it that you think?" "Oh," said Scott, "I lie *simmering* over things for an hour or so before I get up — and there's the time I am dressing to overhaul my half-sleeping, half-waking *projet de chapitre* — and when I get the paper before me, it commonly runs off pretty easily. — Besides, I often take a doze in the plantations, and while Tom marks out a dyke or a drain as I have directed, one's fancy may be running its ain riggs in some other world."

It was in the month following that I first saw Abbotsford. He invited my friend John Wilson (now Professor of Moral Philosophy at Edinburgh) and myself to visit him for a day or two on our return from an excursion to Mr. Wilson's beautiful villa on the Lake of Windermere, but named the particular day (October 8) on which it would be most convenient for him to receive us; and we discovered on our arrival that he had fixed it from a good-natured motive. We found him walking in one of his plantations, at no great distance from the house, with five or six young people, and his friends Lord Melville and Captain Ferguson. Having presented us to the First Lord of the Admiralty, he fell back a little and said, "I am glad you came to-day, for I thought it might be of use to you both, some time or other, to be known to my old schoolfellow here, who is, and I hope

will long continue to be, the great giver of good things
in the Parliament House. I trust you have had enough
of certain pranks with your friend Ebony, and if so,
Lord Melville will have too much sense to remember
them."[1] We then walked round the plantation, as yet
in a very young state, and came back to the house by
a formidable work which he was constructing for the defence of his *haugh* against the wintry violences of the
Tweed; and he discoursed for some time with keen interest upon the comparative merits of different methods of
embankment, but stopped now and then to give us the
advantage of any point of view in which his new building
on the eminence above pleased his eye. It had a fantastic appearance — being but a fragment of the existing
edifice — and not at all harmonizing in its outline with
"Mother Retford's" original tenement to the eastward.
Scott, however, expatiated *con amore* on the rapidity with
which, being chiefly of darkish granite, it was assuming a "time-honored" aspect. Ferguson, with a grave
and respectful look, observed, "Yes, it really has much
the air of some old fastness hard by the river Jordan."
This allusion to the Chaldee MS., already quoted, in
the manufacture of which Ferguson fancied Wilson and
myself to have had a share, gave rise to a burst of laughter among Scott's merry young folks and their companions, while he himself drew in his nether lip, and rebuked
the Captain with "Toots, Adam! toots, Adam!" He
then returned to his embankment, and described how a
former one had been entirely swept away in one night's
flood. But the Captain was ready with another verse
of the Chaldee MS., and groaned out, by way of echo,
"Verily my fine gold hath perished!" Whereupon the
"Great Magician" elevated his huge oaken staff as if to

[1] *Ebony* was Mr. Blackwood's own usual designation in the *jeux d'esprit* of his young Magazine, in many of which the persons thus addressed
by Scott were conjoint culprits. They both were then, as may be inferred, sweeping the boards of the Parliament House as "briefless barristers."

lay it on the waggish soldier's back — but flourished it
gayly over his own head, and laughed louder than the
youngest of the company. As we walked and talked,
the Pepper and Mustard terriers kept snuffing about
among the bushes and heather near us, and started every
five minutes a hare, which scudded away before them and
the ponderous stag-hound Maida — the Sheriff and all
his tail hollowing and cheering, in perfect confidence
that the dogs could do no more harm to poor puss than
the venerable tom-cat, Hinse of Hinsfeldt, who pursued
the vain chase with the rest.

At length we drew near *Peterhouse*, and found sober
Peter himself, and his brother-in-law, the facetious facto-
tum Tom Purdie, superintending, pipe in mouth, three
or four sturdy laborers busy in laying down the turf for
a bowling-green. "I have planted hollies all round it,
you see," said Scott, "and laid out an arbor on the right-
hand side for the laird; and here I mean to have a game
at bowls after dinner every day in fine weather — for I
take that to have been among the indispensables of our
old *vie de château*." But I must not forget the reason
he gave me some time afterwards for having fixed on
that spot for his bowling-green. "In truth," he then
said, "I wished to have a smooth walk, and a canny seat
for myself within ear-shot of Peter's evening psalm."
The coachman was a devout Presbyterian, and many a
time have I in after-years accompanied Scott on his evening stroll, when the principal object was to enjoy, from
the bowling-green, the unfailing melody of this good
man's family worship — and heard him repeat, as Peter's
manly voice led the humble choir within, that beautiful
stanza of Burns's Saturday Night: —

> " They chaunt their artless notes in simple guise ;
> They tune their hearts, by far the noblest aim," etc.

It was near the dinner-hour before we reached the
house, and presently I saw assembled a larger company
than I should have fancied to be at all compatible with

the existing accommodations of the place; but it turned
out that Captain Ferguson, and the friends whom I have
not as yet mentioned, were to find quarters elsewhere for
the night. His younger brother, Captain John Ferguson of the Royal Navy (a favorite lieutenant of Lord
Nelson's), had come over from Huntly Burn; there were
present, also, Mr. Scott of Gala, whose residence is within
an easy distance; Sir Henry Hay Macdougal of Macker-
stoun, an old baronet, with gay, lively, and highly polished manners, related in the same degree to both Gala
and the Sheriff; Sir Alexander Don, the member for
Roxburghshire, whose elegant social qualities have been
alluded to in the preceding chapter: and Dr. Scott of
Darnlee, a modest and intelligent gentleman, who having
realized a fortune in the East India Company's medical
service, had settled within two or three miles of Abbotsford, and, though no longer practising his profession,
had kindly employed all the resources of his skill in the
endeavor to counteract his neighbor's recent liability to
attacks of cramp. Our host and one or two others appeared, as was in those days a common fashion with
country gentlemen, in the lieutenancy uniform of their
county. How fourteen or fifteen people contrived to be
seated in the then dining-room of Abbotsford I know not
— for it seemed quite full enough when it contained only
eight or ten; but so it was — nor, as Sir Harry Macdougal's fat valet, warned by former experience, did not
join the train of attendants, was there any perceptible
difficulty in the detail of the arrangements. Everything
about the dinner was, as the phrase runs, in excellent
style; and in particular the *potage à la Meg Merrilies*,
announced as an attempt to imitate a device of the Duke
of Buccleuch's celebrated cook, — by name Monsieur
Florence, — seemed, to those at least who were better
acquainted with the Kaim of Derncleugh than with the
cuisine of Bowhill,[1] a very laudable specimen of the art.

[1] I understand that this now celebrated soup was *extemporized* by M. Flor-

The champagne circulated nimbly — and I never was
present at a gayer dinner. It had advanced a little
beyond the soup when it received an accompaniment
which would not, perhaps, have improved the satisfaction
of southern guests, had any such been present. A tall
and stalwart bagpiper, in complete Highland costume,
appeared pacing to and fro on the green before the house,
and the window being open, it seemed as if he might as
well have been straining his lungs within the parlor.
At a pause of his strenuous performance, Scott took
occasion to explain that *John of Skye* was a recent acquisition to the rising hamlet of Abbotstown; that the
man was a capital hedger and ditcher, and only figured
with the pipe and philabeg on high occasions in the after-
part of the day; "but indeed," he added, laughing, "I
fear John will soon be discovering that the hook and
mattock are unfavorable to his chanter hand." When
the cloth was drawn, and the never-failing salver of
quaighs introduced, John of Skye, upon some well-
known signal, entered the room, but *en militaire*, without removing his bonnet, and taking his station behind
the landlord, received from his hand the largest of the
Celtic bickers brimful of Glenlivet. The man saluted
the company in his own dialect, tipped off the contents
(probably a quarter of an English pint of raw aqua vitæ)
at a gulp, wheeled about as solemnly as if the whole ceremony had been a movement on parade, and forthwith
recommenced his pibrochs and gatherings, which continued until long after the ladies had left the table, and the
autumnal moon was streaming in upon us so brightly as
to dim the candles.

I had never before seen Scott in such buoyant spirits
as he showed this evening — and I never saw him in

ence on Scott's first visit to Bowhill after the publication of *Guy Manner-*
ing. Florence had *served* — and Scott having on some sporting party made
his personal acquaintance, he used often afterwards to gratify the poet's
military propensities by sending up magnificent representations in pastry,
of citadels taken by the Emperor, etc.

higher afterwards; and no wonder, for this was the first time that he, Lord Melville, and Adam Ferguson, daily companions at the High School of Edinburgh, and part-ners in many joyous scenes of the early volunteer period, had met since the commencement of what I may call the serious part of any of their lives. The great poet and novelist was receiving them under his own roof, when his fame was at its *acme*, and his fortune seemed culmi-nating to about a corresponding height — and the gener-ous exuberance of his hilarity might have overflowed without moving the spleen of a Cynic. Old stories of *the Yards* and *the Cross-causeway* were relieved by sketches of real warfare, such as none but Ferguson (or Charles Mathews, had he been a soldier) could ever have given; and they toasted the memory of *Green-breeks* and the health of *the Beau* with equal devotion.

When we rose from table, Scott proposed that we should all ascend his western turret, to enjoy a moonlight view of the valley. The younger part of his company were too happy to do so: some of the seniors, who had tried the thing before, found pretexts for hanging back. The stairs were dark, narrow, and steep; but the Sheriff piloted the way, and at length there were as many on the top as it could well afford footing for. Nothing could be more lovely than the panorama; all the harsher and more naked features being lost in the delicious moon-light; the Tweed and the Gala winding and sparkling beneath our feet; and the distant ruins of Melrose ap-pearing, as if carved of alabaster, under the black mass of the Eildons. The poet, leaning on his battlement, seemed to hang over the beautiful vision as if he had never seen it before. "If I live," he exclaimed, "I will build me a higher tower, with a more spacious platform, and a staircase better fitted for an old fellow's scram-bling." The piper was heard re-tuning his instrument below, and he called to him for Lochaber no More. John of Skye obeyed, and as the music rose, softened by the distance, Scott repeated in a low key the melancholy words of the song of exile.

On descending from the tower, the whole company were assembled in the new dining-room, which was still under the hands of the carpenters, but had been brilliantly illuminated for the occasion. Mr. Bruce took his station, and old and young danced reels to his melodious accompaniment until they were weary, while Scott and the Dominie looked on with gladsome faces, and beat time now and then, the one with his staff, the other with his wooden leg. A tray with mulled wine and whiskey punch was then introduced, and Lord Melville proposed a bumper, with all the honors, to the *Roof-tree*. Captain Ferguson having sung Johnnie Cope, called on the young ladies for Kenmure 's On and Awa'; and our host then insisted that the whole party should join, standing in a circle hand-in-hand *more majorum*, in the hearty chorus of

> " Weel may we a' be,
> Ill may we never see,
> God bless the king and the gude companie ! "

— which being duly performed, all dispersed. Such was *the handsel* (for Scott protested against its being considered as *the house-heating*) of the new Abbotsford.

When I began this chapter, I thought it would be a short one, but it is surprising how, when one digs into his memory, the smallest details of a scene that was interesting at the time, shall by degrees come to light again. I now recall, as if I had seen and heard them yesterday, the looks and words of eighteen years ago. Awakening between six and seven next morning, I heard Scott's voice close to me, and looking out of the little latticed window of the then detached cottage called *the chapel*, saw him and Tom Purdie pacing together on the green before the door, in earnest deliberation over what seemed to be a rude daub of a drawing; and every time they approached my end of their parade, I was sure to catch the words *Blue Bank*.　It turned out in the course of the day, that a field of clay near Toftfield went by this name, and that the draining of it was one of the chief operations then in hand.　My friend Wilson meanwhile, who lodged also in the chapel, tapped at my door, and asked me to rise and take a walk with him by the river, for he had some angling project in his head.　He went out and joined in the consultation about the Blue Bank, while I was dressing; presently Scott hailed me at the casement, and said he had observed a volume of a new edition of Goethe on my table — would I lend it him for a little?　He carried off the volume accordingly, and retreated with it to his den.　It contained the Faust, and, I believe, in a more complete shape than he had before seen that masterpiece of his old favorite.　When we met at breakfast, a couple of hours after, he was full of the poem — dwelt with enthusiasm on the airy beauty of its lyrics, the terrible pathos of the scene before the *Mater Dolorosa*, and the deep skill shown in the various subtle shadings of character between Mephistopheles and poor Margaret.　He remarked, however, of the Introduction (which I suspect was new to him), that blood would out — that, consummate artist as he was, Goethe was a German, and that nobody but a German would ever have provoked a comparison with the Book of Job, "the grandest poem that ever was written."　He added, that he suspected the end of the story had been left *in obscuro*, from despair to match the closing scene of our own Marlowe's Doctor Faustus.　Mr. Wilson mentioned a report that Coleridge was engaged on a translation of the Faust.　"I hope it is so," said Scott; "Coleridge made Schiller's Wallenstein far finer than he found it, and so he will do by this.　No man has all the resources of poetry in such profusion, but he cannot manage them so as to bring out anything of his own on a large scale at all worthy of his genius.　He is like a lump of coal rich with gas, which lies expending itself in puffs and gleams, unless some shrewd body will clap it into a cast-iron box, and compel the compressed element to do itself justice. His fancy and diction would have long ago placed him above all his contemporaries, had they been under the direction of a sound judgment and a steady will.[1] I don't now expect a great original poem from Coleridge, but he might easily make a sort of fame for himself as a poetical translator, — that would be a thing completely unique and *sui generis*."

While this criticism proceeded, Scott was cutting away at his brown loaf and a plate of kippered salmon, in a style which strongly reminded me of Dandie Dinmont's luncheon at Mump's Hall; nor was his German topic at all the predominant one. On the contrary, the sentences which have dwelt on my memory dropt from him now and then, in the pauses, as it were, of his main talk; — for though he could not help recurring, ever and anon, to the subject, it would have been quite out of his way to make any literary matter the chief theme of his conversation, when there was a single person present who was not likely to feel much interested in its discussion. — How often have I heard him quote on such occasions Mr. Vellum's advice to the butler in Addison's excellent play of The Drummer: "Your conjuror, John, is indeed a twofold personage — but he *eats and drinks like other people!* "

[1] In the Introduction to *The Lay of the Last Minstrel*, 1830, Sir Walter says : " Were I ever to take the unbecoming freedom of censuring a man of Mr. Coleridge's extraordinary talents, it would be on account of the caprice and indolence with which he has thrown from him, as in mere wantonness, those unfinished scraps of poetry, which, like the Torso of antiquity, defy the skill of his poetical brethren to complete them. The charming fragments which the author abandons to their fate are surely too valuable to be treated like the proofs of careless engravers, the sweepings of whose studios often make the fortune of some painstaking collector." And in a note to *The Abbot*, alluding to Coleridge's beautiful and tantalizing fragment of *Christabel*, he adds : " Has not our own imaginative poet cause to fear that future ages will desire to summon him from his place of rest, as Milton longed

' To call up him who left half told
The story of Cambuscan bold ' ? "

I may, however, take this opportunity of observing, that nothing could have been more absurdly unfounded than the statement which I have seen repeated in various sketches of his Life and Manners, that he habitually abstained from conversation on literary topics. In point of fact, there were no topics on which he talked more openly or more earnestly; but he, when in society, lived and talked for the persons with whom he found himself surrounded, and if he did not always choose to enlarge upon the subjects which his companions for the time suggested, it was simply because he thought or fancied that these had selected, out of deference or flattery, subjects about which they really cared little more than they knew. I have already repeated, over and again, my conviction that Scott considered literature, *per se*, as a thing of far inferior importance to the high concerns of political or practical life; but it would be too ridiculous to question that literature nevertheless engrossed, at all times and seasons, the greater part of his own interest and reflection: nor can it be doubted that his general preference of the society of men engaged in the active business of the world, rather than that of, so-called, literary people, was grounded substantially on his feeling that literature, worthy of the name, was more likely to be fed and nourished by the converse of the former than by that of the latter class.

Before breakfast was over, the post-bag arrived, and its contents were so numerous, that Lord Melville asked Scott what election was on hand — not doubting that there must be some very particular reason for such a shoal of letters. He answered that it was much the same most days, and added, "though no one has kinder friends in the franking line, and though Freeling and Croker especially are always ready to stretch the point of privilege in my favor, I am nevertheless a fair contributor to the revenue, for I think my bill for letters seldom comes under £150 a year; and as to coach-parcels, they

are a perfect ruination." He then told with high merriment a disaster that had lately befallen him. "One
morning last spring," he said, "I opened a huge lump
of a despatch, without looking how it was addressed,
never doubting that it had travelled under some omnipo-
tent frank like the First Lord of the Admiralty's, when,
lo and behold, the contents proved to be a MS. play, by
a young lady of New York, who kindly requested me to
read and correct it, equip it with prologue and epilogue,
procure for it a favorable reception from the manager
of Drury Lane, and make Murray or Constable bleed
handsomely for the copyright; and on inspecting the
cover, I found that I had been charged five pounds odd
for the postage. This was bad enough — but there was
no help, so I groaned and submitted. A fortnight or so
after, another packet, of not less formidable bulk, arrived, and I was absent enough to break its seal, too, without examination. Conceive my horror when out jumped
the same identical tragedy of The Cherokee Lovers, with
a second epistle from the authoress, stating that, as the
winds had been boisterous, she feared the vessel entrusted
with her former communication might have foundered,
and therefore judged it prudent to forward a duplicate."

Scott said he must retire to answer his letters, but that
the sociable and the ponies would be at the door by one
o'clock, when he proposed to show Melrose and Dryburgh
to Lady Melville and any of the rest of the party that
chose to accompany them; adding that his son Walter
would lead anybody who preferred a gun to the likeliest
place for a blackcock, and that Charlie Purdie (Tom's
brother) would attend upon Mr. Wilson, and whoever
else chose to try a cast of the salmon-rod. He withdrew
when all this was arranged, and appeared at the time
appointed, with perhaps a dozen letters sealed for the
post, and a coach-parcel addressed to James Ballantyne,
which he dropt at the turnpike-gate as we drove to Melrose. Seeing it picked up by a dirty urchin, and carried

into a hedge pot-house, where half-a-dozen nondescript wayfarers were smoking and tippling, I could not but wonder that it had not been the fate of some one of those innumerable packets to fall into unscrupulous hands, and betray the grand secret. That very morning we had seen two post-chaises drawn up at his gate, and the enthusiastic travellers, seemingly decent tradesmen and their families, who must have been packed in a manner worthy of Mrs. Gilpin, lounging about to catch a glimpse of him at his going forth. But it was impossible in those days to pass between Melrose and Abbotsford without encountering some odd figure, armed with a sketch-book, evidently bent on a peep at the Great Unknown; and it must be allowed that many of these pedestrians looked as if they might have thought it very excusable to make prize, by hook or by crook, of a MS. chapter of the Tales of my Landlord.

Scott showed us the ruins of Melrose in detail; and as we proceeded to Dryburgh, descanted learnedly and sagaciously on the good effects which must have attended the erection of so many great monastic establishments in a district so peculiarly exposed to the inroads of the English in the days of the Border wars. "They were now and then violated," he said, "as their aspect to this hour bears witness; but for once that they suffered, any lay property similarly situated must have been *harried* a dozen times. The bold Dacres, Liddells, and Howards, that could get easy absolution at York or Durham for any ordinary breach of a truce with the Scots, would have had *to dree a heavy dole* had they confessed plundering from the fat brothers, of the same order perhaps, whose lines had fallen to them on the wrong side of the Cheviot." He enlarged, too, on the heavy penalty which the Crown of Scotland had paid for its rash acquiescence in the wholesale robbery of the Church at the Reformation. "The proportion of the soil in the hands of the clergy had," he said, "been very great — too great to be

continued. If we may judge by their share in the public
burdens, they must have had nearly a third of the land
in their possession. But this vast wealth was now distributed among a turbulent nobility, too powerful before;
and the Stuarts soon found, that in the bishops and lord
abbots they had lost the only means of balancing their
factions, so as to turn the scale in favor of law and order;
and by and by the haughty barons themselves, who had
scrambled for the worldly spoil of the church, found that
the spiritual influence had been concentrated in hands
as haughty as their own, and connected with no feelings
likely to buttress their order any more than the Crown
— a new and sterner monkery, under a different name,
and essentially plebeian. Presently the Scotch were on
the verge of republicanism, in state as well as kirk, and
I have sometimes thought it was only the accession of
King Jamie to the throne of England that could have
given monarchy a chance of prolonging its existence
here." One of his friends asked what he supposed might
have been the annual revenue of the abbey of Melrose in
its best day. He answered that he suspected, if all the
sources of their income were now in clever hands, the
produce could hardly be under £100,000 a year; and
added: "Making every allowance for modern improvements, there can be no question that the sixty brothers
of Melrose divided a princely rental. The superiors
were often men of very high birth, and the great majority of the rest were younger brothers of gentlemen's
families. I fancy they may have been, on the whole,
pretty near akin to your Fellows of All Souls — who,
according to their statute, must be *bene nati, bene vestiti,
et mediocriter docti.* They had a good house in Edinburgh, where, no doubt, my lord abbot and his chaplains
maintained a hospitable table during the sittings of Parliament." Some one regretted that we had no lively
picture of the enormous revolution in manners that must
have followed the downfall of the ancient Church in

Scotland. He observed that there were, he fancied,
materials enough for constructing such a one, but that
they were mostly scattered in records — "of which," said
he, "who knows anything to the purpose except Tom
Thomson and John Riddell? It is common to laugh at
such researches, but they pay the good brains that meddle with them; — and had Thomson been as diligent in
setting down his discoveries as he has been in making
them, he might, long before this time of day, have placed
himself on a level with Ducange or Camden. The
change in the country-side," he continued, "must indeed
have been terrific; but it does not seem to have been felt
very severely by a certain Boniface of St. Andrews, for
when somebody asked him, on the subsidence of the
storm, what he thought of all that had occurred, —
'Why,' answered mine host, 'it comes to this, that the
moderautor sits in my meikle chair, where the dean sat
before, and in place of calling for the third stoup of
Bordeaux, bids Jenny bring ben anither bowl of toddy.'"

At Dryburgh, Scott pointed out to us the sepulchral
aisle of his Haliburton ancestors, and said he hoped, in
God's appointed time, to lay his bones among their dust.
The spot was, even then, a sufficiently interesting and
impressive one; but I shall not say more of it at present.

On returning to Abbotsford, we found Mrs. Scott and
her daughters doing penance under the merciless curiosity
of a couple of tourists who had arrived from Selkirk soon
after we set out for Melrose. They were rich specimens
— tall, lanky young men, both of them rigged out in new
jackets and trousers of the Macgregor tartan; the one,
as they had revealed, being a lawyer, the other a Unita-
rian preacher, from New England. These gentlemen,
when told on their arrival that Mr. Scott was not at
home, had shown such signs of impatience, that the servant took it for granted they must have serious business,
and asked if they would wish to speak a word with his

lady. They grasped at this, and so conducted themselves
in the interview, that Mrs. Scott never doubted they had
brought letters of introduction to her husband, and invited them accordingly to partake of her luncheon. They
had been walking about the house and grounds with her
and her daughters ever since that time, and appeared at
the porch, when the Sheriff and his party returned to
dinner, as if they had been already fairly enrolled on his
visiting list. For the moment, he too was taken in — he
fancied that his wife must have received and opened their
credentials — and shook hands with them with courteous
cordiality. But Mrs. Scott, with all her overflowing
good-nature, was a sharp observer; and she, before a
minute had elapsed, interrupted the ecstatic compliments
of the strangers, by reminding them that her husband
would be glad to have the letters of the friends who had
been so good as to write by them. It then turned out
that there were no letters to be produced — and Scott,
signifying that his hour for dinner approached, added,
that as he supposed they meant to walk to Melrose, he
could not trespass further on their time. The two lion-
hunters seemed quite unprepared for this abrupt escape.
But there was about Scott, in perfection, when he chose
to exert it, the power of civil repulsion; he bowed the
overwhelmed originals to his door, and on reëntering the
parlor, found Mrs. Scott complaining very indignantly
that they had gone so far as to pull out their note-book,
and beg an exact account, not only of his age — but of
her own. Scott, already half relenting, laughed heartily
at this misery. He observed, however, that, "if he were
to take in all the world, he had better put up a sign-post
at once, —

> ' Porter, ale, and British spirits,
> Painted bright between twa trees; ' [1]

and that no traveller of respectability could ever be at
a loss for such an introduction as would insure his best

[1] Macneill's *Will and Jean*.

hospitality." Still he was not quite pleased with what had happened — and as we were about to pass, half an hour afterwards, from the drawing-room to the dining-room, he said to his wife, "Hang the Yahoos, Charlotte — but we should have bid them stay dinner." "Devil a bit," quoth Captain John Ferguson, who had again come over from Huntly Burn, and had been latterly assisting the lady to amuse her Americans, "Devil a bit, my dear, — they were quite in a mistake, I could see. The one asked Madame whether she deigned to call her new house Tully-Veolan or Tillietudlem; and the other, when Maida happened to lay his nose against the window, exclaimed *pro-di-gi-ous!* In short, they evidently meant all their humbug not for you, but for the culprit of Waverley, and the rest of that there rubbish." "Well, well, Skipper," was the reply, "for a' that, the loons would hae been nane the waur o' their kail."

From this banter it may be inferred that the younger Ferguson had not as yet been told the Waverley secret — which to any of that house could never have been any mystery. Probably this, or some similar occasion soon afterwards, led to his formal initiation; for during the many subsequent years that the veil was kept on, I used to admire the tact with which, when in their topmost high-jinks humor, both "Captain John" and "The Auld Captain" eschewed any the most distant allusion to the affair.

And this reminds me, that at the period of which I am writing, none of Scott's own family, except of course his wife, had the advantage in that matter of the Skipper.[1]

[1] [Among the American visitors who brought their credentials with them, during this summer, was Edward Everett, then a very young man, who was introduced by Gifford. A little incident mentioned by him in a letter written to Scott not long afterward shows how Abbotsford was already besieged by tourists : "Just before I had the happiness of visiting Abbotsford," he writes, "a party of ladies and gentlemen travelling into Scotland, and determined to see you, wandered into your enclosure and surprised you seated before your door, in that condition into which Horace says your great master Homer sometimes fell. This fact I have upon the authority

Some of them, too, were apt, like him, so long as no
regular confidence had been reposed in them, to avail
themselves of the author's reserve for their own sport
among friends. Thus one morning, just as Scott was
opening the door of the parlor, the rest of the party
being already seated at the breakfast-table, the Dominie
was in the act of helping himself to an egg, marked with
a peculiar hieroglyphic by Mrs. Thomas Purdie, upon
which Anne Scott, then a lively rattling girl of sixteen, lisped out, "That 's a mysterious-looking egg, Mr.
Thomson — what if it should have been meant for *the
Great Unknown?*" Ere the Dominie could reply, her
father advanced to the foot of the table, and having
seated himself and deposited his stick on the carpet beside him, with a sort of whispered whistle — "What 's
that Lady Anne 's [1] saying?" quoth he; "I thought it
had been well known that the *keelavined* egg must be
a soft one for *the Sherra.*" And so he took his egg,
and while all smiled in silence, poor Anne said gayly,

of Miss Sophia, who came out and found them all standing round you in a
ring, without breaking the quiet of your siesta." And the writer goes on
to tell how certain pilgrims who came with him in the coach to Melrose
wandered over the estate for days, hoping to fall in with its master.   See
Familiar Letters, vol. ii. p. 24.

Forty years later Mr. Everett, in writing to Mr. Allibone, recalls the
days of his visit as among the happiest of his life. At that time, he says,
the opinion was not uncommon that Mr. Thomas Scott was the Author of
Waverley, and one day he remarked jestingly to Miss Scott that after all
America could claim the honor of the novels, as it was said her uncle was
the writer. She answered with some warmth that the saying was untrue,
and then added: " I ought in candor to tell you that we all believe that our
father is the author; but we do not know it." Later she said with gentle
dignity, that things occasionally took place which might awaken suspicion ;
" that if they chose to be inquisitive they might perhaps find out how the
case stood ; they believed their father wrote the novels, and that he desired
it to remain concealed, and they respected his supposed wishes too much
to pry into the matter." See Allibone's *Dictionary of Authors*, p. 1966.]

[1] When playing, in childhood, with the young ladies of the Buccleuch
family, she had been overheard saying to her namesake Lady Anne Scott,
" Well, I do wish I were Lady Anne too — it is so much prettier than
Miss ; " thenceforth she was commonly addressed in the family by the coveted title.

in the midst of her blushes, "Upon my word, papa, I
thought Mr. John Ballantyne might have been expected." This allusion to Johnny's glory in being considered as the accredited representative of Jedediah
Cleishbotham produced a laugh, — at which the Sheriff
frowned — and then laughed too.

I remember nothing particular about our second day's
dinner, except that it was then I first met my dear and
honored friend William Laidlaw. The evening passed
rather more quietly than the preceding one. Instead of
the dance in the new dining-room, we had a succession
of old ballads sung to the harp and guitar by the young
ladies of the house; and Scott, when they seemed to have
done enough, found some reason for taking down a volume of Crabbe, and read us one of his favorite tales, —

> " Grave Jonas Kindred, Sibyl Kindred's sire,
>   Was six feet high, and looked six inches higher," etc.

But jollity revived in full vigor when the supper-tray
was introduced; and to cap all merriment, Captain Ferguson dismissed us with The Laird of Cockpen. Lord
and Lady Melville were to return to Melville Castle next
morning, and Mr. Wilson and I happened to mention
that we were engaged to dine and sleep at the seat of my
friend and relation, Mr. Pringle of Torwoodlee, on our
way to Edinburgh. Scott immediately said that he
would send word in the morning to the Laird, that he
and Adam Ferguson meant to accompany us — such
being the unceremonious style in which country neighbors in Scotland visit each other. Next day, accordingly,
we all rode over together to Mr. Pringle's beautiful seat
— the "distant Torwoodlee" of The Lay of the Last
Minstrel, but distant not above five or six miles from
Abbotsford — coursing hares as we proceeded, but inspecting the antiquities of the *Catrail* to the interruption
of our sport. We had another joyous evening at Torwoodlee. Scott and Ferguson returned home at night,
and the morning after, as Wilson and I mounted for

Edinburgh, our kind old host, his sides still sore with laughter, remarked that "the Sheriff and the Captain together were too much for any company."

There was much talk between the Sheriff and Mr. Pringle about the Selkirkshire Yeomanry Cavalry, of which the latter had been the original commandant. Young Walter Scott had been for a year or more Cornet in the corps, and his father was consulting Torwoodlee about an entertainment which he meant to give them on his son's approaching birthday. It was then that the new dining-room was to be first *heated* in good earnest; and Scott very kindly pressed Wilson and myself, at parting, to return for the occasion — which, however, we found it impossible to do. The reader must therefore be satisfied with what is said about it in one of the following letters: —

TO J. B. S. MORRITT, ESQ., M. P., ROKEBY.

ABBOTSFORD, 5th November, 1818.

MY DEAR MORRITT, — Many thanks for your kind letter of 29th October. The matter of the colts being as you state, I shall let it lie over until next year, and then avail myself of your being in the neighborhood to get a good pair of four-year-olds, since it would be unnecessary to buy them a year younger, and incur all the risks of disease and accident, unless they could have been had at a proportional under-value.

* * * * * * leaves us this morning after a visit of about a week. He improves on acquaintance, and especially seems so pleased with everything, that it would be very hard to quarrel with him. Certainly, as the Frenchman said, *il a un grand talent pour le silence.* I take the opportunity of his servant going direct to Rokeby to charge him with this letter, and a plaid which my daughters entreat you to accept of as a token of their *warm* good wishes. Seriously you will find it a good bosom friend in an easterly wind, a black frost, or when your

country avocations lead you to face a *dry wap of snow*. I find it by far the lightest and most comfortable integument which I can use upon such occasions.

We had a grand jollification here last week; — the whole troop of Forest Yeomanry dining with us. I assure you the scene was gay and even grand, with glittering sabres, waving standards, and screaming bagpipes; and that it might not lack spectators of taste, who should arrive in the midst of the hurricane, but Lord and Lady Compton, whose presence gave a great zest to the whole affair. Everything went off very well, and as cavalry have the great advantage over infantry, that their *legs* never get drunk, they retired in decent disorder about ten o'clock. I was glad to see Lord and Lady Compton so very comfortable, and surrounded with so fine a family, the natural bond of mutual regard and affection. She has got very jolly, but otherwise has improved on her travels. I had a long chat with her, and was happy to find her quite contented and pleased with the lot she has drawn in life. It is a brilliant one in many respects, to be sure; but still I have seen the story of the poor woman, who, after all rational subjects of distress had been successively remedied, tormented herself about the screaming of a neighbor's peacock — I say, I have seen this so often realized in actual life, that I am more afraid of my friends making themselves uncomfortable, who have only imaginary evils to indulge, than I am for the peace of those who, battling magnanimously with real inconvenience and danger, find a remedy in the very force of the exertions to which their lot compels them.

I sympathize with you for the *dole* which you are *dreeing* under the inflictions of your honest proser. Of all the boring machines ever devised, your regular and determined story-teller is the most peremptory and powerful in his operations. This is a rainy day, and my present infliction is an idle cousin, a great amateur of the pipes, who is performing incessantly in the next room for the benefit of a probationary minstrel, whose pipes scream *à la distance*, as the young hoarse cock-chicken imitates the gallant and triumphant screech of a veteran Sir Chanticleer. Yours affectionately,

W. Scott.

CHAPTER XLIII

DECLINING HEALTH OF CHARLES, DUKE OF BUCCLEUCH.
— LETTER ON THE DEATH OF QUEEN CHARLOTTE. —
PROVINCIAL ANTIQUITIES, ETC. — EXTENSIVE SALE
OF COPYRIGHTS TO CONSTABLE AND CO. — DEATH OF
MR. CHARLES CARPENTER. — SCOTT ACCEPTS THE OF-
FER OF A BARONETCY. — HE DECLINES TO RENEW
HIS APPLICATION FOR A SEAT ON THE EXCHEQUER
BENCH. — LETTERS TO MORRITT, RICHARDSON, MISS
BAILLIE, THE DUKE OF BUCCLEUCH, LORD MONTAGU,
AND CAPTAIN FERGUSON. — ROB ROY PLAYED AT
EDINBURGH. — LETTER FROM JEDEDIAH CLEISHBOTHAM
TO MR. CHARLES MACKAY

1818–1819

I HAVE now to introduce a melancholy subject — one
of the greatest afflictions that ever Scott encountered.
The health of Charles, Duke of Buccleuch was by this
time beginning to give way, and Scott thought it his
duty to intimate his very serious apprehensions to his
noble friend's brother.

TO THE RIGHT HON. LORD MONTAGU, DITTON PARK, WINDSOR.

EDINBURGH, 12th November, 1818.

MY DEAR LORD, — I am about to write to you with
feelings of the deepest anxiety. I have hesitated for two
or three days whether I should communicate to your
Lordship the sincere alarm which I entertain on account
of the Duke's present state of health, but I have come

to persuade myself, that it will be discharging a part of the duty which I owe to him, to mention my own most distressing apprehensions. I was at the cattle-show on the 6th, and executed the delegated task of toast-master, and so forth. I was told by * * * * that the Duke is under the influence of the muriatic bath, which occasions a good deal of uneasiness when the medicine is in possession of the system. The Duke observed the strictest diet, and remained only a short time at table, leaving me to do the honors, which I did with a sorrowful heart, endeavoring, however, to persuade myself that * * * *'s account, and the natural depression of spirits incidental to his finding himself unable for the time to discharge the duty to his guests, which no man could do with so much grace and kindness, were sufficient to account for the alteration of his manner and appearance. I spent Monday with him quietly and alone, and I must say that all I saw and heard was calculated to give me the greatest pain. His strength is much less, his spirits lower, and his general appearance far more unfavorable than when I left him at Drumlanrig a few weeks before. What * * * *, and indeed what the Duke himself, says of the medicine, may be true — but * * * * is very sanguine, and, like all the personal physicians attached to a person of such consequence, he is too much addicted to the *placebo* — at least I think so — too apt to fear to give offence by contradiction, or by telling that sort of truth which may controvert the wishes or habits of his patient. I feel I am communicating much pain to your Lordship, but I am sure that, excepting yourself, there is not a man in the world whose sorrow and apprehension could exceed mine in having such a task to discharge; for, as your Lordship well knows, the ties which bind me to your excellent brother are of a much stronger kind than usually connect persons so different in rank. But the alteration in voice and person, in features, and in spirits, all argue the decay of natural strength, and the increase of some internal disorder, which is gradually triumphing over the system. Much has been done in these cases by change of climate. I hinted this to the Duke at Drumlanrig, but I found his mind totally averse to it. But he made some inquiries of Harden (just returned from Italy), which seemed to imply that at least the idea of a winter in Italy or the south of France was not altogether out of his consideration. Your Lordship will consider whether he can or ought to be pressed upon this point. He is partial to Scotland, and feels the many high duties which bind him to it. But the air of this country, with its alternations of moisture and dry frost, although excellent for a healthy person, is very trying to a valetudinarian.

I should not have thought of volunteering to communicate such unpleasant news, but that the family do not seem alarmed. I am not surprised at this, because, where the decay of health is very gradual, it is more easily traced by a friend who sees the patient from interval to interval, than by the affectionate eyes which are daily beholding him.

Adieu, my dear Lord. God knows you will scarce read this letter with more pain than I feel in writing it. But it seems indispensable to me to communicate my sentiments of the Duke's present situation to his nearest relation and dearest friend. His life is invaluable to his country and to his family, and how dear it is to his friends can only be estimated by those who know the soundness of his understanding, the uprightness and truth of his judgment, and the generosity and warmth of his feelings.

I am always, my dear Lord, most truly yours,
WALTER SCOTT.

Scott's letters of this and the two following months are very much occupied with the painful subject of the Duke of Buccleuch's health; but those addressed to his

Grace himself are, in general, in a more jocose strain than usual. His friend's spirits were sinking, and he exerted himself in this way, in the hope of amusing the hours of languor at Bowhill. These letters are headed "Edinburgh Gazette Extraordinary," No. 1, No. 2, and so on; but they deal so much in laughable gossip about persons still living, that I find it difficult to make any extracts from them. The following paragraphs, however, from the Gazette of November the 20th, give a little information as to his own minor literary labors: —

"The article on Gourgaud's Narrative [1] *is* by a certain *Vieux Routier* of your Grace's acquaintance, who would willingly have some military hints from you for the continuation of the article, if at any time you should feel disposed to amuse yourself with looking at the General's most marvellous performance. His lies are certainly like the father who begot them. Do not think that at any time the little trumpery intelligence this place affords can interrupt my labors, while it amuses your Grace. I can scribble as fast in the Court of Session as anywhere else, without the least loss of time or hindrance of business. At the same time, I cannot help laughing at the miscellaneous trash I have been putting out of my hand, and the various motives which made me undertake the jobs. An article for the Edinburgh Review [2] — this for the love of Jeffrey, the editor — the first for ten years. Do., being the article *Drama* for the Encyclopædia — this for the sake of Mr. Constable, the publisher. Do. for the Blackwoodian Magazine — this for love of the cause I espoused. Do. for the Quarterly Review [3] — this for the love of myself, I believe, or, which is the same

---

[1] Article on *General Gourgaud's Memoirs* in *Blackwood's Magazine* for November, 1818.

[2] Article on Maturin's *Women, or Pour et Contre.* (*Miscellaneous Prose Works,* vol. xviii.)

[3] Article on *Childe Harold*, Canto IV. (*Miscellaneous Prose Works,* vol. xvii.)

thing, for the love of £100, which I wanted for some odd purpose. As all these folks fight like dog and cat among themselves, my situation is much like the *Suave mare magno*, and so forth. . . .

"I hope your Grace will never think of answering the Gazettes at all, or even replying to letters of business, until you find it quite convenient and easy. The Gazette will continue to appear as materials occur. Indeed I expect, in the end of next week, to look in upon Bowhill, per the Selkirk mail, about eight at night, with the hope of spending a day there, which will be more comfortable than at Abbotsford, where I should feel like a mouse below a firlot. If I find the Court can spare so important a person for one day, I shall order my pony up to meet me at Bowhill, and, supposing me to come on Friday night, I can easily return by the Blucher on Monday, dining and sleeping at Huntly Burn on the Sunday. So I shall receive all necessary reply in person."

Good Queen Charlotte died on the 17th of this month; and in writing to Mr. Morritt on the 21st, Scott thus expresses what was, I believe, the universal feeling at the moment: —

"So we have lost the old Queen. She has only had the sad prerogative of being kept alive by nursing for some painful weeks, whereas perhaps a subject might have closed the scene earlier. I fear the effect of this event on public manners — were there but a weight at the back of the drawing-room door, which would slam it in the face of w——s, its fall ought to be lamented; and I believe that poor Charlotte really adopted her rules of etiquette upon a feeling of duty. If we should suppose the Princess of Wales to have been at the head of the matronage of the land for these last ten years, what would have been the difference on public opinion! No man of experience will ever expect the breath of a court to be favorable to correct morals — *sed si non caste caute*

tamen. One half of the mischief is done by the pub-
licity of the evil, which corrupts those which are near its
influence, and fills with disgust and apprehension those
to whom it does not directly extend. Honest old Eve-
lyn's account of Charles the Second's court presses on
one's recollection, and prepares the mind for anxious
apprehensions."

Towards the end of this month Scott received from his
kind friend Lord Sidmouth, then Secretary of State for
the Home Department, the formal announcement of the
Prince Regent's desire (which had been privately communicated some months earlier through the Lord Chief
Commissioner Adam) to confer on him the rank of Baronet. When Scott first heard of the Regent's gracious
intention, he had signified considerable hesitation about
the prudence of his accepting any such accession of rank;
for it had not escaped his observation, that such airy
sounds, however modestly people may be disposed to
estimate them, are apt to entail in the upshot additional
cost upon their way of living, and to affect accordingly
the plastic fancies, feelings, and habits of their children.
But Lord Sidmouth's letter happened to reach him a few
days after he had heard of the sudden death of his wife's
brother, Charles Carpenter, who had bequeathed the
reversion of his fortune to his sister's family; and this
circumstance disposed Scott to waive his scruples, chiefly
with a view to the professional advantage of his eldest
son, who had by this time fixed on the life of a soldier.
As is usually the case, the estimate of Mr. Carpenter's
property transmitted at the time to England proved to
have been an exaggerated one; as nearly as my present
information goes, the amount was doubled. But as to
the only question of any interest, to wit, how Scott himself felt on all these matters at the moment, the following letter to one whom he had long leaned to as a brother, will be more satisfactory than anything else it is
in my power to quote: —

EDINBURGH, 7th December, 1818.

My DEAR MORRITT, — I know you are indifferent to nothing that concerns us, and therefore I take an early opportunity to acquaint you with the mixture of evil and good which has very lately befallen us. On Saturday last we had the advice of the death of my wife's brother, Charles Carpenter, commercial resident at Salem, in the Madras Establishment. This event has given her great distress. She has not, that we know of, a single blood-relation left in the world, for her uncle, the Chevalier de la Volere,[1] colonel of a Russian regiment, is believed to have been killed in the campaign of 1813. My wife has been very unwell for two days, and is only now sitting up and mixing with us. She has that sympathy which we are all bound to pay, but feels she wants that personal interest in her sorrow which could only be grounded on a personal acquaintance with the deceased.

Mr. Carpenter has, with great propriety, left his property in life-rent to his wife — the capital to my children. It seems to amount to about £40,000. Upwards of £30,000 is in the British funds; the rest, to an uncertain value, in India. I hope this prospect of independence will not make my children different from that which they have usually been — docile, dutiful, and affectionate. I trust it will not. At least, the first expression of their feelings was honorable, for it was a unanimous wish to give up all to their mother. This I explained to them was out of the question; but that, if they should be in possession at any time of this property, they ought, among them, to settle an income of £400 or £500 on their mother for her life, to supply her with a fund at her own uncontrolled disposal, for any indulgence

---

[1] I know nothing of the history or fate of this gentleman, except that he was an ardent Royalist, and emigrated from France early in the Revolution.

or useful purpose that might be required. Mrs. Scott will stand in no need of this; but it is a pity to let kind affections run to waste; and if they never have it in their power to pay such a debt, their willingness to have done so will be a pleasant reflection. I am Scotchman enough to hate the breaking up of family ties, and the too close adherence to personal property. For myself, this event makes me neither richer nor poorer *directly;* but indirectly it will permit me to do something for my poor brother Tom's family, besides pleasing myself in "*plantings,* and *policies,* and *biggings,*"[1] with a safe conscience.

There is another thing I have to whisper to your faithful ear. Our fat friend, being desirous to honor Literature in my unworthy person, has intimated to me, by his organ the Doctor,[2] that, with consent ample and unanimous of all the potential voices of all his ministers, each more happy than another of course on so joyful an occasion, he proposes to dub me Baronet. It would be easy saying a parcel of fine things about my contempt of rank, and so forth; but although I would not have gone a step out of my way to have asked, or bought, or begged or borrowed a distinction, which to me personally will rather be inconvenient than otherwise, yet, coming as it does directly from the source of feudal honors, and as an honor, I am really gratified with it; — especially as it is intimated that it is his Royal Highness's pleasure to heat the oven for me expressly, without waiting till he has some new *batch* of Baronets ready in dough. In plain English, I am to be gazetted *per se.* My poor friend Carpenter's bequest to my family has taken away

---

[1] I believe this is a quotation from some old Scotch chronicler on the character of King James V.

[2] *The Doctor* was Mr. Canning's nickname for Lord Sidmouth, the son of an accomplished physician, the intimate friend of the great Lord Chatham. Mr. Sheridan, when the Scotch Members deserted the Addington administration upon a trying vote, had the grace to say to the Premier, across the table of the House of Commons, — "Doctor! the Thanes fly from thee!"

a certain degree of *impecuniosity*, a necessity of saving cheese-parings and candle-ends, which always looks inconsistent with any little pretension to rank. But as things now stand, Advance banners in the name of God and Saint Andrew. Remember, I anticipate the jest, "I like not such grinning honor as Sir Walter hath." [1] After all, if one must speak for himself, I have my quarters and emblazonments, free of all stain but Border theft and High Treason, which I hope are gentlemanlike crimes; and I hope Sir Walter Scott will not sound worse than Sir Humphry Davy, though my merits are as much under his, in point of utility, as can well be imagined. But a name is something, and mine is the better of the two. Set down this flourish to the account of national and provincial pride, for you must know we have more Messieurs de Sotenville [2] in our Border counties than anywhere else in the Lowlands — I cannot say for the Highlands. The Duke of Buccleuch, greatly to my joy, resolves to go to France for a season. Adam Ferguson goes with him, to glad him by the way. Charlotte and the young folks join in kind compliments.

Most truly yours,   WALTER SCOTT.

A few additional circumstances are given in a letter of the same week to Joanna Baillie. To her, after mentioning the testamentary provisions of Mr. Carpenter, Scott says: —

MY DEAR FRIEND, — I am going to tell you a little secret. I have changed my mind, or rather existing circumstances have led to my altering my opinions in a case of sublunary honor. I have now before me Lord Sidmouth's letter, containing the Prince's gracious and unsolicited intention to give me a Baronetcy. It will neither make me better nor worse than I feel myself — in

---

[1] Sir Walter Blunt — *1st King Henry IV.*, Act V. Scene 3.

[2] See Molière's *George Dandin.*

fact it will be an incumbrance rather than otherwise; but it may be of consequence to Walter, for the title is worth something in the army, although not in a learned profession. The Duke of Buccleuch and Scott of Harden, who, as the heads of my clan and the sources of my gentry, are good judges of what I ought to do, have both given me their earnest opinion to accept of an honor directly derived from the source of honor, and neither begged nor bought, as is the usual fashion. Several of my ancestors bore the title in the seventeenth century; and were it of consequence, I have no reason to be ashamed of the decent and respectable persons who connect me with that period when they carried into the field, like Madoc —

> " The crescent, at whose gleam the *Cambrian* oft,
> Cursing his perilous tenure, wound his horn " —

so that, as a gentleman, I may stand on as good a footing as other new creations. Respecting the reasons peculiar to myself which have made the Prince show his respect for general literature in my person, I cannot be a good judge, and your friendly zeal will make you a partial one: the purpose is fair, honorable, and creditable to the Sovereign, even though it should number him among the monarchs who made blunders in literary patronage. You know Pope says: —

> " The Hero William, and the Martyr Charles,
> One knighted Blackmore, and one pensioned Quarles." [1]

So let the intention sanctify the error, if there should be one on this great occasion. The time of this grand affair is uncertain: it is coupled with an invitation to London, which it would be inconvenient to me to accept, unless it should happen that I am called to come up by the affairs of poor Carpenter's estate. Indeed, the prospects of my children form the principal reason for a change of sentiments upon this flattering offer, joined to my belief that, though I may still be a scribbler from inveterate habit, I shall hardly engage again in any work of consequence.

[1] *Imitations of Horace.* B. ii. Ep. 1. v. 386.

We had a delightful visit from the Richardsons, only rather too short. He will give you a picture of Abbotsford, but not as it exists in my mind's eye, waving with all its future honors. The pinasters are thriving very well, and in a year or two more Joanna's Bower will be worthy of the name. At present it is like Sir Roger de Coverley's portrait, which hovered between its resemblance to the good knight and to a Saracen. Now the said bower has still such a resemblance to its original character of a gravel pit, that it is not fit to be shown to "bairns and fools," who, according to our old canny proverb, should never see half-done work; but Nature, if she works slowly, works surely, and your laurels at Abbotsford will soon flourish as fair as those you have won on Parnassus. I rather fear that a quantity of game, which was shipped awhile ago at Inverness for the Doctor, never reached him: it is rather a transitory commodity in London; there were ptarmigan, grouse, and black game. I shall be grieved if they have miscarried. — My health, thank God, continues as strong as at any period in my life; only I think of rule and diet more than I used to do, and observe as much as in me lies the advice of my friendly physician, who took such kind care of me: my best respects attend him, Mrs. Baillie, and Mrs. Agnes. Ever, my dear friend, most faithfully yours,   W. S.

In the next of these letters Scott alludes, among other things, to a scene of innocent pleasure which I often witnessed afterwards. The whole of the ancient ceremonial of the *daft days*, as they are called in Scotland, obtained respect at Abbotsford. He said it was *uncanny*, and would certainly have felt it very uncomfortable, not to welcome the new year in the midst of his family and a few old friends, with the immemorial libation of a *het pint;* but of all the consecrated ceremonies of the time, none gave him such delight as the visit which he received as *Laird* from all the children on his estate, on the last morning of every December — when, in the words of an obscure poet often quoted by him,

> " The cottage bairns sing blithe and gay,
> At the ha' door for *hogmanay*."

TO MISS JOANNA BAILLIE, HAMPSTEAD.

ABBOTSFORD, 1st January, 1819.

My dear Friend, — Many thanks for your kind letter. Ten brace of ptarmigan sailed from Inverness about the 24th, directed for Dr. Baillie ; — if they should have reached, I hope you would seize some for yourself and friends, as I learn the Doctor is on duty at Windsor. I do not know the name of the vessel, but they were addressed to Dr. Baillie, London, which I trust was enough, for there are not *two*. The Doctor has been exercising his skill upon my dear friend and chief, the Duke of Buccleuch, to whom I am more attached than to any person beyond the reach of my own family, and has advised him to do what, by my earnest advice, he ought to have done three years ago — namely, to go to Lisbon : he left this vicinity with much reluctance to go to Toulouse, but if he will be advised, should not stop save in Portugal or the south of Spain. The Duke is one of those retired and high-spirited men who will never be known until the world asks what became of the huge oak that grew on the brow of the hill, and sheltered such an extent of ground. During the late distress, though his own immense rents remained in arrears, and though I know he was pinched for money, as all men were, but more especially the possessors of entailed estates, he absented himself from London in order to pay with ease to himself the laborers employed on his various estates. These amounted (for I have often seen the roll and helped to check it) to nine hundred and fifty men, working at day wages, each of whom on a moderate average might maintain three persons, since the single men have

mothers, sisters, and aged or very young relations to protect and assist. Indeed it is wonderful how much even
a small sum, comparatively, will do in supporting the
Scottish laborer, who is in his natural state perhaps one
of the best, most intelligent, and kind-hearted of human
beings; and in truth I have limited my other habits of
expense very much since I fell into the habit of employ-
ing mine honest people. I wish you could have seen
about a hundred children, being almost entirely supported by their fathers' or brothers' labor, come down
yesterday to dance to the pipes, and get a piece of cake
and bannock, and pence apiece (no very deadly largess)
in honor of *hogmanay*. I declare to you, my dear friend,
that when I thought the poor fellows who kept these children so neat, and well taught, and well behaved, were
slaving the whole day for eighteen-pence or twenty-pence
at the most, I was ashamed of their gratitude, and of
their becks and bows. But, after all, one does what one
can, and it is better twenty families should be comfortable according to their wishes and habits, than half that
number should be raised above their situation. Besides,
like Fortunio in the fairy tale, I have my gifted men —
the best wrestler and cudgel-player — the best runner
and leaper — the best shot in the little district; and as
I am partial to all manly and athletic exercises, these are
great favorites, being otherwise decent persons, and bearing their faculties meekly. All this smells of sad ego-
tism, but what can I write to you about, save what is
uppermost in my own thoughts: and here am I, thinning
old plantations and planting new ones; now undoing
what has been done, and now doing what I suppose no
one would do but myself, and accomplishing all my
magical transformations by the arms and legs of the
aforesaid genii, conjured up to my aid at eighteen-pence
a day. There is no one with me but my wife, to whom
the change of scene and air, with the facility of easy and
uninterrupted exercise, is of service. The young people

remain in Edinburgh to look after their lessons, and Walter, though passionately fond of shooting, only stayed three days with us, his mind running entirely on mathematics and fortification, French and German. One of the excellencies of Abbotsford is very bad pens and ink; and besides, this being New Year's Day, and my writing-room above the servants' hall, the progress of my correspondence is a little interrupted by the Piper singing Gaelic songs to the servants, and their applause in consequence. Adieu, my good and indulgent friend: the best influences of the New Year attend you and yours, who so well deserve all that they can bring. Most affectionately yours,

WALTER SCOTT.

Before quitting the year 1818, I ought to have mentioned that among Scott's miscellaneous occupations in its autumn, he found time to contribute some curious materials toward a new edition of Burt's Letters from the North of Scotland, which had been undertaken by his old acquaintance, Mr. Robert Jameson. During the winter session he appears to have made little progress with his novel; his painful seizures of cramp were again recurring frequently, and he probably thought it better to allow the story of Lammermoor to lie over until his health should be reëstablished. In the mean time he drew up a set of topographical and historical essays, which originally appeared in the successive numbers of the splendidly illustrated work, entitled Provincial Antiquities of Scotland.[1] But he did this merely to gratify his own love of the subject, and because, well or ill, he must be doing something. He declined all pecuniary recompense; but afterwards, when the success of the publication was secure, accepted from the proprietors some of the beautiful drawings by Turner, Thomson, and other artists, which had been prepared to accompany his

[1] These charming essays are now reprinted in his *Miscellaneous Prose Works* (Edition 1834) vol. vii.

text. These drawings are now in the little breakfast-room at Abbotsford — the same which had been constructed for his own den, and which I found him occupying as such in the spring of 1819.

In the course of December, 1818, he also opened an important negotiation with Messrs. Constable, which was completed early in the ensuing year. The cost of his building had, as is usual, exceeded his calculation; and he had both a large addition to it, and some new purchases of land, in view. Moreover, his eldest son had now fixed on the cavalry, in which service every step infers very considerable expense. The details of this negotiation are remarkable: — Scott considered himself as a very fortunate man when Constable, who at first offered £10,000 for all his then existing copyrights, agreed to give for them £12,000. Meeting a friend in the street, just after the deed had been executed, he said he wagered no man could guess at how large a price Constable had estimated his "eild kye" (cows barren from age). The copyrights thus transferred were, as specified in the instrument: —

" The said Walter Scott, Esq.'s present share, being the entire copyright, of Waverley.

Do.	do.	Guy Mannering.
Do.	do.	Antiquary.
Do.	do.	Rob Roy.
Do.	do.	Tales of My Landlord, 1st Series.
Do.	do.	do. 2d Series.
Do.	do.	do. 3d Series.
Do.	do.	Bridal of Triermain.
Do.	do.	Harold the Dauntless.
Do.	do.	Sir Tristrem.
Do.	do.	Roderick Collection.
Do.	do.	Paul's Letters.
Do.	being one eighth of	The Lay of the Last Minstrel.
Do.	being one half of	The Lady of the Lake.
Do.	being one half of	Rokeby.
Do.	being one half of	The Lord of the Isles."

The instrument contained a clause binding Messrs. Constable never to divulge the name of the Author of Waverley during his life, under a penalty of £2000.

I may observe, that had these booksellers fulfilled their part of this agreement, by paying off, prior to their insolvency in 1826, the whole bonds for £12,000, which they signed on the 2d of February, 1819, no interest in the copyrights above specified could have been expected to revert to the Author of Waverley: but more of this in due season.

He alludes to the progress of the treaty in the following letter to Captain Adam Ferguson, who had, as has already appeared, left Scotland with the Duke of Buccleuch. His Grace hearing, when in London, that one of the Barons of Exchequer at Edinburgh meant speedily to resign, the Captain had, by his desire, written to urge on Scott the propriety of renewing his application for a seat on that bench; which, however, Scott at once refused to do. There were several reasons for this abstinence; among others, he thought such a promotion at this time would interfere with a project which he had formed of joining "the Chief and the Aide-de-Camp" in the course of the spring, and accomplishing in their society the tour of Portugal and Spain — perhaps of Italy also. Some such excursion had been strongly recommended to him by his own physicians, as the likeliest means of interrupting those habits of sedulous exertion at the desk, which they all regarded as the true source of his recent ailments, and the only serious obstacle to his cure; and his standing as a Clerk of Session, considering how largely he had labored in that capacity for infirm brethren, would have easily secured him a twelvemonth's leave of absence from the Judges of his Court. But the principal motive was, as we shall see, his reluctance to interfere with the claims of the then Sheriff of Mid-Lothian, his own and Ferguson's old friend and schoolfellow, Sir William Rae — who, however, accepted the more ambitious post of Lord Advocate, in the course of the ensuing summer.

TO CAPTAIN ADAM FERGUSON, DITTON PARK, WINDSOR.

15th January, 1819.

DEAR ADAM, — Many thanks for your kind letter, this moment received. I would not for the world stand in Jackie (I beg his pardon, Sir John) Peartree's way.[1] He has merited the cushion *en haut*, and besides he needs it. To me it would make little difference in point of income. The *otium cum dignitate*, if it ever come, will come as well years after this as now. Besides, I am afraid the opening will be soon made, through the death of our dear friend the Chief Baron, of whose health the accounts are unfavorable.[2] Immediate promotion would be inconvenient to me, rather than otherwise, because I have the desire, like an old fool as I am, *courir un peu le monde*. I am beginning to draw out from my literary commerce. Constable has offered me £10,000 for the copyrights of published works which have already produced more than twice the sum. I stand out for £12,000. Tell this to the Duke; he knows how I managed to keep the hen till the rainy day was past. I will write two lines to Lord Melville, just to make my bow for the present, resigning any claims I have through the patronage of my kindest and best friend, for I have no other, till the next opportunity. I should have been truly vexed if the Duke had thought of writing about this. I don't wish to hear from him till I can have his account of the lines of Torres Vedras. I care so little how or where I travel, that I am not sure at all whether I shall not come to Lisbon and surprise you, instead of going to Italy by Switzerland; that is, providing the state of Spain will allow me, without any unreasonable danger of my throat, to get from Lisbon to Madrid, and thence to Gibraltar.

---

[1] *Jackie Peartree* had, it seems, been Sir William Rae's nickname at the High School. He probably owed it to some exploit in an orchard.

[2] The Right Honorable Robert Dundas of Arniston, Chief Baron of the Scotch Exchequer, died 17th June, 1819. See *post*, p. 417.

I am determined to roll a little about, for I have lost much of my usual views of summer pleasure here. But I trust we shall have one day the Maid of Lorn (recovered of her lameness), and Charlie Stuart (reconciled to bogs), and Sibyl Grey (no longer retrograde), and the Duke set up by a southern climate, and his military and civil aides-de-camp, with all the rout of younkers and dogs, and a brown hillside, introductory to a good dinner at Bowhill or Drumlanrig, and a merry evening. Amen, and God send it. As to my mouth being stopped with the froth of the title, that is, as the learned Partridge says, a *non sequitur*. You know the schoolboy's expedient of first asking mustard for his beef, and then beef for his mustard. Now, as they put the mustard on my plate, without my asking it, I shall consider myself, time and place serving, as entitled to ask a slice of beef; that is to say, I would do so if I cared much about it; but as it is, I trust it to time and chance, which, as you, dear Adam, know, have (added to the exertions of kind friends) been wonderful allies of mine. People usually wish their letters to come to hand, but I hope you will not receive this in Britain. I am impatient to hear you have sailed. All here are well and hearty. The Baronet[1] and I propose to go up to the Castle to-morrow to fix on the most convenient floor of the Crown House for your mansion, in hopes you will stand treat for gin-grog and Cheshire cheese on your return, to reward our labor. The whole expense will fall within the Treasury order, and it is important to see things made convenient. I will write a long letter to the Duke to Lisbon. Yours ever,   WALTER SCOTT.

P. S. — No news here, but that the goodly hulk of conceit and tallow, which was called Macculloch, of the Royal Hotel, Prince's Street, was put to bed dead-drunk on Wednesday night, and taken out the next morning dead-by-itself-dead. Mair skaith at Sheriffmuir.

[1] Mr. William Clerk.

EDINBURGH, 18th January, 1819.

MY DEAR RICHARDSON, — Many thanks for your kind letter. I own I did mystify Mrs. * * * * a little about the report you mention; and I am glad to hear the finesse succeeded.[1] She came up to me with a great overflow of gratitude for the delight and pleasure, and so forth, which she owed to me on account of these books. Now, as she knew very well that I had never owned myself the author, this was not *polite* politeness, and she had no right to force me up into a corner and compel me to tell her a word more than I chose, upon a subject which concerned no one but myself — and I have no notion of being pumped by any old dowager Lady of Session, male or female. So I gave in dilatory defences, under protestation to add and eik; for I trust, in learning a new slang, you have not forgot the old. In plain words, I denied the charge, and as she insisted to know who else *could* write these novels, I suggested Adam Ferguson as a person having all the information and capacity necessary for that purpose. But the inference that he *was* the author was of her own deducing; and thus ended her attempt, notwithstanding her having primed the pump with a good dose of flattery. It is remarkable, that among all my real friends to whom I did not choose to communicate this matter, not one ever thought it proper or delicate to tease me about it. Respecting the knighthood, I can only say, that coming as it does, and I finding myself and my family in circumstances which will not render the *petit titre* ridiculous, I think there would be more vanity in declining than in accepting what is offered to me by the express wish of the Sovereign as a mark of favor and distinction. Will you be so kind as to inquire and let me know what the fees, etc., of a baronetcy amount to — for I must provide

[1] The wife of one of the Edinburgh Judges is alluded to.

myself accordingly, not knowing exactly when this same title may descend upon me. I am afraid the sauce is rather smart. I should like also to know what is to be done respecting registration of arms and so forth. Will you make these inquiries for me *sotto voce?* I should not suppose, from the persons who sometimes receive this honor, that there is any inquiry about descent or genealogy; mine were decent enough folks, and enjoyed the honor in the seventeenth century, so I shall not be first of the title; and it will sound like that of a Christian knight, as Sir Sidney Smith said.

I had a letter from our immortal Joanna some fortnight since, when I was enjoying myself at Abbotsford. Never was there such a season, flowers springing, birds singing, grubs eating the wheat — as if it was the end of May. After all, nature had a grotesque and inconsistent appearance, and I could not help thinking she resembled a withered beauty who persists in looking youthy, and dressing conform thereto. I thought the loch should have had its blue frozen surface, and russet all about it, instead of an unnatural gayety of green. So much are we the children of habit, that we cannot always enjoy thoroughly the alterations which are most for our advantage. — They have filled up the historical chair here. I own I wish it had been with our friend Campbell, whose genius is such an honor to his country. But he has cast anchor I suppose in the south. Your friend, Mrs. Scott, was much cast down with her brother's death. His bequest to my family leaves my own property much at my own disposal, which is pleasant enough. I was foolish enough sometimes to be vexed at the prospect of my library being sold *sub hasta*, which is now less likely to happen. I always am, most truly yours,   WALTER SCOTT.

On the 15th of February, 1819, Scott witnessed the first representation, on the Edinburgh boards, of the most meritorious and successful of all the *Terryfications*, though Terry himself was not the manufacturer. The drama of Rob Roy will never again be got up so well, in all its parts, as it then was by William Murray's company; the manager's own *Captain Thornton* was excellent — and so was the *Dugald Creature* of a Mr. Duff — there was also a good *Mattie* — (about whose equipment, by the bye, Scott felt such interest that he left his box between the acts to remind Mr. Murray that she "must have a mantle with her lanthorn;") — but the great and unrivalled attraction was the personification of *Bailie Jarvie*, by Charles Mackay, who, being himself a native of Glasgow, entered into the minutest peculiarities of the character with high *gusto*, and gave the west-country dialect in its most racy perfection. It was extremely diverting to watch the play of Scott's features during this admirable realization of his conception; and I must add, that the behavior of the Edinburgh audience on all such occasions, while the secret of the novels was preserved, reflected great honor on their good taste and delicacy of feeling. He seldom, in those days, entered his box without receiving some mark of general respect and admiration; but I never heard of any pretext being laid hold of to connect these demonstrations with the piece he had come to witness, or, in short, to do or say anything likely to interrupt his quiet enjoyment of the evening in the midst of his family and friends. The Rob Roy had a continued run of forty-one nights, during February and March; and it was played once a week, at least, for many years afterwards.[1] Mackay, of course, always selected it for his benefit; — and I now print from Scott's MS. a letter, which, no doubt, reached the mimic Bailie

---

[1] "Between February 15, 1819, and March 14, 1837, *Rob Roy* was played in the Theatre-Royal, Edinburgh, 285 times." — *Letter from Mr. W. Murray.* [Nicol Jarvie remained Mr. Mackay's masterpiece, but his Dominie Sampson and Meg Dods in the dramas founded on *Guy Mannering* and *St. Ronan's Well* were very successful. He died in Glasgow in 1857.]

in the handwriting of one of the Ballantynes, on the first
of these occurrences: —

(*Private.*)

FRIEND MACKAY, — My lawful occasions having
brought me from my residence at Gandercleuch to this
great city, it was my lot to fall into company with certain
friends, who impetrated from me a consent to behold the
stage-play, which hath been framed forth of an history
entitled Rob (*seu potius* Robert) Roy; which history,
although it existeth not in mine erudite work, entitled
Tales of my Landlord, hath nathless a near relation in
style and structure to those pleasant narrations. Wherefore, having surmounted those arguments whilk were
founded upon the unseemliness of a personage in my
place and profession appearing in an open stage-play
house, and having buttoned the teminations of my cravat
into my bosom, in order to preserve mine incognito, and
indued an outer coat over mine usual garments, so that
the hue thereof might not betray my calling, I did place
myself (much elbowed by those who little knew whom
they did incommode) in that place of the Theatre called
the two-shilling gallery, and beheld the show with great
delectation, even from the rising of the curtain to the
fall thereof.

Chiefly, my facetious friend, was I enamored of the
very lively representation of Bailie Nicol Jarvie, in so
much that I became desirous to communicate to thee my
great admiration thereof, nothing doubting that it will
give thee satisfaction to be apprised of the same. Yet
further, in case thou shouldst be of that numerous class
of persons who set less store by good words than good
deeds, and understanding that there is assigned unto
each stage-player a special night, called a benefit (it will
do thee no harm to know that the phrase cometh from
two Latin words, *bene* and *facio*), on which their friends

and patrons show forth their benevolence, I now send thee mine in the form of a five-ell web (*hoc jocose*, to express a note for £5), as a meet present for the Bailie, himself a weaver, and the son of a worthy deacon of that craft. The which propine I send thee in token that it is my purpose, business and health permitting, to occupy the central place of the pit on the night of thy said beneficiary or benefit.

Friend Mackay! from one, whose profession it is to teach others, thou must excuse the freedom of a caution. I trust thou wilt remember that, as excellence in thine art cannot be attained without much labor, so neither can it be extended, or even maintained, without constant and unremitted exertion; and further, that the decorum of a performer's private character (and it gladdeth me to hear that thine is respectable) addeth not a little to the value of his public exertions.

Finally, in respect there is nothing perfect in this world, — at least I have never received a wholly faultless version from the very best of my pupils — I pray thee not to let Rob Roy twirl thee around in the ecstasy of thy joy, in regard it oversteps the limits of nature, which otherwise thou so sedulously preservest in thine admirable national portraiture of Bailie Nicol Jarvie. — I remain thy since e friend and well-wisher,

JEDEDIAH CLEISHBOTHAM.

CHAPTER XLIV

RECURRENCE OF SCOTT'S ILLNESS. — DEATH OF THE
DUKE OF BUCCLEUCH. — LETTERS TO CAPTAIN FER-
GUSON, LORD MONTAGU, MR. SOUTHEY, AND MR.
SHORTREED. — SCOTT'S SUFFERINGS WHILE DICTATING
THE BRIDE OF LAMMERMOOR. — ANECDOTES BY
JAMES BALLANTYNE, ETC. — APPEARANCE OF THE
THIRD SERIES OF TALES OF MY LANDLORD. — ANEC-
DOTE OF THE EARL OF BUCHAN

1819

IT had been Scott's purpose to spend the Easter vacation in London, and receive his baronetcy; but this was
prevented by the serious recurrence of the malady which
so much alarmed his friends in the early part of the year
1817, and which had continued ever since to torment him
at intervals. The subsequent correspondence will show
that afflictions of various sorts were accumulated on his
head at the same period: —

TO THE LORD MONTAGU, DITTON PARK, WINDSOR.

EDINBURGH, 4th March, 1819.

MY DEAR LORD, — The Lord President tells me he
has a letter from his son, Captain Charles Hope, R. N.,
who had just taken leave of our High Chief, upon the
deck of the Liffey. He had not seen the Duke for a
fortnight, and was pleasingly surprised to find his health
and general appearance so very much improved. For my
part, having watched him with such unremitting attention, I feel very confident in the effect of a change of air
and of climate. It is with great pleasure that I find the

Duke has received an answer from me respecting a matter about which he was anxious, and on which I could make his mind quite easy. His Grace wished Adam Ferguson to assist him as his confidential secretary; and with all the scrupulous delicacy that belongs to his character, he did not like to propose this, except through my medium as a common friend. Now, I can answer for Adam, as I can for myself, that he will have the highest pleasure in giving assistance in every possible way the Duke can desire; and if forty years' intimacy can entitle one man to speak for another, I believe the Duke can find nowhere a person so highly qualified for such a confidential situation. He was educated for business, understands it well, and was long a military secretary; — his temper and manners your Lordship can judge as well as I can, and his worth and honor are of the very first water. I confess I should not be surprised if the Duke should wish to continue the connection even afterwards, for I have often thought that two hours' letter-writing, which is his Grace's daily allowance, is rather worse than the duty of a Clerk of Session, because there is no vacation. Much of this might surely be saved by an intelligent friend, on whose style of expression, prudence, and secrecy, his Grace could put perfect reliance. Two words marked on any letter by his own hand would enable such a person to refuse more or less positively — to grant directly or conditionally — or, in short, to maintain the exterior forms of the very troublesome and extensive correspondence which his Grace's high situation entails upon him. I think it is Monsieur le Duc de Saint-Simon who tells us of one of Louis XIV.'s ministers *qu'il avoit la plume* — which he explains by saying that it was his duty to imitate the King's handwriting so closely, as to be almost undistinguishable, and make him on all occasions *parler très noblement*. I wonder how the Duke gets on without such a friend. In the mean time, however, I am glad I can assure him of Ferguson's willing and ready assistance while abroad; and I am happy to find still further that he had got that assurance before they sailed, for tedious hours occur on board of ship, when it will serve as a relief to talk over any of the private affairs which the Duke wishes to entrust to him.

I have been very unwell from a visitation of my old enemy, the cramp in my stomach, which much resembles, as I conceive, the process by which *the deil* would make one's *king's-hood* into a *spleuchan*,[1] according to the anathema of Burns. Unfortunately, the opiates which the medical people think indispensable to relieve spasms, bring on a habit of body which has to be counteracted by medicines of a different tendency, so as to produce a most disagreeable see-saw — a kind of pull-devil, pull-baker contention, the field of battle being my unfortunate *præcordia*. I am better to-day, and I trust shall be able to dispense with these alternations. I still hope to be in London in April.

I will write to the Duke regularly, for distance of place acts in a contrary ratio on the mind and on the eye: trifles, instead of being diminished, as in prospect, become important and interesting, and therefore he shall have a budget of them. Hogg is here busy with his Jacobite songs. I wish he may get handsomely through, for he is profoundly ignorant of history, and it is an awkward thing to read in order that you may write.[2] I give him all the help I can, but he sometimes poses me. For instance, he came yesterday, open mouth, inquiring

---

[1] *King's-Hood* — " The second of the four stomachs of ruminating animals." JAMIESON. — *Spleuchan* — The Gaelic name of the Highlander's tobacco-pouch.

[2] " I am sure I produced two volumes of Jacobite Relics, such as no man in Scotland or England could have produced but myself." So says Hogg, *ipse* — see his *Autobiography*, 1832, p. 88. I never saw the Shepherd so elated as he was on the appearance of a very severe article on this book in the *Edinburgh Review;* for, to his exquisite delight, the hostile critic selected for *exceptive* encomium one " old Jacobite strain," namely, *Donald M'Gillavry*, which Hogg had fabricated the year before. Scott, too, enjoyed this joke almost as much as the Shepherd.

what great dignified clergyman had distinguished himself at Killiecrankie — not exactly the scene where one would have expected a churchman to shine — and I found, with some difficulty, that he had mistaken Major-General Canon, called, in Kennedy's Latin Song, *Canonicus Gallovidiensis*, for the canon of a cathedral. *Ex ungue leonem.* Ever, my dear Lord, your truly obliged and faithful   WALTER SCOTT.

Before this letter reached Lord Montagu, his brother had sailed for Lisbon. The Duke of Wellington had placed his house in that capital (the Palace *das Necessidades*) at the Duke of Buccleuch's disposal; and in the affectionate care and cheerful society of Captain Ferguson, the invalid had every additional source of comfort that his friends could have wished for him. But the malady had gone too far to be arrested by a change of climate; and the letter which he had addressed to Scott, when about to embark at Portsmouth, is endorsed with these words: "*The last I ever received from my dear friend the Duke of Buccleuch. — Alas! alas!*" The principal object of this letter was to remind Scott of his promise to sit to Raeburn for a portrait, to be hung up in that favorite residence where the Duke had enjoyed most of his society. "My prodigious undertaking," writes his Grace, "of a west wing at Bowhill, is begun. A library of forty-one feet by twenty-one is to be added to the present drawing-room. A space for one picture is reserved over the fireplace, and in this warm situation I intend to place the Guardian of Literature. I should be happy to have my friend Maida appear. It is now almost proverbial, ' Walter Scott and his Dog.' Raeburn should be warned that I am as well acquainted with my friend's hands and arms as with his nose — and Vandyke was of my opinion. Many of R.'s works are shamefully finished — the face studied, but everything else neglected. This is a fair opportunity of producing something really worthy of his skill."

I shall insert by and by Scott's answer — which never reached the Duke's hand — with another letter of the same date to Captain Ferguson; but I must first introduce one, addressed a fortnight earlier to Mr. Southey, who had been distressed by the accounts he received of Scott's health from an American traveller, Mr. George Ticknor of Boston — a friend, and worthy to be such, of Mr. Washington Irving.[1] The Poet Laureate, by the way, had adverted also to an impudent trick of a London bookseller, who shortly before this time announced certain volumes of Grub Street manufacture, as "A New Series of the Tales of my Landlord," and who, when John Ballantyne, as the "agent for the Author of Waverley," published a declaration that the volumes thus advertised were not from that writer's pen, met John's declaration by an audacious rejoinder — impeaching his authority, and asserting that nothing but the personal appearance in the field of the gentleman for whom Ballantyne pretended to act, could shake his belief that he was himself in the confidence of the true Simon Pure.[2] This affair gave considerable uneasiness at the time, and for a moment the dropping of Scott's mask seems to have been pronounced advisable by both Ballantyne and Constable. But he was not to be worked upon by such means as these. He calmly replied, "The author who lends himself to such a trick must be a blockhead — let them publish, and that will serve our purpose

[1] [In *The Life, Letters, and Journals of George Ticknor* will be found some interesting notes regarding his visits to Castle Street, and two days spent at Abbotsford in March, 1819.]

[2] June, 1839. — A friend has sent me the following advertisement from an Edinburgh newspaper of 1819 : —

TALES OF MY LANDLORD.

"The Public are respectfully informed, that the Work announced for publication under the title of ' TALES OF MY LANDLORD, Fourth Series, containing *Pontefract Castle*,' is not written by the Author of the First, Second, and Third Series of TALES OF MY LANDLORD, of which we are the Proprietors and Publishers.

ARCHIBALD CONSTABLE & Co."

better than anything we ourselves could do." I have forgotten the names of the "tales," which, being published accordingly, fell still-born from the press. Mr. Southey had likewise dropped some allusions to another newspaper story of Scott's being seriously engaged in a dramatic work — a rumor which probably originated in the assistance he had lent to Terry in some of the recent highly popular adaptations of his novels to the purposes of the stage; though it is not impossible that some hint of the *Devorgoil* matter may have transpired. "It is reported," said the Laureate, "that you are about to bring forth a play, and I am greatly in hopes it may be true; for I am verily persuaded that in this course you might run as brilliant a career as you have already done in narrative — both in prose and rhyme; — for as for believing that you have a double in the field — not I! Those same powers would be equally certain of success in the drama, and were you to give them a dramatic direction, and reign for a third seven years upon the stage, you would stand alone in literary history. Indeed already I believe that no man ever afforded so much delight to so great a number of his contemporaries in this or in any other country. God bless you, my dear Scott, and believe me ever yours affectionately, R. S." Mr. Southey's letter had further announced his wife's safe delivery of a son; the approach of the conclusion of his History of Brazil; and his undertaking of the Life of Wesley.

TO ROBERT SOUTHEY, ESQ., KESWICK.

ABBOTSFORD, 4th April, 1819.

MY DEAR SOUTHEY, — Tidings from you must be always acceptable, even were the bowl in the act of breaking at the fountain — and my health is at present very *totterish*. I have gone through a cruel succession of spasms and sickness, which have terminated in a special fit of the jaundice, so that I might sit for the image of

Plutus, the god of specie, so far as complexion goes. I shall like our American acquaintance the better that he has sharpened your remembrance of me, but he is also a wondrous fellow for romantic lore and antiquarian research, considering his country. I have now seen four or five well-lettered Americans, ardent in pursuit of knowledge, and free from the ignorance and forward presumption which distinguish many of their country-men. I hope they will inoculate their country with a love of letters, so nearly allied to a desire of peace and a sense of public justice — virtues to which the great Transatlantic community is more strange than could be wished. Accept my best and most sincere wishes for the health and strength of your latest pledge of affection. When I think what you have already suffered, I can imagine with what mixture of feelings this event must necessarily affect you; but you need not to be told that we are in better guidance than our own. I trust in God this late blessing will be permanent, and inherit your talents and virtues. When I look around me, and see how many men seem to make it their pride to misuse high qualifications, can I be less interested than I truly am in the fate of one who has uniformly dedicated his splendid powers to maintaining the best interests of hu-manity? I am very angry at the time you are to be in London, as I must be there in about a fortnight, or so soon as I can shake off this depressing complaint, and it would add not a little that I should meet you there. My chief purpose is to put my eldest son into the army. I could have wished he had chosen another profession, but have no title to combat a choice which would have been my own had my lameness permitted. Walter has appar-ently the dispositions and habits fitted for the military profession, a very quiet and steady temper, an attach-ment to mathematics and their application, good sense, and uncommon personal strength and activity, with ad-dress in most exercises, particularly horsemanship.

— I had written thus far last week when I was interrupted, first by the arrival of our friend Ticknor with Mr. Cogswell, another well-accomplished Yankee — (by the bye, we have them of all sorts, *e. g.*, one Mr. * * * *, rather a fine man, whom the girls have christened, with some humor, the Yankee Doodle *Dandie*). They have had Tom Drum's entertainment, for I have been seized with one or two successive *crises* of my cruel malady, lasting in the utmost anguish from eight to ten hours. If I had not the strength of a team of horses, I could never have fought through it, and through the heavy fire of medical artillery, scarce less exhausting — for bleeding, blistering, calomel, and ipecacuanha have gone on without intermission — while, during the agony of the spasms, laudanum became necessary in the most liberal doses, though inconsistent with the general treatment. I did not lose my senses, because I resolved to keep them, but I thought once or twice they would have gone overboard, top and top-gallant. I should be a great fool, and a most ungrateful wretch, to complain of such inflictions as these. My life has been, in all its private and public relations, as fortunate perhaps as was ever lived, up to this period; and whether pain or misfortune may lie behind the dark curtain of futurity, I am already a sufficient debtor to the bounty of Providence to be resigned to it. Fear is an evil that has never mixed with my nature, nor has even unwonted good fortune rendered my love of life tenacious; and so I can look forward to the possible conclusion of these scenes of agony with reasonable equanimity, and suffer chiefly through the sympathetic distress of my family.

— Other ten days have passed away, for I would not send this Jeremiad to tease you, while its termination seemed doubtful. For the present,

> " The game is done — I 've won, I 've won,
> Quoth she, and whistles thrice." [1]

---

[1] These lines are from Coleridge's *Ancient Mariner.*

I am this day, for the first time, free from the relics of
my disorder, and, except in point of weakness, perfectly
well. But no broken-down hunter had ever so many
sprung sinews, whelks, and bruises. I am like Sancho
after the doughty affair of the Yanguesian Carriers,
and all through the unnatural twisting of the muscles
under the influence of that *Goule*, the cramp. I must
be swathed in Goulard and Rosemary spirits — *probatum
est*.

I shall not fine and renew a lease of popularity upon
the theatre. To write for low, ill-informed, and conceited actors, whom you must please, for your success is
necessarily at their mercy, I cannot away with. How
would you, or how do you think I should relish being
the object of such a letter as Kean[1] wrote t'other day to
a poor author, who, though a pedantic blockhead, had at
least the right to be treated as a gentleman by a copper-
laced, twopenny tearmouth, rendered mad by conceit and
success? Besides, if this objection were out of the way,
I do not think the character of the audience in London
is such that one could have the least pleasure in pleasing
them. One half come to prosecute their debaucheries,
so openly that it would degrade a bagnio. Another set
to snooze off their beef-steaks and port wine; a third are
critics of the fourth column of the newspaper; fashion,
wit, or literature, there is not; and, on the whole, I
would far rather write verses for mine honest friend
Punch and his audience. The only thing that could
tempt me to be so silly, would be to assist a friend in
such a degrading task who was to have the whole profit
and shame of it.

Have you seen decidedly the most full and methodized
collection of Spanish romances (ballads) published by
the industry of Depping (Altenburgh and Leipsic),

---

[1] The reader will find something about this actor's quarrel with Mr.
Bucke, author of *The Italians*, in Barry Cornwall's *Life of Kean*, vol. ii.
p. 178.

1817? It is quite delightful. Ticknor had set me agog to see it, without affording me any hope it could be had in London, when by one of these fortunate chances which have often marked my life, a friend, who had been lately on the Continent, came unexpectedly to inquire for me, and plucked it forth *par manière de cadeau*. God prosper you, my dear Southey, in your labors; but do not work too hard — *experto crede*. This conclusion, as well as the confusion of my letter, like the Bishop of Grenada's sermon, savors of the apoplexy. My most respectful compliments attend Mrs. S. Yours truly,

WALTER SCOTT.

P. S. — I shall long to see the conclusion of the Brazil history, which, as the interest comes nearer, must rise even above the last noble volume. Wesley you alone can touch; but will you not have the hive about you? When I was about twelve years old, I heard him preach more than once, standing on a chair, in Kelso churchyard. He was a most venerable figure, but his sermons were vastly too colloquial for the taste of Saunders. He told many excellent stories. One I remember, which he said had happened to him at Edinburgh. "A drunken dragoon," said Wesley, "was commencing an assertion in military fashion, G—d eternally d—n me, just as I was passing. I touched the poor man on the shoulder, and when he turned round fiercely, said calmly, you mean *God bless you*." In the mode of telling the story he failed not to make us sensible how much his patriarchal appearance, and mild yet bold rebuke, overawed the soldier, who touched his hat, thanked him, and, I think, came to chapel that evening.

TO ROBERT SHORTREED, ESQ.. SHERIFF-SUBSTITUTE, ETC.,
JEDBURGH.

ABBOTSFORD, 13th April, 1819.

DEAR BOB, — I am very desirous to procure, and as soon as possible, Mrs. Shortreed's excellent receipt for making yeast. The Duke of Buccleuch complains extremely of the sour yeast at Lisbon as disagreeing with his stomach, and I never tasted half such good bread as Mrs. Shortreed has baked at home. I am sure you will be as anxious as I am that the receipt should be forwarded to his Grace as soon as possible. I remember Mrs. Shortreed giving a most distinct account of the whole affair. It should be copied over in a very distinct hand, lest Monsieur Florence makes blunders.

I am recovering from my late indisposition, but as weak as water. To write these lines is a fatigue. I scarce think I can be at the circuit at all — certainly only for an hour or two. So on this occasion I will give Mrs. Shortreed's kind hospitality a little breathing time. I am tired even with writing these few lines. Yours ever,   WALTER SCOTT.[1]

TO HIS GRACE THE DUKE OF BUCCLEUCH, ETC., LISBON.

ABBOTSFORD, 15th April, 1819.

MY DEAR LORD DUKE, — How very strange it seems that this should be the first letter I address to your Grace, and you so long absent from Scotland, and looking for all the news and nonsense of which I am in general such a faithful reporter. Alas, I have been ill — very — very ill — only Dr. Baillie says there is nothing of consequence about my malady *except the pain* — a pretty exception — said pain being intense enough to keep me roaring as loud as your Grace's *ci-devant* John of Lorn, and of, generally speaking, from six to eight hours' incessant duration, only varied by intervals of deadly sickness. Poor Sophia was alone with me for some time, and managed a half-distracted pack of servants with spirit, and sense, and presence of mind, far

---

[1] "Sir Walter got not only the recipe for making bread from us — but likewise learnt the best mode of cutting it ' in a family way.' The breadboard and large knife used at Abbotsford at breakfast-time were adopted by Sir Walter. after seeing them ' work well ' in our family." — *Note by Mr. Andrew Shortreed.*

beyond her years, never suffering her terror at seeing me in a state so new to her, and so alarming, to divert her mind an instant from what was fit and proper to be done. Pardon this side compliment to your Grace's little Jacobite, to whom you have always been so kind. If sympathy could have cured me, I should not have been long ill. Gentle and simple were all equally kind, and even old Tom Watson crept down from Falshope to see how I was coming on, and to ejaculate "if anything ailed the Shirra, it would be sair on the Duke." The only unwelcome resurrection was that of old * * * *, whose feud with me (or rather dryness) I had well hoped was immortal; but he came jinking over the moor with daughters and ponies, and God knows what, to look after my precious health. I cannot tolerate that man; it seems to me as if I hated him for things not only past and present, but for some future offence, which is as yet in the womb of fate.

I have had as many remedies sent me for cramp and jaundice as would set up a quack doctor: three from Mrs. Plummer, each better than the other — one at least from every gardener in the neighborhood — besides all sorts of recommendations to go to Cheltenham, to Harrowgate, to Jericho for aught I know. Now if there is one thing I detest more than another, it is a watering-place, unless a very pleasant party be previously formed, when, as Tony Lumpkin says, "a gentleman may be in a concatenation." The most extraordinary recipe was that of my Highland piper, John Bruce, who spent a whole Sunday in selecting twelve stones from twelve *south-running* streams, with the purpose that I should sleep upon them, and be whole. I caused him to be told that the recipe was infallible, but that it was absolutely necessary to success that the stones should be wrapt up in the petticoat of a widow who had never wished to marry again; upon which the piper renounced all hope of completing the charm. I had need of a softer couch

than Bruce had destined me, for so general was the ten-
sion of the nerves all over the body, although the pain
of the spasms in the stomach did not suffer the others to
be felt, that my whole left leg was covered with swelling
and inflammation, arising from the unnatural action of
the muscles, and I had to be carried about like a child.
My right leg escaped better, the muscles there having
less irritability, owing to its lame state. Your Grace
may imagine the energy of pain in the nobler parts, when
cramps in the extremities, sufficient to produce such
effects, were unnoticed by me during their existence.
But enough of so disagreeable a subject.

Respecting the portrait, I shall be equally proud and
happy to sit for it, and hope it may be so executed as to
be in some degree worthy of the preferment to which it
is destined.[1] But neither my late golden hue (for I was
covered with jaundice), nor my present silver complexion
(looking much more like a spectre than a man), will present any idea of my quondam beef-eating physiognomy.
I must wait till the *age of brass*, the true juridical bronze
of my profession, shall again appear on my frontal. I
hesitate a little about Raeburn, unless your Grace is
quite determined. He has very much to do; works just
now chiefly for cash, poor fellow, as he can have but a
few years to make money; and has twice already made
a very chowder-headed person of me. I should like
much (always with your approbation) to try Allan, who
is a man of real genius, and has made one or two glorious
portraits, though his predilection is to the historical
branch of the art. We did rather a handsome thing for
him, considering that in Edinburgh we are neither very
wealthy nor great amateurs. A hundred persons subscribed ten guineas apiece to raffle[2] for his fine picture

---

[1] The position in the Library at Bowhill, originally destined by the late
Duke of Buccleuch for a portrait that never was executed, is now filled
by that which Raeburn painted in 1808 for Constable.

[2] Three pictures were ultimately raffled for; and the following note,

of the Circassian Chief selling Slaves to the Turkish Pacha — a beautiful and highly poetical picture. There was another small picture added by way of second prize, and, what is curious enough, the only two peers on the list, Lord Wemyss and Lord Fife, both got prizes. Allan has made a sketch which I shall take to town with me when I can go, in hopes Lord Stafford, or some other picture-buyer, may fancy it, and order a picture. The subject is the murder of Archbishop Sharp on Magus Moor, prodigiously well treated. The savage ferocity of the assassins, crowding one on another to strike at the old prelate on his knees — contrasted with the old man's figure — and that of his daughter endeavoring to interpose for his protection, and withheld by a ruffian of milder mood than his fellows: — the dogged fanatical severity of Rathillet's countenance, who remained on

dated April the 1st, 1819, shows how keenly and practically Scott, almost in the crisis of his malady, could attend to the details of such a business: —

TO J. G. LOCKHART, ESQ., ADVOCATE, EDINBURGH.

. . . I have been dreadfully ill since I wrote to you, but I think I have now got the turn fairly. It was quite time, for though the doctors say the disease is not dangerous, yet I could not have endured six days more agony. I have a summons from the ingenious Mr. David Bridges to attend to my interests at his shop next Saturday, or send some qualified person to act on my behalf. I suppose that this mysterious missive alludes to the plan about Allan's pictures, and at any rate I hope you will act for me. I should think a raffle with dice would give more general satisfaction than a lottery. You would be astonished what unhandsome suspicions well-educated and sensible persons will take into their heads, when a selfish competition awakens the mean and evil passions of our nature. Let each subscriber throw the dice in person or by proxy, leaving out all who throw under a certain number, and let this be repeated till the number is so far reduced that the three who throw highest may hold the prizes. I have much to say to you, and should you spare me a day about the end of next week, I trust you will find me pretty *bobbish*.

Always yours affectionately,

W. S.

The Mr. David Bridges here mentioned has occurred already. — See *ante*, p. 262. The jokers in *Blackwood* made him happy by dubbing him, "The Director-General of the Fine Arts for Scotland." — He says the subscribers for the Allan-Raffle were not so numerous as Scott had supposed. (Mr. Bridges died in November, 184·), in his 64th year.)

horseback, witnessing, with stern fanaticism, the murder
he did not choose to be active in, lest it should be said
that he struck out of private revenge — are all amazingly
well combined in the sketch. I question if the artist can
bring them out with equal spirit in the painting which
he meditates.[1] Sketches give a sort of fire to the imagination of the spectator, who is apt to fancy a great deal
more for himself, than the pencil, in the finished picture,
can possibly present to his eye afterwards. — Constable
has offered Allan three hundred pounds to make sketches
for an edition of the Tales of my Landlord, and other
novels of that cycle, and says he will give him the same
sum next year, so, from being pinched enough, this very
deserving artist suddenly finds himself at his ease. He
was long at Odessa with the Duke of Richelieu, and is
a very entertaining person.

I saw with great pleasure Wilkie's sketch of your
Grace, and I think when I get to town I shall coax him
out of a copy, to me invaluable. I hope, however, when
you return, you will sit to Lawrence. We should have
at least one picture of your Grace from the real good
hand. Sooth to speak, I cannot say much for the juvenile representations at Bowhill and in the library at
Dalkeith. Return, however, with the original features
in good health, and we shall not worry you about portraits. The library at Bowhill will be a delightful room,
and will be some consolation to me who must, I fear, lose
for some time the comforts of the eating-room, and sub-
stitute panada and toast and water for the bonny haunch
and buxom bottle of claret. Truth is, I must make
great restrictions on my creature-comforts, at least till
my stomach recovers its tone and ostrich-like capacity of
digestion. Our spring here is slow, but not unfavorable: the country looking very well, and my plantings
for the season quite completed. I have planted quite up

---

[1] The fine picture which Allan executed is in the possession of Mr.
Lockhart of Milton-Lockhart, and has been well engraved.

two little glens, leading from the Aide-de-Camp's habitation up to the little loch, and expect the blessings of posterity for the shade and shelter I shall leave, where, God knows, I found none.

It is doomed this letter is not to close without a request. I conclude your Grace has already heard from fifty applicants that the kirk of Middlebie is vacant, and I come forward as the fifty-first (always barring prior engagements and better claims) in behalf of George Thomson, a son of the minister of Melrose, being the grinder of my boys, and therefore deeply entitled to my gratitude and my good offices, as far as they can go. He is nearer Parson Abraham Adams than any living creature I ever saw — very learned, very religious, very simple, and extremely absent. His father, till very lately, had but a sort of half stipend, during the incumbency of a certain notorious Mr. MacLagan, to whom he acted only as assistant. The poor devil was brought to the grindstone (having had the want of precaution to beget a large family), and became the very figure of a fellow who used to come upon the stage to sing "Let us all be unhappy together." This poor lad George was his saving angel, not only educating himself, but taking on him the education of two of his brothers, and maintaining them out of his own scanty pittance. He is a sensible lad, and by no means a bad preacher, a stanch Anti-Gallican, and orthodox in his principles. Should your Grace find yourself at liberty to give countenance to this very innocent and deserving creature, I need not say it will add to the many favors you have conferred on me; but I hope the parishioners will have also occasion to say, "Weel bobbit, George of Middlebie." Your Grace's Aide-de-Camp, who knows young Thomson well, will give you a better idea of him than I can do. He lost a leg by an accident in his boyhood, which spoiled as bold and fine-looking a grenadier as ever charged bayonet against a Frenchman's throat. I think your Grace will not like him the worse for having a spice of military and loyal spirit about him. If you knew the poor fellow, your Grace would take uncommon interest in him, were it but for the odd mixture of sense and simplicity, and spirit and good morals. Somewhat too much of him.

I conclude you will go to Mafra, Cintra, or some of these places, which Baretti describes so delightfully, to avoid the great heats, when the Palace de las Necessidades must become rather oppressive. By the bye, though it were only for the credit of the name, I am happy to learn it has that useful English comfort, a water-closet. I suppose the armorer of the Liffey has already put it in complete repair. Your Grace sees the most secret passages respecting great men cannot be hidden from their friends. There is but little news here but death in the clan. Harden's sister is dead — a cruel blow to Lady Die,[1] who is upwards of eighty-five, and accustomed to no other society. Again, Mrs. Frank Scott, his uncle's widow, is dead, unable to survive the loss of two fine young men in India, her sons, whose death closely followed each other. All this is sad work; but it is a wicked and melancholy world we live in. God bless you, my dear, dear Lord. Take great care of your health for the sake of all of us. You are the breath of our nostrils, useful to thousands, and to many of these thousands indispensable. I will write again very soon, when I can keep my breast longer to the desk without pain, for I am not yet without frequent relapses, when they souse me into scalding water without a moment's delay, where I lie, as my old *grieve* Tom Purdie said last night, being called to assist at the operation, "like a *haulded saumon*." I write a few lines to the Aide-de-Camp, but I am afraid of putting this letter beyond the bounds of Lord Montagu's frank. When I can do anything for your Grace here, you know I am most

[1] See *ante*, vol. i. p. 230.

pleased and happy. — Ever respectfully and affectionately your Grace's　　WALTER SCOTT.

TO CAPTAIN ADAM FERGUSON, ETC., ETC., ETC.

ABBOTSFORD, April 16, 1819.

MY DEAR ADAM, — Having only been able last night
to finish a long letter to the Chief, I now add a few lines
for the Aide-de-Camp. I have had the pleasure to hear
of you regularly from Jack,[1] who is very regular in steer-
ing this way when packets arrive; and I observe with
great satisfaction that you think our good Duke's health
is on the mending hand. Climate must operate as an
alterative, and much cannot perhaps be expected from it
at first. Besides, the great heat must be a serious draw-
back. But I hope you will try by and by to get away to
Cintra, or some of those sequestered retreats where there
are shades and cascades to cool the air. I have an idea
the country there is eminently beautiful. I am afraid
the Duke has not yet been able to visit Torres Vedras,
but *you* must be meeting with things everywhere to put
you in mind of former scenes. As for the Senhoras, I
have little doubt that the difference betwixt your military
hard fare and Florence's high sauces and jellies will
make them think that time has rather improved an old
friend than otherwise. Apropos of these ticklish subjects. I am a suitor to the Duke, with little expectation
of success (for I know his engagements), for the kirk of
Middlebie to George Thomson, the very Abraham Adams
of Presbytery. If the Duke mentions him to you (not
otherwise) pray lend him a lift. With a kirk and a
manse the poor fellow might get a good farmer's daughter, and beget grenadiers for his Majesty's service. But
as I said before, I dare say all St. Hubert's black pack
are in full cry upon the living, and that he has little or
no chance. It is something, however, to have tabled
him, as better may come of it another day.

[1] Captain John Ferguson, R. N.

All at Huntly Burn well and hearty, and most kind in their attentions during our late turmoils. Bauby [1] came over to offer her services as sick-nurse, and I have drunk scarce anything but delicious ginger-beer of Miss Bell's brewing, since my troubles commenced. They have been, to say the least, damnable; and I think you would hardly know me. When I crawl out on Sibyl Grey, I am the very image of Death on the pale horse — lanthorn-jawed, decayed in flesh, stooping as if I meant to eat the pony's ears, and unable to go above a footpace. But although I have had, and must expect, frequent relapses, yet the attacks are more slight, and I trust I shall mend with the good weather. Spring sets in very pleasantly, and in a settled fashion. I have planted a number of shrubs, etc., at Huntly Burn, and am snodding up the drive of the old farmhouse, enclosing the Toftfield, and making a good road from the parish road to your gate. This I tell you to animate you to pick up a few seeds both of forest trees, shrubs, and vegetables; we will rear them in the hot-house, and divide honorably. *Avis au lecteur.* I have been a good deal entrusted to the care of Sophia, who is an admirable sick-nurse. Mamma has been called to town by two important avocations: to get a cook — no joking matter, — and to see Charles, who was but indifferent, but has recovered. You must have heard of the death of Joseph Hume, David's only son. Christ! what a calamity! — just entering life with the fairest prospects — full of talent, and the heir of an old and considerable family — a fine career before him: all this he was one day, or rather one hour — or rather in the course of five minutes — so sudden was the death — and then — a heap of earth. His disease is unknown; something about the heart, I believe; but it had no alarming appearance, nothing worse than a cold and sore throat, when convulsions came, and death ensued. It is

[1] Bauby — *i. e.*, Barbara, was a kind old housekeeper of the Miss Fergusons.

a complete smash to poor David, who had just begun to hold his head up after his wife's death. But he bears it stoutly, and goes about his business as usual. A woeful case. London is now out of the question with me; I have no prospect of being now able to stand the journey by sea or land; but the best is, I have no pressing business there. The Commie [1] takes charge of Walter's matters — cannot, you know, be in better hands; and Lord Melville talks of gazetting *quam primum.* I will write a long letter very soon, but my back, fingers, and eyes ache with these three pages. All here send love and fraternity. Yours ever most truly,

WALTER SCOTT.

P. S. — By the bye, old Kennedy, the tinker, swam for his life at Jedburgh, and was only, by the sophisticated and timid evidence of a seceding doctor, who differed from all his brethren, saved from a well-deserved gibbet. He goes to botanize for fourteen years. Pray tell this to the Duke, for he was

> "An old soldier of the Duke's,
> And the Duke's old soldier."

Six of his brethren, I am told, were in court, and kith and kin without end. I am sorry so many of the clan are left. The cause of quarrel with the murdered man was an old feud between two gypsy clans, the Kennedies and Irvings, which, about forty years since, gave rise to a desperate quarrel and battle on Hawick Green, in which the grandfathers of both Kennedy, and Irving whom he murdered, were engaged.

In the next of these letters there is allusion to a drama, on the story of The Heart of Mid-Lothian, of which Mr. Terry had transmitted the MS. to Abbotsford — and which ultimately proved very successful. Terry had, shortly before this time, become the acting manager of the Haymarket Theatre.

[1] The Lord Chief-Commissioner Adam.

ABBOTSFORD, 18th April, 1819.

DEAR TERRY, — I am able (though very weak) to answer your kind inquiries. I have thought of you often, and been on the point of writing or dictating a letter, but till very lately I could have had little to tell you of but distress and agony, with constant relapses into my unhappy malady, so that for weeks I seemed to lose rather than gain ground, all food nauseating on my stomach, and my clothes hanging about me like a potato-bogle,[1] with from five or six to ten hours of mortal pain every third day; latterly the fits have been much milder, and have at last given way to the hot bath without any use of opiates; an immense point gained, as they hurt my general health extremely. Conceive my having taken, in the course of six or seven hours, six grains of opium, three of hyoscyamus, near 200 drops of laudanum — and all without any sensible relief of the agony under which I labored. My stomach is now getting confirmed, and I have great hopes the bout is over; it has been a dreadful set-to. I am sorry to hear Mrs. Terry is complaining; you ought not to let her labor, neither at Abbotsford sketches nor at anything else, but to study to keep her mind amused as much as possible. As for Walter, he is a shoot of an *Aik*,[2] and I have no fear of him: I hope he remembers Abbotsford and his soldier namesake.

I send the MS. — I wish you had written for it earlier. My touching, or even thinking of it, was out of the question; my corrections would have smelled as cruelly of the cramp as the Bishop of Grenada's homily did of the apoplexy. Indeed I hold myself inadequate to estimate those criticisms which rest on stage effect, having been of late very little of a play-going person. Would to Heaven these sheets could do for you what

[1] *Anglice* — Scarecrow.   [2] *Anglice* — an Oak.

Rob Roy has done for Murray; he has absolutely netted upwards of £3000: to be sure, the man who played the Bailie made a piece of acting equal to whatever has been seen in the profession. For my own part, I was actually electrified by the truth, spirit, and humor which he threw into the part. It was the living Nicol Jarvie: conceited, pragmatical, cautious, generous, proud of his connection with Rob Roy, frightened for him at the same time, and yet extremely desirous to interfere with him as an adviser: the tone in which he seemed to give him up for a lost man after having provoked him into some burst of Highland violence, "Ah Rab! Rab!" was quite inimitable. I do assure you I never saw a thing better played. It is like it may be his only part, for no doubt the Patavinity and knowledge of the provincial character may have aided him much; but still he must be a wonderful fellow; and the houses he drew were tremendous.

I am truly glad you are settled in London — "a rolling stone" — "the proverb is something musty:"[1] it is always difficult to begin a new profession; I could have wished you quartered nearer us, but we shall always hear of you. The becoming stage-manager at the Haymarket I look upon as a great step: well executed, it cannot but lead to something of the same kind elsewhere. You must be aware of stumbling over a propensity which easily besets you from the habit of not having your time fully employed — I mean what the women very expressively call *dawdling*. Your motto must be *Hoc age*. Do instantly whatever is to be done, and take the hours of reflection or recreation after business, and never before it. When a regiment is under march, the rear is often thrown into confusion because the front do not move steadily and without interruption. It is the same thing with business. If that which is first in hand is not instantly, steadily, and regularly despatched, other things accumulate behind till affairs begin to press all at once,

---

[1] *Hamlet*, Act III. Scene 2.

and no human brain can stand the confusion: pray mind this, it is one of your few weak points — ask Mrs. Terry else. A habit of the mind it is which is very apt to beset men of intellect and talent, especially when their time is not regularly filled up, but left at their own ar- rangement. But it is like the ivy round the oak, and ends by limiting, if it does not destroy, the power of manly and necessary exertion. I must love a man so well to whom I offer such a word of advice, that I will not apologize for it, but expect to hear you are become as regular as a Dutch clock — hours, quarters, minutes, all marked and appropriated. This is a great cast in life, and must be played with all skill and caution.

We wish much to have a plan of the great bed, that we may hang up the tester. Mr. Atkinson offered to have it altered or exchanged; but with the expense of land-carriage and risk of damage, it is not to be thought of. I enclose a letter to thank him for all his kindness. I should like to have the invoice when the things are shipped. I hope they will send them to Leith, and not to Berwick. The plasterer has broke a pane in the armory. I enclose a sheet with the size, the black lines being traced within the lead; and I add a rough drawing of the arms, which are those of my mother. I should like it replaced as soon as possible, for I will set the expense against the careless rascal's account.

I have got a beautiful scarlet paper, inlaid with gold (rather crimson than scarlet) in a present from India, which will hang the parlor to a T; but we shall want some articles from town to enable us to take possession of the parlor — namely, a *carpet* — you mentioned a *wainscot pattern*, which would be delightful — item, *grates* for said parlor and armory — a plain and unex- pensive pattern, resembling that in my room (which vents most admirably), and suited by half-dogs for burning wood. The sideboard and chairs you have mentioned. I see Mr. Bullock (George's brother) advertises his museum for sale. I wonder if a good set of *real tilting* armor could be got cheap there. James Ballantyne got me one very handsome bright steel cuirassier of Queen Elizabeth's time, and two less perfect, for £20 — dog cheap; they make a great figure in the armory. Hangings, curtains, etc., I believe we shall get as well in Edinburgh as in London; it is in your joiner and cabinet work that your infinite superiority lies.

Write to me if I can do aught about the play — though I fear not: much will depend on Dumbiedikes, in whom Liston will be strong. Sophia has been chiefly my nurse, as an indisposition of little Charles called Charlotte to town. She returned yesterday with him. All beg kind compliments to you and Mrs. Terry and little Walter. I remain your very feeble but convalescent to command, WALTER SCOTT.

P. S. — We must not forget the case for the leaves of the table while out of use; without something of the kind, I am afraid they will be liable to injury, which is a pity, as they are so very beautiful.[1]

The accounts of Scott's condition circulated in Edinburgh in the course of this April were so alarming, that I should not have thought of accepting his invitation to revisit Abbotsford, unless John Ballantyne had given me better tidings about the end of the month.[2] He informed

---

[1] The Duke of Buccleuch gave Scott some old oak-roots from Drumlanrig, out of which a very beautiful set of dinner-tables were manufactured by Messrs. Bullock.

[2] [An extract from a letter of March 23 will show how warm a regard Scott already felt for Lockhart: " I am but just on my feet after a fourth very severe spasmodic affection, which held me from half-past six last night to half-past three this morning in a state little short of the extreme agony, during which time, to the infinite consternation of my terrified family, I waltzed with Madam Cramp to my own sad music.

> I sighed and howl'd,
> And groaned and growl'd,
> A wild and wondrous sound;

incapable of lying in one posture, yet unable to find any possible means of

me that his "illustrious friend" (for so both the Ballantynes usually spoke of him) was so much recovered as to
have resumed his usual literary tasks, though with this
difference, that he now, for the first time in his life,
found it necessary to employ the hand of another. I
have now before me a letter of the 8th April, in which
Scott says to Constable: "Yesterday I began to dictate,
and did it easily and with comfort. This is a great point,
but I must proceed by little and little; last night I had
a slight return of the enemy, but baffled him;" — and
he again writes to the bookseller on the 11th, "John
Ballantyne is here, and returns with copy, which my increasing strength permits me to hope I may now furnish
regularly."

The *copy* (as MS. for the press is technically called)
which Scott was thus dictating, was that of The Bride of
Lammermoor, and his amanuenses were William Laidlaw
and John Ballantyne; — of whom he preferred the latter,
when he could be at Abbotsford, on account of the superior rapidity of his pen; and also because John kept his
pen to the paper without interruption, and, though with
many an arch twinkle in his eyes, and now and then an
audible smack of his lips, had resolution to work on like
a well-trained clerk; whereas good Laidlaw entered with

changing it. I thought of you amid all this agony, and of the great game
which with your parts and principles lies before you in Scotland, and having been for very many years the only man of letters who at least stood by,
if he could not support, the banner of ancient faith and loyalty, I was men-
tally bequeathing to you my baton, like old Douglas: —

> ' Take *thou* the vanguard of the three
>   And bury me by the bracken bush,
>   That grows upon yon lily lea.'

"I believe the women thought I was growing light-headed as they heard
me repeat a rhyme apparently so little connected with my situation. I
have much to say to you on these subjects, for which I hope we shall have
a fit time; for, like old Sir Anthony Absolute, I hope still to live long
and be very troublesome to you. Indeed, the surgeon could not help expressing his astonishment at the great strength of my temperament, and
I think had an eye to my ribs as glorious hoops for a skeleton." — *Familiar Letters*, vol. ii. p. 38.]

such keen zest into the interest of the story as it flowed from the author's lips, that he could not suppress exclamations of surprise and delight: — "Gude keep us a'! — the like o' that! — eh sirs! eh sirs!" — and so forth — which did not promote despatch. I have often, however, in the sequel, heard both these secretaries describe the astonishment with which they were equally affected when Scott began this experiment. The affectionate Laidlaw beseeching him to stop dictating, when his audible suffering filled every pause, "Nay, Willie," he answered, "only see that the doors are fast. I would fain keep all the cry as well as all the wool to ourselves; but as to giving over work, that can only be when I am in woollen." John Ballantyne told me, that after the first day he always took care to have a dozen of pens made before he seated himself opposite to the sofa on which Scott lay, and that though he often turned himself on his pillow with a groan of torment, he usually continued the sentence in the same breath. But when dialogue of peculiar animation was in progress, spirit seemed to triumph altogether over matter — he arose from his couch and walked up and down the room, raising and lowering his voice, and as it were acting the parts. It was in this fashion that Scott produced the far greater portion of The Bride of Lammermoor — the whole of the Legend of Montrose — and almost the whole of Ivanhoe. Yet, when his health was fairly reëstablished, he disdained to avail himself of the power of dictation, which he had thus put to the sharpest test, but resumed, and for many years resolutely adhered to, the old plan of writing everything with his own hand. When I once, some time afterwards, expressed my surprise that he did not consult his ease, and spare his eyesight at all events, by occasionally dictating, he answered, "I should as soon think of getting into a sedan chair while I can use my legs."

On one of the envelopes in which a chapter of The Bride of Lammermoor reached the printer in the Canongate about this time (May 2, 1819), there is this note in the author's own handwriting: —

DEAR JAMES, — These matters will need more than your usual carefulness. Look sharp — double sharp — my trust is constant in thee: —

> " Tarry woo, tarry woo,
> Tarry woo is ill to spin;
> Card it weel, card it weel,
> Card it weel ere ye begin.
> When 't is carded, row'd, and spun,
> Then the work is hafflins done;
> But when woven, drest, and clean,
> It may be cleading for a queen."

So be it, — W. S.

But to return: I rode out to Abbotsford with John Ballantyne towards the end of the spring vacation, and though he had warned me of a sad change in Scott's appearance, it was far beyond what I had been led to anticipate. He had lost a great deal of flesh — his clothes hung loose about him — his countenance was meagre, haggard, and of the deadliest yellow of the jaundice — and his hair, which a few weeks before had been but slightly sprinkled with gray, was now almost literally snow-white. His eye, however, retained its fire unquenched; indeed it seemed to have gained in brilliancy from the new languor of the other features; and he received us with all the usual cordiality, and even with little perceptible diminishment in the sprightliness of his manner. He sat at the table while we dined, but partook only of some rice pudding; and after the cloth was drawn, while sipping his toast and water, pushed round the bottles in his old style, and talked with easy cheerfulness of the stout battle he had fought, and which he now seemed to consider as won.

"One day there was," he said, "when I certainly began to have great doubts whether the mischief was not getting at my mind — and I'll tell you how I tried to reassure myself on that score. I was quite unfit for anything like original composition; but I thought if I could turn an old German ballad I had been reading into decent rhymes, I might dismiss my worst apprehensions — and you shall see what came of the experiment." He then desired his daughter Sophia to fetch the MS. of The Noble Moringer, as it had been taken down from his dictation, partly by her and partly by Mr. Laidlaw, during one long and painful day while he lay in bed. He read it to us as it stood, and seeing that both Ballantyne and I were much pleased with the verses, he said he should copy them over, — make them a little "tighter about the joints," — and give me them to be printed in the Edinburgh Annual Register for 1816, — to consult him about which volume had partly been the object of my visit; and this promise he redeemed before I left him.

The reading of this long ballad, however (it consists of forty-three stanzas),[1] seemed to have exhausted him: he retired to his bedroom; and an hour or two after, when we were about to follow his example, his family were distressed by the well-known symptoms of another sharp recurrence of his affliction. A large dose of opium and the hot bath were immediately put in requisition. His good neighbor, Dr. Scott of Darnlee, was sent for, and soon attended; and in the course of three or four hours we learned that he was once more at ease. But I can never forget the groans which, during that space, his agony extorted from him. Well knowing the iron strength of his resolution, to find him confessing its extremity, by cries audible not only all over the house, but even to a considerable distance from it (for Ballantyne and I, after he was put into his bath, walked forth to be out of the way, and heard him distinctly at

---

[1] See Scott's *Poetical Works* (Ed. 1834), vol. vi. p. 343 [Cambridge Ed. p. 444].

the bowling-green), it may be supposed that this was sufficiently alarming, even to my companion; how much
more to me, who had never before listened to that voice,
except in the gentle accents of kindness and merriment.

I told Ballantyne that I saw this was nò time for my
visit, and that I should start for Edinburgh again at an
early hour — and begged he would make my apologies —
in the propriety of which he acquiesced. But as I was
dressing, about seven next morning, Scott himself tapped
at my door, and entered, looking better I thought than
at my arrival the day before. "Don't think of going,"
said he; "I feel hearty this morning, and if my devil
does come back again, it won't be for three days at any
rate. For the present, I want nothing to set me up
except a good trot in the open air, to drive away the
accursed vapors of the laudanum I was obliged to swallow last night. You have never seen Yarrow, and when
I have finished a little job I have with Jocund Johnny,
we shall all take horse and make a day of it." When I
said something about a ride of twenty miles being rather
a bold experiment after such a night, he answered that
he had ridden more than forty, a week before, under
similar circumstances, and felt nothing the worse. He
added, that there was an election on foot, in consequence
of the death of Sir John Riddell, of Riddell, Member of
Parliament for the Selkirk district of Burghs, and that
the bad health and absence of the Duke of Buccleuch
rendered it quite necessary that he should make exertions
on this occasion. "In short," said he, laughing, "I
have an errand which I shall perform — and as I must
pass Newark, you had better not miss the opportunity of
seeing it under so excellent a cicerone as the old minstrel,

'Whose withered cheek and tresses grey
Shall yet see many a better day.'"

About eleven o'clock, accordingly, he was mounted,
by the help of Tom Purdie, upon a stanch, active cob,
yclept Sibyl Grey, — exactly such a creature as is

described in Mr. Dinmont's *Dumple* — while Ballantyne sprang into the saddle of noble *Old Mortality*, and we proceeded to the town of Selkirk, where Scott halted to do business at the Sheriff-Clerk's, and begged us to move onward at a gentle pace until he should overtake us. He came up by and by at a canter, and seemed in high glee with the tidings he had heard about the canvass. And so we rode by Philiphaugh, Carterhaugh, Bowhill, and Newark, he pouring out all the way his picturesque anecdotes of former times — more especially of the fatal field where Montrose was finally overthrown by Leslie. He described the battle as vividly as if he had witnessed it; the passing of the Ettrick at daybreak by the Covenanting General's heavy cuirassiers, many of them old soldiers of Gustavus Adolphus, and the wild confusion of the Highland host when exposed to their charge on an extensive *haugh* as flat as a bowling-green. He drew us aside at *Slain-men's-lee*, to observe the green mound that marks the resting-place of the slaughtered royalists; and pointing to the apparently precipitous mountain, Minchmoor, over which Montrose and his few cavaliers escaped, mentioned that, rough as it seemed, his mother remembered passing it in her early days in a coach and six, on her way to a ball at Peebles — several footmen marching on either side of the carriage to prop it up, or drag it through bogs, as the case might require. He also gave us, with all the dramatic effect of one of his best chapters, the history of a worthy family who, inhabiting at the time of the battle a cottage on his own estate, had treated with particular kindness a young officer of Leslie's army quartered on them for a night or two before. When parting from them to join the troops, he took out a purse of gold, and told the good woman that he had a presentiment he should not see another sun set, and in that case would wish his money to remain in her kind hands; but, if he should survive, he had no doubt she would restore it honestly. The young man returned mortally wounded, but lingered awhile under her roof, and finally bequeathed to her and hers his purse and his blessing. "Such," he said, "was the origin of the respectable lairds of ——, now my good neighbors."

The prime object of this expedition was to talk over the politics of Selkirk with one of the Duke of Buccleuch's great store-farmers, who, as the Sheriff had learned, possessed private influence with a doubtful bailie or deacon among the Souters. I forget the result, if ever I heard it. But next morning, having, as he assured us, enjoyed a good night in consequence of this ride, he invited us to accompany him on a similar errand across Bowden Moor, and up the Valley of the Ayle; and when we reached a particularly bleak and dreary point of that journey, he informed us that he perceived in the waste below a wreath of smoke, which was the appointed signal that a *wavering* Souter of some consequence had agreed to give him a personal interview where no Whiggish eyes were likely to observe them; — and so, leaving us on the road, he proceeded to thread his way westward, across moor and bog, until we lost view of him. I think a couple of hours might have passed before he joined us again, which was, as had been arranged, not far from the village of Lilliesleaf. In that place, too, he had some negotiation of the same sort to look after; and when he had finished it, he rode with us all round the ancient woods of Riddell, but would not go near the house; I suppose lest any of the afflicted family might still be there. Many were his lamentations over the catastrophe which had just befallen them. "They are," he said, "one of the most venerable races in the south of Scotland — they were here long before these glens had ever heard the name of Soulis or of Douglas — to say nothing of Buccleuch: they can show a Pope's bull of the tenth century, authorizing the then Riddell to marry a relation within the forbidden degrees. Here they have been for a thousand years at least; and now all the inher-

itance is to pass away, merely because one good worthy
gentleman would not be contented to enjoy his horses,
his hounds, and his bottle of claret, like thirty or forty
predecessors, but must needs turn scientific agriculturist,
take almost all his fair estate into his own hand, superintend for himself perhaps a hundred ploughs, and try
every new nostrum that has been tabled by the quackish
improvers of the time. And what makes the thing ten
times more wonderful is, that he kept day-book and
ledger, and all the rest of it, as accurately as if he had
been a cheesemonger in the Grassmarket.'' Some of the
most remarkable circumstances in Scott's own subsequent
life have made me often recall this conversation — with
more wonder than he expressed about the ruin of the
Riddells.

I remember he told us a world of stories, some tragical, some comical, about the old lairds of this time-honored lineage; and among others, that of the seven Bibles
and the seven bottles of ale, which he afterwards inserted
in a note to The Bride of Lammermoor.[1] He was also

---

[1] " It was once the universal custom to place ale, wine, or some strong
liquor, in the chamber of an honored guest, to assuage his thirst should he
feel any on awakening in the night, which, considering that the hospitality
of that period often reached excess, was by no means unlikely. The author has met some instances of it in former days, and in old-fashioned families. It was, perhaps, no poetic fiction that records how

> ' My cummer and I lay down to sleep
> With two pint stoups at our bed feet ;
> And aye when we waken'd we drank them dry;
> What think you o' my cummer and I ? '

" It is a current story in Teviotdale, that in the house of an ancient
family of distinction, much addicted to the Presbyterian cause, a Bible
was always put into the sleeping apartment of the guests, along with a
bottle of strong ale. On some occasion there was a meeting of clergymen
in the vicinity of the castle, all of whom were invited to dinner by the
worthy Baronet, and several abode all night. According to the fashion of
the times, seven of the reverend guests were allotted to one large barrack-
room, which was used on such occasions of extended hospitality. The
butler took care that the divines were presented, according to custom, each
with a Bible and a bottle of ale. But after a little consultation among
themselves, they are said to have recalled the domestic as he was leaving

full of anecdotes about a friend of his father's, a minister
of Lilliesleaf, who reigned for two generations the most
popular preacher in Teviotdale; but I forget the orator's
name. When the original of Saunders Fairford congratulated him in his latter days on the undiminished
authority he still maintained — every kirk in the neighborhood being left empty when it was known he was to
mount the *tent* at any country sacrament — the shrewd
divine answered: "Indeed, Mr. Walter, I sometimes
think it's vera surprising. There's aye a talk of this
or that wonderfully gifted young man frae the college;
but whenever I'm to be at the same *occasion* with ony
o' them, I e'en mount the white horse in the Revelations,
and he dings them a'."

Thus Scott amused himself and us as we jogged homewards: and it was the same the following day, when (no
election matters pressing) he rode with us to the western
peak of the Eildon hills, that he might show me the
whole panorama of his Teviotdale, and expound the direction of the various passes by which the ancient forayers
made their way into England, and tell the names and the
histories of many a monastic chapel and baronial peel,
now mouldering in glens and dingles that escape the eye
of the traveller on the highways. Among other objects
on which he descanted with particular interest, were the
ruins of the earliest residence of the Kerrs of Cessford,
so often opposed in arms to his own chieftains of Branksome, and a desolate little kirk on the adjoining moor,
where the Dukes of Roxburghe are still buried in the

the apartment. 'My friend,' said one of the venerable guests, 'you must
know, when we meet together as brethren, the youngest minister reads
aloud a portion of Scripture to the rest; — only one Bible, therefore,
is necessary; take away the other six, and in their place bring six more
bottles of ale.'

"This synod would have suited the 'hermit sage' of Johnson, who
answered a pupil who inquired for the real road to happiness with the
celebrated line,

'Come, my lad, and drink some beer!'"

— See *The Bride of Lammermoor*, note to chap. xiv.

same vault with the hero who fell at Turn-again. Turn-ing to the northward, he showed us the crags and tower of Smailholm, and behind it the shattered fragment of Ercildoune — and repeated some pretty stanzas ascribed to the last of the real wandering minstrels of this district, by name *Burn:* —

> " Sing Erceldoune, and Cowdenknowes,
>   Where Homes had ance commanding,
> And Drygrange, wi' the milk-white ewes,
>   'Twixt Tweed and Leader standing.
> The bird that flees through Redpath trees
>   And Gledswood banks each morrow,
> May chaunt and sing — *sweet Leader's haughs*
>   And *Bonny howms of Yarrow.*
>
> " But Minstrel Burn cannot assuage
>   His grief while life endureth,
> To see the changes of this age
>   Which fleeting time procureth ;
> For mony a place stands in hard case,
>   Where blythe folks kent nae sorrow,
> With Homes that dwelt on Leader side,
>   And Scotts that dwelt on Yarrow." [1]

That night he had again an attack of his cramp, but not so serious as the former. Next morning he was again at work with Ballantyne at an early hour; and when I parted from him after breakfast, he spoke cheerfully of being soon in Edinburgh for the usual business of his Court. I left him, however, with dark prognostications; and the circumstances of this little visit to Abbotsford have no doubt dwelt on my mind the more distinctly, from my having observed and listened to him throughout under the painful feeling that it might very probably be my last.

On the 5th of May he received the intelligence of the death of the Duke of Buccleuch, which had occurred at Lisbon on the 20th April; and next morning he wrote as follows to his Grace's brother: —

[1] [See *ante*, vol. i. p. 378, note.]

ABBOTSFORD, 6th May, 1819.

MY DEAR LORD, — I heard from Lord Melville, by yesterday's post, the calamitous news which your Lordship's very kind letter this moment confirmed, had it required confirmation. For this fortnight past, my hopes have been very faint indeed, and on Wednesday, when I had occasion to go to Yarrow, and my horse turned from habit to go up the avenue at Bowhill, I felt deeply impressed that it was a road I should seldom travel for a long time at least. To your Lordship — let me add, to myself — this is an irreparable loss; for such a fund of excellent sense, high principle, and perfect honor have been rarely combined in the same individual. To the country the inestimable loss will be soon felt, even by those who were insensible to his merits, or wished to detract from them, when he was amongst us. In my opinion he never recovered from his domestic calamity. He wrote to me, a few days after that cruel event, a most affectionate and remarkable letter, explaining his own feelings, and while he begged that I would come to him, assuring me that I should find him the same he would be for the future years of his life. He kept his word; but I could see a grief of that calm and concentrated kind which claims the hours of solitude and of night for its empire, and gradually wastes the springs of life.

Among the thousand painful feelings which this melancholy event had excited, I have sometimes thought of his distance from home. Yet this was done with the best intention, and upon the best advice, and was perhaps the sole chance which remained for reëstablishment. It has pleased God that it has failed; but the best means were used under the best direction, and mere mortality can do no more. I am very anxious about the dear young ladies, whose lives were so much devoted to their father, and shall be extremely desirous of knowing how they are. The Duchess has so much firmness of mind, and Lady M. so much affectionate prudence, that they will want no support that example and kindness can afford. To me the world seems a sort of waste without him. We had many joint objects, constant intercourse, and unreserved communication, so that through him and by him I took interest in many things altogether out of my own sphere, and it seems to me as if the horizon were narrowed and lowered around me. But God's will be done; it is all that brother or friend can or dare say. — I have reluctance to mention the trash which is going on here. Indeed, I think little is altered since I wrote to your Lordship fully, excepting that last night late, Chisholm [1] arrived at Abbotsford from Lithgow, recalled by the news which had somehow reached Edinburgh, — as I suspect by some officiousness of * * * *. He left Lithgow in such a state that there is no doubt he will carry that burgh, unless Pringle [2] gets Selkirk. He is gone off this morning to try the possible and impossible to get the single vote which he wants, or to prevail on one person to stand neuter. It is possible he may succeed, though this event, when it becomes generally known, will be greatly against his efforts. I should care little more about the matter, were it not for young Walter, [3] and for the despite I feel at the success of speculations which were formed on the probability of the event which has happened. Two sons of * * * * * * * came here yesterday, and with their father's philosophical spirit of self-accommodation, established themselves for the night. Betwixt them and Chisholm's noise, my head and my stomach suffered so much (under the necessity of drowning feelings which I could not express), that I had a return of the spasms, and I felt as if a phantasmagoria was going on around me. Quiet, and some indul-

---

[1] Mr. Chisholm was the Tory candidate for the Selkirk burghs.
[2] Mr. Pringle of Clifton, the Whig candidate.
[3] Walter Francis, the present Duke of Buccleuch.

gence of natural and solitary sorrow, have made me well. To-day I will ride up to Selkirk and see the magistrates, or the chief of them. It is necessary they should not think the cause deserted. If it is thought proper to suspend the works at Bowhill, perhaps the measure may be delayed till the decision of this matter.

I am sure, my dear Lord, you will command me in all I can do. I have only to regret it is so little. But to show that my gratitude has survived my benefactor, would be the pride and delight of my life. I never thought it possible that a man could have loved another so much, where the distance of rank was so very great. But why recur to things so painful? I pity poor Adam Ferguson, whose affections were so much engaged by the Duke's kindness, and who has with his gay temper a generous and feeling heart. The election we may lose, but not our own credit, and that of the family — that you may rest assured of. My best respects and warmest sympathy attend the dear young ladies, and Lady Montagu. I shall be anxious to know how the Duchess-Dowager does under this great calamity. The poor boy — what a slippery world is before him, and how early a dangerous, because a splendid, lot is presented to him! But he has your personal protection. Believe me, with a deep participation in your present distress, your Lordship's most faithfully,

WALTER SCOTT.

Scott drew up for Ballantyne's newspaper of that week the brief character of Charles, Duke of Buccleuch, which has since been included in his Prose Miscellanies (vol. iv.); and the following letter accompanied a copy of it to Ditton Park: —

TO THE LORD MONTAGU, ETC., ETC., ETC.

MY DEAR LORD, — I send you the newspaper article under a different cover. I have studied so much to suppress my own feelings, and so to give a just, calm, and temperate view of the excellent subject of our present sorrow, such as I conceive might be drawn by one less partially devoted to him, that it has to my own eye a cold and lifeless resemblance of an original so dear to me. But I was writing to the public, and to a public less acquainted with him than a few years' experience would have made them. Even his own tenantry were but just arrived at the true estimation of his character. I wrote, therefore, to insure credit and belief, in a tone greatly under my own feelings. I have ordered twenty-five copies to be put in a different shape, of which I will send your Lordship twenty. It has been a painful task, but I feel it was due from me. I am just favored with your letter. I beg your Lordship will not write more frequently than you find quite convenient, for you must have now more than enough upon you. The arrangement respecting Boughton [1] is what I expected — the lifeless remains will be laid where the living thoughts had long been. I grieve that I shall not see the last honors, yet I hardly know how I could have gone through the scene.

Nothing in the circumstances could have given me the satisfaction which I receive from your Lordship's purpose of visiting Scotland, and bringing down the dear young ladies, who unite so many and such affecting ties upon the regard and affection of every friend of the family. It will be a measure of the highest necessity for the political interest of the family, and your Lordship will have an opportunity of hearing much information of importance, which really could not be made the subject of writing. The extinction of fire on the hearths of this great house would be putting out a public light and a

[1] Boughton, in Northamptonshire. This seat came into the possession of Henry, Duke of Buccleuch, by his marriage with the daughter and heiress of John, the last Duke of Montagu, who survived for many years her son, Duke Charles. At Boughton, as the reader will see, Scott's early friend, the Duchess Harriet of Buccleuch, had been buried in 1814.

public beacon in the time of darkness and storms. Ever your most faithful   **W. S.**

On the 11th of May, Scott returned to Edinburgh, and was present next day at the opening of the Court of Session; when all who saw him were as much struck as I had been at Abbotsford with the lamentable change his illness had produced in his appearance. He was unable to persist in attendance at the Clerks' Table — for several weeks afterwards I think he seldom if ever attempted it; — and I well remember that, when the Third Series of the Tales of my Landlord at length came out (which was on the 10th of June), he was known to be confined to bed, and the book was received amidst the deep general impression that we should see no more of that parentage. On the 13th he wrote thus to Captain Ferguson, who had arrived in London with the remains of the Duke of Buccleuch: —

TO CAPTAIN ADAM FERGUSON, ETC., ETC., MONTAGU HOUSE, WHITEHALL.

MY DEAR ADAM, — I am sorry to say I have had another eight days' visit of my disorder, which has confined me chiefly to my bed. It is not attended with so much acute pain as in spring, but with much sickness and weakness. It will perhaps shade off into a mild chronic complaint — if it returns frequently with the same violence, I shall break up by degrees, and follow my dear Chief. I do not mean that there is the least cause for immediate apprehension, but only that the constitution must be injured at last, as well by the modes of cure, or rather of relief, as by the pain. My digestion as well as my appetite are for the present quite gone — a change from former days of Leith and Newhaven parties. I thank God I can look at this possibility without much anxiety, and without a shadow of fear.

Will you, if your time serves, undertake two little

commissions for me? One respects a kind promise of
Lord Montagu to put George Thomson's name on a list
for kirk preferment. I don't like to trouble him with
letters — he must be overwhelmed with business, and has
his dear brother's punctuality in replying even to those
which require none. I would fain have that Scottish
Abraham Adams provided for if possible. My other
request is, that you will, if you can, see Terry, and ask
him what is doing about my dining-room chairs, and
especially about the carpet, for I shall not without them
have the use of what Slender calls "mine own great
parlor" this season. I should write to him, but am
really unable. I hope you will soon come down — a
sight of you would do me good at the worst turn I have
yet had. The Baronet [1] is very kind, and comes and sits
by me. Everybody likes the Regalia, and I have heard
of no one grudging their *hog* [2] — but you must get something better. I have been writing to the Commie [3] about
this. He has been inexpressibly kind in Walter's matter, and the Duke of York has promised an early commission. When you see our friend, you can talk over
this, and may perhaps save him the trouble of writing
particular directions what further is to be done. Iago's
rule, I suppose — "put money in thy purse." I wish
in passing you would ask how the ladies are in Piccadilly. Yours ever,

W. SCOTT.

The Bride of Lammermoor, and A Legend of Montrose, would have been read with indulgence had they
needed it; for the painful circumstances under which
they must have been produced were known wherever an
English newspaper made its way; but I believe that,
except in numerous typical errors, which sprung of necessity from the author's inability to correct any proof

---

[1] Mr. William Clerk.   [2] A shilling.
[3] The Lord Chief-Commissioner Adam.

sheets, no one ever affected to perceive in either tale the slightest symptom of his malady. Dugald Dalgetty was placed by acclamation in the same rank with Bailie Jarvie — a conception equally new, just, and humorous, and worked out in all the details, as if it had formed the luxurious entertainment of a chair as easy as was ever shaken by Rabelais; and though the character of Montrose himself seemed hardly to have been treated so fully as the subject merited, the accustomed rapidity of the novelist's execution would have been enough to account for any such defect. Of Caleb Balderstone — (the hero of one of the many ludicrous delineations which he owed to the late Lord Haddington, a man of rare pleasantry, and one of the best tellers of old Scotch stories that I ever heard) — I cannot say that the general opinion was then, nor do I believe it ever since has been, very favorable. It was pronounced at the time, by more than one critic, a mere caricature; and though Scott himself would never in after-days admit this censure to be just, he allowed that "he might have sprinkled rather too much parsley over his chicken." But even that blemish, for I grant that I think it a serious one, could not disturb the profound interest and pathos of The Bride of Lammermoor — to my fancy the most pure and powerful of all the tragedies that Scott ever penned. The reader will be well pleased, however, to have, in place of any critical observations on this work, the following particulars of its composition from the notes which its printer dictated when stretched on the bed from which he well knew he was never to rise.

"The book" (says James Ballantyne) "was not only written, but published, before Mr. Scott was able to rise from his bed; and he assured me, that when it was first put into his hands in a complete shape, he did not recollect one single incident, character, or conversation it contained! He did not desire me to understand, nor did I understand, that his illness had erased from his memory the original incidents of the story, with which he had been acquainted from his boyhood. These remained rooted where they had ever been ; or, to speak more explicitly, he remembered the general facts of the existence of the father and mother, of the son and daughter, of the rival lovers, of the compulsory marriage, and the attack made by the bride upon the hapless bridegroom,[1] with the general catastrophe of the whole. All these things he recollected just as he did before he took to his bed : but he literally recollected nothing else — not a single character woven by the romancer, not one of the many scenes and points of humor, nor anything with which he was connected as the writer of the work. 'For a long time,' he said, ' I felt myself very uneasy in the course of my reading, lest I should be startled by meeting something altogether glaring and fantastic. However, I recollected that you had been the printer, and I felt sure that you would not have permitted anything of this sort to pass.' 'Well,' I said, 'upon the whole, how did you like it ? ' 'Why,' he said, 'as a whole, I felt it monstrous gross and grotesque ; but still the worst of it made me laugh, and I trusted the good-natured public would not be less indulgent.' I do not think I ever ventured to lead to the discussion of this singular phenomenon again ; but you may depend upon it, that what I have now said is as distinctly reported as if it had been taken down in short-hand at the moment ; I should not otherwise have ventured to allude to the matter at all. I believe you will agree with me in thinking that the history of the human mind contains nothing more wonderful."

Soon after Scott reappeared in the Parliament House, he came down one Saturday to the vaulted chambers below, where the Advocates' Library was then kept, to

[1] There appeared in the *Edinburgh Evening Post* of October 10, 1840, a letter dated September 5, 1823, addressed by Sir J. Horne Dalrymple Elphinstone, Bart., to the late Sir James Stewart Denham of Coltness, Bart., both descendants of the Lord President Stair, whose daughter was the original of the Bride of Lammermoor, from which it appears that, according to the traditional creed of the Dalrymple family, the lady's unhappy lover, Lord Rutherford, had found means to be secreted in the nuptial chamber, and that the wound of the bridegroom, Sir David Dunbar of Baldoon, was inflicted by his Lordship's hand. The letter in question will be appended to future editions of the novel. — (1841.)

attend a meeting of the Faculty, and as the assembly was breaking up, he asked me to walk home with him, taking Ballantyne's printing-office in our way. He moved languidly, and said, if he were to stay in town many days, he must send for Sibyl Grey; but his conversation was heart-whole; and, in particular, he laughed till, despite his weakness, the stick was flourishing in his hand, over the following almost incredible specimen of that most absurd personage the late Earl of Buchan.

Hearing one morning shortly before this time, that Scott was actually *in extremis*, the Earl proceeded to Castle Street, and found the knocker tied up. He then descended to the door in the area, and was there received by honest Peter Mathieson, whose face seemed to confirm the woeful tidings, for in truth his master was ill enough. Peter told his Lordship that he had the strictest orders to admit no visitor; but the Earl would take no denial, pushed the bashful coachman aside, and elbowed his way upstairs to the door of Scott's bedchamber. He had his fingers upon the handle before Peter could give warning to Miss Scott; and when she appeared to remonstrate against such an intrusion, he patted her on the head like a child, and persisted in his purpose of entering the sick-room so strenuously, that the young lady found it necessary to bid Peter see the Earl downstairs again, at whatever damage to his dignity. Peter accordingly, after trying all his eloquence in vain, gave the tottering, bustling, old, meddlesome coxcomb a single shove, — as respectful, doubt not, as a shove can ever be, — and he accepted that hint, and made a rapid exit. Scott, meanwhile, had heard the confusion, and at length it was explained to him; when, fearing that Peter's gripe might have injured Lord Buchan's feeble person, he desired James Ballantyne, who had been sitting by his bed, to follow the old man home — make him comprehend, if he could, that the family were in such bewilderment of alarm, that the ordinary rules of civility were out of the question — and, in fine, inquire what had been the object of his Lordship's intended visit. James proceeded forthwith to the Earl's house in George Street and found him strutting about his library in a towering indignation. Ballantyne's elaborate demonstrations of respect, however, by degrees softened him, and he condescended to explain himself. "I wished," said he, "to embrace Walter Scott before he died, and inform him that I had long considered it as a satisfactory circumstance that he and I were destined to rest together in the same place of sepulture. The principal thing, however, was to relieve his mind as to the arrangements of his funeral — to show him a plan which I had prepared for the procession — and, in a word, to assure him that I took upon myself the whole conduct of the ceremonial at Dryburgh." He then exhibited to Ballantyne a formal programme, in which, as may be supposed, the predominant feature was not Walter Scott, but David, Earl of Buchan. It had been settled, *inter alia*, that the said Earl was to pronounce an eulogium over the grave, after the fashion of French Academicians in the *Père la Chaise*.

And this silliest and vainest of busybodies was the elder brother of Thomas and Henry Erskine! But the story is well known of his boasting one day to the late Duchess of Gordon of the extraordinary talents of his family — when her unscrupulous Grace asked him, very coolly, whether the wit had not come by the mother, and been all settled on the younger branches?

Scott, as his letters to be quoted presently will show, had several more attacks of his disorder, and some very severe ones, during the autumn of 1819; nor, indeed, had it quite disappeared until about Christmas. But from the time of his return to Abbotsford in July, when he adopted the system of treatment recommended by a skilful physician (Dr. Dick), who had had large experience in maladies of this kind during his Indian life, the seizures gradually became less violent, and his confidence that he was ultimately to baffle the enemy remained unshaken.[1]

As I had no opportunity of seeing him again until he was almost entirely reëstablished, I shall leave the progress of his restoration to be collected from his correspondence. But I must not forget to set down what his daughter Sophia afterwards told me of his conduct upon one night in June, when he really did despair of himself. He then called his children about his bed, and took leave of them with solemn tenderness. After giving them, one by one, such advice as suited their years and characters, he added: "For myself, my dears, I am unconscious of ever having done any man an injury, or omitted any fair opportunity of doing any man a benefit. I well know that no human life can appear otherwise than weak and filthy in the eyes of God: but I rely on the merits and intercession of our Redeemer." He then laid his hand on their heads, and said, "God bless you! Live so that you may all hope to meet each other in a better place hereafter. And now leave me, that I may turn my face to the wall." They obeyed him; but he presently fell into a deep sleep; and when he awoke from it after many hours, the crisis of extreme danger was felt by himself, and pronounced by his physician, to have been overcome.

[1] ["For nearly two years he had to struggle for his life with that severe illness, which the natural strength of his constitution at length proved sufficient to throw off. With its disappearance, although restored to health, disappeared also much of his former vigor of body, activity, and power of undergoing fatigue, while in personal appearance he had advanced twenty years in the downward course of life; his hair had become bleached to pure white and scanty locks; the fire of his eye quenched; and his step, more uncertain, had lost the vigorous swinging gait with which he was used to proceed; in fact, old age had by many years anticipated its usual progress and marked how severely he had suffered." — James Skene's *Reminiscences.* — See *Journal*, vol. ii. p. 97, note.]

CHAPTER XLV

1819

BEFORE Scott left Edinburgh, on the 12th of July, he had not only concluded his bargain with Constable for another novel, but, as will appear from some of his letters, made considerable progress in the dictation of Ivanhoe.

That he already felt great confidence on the score of his health may be inferred from his allowing his son, Walter, about the middle of the month, to join the 18th regiment of Hussars in which he had, shortly before, received his commission as Cornet.

Scott's letters to his son, the first of his family that left the house, will merit henceforth a good deal of the reader's attention. Walter was, when he thus quitted Abbotsford to try his chances in the active world, only in the eighteenth year of his age; and the fashion of education in Scotland is such, that he had scarcely ever slept a night under a different roof from his parents, until this separation occurred. He had been treated from his cradle with all the indulgence that a man of sense can ever permit himself to show to any of his children; and for several years he had now been his father's daily companion in all his out-of-doors occupations and amusements. The parting was a painful one; but Scott's ambition centred in the heir of his name, and instead of fruitless pinings and lamentings, he henceforth made it his constant business to keep up such a frank correspondence with the young man as might enable himself to exert over him, when at a distance, the gentle influence of kindness, experience, and wisdom. The series of his letters to his son is, in my opinion, by far the most interesting and valuable, as respects the personal character and temper of the writer. It will easily be supposed that, as the young officer entered fully into his father's generous views of what their correspondence ought to be, and detailed every little incident of his new career with the same easy confidence as if he had been writing to a friend or elder brother not very widely differing from himself in standing, the answers abound with opinions on subjects with which I have no right to occupy or entertain my readers: but I shall introduce in the prosecution of this work, as many specimens of Scott's paternal advice as I can hope to render generally intelligible without indelicate explanations — and more especially such as may prove serviceable to other young persons when first embarking under their own pilotage upon the sea of life. Scott's manly kindness to his boy, whether he is expressing approbation or censure of his conduct, can require no pointing out; and his practical wisdom was of that liberal order, based on such comprehensive views of man and the world, that I am persuaded it will often be found available to the circumstances of their own various cases, by young men of whatever station or profession.

I shall, nevertheless, adhere as usual to the chronological order; and one or two miscellaneous letters must accordingly precede the first article of his correspondence with the Cornet. He alludes, however, to the youth's departure in the following: —

TO MRS. MACLEAN CLEPHANE OF TORLOISK.

ABBOTSFORD, July 15, 1819.

DEAR MRS. CLEPHANE, — Nothing could give me more pleasure than to hear you are well, and thinking of looking this way. You will find all my things in very different order from when you were here last, and plenty of room for matron and miss, man and maid. We have no engagements, except to Newton Don about the 20th August — if we be alive — no unreasonable proviso in so long an engagement. My health, however, seems in a fair way of being perfectly restored. It is a joke to talk of any other remedy than that forceful but most unpleasant one — *calomel*. I cannot say I ever felt advantage from anything else; and I am perfectly satisfied that, used as an alterative, and taken in very small quantities for a long time, it must correct all the inaccuracies of the biliary organs. At least it has done so in my case more radically than I could have believed possible. I have intermitted the régime for some days, but begin a new course next week for precaution. Dr. Dick, of the East India Company's service, has put me on this course of cure,[1] and says he never knew it fail unless when the

---

[1] [An interesting letter from Dr. Dick to Scott will be found in *Familiar Letters* (vol. ii. p. 53), in which he speaks of their common friend, Leyden, and expresses sorrow at the tone regarding him taken by some of the Edinburgh periodicals, which ridiculed the idea of comparing him with Sir William Jones as a linguist. The writer, who knew both, shows Leyden to have been in this respect much the greater of the two. The Doctor makes light of his efficient services in Scott's case, and says : " I have only to offer my grateful thanks for your intended present, which, however, I must beg leave to decline, because I am rewarded already a thousandfold, by being allowed the honor of prescribing for you, and by being assured, under your own hand, that you are so well. . . . But if you will send me one volume of any kind, and write on it that it is from yourself, I shall consider it a great favor. I have the vanity to wish that my son and his descendants may have it to show as a proof that I was honored with the friendship of the author."]

liver was irreparably injured. I believe I shall go to
Carlsbad next year. If I must go to a watering-place,
I should like one where I might hope to see and learn
something new myself, instead of being hunted down by
some of the confounded lion-catchers who haunt English
spas. I have not the art of being savage to those people,
though few are more annoyed by them. I always think
of Snug the Joiner —

> "—— If I should as lion *come in strife*
> Into such place, 't were pity on my life."

I have been delayed in answering your kind letter by
Walter's departure from us to join his regiment, the 18th
Dragoons. He has chosen a profession for which he is
well suited, being of a calm but remarkably firm temper
— fond of mathematics, engineering, and all sorts of calculation — clear-headed, and good-natured. When you
add to this a good person and good manners, with great
dexterity in horsemanship and all athletic exercises, and
a strong constitution, one hopes you have the grounds of
a good soldier. My own selfish wish would have been
that he should have followed the law; but he really had
no vocation that way, wanting the acuteness and liveliness of intellect indispensable to making a figure in that
profession. So I am satisfied all is for the best, only
I shall miss my gamekeeper and companion in my rides
and walks. But so it was, is, and must be — the young
must part from the nest, and learn to wing their own
way against the storm.

I beg my best and kindest compliments to Lady Compton. Stooping to write hurts me, or I would have sent
her a few lines. As I shall be stationary here for all
this season, I shall not see her, perhaps, for long enough.
Mrs. Scott and the girls join in best love, and I am ever,
dear Mrs. Clephane, your faithful and most obedient
servant, WALTER SCOTT.

I have had some hesitation about introducing the next

letter — which refers to the then recent publication of
a sort of mock-tour in Scotland, entitled Peter's Letters
to his Kinsfolk. Nobody but a very young and a very
thoughtless person could have dreamt of putting forth
such a book; yet the Epistles of the imaginary Dr.
Morris have been so often denounced as a mere string
of libels, that I think it fair to show how much more
leniently Scott judged of them at the time. Moreover,
his letter is a good specimen of the liberal courtesy with
which, on all occasions, he treated the humblest aspirants
in literature. Since I have alluded to Peter's Letters at
all, I may as well take the opportunity of adding that
they were not wholly the work of one hand.[1]

TO J. G. LOCKHART, ESQ., CARNBROE HOUSE, HOLLYTOWN.

ABBOTSFORD, July 19, 1819.

MY DEAR SIR, — *Distinguendum est.* When I receive a book *ex dono* of the author, in the general case
I offer my thanks with all haste before I cut a leaf, lest
peradventure I should feel more awkward in doing so
afterwards, when they must not only be tendered for the
well-printed volumes themselves, and the attention which
sent them my way, but moreover for the supposed pleasure I have received from the contents. But with respect to the learned Dr. Morris, the case is totally different, and I formed the immediate resolution not to say a
word about that gentleman's labors without having read
them at least twice over — a pleasant task, which has

---

[1] [The other hand is supposed to have been Wilson's. It is difficult for
any reader of to-day to understand why these clever and interesting
sketches of the men and manners of the Edinburgh of 1819 should have
been so emphatically denounced in certain quarters. This is not the first
occasion on which Scott sent words of praise concerning the *Letters*, which
first appeared in part in *Blackwood's Magazine*. He says of the Pleaders'
portraits [John Clerk, Cranstoun, and Jeffrey], they " are about the best
I ever read, and will preserve these three very remarkable and original
men, for all of whom, however differing in points whereon I wish we had
agreed, I entertain not only deep respect, but sincere friendship and
regard." — *Familiar Letters*, vol. ii. p. 39.]

been interrupted partly by my being obliged to go down the country, partly by an invasion of the Southron, in the persons of Sir John Shelley, famous on the turf, and his lady. I wish Dr. Morris had been of the party, chiefly for the benefit of a little Newmarket man, called Cousins, whose whole ideas, similes, illustrations, etc., were derived from the course and training stable. He was perfectly good-humored, and I have not laughed more this many a day.

I think the Doctor has got over his ground admirably; — only the general turn of the book is perhaps too favorable, both to the state of our public society, and of individual character: —

> " His fools have their follies so lost in a crowd
> Of virtues and feelings, that folly grows proud." [1]

But it was, in every point of view, right to take this more favorable tone, and to throw a Claude Lorraine tint over our northern landscape. We cannot bear the actual bare truth, either in conversation, or that which approaches nearest to conversation, in a work like the Doctor's, published within the circle to which it refers.

For the rest, the Doctor has fully maintained his high character for force of expression, both serious and comic, and for acuteness of observation — *rem acu tetigit* — and his scalpel has not been idle, though his lenient hand has cut sharp and clean, and poured balm into the wound. What an acquisition it would have been to our general information to have had such a work written, I do not say fifty, but even five-and-twenty years ago; and how much of grave and gay might then have been preserved, as it were, in amber, which have now mouldered away. When I think that at an age not much younger than yours I knew Black, Ferguson, Robertson, Erskine, Adam Smith, John Home, etc., etc., and at least saw Burns, I can appreciate better than any one the value of a work which, like this, would have handed them down

[1] Goldsmith's *Retaliation.*

to posterity in their living colors. Dr. Morris ought, like Nourjahad, to revive every half century, to record the fleeting manners of the age, and the interesting features of those who will be only known to posterity by their works. If I am very partial to the Doctor, which I am not inclined to deny, remember I have been bribed by his kind and delicate account of his visit to Abbotsford. Like old Cumberland, or like my own gray cat, I will e'en purr and put up my back, and enjoy his kind flattery, even when I know it goes beyond my merits.

I wish you would come and spend a few days here, while this delightful weather lasts. I am now so well as quite to enjoy the society of my friends, instead of the woeful pickle in which I was in spring, when you last favored me. It was, however, *dignus vindice nodus*, for no less a deity descended to my aid than the potent Mercury himself, in the shape of calomel, which I have been obliged to take daily, though in small quantities, for these two months past. Notwithstanding the inconveniences of this remedy, I thrive upon it most marvellously, having recovered both sleep and appetite; so when you incline to come this way, you will find me looking pretty *bobbishly*. Yours very truly,

WALTER SCOTT.

On the same day, Scott wrote as follows to John Ballantyne, who had started for London, on his route to Paris in quest of articles for next winter's auction-room — and whose good offices he was anxious to engage on behalf of the Cornet, in case they should happen to be in the metropolis at the same time: —

TO MR. JOHN BALLANTYNE, CARE OF MESSRS. LONGMAN & CO., LONDON.

ABBOTSFORD, July 19, 1819.

DEAR JOHN, — I have only to say, respecting matters here, that they are all going on quietly. The first volume is very nearly finished, and the whole will be out in the first or second week of September. It will be well if you can report yourself in Britain by that time at farthest, as something must be done on the back of this same Ivanhoe.

Walter left us on Wednesday night, and will be in town by the time this reaches you, looking, I fancy, very like a cow in a fremd loaning.[1] He will be heard of at Miss Dumergue's. Pray look after him, and help him about his purchases.

I hope you will be so successful in your foreign journey as to diddle the Edinburgh folk out of some cash this winter. But don't forget September, if you wish to partake the advantages thereof.

I wish you would see what good reprints of old books are come out this year at Triphook's, and send me a note of them. — Yours very truly,

W. SCOTT.

John Ballantyne found the Cornet in London, and did for him what his father had requested.

TO MR. JOHN BALLANTYNE.

ABBOTSFORD, July 26, 1819.

DEAR JOHN, — I have yours with the news of Walter's rattle-traps, which are abominably extravagant. But there is no help for it but submission. The things seem all such as cannot well be wanted. How the devil they mount them to such a price, the tailors best know. They say it takes *nine* tailors to make a man — apparently, one is sufficient to ruin him. We shall rub through here well enough, though James is rather glumpy and dumpy — chiefly, I believe, because his child is unwell. If you can make any more money for me in London, good and well. I have no spare cash till Ivanhoe comes forth. Yours truly,   W. SCOTT.

[1] *Anglice* — a strange pasture.

P. S. — Enclosed are sundry letters of introduction for the *ci-devant* Laird of Gilnockie.

TO MISS EDGEWORTH OF EDGEWORTHSTOWN.

ABBOTSFORD, July 21, 1819.

MY DEAR MISS EDGEWORTH, — When this shall happen to reach your hands, it will be accompanied by a second edition of Walter Scott, a *tall* copy, as collectors say, and bound in Turkey leather, garnished with all sorts of fur and frippery — not quite so well *lettered*, however, as the old and vamped original edition. In other and more intelligible phrase, the tall Cornet of Hussars, whom this will introduce to you, is my eldest son, who is now just leaving me to join his regiment in Ireland. I have charged him, and he is himself sufficiently anxious, to avoid no opportunity of making your acquaintance, as to be known to the good and the wise is by far the best privilege he can derive from my connection with literature. I have always felt the value of having access to persons of talent and genius to be the best part of a literary man's prerogative, and you will not wonder, I am sure, that I should be desirous this youngster should have a share of the same benefit.

I have had dreadful bad health for many months past and have endured more pain than I thought was consistent with life. But the thread, though frail in some respects, is tough in others; and here am I with renewed health, and a fair prospect of regaining my strength, much exhausted by such a train of suffering.

I do not know when this will reach you, my son's motions being uncertain. But, find you where or when it will, it comes, dear Miss Edgeworth, from the sincere admirer of your genius, and of the patriotic and excellent manner in which it has always been exerted. In which character I subscribe myself ever yours truly,

WALTER SCOTT.

I believe, at the time when the foregoing letter was written, Scott and Miss Edgeworth had never met. The next was addressed to a gentleman whose acquaintance the poet had formed when collecting materials for his edition of Swift. On that occasion Mr. Hartstonge was of great service to Scott — and he appears to have paid him soon afterwards a visit at Abbotsford. Mr. Hartstonge was an amiable and kind-hearted man, and enthusiastically devoted to literature; but his own poetical talents were undoubtedly of the sort that finds little favor either with gods or columns. He seems to have written shortly before this time to inquire about his old acquaintance's health.

TO MATTHEW WELD HARTSTONGE, ESQ., MOLESWORTH STREET, DUBLIN.

ABBOTSFORD, July 21, 1819.

MY DEAR SIR, — . . . Fortunately at present my system is pretty strong. In the mean while my family are beginning to get forwards. Walter·(you remember my wading into Cauldshiels Loch to save his little frigate from wreck) is now a Cornet of six feet two inches in your Irish 18th Hussars; the regiment is now at Cork, and will probably be next removed to Dublin, so you will see your old friend with a new face; be-furred, be-feathered, and be-whiskered in the highest military *ton*. I have desired him to call upon you, should he get to Dublin on leave, or come there upon duty. I miss him here very much, for he was my companion, gamekeeper, etc., etc., and when one loses one's own health and strength, there are few things so pleasant as to see a son enjoying both in the vigor of hope and promise. Think of this, my good friend, and as you have kind affections to make some good girl happy, settle yourself in life while you are young, and lay up, by so doing, a stock of domestic happiness, against age or bodily decay. There are many good things in life, whatever satirists and misanthropes may say to the contrary; but probably the best of all, next to a conscience void of offence (without which, by the bye, they can hardly exist), are the quiet exercise and enjoyment of the social feelings, in which we are at once happy ourselves, and the cause of happiness to them who are dearest to us.

I have no news to send you from hence. The addition to my house is completed with battlement and bartisan, but the old cottage remains hidden among creepers, until I shall have leisure — *i. e.*, time and money — to build the rest of my mansion — which I will not do hastily, as the present is amply sufficient for accommodation. Adieu, my dear sir; never reckon the degree of my regard by the regularity of my correspondence, for besides the vile diseases of laziness and procrastination, which have always beset me, I have had of late both pain and languor sufficient to justify my silence. Believe me, however, always most truly yours,

WALTER SCOTT.

The first letter the young Cornet received from his father after mounting his "rattle-traps" was the following: —

TO CORNET WALTER SCOTT, 18TH HUSSARS, CORK.

ABBOTSFORD, August 1, 1819.

DEAR WALTER, — I was glad to find you got safe to the hospitable quarters of Piccadilly, and were put on the way of achieving your business well and expeditiously. You would receive a packet of introductory letters by John Ballantyne, to whom I addressed them.

I had a very kind letter two days ago from your Colonel.[1] Had I got it sooner it would have saved some expense in London, but there is no help for it now. As you are very fully provided with all these appointments,

---

[1] The then commandant of the 18th Hussars was Lieutenant-Colonel the Hon. Henry Murray, brother to the Earl of Mansfield.

you must be particular in taking care of them, otherwise the expense of replacing them will be a great burden. Colonel Murray seems disposed to show you much attention. He is, I am told, rather a reserved man, which indeed is the manner of his family. You will, therefore, be the more attentive to what he says, as well as to answer all advances he may make to you with cordiality and frankness; for if you be shy on the one hand, and he reserved on the other, you cannot have the benefit of his advice, which I hope and wish you may gain. I shall be guided by his opinion respecting your allowance: he stipulates that you shall have only two horses (not to be changed without his consent), and on no account keep a gig. You know of old how I detest that mania of driving wheel-barrows up and down, when a man has a handsome horse, and can ride him. They are both foolish and expensive things, and, in my opinion, are only fit for English bagmen — therefore gig it not, I pray you.

In buying your horses you will be very cautious. I see Colonel Murray has delicacy about assisting you directly in the matter — for he says very truly that some gentlemen make a sort of traffic in horse-flesh — from which his duty and inclination equally lead him to steer clear. But he will take care that you don't buy any that are unfit for service, as in the common course they must be approved by the commandant as *chargers*. Besides which, he will probably give you some private hints, of which avail yourself, as there is every chance of your needing much advice in this business. Two things I preach on my own experience: 1*st*, Never to buy an aged horse, however showy. He must have done work, and, at any rate, will be unserviceable in a few years. 2*dly*, To buy rather when the horse is something low in condition, that you may the better see all his points. Six years is the oldest at which I would purchase. You will run risk of being jockeyed by knowing gentlemen of your own corps parting with their *experienced* chargers to *oblige* you. Take care of this. Any good-tempered horse learns the dragoon duty in wonderfully short time, and you are rider enough not to want one quite broke in. Look well about you, and out into the country. Excellent horses are bred all through Munster, and better have a clever young one than an old regimental brute foundered by repeated charges and bolts. If you see a brother-officer's horse that pleases you much, and seems reasonable, look particularly how he stands on his forelegs, and for that purpose see him in the stable. If he shifts and shakes a little, have nothing to say to him. This is the best I can advise, not doubting you will be handsomely excised after all. The officer who leaves his corps may be disposing of good horses, and perhaps selling reasonable. One who continues will not, at least should not, part with a good horse without some great advantage.

You will remain at Cork till you have learned your regimental duty, and then probably be despatched to some outquarter. I need not say how anxious I am that you should keep up your languages, mathematics, and other studies. To have lost that which you already in some degree possess — and that which we don't practise we soon forget — would be a subject of unceasing regret to you hereafter. You have good introductions, and don't neglect to avail yourself of them. Something in this respect your name may do for you — a fair advantage, if used with discretion and propriety. By the way, I suspect you did not call on John Richardson.

The girls were very dull after you left us; indeed the night you went away, Anne had hysterics, which lasted some time. Charles also was down in the mouth, and papa and mamma a little grave and dejected. I would not have you think yourself of too great importance neither, for the greatest personages are not always long missed, and to make a bit of a parody, —

> " Down falls the rain, up gets the sun,
> Just as if Walter were not gone."

We comfort ourselves with the hopes that you are to be happy in the occupation you have chosen, and in your new society. Let me know if there are any well-informed men among them, though I don't expect you to find out that for some time. Be civil to all, till you can by degrees find out who are really best deserving.

I enclose a letter from Sophia, which doubtless contains all the news. St. Boswell's Fair rained miserably, and disappointed the misses. The weather has since been delightful, and harvest advances fast. All here goes its old round — the habits of age do not greatly change, though those of youth do. Mamma has been quite well, and so have I — but I still take calomel. I was obliged to drink some claret with Sir A. Don, Sir John Shelley, and a funny little Newmarket quizzy, called Cousins, whom they brought here with them the other day, but I was not the worse. I wish you had Sir J. S. at your elbow when you are buying your horses — he is a very knowing man on the turf. I like his lady very much. She is perfectly feminine in her manners, has good sense, and plays divinely on the harp; besides all which, she shoots wild boars, and is the boldest horsewoman I ever saw. I saw her at Paris ride like a lapwing, in the midst of all the aide-de-camps and suite of the Duke of Wellington.

Write what your horses come to, etc. Your outfit will be an expensive matter; but once settled, it will be fairly launching you into life in the way you wished, and I trust you will see the necessity of prudence and a gentlemanlike economy, which consists chiefly in refusing one's self trifling indulgences until we can easily pay for them. Once more, I beg you to be attentive to Colonel Murray and to his lady. I hear of a disease among the moorfowl. I suppose they are dying for grief at your departure.

Ever, my dear boy, your affectionate father,

WALTER SCOTT.

7th August, 1819.

DEAR WALTER, — . . . I shall be curious to know how you like your brother-officers, and how you dispose of your time. The drills and riding-school will, of course, occupy much of your mornings for some time. I trust, however, you will keep in view drawing, languages, etc. It is astonishing how far even half an hour a day, regularly bestowed on one object, will carry a man in making himself master of it. The habit of dawdling away time is easily acquired, and so is that of putting every moment either to use or to amusement.

You will not be hasty in forming intimacies with any of your brother-officers, until you observe which of them are most generally respected, and likely to prove most creditable friends. It is seldom that the people who put themselves hastily forward to please are those most worthy of being known. At the same time you will take care to return all civility which is offered, with readiness and frankness. The Italians have a proverb, which I hope you have not forgot poor Pierrotti's lessons so far as not to comprehend, " *Volto sciolto e pensieri stretti.*" There is no occasion to let any one see what you exactly think of him; and it is the less prudent, as you will find reason, in all probability, to change your opinion more than once.

I shall be glad to hear of your being fitted with a good servant. Most of the Irish of that class are scapegraces — drink, steal, and lie like the devil. If you could pick up a canny Scot, it would be well. Let me know about your mess. To drink hard is none of your habits; but even drinking what is called a certain quantity every day, hurts the stomach, and by hereditary descent yours is delicate. I believe the poor Duke of Buccleuch laid the foundation of that disease which occasioned his premature death in the excesses of Villars's regiment; and

I am sorry and ashamed to say, for your warning, that the habit of drinking wine, so much practised when I was a young man, occasioned, I am convinced, many of my cruel stomach complaints. You had better drink a bottle of wine on any particular occasion, than sit and soak and sipple at an English pint every day.

All our bipeds are well. Hamlet had an inflammatory attack, and I began to think he was going mad, after the example of his great namesake, but Willie Laidlaw bled him, and he has recovered. Pussy is very well. Mamma, the girls, and Charlie, join in love. Yours affectionately,

W. S.

P. S. — Always mention what letters of mine you have received, and write to me whatever comes into your head. It is the privilege of great boys when distant that they cannot tire papas by any length of detail upon any subject.

TO THE SAME.

ABBOTSFORD, 13th August, 1819.

MY DEAREST WALTER, — I am very much obliged to Colonel Murray for the trouble he has taken on your behalf. I hope he has received the letter which I wrote to him a fortnight since under Mr. Freeling's cover. It enclosed a parcel of letters to you. I took the liberty of asking his advice what allowance you should have to assist you. You know pretty well my circumstances and your own, and that I wish you to be comfortable, but not in any respect extravagant; and this for your own sake, and not for that of money, which I never valued very much, perhaps not so much as I ought to have done. I think by speaking to Colonel Murray you may get at his opinion, and I have so much trust in your honor and affection as to confide in your naming your own allowance. Meantime, lest the horse should starve while the grass grows, I enclose a cheque upon Messrs. Coutts for £50, to accompt of your first year's allowance. Your paymaster will give you the money for it I dare say.

You have to endorse the bill, *i. e.*, write your name on the back of it.

All concerned are pleased with your kind tokens of remembrance from London. Mamma and I like the caricatures very much. I think, however, scarce any of them shows the fancy and talent of old Gilray: he became insane, I suppose by racking his brain in search of extravagant ideas, and was supported in his helpless condition by the woman who keeps the great print-shop in St. James's Street, who had the generosity to remember that she had made thousands by his labor.

Everything here goes on in the old fashion, and we are all as well as possible, saving that Charles rode to Lawrence fair yesterday in a private excursion, and made himself sick with eating gingerbread, whereby he came to disgrace.

Sophia has your letter of the 4th, which she received yesterday. The enclosed will help you to set up shop and to get and pay whatever is necessary. I wish we had a touch of your hand to make the parties rise in the morning, at which they show as little alertness as usual.

I beg you will keep an account of money received and paid. Buy a little book ruled for the purpose, for pounds, shillings, and pence, and keep an account of cash received and expended. The balance ought to be cash in purse, if the book is regularly kept. But any very small expenses you can enter as "Sundries, £0: 3: 6," which saves trouble.

You will find this most satisfactory and useful. But, indeed, arithmetic is indispensable to a soldier who means to rise in his profession. All military movements depend upon calculation of time, numbers, and distance.

Dogs all well — cat sick — supposed with eating birds in their feathers. Sisters, brother, and mamma join in love to the "poor wounded hussa-a-r;" — I dare say you have heard the song; if not, we shall send it for the benefit of the mess. Yours affectionately,

WALTER SCOTT.

P. S. — Yesterday, *the* 12*th*, would, I suppose, produce some longings after the Peel heights.

In the following letter to Mr. Richardson, we see Scott busied about certain little matters of heraldic importance which had to be settled before his patent of baronetcy could be properly made out. He also alludes to two little volumes, which he edited during this autumn — the Memorials of the Haliburtons, a thin quarto (never published) — and the poems of Patrick Carey, of which he had given specimens some years before in the Annual Register.

TO JOHN RICHARDSON, ESQ., FLUDYER STREET, WESTMINSTER.

ABBOTSFORD, 22d August, 1819.

MY DEAR RICHARDSON, — I am sorry Walter did not get to your kind domicile. But he stayed but about five or six days in London, and great was his haste, as you may well suppose. He had a world of trinkums to get, for you know there goes as much to the man-millinery of a young officer of hussars as to that of an heiress on her bridal day. His complete equipage, horses not included, cost about £360, and if you add a couple of blood horses, it will be £200 more, besides the price of his commission, for the privilege of getting the hardness of his skull tried by a brick-bat at the next meeting of Radical Reformers. I am not much afraid of these folks, however, because I remember 1793 and 1794, when the same ideas possessed a much more formidable class of the people, being received by a large proportion of farmers, shopkeepers, and others, possessed of substance. A mere mob will always be a fire of loose straw; but it is melancholy to think of the individual mischief that may be done. I did not find it quite advisable to take so long a journey as London this summer. I am quite recovered; but my last attack was of so dreadful a nature, that I wish to be quite insured against another — *i. e.*, as much as one can be insured against such a circumstance — before leaving home for any length of time.

To return to the vanities of this world, from what threatened to hurry me to the next: I enclose a drawing of my arms, with the supporters which the heralds here assign me. Our friend Harden seems to wish I would adopt one of his Mer-maidens, otherwise they should be both Moors, as on the left side. I have also added an impression of my seal. You can furnish Sir George Naylor with as much of my genealogy as will serve the present purpose. I shall lose no time in connecting myself by a general service with my grand-uncle, the last Haliburton of Dryburgh Abbey, or Newmains, as they call it. I spoke to the Lyon-office people in Edinburgh. I find my entry there will be an easy matter, the proofs being very pregnant and accessible. I would not stop for a trifling expense to register my pedigree in England, as far as you think may be necessary, to show that it is a decent one. My ancestors were brave and honest men, and I have no reason to be ashamed of them, though they were neither wealthy nor great.

As something of an antiquary and genealogist, I should not like there were any mistakes in this matter, so I send you a small note of my descent by my father and my paternal grandmother, with a memorandum of the proofs by which they may be supported, to which I might add a whole cloud of oral witnesses. I hate the being suspected of fishing for a pedigree, or bolstering one up with false statements. How people can bring themselves to this, I cannot conceive. I send you a copy of the Haliburton MS., of which I have printed twenty for the satisfaction of a few friends. You can have any part of them copied in London which ought to be registered. I should like if Sir George Naylor would take the trouble of looking at the proofs, which are chiefly extracts from the public records. I take this opportunity to send you also a copy of a little amateur-book — Carey's Poems —

a thoroughbred Cavalier, and, I think, no bad versifier. Kind compliments to Mrs. Richardson. Yours, my dear Richardson, most truly,   WALTER SCOTT.

TO CORNET W. SCOTT, 18TH HUSSARS, CORK.

ABBOTSFORD, 4th September, 1819.

DEAR WALTER, — Your very acceptable letter of the 26th reached me to-day. I had begun to be apprehensive that the draft had fallen into the hands of the Philistines, but the very long calm must have made the packets slow in their progress, which I suppose was the occasion of the delay. Respecting the allowance, Colonel Murray informs me that from £200 to £250, in addition to the pay of a Cornet, ought to make a young man very comfortable. He adds, which I am much pleased to hear, that your officers are, many of them, men of moderate fortune, and disposed to be economical. I had thought of £200 as what would suit us both, but when I see the account which you very properly keep, I shall be better able to determine. It must be considered that any uncommon expense, as the loss of a horse or the like, may occasion an extra draft over and above the allowance. I like very much your methodical arrangement as to expenses; it is rather a tiresome thing at first to keep an accompt of pounds, shillings, and pence, but it is highly necessary, and enables one to see how the money actually goes. It is, besides, a good practical way of keeping up acquaintance with arithmetic, and you will soon find that the principles on which all military movements turn are arithmetical, and that though one may no doubt learn to do them by rote, yet to *understand* them, you must have recourse to numbers. Your adjutant will explain this to you. By the way, as he is a foreigner, you will have an opportunity to keep up a little of your French and German. Both are highly necessary to you; the knowledge of the last, with few other qualifications, made several officers' fortunes last war.

I observe with pleasure you are making acquaintances among the gentry, which I hope you will not drop for want of calling, etc. I trust you have delivered all your recommendations, for it is an affront to omit doing so, both to the person who writes them, and those for whom they are designed. On the other hand, one always holds their head a little better up in the world when they keep good society. Lord and Lady Melville are to give you recommendations when you go to Dublin. I was at Melville Castle for two days, and found them both well. I was also one day at Langholm Lodge to meet Lord Montagu. Possibly, among your Irish friends, you may get some shooting. I shall be glad you avail yourself of any such opportunities, and also that, when you get your own horses, you hunt in the winter, if you be within the reach of hounds. Nothing confirms a man in horseman-ship so well as hunting, though I do not recommend it to beginners, who are apt to learn to ride like grooms. Besides the exercise, field-sports make a young soldier acquainted with the country, and habituate him to have a good eye for distance and for taking up the *carte de pays* in general, which is essential to all, but especially to officers of light troops, who are expected to display both alertness and intelligence in reporting the nature of the country, being in fact the *eyes* of the army. In every point of view, field-sports are preferable to the in-doors amusement of a billiard-table, which is too often the lounging-place for idle young officers, where there is nothing to be got but a habit of throwing away time, and an acquaintance with the very worst society — I mean at public billiard-rooms — for unquestionably the game itself is a pretty one, when practised among gentlemen, and not made a constant habit of. But public billiard-tables are almost always the resort of blacklegs and sharpers, and all that numerous class whom the French call *chevaliers d'industrie*, and we, *knights of the whip-ping-post*.

I am glad you go to the anatomical lectures. An acquaintance with our own very extraordinary frame is a useful branch of general knowledge, and as you have some turn for drawing, it will also enable you to judge of the proper mode of disposing the limbs and muscles of your figures, should you prosecute the art so far. In fact, there is no branch of study can come much amiss to a young man, providing he does study, and very often the precise occupation of the time must be trusted to taste and opportunity.

The White Boys made a great noise when I was a boy. But Ireland (the more is the pity) has never been without White Boys, or Right Boys, or Defenders, or Peep-of-day Boys, or some wild association or another for disturbing the peace of the country. We shall not be many degrees better if the Radical Reformers be not checked. The Manchester Yeomen behaved very well, upsetting the most immense crowd ever was seen, and notwithstanding the lies in the papers, without any unnecessary violence. Mr. Hunt pretends to have had several blows on his head with sabres, but has no wound to show for it. I am disposed to wish he had got such a one as once on a day I could have treated him to. I am apt to think his politic pate would have broached no more sedition.

Miss Rutherford and Eliza Russell are now with us. We were also favored with a visit of the Miss ——s, who are rather empty canisters, though I dare say very good girls. Anne tired of them most inhospitably. Mrs. Maclean Clephane and her two unmarried daughters are now here; being, as we say, pears of another tree. Your sisters seem very fond of the young ladies, and I am glad of it, for they will see that a great deal of accomplishment and information may be completely reconciled with liveliness, fun, good-humor, and good-breeding.

All here send love. Dogs and cat are well. I dare say you have heard from some other correspondent that poor Lady Wallace died of an inflammation, after two days' illness. Trout[1] has returned here several times, poor fellow, and seems to look for you; but Henry Scott is very kind to him, and he is a great favorite.

As you Hussars smoke, I will give you one of my pipes, but you must let me know how I can send it safely. It is a very handsome one, though not my best. I will keep my *Meerschaum* until I make my Continental tour, and then you shall have that also. I hope you will get leave for a few months, and go with me. Yours very affectionately,   WALTER SCOTT.

About this time, as the succeeding letters will show, Abbotsford had the honor of a short visit from Prince Leopold of Saxe-Coburg, now King of the Belgians. Immediately afterwards Scott heard of the death of Mrs. William Erskine, and repaired to Edinburgh to condole with his afflicted friend.[2] His allusions, meanwhile, to views of buying more land on Tweedside, are numerous. These speculations are explained in a most characteristic style to the Cornet; and we see that one of them was cut short by the tragical death of a *bonnet-laird* already introduced to the reader's notice — namely, *Lauchie Longlegs*, the admired of Geoffrey Crayon.

TO CORNET WALTER SCOTT, 18TH HUSSARS, CORK.

ABBOTSFORD, 27th September, 1819.

MY DEAR WALTER, — Your letter of the 10th gave me the pleasant assurance that you are well and happy, and attending to your profession. We have been jogging on here in the old fashion, somewhat varied by an unexpected visit, on Friday last, from no less a person than Prince Leopold. I conclude you will have all the

[1] *Lady Wallace* was a pony; *Trout* a favorite pointer which the Cornet had given, at leaving home, to the young Laird of Harden, now the Master of Polwarth.

[2] For Scott's Epitaph for Mrs. Erskine, see his *Poetical Works* (Ed. 1834), vol. xi. p. 347 [Cambridge Ed. p. 447].

particulars of this important event from the other members of the family, so I shall only say that when I mentioned the number of your regiment, the Prince said he had several friends in the 18th, and should now think he had one more, which was very polite. By the way, I hear an excellent character of your officers for regularity and gentlemanlike manners. This report gives me great pleasure, for to live in bad society will deprave the best manners, and to live in good will improve the worst.

I am trying a sort of bargain with neighbor Nicol Milne at present. He is very desirous of parting with his estate of Faldonside, and if he will be contented with a reasonable price, I am equally desirous to be the purchaser. I conceive it will come to about £30,000 at least. I will not agree to give a penny more; and I think that sum is probably £2000 and more above its actual marketable value. But then it lies extremely convenient for us, and would, joined to Abbotsford, make a very gentlemanlike property, worth at least £1800 or £2000 a year. I can command about £10,000 of my own, and if I be spared life and health, I should not fear rubbing off the rest of the price, as Nicol is in no hurry for payment. As you will succeed me in my landed property, I think it right to communicate my views to you. I am much moved by the prospect of getting at about £2000 or £3000 worth of marle, which lies on Milne's side of the loch, but which can only be drained on my side, so that he can make no use of it. This would make the lands of Abbotsford worth 40s. an acre over-head, excepting the sheep farm. I am sensible I might dispose of my money to more advantage, but probably to none which, in the long run, would be better for you — certainly to none which would be productive of so much pleasure to myself. The woods are thriving, and it would be easy, at a trifling expense, to restore Faldonside loch, and stock it with fish. In fact, it would require but a small dam-head. By means of a little judicious planting, added to what is already there, the estate might be rendered one of the most beautiful in this part of Scotland. Such are my present plans, my dear boy, having as much your future welfare and profit in view as the immediate gratification of my own wishes.

I am very sorry to tell you that poor Mrs. William Erskine is no more. She was sent by the medical people on a tour to the lakes of Cumberland, and was taken ill at Lowood, on Windermere. Nature, much exhausted by her previous indisposition, sunk under four days' illness. Her husband was with her, and two of her daughters — he is much to be pitied.

Mr. Rees, the bookseller, told me he had met you in the streets of Cork, and reported well of the growth of your *Schnurr-bart*. I hope you know what that means. Pray write often, as the post comes so slow. I keep all your letters, and am much pleased with the frankness of the style. No word of your horses yet? but it is better not to be impatient, and to wait for good ones. I have been three times on Newark, and killed six hares each time. The two young dogs are capital good.

I must not omit to tell you our old, and, I may add, our kind neighbor Lauchie, has departed, or, as Tom expresses it, has been fairly *flytten out o' the warld*. You know the old quarrel betwixt his brother and him about the wife: in an ill-fated hour Jock the brother came down to Lochbreist with a sister from Edinburgh, who was determined to have her share of the scolding-match; they attacked poor old Lauchie like mad folks, and reviled his wife in all sort of evil language. At length his passion was wrought up to a great pitch, and he answered with much emotion, that if she were the greatest —— in Edinburgh, it was not their business, and as he uttered this speech, he fell down on his back, and lay a dead man before them. There is little doubt the violence of the agitation had broke a blood-vessel in the heart or brain. A very few days since he was run-

ning up and down calling for a coffin, and wishing to
God he was in one; to which Swanston,[1] who was present,
answered, he could not apply to a better hand, and he
would make him one if he had a mind. He has left a
will of his own making, but from some informality I
think it will be set aside. His land cannot come into
the market until his girl comes of age, which, by the
way, makes me more able for the other bargain. . . .
The blackcocks are very plenty. I put up fourteen cocks
and hens in walking up the Clappercleuch to look at the
wood. Do you not wish you had been on the outside
with your gun? Tom has kept us well supplied with
game; he boasts that he shot fifteen times without a
miss. I shall be glad to hear that you do the same on
Mr. Newenham's grounds. Mamma, the girls, and
Charles, all join in love and affection. Believe me ever,
dear Walter, your affectionate father,

WALTER SCOTT.

TO THE LORD MONTAGU, ETC., ETC., ETC.

ABBOTSFORD, 3d October. 1819.

MY DEAR LORD, — I am honored with your Buxton
letter. . . . Anent Prince Leopold, I only heard of his
approach at eight o'clock in the morning, and he was to
be at Selkirk by eleven. The magistrates sent to ask
me to help them to receive him. It occurred to me he
might be coming to Melrose to see the Abbey, in which
case I could not avoid asking him to Abbotsford, as he
must pass my very door. I mentioned this to Mrs.
Scott, who was lying quietly in bed, and I wish you had
heard the scream she gave on the occasion. "What have
we to offer him?" — "Wine and cake," said I, thinking
to make all things easy; but she ejaculated, in a tone
of utter despair, "Cake!! where am I to get cake?"

---

[1] John Swanston had then the care of the sawmill at Toftfield; he was
one of Scott's most valued dependents, and in the sequel succeeded Tom
Purdie as his henchman.

However, being partly consoled with the recollection that
his visit was a very improbable incident, and curiosity,
as usual, proving too strong for alarm, she set out with
me in order not to miss a peep of the great man.   James
Skene and his lady were with us, and we gave our car-
riages such additional dignity as a pair of leaders could
add, and went to meet him in full puff.   The Prince
very civilly told me, that, though he could not see Melrose on this occasion, he wished to come to Abbotsford
for an hour.   New despair on the part of Mrs. Scott,
who began to institute a domiciliary search for cold meat
through the whole city of Selkirk, which produced *one
shoulder of cold lamb*.   In the mean while, his Royal
Highness received the civic honors of the BIRSE [1] very
graciously.   I had hinted to Bailie Lang, [2] that it ought
only to be licked *symbolically* on the present occasion;
so he flourished it three times before his mouth, but without touching it with his lips, and the Prince followed his
example as directed.   Lang made an excellent speech —
sensible, and feeling, and well delivered.   The Prince
seemed much surprised at this great propriety of expression and behavior in a magistrate, whose people seemed
such a rabble, and whose whole band of music consisted
in a drum and fife.   He noticed to Bailie Anderson that
Selkirk seemed very populous in proportion to its extent.
"On an occasion like this it seems so," answered the
Bailie, — neatly enough, I thought.   I question if any
magistrates in the kingdom, lord mayors and aldermen
not excepted, could have behaved with more decent and
quiet good-breeding.   Prince Leopold repeatedly alluded
to this during the time he was at Abbotsford.   I do not
know how Mrs. Scott ultimately managed; but with
broiled salmon, and blackcock, and partridges, she gave

[1] See *ante*, p. 88.
[2] Scott's good friend, Mr. Andrew Lang, Sheriff-Clerk for Selkirkshire.
was then chief magistrate of the county town.   [He was the grandfather of the accomplished man of letters who bears his name.]

him a very decent lunch; and I chanced to have some very fine old hock, which was mighty germane to the matter.

The Prince seems melancholy, whether naturally or from habit, I do not pretend to say; but I do not remember thinking him so at Paris, where I saw him frequently, then a much poorer man than myself; yet he showed some humor, for, alluding to the crowds that followed him everywhere, he mentioned some place where he had gone out to shoot, but was afraid to proceed for fear of "bagging a boy." He said he really thought of getting some shooting-place in Scotland, and promised me a longer visit on his return. If I had had a day's notice to have *warned the waters*, we could have met him with a very respectable number of the gentry; but there was no time for this, and probably he liked it better as it was. There was only young Clifton who could have come, and he was shy and cubbish, and would not, though requested by the Selkirk people. He was perhaps ashamed to march through Coventry with them. It hung often and sadly on my mind that *he* was wanting who could and would have received him like a Prince indeed; and yet the meeting betwixt them, had they been fated to meet, would have been a very sad one. I think I have now given your Lordship a very full, true, and particular account of our royal visit, unmatched even by that of King Charles at the Castle of Tillietudlem. That we did not speak of it for more than a week after it happened, and that that emphatic monosyllable, *The Prince*, is not heard amongst us more than ten times a day, is, on the whole, to the credit of my family's understanding. The piper is the only one whose brain he seems to have endangered; for, as the Prince said he preferred him to any he had heard in the Highlands — (which, by the way, shows his Royal Highness knows nothing of the matter) — the fellow seems to have become incapable of his ordinary occupation as a forester, and

has cut stick and stem without remorse to the tune of
Phail Phranse, i. e., the Prince's Welcome.

I am just going to the head-court with Donaldson, and
go a day sooner to exhume certain old monuments of the
Rutherfords at Jedburgh. Edgerstone[1] is to meet me
at Jedburgh for this research, and then we shall go up
with him to dinner. My best respects attend Lady
Montagu. I wish this letter may reach you on a more
lively day than it is written in, for it requires little to
add to its dulness. Tweed is coming down very fast, the
first time this summer. Believe me, my dear Lord, most
truly yours,   WALTER SCOTT.

TO W. SCOTT, ESQ., 18TH HUSSARS, CORK.

ABBOTSFORD, 14th October, 1819.

DEAR WALTER, — I had your last letter, and am very
glad you find pleasant society. Mrs. Dundas of Arniston
is so good as to send you some introductions, which you
will deliver as soon as possible. You will be now in
some degree accustomed to meet with strangers, and to
form your estimate of their character and manners. I
hope, in the mean time, the French and German are
attended to; please to mention in your next letter what
you are reading, and in what languages. The hours of
youth, my dear Walter, are too precious to be spent all
in gayety. We must lay up in that period when our
spirit is active, and our memory strong, the stores of information which are not only to facilitate our progress
through life, but to amuse and interest us in our later
stage of existence. I very often think what an unhappy
person I should have been, if I had not done something
more or less towards improving my understanding when

---

[1] The late John Rutherford of Edgerstone, long M. P. for Roxburghshire, was a person of high worth, and universally esteemed. Scott used
to say Edgerstone was his *beau ideal* of the character of a country gentleman. He was, I believe, the head of the once great and powerful clan of
Rutherford.

I was at your age; and I never reflect, without severe
self-condemnation, on the opportunities of acquiring
knowledge which I either trifled with, or altogether neglected. I hope you will be wiser than I have been, and
experience less of that self-reproach.

My last acquainted you with Mrs. Erskine's death,
and I grieve to say we have just received intelligence
that our kind neighbor and good friend Lord Somerville
is at the very last gasp. His disease is a dysentery, and
the symptoms, as his brother writes to Mr. Samuel Somerville, are mortal. He is at Vevay, upon his road, I
suppose, to Italy, where he had purposed spending the
winter. His death, for I understand nothing else can
be expected, will be another severe loss to me; for he
was a kind, good friend, and at my time of day men do
not readily take to new associates. I must own this has
been one of the most melancholy years I ever passed.
The poor Duke, who loved me so well — Mrs. Erskine —
Lord Somerville — not to mention others with whom I
was less intimate, make it one year of mourning. I
should not forget the Chief Baron, who, though from ill
health we met of late seldom, was always my dear friend,
and indeed very early benefactor. I must look forwards
to seeing in your success and respectability, and in the affection and active improvement of all of you, those pleasures which are narrowed by the death of my contemporaries. Men cannot form new intimacies at my period
of life, but must be happy or otherwise according to the
good fortune and good conduct of those near relatives
who rise around them.

I wish much to know if you are lucky in a servant.
Trust him with as little cash as possible, and keep short
accounts. Many a good servant is spoiled by neglecting
this simple precaution. The man is tempted to some
expense of his own, gives way to it, and then has to make
it up by a system of overcharge and peculation; and thus
mischief begins, and the carelessness of the master makes

a rogue out of an honest lad, and cheats himself into the bargain.

I have a letter from your uncle Tom, telling me his eldest daughter is to be forthwith married to a Captain Huxley of his own regiment. As he has had a full opportunity of being acquainted with the young gentleman, and approves of the match, I have to hope that it will be a happy one. I fear there is no great fortune in the case on either side, which is to be regretted.

Of domestic affairs I have little to tell you. The harvest has been excellent, the weather delightful; but this I must often have repeated. To-day I was thinning out fir-trees in the thicket, and the men were quite exhausted with the heat, and I myself, though only marking the trees, felt the exercise sufficiently warm. The wood is thriving delightfully. On the 28th we are to have a dance in honor of your birthday. I wish you could look in upon us for the day at least — only I am afraid we could not part with you when it was over, and so you would be in the guise of Cinderella, when she outstayed her time at the ball, and all her finery returned into its original base materials. Talking of balls, the girls would tell you the Melrose hop, where mamma presided, went off well.

I expect poor Erskine and his daughter next week, or the week after. I went into town to see him — and found him bearing his great loss with his natural gentleness and patience. But he was sufficiently distressed, as he has great reason to be. I also expect Lord and Lady Melville here very soon. Sir William Rae (now Lord Advocate) and his lady came to us on Saturday. On Sunday Maida walked with us, and in jumping the paling at the Greentongue park contrived to hang himself up by the hind leg. He howled at first, but seeing us making towards him he stopped crying, and waved his tail, by way of signal, it was supposed, for assistance. He sustained no material injury, though his leg was strangely twisted into the bars, and he was nearly hanging by it. He showed great gratitude, in his way, to his deliverers.

This is a long letter, and little in it; but that is nothing extraordinary. All send best love — and I am ever, dear Walter, your affectionate father,

WALTER SCOTT.

TO THOMAS SCOTT, ESQ., PAYMASTER, 70TH REGIMENT, CANADA.

ABBOTSFORD, 16th October, 1819.

DEAR TOM, — I received yesterday your very acceptable letter, containing the news of Jessie's approaching marriage, in which, as a match agreeable to her mother and you, and relieving your minds from some of the anxious prospects which haunt those of parents, I take the most sincere interest. Before this reaches you the event will probably have taken place. Meantime, I enclose a letter to the bride or wife, as the case may happen to be. I have sent a small token of good-will to ballast my good wishes, which you will please to value for the young lady, that she may employ it as most convenient or agreeable to her. A little more fortune would perhaps have done the young folks no harm; but Captain Huxley, being such as you describe him, will have every chance of getting forward in his profession; and the happiest marriages are often those in which there is, at first, occasion for prudence and economy. I do certainly feel a little of the surprise which you hint at, for time flies over our heads one scarce marks how, and children become marriageable ere we consider them as out of the nursery. My eldest son, Walter, has also wedded himself — but it is to a regiment of hussars. He is at present a cornet in the 18th, and quartered in Cork barracks. He is capital at most exercises, but particularly as a horseman. I do not intend he shall remain in the cavalry, however, but shall get him into the line when he is capable of promotion. Since he has chosen this profession, I shall be desirous that he follows it out in good earnest, and that can only be done by getting into the infantry.

My late severe illness has prevented my going up to London to receive the honor which the Prince Regent has announced his intention to inflict upon me. My present intention is, if I continue as well as I have been, to go up about Christmas to get this affair over. My health was restored (I trust permanently) by the use of calomel, a very severe and painful remedy, especially in my exhausted state of body, but it has proved a radical one. By the way, *Radical* is a word in very bad odor here, being used to denote a set of blackguards a hundred times more mischievous and absurd than our old friends in 1794 and 1795. You will learn enough of the doings of the *Radical Reformers* from the papers. In Scotland we are quiet enough, excepting in the manufacturing districts, and we are in very good hands, as Sir William Rae, our old commander, is Lord Advocate. Rae has been here two or three days, and left me yesterday; he is the old man, sensible, cool-headed, and firm, always thinking of his duty, never of himself. He inquired kindly after you, and I think will be disposed to serve you, should an opportunity offer. Poor William Erskine has lost his excellent wife, after a long and wasting illness. She died at Lowood on Windermere, he having been recommended to take her upon a tour about three weeks before her death. I own I should scarce forgive a physician who should contrive to give me this addition to family distress. I went to town last week to see him, and found him, upon the whole, much better than I expected. I saw my mother on the same occasion, admirably well indeed. She is greatly better than this time two years, when she rather quacked herself a little too much. I have sent your letter to our mother, and will not fail to transmit to our other friends the agreeable news of your daughter's settlement. Our cousin, Sir Harry Macdougal, is marrying his eldest daughter to Sir

Thomas Brisbane, a very good match on both sides. I have been paying a visit on the occasion, which suspends my closing this letter. I hope to hear very soon from you. Respecting our silence, I, like a ghost, only waited to be spoken to, and you may depend on me as a regular correspondent, when you find time to be one yourself. Charlotte and the girls join in kind love to Mrs. Scott and all the family. I should like to know what you mean to do with young Walter, and whether I can assist you in that matter. Believe me, dear Tom, ever your affectionate brother,

W. SCOTT.

TO DANIEL TERRY, ESQ., LONDON.

ABBOTSFORD, November 10, 1819.

MY DEAR TERRY, — I should be very sorry if you thought the interest I take in you and yours so slight as not to render your last letter extremely interesting. We have all our various combats to fight in this best of all possible worlds, and, like brave fellow-soldiers, ought to assist one another as much as possible. I have little doubt, that if God spares me till my little namesake be fit to take up his share of the burden, I may have interest enough to be of great advantage to him in the entrance of life. In the present state of your own profession, you would not willingly, I suppose, choose him to follow it; and, as it is very seductive to young people of a lively temper and good taste for the art, you should, I think, consider early how you mean to dispose of little Walter, with a view, that is, to the future line of life which you would wish him to adopt. Mrs. Terry has not the good health which all who know her amiable disposition and fine accomplishments would anxiously wish her; yet, with impaired health and the caution which it renders necessary, we have very frequently instances of the utmost verge of existence being attained, while robust strength is cut off in the middle career. So you must be of good heart, and hope the best in this as in other cases of a like affecting nature. I go to town on Monday, and will forward under Mr. Freeling's cover as much of Ivanhoe as is finished in print. It is completed, but in the hands of a very slow transcriber; when I can collect it, I will send you the MS., which you will please to keep secret from every eye. I think this will give a start, if it be worth taking, of about a month, for the work will be out on the 20th of December. It is certainly possible to adapt it to the stage, but the expense of scenery and decorations would be great, this being a tale of chivalry, not of character. There is a tale in existence, by dramatizing which, I am certain, a most powerful effect might be produced: it is called Undine, and I believe has been translated into French by Mademoiselle Montolieu, and into English from her version: do read it, and tell me your opinion: in German the character of Undine is exquisite. The only objection is, that the catastrophe is unhappy, but this might be altered. I hope to be in London for ten days the end of next month; and so good-by for the present, being in great haste, most truly yours,

W. SCOTT.

I conclude this chapter with a letter written two or three days before Scott quitted Abbotsford for the winter session. It is addressed to his friend Hartstonge, who had taken the opportunity of the renewal of Scott's correspondence to solicit his opinion and assistance touching a MS. drama; and the reader will be diverted with the style in which the amiable tragedian is treated to his *quietus:* —

TO MATTHEW WELD HARTSTONGE, ESQ., DUBLIN.

ABBOTSFORD, 11th November, 1819.

MY DEAR SIR, — I was duly favored with your packet, containing the play, as well as your very kind letter. I will endeavor (though extremely unwilling to offer criticism on most occasions) to meet your confidence with perfect frankness. I do not consider the Tragedy as likely to make that favorable impression on the public which I would wish that the performance of a friend should effect — and I by no means recommend to you to hazard it upon the boards. In other compositions, the neglect of the world takes nothing from the merit of the author; but there is something ludicrous in being *affiché* as the author of an unsuccessful play. Besides, you entail on yourself the great and eternal plague of altering and retrenching to please the humors of performers, who are, speaking generally, extremely ignorant, and capricious in proportion. These are not vexations to be voluntarily undertaken; and the truth is, that in the present day there is only one reason which seems to me adequate for the encountering the plague of trying to please a set of conceited performers and a very motley audience, — I mean the want of money, from which, fortunately, you are exempted. It is very true that some day or other a great dramatic genius may arise to strike out a new path; but I fear till this happens no great effect will be produced by treading in the old one. The reign of Tragedy seems to be over, and the very considerable poetical abilities which have been lately applied to it, have failed to revive it. Should the public ever be indulged with small theatres adapted to the hours of the better ranks in life, the dramatic art may recover; at present it is in abeyance — and I do therefore advise you in all sincerity to keep the Tragedy (which I return under cover) safe under your own charge. Pray think of this as one of the most unpleasant offices of friendship — and be not angry with me for having been very frank, upon an occasion when frankness may be more useful than altogether palatable.

I am much obliged to you for your kind intentions towards my young Hussar. We have not heard from

him for three weeks. I believe he is making out a meditated visit to Killarney. I am just leaving the country
for Edinburgh, to attend my duty in the courts; but the
badness of the weather in some measure reconciles me
to the unpleasant change. I have the pleasure to continue the most satisfactory accounts of my health; it is,
to external appearance, as strong as in my strongest days
— indeed, after I took once more to Sancho's favorite
occupations of eating and sleeping, I recovered my losses
wonderfully. Very truly yours,

WALTER SCOTT.

CHAPTER XLVI

POLITICAL ALARMS. — THE RADICALS. — LEVIES OF
VOLUNTEERS. — PROJECT OF THE BUCCLEUCH LE-
GION. — DEATH OF SCOTT'S MOTHER, HER BROTHER
DR. RUTHERFORD, AND HER SISTER CHRISTIAN. —
LETTERS TO LORD MONTAGU, MR. THOMAS SCOTT,
CORNET SCOTT, MR. LAIDLAW, AND LADY LOUISA
STUART. — PUBLICATION OF IVANHOE

1819

TOWARDS the winter of 1819 there prevailed a spirit
of alarming insubordination among the mining population of Northumberland and the weavers of the West of
Scotland; and Scott was particularly gratified with finding that his own neighbors at Galashiels had escaped the
contagion. There can be little doubt that this exemption
was principally owing to the personal influence and authority of the Laird of Abbotsford and Sheriff of the
Forest; but the people of Galashiels were also fortunate
in the qualities of their own beneficent landlords, Mr.
Scott of Gala, and Mr. Pringle of Torwoodlee. The
progress of the western *Reformers* by degrees led even
the most important Whigs in that district to exert themselves in the organization of volunteer regiments, both
mounted and dismounted; and, when it became generally suspected that Glasgow and Paisley maintained a
dangerous correspondence with the refractory colliers
of Northumberland — Scott, and his friends the Lairds of
Torwoodlee and Gala, determined to avail themselves of
the loyalty and spirit of the men of Ettrick and Teviotdale, and proposed first raising a company of sharpshoot-

ers among their own immediate neighbors, and afterwards
— this plan receiving every encouragement — a legion or
brigade upon a large scale, to be called the Buccleuch
Legion. During November and December, 1819, these
matters formed the chief daily care and occupation of the
author of Ivanhoe; and though he was still obliged to
dictate most of the chapters of his novel, we shall see
that, in case it should be necessary for the projected levy
of Foresters to march upon Tynedale, he was prepared
to place himself at their head.

He had again intended, as soon as he should have
finished Ivanhoe, to proceed to London, and receive his
baronetcy; but as that affair had been crossed at Easter
by his own illness, so at Christmas it was again obliged
to be put off in consequence of a heavy series of domestic
afflictions. Within one week Scott lost his excellent
mother, his uncle Dr. Daniel Rutherford, Professor of
Botany in the University of Edinburgh — and their
sister, Christian Rutherford, already often mentioned as
one of the dearest and most esteemed of all his friends
and connections. .

The following letters require no further introduction
or comment: —

TO THE LORD MONTAGU, BUXTON.

ABBOTSFORD, 12th November, 1819.

MY DEAR LORD, — . . . I wish I had any news to
send your Lordship; but the best is, we are all quiet
here. The Galashiels weavers, both men and masters,
have made their political creed known to me, and have
sworn themselves anti-radical. They came in solemn
procession, with their banners, and my own piper at their
head, whom they had borrowed for the nonce. But the
Tweed being in flood, we could only communicate like
Wallace and Bruce across the Carron. However, two
deputies came through in the boat, and made me acquainted with their loyal purposes. The evening was

crowned with two most distinguished actions — the weavers refusing, in the most peremptory manner, to accept of a couple of guineas to buy whiskey, and the renowned John of Skye, piper in ordinary to the Laird of Abbotsford, no less steadily refusing a very handsome collection, which they offered him for his minstrelsy. All this sounds very nonsensical, but the people must be humored and countenanced when they take the right turn, otherwise they will be sure to take the wrong. The accounts from the West sometimes make me wish our little Duke five or six years older, and able to get on horseback. It seems approaching to the old song —

> " Come fill up our cup, come fill up our can,
> Come saddle the horses, and call up our men,
> Come open the gates, and let us go free,
> And we 'll show them the bonnets of bonny Dundee." [1]

I am rather too old for that work now, and I cannot look forward to it with the sort of feeling that resembled pleasure — as I did in my younger and more healthy days. However, I have got a good following here, and will endeavor to keep them together till times mend.

My respectful compliments attend Lady Montagu, and I am always, with the greatest regard, your Lordship's very faithful   WALTER SCOTT.

TO CORNET WALTER SCOTT, 18TH HUSSARS.

EDINBURGH, 13th November, 1819.

DEAR WALTER, — I am much surprised and rather hurt at not hearing from you for so long a while. You ought to remember that, however pleasantly the time may be passing with you, we at home have some right to expect that a part of it (a very small part will serve the turn) should be dedicated, were it but for the sake of propriety, to let us know what you are about. I cannot say I shall be flattered by finding myself under the necessity of again complaining of neglect. To write once a

[1] See Scott's *Poetical Works*, vol. xii. p. 195 [Cambridge Ed. p. 485].

week, to one or other of us, is no great sacrifice, and it
is what I earnestly pray you to do.

We are to have great doings in Edinburgh this winter.
No less than Prince Gustavus of Sweden is to pass the
season here, and do what Princes call studying. He is
but half a Prince either, for this Northern Star is somewhat shorn of his beams. His father was, you know,
dethroned by Buonaparte, at least by the influence of his
arms, and one of his generals, Bernadotte, made heir of
the Swedish throne in his stead. But this youngster, I
suppose, has his own dreams of royalty, for he is nephew
to the Emperor of Russia (by the mother's side), and
that is a likely connection to be of use to him, should the
Swedish nobles get rid of Bernadotte, as it is said they
wish to do. Lord Melville has recommended the said
Prince particularly to my attention, though I do not see
how I can do much for him.

I have just achieved my grand remove from Abbotsford to Edinburgh — a motion which you know I do not
make with great satisfaction. We had the Abbotsford
hunt last week. The company was small, as the newspapers say, but select, and we had excellent sport, killing
eight hares. We coursed on Gala's ground, and he was
with us. The dinner went off with its usual alacrity,
but we wanted you and Sally to ride and mark for us.

I enclose another letter from Mrs. Dundas of Arniston. I am afraid you have been careless in not delivering those I formerly forwarded, because in one of them,
which Mrs. Dundas got from a friend, there was enclosed
a draft for some money. I beg you will be particular
in delivering any letters entrusted to you, because though
the good-nature of the writers may induce them to write
to be of service to you, yet it is possible that they may,
as in this instance, add things which are otherwise of
importance to their correspondents. It is probable that
you may have picked up among your military friends the
idea that the mess of a regiment is all in all sufficient to

itself; but when you see a little of the world you will be satisfied that none but pedants — for there is pedantry in all professions — herd exclusively together, and that those who do so are laughed at in real good company. This you may take on the authority of one who has seen more of life and society, in all its various gradations, from the highest to the lowest, than a whole hussar regimental mess, and who would be much pleased by knowing that you reap the benefit of an experience which has raised him from being a person of small consideration to the honor of being father of an officer of hussars. I therefore enclose another letter from the same kind friend, of which I pray you to avail yourself. In fact, those officers who associate entirely among themselves see and know no more of the world than their messman, and get conceited and disagreeable by neglecting the opportunities offered for enlarging their understanding. Every distinguished soldier whom I have known, and I have known many, was a man of the world, and accustomed to general society.

To sweeten my lecture, I have to inform you that, this being quarter-day, I have a remittance of £50 to send you whenever you are pleased to let me know it will be acceptable — for, like a ghost, I will not speak again till I am spoken to.

I wish you not to avail yourself of your leave of absence this winter, because, if my health continues good, I shall endeavor to go on the Continent next summer, and should be very desirous to have you with me; therefore, I beg you to look after your French and German. We had a visit from a very fine fellow indeed at Abbotsford, — Sir Thomas Brisbane, who long commanded a brigade in the Peninsula. He is very scientific, but bores no one with it, being at the same time a well-informed man on all subjects, and particularly alert in his own profession, and willing to talk about what he has seen. Sir Harry Hay Macdougal, whose eldest daughter he is to marry, brought him to Abbotsford on a sort of wedding visit, as we are cousins according to the old fashion of country kin; Beardie, of whom Sir Harry has a beautiful picture, being a son of an Isabel Macdougal, who was, I fancy, grand-aunt to Sir Harry.

Once more, my dear Walter, write more frequently, and do not allow yourself to think that the first neglect in correspondence I have ever had to complain of has been on your part. I hope you have received the Meerschaum pipe. — I remain your affectionate father,

WALTER SCOTT.

TO THE SAME.

EDINBURGH, 3d December, 1819.

MY DEAR WALTER, — I hope your servant proves careful and trusty. Pray let me know this. At any rate, do not trust him a bit further than you can help it, for in buying anything you will get it much cheaper yourself than he will. We are now settled for the winter; that is, all of them excepting myself, who must soon look southwards. On Saturday we had a grand visitor, i. e., the Crown Prince of Sweden, under the name of Count Itterburg. His travelling companion or tutor is Baron de Polier, a Swiss of eminence in literature and rank. They took a long look at King Charles XII., who, you cannot have forgotten, keeps his post over the dining-room chimney; and we were all struck with the resemblance betwixt old Ironhead, as the janissaries called him, and his descendant. The said descendant is a very fine lad, with very soft and mild manners, and we passed the day very pleasantly. They were much diverted with Captain Adam,[1] who outdid his usual outdoings, and, like the Barber of Bagdad, danced the dance and sung the song of every person he spoke of.

I am concerned I cannot give a very pleasant account of things here. Glasgow is in a terrible state. The

---

[1] Sir Adam Ferguson.

Radicals had a plan to seize on 1000 stand of arms, as well as a depôt of ammunition, which had been sent from Edinburgh Castle for the use of the volunteers. The Commander-in-Chief, Sir Thomas Bradford, went to Glasgow in person, and the whole city was occupied with patrols of horse and foot, to deter them from the meditated attack on the barracks. The arms were then delivered to the volunteers, who are said to be 4000 on paper; how many effective and trustworthy, I know not. But it was a new sight in Scotland on a Sunday to see all the inhabitants in arms, soldiers patrolling the streets, and the utmost precaution of military service exacted and observed in an apparently peaceful city.

The Old Blue Regiment of volunteers was again summoned together yesterday. They did not muster very numerous, and looked most of them a little *ancient*. However, they are getting recruits fast, and then the veterans may fall out of the ranks. The Commander-in-Chief has told the President that he may soon be obliged to leave the charge of the Castle to these armed citizens. This looks serious. The President[1] made one of the most eloquent addresses that ever was heard, to the Old Blues. The Highland Chiefs have offered to raise their clans, and march them to any point in Scotland where their services shall be required. To be sure, the Glasgow folks would be a little surprised at the arrival of Dugald Dhu, "brogues an' brochan an' a'." I shall, I think, bid Ballantyne send you a copy of his weekly paper, which often contains things you would like to see, and will keep you in mind of Old Scotland.

They are embodying a troop of cavalry in Edinburgh — nice young men and good horses. They have paid me the compliment to make me an honorary member of

---

[1] The Right Honorable Charles Hope, Lord President of the Court of Session, was Colonel-commandant of the Old Blues, or First Regiment of Edinburgh Volunteers.

the corps, as my days of active service have been long over. Pray take care, however, of my sabre, in case the time comes which must turn out all.

I have almost settled that, if things look moderately tranquil in Britain in spring and summer, I will go abroad, and take Charles, with the purpose of leaving him, for two or three years, at the famous institution of Fellenborg, near Berne, of which I hear very highly. Two of Fraser Tytler's sons are there, and he makes a very favorable report of the whole establishment. I think that such a residence abroad will not only make him well acquainted with French and German, as indeed he will hear nothing else, but also prevent his becoming an Edinburgh *petit-maître* of fourteen or fifteen, which he could otherwise scarce avoid. I mentioned to you that I should be particularly glad to get you leave of absence, providing it does not interfere with your duty, in order that you may go with us. If I have cash enough, I will also take your sister and mamma, and you might return home with them by Paris, in case I went on to Italy. All this is doubtful, but I think it is almost certain that Charles and I go, and hope to have you with us. This will be probably about July next, and I wish you particularly to keep it in view. If these dark prospects become darker, which God forbid! neither you nor I will have it in our power to leave the post to which duty calls us.

Mamma and the girls are quite well, and so is Master Charles, who is of course more magnificent, as being the only specimen of youthhead at home. He has got an old broadsword hanging up at his bed-head, which, to be the more ready for service, hath no sheath. To this I understand we are to trust for our defence against the Radicals. Anne (notwithstanding the assurance) is so much afraid of the disaffected, that last night, returning with Sophia from Portobello, where they had been dancing with the Scotts of Harden, she saw a Radical in every man that the carriage passed. Sophia is of course wise and philosophical, and mamma has not yet been able to conceive why we do not catch and hang the whole of them, untried and unconvicted. Amidst all their various emotions, they join in best love to you; and I always am very truly yours,   W. SCOTT.

P. S. — I shall set off for London on the 25th.

TO THE SAME.

EDINBURGH, 17th December, 1819.

MY DEAR WALTER, — I have a train of most melancholy news to acquaint you with. On Saturday I saw your grandmother perfectly well, and on Sunday the girls drank tea with her, when the good old lady was more than usually in spirits; and, as if she had wished to impress many things on their memory, told over a number of her old stories with her usual alertness and vivacity. On Monday she had an indisposition, which proved to be a paralytic affection, and on Tuesday she was speechless, and had lost the power of one side, without any hope of recovery, although she may linger some days. But what is very remarkable, and no less shocking, Dr. Rutherford, who attended his sister in perfect health upon Tuesday, died himself upon the Wednesday morning. He had breakfasted without intimating the least illness, and was dressed to go out, and particularly to visit my mother, when he sunk backwards, and died in his daughter Anne's arms, almost without a groan. To add to this melancholy list, our poor friend, Miss Christie, is despaired of. She was much affected by my mother's fatal indisposition, but does not know as yet of her brother's death.

Dr. Rutherford was a very ingenious as well as an excellent man, more of a gentleman than his profession too often are, for he could not take the back-stairs mode of rising in it, otherwise he might have been much more wealthy. He ought to have had the Chemistry class, as he was one of the best chemists in Europe; [1] but superior interest assigned it to another, who, though a neat experimentalist, is not to be compared to poor Daniel for originality of genius. Since you knew him, his health was broken and his spirits dejected, which may be traced to the loss of his eldest son on board an East Indiaman, and also, I think, to a slight paralytic touch which he had some years ago.

To all this domestic distress I have to add the fearful and unsettled state of the country. All the regular troops are gone to Glasgow. The Mid-Lothian Yeomanry and other corps of volunteers went there on Monday, and about 5000 men occupied the town. In the mean while, we were under considerable apprehension here, the Castle being left in the charge of the city volunteers and a few veterans.

All our corner, high and low, is loyal. Torwoodlee, Gala, and I, have offered to raise a corps, to be called the Loyal Foresters, to act anywhere south of the Forth. If matters get worse, I will ask leave of absence for you from the Commander-in-Chief, because your presence will be materially useful to levy men, and you can only be idle where you are, unless Ireland should be disturbed. Your old corps of the Selkirkshire Yeomanry have been under orders, and expect to be sent either to Dumfries or Carlisle. Berwick is dismantled, and they are removing the stores, cannon, etc., from one of the strongest places here, for I defy the devil to pass the bridge at Berwick, if reasonably well kept by 100 men. But there

---

[1] " The subject of his *Thesis* is singular, and entitles Rutherford to rank very high among the chemical philosophers of modern times. Its title is *De Aere Mephitico*, etc. — It is universally admitted that Dr. Rutherford first discovered this gas — the reputation of his discovery being speedily spread through Europe, his character as a chemist of the first eminence was firmly established, and much was augured from a young man in his twenty-second year having distinguished himself so remarkably." — Bower's *History of the University of Edinburgh*, vol. iii. (1830), pp. 260, 261.

is a spirit of consternation implied in many of the orders, which, *entre nous*, I like worse than what I see or know of the circumstances which infer real danger. For myself I am too old to fight, but nobody is too old to die, like a man of virtue and honor, in defence of the principles he has always maintained.

I would have you to keep yourself ready to return here suddenly, in case the Duke of York should permit your temporary services in your own country, which, if things grow worse, I will certainly ask. The fearful thing is the secret and steady silence observed by the Radicals in all they do. Yet, without anything like effective arms or useful discipline, without money and without a commissariat, what can they do, but, according to their favorite toast, have blood and plunder? Mamma and the girls, as well as Charles, send kind love. Your affectionate father,

WALTER SCOTT.

TO MR. WILLIAM LAIDLAW, KAESIDE.

EDINBURGH, December 20, 1819.

MY DEAR WILLIE, — Distress has been very busy with me since I wrote to you. I have lost, in the course of one week, my valued relations, Dr. and Miss Rutherford — happy in this, that neither knew of the other's dissolution. My dear mother has offered me deeper subject of affliction, having been struck with the palsy, and being now in such a state that I scarce hope to see her again.

But the strange times compel me, under this pressure of domestic distress, to attend to public business. I find Mr. Scott of Gala agrees with me in thinking we should appeal at this crisis to the good sense and loyalty of the lower orders, and we have resolved to break the ice, and be the first in the Lowlands, so far as I have yet heard of, to invite our laborers and those over whom circumstances and fortune give us influence, to rise with us in arms, and share our fate. You know, as well as any one, that I have always spent twice the income of my property in giving work to my neighbors, and I hope they will not be behind the Galashiels people, who are very zealous. Gala and I go hand in hand, and propose to raise at least a company each of men, to be drilled as sharpshooters or infantry, which will be a lively and interesting amusement for the young fellows. The dress we propose to be as simple, and at the same time as serviceable, as possible; — a jacket and trousers of Galashiels gray cloth, and a smart bonnet with a small feather, or, to save even that expense, a sprig of holly. And we will have shooting at the mark, and prizes, and fun, and a little whiskey, and daily pay when on duty or drill. I beg of you, dear Willie, to communicate my wish to all who have received a good turn at my hand, or may expect one, or may be desirous of doing me one — (for I should be sorry Darnick and Brigend were beat) — and to all other free and honest fellows who will take share with me on this occasion. I do not wish to take any command farther than such as shall entitle me to go with the corps, for I wish it to be distinctly understood that, in whatever capacity, *I go with them,* and take a share in good or bad as it casts up. I cannot doubt that I will have your support, and I hope you will use all your enthusiasm in our behalf. Morrison volunteers as our engineer. Those who I think should be spoke to are the following, among the higher class: —

John Usher.[1] He should be lieutenant, or his son ensign.

Sam Somerville.[2] I will speak to him — he may be

---

[1] Mr. Usher has already been mentioned as Scott's predecessor in the property of Toftfield. He now resided near those lands, and was Scott's tenant on the greater part of them.

[2] Samuel Somerville, W. S. (a son of the historian of Queen Anne), had a pretty villa at Lowood, on the Tweed, immediately opposite the seat of his relation, Lord Somerville, of whose estate he had the management.

lieutenant, if Usher declines; but I think, in that case, Usher should give us his son.

Young Nicol Milne[1] is rather young, but I will offer to his father to take him in.

Harper[2] is a *sine qua non*. Tell him I depend on him for the honor of Darnick. I should propose to him to take a gallant halbert.

Adam Ferguson thinks you should be our adjutant. John Ferguson I propose for captain. He is steady, right bold, and has seen much fire. The auld captain will help us in one shape or other. For myself, I know not what they propose to make of me, but it cannot be anything very active. However, I should like to have a steady quiet horse, drilled to stand fire well, and if he has these properties, no matter how stupid, so he does not stumble. In this case the price of such a horse will be no object.

These, my dear friend, are your beating orders. I would propose to raise about sixty men, and not to take old men. John the Turk[3] will be a capital corporal; and I hope in general that all my young fellows will go with me, leaving the older men to go through necessary labor. Sound Tom what he would like. I think, perhaps, he would prefer managing matters at home in your absence and mine at drill.

John of Skye is cock-a-hoop upon the occasion, and I suppose has made fifty blunders about it by this time. You must warn Tom Jamieson, Gordon Winness, John Swanston (who will carry off all the prizes at shooting), Davidson, and so forth.

If you think it necessary, a little handbill might be

[1] Nicol Milne, Esq. (now advocate), eldest son of the Laird of Faldonside.

[2] Harper, keeper of a little inn at Darnick, was a gallant and spirited yeoman — uniformly the gainer of the prizes at every contest of strength and agility in that district.

[3] One of Scott's foresters — thus designated as being, in all senses of the word, a *gallant* fellow.

circulated. But it may be better to see if Government will accept our services; and I think, in the situation of the country, when work is scarce, and we offer pay for their playing themselves, we should have choice of men. But I would urge no one to do what he did not like.

The very precarious state of my poor mother detains me here, and makes me devolve this troublesome duty upon you. All you have to do, however, is to sound the men, and mark down those who seem zealous. They will perhaps have to fight with the pitmen and colliers of Northumberland for defence of their firesides, for these literal *blackguards* are got beyond the management of their own people. And if such is the case, better keep them from coming into Scotland, than encounter the mischief they might do there.

Yours always most truly,
WALTER SCOTT.

TO THOMAS SCOTT, ESQ., 70TH REGIMENT, KINGSTON, CANADA.

EDINBURGH, 22d December, 1819.

MY DEAR TOM, — I wrote you about ten days since, stating that we were all well here. In that very short space a change so sudden and so universal has taken place among your friends here, that I have to communicate to you a most miserable catalogue of losses. Our dear mother was on Sunday the 12th December in all her usual strength and alertness of mind. I had seen and conversed with her on the Saturday preceding, and never saw her better in my life of late years. My two daughters drank tea with her on Sunday, when she was uncommonly lively, telling them a number of stories, and being in rather unusual spirits, probably from the degree of excitation which sometimes is remarked to precede a paralytic affection. In the course of Monday she received that fatal summons, which at first seemed slight; but in the night betwixt Monday and Tuesday our mother lost the use both of speech and of one side. Since that time she has lain in bed constantly, yet so sensible as to see me and express her earnest blessing on all of us. The power of speech is totally lost; nor is there any hope, at her advanced age, that the scene can last long. Probably a few hours will terminate it. At any rate, life is not to be wished, even for our nearest and dearest, in those circumstances. But this heavy calamity was only the commencement of our family losses. Dr. Rutherford, who had seemed perfectly well, and had visited my mother upon Tuesday the 14th, was suddenly affected with gout in his stomach, or some disease equally rapid, on Wednesday the 15th, and, without a moment's warning or complaint, fell down a dead man, almost without a single groan. You are aware of his fondness for animals: he was just stroking his cat after eating his breakfast, as usual, when, without more warning than a half-uttered exclamation, he sunk on the ground, and died in the arms of his daughter Anne. Though the Doctor had no formed complaint, yet I have thought him looking poorly for some months; and though there was no failure whatever in intellect, or anything which approached it, yet his memory was not so good; and I thought he paused during the last time he attended me, and had difficulty in recollecting the precise terms of his recipe. Certainly there was a great decay of outward strength. We were very anxious about the effect this fatal news was likely to produce on the mind and decayed health of our aunt, Miss C. Rutherford, and resolved, as her health had been gradually falling off ever since she returned from Abbotsford, that she should never learn anything of it until it was impossible to conceal it longer. But God had so ordered it that she was never to know the loss she had sustained, and which she would have felt so deeply. On Friday the 17th December, the second day after her brother's death, she expired, without a groan and without suffering, about six in the morning. And so we lost an excellent and warm-hearted relation, one of the few women I ever knew whose strength of mental faculties enabled her, at a mature period of life, to supply the defects of an imperfect education. It is a most uncommon and afflicting circumstance, that a brother and two sisters should be taken ill the same day — that two of them should die, without any rational possibility of the survivance of the third — and that no one of the three could be affected by learning the loss of the other. The Doctor was buried on Monday the 20th, and Miss Rutherford this day (Wednesday the 22d), in the burial-place adjoining to and surrounding one of the new Episcopal chapels,[1] where Robert Rutherford[2] had purchased a burial-ground of some extent, and parted with one half to the Russells. It is surrounded with a very high wall, and all the separate burial-grounds (five, I think, in number) are separated by party-walls going down to the depth of twelve feet, so as to prevent the possibility either of encroachment, or of disturbing the relics of the dead. I have purchased one half of Miss Russell's interest in this sad spot, moved by its extreme seclusion, privacy, and security. When poor Jack was buried in the Greyfriars' Churchyard, where my father and Anne lie,[3] I thought their graves more encroached upon than I liked to witness; and in this new place I intend to lay our poor mother when the scene shall close; so that the brother and the two sisters, whose fate has been so very closely entwined in death, may not be divided in the grave, — and this I hope you will approve of.

Thursday, December 23d. — My mother still lingers this morning, and as her constitution is so excellent, she may perhaps continue to exist some time, or till another stroke. It is a great consolation that she is perfectly easy. All her affairs of every sort have been very long

[1] St. John's Chapel.

[2] Robert Rutherford, Esq., W. S., son to the Professor of Botany.

[3] " Our family heretofore buried in the Greyfriars' Churchyard, close by the entrance to Heriot's Hospital, and on the southern or left-hand side as you pass from the churchyard." — *MS. Memorandum.*

arranged for this great change, and with the assistance of Donaldson and Macculloch, you may depend, when the event takes place, that your interest will be attended to most pointedly. — I hope our civil tumults here are like to be ended by the measures of Parliament. I mentioned in my last that Kinloch of Kinloch was to be tried for sedition. He has forfeited his bail, and was yesterday laid under outlawry for non-appearance. Our neighbors in Northumberland are in a deplorable state; upwards of 50,000 blackguards are ready to rise between Tyne and Wear.[1] On the other hand, the Scottish frontiers are steady and loyal, and arming fast. Scott of Gala and I have offered 200 men, all fine strapping young fellows, and good marksmen, willing to go anywhere with us. We could easily double the number. So the necessity of the times has made me get on horseback once more. Our mother has at different times been perfectly conscious of her situation, and knew every one, though totally unable to speak. She seemed to take a very affectionate farewell of me the last time I saw her, which was the day before yesterday; and as she was much agitated, Dr. Keith advised I should not see her again, unless she seemed to desire it, which hitherto she has not done. She sleeps constantly, and will probably be so removed. Our family sends love to yours. Yours most affectionately: —

WALTER SCOTT.

Scott's excellent mother died on the 24th December — the day after he closed the foregoing letter to his brother.

On the 18th, in the midst of these accumulated afflictions, the romance of Ivanhoe made its appearance. The date has been torn from the following letter, but it was evidently written while all these events were fresh and recent: —

[1] This was a ridiculously exaggerated report of that period of alarm.

TO THE LADY LOUISA STUART, DITTON PARK, WINDSOR.

DEAR LADY LOUISA, — I am favored with your letter from Ditton, and am glad you found anything to entertain you in Ivanhoe.[1] Novelty is what this giddy-paced time demands imperiously, and I certainly studied as much as I could to get out of the old beaten track, leaving those who like to keep the road, which I have rutted pretty well. I have had a terrible time of it this year, with the loss of dear friends and near relations; it is almost fearful to count up my losses, as they make me bankrupt in society. My brother-in-law; our never-to-be-enough regretted Duke; Lord Chief Baron, my early, kind, and constant friend, who took me up when I was a young fellow of little mark or likelihood; the wife of my intimate friend William Erskine; the only son of my friend David Hume, a youth of great promise, and just entering into life, who had grown up under my eye from childhood; my excellent mother; and, within a few days, her surviving brother and sister. My mother was the only one of these whose death was the natural

---

[1] [Lady Louisa's letter was written January 16, 1820, and can be found in *Familiar Letters*, vol. ii. p. 71. In it she says : —

" Everybody in this house has been reading an odd new kind of a book called *Ivanhoe*, and nobody, as far as I have observed, has willingly laid it down again till finished. By this, I conclude that its success will be fully equal to that of its predecessors, notwithstanding it has quite abandoned their ground and ploughed up a field hitherto untouched. The interest of it, indeed, is most powerful ; few things in prose or verse seize upon one's mind so strongly, or are read with such breathless eagerness, as the storming of the castle, related by Rebecca, and her trial at Templestowe. Few characters ever were so forcibly painted as hers : the Jew, too, the Templar, the courtly knight De Bracy, the wavering, inconstant wickedness of John, are all worthy of Shakespeare. I must not omit paying my tribute to Cedric, that worthy forefather of the genuine English country gentleman. . . . And according to what has been alleged against the author in some other instances, the hero and the heroine are the people one cares least about. But provided one does but care enough about somebody, it is all one to me ; and I think the cavil is like that against Milton for making the Devil his hero."]

consequence of very advanced life. And our sorrows are
not at an end. A sister of my mother's, Mrs. Russell
of Ashestiel, long deceased, had left (besides several sons,
of whom only one now survives and is in India) three
daughters, who lived with her youngest sister, Miss
Rutherford, and were in the closest habits of intimacy
with us. The eldest of these girls, and a most excellent
creature she is, was in summer so much shocked by the
sudden news of the death of one of the brothers I have
mentioned, that she was deprived of the use of her limbs
by an affection either nervous or paralytic. She was
slowly recovering from this afflicting and helpless situation, when the sudden fate of her aunts and uncle, particularly of her who had acted as a mother to the family,
brought on a new shock; and though perfectly possessed
of her mind, she has never since been able to utter a
word. Her youngest sister, a girl of one or two and
twenty, was so much shocked by this scene of accumulated distress, that she was taken very ill, and having
suppressed and concealed her disorder, relief came too
late, and she has been taken from us also. She died in
the arms of the elder sister, helpless as I have described
her; and to separate the half dead from the actual corpse
was the most melancholy thing possible. You can hardly
conceive, dear Lady Louisa, the melancholy feeling of
seeing the place of last repose belonging to the devoted
family open four times within so short a space, and to
meet the same group of sorrowing friends and relations
on the same sorrowful occasion. Looking back on those
whom I have lost, all well known to me excepting my
brother-in-law, whom I could only judge of by the general report in his favor, I can scarce conceive a group
possessing more real worth and amiable qualities, not to
mention talents and accomplishments. I have never felt
so truly what Johnson says so well, —

> " Condemn'd to Hope's delusive mine,
> As on we toil from day to day,

By sudden blasts, or slow decline,
Our social comforts drop away." [1]

I am not sure whether it was your Ladyship, or the poor Duchess of Buccleuch, who met my mother once, and flattered me by being so much pleased with the good old lady. She had a mind peculiarly well stored with much acquired information and natural talent, and as she was very old, and had an excellent memory, she could draw without the least exaggeration or affectation the most striking pictures of the past age. If I have been able to do anything in the way of painting the past times, it is very much from the studies with which she presented me. She connected a long period of time with the present generation, for she remembered, and had often spoken with, a person who perfectly recollected the battle of Dunbar, and Oliver Cromwell's subsequent entry into Edinburgh. She preserved her faculties to the very day before her final illness; for our friends Mr. and Mrs. Scott of Harden visited her on the Sunday; and, coming to our house after, were expressing their surprise at the alertness of her mind, and the pleasure which she had in talking over both ancient and modern events. She had told them with great accuracy the real story of the Bride of Lammermuir, and pointed out wherein it differed from the novel. She had all the names of the parties, and detailed (for she was a great genealogist) their connection with existing families. On the subsequent Monday she was struck with a paralytic affection, suffered little, and that with the utmost patience; and what was God's reward, and a great one to her innocent and benevolent life, she never knew that her brother and sister, the last thirty years younger than herself, had trodden the dark path before her. She was a strict economist, which she said enabled her to be liberal; out of her little income of about £300 a year, she bestowed at least a third in well-chosen charities, and with the

[1] *Lines on the Death of Mr. Robert Levett.*

rest lived like a gentlewoman, and even with hospitality
more general than seemed to suit her age; yet I could
never prevail on her to accept of any assistance. You
cannot conceive how affecting it was to me to see the
little preparations of presents which she had assorted for
the New Year — for she was a great observer of the old
fashions of her period — and to think that the kind heart
was cold which delighted in all these acts of kindly affection. I should apologize, I believe, for troubling your
ladyship with these melancholy details; but you would
not thank me for a letter written with constraint, and
my mind is at present very full of this sad subject,
though I scarce know any one to whom I would venture
to say so much. I hear no good news of Lady Anne,
though Lord Montagu writes cautiously. The weather
is now turning milder, and may, I hope, be favorable to
her complaint. After my own family, my thought most
frequently turns to these orphans, whose parents I loved
and respected so much. — I am always, dear Lady Louisa, your very respectful and obliged

                                        WALTER SCOTT.

There is in the library at Abbotsford a fine copy of
Baskerville's folio Bible, two volumes, printed at Cambridge in 1763; and there appears on the blank leaf, in
the trembling handwriting of Scott's mother, this inscription: "*To my dear son, Walter Scott, from his
affectionate mother, Anne Rutherford, — January 1st,
1819.*" Under these words her son has written as follows:
"This Bible was the gift of my grandfather Dr. John
Rutherford, to my mother, and presented by her to me;
being, alas, the last gift which I was to receive from
that excellent parent, and, as I verily believe, the thing
which she most loved in the world, — not only in humble
veneration of the sacred contents, but as the dearest
pledge of her father's affection to her. As such she gave
it to me; and as such I bequeath it to those who may

represent me — charging them carefully to preserve the same, in memory of those to whom it has belonged. 1820."

If literary success could have either filled Scott's head or hardened his heart, we should have no such letters as those of December, 1819. Ivanhoe was received throughout England with a more clamorous delight than any of the Scotch novels had been. The volumes (three in number) were now, for the first time, of the post 8vo form, with a finer paper than hitherto, the press-work much more elegant, and the price accordingly raised from eight shillings the volume to ten; yet the copies sold in this original shape were twelve thousand.

I ought to have mentioned sooner, that the original intention was to bring out Ivanhoe as the production of a new hand, and that, to assist this impression, the work was printed in a size and manner unlike the preceding ones; but Constable, when the day of publication approached, remonstrated against this experiment, and it was accordingly abandoned.

The reader has already been told that Scott dictated the greater part of this romance. The portion of the MS. which is his own, appears, however, not only as well and firmly executed as that of any of the Tales of my Landlord, but distinguished by having still fewer erasures and interlineations, and also by being in a smaller hand. The fragment is beautiful to look at — many pages together without one alteration.[1] It is, I suppose, superfluous to add, that in no instance did Scott rewrite his prose before sending it to the press. Whatever may have been the case with his poetry, the world uniformly received the *prima cura* of the novelist.

As a work of art, Ivanhoe is perhaps the first of all Scott's efforts, whether in prose or in verse; nor have

---

[1] Three of these MS. pages were a fair day's work in the author's estimation — equal to fifteen or sixteen of the original impression.

the strength and splendor of his imagination been displayed to higher advantage than in some of the scenes of this romance. But I believe that no reader who is capable of thoroughly comprehending the author's Scotch character and Scotch dialogue will ever place even Ivanhoe, as a work of genius, on the same level with Waverley, Guy Mannering, or The Heart of Mid-Lothian.

There is, to me, something so remarkably characteristic of Scott's mind and manner in a particular passage of the Introduction, which he penned ten years afterwards for this work, that I must be pardoned for extracting it here. He says: "The character of the fair Jewess found so much favor in the eyes of some fair readers, that the writer was censured, because, when arranging the fates of the characters of the drama, he had not assigned the hand of Wilfred to Rebecca, rather than the less interesting Rowena. But, not to mention that the prejudices of the age rendered such a union almost impossible, the author may, in passing, observe that he thinks a character of a highly virtuous and lofty stamp is degraded rather than exalted by an attempt to reward virtue with temporal prosperity. Such is not the recompense which Providence has deemed worthy of suffering merit; and it is a dangerous and fatal doctrine to teach young persons, the most common readers of romance, that rectitude of conduct and of principle are either naturally allied with, or adequately rewarded by, the gratification of our passions, or attainment of our wishes. In a word, if a virtuous and self-denied character is dismissed with temporal wealth, greatness, rank, or the indulgence of such a rashly formed or ill-assorted passion as that of Rebecca for Ivanhoe, the reader will be apt to say, verily Virtue has had its reward. But a glance on the great picture of life will show that the duties of self-denial, and the sacrifice of passion to principle, are seldom thus remunerated; and that the internal consciousness of their high-minded discharge of duty produces on their own reflections a more adequate recompense, in the form of that peace which the world cannot give or take away."

The introduction of the charming Jewess and her father originated, I find, in a conversation that Scott held with his friend Skene during the severest season of his bodily sufferings in the early part of this year. "Mr. Skene," says that gentleman's wife, "sitting by his bedside, and trying to amuse him as well as he could in the intervals of pain, happened to get on the subject of the Jews, as he had observed them when he spent some time in Germany in his youth. Their situation had naturally made a strong impression; for in those days they retained their own dress and manners entire, and were treated with considerable austerity by their Christian neighbors, being still locked up at night in their own quarter by great gates; and Mr. Skene, partly in seriousness, but partly from the mere wish to turn his mind at the moment upon something that might occupy and divert it, suggested that a group of Jews would be an interesting feature if he could contrive to bring them into his next novel." Upon the appearance of Ivanhoe, he reminded Mr. Skene of this conversation, and said, "You will find this book owes not a little to your German reminiscences." Mrs. Skene adds: "Dining with us one day, not long before Ivanhoe was begun, something that was mentioned led him to describe the sudden death of an advocate of his acquaintance, a Mr. Elphinstone, which occurred in the *Outer-house* soon after he was called to the Bar. It was, he said, no wonder that it had left a vivid impression on his mind, for it was the first sudden death he ever witnessed; and he now related it so as to make us all feel as if we had the scene passing before our eyes. In the death of the Templar in Ivanhoe, I recognized the very picture — I believe I may safely say the very words." [1]

[1] See *Ivanhoe*, end of chap. xliv.

By the way, before Ivanhoe made its appearance, I had myself been formally admitted to the author's secret; but had he favored me with no such confidence, it would have been impossible for me to doubt that I had been present some months before at the conversation which suggested, and indeed supplied all the materials of, one of its most amusing chapters. I allude to that in which our Saxon terms for animals in the field, and our Norman equivalents for them as they appear on the table, and so on, are explained and commented on. All this Scott owed to the after-dinner talk one day in Castle Street of his old friend Mr. William Clerk, — who, among other elegant pursuits, has cultivated the science of philology very deeply.[1]

I cannot conclude this chapter without observing that the publication of Ivanhoe marks the most brilliant epoch in Scott's history as the literary favorite of his contemporaries. With the novel which he next put forth, the immediate sale of these works began gradually to decline; and though, even when that had reached its lowest declension, it was still far above the most ambitious dreams of any other novelist, yet the publishers were afraid the announcement of anything like a falling-off might cast a damp over the spirits of the author. He was allowed to remain, for several years, under the impression that whatever novel he threw off commanded at

---

[1] [It is said that the character of Rebecca was suggested to Scott by Washington Irving's description of Rebecca Gratz of Philadelphia, a lady belonging to a Jewish family of high position in that city, with whom Irving was intimate. Miss Gratz had been a friend of his betrothed, Matilda Hoffman, and in her youth had loved devotedly a man in every way worthy of her, but the difference of religion made their union impossible. During a conversation with Scott, Irving spoke with much feeling of Rebecca Gratz, of her extraordinary beauty, of her adherence to her faith under most trying circumstances, of her nobility, distinction, and loveliness of character, and her untiring zeal in works of charity, greatly interesting his host, as the guest recalled when Ivanhoe appeared.

Rebecca Gratz died in 1869 in her eighty-ninth year. A sketch of her, with a portrait after a miniature by Malbone, was published in the Century Magazine for September, 1882.]

once the old triumphant sale of ten or twelve thousand, and was afterwards, when included in the collective edition, to be circulated in that shape also as widely as Waverley or Ivanhoe. In my opinion, it would have been very unwise in the booksellers to give Scott any unfavorable tidings upon such subjects after the commencement of the malady which proved fatal to him, — for that from the first shook his mind; but I think they took a false measure of the man when they hesitated to tell him exactly how the matter stood, throughout 1820 and the three or four following years, when his intellect was as vigorous as it ever had been, and his heart as courageous; and I regret their scruples (among other reasons), because the years now mentioned were the most costly ones in his life; and for every twelvemonth in which any man allows himself, or is encouraged by others, to proceed in a course of unwise expenditure, it becomes proportionably more difficult for him to pull up when the mistake is at length detected or recognized.

CHAPTER XLVII

THE VISIONARY. — THE PEEL OF DARNICK. — SCOTT'S
SATURDAY EXCURSIONS TO ABBOTSFORD. — A SUN-
DAY THERE IN FEBRUARY. — CONSTABLE. — JOHN
BALLANTYNE. — THOMAS PURDIE, ETC. — PRINCE
GUSTAVUS VASA. — PROCLAMATION OF KING GEORGE
IV. — PUBLICATION OF THE MONASTERY

1820

In the course of December, 1819 and January, 1820,
Scott drew up three essays, under the title of The Visionary, upon certain popular doctrines or delusions, the
spread of which at this time filled with alarm, not only
Tories like him, but many persons who had been distinguished through life for their adherence to political liberalism. These papers appeared successively in James
Ballantyne's Edinburgh Weekly Journal, and their parentage being obvious, they excited much attention in
Scotland. Scott collected them into a pamphlet, which
had also a large circulation; and I remember his showing very particular satisfaction when he observed a mason
reading it to his comrades, as they sat at their dinner, by
a new house on Leith Walk. During January, however,
his thoughts continued to be chiefly occupied with the
details of the proposed corps of Foresters; of which, I
believe it was at last settled, as far as depended on the
other gentlemen concerned in it, that he should be the
Major. He wrote and spoke on this subject with undiminished zeal, until the whole fell to the ground in consequence of the Government's ultimately declining to
take on itself any part of the expense; a refusal which

must have been fatal to any such project when the Duke
of Buccleuch was a minor. He felt the disappointment
keenly; but, in the mean time, the hearty alacrity with
which his neighbors of all classes gave in their adhesion
had afforded him much pleasure, and, as regarded his
own immediate dependents, served to rivet the bonds
of affection and confidence, which were to the end maintained between him and them. Darnick had been especially ardent in the cause, and he thenceforth considered
its volunteers as persons whose individual fortunes closely
concerned him. I could fill many a page with the letters
which he wrote at subsequent periods, with the view of
promoting the success of these spirited young fellows in
their various departments of industry: they were proud
of their patron, as may be supposed, and he was highly
gratified, as well as amused, when he learned that —
while the rest of the world were talking of "The Great
Unknown" — his usual *sobriquet* among these villagers
was "The Duke of Darnick." Already his possessions
almost encircled this picturesque and thriving hamlet;
and there were few things on which he had more strongly
fixed his fancy than acquiring a sort of symbol of seign-
iory there, by becoming the purchaser of a certain then
ruinous tower that predominated, with a few coeval trees,
over the farmhouses and cottages of his *ducal* vassals.
A letter, previously quoted, contains an allusion to this
Peelhouse of Darnick; which is moreover exactly described in the novel which he had now in hand — The
Monastery. The interest Scott seemed to take in the
Peel awakened, however, the pride of its hereditary
proprietor: and when that worthy person, who had made
some money by trade in Edinburgh, resolved on fitting
it up for the evening retreat of his own life, *his Grace
of Darnick* was too happy to waive his pretensions.

This was a winter of uncommon severity in Scotland;
and the snow lay so deep and so long as to interrupt
very seriously all Scott's country operations. I find, in

his letters to Laidlaw, various paragraphs expressing the concern he took in the hardships which his poor neighbors must be suffering. Thus, on the 19th of January, he says: —

DEAR WILLIE, — I write by the post that you may receive the enclosed, or rather subjoined, cheque for £60, in perfect safety. This dreadful morning will probably stop Mercer.[1] It makes me shiver in the midst of superfluous comforts to think of the distress of others. £10 of the £60 I wish you to distribute among our poorer neighbors, so as may best aid them. I mean not only the actually indigent, but those who are, in our phrase, *ill aff*. I am sure Dr. Scott[2] will assist you with his advice in this labor of love. I think part of the wood-money,[3] too, should be given among the Abbotstown folks if the storm keeps them off work, as is like. Yours truly,   WALTER SCOTT.

Deep, deep snow lying here. How do the goodwife and bairns? The little bodies will be half-buried in snow-drift.

And again, on the 25th, he writes thus: —

DEAR WILLIE, — I have yours with the news of the inundation, which, it seems, has done no damage. I hope *Mai* will be taken care of. He should have a bed in the kitchen, and always be called indoors after it is dark, for all the kind are savage at night. Please cause Swanston to knock him up a box, and fill it with straw from time to time. I enclose a cheque for £50 to pay accounts, etc. Do not let the poor bodies want for a £5, or even a £10, more or less; —

---

[1] The weekly Darnick carrier.
[2] Dr. Scott of Darnlee. — See *ante*, p. 277. This very amiable, modest, and intelligent friend of Sir Walter Scott's died in 1837.
[3] Some money expected from the sale of larches.

"We 'll get a blessing wi' the lave,
    And never miss 't." [1]

Yours,   W. S.

In the course of this month, through the kindness of
Mr. Croker, Scott received from the late Earl Bathurst,
then Colonial Secretary of State, the offer of an appointment in the civil service of the East India Company for
his second son: and this seemed at the time too good
a thing not to be gratefully accepted; though the apparently increasing prosperity of his fortunes induced him,
a few years afterwards, to indulge his parental feelings
by throwing it up. He thus alludes to this matter in
a letter to his good old friend at Jedburgh:—

TO ROBERT SHORTREED, ESQ., SHERIFF-SUBSTITUTE OF
ROXBURGHSHIRE, JEDBURGH.

EDINBURGH, 19th January, 1820.

MY DEAR SIR, — I heartily congratulate you on getting the appointment for your son William in a manner
so very pleasant to your feelings, and which is, like all
Whytbank does, considerate, friendly, and generous.[2]
I am not aware that I have any friends at Calcutta, but
if you think letters to Sir John Malcolm and Lieut.-Colo-
nel Russell would serve my young friend, he shall have
my best commendations to them.

It is very odd that almost the same thing has happened
to me; for about a week ago I was surprised by a letter,
saying that an unknown friend (who since proves to be
Lord Bathurst, whom I never saw or spoke with) would
give my second son a Writer's situation for India.
Charles is two years too young for this appointment; but
I do not think I am at liberty to decline an offer so

---

[1] Burns — *Lines to a Mouse.*

[2] "An India appointment, with the name blank, which the late Mr.
Pringle of Whytbank sent unsolicited, believing it might be found useful
to a family where there were seven sons to provide for." — *Note by Mr.
A. Shortreed.*

advantageous, if it can be so arranged that, by exchange or otherwise, it can be kept open for him. Ever yours faithfully,   WALTER SCOTT.

About the middle of February — it having been ere that time arranged that I should marry his eldest daughter[1] in the course of the spring — I accompanied him and part of his family on one of those flying visits to Abbotsford, with which he often indulged himself on a Saturday during term. Upon such occasions Scott appeared at the usual hour in Court, but wearing, instead of the official suit of black, his country morning dress — green jacket and so forth — under the clerk's gown; a license of which many gentlemen of the long

[1] [Of Miss Scott, not long before her marriage, Mr. George Ticknor writes : —

"Sophia Scott is a remarkable girl, with great simplicity and naturalness of manners, full of enthusiasm, with tact in everything, a lover of old ballads, a Jacobite, and, in short, in all respects, such a daughter as Scott ought to have and ought to be proud of. And he is proud of her, as I saw again and again when he could not conceal it.

"One evening, after dinner, he told her to take her harp and play five or six ballads he mentioned to her, as a specimen of the different ages of Scottish music. I hardly ever heard anything of the kind that moved me so much. And yet, I imagine, many sing better ; but I never saw such an air and manner, such spirit and feeling, such decision and power. . . . I was so much excited that I turned round to Mr. Scott and said to him, probably with great emphasis, 'I never heard anything so fine ;' and he, seeing how involuntarily I had said it, caught me by the hand, and replied, very earnestly, 'Everybody says so, sir,' but added in an instant, blushing a little, 'but I must not be too vain of her.'

"I was struck, too, with another little trait in her character and his, that exhibited itself the same evening. Lady Hume asked her to play *Rob Roy*, an old ballad. A good many persons were present, and she felt a little embarrassed by the recollection of how much her father's name had been mentioned in connection with this strange Highlander's ; but, as upon all occasions, she took the most direct means to settle her difficulties ; . . . she ran across the room to her father, and, blushing pretty deeply, whispered to him. 'Yes, my dear,' he said, loud enough to be heard, 'play it, to be sure, if you are asked, and *Waverley* and the *Antiquary*, too, if there be any such ballads.' . . . She is as perfectly right-minded as I ever saw one so young, and, indeed, perhaps right-mindedness is the prevailing feature in her character." — *Life of George Ticknor*, vol. i. pp. 281, 283.]

robe had been accustomed to avail themselves in the days
of his youth — it being then considered as the authentic
badge that they were lairds as well as lawyers — but
which, to use the dialect of the place, had fallen into
desuetude before I knew the Parliament House. He
was, I think, one of the two or three, or at most the half
dozen, who still adhered to this privilege of their order;
and it has now, in all likelihood, become quite obsolete,
like the ancient custom, a part of the same system, for
all Scotch barristers to appear without gowns or wigs,
and in colored clothes, when upon circuit. At noon,
when the Court broke up, Peter Mathieson was sure to
be in attendance in the Parliament Close, and five minutes after, the gown had been tossed off, and Scott, rubbing his hands for glee, was under weigh for Tweedside.
On this occasion, he was, of course, in mourning; but I
have thought it worth while to preserve the circumstance
of his usual Saturday's costume. As we proceeded, he
talked without reserve of the novel of The Monastery, of
which he had the first volume with him; and mentioned,
what he had probably forgotten when he wrote the Introduction of 1830, that a good deal of that volume had
been composed before he concluded Ivanhoe. "It was
a relief," he said, "to interlay the scenery most familiar
to me with the strange world for which I had to draw so
much on imagination."

Next morning there appeared at breakfast John Ballantyne, who had at this time a shooting or hunting box
a few miles off, in the vale of the Leader, and with him
Mr. Constable, his guest; and it being a fine clear day,
as soon as Scott had read the Church service and one of
Jeremy Taylor's sermons, we all sallied out, before noon,
on a perambulation of his upland territories; Maida and
the rest of the favorites accompanying our march. At
starting we were joined by the constant henchman, Tom
Purdie — and I may save myself the trouble of any
attempt to describe his appearance, for his master has

given us an inimitably true one in introducing a certain personage of his Redgauntlet: "He was, perhaps, sixty years old; yet his brow was not much furrowed, and his jet black hair was only grizzled, not whitened, by the advance of age. All his motions spoke strength unabated; and, though rather undersized, he had very broad shoulders, was square-made, thin-flanked, and apparently combined in his frame muscular strength and activity; the last somewhat impaired, perhaps, by years, but the first remaining in full vigor. A hard and harsh countenance; eyes far sunk under projecting eyebrows, which were grizzled like his hair: a wide mouth, furnished from ear to ear with a range of unimpaired teeth of uncommon whiteness, and a size and breadth which might have become the jaws of an ogre, completed this delightful portrait." Equip this figure in Scott's cast-off green jacket, white hat and drab trousers; and imagine that years of kind treatment, comfort, and the honest consequence of a confidential *grieve*, had softened away much of the hardness and harshness originally impressed on the visage by anxious penury and the sinister habits of a *black-fisher*, — and the Tom Purdie of 1820 stands before us.

We were all delighted to see how completely Scott had recovered his bodily vigor, and none more so than Constable, who, as he puffed and panted after him up one ravine and down another, often stopped to wipe his forehead, and remarked that "it was not every author who should lead him such a dance." But Purdie's face shone with rapture as he observed how severely the swag-bellied bookseller's activity was tasked. Scott exclaiming exultingly, though perhaps for the tenth time, "This will be a glorious spring for our trees, Tom!" — "You may say that, Shirra," quoth Tom, — and then lingering a moment for Constable — "My certy," he added, scratching his head, "and I think it will be a grand season for *our buiks* too." But indeed Tom always talked of *our*

buiks as if they had been as regular products of the soil
as *our aits* and *our birks*.[1] Having threaded, first the
Haxelcleugh, and then the Rhymer's Glen, we arrived
at Huntly Burn, where the hospitality of the kind *Weird-
Sisters*, as Scott called the Miss Fergusons, reanimated
our exhausted Bibliopoles, and gave them courage to
extend their walk a little further down the same famous
brook.   Here there was a small cottage in a very sequestered situation, by making some little additions to
which Scott thought it might be converted into a suitable
summer residence for his daughter and future son-in-law.
The details of that plan were soon settled — it was agreed
on all hands that a sweeter scene of seclusion could not
be fancied. He repeated some verses of Rogers's
Wish, which paint the spot: —

> " Mine be a cot beside the hill —
> A bee-hive's hum shall soothe my ear ;
> A willowy brook that turns a mill,
> With many a fall shall linger near : " etc.

But when he came to the stanza, —

> " And Lucy at her wheel shall sing,
> In russet-gown and apron blue,"

he departed from the text, adding, —

[1] [Mr. Skene, in his *Reminiscences*, says of Tom Purdie : —
" He used to talk of Sir Walter's publications as our books, and said that
the reading of them was the greatest comfort to him, for whenever he was
off his sleep, which sometimes happened, he had only to take one of the
novels, and before he read two pages it was sure to set him asleep. Tom,
with the usual shrewdness common to his countrymen in that class of life,
joined a quaintness and drollery in his notions and mode of expressing
himself that was very amusing ; he was familiar, but at the same time
perfectly respectful, although he was sometimes tempted to deal sharp
cuts, particularly at Sir Adam Ferguson. whom he seemed to take a pleasure
in assailing. When Sir Walter obtained the honor of knighthood for Sir
Adam, upon the plea of his being Custodier of the Regalia of Scotland,
Tom was very indignant, because, he said, ' It would take some of the
shine out of us,' meaning Sir Walter. . . . He was remarkably fastidious
in his care of the Library, and it was exceedingly amusing to see a clod-
hopper (for he was always in the garb of a ploughman) moving about in
the splendid apartment, scrutinizing the state of the books, putting de-
rangement to rights, remonstrating when he observed anything that indicated carelessness." — See *Journal*, vol. ii. p. 318, note.]

" But if Bluestockings here you bring,
The Great Unknown won't dine with you."

Johnny Ballantyne, a projector to the core, was particularly zealous about this embryo establishment. Foreseeing that he should have had walking enough ere he
reached Huntly Burn, his dapper little Newmarket groom
had been ordered to fetch Old Mortality thither, and
now, mounted on his fine hunter, he capered about us,
looking pallid and emaciated as a ghost, but as gay and
cheerful as ever, and would fain have been permitted to
ride over hedge and ditch to mark out the proper line of
the future avenue.   Scott admonished him that the coun-
try-people, if they saw him at such work, would take the
whole party for heathens; and clapping spurs to his
horse, he left us.   "The deil's in the body," quoth Tom
Purdie; "he'll be ower every *yett* atween this and Turn-
again, though it be the Lord's day.   I wadna wonder if
he were to be *ceeted* before the Session."   "Be sure,
Tam," cries Constable, "that ye egg on the Dominie to
blaw up his father — I wouldna grudge a hundred miles
o' gait to see the ne'er-do-weel on the stool, and neither,
I'll be sworn, would the Sheriff." — "Na, na," quoth
the Sheriff; "we'll let sleeping dogs be, Tam."

As we walked homeward, Scott, being a little fatigued,
laid his left hand on Tom's shoulder, and leaned heavily
for support, chatting to his "Sunday pony," as he called
the affectionate fellow, just as freely as with the rest of
the party, and Tom put in his word shrewdly and manfully, and grinned and grunted whenever the joke
chanced to be within his apprehension.   It was easy to
see that his heart swelled within him from the moment
that the Sheriff got his collar in his gripe.

There arose a little dispute between them about what
tree or trees ought to be cut down in a hedge-row that
we passed, and Scott seemed somewhat ruffled with finding that some previous hints of his on that head had not
been attended to.   When we got into motion again, his

hand was on Constable's shoulder — and Tom dropped a pace or two to the rear, until we approached a gate, when he jumped forward and opened it. "Give us a pinch of your snuff, Tom," quoth the Sheriff. Tom's mull was produced, and the hand resumed its position. I was much diverted with Tom's behavior when we at length reached Abbotsford. There were some garden chairs on the green in front of the cottage porch. Scott sat down on one of them to enjoy the view of his new tower as it gleamed in the sunset, and Constable and I did the like. Mr. Purdie remained lounging near us for a few minutes, and then asked the Sheriff "to speak a word." They withdrew together into the garden — and Scott presently rejoined us with a particularly comical expression of face. As soon as Tom was out of sight, he said — "Will ye guess what he has been saying, now? — Well, this is a great satisfaction! Tom assures me that he has thought the matter over, and *will take my advice* about the thinning of that clump behind Captain Ferguson's."[1]

---

[1] I am obliged to my friend Mr. Scott of Gala for reminding me of the following trait of Tom Purdie. The first time Mr. John Richardson of Fludyer Street came to Abbotsford, Tom (who took him for a Southron) was sent to attend upon him while he tried for a *fish* (*i. e.*, a salmon) in the neighborhood of Melrose Bridge. As they walked thither, Tom boasted grandly of the size of the fish he had himself caught there, evidently giving the stranger no credit for much skill in the Waltonian craft. By and by, however, Richardson, who is an admirable angler, hooked a vigorous fellow, and after a beautiful exhibition of the art, landed him in safety. " A fine *fish*, Tom." — " Oo, aye, Sir," quoth Tom, " it 's a bonny grilse." " A *grilse*, Tom ! " says Mr. R., " it 's as heavy a *salmon* as the heaviest you were telling me about." Tom showed his teeth in a smile of bitter incredulity ; but while they were still debating, Lord Somerville's fisherman came up with scales in his basket, and Richardson insisted on having his victim weighed. The result was triumphant for the captor. " Weel," says Tom, letting the salmon drop on the turf, " weel, ye *are* a meikle fish, mon — and a meikle *fule*, too " (he added in a lower key), " to let yoursell be kilt by an Englander." — (1839.)

[Mr. Richardson's own account of this incident can be found in the memorial sketch of him in the *North British Review* for November, 1864. The scene was not Abbotsford, but Ashestiel, in September, 1810.]

I must not forget that, whoever might be at Abbotsford, Tom always appeared at his master's elbow on
Sunday, when dinner was over, and drank long life to
the Laird and the Lady and all the good company, in
a quaigh of whiskey, or a tumbler of wine, according to
his fancy. I believe Scott has somewhere expressed in
print his satisfaction that, among all the changes of our
manners, the ancient freedom of personal intercourse
may still be indulged between a master and an *out-of-
doors* servant; but in truth he kept by the old fashion
even with domestic servants, to an extent which I have
hardly seen practised by any other gentleman. He conversed with his coachman if he sat by him, as he often
did on the box — with his footman, if he happened to be
in the rumble; and when there was any very young lad
in the household, he held it a point of duty to see that
his employments were so arranged as to leave time for
advancing his education, made him bring his copy-book
once a week to the library, and examined him as to all
that he was doing. Indeed he did not confine this humanity to his own people. Any steady servant of a
friend of his was soon considered as a sort of friend too,
and was sure to have a kind little colloquy to himself at
coming and going. With all this, Scott was a very
rigid enforcer of discipline — contrived to make it thoroughly understood by all about him, that they must do
their part by him as he did his by them; and the result
was happy. I never knew any man so well served as he
was — so carefully, so respectfully, and so silently; and
I cannot help doubting if, in any department of human
operations, real kindness ever compromised real dignity.

In a letter, already quoted, there occurs some mention
of the Prince Gustavus Vasa, who was spending this
winter in Edinburgh, and his Royal Highness's accomplished attendant, the Baron Polier. I met them frequently in Castle Street, and remember as especially
interesting the first evening that they dined there. The

only portrait in Scott's Edinburgh dining-room was one
of Charles XII. of Sweden, and he was struck, as indeed
every one must have been, with the remarkable resemblance which the exiled Prince's air and features presented to the hero of his race.   Young Gustavus, on his
part, hung with keen and melancholy enthusiasm on
Scott's anecdotes of the expedition of Charles Edward
Stewart. — The Prince, accompanied by Scott and myself, witnessed the ceremonial of the proclamation of
King George IV. on the 2d of February at the Cross
of Edinburgh, from a window over Mr. Constable's shop
in the High Street; and on that occasion, also, the air
of sadness that mixed in his features with eager curiosity
was very affecting.   Scott explained all the details to
him, not without many lamentations over the barbarity of
the Auld Reekie bailies, who had removed the beautiful
Gothic Cross itself, for the sake of widening the thor-
oughfare.   The weather was fine, the sun shone bright;
and the antique tabards of the heralds, the trumpet notes
of *God save the King*, and the hearty cheerings of the
immense uncovered multitude that filled the noble old
street, produced altogether a scene of great splendor and
solemnity.   The Royal Exile surveyed it with a flushed
cheek and a watery eye, and Scott, observing his emotion, withdrew with me to another window, whispering:
"Poor lad! poor lad! God help him."   Later in the
season, the Prince spent a few days at Abbotsford; but
I have said enough to explain some allusions in the next
letter to Lord Montagu, in which Scott also adverts to
several public events of January and February, 1820, —
the assassination of the Duke of Berri, the death of
King George III., the general election which followed
the royal demise, and its more unhappy consequence,
the reagitation of the old disagreement between George
IV. and his wife, who, as soon as she learned his accession to the throne, announced her resolution of returning
from the Continent (where she had been leading for some

years a wandering life), and asserting her rights as Queen. The Tory gentleman, in whose canvass of the Selkirk boroughs Scott was now earnestly concerned, was his worthy friend, Mr. Henry Monteith of Carstairs, who ultimately carried the election.

TO THE LORD MONTAGU, ETC., DITTON PARK.

EDINBURGH, 22d February, 1820.

MY DEAR LORD, — I have nothing to say, except that Selkirk has declared decidedly for Monteith, and that his calling and election seem to be sure. Roxburghshire is right and tight. Harden will not stir for Berwickshire. In short, within my sphere of observation, there is nothing which need make you regret your personal absence; and I hope my dear young namesake and chief will not find his influence abated while he is unable to head it himself. It is but little I can do, but it shall always be done with a good will — and merits no thanks, for I owe much more to his father's memory than ever I can pay a tittle of. I often think what he would have said or wished, and, within my limited sphere, *that* will always be a rule to me while I have the means of advancing in any respect the interest of his son; — certainly, if anything could increase this desire, it would be the banner being at present in your Lordship's hand. I can do little but look out ahead, but that is always something. When I look back on the house of Buccleuch, as I once knew it, it is a sad retrospect. But we must look forward, and hope for the young blossom of so goodly a tree. I think your Lordship judged quite right in carrying Walter in his place to the funeral.[1] He will long remember it, and may survive many occasions of the same kind, to all human appearance. — Here is a horrid business of the Duke de Berri. It was first told me yesterday by Count Itterburg (*i. e.*, Prince Gustavus

[1] The funeral of George III. at Windsor : the young Duke of Buccleuch was at this time at Eton.

of Sweden, son of the ex-King), who comes to see me
very often. No fairy tale could match the extravagance
of such a tale being told to a private Scotch gentleman
by such a narrator, his own grandfather having perished
in the same manner. But our age has been one of complete revolution, baffling all argument and expectation.
As to the King and Queen, or, to use the abbreviation
of an old Jacobite of my acquaintance, who, not loving
to hear them so called at full length, and yet desirous to
have the newspapers read to him, commanded these
words always to be pronounced as the letters K. and Q.
— I say then, as to the K. and the Q., I venture to
think, that whichever strikes the first blow will lose the
battle. The sound, well-judging, and well-principled
body of the people will be much shocked at the stirring
such a hateful and disgraceful question. If the K. urges
it unprovoked, the public feeling will put him in the
wrong: if he lets her alone, her own imprudence, and that
of her hot-headed adviser Harry Brougham, will push on
the discussion; and, take a fool's word for it, as Sancho
says, the country will never bear her coming back, foul
with the various kinds of infamy she has been stained
with, to force herself into the throne. On the whole, it
is a discussion most devoutly to be deprecated by those
who wish well to the Royal family.

Now for a very different subject. I have a report that
there is found on the farm of Melsington, in a bog, the
limb of a bronze figure, full size, with a spur on the
heel. This has been reported to Mr. Riddell, as Commissioner, and to me as Antiquary in chief, on the estate.
I wish your Lordship would permit it to be sent provi-
sionally to Abbotsford, and also allow me, if it shall
seem really curious, to make search for the rest of the
statue. Clarkson[1] has sent me a curious account of it;
and that a Roman statue (for such it seems) of that size

---

[1] Ebenezer Clarkson, Esq., a surgeon of distinguished skill at Selkirk,
and through life a trusty friend and crony of the Sheriff's.

should be found in so wild a place, has something very irritating to the curiosity. I do not of course desire to have anything' more than the opportunity of examining the relique. It may be the foundation of a set of bronzes, if stout Lord Walter should turn to *virtu*.

Always, my dear Lord, most truly yours,

WALTER SCOTT.

The novel of The Monastery was published by Messrs. Longman and Company in the beginning of March. It appeared, not in the post 8vo form of Ivanhoe, but in three volumes 12mo, like the earlier works of the series. In fact, a few sheets of The Monastery had been printed before Scott agreed to let Ivanhoe have "By the Author of Waverley" on its title-page; and the different shapes of the two books belonged to the abortive scheme of passing off "Mr. Laurence Templeton" as a hitherto unheard-of candidate for literary success.

CHAPTER XLVIII

SCOTT REVISITS LONDON. — HIS PORTRAIT BY LAW-
RENCE, AND BUST BY CHANTREY. — ANECDOTES BY
ALLAN CUNNINGHAM. — LETTERS TO MRS. SCOTT,
LAIDLAW, ETC. — HIS BARONETCY GAZETTED. — MAR-
RIAGE OF HIS DAUGHTER SOPHIA. — LETTER TO "THE
BARON OF GALASHIELS." — VISIT OF PRINCE GUS-
TAVUS VASA AT ABBOTSFORD. — TENDERS OF HON-
ORARY DEGREES FROM OXFORD AND CAMBRIDGE. —
LETTER TO MR. THOMAS SCOTT

1820

At the rising of his Court on the 12th of March, Scott
proceeded to London, for the purpose of receiving his
baronetcy, which he had been prevented from doing in
the spring of the preceding year by his own illness, and
again at Christmas by accumulated family afflictions.
On his arrival in town, his son, the Cornet, met him; and
they both established themselves at Miss Dumergue's.

One of his first visitors was Sir Thomas Lawrence,
who informed him that the King had resolved to adorn
the great gallery, then in progress at Windsor Castle,
with portraits by his hand of his Majesty's most distinguished contemporaries; all the reigning monarchs of
Europe, and their chief ministers and generals, had already sat for this purpose: on the same walls the King
desired to see exhibited those of his own subjects who
had attained the highest honors of literature and science
— and it was his pleasure that this series should commence with Walter Scott. The portrait was of course
begun immediately, and the head was finished before

Scott left town.   Sir Thomas has caught and fixed with admirable skill one of the loftiest expressions of Scott's countenance at the proudest period of his life: to the perfect truth of the representation, every one who ever surprised him in the act of composition at his desk, will bear witness.   The expression, however, was one with which many who had seen the man often were not familiar; and it was extremely unfortunate that Sir Thomas filled in the figure from a separate sketch after he had quitted London.   When I first saw the head, I thought nothing could be better; but there was an evident change for the worse when the picture appeared in its finished state — for the rest of the person had been done on a different scale, and this neglect of proportion takes considerably from the majestic effect which the head itself, and especially the mighty pile of forehead, had in nature.   I hope one day to see a good engraving of the head alone, as I first saw it floating on a dark sea of canvas.

Lawrence told me, several years afterwards, that, in his opinion, the two greatest men he had painted were the Duke of Wellington and Sir Walter Scott; "and it was odd," said he, "that they both chose usually the same hour for sitting — seven in the morning.   They were both as patient sitters as I ever had.   Scott, however, was, in my case at least, a very difficult subject. I had selected what struck me as his noblest look; but when he was in the chair before me, he talked away on all sorts of subjects in his usual style, so that it cost me great pains to bring him back to solemnity, when I had to attend to anything beyond the outline of a subordinate feature.   I soon found that the surest recipe was to say something that would lead him to recite a bit of poetry. I used to introduce, by hook or by crook, a few lines of Campbell or Byron — he was sure to take up the passage where I left it, or *cap* it by something better — and then, when he was, as Dryden says of one of his heroes, —

'Made up of three parts fire — so full of heaven
It sparkled at his eyes ' —

then was my time — and I made the best use I could of
it. The hardest day's work I had with him was once
when * * * * *[1] accompanied him to my painting room.
* * * * * was in particularly gay spirits, and nothing
would serve him but keeping both artist and sitter in a
perpetual state of merriment by anecdote upon anecdote
about poor Sheridan. The anecdotes were mostly in
themselves black enough — but the style of the *conteur*
was irresistibly quaint and comical. When Scott came
next, he said he was ashamed of himself for laughing so
much as he listened to them; ' for truly,' quoth he, ' if
the tithe was fact, * * * * * might have said to Sherry
— as Lord Braxfield once said to an eloquent culprit at
the Bar — "Ye 're a vera clever chiel', man, but ye wad
be nane the waur o' a hanging." ' "

It was also during this visit to London that Scott sat
to Mr. (now Sir Francis) Chantrey for that bust which
alone preserves for posterity the cast of expression most
fondly remembered by all who ever mingled in his domestic circle. Chantrey's request that Scott would sit
to him was communicated through Mr. Allan Cunningham, then (as now) employed as Clerk of the Works in
our great Sculptor's establishment. Mr. Cunningham,
in his early days, when gaining his bread as a stone-
mason in Nithsdale, made a pilgrimage on foot into
Edinburgh, for the sole purpose of seeing the author of
Marmion as he passed along the street. He was now in
possession of a celebrity of his own, and had mentioned
to his patron his purpose of calling on Scott to thank
him for some kind message he had received, through a
common friend, on the subject of those Remains of Nithsdale and Galloway Song, which first made his poetical
talents known to the public. Chantrey embraced this
opportunity of conveying to Scott his own long-cher-

[1] A distinguished Whig friend.

ished ambition of modelling his head; and Scott at once assented to the flattering proposal. "It was about nine in the morning," says Mr. Cunningham, "that I sent in my card to him at Miss Dumergue's in Piccadilly. It had not been gone a minute, when I heard a quick heavy step coming, and in he came, holding out both hands, as was his custom, and saying, as he pressed mine, 'Allan Cunningham, I am glad to see you.' I said something," continues Mr. C., "about the pleasure I felt in touching the hand that had charmed me so much. He moved his hand, and with one of his comic smiles, said, ' Ay — and a big brown hand it is.' I was a little abashed at first: Scott saw it, and soon put me at my ease; he had the power — I had almost called it the art, but art it was not — of winning one's heart and restoring one's confidence beyond any man I ever met." Then ensued a little conversation, in which Scott complimented Allan on his ballads, and urged him to try some work of more consequence, quoting Burns's words, "for dear auld Scotland's sake;" but being engaged to breakfast in a distant part of the town, he presently dismissed his visitor, promising to appear next day at an early hour, and submit himself to Mr. Chantrey's inspection.

Chantrey's purpose had been the same as Lawrence's — to seize a poetical phasis of Scott's countenance; and he proceeded to model the head as looking upwards, gravely and solemnly. The talk that passed, meantime, had equally amused and gratified both, and fortunately, at parting, Chantrey requested that Scott would come and breakfast with him next morning before they recommenced operations in the studio. Scott accepted the invitation, and when he arrived again in Ecclestone Street, found two or three acquaintances assembled to meet him, — among others, his old friend Richard Heber. The breakfast was, as any party in Sir Francis Chantrey's house is sure to be, a gay and joyous one, and not having seen Heber in particular for several years, Scott's spirits were unusually excited by the presence of an intimate associate of his youthful days. I transcribe what follows from Mr. Cunningham's Memorandum: —

" Heber made many inquiries about old friends in Edinburgh, and old books and old houses, and reminded the other of their early socialities. ' Ay,' said Mr. Scott, ' I remember we once dined out together, and sat so late that when we came away the night and day were so neatly balanced, that we resolved to walk about till sunrise. The moon was not down, however, and we took advantage of her Ladyship's lantern, and climbed to the top of Arthur's Seat ; when we came down we had a rare appetite for breakfast.' — ' I remember it well,' said Heber ; ' Edinburgh was a wild place in those days, — it abounded in clubs — convivial clubs.' — ' Yes,' replied Mr. Scott, ' and abounds still ; but the conversation is calmer, and there are no such sallies now as might be heard in other times. One club, I remember, was infested with two Kemps, father and son ; when the old man had done speaking, the young one began, — and before he grew weary, the father was refreshed, and took up the song. John Clerk, during a pause, was called on for a stave ; he immediately struck up, in a psalm-singing tone, and electrified the club with a verse which sticks like a burr to my memory, —

> " Now, God Almighty judge James Kemp,
>   And likewise his son John,
> And hang them over Hell in hemp,
>   And burn them in brimstone." ' —

" In the midst of the mirth which this specimen of psalmody raised, John (commonly called *Jack*) Fuller, the member for Surrey, and standing jester of the House of Commons, came in. Heber, who was well acquainted with the free and joyous character of that worthy, began to lead him out by relating some festive anecdotes : Fuller growled approbation, and indulged us with some of his odd sallies ; things which he assured us ' were damned good, and true too, which was better.' Mr. Scott, who was standing when Fuller came in, eyed him at first with a look grave and considerate ; but as the stream of con-

versation flowed, his keen eye twinkled brighter and brighter;
his stature increased, for he drew himself up, and seemed to
take the measure of the hoary joker, body and soul. An hour
or two of social chat had meanwhile induced Mr. Chantrey to
alter his views as to the bust, and when Mr. Scott left us, he
said to me privately, 'This will never do — I shall never be
able to please myself with a perfectly serene expression. I
must try his conversational look, take him when about to break
out into some sly funny old story.' As Chantrey said this, he
took a string, cut off the head of the bust, put it into its present
position, touched the eyes and the mouth slightly, and wrought
such a transformation upon it, that when Scott came to his
third sitting, he smiled and said, — 'Ay, ye 're mair like your-
sel now! — Why, Mr. Chantrey, no witch of old ever performed
such cantrips with clay as this.' " [1]

These sittings were seven in number; but when Scott
revisited London a year afterwards, he gave Chantrey
several more, the bust being by that time in marble.
Allan Cunningham, when he called to bid him farewell,
as he was about to leave town on the present occasion,
found him in court dress, preparing to kiss hands at
the Levee, on being gazetted as Baronet. "He seemed
anything but at his ease," says Cunningham, "in that
strange attire; he was like one in armor — the stiff cut
of the coat — the large shining buttons and buckles — the
lace ruffles — the queue — the sword — and the cocked
hat, formed a picture at which I could not forbear smiling. He surveyed himself in the glass for a moment, and
burst into a hearty laugh. 'O Allan,' he said, 'O
Allan, what creatures we must make of ourselves in obe-

---

[1] [Mr. C. R. Leslie, himself the painter of an admirable portrait of
Scott, says of Chantrey's work: —

"Of the many portraits of him, Chantrey's bust is, to my mind, the
most perfect; . . . the gentle turn of the head, inclined a little forwards
and down, and the lurking humor in the eye and about the mouth, are
Scott's own. Chantrey watched Sir Walter in company, and invited him
to breakfast previous to the sittings, and by these means caught the expression that was most characteristic." — *Leslie's Autobiographical Recollections.*]

dience to Madam Etiquette!   Seest thou not, I say, what a deformed thief this fashion is? how giddily she turns about all the hot bloods between fourteen and five-and-thirty?' " [1]

Scott's baronetcy was conferred on him, not in consequence of any Ministerial suggestion, but by the King personally, and of his own unsolicited motion; and when the poet kissed his hand, he said to him, "I shall always reflect with pleasure on Sir Walter Scott's having been the first creation of my reign."

The Gazette announcing his new dignity was dated March 30, and published on the 2d of April, 1820; and the Baronet, as soon afterwards as he could get away from Lawrence, set out on his return to the North; for he had such respect for the ancient prejudice (a classical as well as a Scottish one) against marrying in May, that he was anxious to have the ceremony in which his daughter was concerned over before that unlucky month should commence.[2]   It is needless to say, that during this stay

---

[1] *Much Ado about Nothing*, Act III. Scene 3.

[2] [On March 15 Scott had written to Lady Abercorn: "Sophia is going to be married, and to a young man of uncommon talents, — indeed of as promising a character as I know. He is highly accomplished, a beautiful poet and fine draughtsman, and, what is better, of a most honorable and gentlemanlike disposition. He is handsome besides, and I like everything about him, except that he is more grave and retired than I (who have been all my life something of an *étourdi*) like particularly, but it is better than the opposite extreme. In point of situation they have enough to live upon, and ' the world for the winning.' . . . Your Ladyship will see some beautiful lines of his writing in the last number of a very clever periodical publication called *Blackwood's Edinburgh Magazine*. The verses are in an essay on the ballad poetry of the Spaniards, which he illustrates by some beautiful translations which — to speak truth — are much finer than the originals. . . . The youngster's name is John Gibson Lockhart; he comes of a good Lanarkshire family, and is very well connected. His father is a clergyman."

Two months later, in a letter to Morritt, Sir Walter says: —

" To me, as it seems neither of my sons have a strong literary turn, the society of a son-in-law possessed of learning and talent must be a very great acquisition, and relieve me from some anxiety with respect to a valuable part of my fortune, consisting of copyrights, etc., which, though advantageous in my lifetime, might have been less so at my decease, unless

in London he had again experienced, in its fullest measure, the enthusiasm of all ranks of his acquaintance; and I shall now transcribe a few paragraphs from domestic letters, which will show, among other things, how glad he was when the hour came that restored him to his ordinary course of life.

TO MRS. SCOTT, 39 CASTLE STREET, EDINBURGH.

PICCADILLY, 20th March, 1820.

MY DEAR CHARLOTTE, — I have got a delightful plan for the addition at Abb——, which I think will make it quite complete, and furnish me with a handsome library, and you with a drawing-room and better bedroom, with good bedrooms for company, etc. It will cost me a little hard work to meet the expense, but I have been a good while idle. I hope to leave this town early next week, and shall hasten back with great delight to my own household gods.

I hope this will find you from under Dr. Ross's charge. I expect to see you quite in beauty when I come down, for I assure you I have been coaxed by very pretty ladies here, and look for merry faces at home. My picture comes on, and will be a grand thing, but the sitting is a great bore. Chantrey's bust is one of the finest things he ever did. It is quite the fashion to go to see it — there 's for you. Yours, my dearest love, with the most sincere affection,   WALTER SCOTT.

TO THE SAME.

PICCADILLY, March 27.

MY DEAR CHARLOTTE, — I have the pleasure to say that Lord Sidmouth has promised to dismiss me in all

under the management of a person acquainted with the nature of such property. All I have to fear on Lockhart's part, is a certain rashness, which I trust has been the effect of youth and high spirits, joined to lack of good advice, as he seems perfectly good-humored and very docile. So I trust your little friend Sophia, who I know has an interest in your bosom, has a very fair chance for such happiness as this motley world can afford." — *Familiar Letters*, vol. ii. pp. 73, 77.]

my honors by the 30th, so that I can easily be with you by the end of April; and you and Sophia may easily select the 28th, 29th, or 30th, for the ceremony. I have been much fêted here, as usual, and had a very quiet dinner at Mr. Arbuthnot's yesterday with the Duke of Wellington, where Walter heard the great Lord in all his glory talk of war and Waterloo. Here is a hellish — yes, literally a hellish bustle. My head turns round with it. The whole mob of the Middlesex blackguards pass through Piccadilly twice a day, and almost drive me mad with their noise and vociferation.[1] Pray do, my dear Charlotte, write soon. You know those at a distance are always anxious to hear from home. I beg you to say what would give you pleasure that I could bring from this place, and whether you want anything from Mrs. Arthur for yourself, Sophia, or Anne; also what would please little Charles. You know you may stretch a point on this occasion. Richardson says your honors will be gazetted on Saturday; certainly very soon, as the King, I believe, has signed the warrant. When, or how I shall see him, is not determined, but I suppose I shall have to go to Brighton. My best love attends the girls, little Charles, and all the quadrupeds.

I conclude that the marriage will take place in Castle Street, and want to know where they go, etc. All this you will have to settle without my wise head; but I shall be terribly critical — so see you do all right. I am always, dearest Charlotte, most affectionately yours,

WALTER SCOTT.

(For the Lady Scott of Abbotsford — to be.)

TO MR. JAMES BALLANTYNE, PRINTER, ST. JOHN'S STREET,
EDINBURGH.

96 PICCADILLY, 28th March.

DEAR JAMES, — I am much obliged by your attentive letter. Unquestionably Longman and Co. sell their books

---

[1] The general election was going on.

at subscription price, because they have the first of the
market, and only one third of the books; so that, as
they say with us, "let them care that come ahint." This
I knew and foresaw, and the ragings of the booksellers,
considerably aggravated by the displeasure of Constable
and his house, are ridiculous enough; and as to their
injuring the work, if it have a principle of locomotion in
it, they cannot stop it — if it has not, they cannot make it
move. I care not a bent twopence about their quarrels;
only I say now, as I always said, that Constable's management is best, both for himself and the author; and,
had we not been controlled by the narrowness of discount, I would put nothing past him. I agree with the
public in thinking the work not very interesting; but it
was written with as much care as the others — that is,
with no care at all; and,

"If it is na weil bobbit, we 'll bobb it again."

On these points I am Atlas. I cannot write much in
this bustle of engagements, with Sir Francis's mob hol-
loing under the windows. I find that even this light
composition demands a certain degree of silence, and I
might as well live in a cotton-mill. Lord Sidmouth tells
me I will obtain leave to quit London by the 30th, which
will be delightful news, for I find I cannot bear late
hours and great society so well as formerly; and yet it
is a fine thing to hear politics talked of by Ministers of
State, and war discussed by the Duke of Wellington.[1]

[1] [Soon after his return, Scott writes to Morritt: —

"London I thought incredibly tiresome; I wanted my sheet anchors, —
you and poor George Ellis, — by whom I could ride at quiet moorings
without mixing entirely in the general vortex. The great lion — great in
every sense — was the gigantic Belzoni, the handsomest man (for a giant)
I ever saw or could suppose to myself. He is said completely to have
overawed the Arabs, your old friends, by his great strength, height, and
energy. I had one delightful evening in company with the Duke of
Wellington, and heard him fight over Waterloo and his other battles with
the greatest good-humor. It is odd, he says, that the most distinct
writer on military affairs whose labors he has perused is James II., in the

My occasions here will require that John or you send me two notes payable at Coutts's for £300 each, at two and three months' date. I will write to Constable for one at £350, which will settle my affairs here — which, with fees and other matters, come, as you may think, pretty heavy. Let the bills be drawn payable at Coutts's, and sent without delay. I will receive them safe if sent under Mr. Freeling's cover. Mention particularly what you are doing, for now is your time to push miscellaneous work. Pray take great notice of inaccuracies in the Novels. They are very, very many — some mine, I dare say — but all such as you may and ought to correct. If you would call on William Erskine (who is your well-wisher, and a little mortified he never sees you), he would point out some of them.

Do you ever see Lockhart? You should consult him on every doubt where you would refer to me if present. Yours very truly,   W. S.

You say nothing of John, yet I am anxious about him.

TO MR. LAIDLAW, KAESIDE, MELROSE.

LONDON, April 2, 1820.

DEAR WILLIE, — I had the great pleasure of your letter, which carries me back to my own braes, which I love so dearly, out of this place of bustle and politics. When I can see my Master — and thank him for many acts of favor — I think I will bid adieu to London forever; for neither the hours nor the society suit me so well as a few years since. There is too much necessity for exertion, too much brilliancy and excitation from morning till night.

I am glad the sheep are away, though at a loss. I should think the weather rather too dry for planting, judging by what we have here. Do not let Tom go on

warlike details given in his own Memoirs. I have not read over these Memoirs lately, but I think I do not recollect much to justify the eulogium of so great a master." — *Familiar Letters*, vol. ii. p. 77.]

sticking in plants to no purpose — better put in firs in a rainy week in August. Give my service to him. I expect to be at Edinburgh in the end of this month, and to get a week at Abbotsford before the Session sits down. I think you are right to be in no hurry to let Broomielees. There seems no complaint of wanting money here just now, so I hope things will come round.

Ever yours truly,

WALTER SCOTT.

TO MISS SCOTT, CASTLE STREET, EDINBURGH.

LONDON, April 3, 1820.

DEAR SOPHIA, — I have no letter from any one at home excepting Lockhart, and he only says you are all well; and I trust it is so. I have seen most of my old friends, who are a little the worse for the wear, like myself. A five years' march down the wrong side of the hill tells more than ten on the right side. Our good friends here are kind as kind can be, and no frumps. They lecture the Cornet a little, which he takes with becoming deference and good-humor. There is a certain veil of Flanders lace floating in the wind for a certain occasion, from a certain godmother, but that is more than a dead secret.

We had a very merry day yesterday at Lord Melville's, where we found Lord Huntly [1] and other friends, and had a bumper to the new Baronet, whose name was Gazetted that evening. Lady Huntly plays Scotch tunes like a Highland angel. She ran a set of variations on " Kenmure's on and awa'," which I told her were enough to raise a whole country-side. I never in my life heard such fire thrown into that sort of music. I am now laying anchors to windward, as John Ferguson says, to get Walter's leave extended. We saw the Duke of York, who was very civil, but wants altogether the courtesy of the King. I have had a very gracious message from the King. He is expected up very soon, so I don't go to

[1] The late Duke of Gordon.

Brighton, which is so far good. I fear his health is not strong. Meanwhile all goes forward for the Coronation. The expense of the robes for the peers may amount to £400 apiece. All the ermine is bought up at the most extravagant prices. I hear so much of it, that I really think, like Beau Tibbs,[1] I shall be tempted to come up and see it, if possible. Indeed, I don't see why I should not stay here, as I seem to be forgotten at home. The people here are like to smother me with kindness, so why should I be in a great hurry to leave them?

I write, wishing to know what I could bring Anne and you and mamma down, that would be acceptable; and I shall be much obliged to you to put me up to that matter. To little Charles also I promised something, and I wish to know what he would like. I hope he pays attention to Mr. Thomson, to whom remember my best compliments. I hope to get something for him soon.

To-day I go to spend my Sabbath quietly with Joanna Baillie and John Richardson, at Hampstead. The long Cornet goes with me. I have kept him amongst the seniors; nevertheless he seems pretty well amused. He is certainly one of the best-conditioned lads I ever saw, in point of temper.

I understand you and Anne have gone through the ceremony of confirmation. Pray write immediately, and let me know how you are all going on, and what you would like to have, all of you. You know how much I would like to please you.

Yours, most affectionately,

WALTER SCOTT.

While Scott remained in London, the Professorship of Moral Philosophy in the University of Edinburgh became vacant by the death of Dr. Thomas Brown; and among others who proposed themselves as candidates to fill it, was the author of the Isle of Palms. He was opposed

[1] See Goldsmith's *Citizen of the World*, No. 105.

in the Town Council (who are the patrons of most of the
Edinburgh Chairs), on various pretences, but solely, in
fact, on party grounds, — certain humorous political
pieces having much exacerbated the Whigs of the North
against him; and I therefore wrote to Scott, requesting
him to animate the Tory Ministers in his behalf. Sir
Walter did so, and Mr. Wilson's canvass was successful.[1]
The answer to my communication was in these terms: —

---

[1] [This academic struggle was as fiercely contested as though it had
been a political contest, which in truth it was. Lockhart celebrated Wilson's victory in the *Testimonium* (prefacing the seventh volume of *Blackwood*), thus keeping alive the passion of the hour. In July Scott wrote
to his son-in-law, and through him to Wilson, a letter which is especially
interesting, as showing the writer's attitude in regard to the personalities
of *Maga*, which his political opponents were inclined to believe had at
least his tacit approval. The letter, from which these extracts are taken,
will be found in Lang's *Life of Lockhart* (vol. i. pp. 239-245), where it
was published for the first time: —

. . . "I am sure our friend has been taught the danger of giving way to
high spirits in mixed society, where there is some one always ready to
laugh at the joke and to put it into his pocket to throw in the jester's face
on some future occasion. It is plain Wilson must have walked the course
had he been cautious in selecting the friends of his lighter hours, and now,
clothed with philosophical dignity, his friends will really expect he should
be on his guard in this respect, and add to his talents and amiable disposition the proper degree of *retenue* becoming a moral teacher. Try to express all this to him in your own way, and believe that, as I have said it
from the best motives, so I would wish it conveyed in the most delicate
terms, as from one who equally honors Wilson's genius and loves his
benevolent, ardent, and amiable disposition, but who would willingly see
them mingled with the caution which leaves calumny no pin to hang her
infamous accusations upon.

"For the reasons above mentioned I wish you had not published the
Testimonium. It is very clever, but descends to too low game. If Jeffrey
or Cranstoun, or any of the dignitaries, chose to fight such skirmishes,
there would be some credit in it; but I do not like to see you turn out as
a sharpshooter with * * * *. 'What does thou drawn among these heart-
less hinds?' . . . I have hitherto avoided saying anything on this subject,
though some little turn towards personal satire is, I think, the only draw-
back to your great and powerful talents, and I think I may have hinted
as much to you. But I wished to see how this matter of Wilson's would
turn, before making a clean breast upon this subject. It might have
so happened that you could not handsomely or kindly have avoided a
share in his defence, if the enemy had prevailed, and where friendship, or
country, or any strong call demands the use of satiric talent, I hope I

TO J. G. LOCKHART, ESQ., GREAT KING STREET, EDINBURGH.

LONDON, 30th March, 1820.

DEAR LOCKHART, — I have yours of the Sunday morning, which has been terribly long of coming. There needed no apology for mentioning anything in which I could be of service to Wilson; and, so far as good words and good wishes *here* can do, I think he will be success-

should neither fear risk myself or desire a friend to shun it. But now that he has triumphed, I think it would be bad taste to cry out, —

' Strike up our drums — pursue the scattered stray.'

Besides, the natural consequence of his new situation must be his relinquishing his share in these compositions — at least, he will injure himself in the opinion of many friends, and expose himself to a continuation of galling and vexatious disputes to the embittering of his life, should he do otherwise. In that case I really hope you will pause before you undertake to be the Boaz of the *Maga*; I mean in the personal and satirical department, when the Jachin has seceded.

" Besides all other objections of personal enemies, personal quarrels, constant obloquy, and all uncharitableness, such an occupation will fritter away your talents, hurt your reputation both as a lawyer and a literary man, and waste away your time in what at best will be but a monthly wonder. What has been done in this department will be very well as a frolic of young men, but let it suffice, ' the gambol has been shown ' — the frequent repetition will lose its effect even as pleasantry, for Peter Pindar, the sharpest of personal satirists, wrote himself down, and wrote himself out, and is forgotten. . . .

" Revere yourself, my dear boy, and think you were born to do your country better service than in this species of warfare. I make no apology (I am sure you will require none) for speaking plainly what my anxious affection dictates. As the old warrior says, ' May the name of Mevni be forgotten among the people, and may they only say, Behold the father of Gaul.' I wish you to have the benefit of my experience without purchasing it; and be assured, that the consciousness of attaining complete superiority over your calumniators and enemies by the force of your general character, is worth a dozen of triumphs over them by the force of wit and raillery. I am sure Sophia, as much as she can or ought to form any judgment respecting the line of conduct you have to pursue in your new character of a man married and settled, will be of my opinion in this matter, and that you will consider her happiness and your own, together with the respectability of both, by giving what I have said your anxious consideration."

Lockhart's reply to this letter, expressing gratitude, and promising amendment, can be found in *Familiar Letters*, vol. ii. p. 86.]

ful; but the battle must be fought in Edinburgh. You are aware that the only point of exception to Wilson may be, that, with the fire of genius, he has possessed some of its eccentricities; but, did he ever approach to those of Henry Brougham, who is the god of Whiggish idolatry? If the high and rare qualities with which he is invested are to be thrown aside as useless, because they may be clouded by a few grains of dust which he can blow aside at pleasure, it is less a punishment on Mr. Wilson than on the country. I have little doubt he would consider success in this weighty matter as a pledge for binding down his acute and powerful mind to more regular labor than circumstances have hitherto required of him, for indeed, without doing so, the appointment could in no point of view answer his purpose. He must stretch to the oar for his own credit, as well as that of his friends; and if he does so, there can be no doubt that his efforts will be doubly blessed, in reference both to himself and to public utility. He must make every friend he can amongst the Council. Palladio Johnstone should not be omitted. If my wife canvasses him, she may do some good.[1]

You must, of course, recommend to Wilson great temper in his canvass — for wrath will do no good. After all, he must leave off sack, purge and live cleanly as a gentleman ought to do; otherwise people will compare his present ambition to that of Sir Terry O'Fag, when he wished to become a judge. "Our pleasant follies are made the whips to scourge us," as Lear says; for otherwise, what could possibly stand in the way of his nomination? I trust it will take place, and give him the

---

[1] Mr. Robert Johnstone, a grocer on a large scale on the North Bridge of Edinburgh, and long one of the leading Bailies, was about this time the prominent patron of some architectural novelties in Auld Reekie, which had found no favor with Scott; — hence his prænomen of *Palladio* — which he owed, I believe, to a song in *Blackwood's Magazine.* The good Bailie had been at the High School with Sir Walter, and their friendly intercourse was never interrupted but by death.

consistence and steadiness which are all he wants to make him the first man of the age.

I am very angry with Castle Street — not a soul has written me, save yourself, since I came to London.

Yours very truly,

WALTER SCOTT.

Sir Walter, accompanied by the Cornet, reached Edinburgh late in April, and on the 29th of that month he gave me the hand of his daughter Sophia. The wedding, *more Scotico*, took place in the evening; and adhering on all such occasions to ancient modes of observance with the same punctiliousness which he mentions as distinguishing his worthy father, he gave a jolly supper afterwards to all the friends and connections of the young couple.[1]

His excursions to Tweedside during Term-time were, with very rare exceptions, of the sort which I have described in the preceding chapter; but he departed from his rule about this time in honor of the Swedish Prince, who had expressed a wish to see Abbotsford before leaving Scotland, and assembled a number of his friends and neighbors to meet his Royal Highness. Of the invitations which he distributed on this occasion, I insert one specimen — that addressed to Mr. Scott of Gala: —

To the Baron of Galashiels
The Knight of Abbotsford sends greeting.

Trusty and well-beloved, — Whereas Gustavus, Prince Royal of Sweden, proposeth to honor our poor house of Abbotsford with his presence on Thursday next, and to

---

[1] [" On Friday evening I gave away Sophia to Mr. Lockhart. . . . I own my house seems lonely to me since she left us, but that is a natural feeling, which will soon wear off. I have every reason to think I have consulted her happiness in the match, as became the father of a most attached and dutiful daughter, who never in her life gave me five minutes' vexation. In the mean time the words run strangely in my ear : —

' Ah me ! the flower and blossom of my house
The wind has blown away to other towers.' "

— Scott to Lady Abercorn — *Familiar Letters*, vol. ii. p. 75.]

repose himself there for certain days, We do heartily pray you, out of the love and kindness which is and shall abide betwixt us, to be aiding to us at this conjuncture, and to repair to Abbotsford with your lady, either upon Thursday or Friday, as may best suit your convenience and pleasure, looking for no denial at your hands. Which loving countenance we will, with all thankfulness, return to you at your mansion of Gala. The hour of appearance being five o'clock, we request you to be then and there present, as you love the honor of the name; and so advance banners in the name of God and St. Andrew.

WALTER SCOTT.

Given at EDINBURGH,
20th May, 1820.

The visit of Count Itterburg is alluded to in this letter to the Cornet, who had now rejoined his regiment in Ireland. It appears that on reaching headquarters he had found a charger *hors de combat*.

TO WALTER SCOTT, ESQ., 18TH HUSSARS, CORK.

CASTLE STREET, May 31, 1820.

DEAR WALTER, — I enclose the cheque for the allowance; pray take care to get good notes in exchange. You had better speak to the gentleman whom Lord Shannon introduced you to, for, when banks take a-breaking, it seldom stops with the first who go. I am very sorry for your loss. You must be economical for a while, and bring yourself round again, for at this moment I cannot so well assist as I will do by and by. So do not buy anything but what you *need*.

I was at Abbotsford for three days last week, to receive Count Itterburg, who seemed very happy while with us, and was much affected when he took his leave. I am sorry for him — his situation is a very particular one, and his feelings appear to be of the kindest order. When he took leave of me, he presented me with a beautiful seal, with all our new blazonries cut on a fine amethyst; and what I thought the prettiest part, on one side of the setting is cut my name, on the other the Prince's — *Gustaf*. He is to travel through Ireland, and will probably be at Cork. You will, of course, ask the Count and Baron to mess, and offer all civilities in your power, in which, I dare say, Colonel Murray will readily join. They intend to inquire after you.

I have bought the land adjoining to the Burnfoot cottage, so that we now march with the Duke of Buccleuch all the way round that course. It cost me £2300 — but there is a great deal of valuable fir planting, which you may remember; fine roosting for the black game. Still I think it is £200 too dear, but Mr. Laidlaw thinks it can be made worth the money, and it rounds the property off very handsomely. You cannot but remember the ground; it lies under the Eildon, east of the Chargelaw.

Mamma, Anne, and Charles are all well. Sophia has been complaining of a return of her old sprain. I told her Lockhart would return her on our hands as not being sound wind and limb.

I beg you to look at your French, and have it much at heart that you should study German. Believe me, always affectionately yours,

WALTER SCOTT.

In May, 1820, Scott received from both the English Universities the highest compliment which it was in their power to offer him. The Vice-Chancellors of Oxford and Cambridge communicated to him, in the same week, their request that he would attend at the approaching Commemorations, and accept the honorary degree of Doctor in Civil Law. It was impossible for him to leave Scotland again that season; and on various subsequent renewals of the same flattering proposition from either body, he was prevented, by similar circumstances, from availing himself of their distinguished kindness.

In the course of a few months, Scott's family arrangements had undergone, as we have seen, considerable alteration. Meanwhile he continued anxious to be allowed to adopt, as it were, the only son of his brother Thomas; and the letter, in consequence of which that promising youth was at last committed to his charge, contains so much matter likely to interest parents and guardians, that, though long, I cannot curtail it.

TO THOMAS SCOTT, ESQ., PAYMASTER 70TH REGIMENT.

ABBOTSFORD, 23d July, 1820.

MY DEAR TOM, — Your letter of May, this day received, made me truly happy, being the first I have received from you since our dear mother's death, and the consequent breaches which fate has made in our family. My own health continues quite firm, at no greater sacrifice than bidding adieu to our old and faithful friend John Barleycorn, whose life-blood has become a little too heavy for my stomach. I wrote to you from London concerning the very handsome manner in which the King behaved to me in conferring my *petit titre*, and also of Sophia's intended marriage, which took place in the end of April, as we intended. I got Walter's leave prolonged, that he might be present, and I assure you, that when he attended the ceremony in full regimentals, you have scarce seen a handsomer young man. He is about six feet and an inch, and perfectly well made. Lockhart seems to be everything I could wish, — and as they have enough to live easily upon for the present, and good expectations for the future, life opens well with them. They are to spend their vacations in a nice little cottage, in a glen belonging to this property, with a rivulet in front, and a grove of trees on the east side to keep away the cold wind. It is about two miles distant from this house, and a very pleasant walk reaches to it through my plantations, which now occupy several hundred acres. Thus there will be space enough betwixt the old man of letters and the young one. Charles's destination to India is adjourned till he reaches the proper age: it seems he cannot hold a Writership until he is sixteen years old, and then is admitted to study for two years at Hertford College.

After my own sons, my most earnest and anxious wish will be, of course, for yours, — and with this view I have pondered well what you say on the subject of your Walter; and whatever line of life you may design him for, it is scarce possible but that I can be of considerable use to him. Before fixing, however, on a point so very important, I would have you consult the nature of the boy himself. I do not mean by this that you should ask his opinion, because at so early an age a well bred up child naturally takes up what is suggested to him by his parents; but I think you should consider, with as much impartiality as a parent can, his temper, disposition, and qualities of mind and body. It is not enough that you think there is an opening for him in one profession rather than another, — for it were better to sacrifice the fairest prospects of that kind than to put a boy into a line of life for which he is not calculated. If my nephew is steady, cautious, fond of a sedentary life and quiet pursuits, and at the same time a proficient in arithmetic, and with a disposition towards the prosecution of its highest branches, he cannot follow a better line than that of an accountant. It is highly respectable — and is one in which, with attention and skill, aided by such opportunities as I may be able to procure for him, he must ultimately succeed. I say ultimately — because the harvest is small and the laborers numerous in this as in other branches of our legal practice; and whoever is to dedicate himself to them, must look for a long and laborious tract of attention ere he reaches the reward of his labors. If I live, however, I will do all I can for him, and see him put under a proper person, taking his 'prentice fee, etc., upon myself. But if, which may possibly

be the case, the lad has a decided turn for active life and
adventure, is high-spirited, and impatient of long and
dry labor, with some of those feelings not unlikely to result from having lived all his life in a camp or a bar-
rack, do not deceive yourself, my dear brother — you
will never make him an accountant; you will never be
able to convert such a sword into a pruning-hook, merely
because you think a pruning-hook the better thing of the
two.   In this supposed case, your authority and my recommendation might put him into an accountant's office;
but it would be just to waste the earlier years of his life
in idleness, with all the temptations to dissipation which
idleness gives way to; and what sort of a place a writing-
chamber is, you cannot but remember. So years might
wear away, and at last the youth starts off from his profession, and becomes an adventurer too late in life, and
with the disadvantage, perhaps, of offended friends and
advanced age standing in the way of his future prospects.

This is what I have judged fittest in my own family,
for Walter would have gone to the Bar had I liked; but
I was sensible (with no small reluctance did I admit the
conviction) that I should only spoil an excellent soldier
to make a poor and undistinguished gownsman. On the
same principle I shall send Charles to India, — not, God
knows, with my will, for there is little chance of my
living to see him return; but merely that, judging by
his disposition, I think the voyage of his life might be
otherwise lost in shallows. He has excellent parts, but
they are better calculated for intercourse with the world
than for hard and patient study.   Having thus sent one
son abroad from my family, and being about to send off
the other in due time, you will not, I am sure, think that
I can mean disregard to your parental feelings in stating
what I can do for your Walter. Should his temper and
character incline for active life, I think I can promise to
get him a cadetship in the East India Company's service;
so soon as he has had the necessary education, I will be

at the expense of his equipment and passage-money; and when he reaches India, there he is completely provided, secure of a competence if he lives, and with great chance of a fortune if he thrives. I am aware this would be a hard pull at Mrs. Scott's feelings and yours; but recollect, your fortune is small, and the demands on it numerous, and pagodas and rupees are no bad things. I can get Walter the first introductions, and if he behaves himself as becomes your son, and my nephew, I have friends enough in India, and of the highest class, to insure his success, even his rapid success — always supposing my recommendations to be seconded by his own conduct. If, therefore, the youth has anything of your own spirit, for God's sake do not condemn him to a drudgery which he will never submit to — and remember, to sacrifice his fortune to your fondness will be sadly mistaken affection. As matters stand, unhappily you must be separated; and considering the advantages of India, the mere circumstance of distance is completely counterbalanced. Health is what will naturally occur to Mrs. Scott; but the climate of India is now well understood, and those who attend to ordinary precautions live as healthy as in Britain. And so I have said my say. Most heartily will I do my best in any way you may ultimately decide for; and as the decision really ought to turn on the boy's temper and disposition, you must be a better judge by far than any one else. But if he should resemble his father and uncle in certain indolent habits, I fear he will make a better subject for an animating life of enterprise than for the technical labor of an accountant's desk. There is no occasion, fortunately, for forming any hasty resolution. When you send him here, I will do all that is in my power to stand in the place of a father to him, and you may fully rely on my care and tenderness. If he should ultimately stay at Edinburgh, as both my own boys leave me, I am sure I shall have great pleasure in having the nearest in blood after them with me. Pray send him as soon as you can, for at his age, and under imperfect opportunities of education, he must have a good deal to make up. I wish I could be of the same use to you which I am sure I can be to your son.

Of public news I have little to send. The papers will tell you the issue of the Radical row for the present. The yeomanry behaved most gallantly. There is in Edinburgh a squadron as fine as ours was — all young men, and zealous soldiers. They made the western campaign with the greatest spirit, and had some hard and fatiguing duty, long night-marches, surprises of the enemy, and so forth, but no fight, for the whole Radical plot went to the devil when it came to gun and sword. Scarce any blood was shed, except in a trifling skirmish at Bonnymuir, near Carron. The rebels were behind a wall, and fired on ten hussars and as many yeomen — the latter under command of a son of James Davidson, W. S. The cavalry cleared the wall, and made them prisoners to a man. The Commission of Oyer and Terminer is now busy trying them and others. The Edinburgh young men showed great spirit; all took arms, and my daughters say (I was in London at the time) that not a feasible-looking beau was to be had for love or money. Several were like old Beardie; they would not shave their moustaches till the Radicals were put down, and returned with most awful whiskers. Lockhart is one of the cavalry, and a very good trooper. It is high to hear these young fellows talk of the Raid of Airdrie, the trot of Kilmarnock, and so on, like so many mosstroopers.

The Queen is making an awful bustle, and though by all accounts her conduct has been most abandoned and beastly, she has got the whole mob for her partisans, who call her injured innocence, and what not. She has courage enough to dare the worst, and a most decided desire to be revenged of *him*, which, by the way, can scarce be wondered at. If she had as many followers of high as of low degree (in proportion), and funds to equip them, I should not be surprised to see her fat bottom in a pair of buckskins, and at the head of an army — God mend all. The things said of her are beyond all usual profligacy. Nobody of any fashion visits her. I think myself monstrously well clear of London and its intrigues, when I look round my green fields, and recollect I have little to do, but to

> —— " make my grass mow,
> And my apple-tree grow."

I beg my kind love to Mrs. Huxley. I have a very acceptable letter from her, and I trust to retain the place she promises me in her remembrance. Sophia will be happy to hear from Uncle Tom, when Uncle Tom has so much leisure. My best compliments attend your wife and daughters, not forgetting Major Huxley and Walter. My dear Tom, it will be a happy moment when circumstances shall permit us a meeting on this side Jordan, as Tabitha says, to talk over old stories, and lay new plans. So many things have fallen out which I had set my heart upon strongly, that I trust this may happen amongst others. — Believe me, yours very affectionately,

WALTER SCOTT.[1]

[1] Here ended Vol. IV. of the Original Edition. — (1839.)

CHAPTER XLIX

AUTUMN AT ABBOTSFORD. — SCOTT'S HOSPITALITY. —
VISIT OF SIR HUMPHRY DAVY, HENRY MACKENZIE,
DR. WOLLASTON, AND WILLIAM STEWART ROSE. —
COURSING ON NEWARK HILL. — SALMON-FISHING. —
THE FESTIVAL AT BOLDSIDE. — THE ABBOTSFORD
HUNT. — THE KIRN, ETC.

1820

ABOUT the middle of August, my wife and I went to
Abbotsford; and we remained there for several weeks,
during which I became familiarized to Sir Walter Scott's
mode of existence in the country. It was necessary to
observe it, day after day, for a considerable period, before
one could believe that such was, during nearly half the
year, the routine of life with the most productive author
of his age. The humblest person who stayed merely for
a short visit, must have departed with the impression
that what he witnessed was an occasional variety; that
Scott's courtesy prompted him to break in upon his
habits when he had a stranger to amuse; but that it was
physically impossible that the man who was writing the
Waverley romances at the rate of nearly twelve volumes
in the year, could continue, week after week, and month
after month, to devote all but a hardly perceptible fraction of his mornings to out-of-doors occupations, and
the whole of his evenings to the entertainment of a constantly varying circle of guests.

The hospitality of his afternoons must alone have been
enough to exhaust the energies of almost any man; for
his visitors did not mean, like those of country-houses in

general, to enjoy the landlord's good cheer and amuse each other; but the far greater proportion arrived from a distance, for the sole sake of the Poet and Novelist himself, whose person they had never before seen, and whose voice they might never again have any opportunity of hearing. No other villa in Europe was ever resorted to from the same motives, and to anything like the same extent, except Ferney; and Voltaire never dreamt of being visible to his *hunters*, except for a brief space of the day; — few of them even dined with him, and none of them seem to have slept under his roof. Scott's establishment, on the contrary, resembled in every particular that of the affluent idler, who, because he has inherited, or would fain transmit, political influence in some province, keeps open house — receives as many as he has room for, and sees their apartments occupied, as soon as they vacate them, by another troop of the same description. Even on gentlemen guiltless of inkshed, the exercise of hospitality upon this sort of scale is found to impose a heavy tax; few of them, nowadays, think of maintaining it for any large portion of the year: very few indeed below the highest rank of the nobility — in whose case there is usually a staff of led-captains, led-chaplains, servile dandies, and semi-professional talkers and jokers from London, to take the chief part of the burden. Now, Scott had often in his mouth the pithy verses, —

> " Conversation is but carving : —
> Give no more to every guest,
> Than he 's able to digest ;
> Give him always of the prime,
> And but little at a time ;
> Carve to all but just enough,
> Let them neither starve nor stuff,
> *And that you may have your due,*
> *Let your neighbors carve for you : "* —

and he, in his own familiar circle always, and in other circles where it was possible, furnished a happy exemplification of these rules and regulations of the Dean of St.

Patrick's. But the same sense and benevolence which dictated adhesion to them among his old friends and acquaintance, rendered it necessary to break them when he was receiving strangers of the class I have described above at Abbotsford: he felt that their coming was the best homage they could pay to his celebrity, and that it would have been as uncourteous in him not to give them their fill of his talk, as it would be in your every-day lord of manors to make his casual guests welcome indeed to his venison, but keep his grouse-shooting for his immediate allies and dependents.

Every now and then he received some stranger who was not indisposed to take his part in the *carving ;* and how good-humoredly he surrendered the lion's share to any one that seemed to covet it — with what perfect placidity he submitted to be bored even by bores of the first water, must have excited the admiration of many besides the daily observers of his proceedings. I have heard a spruce Senior Wrangler lecture him for half an evening on the niceties of the Greek epigram; I have heard the poorest of all parliamentary blunderers try to detail to him the *pros* and *cons* of what he called the *Truck System ;* and in either case the same bland eye watched the lips of the tormentor. But, with such ludicrous exceptions, Scott was the one object of the Abbotsford pilgrims; and evening followed evening only to show him exerting, for their amusement, more of animal spirits, to say nothing of intellectual vigor, than would have been considered by any other man in the company as sufficient for the whole expenditure of a week's existence. Yet this was not the chief marvel; he talked of things that interested himself, because he knew that by doing so he should give most pleasure to his guests. But how vast was the range of subjects on which he could talk with unaffected zeal; and with what admirable delicacy of instinctive politeness did he select his topic according to the peculiar history, study, pursuits, or social

habits of the stranger! — How beautifully he varied his
style of letter-writing, according to the character and
situation of his multifarious correspondents, the reader
has already been enabled to judge; but to carry the same
system into practice *at sight* — to manage utter strangers, of many and widely different classes, in the same
fashion, and with the same effect — called for a quickness of observation, and fertility of resource, such as no
description can convey the slightest notion of to those
who never witnessed the thing for themselves. And all
this was done without approach to the unmanly trickery
of what is called *catching the tone* of the person one
converses with. Scott took the subject on which he
thought such a man or woman would like best to hear
him speak — but not to handle it in their way, or in any
way but what was completely, and most simply his own;
— not to flatter them by embellishing, with the illustration of his genius, the views and opinions which they
were supposed to entertain, — but to let his genius play
out its own variations, for his own delight and theirs, as
freely and easily, and with as endless a multiplicity of
delicious novelties, as ever the magic of Beethoven or
Mozart could fling over the few primitive notes of a village air.

It is the custom in some, perhaps in many country-
houses, to keep a register of the guests, and I have often
regretted that nothing of the sort was ever attempted at
Abbotsford. It would have been a curious record —
especially if so contrived (as I have seen done) that
the names of each day should, by their arrangement on
the page, indicate the exact order in which the company
sat at dinner. It would hardly, I believe, be too much
to affirm, that Sir Walter Scott entertained, under his
roof, in the course of the seven or eight brilliant seasons
when his prosperity was at its height, as many persons
of distinction in rank, in politics, in art, in literature,
and in science, as the most princely nobleman of his age

ever did in the like space of time. — I turned over, since I wrote the preceding sentence, Mr. Lodge's compendium of the British Peerage, and on summing up the titles which suggested *to myself* some reminiscence of this kind, I found them nearly as one out of six. — I fancy it is not beyond the mark to add, that of the eminent foreigners who visited our island within this period, a moiety crossed the Channel mainly in consequence of the interest with which his writings had invested Scotland — and that the hope of beholding the man under his own roof was the crowning motive with half that moiety. As for countrymen of his own, like him ennobled, in the higher sense of that word, by the display of their intellectual energies, if any one such contemporary can be pointed out as having crossed the Tweed, and yet not spent a day at Abbotsford, I shall be surprised.

It is needless to add, that Sir Walter was familiarly known, long before the days I am speaking of, to almost all the nobility and higher gentry of Scotland; and consequently, that there seldom wanted a fair proportion of them to assist him in doing the honors of his country. It is still more superfluous to say so respecting the heads of his own profession at Edinburgh: *Sibi et amicis* — Abbotsford was their villa whenever they pleased to resort to it, and few of them were ever absent from it long. He lived meanwhile in a constant interchange of easy visits with the gentlemen's families of Teviotdale and the Forest; so that, mixed up with his superfine admirers of the Mayfair breed, his staring worshippers from foreign parts, and his quick-witted coevals of the Parliament House — there was found generally some hearty homespun laird, with his dame — the young laird, a bashful bumpkin, perhaps, whose ideas did not soar beyond his gun and pointer — or perhaps a little pseudo-dandy, for whom the Kelso race-course and the Jedburgh ball were "Life," and "the World;" and not forgetting a brace of "Miss Rawbolds,"[1] in whom, as their mamma prognosticated, some of Sir Walter's young Waverleys or Osbaldistones might peradventure discover a Flora MacIvor or a Die Vernon. To complete the *olla podrida*, we must remember that no old acquaintance, or family connections, however remote their actual station or style of manners from his own, were forgotten or lost sight of. He had some, even near relations, who, except when they visited him, rarely, if ever, found admittance to what the haughty dialect of the upper world is pleased to designate exclusively as *society*. These were welcome guests, let who might be under that roof; and it was the same with many a worthy citizen of Edinburgh, habitually moving in the obscurest of circles, who had been in the same class with Scott at the High School, or his fellow-apprentice when he was proud of earning three-pence a page by the use of his pen. To dwell on nothing else, it was surely a beautiful perfection of real universal humanity and politeness, that could enable this great and good man to blend guests so multifarious in one group, and contrive to make them all equally happy with him, with themselves, and with each other.

I remember saying to William Allan one morning as the whole party mustered before the porch after breakfast, "A faithful sketch of what you at this moment see would be more interesting a hundred years hence, than the grandest so-called historical picture that you will ever exhibit at Somerset House;" and my friend agreed with me so cordially, that I often wondered afterwards he had not attempted to realize the suggestion. The subject ought, however, to have been treated conjointly by him (or Wilkie) and Edwin Landseer. It was a clear, bright September morning, with a sharpness

---

[1] " There were the six Miss Rawbolds — pretty dears!
   All song and sentiment; whose hearts were set
   Less on a convent than a coronet."
                                   Don Juan, canto xiii. st. 85.

in the air that doubled the animating influence of the
sunshine, and all was in readiness for a grand coursing-
match on Newark Hill. The only guest who had chalked
out other sport for himself was the stanchest of anglers,
Mr. Rose — but he, too, was there on his *shelty*, armed
with his salmon-rod and landing-net, and attended by his
humorous squire Hinves, and Charlie Purdie, a brother
of Tom, in those days the most celebrated fisherman of
the district. This little group of Waltonians, bound for
Lord Somerville's preserve, remained lounging about to
witness the start of the main cavalcade. Sir Walter,
mounted on Sibyl, was marshalling the order of procession with a huge hunting-whip; and among a dozen frolicsome youths and maidens, who seemed disposed to
laugh at all discipline, appeared, each on horseback, each
as eager as the youngest sportsman in the troop, Sir
Humphry Davy, Dr. Wollaston, and the patriarch of
Scottish belles-lettres, Henry Mackenzie. The Man of
Feeling, however, was persuaded with some difficulty to
resign his steed for the present to his faithful negro follower, and to join Lady Scott in the sociable, until we
should reach the ground of our *battue*. Laidlaw, on a
long-tailed wiry Highlander, yclept *Hoddin Grey*, which
carried him nimbly and stoutly, although his feet almost
touched the ground as he sat, was the adjutant. But
the most picturesque figure was the illustrious inventor
of the safety-lamp. He had come for his favorite sport
of angling, and had been practising it successfully with
Rose, his travelling companion, for two or three days
preceding this, but he had not prepared for coursing
fields, or had left Charlie Purdie's troop for Sir Walter's
on a sudden thought; and his fisherman's costume — a
brown hat with flexible brims, surrounded with line upon
line, and innumerable fly-hooks — jack-boots worthy of
a Dutch smuggler, and a fustian surtout dabbled with
the blood of salmon, made a fine contrast with the smart
jackets, white-cord breeches, and well-polished jockey-

boots of the less distinguished cavaliers about him. Dr.
Wollaston was in black, and, with his noble serene dignity of countenance, might have passed for a sporting
archbishop.[1] Mr. Mackenzie, at this time in the seventy-
sixth year of his age, with a white hat turned up with green,
green spectacles, green jacket, and long brown leathern
gaiters buttoned upon his nether anatomy, wore a dog-
whistle round his neck, and had all over the air of as
resolute a devotee as the gay Captain of Huntly Burn.
Tom Purdie and his subalterns had preceded us by a few
hours with all the greyhounds that could be collected at
Abbotsford, Darnick, and Melrose; but the giant Maida
had remained as his master's orderly, and now gambolled
about Sibyl Grey, barking for mere joy like a spaniel
puppy.

The order of march had been all settled, and the sociable was just getting under weigh, when *the Lady Anne*
broke from the line, screaming with laughter, and exclaimed, "Papa, papa, I knew you could never think of
going without your pet." Scott looked round, and I
rather think there was a blush as well as a smile upon
his face, when he perceived a little black pig frisking
about his pony, and evidently a self-elected addition to
the party of the day. He tried to look stern, and
cracked his whip at the creature, but was in a moment
obliged to join in the general cheers. Poor piggy soon
found a strap round its neck, and was dragged into the
background: — Scott, watching the retreat, repeated
with mock pathos the first verse of an old pastoral
song, —

> "What will I do gin my hoggie[2] die ?
> My joy, my pride, my hoggie!
> My only beast, I had nae mae,
> And wow! but I was vogie! "

[1] [William Hyde Wollaston, the distinguished physiologist, chemist,
and physicist.]

[2] *Hog* signifies in the Scotch dialect a young sheep that has never been
shorn. Hence, no doubt, the name of the Poet of Ettrick — derived from

— the cheers were redoubled — and the squadron moved on.

This pig had taken — nobody could tell how — a most sentimental attachment to Scott, and was constantly urging its pretensions to be admitted a regular member of his *tail* along with the greyhounds and terriers; but, indeed, I remember him suffering another summer under the same sort of pertinacity on the part of an affectionate hen. I leave the explanation for philosophers — but such were the facts. I have too much respect for the vulgarly calumniated donkey to name him in the same category of pets with the pig and the hen; but a year or two after this time, my wife used to drive a couple of these animals in a little garden chair, and whenever her father appeared at the door of our cottage, we were sure to see Hannah More and Lady Morgan (as Anne Scott had wickedly christened them) trotting from their pasture to lay their noses over the paling, and, as Washington Irving says of the old white-haired hedger with the Parisian snuff-box, "to have a pleasant crack wi' the laird."

But to return to our *chasse*. On reaching Newark Castle, we found Lady Scott, her eldest daughter, and the venerable Mackenzie, all busily engaged in unpacking a basket that had been placed in their carriage, and arranging the luncheon it contained upon the mossy rocks overhanging the bed of the Yarrow. When such of the company as chose had partaken of this refection, the Man of Feeling resumed his pony, and all ascended the mountain, duly marshalled at proper distances, so as to beat in a broad line over the heather, Sir Walter directing the movement from the right wing — towards Blackandro. Davy, next to whom I chanced to be rid-

a long line of shepherds. Mr. Charles Lamb, however, in one of his sonnets suggests this pretty origin of *his* " Family Name : " —

> " Perhaps some shepherd on Lincolnian plains,
>   In manners guileless as his own sweet flocks,
>   Received it first amid the merry mocks
>   And arch allusions of his fellow swains."

ing, laid his whip about the fern like an experienced hand, but cracked many a joke, too, upon his own jack-boots, and surveying the long eager battalion of bush-rangers, exclaimed, "Good heavens! is it thus that I visit the scenery of The Lay of the Last Minstrel?" He then kept muttering to himself, as his glowing eye (the finest and brightest that I ever saw) ran over the land-scape, some of those beautiful lines from the *Conclusion* of the Lay:—

> —— " But still,
> When summer smiled on sweet Bowhill,
> And July's eve, with balmy breath,
> Waved the blue-bells on Newark heath,
> When throstles sung in Hareheadshaw,
> And corn was green on Carterhaugh,
> And flourished, broad, Blackandro's oak,
> The aged harper's soul awoke," etc.

Mackenzie, spectacled though he was, saw the first sitting hare, gave the word to slip the dogs, and spurred after them like a boy. All the seniors, indeed, did well as long as the course was upwards, but when puss took down the declivity, they halted and breathed themselves upon the knoll — cheering gayly, however, the young people, who dashed at full speed past and below them. Coursing on such a mountain is not like the same sport over a set of fine English pastures. There were gulfs to be avoided and bogs enough to be threaded — many a stiff nag stuck fast — many a bold rider measured his length among the peat-hags — and another stranger to the ground besides Davy plunged neck-deep into a treacherous well-head, which, till they were floundering in it, had borne all the appearance of a piece of delicate green turf. When Sir Humphry emerged from his in-voluntary bath, his habiliments garnished with mud, slime, and mangled water-cresses, Sir Walter received him with a triumphant *encore!* But the philosopher had his revenge, for joining soon afterwards in a brisk gallop, Scott put Sibyl Grey to a leap beyond her prowess, and

lay humbled in the ditch, while Davy, who was better
mounted, cleared it and him at a bound. Happily there
was little damage done — but no one was sorry that the
sociable had been detained at the foot of the hill.

I have seen Sir Humphry in many places, and in company of many different descriptions; but never to such
advantage as at Abbotsford. His host and he delighted
in each other, and the modesty of their mutual admiration was a memorable spectacle. Davy was by nature
a poet — and Scott, though anything but a philosopher
in the modern sense of that term, might, I think it very
likely, have pursued the study of physical science with
zeal and success, had he happened to fall in with such
an instructor as Sir Humphry would have been to him,
in his early life. Each strove to make the other talk —
and they did so in turn more charmingly than I ever
heard either on any other occasion whatsoever. Scott in
his romantic narratives touched a deeper chord of feeling
than usual, when he had such a listener as Davy; and
Davy, when induced to open his views upon any question
of scientific interest in Scott's presence, did so with a
degree of clear energetic eloquence, and with a flow of
imagery and illustration, of which neither his habitual
tone of table-talk (least of all in London), nor any of his
prose writings (except, indeed, the posthumous Consola-
tions of Travel) could suggest an adequate notion. I
say his prose writings — for who that has read his sublime quatrains on the doctrine of Spinoza can doubt that
he might have united, if he had pleased, in some great
didactic poem, the vigorous ratiocination of Dryden and
the moral majesty of Wordsworth? I remember William Laidlaw whispering to me, one night, when their
"rapt talk" had kept the circle round the fire until long
after the usual bedtime of Abbotsford: "Gude preserve
us! this is a very superior occasion! Eh, sirs!" he
added, cocking his eye like a bird, "I wonder if Shakespeare and Bacon ever met to screw ilk other up?"

Since I have touched on the subject of Sir Walter's autumnal diversions in these his later years, I may as well notice here two annual festivals, when sport was made his pretext for assembling his rural neighbors about him — days eagerly anticipated, and fondly remembered by many. One was a solemn bout of salmon-fishing for the neighboring gentry and their families, instituted originally, I believe, by Lord Somerville, but now, in his absence, conducted and presided over by the Sheriff. Charles Purdie, already mentioned, had charge (partly as lessee) of the salmon-fisheries for three or four miles of the Tweed, including all the water attached to the lands of Abbotsford, Gala, and Allwyn; and this festival had been established with a view, besides other considerations, of recompensing him for the attention he always bestowed on any of the lairds or their visitors that chose to fish, either from the banks or the boat, within his jurisdiction. His selection of the day, and other precautions, generally secured an abundance of sport for the great anniversary; and then the whole party assembled to regale on the newly caught prey, boiled, grilled, and roasted in every variety of preparation, beneath a grand old ash, adjoining Charlie's cottage at Boldside, on the northern margin of the Tweed, about a mile above Abbotsford. This banquet took place earlier in the day or later, according to circumstances; but it often lasted till the harvest moon shone on the lovely scene and its revellers. These formed groups that would have done no discredit to Watteau — and a still better hand has painted the background in the Introduction to The Monastery: "On the opposite bank of the Tweed might be seen the remains of ancient enclosures, surrounded by sycamores and ash-trees of considerable size. These had once formed the crofts or arable ground of a village, now reduced to a single hut, the abode of a fisherman, who also manages a ferry. The cottages, even the church which once existed there, have sunk into vestiges hardly to be traced without visiting the spot, the inhabitants having gradually withdrawn to the more prosperous town of Galashiels, which has risen into consideration within two miles of their neighborhood. Superstitious eld, however, has tenanted the deserted grove with aërial beings, to supply the want of the mortal tenants who have deserted it. The ruined and abandoned churchyard of Boldside has been long believed to be haunted by the Fairies, and the deep broad current of the Tweed, wheeling in moonlight round the foot of the steep bank, with the number of trees originally planted for shelter round the fields of the cottagers, but now presenting the effect of scattered and detached groves, fill up the idea which one would form in imagination for a scene that Oberon and Queen Mab might love to revel in. There are evenings when the spectator might believe, with Fathei Chaucer, that the

> —— ' Queen of Faëry,
> With harp, and pipe, and symphony,
> Were dwelling in the place.' "

Sometimes the evening closed with a "burning of the water;" and then the Sheriff, though now not so agile as when he practised that rough sport in the early times of Ashestiel, was sure to be one of the party in the boat, — held a torch, or perhaps took the helm, — and seemed to enjoy the whole thing as heartily as the youngest of his company, —

> " 'T is blithe along the midnight tide,
> With stalwart arm the boat to guide —
> On high the dazzling blaze to rear,
> And heedful plunge the barbed spear ;
> Rock, wood, and scaur, emerging bright,
> Fling on the stream their ruddy light,
> And from the bank our band appears
> Like Genii armed with fiery spears." [1]

The other "superior occasion" came later in the season; the 28th of October, the birthday of Sir Walter's

[1] See *Poetical Works*, vol. xi. pp. 334, 335 [Cambridge Ed. p. 467].

eldest son, was, I think, that usually selected for *the Abbotsford Hunt*. This was a coursing-field on a large scale, including, with as many of the young gentry as pleased to attend, all Scott's personal favorites among the yeomen and farmers of the surrounding country. The Sheriff always took the field, but latterly devolved the command upon his good friend Mr. John Usher, the ex-laird of Toftfield; and he could not have had a more skilful or a better-humored lieutenant. The hunt took place either on the moors above the Cauldshiels Loch, or over some of the hills on the estate of Gala, and we had commonly, ere we returned, hares enough to supply the wife of every farmer that attended, with soup for a week following. The whole then dined at Abbotsford, the Sheriff in the chair, Adam Ferguson croupier, and Dominie Thomson, of course, chaplain. George, by the way, was himself an eager partaker in the preliminary sport; and now he would favor us with a grace, in Burns's phrase, "as long as my arm," beginning with thanks to the Almighty, who had given man dominion over the fowls of the air, and the beasts of the field, and expatiating on this text with so luculent a commentary, that Scott, who had been fumbling with his spoon long before he reached his Amen, could not help exclaiming as he sat down, "Well done, Mr. George! I think we've had everything but the view holla!" The company, whose onset had been thus deferred, were seldom, I think, under thirty in number, and sometimes they exceeded forty. The feast was such as suited the occasion — a baron of beef, roasted, at the foot of the table, a salted round at the head, while tureens of hare-soup, hotch-potch, and cocky-leeky, extended down the centre, and such light articles as geese, turkeys, entire sucking-pigs, a singed sheep's head, and the unfailing haggis, were set forth by way of side dishes. Blackcock and moorfowl, bushels of snipe, *black puddings, white puddings*, and pyramids of pancakes, formed the second course. Ale

was the favorite beverage during dinner, but there was
plenty of port and sherry for those whose stomachs they
suited. The quaighs of Glenlivet were filled brimful,
and tossed off as if they held water. The wine decanters
made a few rounds of the table, but the hints for hot
punch and toddy soon became clamorous. Two or three
bowls were introduced, and placed under the supervision
of experienced manufacturers, — one of these being usually the Ettrick Shepherd, — and then the business of
the evening commenced in good earnest. The faces
shone and glowed like those at Camacho's wedding: the
chairman told his richest stories of old rural life, Lowland or Highland; Ferguson and humbler heroes fought
their peninsular battles o'er again; the stalwart Dandie
Dinmonts lugged out their last winter's snowstorm, the
parish scandal, perhaps, or the dexterous bargain of the
Northumberland *tryste;* and every man was knocked
down for the song that he sung best, or took most pleasure in singing. Sheriff-Substitute Shortreed (a cheerful, hearty, little man, with a sparkling eye and a most
infectious laugh) gave us Dick o' the Cow, or Now
Liddesdale has ridden a Raid; his son Thomas (Sir Walter's assiduous disciple and assistant in Border Heraldry
and Genealogy) shone without a rival in The Douglas
Tragedy and The Twa Corbies; a weather-beaten, stiff-
bearded veteran, *Captain* Ormistoun, as he was called
(though I doubt if his rank was recognized at the Horse-
Guards), had the primitive pastoral of Cowdenknowes in
sweet perfection; Hogg produced The Women Folk, or
The Kye comes Hame; and, in spite of many grinding
notes, contrived to make everybody delighted, whether
with the fun or the pathos of his ballad; the Melrose
doctor sang in spirited style some of Moore's master-
pieces; a couple of retired sailors joined in Bould Admiral Duncan upon the High Sea; — and the gallant croupier crowned the last bowl with Ale, good Ale, thou art
my Darling! Imagine some smart Parisian *savant* —

some dreamy pedant of Halle or Heidelberg — a brace of stray young Lords from Oxford or Cambridge, or perhaps their prim college tutors, planted here and there amidst these rustic wassailers — this being their first vision of the author of Marmion and Ivanhoe, and he appearing as heartily at home in the scene as if he had been a veritable *Dandie* himself — his face radiant, his laugh gay as childhood, his chorus always ready. And so it proceeded until some worthy, who had fifteen or twenty miles to ride home, began to insinuate that his wife and bairns would be getting sorely anxious about the fords, and the Dumples and Hoddins were at last heard neighing at the gate, and it was voted that the hour had come for *doch an dorrach* — the stirrup-cup — to wit, a bumper all round of the unmitigated *mountain dew*. How they all contrived to get home in safety, Heaven only knows — but I never heard of any serious accident except upon one occasion, when James Hogg made a bet at starting that he would leap over his wall-eyed pony as she stood, and broke his nose in this experiment of "o'ervaulting ambition." One comely goodwife, far off among the hills, amused Sir Walter by telling him, the next time he passed her homestead after one of these jolly doings, what her husband's first words were when he alighted at his own door: "Ailie, my woman, I'm ready for my bed, and oh lass (he gallantly added), I wish I could sleep for a towmont, for there's only ae thing in this warld worth living for, and that's the Abbotsford Hunt!"

It may well be supposed that the President of the Boldside Festival and the Abbotsford Hunt did not omit the good old custom of *the Kirn*. Every November, before quitting the country for Edinburgh, he gave a *harvest-home*, on the most approved model of former days, to all the peasantry on his estate, their friends and kindred, and as many poor neighbors besides as his barn could hold. Here old and young danced from sunset to sunrise, — John of Skye's bagpipe being relieved at intervals by the violin of some Wandering Willie; — and the laird and all his family were present during the early part of the evening — he and his wife to distribute the contents of the first tub of whiskey-punch, and his young people to take their due share in the endless reels and hornpipes of the earthen floor. As Mr. Morritt has said of him as he appeared at Laird Nippy's kirn of earlier days, "To witness the cordiality of his reception might have unbent a misanthrope." He had his private joke for every old wife or "gausie carle," his arch compliment for the ear of every bonny lass, and his hand and his blessing for the head of every little *Eppie Daidle* from Abbotstown or Broomielees.

"The notable paradox," he says in one of the most charming of his essays, "that the residence of a proprietor upon his estate is of as little consequence as the bodily presence of a stockholder upon Exchange, has, we believe, been renounced. At least, as in the case of the Duchess of Suffolk's relationship to her own child, the vulgar continue to be of opinion that there is some difference in favor of the next hamlet and village, and even of the vicinage in general, when the squire spends his rents at the manor-house, instead of cutting a figure in France or Italy. A celebrated politician used to say he would willingly bring in one bill to make poaching felony, another to encourage the breed of foxes, and a third to revive the decayed amusements of cock-fighting and bull-baiting — that he would make, in short, any sacrifice to the humors and prejudices of the country gentlemen, in their most extravagant form, provided only he could prevail upon them to ' dwell in their own houses, be the patrons of their own tenantry, and the fathers of their own children.' " [1]

[1] Essay on Landscape Gardening, *Miscellaneous Prose Works*, vol. xxi. p. 77.

CHAPTER L

1820–1821

In the September of 1820, Longman, in conjunction
with Constable, published The Abbot — the continuation,
to a certain extent, of The Monastery, of which I barely
mentioned the appearance under the preceding March.
I had nothing of any consequence to add to the information which the subsequent Introduction affords us respecting the composition and fate of the former of these
novels. It was considered as a failure — the first of the
series on which any such sentence was pronounced; —
nor have I much to allege in favor of the White Lady
of Avenel, generally criticised as the primary blot — or
of Sir Piercie Shafton, who was loudly, though not quite
so generally, condemned. In either case, considered
separately, he seems to have erred from dwelling (in the
German taste) on materials that might have done very
well for a rapid sketch. The phantom with whom we
have leisure to become familiar is sure to fail — even
the witch of Endor is contented with a momentary
appearance and five syllables of the shade she evokes.
And we may say the same of any grotesque absurdity in

human manners. Scott might have considered with advantage how lightly and briefly Shakespeare introduces *his* Euphuism — though actually the prevalent humor of the hour when he was writing. But perhaps these errors might have attracted little notice had the novelist been successful in finding some reconciling medium capable of giving consistence and harmony to his naturally incongruous materials. "These," said one of his ablest critics, "are joined — but they refuse to blend. Nothing can be more poetical in conception, and sometimes in language, than the fiction of the White Maid of Avenel; but when this ethereal personage, who rides on the cloud which ' for Araby is bound ' — who is

> ' Something between heaven and hell,
>   Something that neither stood nor fell,'

whose existence is linked by an awful and mysterious destiny to the fortunes of a decaying family; when such a being as this descends to clownish pranks, and promotes a frivolous jest about a tailor's bodkin, the course of our sympathies is rudely arrested, and we feel as if the author had put upon us the old-fashioned pleasantry of selling a bargain." [1]

The beautiful natural scenery, and the sterling Scotch characters and manners introduced in The Monastery are, however, sufficient to redeem even these mistakes; and, indeed, I am inclined to believe that it will ultimately occupy a securer place than some romances enjoying hitherto a far higher reputation, in which he makes no use of Scottish materials.

Sir Walter himself thought well of The Abbot when he had finished it. When he sent me a complete copy I found on a slip of paper at the beginning of volume first, these two lines from Tom Crib's Memorial to Congress : —

> " Up he rose in a funk, lapped a toothful of brandy,
>   And *to it* again ! — any odds upon Sandy ! " —

[1] Adolphus's *Letters to Heber*, p. 13.

and whatever ground he had been supposed to lose in The Monastery, part at least of it was regained by this tale, and especially by its most graceful and pathetic portraiture of Mary Stuart. "The Castle of Lochleven," says the Chief-Commissioner Adam, "is seen at every turn from the northern side of Blair-Adam. This castle, renowned and attractive above all the others in my neighborhood, became an object of much increased attention, and a theme of constant conversation, after the author of Waverley had, by his inimitable power of delineating character — by his creative poetic fancy in representing scenes of varied interest — and by the splendor of his romantic descriptions, infused a more diversified and a deeper tone of feeling into the history of Queen Mary's captivity and escape."

I have introduced this quotation from a little book privately printed for the amiable Judge's own family and familiar friends, because Sir Walter owned to myself at the time, that the idea of The Abbot had arisen in his mind during a visit to Blair-Adam. In the pages of the tale itself, indeed, the beautiful localities of that estate are distinctly mentioned, with an allusion to the virtues and manners that adorn its mansion, such as must have been intended to satisfy the possessor (if he could have had any doubts on the subject) as to the authorship of those novels.

The Right Honorable William Adam (who must pardon my mentioning him here as the only man I ever knew that rivalled Sir Walter Scott in uniform graciousness of *bonhomie* and gentleness of humor)[1] was appointed, in 1815, to the Presidency of the Court for Jury Trial in Civil Cases, then instituted in Scotland, and he thenceforth spent a great part of his time at his paternal seat in Kinross-shire. Here, about midsummer, 1816, he received a visit from his near relation William Clerk, Adam Ferguson, his hereditary friend and especial favorite, and

[1] See *ante*, p. 34.

their lifelong intimate, Scott. They remained with him
for two or three days, in the course of which they were
all so much delighted with their host, and he with them,
that it was resolved to reassemble the party, with a few
additions, at the same season of every following year.
This was the origin of the Blair-Adam Club, the regular members of which were in number nine; namely,
the four already named — the Chief-Commissioner's son,
Admiral Sir Charles Adam — his son-in-law, the late
Mr. Anstruther Thomson of Charleton, in Fifeshire —
Mr. Thomas Thomson, the Deputy-Register of Scotland
— his brother, the Rev. John Thomson, minister of
Duddingston, who, though a most diligent and affectionate parish priest, has found leisure to make himself
one of the first masters of the British School of Landscape Painting — and the Right Hon. Sir Samuel Shepherd, who, after filling with high distinction the office
of Attorney-General in England, became Chief Baron of
the Court of Exchequer in Scotland, shortly after the
third anniversary of this brotherhood, into which he was
immediately welcomed with unanimous cordiality. They
usually contrived to meet on a Friday; spent the Saturday in a ride to some scene of historical interest within
an easy distance; enjoyed a quiet Sunday at home —
"duly attending divine worship at the Kirk of Cleish
(not Cleishbotham)" — gave Monday morning to another antiquarian excursion, and returned to Edinburgh
in time for the Courts of Tuesday. From 1816 to 1831
inclusive, Sir Walter was a constant attendant at these
meetings. He visited in this way Castle Campbell, Magus Moor, Falkland, Dunfermline, St. Andrews, and
many other scenes of ancient celebrity: to one of those
trips we must ascribe his dramatic sketch of Macduff's
Cross — and to that of the dog-days of 1819, we owe
the weightier obligation of The Abbot.

I expect an easy forgiveness for introducing from the
liber rarissimus of Blair-Adam the page that belongs

to that particular meeting — which, though less numerous
than usual, is recorded as having been "most pleasing
and delightful." "There were," writes the President,
"only five of us; the Chief Baron, Sir Walter, Mr.
Clerk, Charles Adam, and myself. The weather was
sultry, almost beyond bearing. We did not stir beyond
the bounds of the pleasure-ground, indeed not far from
the vicinity of the house; wandering from one shady
place to another, lolling upon the grass, or sitting upon
prostrate trees not yet carried away by the purchaser.
Our conversation was constant, though tranquil; and
what might be expected from Mr. Clerk, who is a superior converser, and whose mind is stored with knowledge;
and from Sir Walter Scott, who has let the public know
what his powers are. Our talk was of all sorts (except
of *beeves*). Besides a display of their historic knowledge,
at once extensive and correct, they touched frequently
on the pleasing reminiscences of their early days. Shepherd and I could not go back to those periods; but we
could trace our own intimacy and constant friendship for
more than forty years back, when in 1783 we began our
professional pursuits on the Circuit. So that if Scott
could describe, with inconceivable humor, their doings
at Mr. Murray's of Simprim, when emerging from boyhood; when he, and Murray, and Clerk, and Adam Ferguson, acted plays in the schoolroom (Simprim making the dominie bear his part) — when Ferguson was
prompter, orchestra, and audience — and as Scott said,
representing the whole pit, kicked up an ' O. P.' row by
anticipation; and many other such recollections — Shepherd and I could tell of our Circuit fooleries, as old
Fielding (the son of the great novelist) called them — of
the Circuit songs which Will Fielding made and sung,
— and of the grave Sir William Grant (then a briefless
barrister), ycleped by Fielding the Chevalier Grant,
bearing his part in those fooleries, enjoying all our
pranks with great zest, and who talked of them with

delight to his dying day. When the conversation took a graver tone, and turned upon literary subjects, the Chief-Baron took a great share in it; for notwithstanding his infirmity of deafness, he is a most pleasing and agreeable converser, and readily picks up what is passing; and having a classical mind and classical information, gives a pleasing, gentlemanly, and well-informed tone to general conversation. — Before I bring these recollections of our social and cheerful doings to a close, let me observe, that there was a characteristic feature attending them, which it would be injustice to the individuals who composed our parties not to mention. The whole set of us were addicted to take a full share of conversation, and to discuss every subject that occurred with sufficient keenness. The topics were multifarious, and the opinions of course various; but during the whole time of our intercourse, for so many years, four days at a time, and always together, except when we were asleep, there never was the least tendency, on any occasion, to any unruly debate, nor to anything that deviated from the pure delight of social intercourse."

The Chief-Commissioner adds the following particulars in his appendix:—

"Our return from Blair-Adam (after the first meeting of the Club) was very early on a Tuesday morning, that we might reach the Courts by nine o'clock. An occurrence took place near the Hawes' Inn, which left little doubt upon my mind that Sir Walter Scott was the author of Waverley, of Guy Mannering, and of The Antiquary, his only novels then published. The morning was prodigiously fine, and the sea as smooth as glass. Sir Walter and I were standing on the beach, enjoying the prospect; the other gentlemen were not come from the boat. The porpoises were rising in great numbers, when Sir Walter said to me, 'Look at them, how they are showing themselves; what fine fellows they are! I have the greatest respect for them: I would as soon kill a man as a phoca.' I could not conceive that the same idea could occur to two men respecting this animal, and set down that it could only be Sir Walter Scott who made the phoca have the better of the battle with the Antiquary's nephew, Captain M'Intyre.[1]

"Soon after, another occurrence quite confirmed me as to the authorship of the novels. On that visit to Blair-Adam, in course of conversation, I mentioned an anecdote about Wilkie, the author of The Epigoniad, who was but a formal poet, but whose conversation was most amusing, and full of fancy. Having heard much of him in my family, where he had been very intimate, I went, when quite a lad, to St. Andrews, where he was a Professor, for the purpose of visiting him. I had scarcely let him know who I was, when he said, 'Mr. William, were you ever in this place before?' I said, no. 'Then, sir, you must go and look at Regulus' Tower, — no doubt you will have something of an eye of an architect about you; — walk up to it at an angle, advance and recede until you get to see it at its proper distance, and come back and tell me whether you ever saw anything so beautiful in building: till I saw that tower and studied it, I thought the beauty of architecture had consisted in curly-wurlies, but now I find it consists in symmetry and proportion.' In the following winter Rob Roy was published, and there I read that the Cathedral of Glasgow was 'a respectable Gothic structure, without any *curly-wurlies.*'

"But what confirmed, and was certainly meant to disclose to me the author (and that in a very elegant manner), was the mention of the Kiery Craigs — a picturesque piece of scenery in the grounds of Blair-Adam — as being in the vicinity of Kelty Bridge, the *howf* of Auchtermuchty, the Kinross carrier. — It was only an intimate friend of the family, in the habit of coming to Blair-Adam, who could know anything of the Kiery Craigs or its name; and both the scenery and the name had attractions for Sir Walter.

"At our first meeting after the publication of The Abbot, when the party was assembled on the top of the rock, the Chief-Baron Shepherd, looking Sir Walter full in the face, and stamping his staff on the ground, said, 'Now, Sir Walter, I think we be upon the top of the Kiery *Craggs.*' Sir Walter preserved profound silence; but there was a conscious looking down, and a considerable elongation of his upper lip."

---

[1] The good Chief-Commissioner makes a little mistake here — a *Phoca* being, not a porpoise, but a *Seal.*

Since I have obtained permission to quote from this private volume, I may as well mention that I was partly moved to ask that favor, by the author's own confession that his "Blair-Adam, from 1733 to 1834," originated in a suggestion of Scott's. "It was," says the Judge, "on a fine Sunday, lying on the grassy summit of Bennarty, above its craggy brow, that Sir Walter said, looking first at the flat expanse of Kinross-shire (on the south side of the Ochils), and then at the space which Blair-Adam fills between the hill of Drumglow (the highest of the Cleish hills) and the valley of Lochore, ' What an extraordinary thing it is, that here to the north so little appears to have been done, when there are so many proprietors to work upon it ; and to the south, here is a district of country entirely made by the efforts of one family, in three generations, and one of them amongst us in the full enjoyment of what has been done by his two predecessors and himself. Blair-Adam, as I have always heard, had a wild, uncomely, and unhospitable appearance, before its improvements were begun. It would be most curious to record in writing its original state, and trace its gradual progress to its present condition.' " Upon this suggestion, enforced by the approbation of the other members present, the President of the Blair-Adam Club commenced arranging the materials for what constitutes a most instructive as well as entertaining history of the agricultural and arboricultural progress of his domains, in the course of a hundred years, under his grandfather, his father (the celebrated architect), and himself. And Sir Walter had only suggested to his friend of Kinross-shire what he was resolved to put into practice with regard to his own improvements on Tweedside ; for he begun at precisely the same period to keep a regular Journal of all his rural transactions, under the title of Sylva Abbotsfordiensis.

For reasons, as we have seen, connected with the affairs of the Ballantynes, Messrs. Longman published the first edition of The Monastery; and similar circumstances induced Sir Walter to associate this house with that of Constable in the succeeding novel. Constable disliked its title, and would fain have had The Nunnery instead: but Scott stuck to his Abbot. The bookseller grumbled a little, but was soothed by the author's reception of his request that Queen Elizabeth might be brought into the field in his next romance, as a companion to the Mary Stuart of The Abbot.[1] Scott would not indeed indulge him with the choice of the particular period of Elizabeth's reign, indicated in the proposed title of The Armada; but expressed his willingness to take up his own old favorite, the legend of Meikle's ballad. He wished to call the novel, like the ballad, Cumnor-Hall, but in further deference to Constable's wishes, substituted Kenilworth. John Ballantyne objected to this title, and told Constable the result would be "something worthy of the kennel;" but Constable had all reason to be satisfied with the child of his christening. His partner, Mr. Cadell, says: "His vanity boiled over so much at this time, on having his suggestion gone into, that when in his high moods, he used to stalk up and down his room, and exclaim, 'By G——, I am all but the author of the Waverley Novels!'" Constable's bibliographical knowledge, however, it is but fair to say, was really of most essential service to Scott upon many of these occasions; and his letter (now before me) proposing the subject of The Armada, furnished the Novelist with such a catalogue of materials for the illustration of the period as may, probably enough, have called forth some very energetic expression of thankfulness.

---

[1] [Scott writes in December to Lady Louisa Stuart: "I do not design any scandal about Queen Bess, whom I admire much, although, like an old *true blue*, I have malice against her on Queen Mary's account. But I think I shall be very fair. The story is the tragedy of Leicester's first wife, and I have made it, as far as my facilities would permit, 'a pleasant tragedy, stuffed with most pitiful mirth.'" — *Familiar Letters*, vol. ii. p. 102.]

Scott's kindness secured for John Ballantyne the usual interest in the profits of Kenilworth, the last of his great works in which this friend was to have any concern. I have already mentioned the obvious drooping of his health and strength; and a document, to be introduced presently, will show that John himself had occasional glimpses, at least, of his danger, before the close of 1819. Nevertheless, his spirits continued, at the time of which I am now treating, to be in general as high as ever; — nay, it was now, after his maladies had taken a very serious shape, and it was hardly possible to look on him without anticipating a speedy termination of his career, that the gay hopeful spirit of the shattered and trembling invalid led him to plunge into a new stream of costly indulgence. It was an amiable point in his character that he had always retained a tender fondness for his native place. He had now taken up the ambition of rivalling his illustrious friend, in some sort, by providing himself with a summer retirement amidst the scenery of his boyhood; and it need not be doubted, at the same time, that in erecting a villa at Kelso, he anticipated and calculated on substantial advantages from its vicinity to Abbotsford.

One fine day of this autumn I accompanied Sir Walter to inspect the progress of this edifice, which was to have the title of Walton Hall. John had purchased two or three old houses of two stories in height, with notched gables and thatched roofs, near the end of the long original street of Kelso, and not far from the gateway of the Duke of Roxburghe's magnificent park, with their small gardens and paddocks running down to the margin of the Tweed. He had already fitted up convenient bachelor's lodgings in one of the primitive tenements, and converted the others into a goodly range of stabling, and was now watching the completion of his new *corps de logis* behind, which included a handsome entrance-hall, or saloon, destined to have old Piscator's bust, on a stand, in the centre, and to be embellished all round with emblems of his sport. Behind this were spacious rooms overlooking the little *pleasance*, which was to be laid out somewhat in the Italian style, with ornamental steps, a fountain and *jet d'eau*, and a broad terrace hanging over the river, and commanding an extensive view of perhaps the most beautiful landscape in Scotland. In these new dominions John received us with pride and hilarity; and we then walked with him over this pretty town, lounged away an hour among the ruins of the Abbey, and closed our perambulation with *the Garden*, where Scott had spent some of the happiest of his early summers, and where he pointed out with sorrowful eyes the site of the Platanus under which he first read Percy's Reliques. Returning to John's villa, we dined gayly, *al fresco*, by the side of his fountain; and after not a few bumpers to the prosperity of Walton Hall, he mounted Old Mortality, and escorted us for several miles on our ride homewards. It was this day that, overflowing with kindly zeal, Scott revived one of the long-forgotten projects of their early connection in business, and offered his services as editor of a Novelists' Library, to be printed and published for the sole benefit of his host. The offer was eagerly embraced, and when, two or three mornings afterwards John returned Sir Walter's visit, he had put into his hands the MS. of that admirable life of Fielding, which was followed at brief intervals, as the arrangements of the projected work required, by others of Smollett, Richardson, Defoe, Sterne, Johnson, Goldsmith, Le Sage, Horace Walpole, Cumberland, Mrs. Radcliffe, Charles Johnstone, Clara Reeve, Charlotte Smith, and Robert Bage. The publication of the first volume of Ballantyne's Novelists' Library did not take place, however, until February, 1821; and the series was closed soon after the proprietor's death in the ensuing summer. In spite of the charming prefaces, in which Scott combines all the graces of his easy narrative with

a perpetual stream of deep and gentle wisdom in com-
menting on the tempers and fortunes of his best predecessors in novel literature, and also with expositions of
his own critical views, which prove how profoundly he
had investigated the principles and practice of those
masters before he struck out a new path for himself — in
spite of these delightful and valuable essays, the publication was not prosperous. Constable, after Ballantyne's
death, would willingly have resumed the scheme. But
Scott had by that time convinced himself that it was in
vain to expect much success for a collection so bulky and
miscellaneous, and which must of necessity include a
large proportion of matter, condemned by the purity,
whether real or affected, of modern taste. He could
hardly have failed to perceive, on reflection, that his
own novels, already constituting an extensive library of
fiction, in which no purist could pretend to discover
danger for the morals of youth, had in fact superseded
the works of less strait-laced days in the only permanently and solidly profitable market for books of this
order. He at all events declined Constable's proposition
for renewing and extending this attempt. What he did,
was done gratuitously for John Ballantyne's sake; and
I have dwelt on it thus long, because, as the reader will
perceive by and by, it was so done during (with one exception) the very busiest period of Scott's literary life.

Shortly before Scott wrote the following letters, he
had placed his second son (at this time in his fifteenth
year) under the care of the Reverend John Williams,
who had been my intimate friend and companion at Oxford, with a view of preparing him for that University.[1]

---

[1] [Writing to Lady Louisa Stuart, December 14, Scott says: "My
youngest son, who is very clever and very idle, I have sent to a learned
clergyman . . . to get more thoroughly grounded in classical learning.
For two years Mr. Williams has undertaken to speak with him in Latin,
and, as everybody else talks Welsh, he will have nobody to show off his
miscellaneous information to, and thus a main obstacle to his improvement
will be removed. It would be a pity any stumbling-block were left for

Mr. Williams was then Vicar of Lampeter, in Cardiganshire, and the high satisfaction with which his care of Charles Scott inspired Sir Walter, induced several other Scotch gentlemen of distinction by and by to send their sons also to his Welsh parsonage; the result of which northern connections was important to the fortunes of one of the most accurate and extensive scholars and most skilful teachers of the present time.

TO WALTER SCOTT, ESQ., 18TH HUSSARS, CORK.

EDINBURGH, 14th November, 1820.

MY DEAR WALTER, — I send you a cheque on Coutts for your quarter's allowance. I hope you manage your cash like a person of discretion — above all, avoid the card-tables of ancient dowagers. Always remember that my fortune, however much my efforts may increase it, and although I am improving it for your benefit, not for any that can accrue in my own time, — yet never can be more than a decent independence, and therefore will make a poor figure unless managed with good sense, moderation, and prudence — which are habits easily acquired in youth, while habitual extravagance is a fault very difficult to be afterwards corrected.

We came to town yesterday, and bade adieu to Abbotsford for the season. Fife,[1] to mamma's great surprise and scandal, chose to stay at Abbotsford with Mai, and plainly denied to follow the carriage — so our canine establishment in Castle Street is reduced to little Ury.[2] We spent two days at Arniston, on the road, — and on coming here, found Sophia as nicely and orderly settled in her house as if she had been a married woman these five years. I believe she is very happy — perhaps unusually so, for her wishes are moderate, and all seem anxious to please her. She is preparing in due time for

him to break his shins over, for he has a most active mind and a good disposition." — *Familiar Letters*, vol. ii. p. 103.]

1 *Finette* — a spaniel of Lady Scott's.

2 *Urisk* [Ourisque] — a small terrier of the long silky-haired Kintail breed.

the arrival of a little stranger, who will make you an uncle, and me (God help me!) a grandpapa.

The Round Towers you mention are very curious, and seem to have been built, as the Irish hackney-coachman said of the Martello one at the Black Rock, "to puzzle posterity." There are two of them in Scotland — both excellent pieces of architecture; one at Brechin, built quite close to the old church, so as to appear united with it, but in fact it is quite detached from the church, and sways from it in a high wind, when it vibrates like a lighthouse. The other is at Abernethy in Perthshire — said to have been the capital city of the Picts. I am glad to see you observe objects of interest and curiosity, because otherwise a man may travel over the universe without acquiring any more knowledge than his horse does.

We had our hunt, and our jollification after it, on last Wednesday. It went off in great style, although I felt a little sorry at having neither Charles nor you in the field. By the way, Charles seems most admirably settled. I had a most sensible letter on the subject from Mr. Williams, who appears to have taken great pains, and to have formed a very just conception both of his merits and foibles. When I have an opportunity, I will hand you his letter; for it will entertain you, it is so correct a picture of Monsieur Charles.

Dominie Thomson has gone to a Mrs. Dennistoun, of Colgrain, to drill her youngsters. I am afraid he will find a change; but I hope to have a nook open to him by and by — as a sort of retreat or harbor on his lee. Adieu, my dear — always believe me your affectionate father,

WALTER SCOTT.

TO MR. CHARLES SCOTT.

Care of the Rev. John Williams, Lampeter.

EDINBURGH, 14th November, 1820.

MY DEAR BOY CHARLES, — Your letters made us all very happy, and I trust you are now comfortably settled and plying your task hard. Mr. Williams will probably ground you more perfectly in the grammar of the classical languages than has hitherto been done, and this you will at first find but dry work. But there are many indispensable reasons why you must bestow the utmost attention upon it. A perfect knowledge of the classical languages has been fixed upon, and not without good reason, as the mark of a well-educated young man; and though people may have scrambled into distinction without it, it is always with the greatest difficulty, just like climbing over a wall, instead of giving your ticket at the door. Perhaps you may think another proof of a youth's talents might have been adopted; but what good will arise from your thinking so, if the general practice of society has fixed on this particular branch of knowledge as the criterion? Wheat or barley were as good grain, I suppose, as *sesamum;* but it was only to *sesamum* that the talisman gave way, and the rock opened; and it is equally certain that, if you are not a well-founded grammatical scholar in Greek and Latin, you will in vain present other qualifications to distinction. Besides, the study of grammar, from its very asperities, is calculated to teach youth that patient labor which is necessary to the useful exertion of the understanding upon every other branch of knowledge; and your great deficiency is want of steadiness and of resolute application to the dry as well as the interesting parts of your learning. But exerting yourself, as I have no doubt you will do, under the direction of so learned a man and so excellent a teacher as Mr. Williams, and being without the temptations to idleness which occurred at home, I have every reason to believe that to your natural quickness you will presently add such a *habit* of application and steadiness, as will make you a respected member of society, perhaps a distinguished one. It is very probable that the whole success of your future life may depend on the manner in which you employ *the next two years;* and I am therefore most anxious you should fully avail yourself of the opportunities now afforded you.

You must not be too much disconcerted with the apparent dryness of your immediate studies. Language is the great mark by which man is distinguished from the beasts, and a strict acquaintance with the manner in which it is composed becomes, as you follow it a little way, one of the most curious and interesting exercises of the intellect.

We had our grand hunt on Wednesday last, a fine day, and plenty of sport. We hunted all over Huntly wood, and so on to Halidon and Prieston — saw twelve hares, and killed six, having very hard runs, and tiring three packs of grews completely. In absence of Walter and you, Stenhouse the horse-couper led the field, and rode as if he had been a piece of his horse, sweltering like a wild-drake all through Marriage-Moss, at a motion betwixt swimming and riding. One unlucky accident befell; — Queen Mab, who was bestrode by Captain Adam, lifted up her heels against Mr. Craig of Galashiels,[1] whose leg she greeted with a thump like a pistol-shot, while by the same movement she very nearly sent the noble Captain over her ears. Mr. Craig was helped from horse, but would not permit his boot to be drawn off, protesting he would faint if he saw the bone of his leg sticking through the stocking. Some thought he was reluctant to exhibit his legs in their primitive and unclothed simplicity, in respect they have an unhappy resemblance to a pair of tongs. As for the Captain, he declared that if the accident had happened *in action*, the surgeon and drum-boys would have had off, not his *boot* only, but his *leg to boot*, before he could have uttered a remonstrance. At length Gala and I prevailed to have the boot drawn, and to my great joy I found the damage was not serious, though the pain must have been severe.

---

[1] Mr. George Craig, factor to the laird of Gala, and manager of a little branch bank at Galashiels. This worthy man was one of the regular members of the Abbotsford Hunt.

On Saturday we left Abbotsford, and dined and spent Sunday at Arniston, where we had many inquiries after you from Robert Dundas, who was so kind to you last year.

I must conclude for the present, requesting your earnest pursuit of such branches of study as Mr. Williams recommends. In a short time, as you begin to comprehend the subjects you are learning, you will find the path turn smoother, and that which at present seems wrapped up in an inextricable labyrinth of thorns and briers, will at once become easy and attractive. — Always, dear Charlie, your affectionate father,   W. S.

On the same day Scott wrote as follows to the manly and amiable author of Sir Marmaduke Maxwell, who had shortly before sent the MS. of that romantic drama to Abbotsford for his inspection: —

TO MR. ALLAN CUNNINGHAM.

Care of F. Chantrey, Esq., R. A., London.

EDINBURGH, 14th November, 1820.

MY DEAR ALLAN, — I have been meditating a long letter to you for many weeks past; but company, and rural business, and rural sports, are very unfavorable to writing letters. I have now a double reason for writing, for I have to thank you for sending me in safety a beautiful specimen of our English Michael's talents in the cast of my venerable friend Mr. Watt: it is a most striking resemblance, with all that living character which we are apt to think life itself alone can exhibit. I hope Mr. Chantrey does not permit his distinguished skill either to remain unexercised, or to be lavished exclusively on subjects of little interest. I would like to see him engaged on some subject of importance completely adapted to the purpose of his chisel, and demanding its highest powers. Pray remember me to him most kindly.

I have perused twice your curious and interesting

manuscript. Many parts of the poetry are eminently beautiful, though I fear the great length of the piece, and some obscurity of the plot, would render it unfit for dramatic representation. There is also a fine tone of supernatural impulse spread over the whole action, which I think a common audience would not be likely to adopt or comprehend — though I own that to me it has a very powerful effect. Speaking of dramatic composition in general, I think it is almost essential (though the rule be most difficult in practice) that the plot, or business of the piece, should advance with every line that is spoken. The fact is, the drama is addressed chiefly to the eyes, and as much as can be, by any possibility, represented on the stage, should neither be told nor described. Of the miscellaneous part of a large audience, many do not understand, nay, many cannot hear, either narrative or description, but are solely intent upon the action exhibited. It is, I conceive, for this reason that very bad plays, written by performers themselves, often contrive to get through, and not without applause; while others, immeasurably superior in point of poetical merit, fail, merely because the author is not sufficiently possessed of the trick of the scene, or enough aware of the importance of a maxim pronounced by no less a performer than Punch himself — (at least he was the last authority from whom I heard it), — *Push on, keep moving!* [1] Now, in your very ingenious dramatic effort, the interest not only stands still, but sometimes retrogrades. It contains, notwithstanding, many passages of eminent beauty, — many specimens of most interesting dialogue; and, on the whole, if it is not fitted for the modern stage, I am not sure that its very imperfections do not render it more fit for the closet, for we certainly do not always read with the greatest pleasure those plays which act best.

If, however, you should at any time wish to become

---

[1] *Punch* had been borrowing from *Young Rapid*, in the *Cure for the Heart-ache.*

a candidate for dramatic laurels, I would advise you, in
the first place, to consult some professional person of
judgment and taste. I should regard friend Terry as
an excellent Mentor, and I believe he would concur with
me in recommending that at least one third of the drama
be retrenched, that the plot should be rendered simpler,
and the motives more obvious, and I think the powerful
language and many of the situations might then have
their full effect upon the audience. I am uncertain if
I have made myself sufficiently understood; but I would
say, for example, that it is ill explained by what means
Comyn and his gang, who land as shipwrecked men, become at once possessed of the old lord's domains, merely
by killing and taking possession. I am aware of what
you mean — namely, that being attached to the then
rulers, he is supported in his ill-acquired power by their
authority. But this is imperfectly brought out, and
escaped me at the first reading. The superstitious motives, also, which induced the shepherds to delay their
vengeance, are not likely to be intelligible to the generality of the hearers. It would seem more probable that
the young Baron should have led his faithful vassals to
avenge the death of his parents; and it has escaped me
what prevents him from taking this direct and natural
course. Besides it is, I believe, a rule (and it seems a
good one) that one single interest, to which every other
is subordinate, should occupy the whole play, — each
separate object having just the effect of a mill-dam, slui-
cing off a certain portion of the sympathy, which should
move on with increasing force and rapidity to the catastrophe. Now, in your work, there are several divided
points of interest; there is the murder of the old Baron
— the escape of his wife — that of his son — the loss of
his bride — the villainous artifices of Comyn to possess
himself of her person — and, finally, the fall of Comyn,
and acceleration of the vengeance due to his crimes. I
am sure your own excellent sense, which I admire as

much as I do your genius, will give me credit for my frankness in these matters; I only know, that I do not know many persons on whose performances I would venture to offer so much criticism.

I will return the manuscript under Mr. Freeling's Post-Office cover, and I hope it will reach you safe. — Adieu, my leal and esteemed friend — yours truly,

WALTER SCOTT.

Shortly afterwards, Mr. Cunningham, thanking his critic, said he had not yet received back his MS.; but that he hoped the delay had been occasioned by Sir Walter's communication of it to some friend of theatrical experience. He also mentioned his having undertaken a collection of The Songs of Scotland, with notes. The answer was in these terms: —

TO MR. ALLAN CUNNINGHAM.

MY DEAR ALLAN, — It was as you supposed — I detained your manuscript to read it over with Terry. The plot appears to Terry, as to me, ill-combined, which is a great defect in a drama, though less perceptible in the closet than on the stage. Still, if the mind can be kept upon one unbroken course of interest, the effect even in perusal is more gratifying. I have always considered this as the great secret in dramatic poetry, and conceive it one of the most difficult exercises of the invention possible, to conduct a story through five acts, developing it gradually in every scene, so as to keep up the attention, yet never till the very conclusion permitting the nature of the catastrophe to become visible, — and all the while to accompany this by the necessary delineation of character and beauty of language. I am glad, however, that you mean to preserve in some permanent form your very curious drama, which, if not altogether fitted for the stage, cannot be read without very much and very deep interest.

I am glad you are about Scottish song. No man — not Robert Burns himself — has contributed more beautiful effusions to enrich it. Here and there I would pluck a flower from your Posy to give what remains an effect of greater simplicity; but luxuriance can only be the fault of genius, and many of your songs are, I think, unmatched. I would instance, It's Hame and it's Hame, which my daughter Mrs. Lockhart sings with such uncommon effect. You cannot do anything either in the way of original composition, or collection, or criticism, that will not be highly acceptable to all who are worth pleasing in the Scottish public — and I pray you to proceed with it.

Remember me kindly to Chantrey. I am happy my effigy is to go with that of Wordsworth,[1] for (differing from him in very many points of taste) I do not know a man more to be venerated for uprightness of heart and loftiness of genius. Why he will sometimes choose to crawl upon all fours, when God has given him so noble a countenance to lift to heaven, I am as little able to account for, as for his quarrelling (as you tell me) with the wrinkles which time and meditation have stamped his brow withal.

I am obliged to conclude hastily, having long letters to write — God wot upon very different subjects. I pray my kind respects to Mrs. Chantrey. — Believe me, dear Allan, very truly yours, etc.,

WALTER SCOTT.

The following letter touches on the dropping of the Bill which had been introduced by Government for the purpose of degrading the consort of George the Fourth; the riotous rejoicings of the Edinburgh mob on that occasion; and Scott's acquiescence in the request of the

[1] Mr. Cunningham had told Scott that Chantrey's bust of Wordsworth (another of his noblest works) was also to be produced at the Royal Academy's Exhibition for 1821.

guardians of the young Duke of Buccleuch, that he should act as chancellor of the jury about to *serve* his grace *heir* (as the law phrase goes) to the Scottish estates of his family.

TO THE LORD MONTAGU.

EDINBURGH, 30th November, 1820.

MY DEAR LORD, — I had your letter some time since, and have now to congratulate you on your two months' spell of labor-in-vain duty being at length at an end. The old sign of the Labor-in-vain Tavern was a fellow attempting to scrub a black-a-moor white; but the present difficulty seems to lie in showing that one *is* black. Truly, I congratulate the country on the issue; for, since the days of Queen Dollalolla[1] and the *Rumti-iddity* chorus in Tom Thumb, never was there so jolly a representative of royalty. A good ballad might be made, by way of parody, on Gay's Jonathan Wild, —

> " Her Majesty's trial has set us at ease,
> And every wife round me may kiss if she please."

We had the Marquis of Bute and Francis Jeffrey, very brilliant in George Street, and I think one grocer besides. I was hard threatened by letter, but I caused my servant to say in the quarter where I thought the threatening came from, that I should suffer my windows to be broken like a Christian, but if anything else was attempted, I should become as great a heathen as the Dey of Algiers. We were passed over, but many houses were terribly *Cossaqué*, as was the phrase in Paris in 1814 and 1815. The next night, being, like true Scots-

---

[1] *Queen.* — " What though I now am half-seas o'er,
    I scorn to baulk this bout ;
    Of stiff rack-punch fetch bowls a score,
    'Fore George, I 'll see them out !

Chorus. — " Rumti-iddity, row, row, row,
    If we 'd a good sup, we 'd take it now."

Fielding's *Tom Thumb.*

men, wise behind the hand, the bailies had a sufficient force sufficiently arranged, and put down every attempt to riot. If the same precautions had been taken before, the town would have been saved some disgrace, and the loss of at least £1000 worth of property. — Hay Donaldson[1] is getting stout again, and up to the throat in business; there is no getting a word out of him that does not smell of parchment and special service. He asked me, as it is to be a mere *law* service, to act as chancellor on the Duke's inquest, which honorable office I will of course undertake with great willingness, and discharge — I mean the *hospitable* part of it — to the best of my power. I think you are right to avoid a more extended service, as £1000 certainly would not clear the expense, as you would have to dine at least four counties, and as sweetly sing, with Duke Wharton on Chevy Chase,

> " Pity it were
> So much good wine to spill,
> As these bold freeholders would drink,
> Before they had their fill."

I hope we shall all live to see our young baron take his own chair, and feast the land in his own way. Ever your Lordship's most truly faithful

WALTER SCOTT.

P S. — In the illumination row, young Romilly was knocked down and robbed by the mob, just while he was in the act of declaiming on the impropriety of having constables and volunteers to interfere with the harmless mirth of the people.

TO MR. CHARLES SCOTT.

Care of the Rev. John Williams, Lampeter.

EDINBURGH, 19th December, 1820.

MY DEAR CHARLES, — We begin to be afraid that, in improving your head, you have lost the use of your

---

[1] This gentleman, Scott's friend and confidential solicitor, had obtained (I believe), on his recommendation, the legal management of the Buccleuch affairs in Scotland.

fingers, or got so deep into the Greek and Latin grammar, that you have forgotten how to express yourself in your own language. To ease our anxious minds in these important doubts, we beg you will write as soon as possible, and give us a full account of your proceedings, as I do not approve of long intervals of silence, or think that you need to stand very rigorously upon the exchange of letters, especially as mine are so much the longest.

I rely upon it that you are now working hard in the classical mine, getting out the rubbish as fast as you can, and preparing yourself to collect the ore. I cannot too much impress upon your mind that *labor* is the condition which God has imposed on us in every station of life — there is nothing worth having, that can be had without it, from the bread which the peasant wins with the sweat of his brow, to the sports by which the rich man must get rid of his ennui. The only difference betwixt them is, that the poor man labors to get a dinner to his appetite, the rich man to get an appetite to his dinner. As for knowledge, it can no more be planted in the human mind without labor, than a field of wheat can be produced without the previous use of the plough. There is indeed this great difference, that chance or circumstances may so cause it that another shall reap what the farmer sows; but no man can be deprived, whether by accident or misfortune, of the fruits of his own studies; and the liberal and extended acquisitions of knowledge which he makes are all for his own use. Labor, my dear boy, therefore, and improve the time. In youth our steps are light, and our minds are ductile, and knowledge is easily laid up; but if we neglect our spring, our summers will be useless and contemptible, our harvest will be chaff, and the winter of our old age unrespected and desolate.

It is now Christmas-tide, and it comes sadly round to me as reminding me of your excellent grandmother, who was taken from us last year at this time. Do you, my dear Charles, pay attention to the wishes of your parents while they are with you, that you may have no self-reproach when you think of them at a future period.

You hear the Welsh spoken much about you, and if you can pick it up without interfering with more important labors, it will be worth while. I suppose you can easily get a grammar and dictionary. It is, you know, the language spoken by the Britons before the invasion of the Anglo-Saxons, who brought in the principal ingredients of our present language, called from thence English. It was afterwards, however, much mingled with Norman French, the language of William the Conqueror and his followers; so if you can pick up a little of the Cambro-British speech, it will qualify you hereafter to be a good philologist, should your genius turn towards languages. Pray, have you yet learned who Howel Dha was? — Glendower you are well acquainted with by reading Shakespeare. The wild mysterious barbaric grandeur with which he has invested that chieftain has often struck me as very fine. I wish we had some more of him.

We are all well here, and I hope to get to Abbotsford for a few days — they cannot be many — in the ensuing vacation, when I trust to see the planting has got well forward. All are well here, and Mr. Cadell[1] is come back, and gives a pleasant account of your journey. Let me hear from you very soon, and tell me if you expect any *skating*, and whether there is any ice in Wales. I presume there will be a merry Christmas, and beg my best wishes on the subject to Mr. Williams, his sister, and family. The Lockharts dine with us, and the Scotts of Harden, James Scott[2] with his pipes, and I hope Captain Adam. We will remember your health in a

---

[1] Mr. Robert Cadell, of the house of Constable, had this year conveyed Charles Scott from Abbotsford to Lampeter.

[2] Sir Walter's cousin, a son of his uncle Thomas. See *ante*, vol. i. p. 62.

glass of claret just about *six* o'clock at night; so that you will know exactly (allowing for variation of time) what we are doing at the same moment.

But I think I have written quite enough to a young Welshman, who has forgot all his Scots kith, kin, and allies. Mamma and Anne send many loves. Walter came like a shadow, and so departed — after about ten days' stay. The effect was quite dramatic, for the door was flung open as we were about to go down to dinner, and Turner announced *Captain Scott*. We could not conceive who was meant, when in walked Walter as large as life. He is positively a new edition of the Irish giant. — I beg my kind respects to Mr. Williams. At his leisure I should be happy to have a line from him. — I am, my dear little boy, always your affectionate father,

WALTER SCOTT.

The next letter contains a brief allusion to an affair, which in the life of any other man of letters would have deserved to be considered as of some consequence. The late Sir James Hall of Dunglass resigned, in November, 1820, the Presidency of the Royal Society of Edinburgh; and the Fellows, though they had on all former occasions selected a man of science to fill that post, paid Sir Walter the compliment of unanimously requesting him to be Sir James's successor in it. He felt and expressed a natural hesitation about accepting this honor — which at first sight seemed like invading the proper department of another order of scholars. But when it was urged upon him that the Society is really a double one, — embracing a section for literature as well as one of science, — and that it was only due to the former to let it occasionally supply the chief of the whole body, — Scott acquiesced in the flattering proposal; and his gentle skill was found effective, so long as he held the Chair, in maintaining and strengthening the tone of good feeling and good manners which can alone render the meetings of such a Society either agreeable or useful.   The new President himself soon began to take a lively interest in many of their discussions — those at least which pointed to any discovery of practical use; — and he by and by added some eminent men of science, with whom his acquaintance had hitherto been slight, to the list of his most valued friends: I may mention in particular Doctor, now Sir David, Brewster.

Sir Walter also alludes to an institution of a far different description, — that called "The Celtic Society of Edinburgh;" a club established mainly for the patronage of ancient Highland manners and customs, especially the use of "the Garb of Old Gaul" — though part of their funds have always been applied to the really important object of extending education in the wilder districts of the north.   At their annual meetings Scott was, as may be supposed, a regular attendant.   He appeared, as in duty bound, in the costume of the Fraternity, and was usually followed by "John of Skye," in a still more complete, or rather incomplete, style of equipment.

TO THE LORD MONTAGU, DITTON PARK.

EDINBURGH, 17th January, 1821.

MY DEAR LORD, — We had a tight day of it on Monday last, both dry and wet.   The dry part was as dry as may be, consisting in rehearsing the whole lands of the Buccleuch estate for five mortal hours, although Donaldson had kindly selected a clerk whose tongue went over baronies, lordships, and regalities, at as high a rate of top speed as ever Eclipse displayed in clearing the course at Newmarket.   The evening went off very well — considering that while looking forward with the natural feelings of hope and expectation on behalf of our young friend, most of us who were present could not help casting looks of sad remembrance on the days we had seen.   However, we did very well, and I kept the chair till eleven, when we had coffee, and departed, "no very fou, but gaily yet."[1] Besides the law gentlemen, and immediate agents of the family, I picked up on my own account Tom Ogilvie,[2] Sir Harry Hay Macdougal, Harden and his son, Gala, and Captain John Ferguson, whom I asked as from myself, stating that the party was to be quite private. I suppose there was no harm in this, and it helped us well on. I believe your nephew and my young chief enters life with as favorable auspices as could well attend him, for to few youths can attach so many good wishes, and *none* can look back to more estimable examples both in his father and grandfather. I think he will succeed to the warm and social affections of his relatives, which, if they sometimes occasion pain to those who possess them, contain also the purest sources of happiness as well as of virtue.

Our late Pitt meeting amounted to about 800, a most tremendous multitude. I had charge of a separate room, containing a detachment of about 250, and gained a headache of two days, by roaring to them for five or six hours almost incessantly. The Foxites had also a very numerous meeting, — 500 at least, but sad scamps. We had a most formidable band of young men, almost all

---

[1] [" It was often remarked as a proof that they [the novels] were all Sir Walter's, that he was never known to refer to them, though they were the constant topic of conversation in every company at the time. I recollect, however, one striking instance to the contrary. In the month of January, 1821, a dinner was given in the Waterloo Rooms, Edinburgh, to a large party of gentlemen, to celebrate the serving Heir, as it is called in Scotland, of a young gentleman, to the large estates of his ancestors. Sir Walter having been Chancellor of the Inquest, also presided at the dinner, and after the usual toasts on such occasions, he rose, and, with a smiling face, spoke to the following effect : ' Gentlemen, I dare say you have read of a man called Dandie Dinmont, and his dogs. He had old Pepper and old Mustard, and young Pepper and young Mustard, and little Pepper and little Mustard ; but he used to say that " beast or body, education should aye be minded ; a dog is good for nothing until it has been weel entered ; I have always had my dogs weel entered." Now, gentlemen, I am sure [the Duke] has been weel entered, and if you please we shall drink to the health of his guardians.' " — Gibson's *Reminiscences of Sir Walter Scott.*]

[2] The late Thomas Elliot Ogilvie, Esq., of Chesters, in Roxburghshire — one of Sir Walter's good friends among his country neighbors.

born gentlemen and zealous proselytes. We shall now begin to look anxiously to London for news. I suppose they will go by the ears in the House of Commons: but I trust Ministers will have a great majority. If not, they should go out, and let the others make the best of it with their acquitted Queen, who will be a ticklish card in their hand, for she is by nature *intrigante* more ways than one. The loss of Canning is a serious disadvantage; many of our friends have good talents and good taste; but I think he alone has that higher order of parts which we call genius. I wish he had had more prudence to guide it. He has been a most unlucky politician. Adieu. Best love to all at ●Ditton, and great respect withal. My best compliments attend my young chief, now seated, to use an Oriental phrase, upon the *Musnud*. I am almost knocked up with public meetings, for the triple Hecate was a joke to my plurality of offices this week. On Friday I had my Pittite stewardship; — on Monday my chancellorship; — yesterday my presidentship of the Royal Society; for I had a meeting of that learned body at my house last night, where mulled wine and punch were manufactured and consumed according to the latest philosophical discoveries. Besides all this, I have before my eyes the terrors of a certain Highland Association, who dine bonneted and *kilted* in the old fashion (all save myself, of course), and armed to the teeth. This is rather severe service; but men who wear broadswords, dirks, and pistols, are not to be neglected in these days; and the Gael are very loyal lads, so it is as well to keep up an influence with them. Once more, my dear Lord, farewell, and believe me always most truly yours, WALTER SCOTT.

In the course of the riotous week commemorated in the preceding letter, appeared Kenilworth, in three volumes post 8vo, like Ivanhoe, which form was adhered to with all the subsequent novels of the series. Kenilworth was one of the most successful of them all at the time of publication; and it continues, and, I doubt not, will ever continue to be placed in the very highest rank of prose fiction.[1] The rich variety of character, and scenery, and incident in this novel, has never indeed been surpassed; nor, with the one exception of The Bride of Lammermoor, has Scott bequeathed us a deeper and more affecting tragedy than that of Amy Robsart.

[1] [Mr. Morritt writes to Scott, January 28, 1821: "I feel that I am leaving Rokeby in your debt, and before I set out for town, amongst other things I have to settle, I may as well discharge my account by paying you a reasonable and no small return of thanks for *Kenilworth*, which was duly delivered, read, re-read, and thumbed with great delight by our fireside. You know, when I first heard that Queen Elizabeth was to be brought forward as a heroine of a novel, how I trembled for her reputation. Well knowing your not over-affectionate regard for that flower of maidenhood, I dreaded lest all her venerable admirers on this side of the Tweed would have been driven to despair by a portrait of her Majesty after the manner of Mr. Sharpe's ingenious sketches The author, however, has been so very fair, and has allowed her so many of her real historical merits, that I think he really has, like Squire Western, a fair right to demand that we should at least allow her to have been a b——. I am not sure that I do not like and enjoy *Kenilworth* quite as much as any of its predecessors. I think it peculiarly happy in the variety and facility of its portraits, and the story is so interesting, and so out of the track of the common sources of novel interest, that perhaps I like it better from its having so little of the commonplace heroes and heroines who adorn all other tales of the sort." — *Familiar Letters*, vol. ii. p. 107.]

CHAPTER LI

VISIT TO LONDON. — PROJECT OF THE ROYAL SOCIETY OF LITERATURE. — AFFAIRS OF THE 18TH HUSSARS. — MARRIAGE OF CAPTAIN ADAM FERGUSON. — LETTERS TO LORD SIDMOUTH, LORD MONTAGU, ALLAN CUNNINGHAM, MRS. LOCKHART, AND CORNET SCOTT

1821

BEFORE the end of January, 1821, Scott went to London at the request of the other Clerks of Session, that he might watch over the progress of an Act of Parliament, designed to relieve them from a considerable part of their drudgery, in attesting recorded deeds by signature; — and his stay was prolonged until near the beginning of the Summer term of his Court. His letters while in London are mostly to his own family, and on strictly domestic topics; but I shall extract a few of them, chiefly (for reasons which I have already sufficiently intimated) those addressed to his son the Cornet. I need not trespass on the reader's attention by any attempt to explain in detail the matters to which these letters refer. It will be seen that Sir Walter had heard some rumors of irregularity in the interior of the 18th Hussars; and that the consequent interference of the then Commander of the Forces in Ireland, the late Sir David Baird, had been received in anything but a spirit of humility. The reports that reached Scott proved to have been most absurdly exaggerated; but nevertheless his observations on them seem well worth quoting. It so happened that the 18th was one of several regiments about to be reduced at this time; and as soon as that event took place, Cornet

Scott was sent to travel in Germany, with a view to his improvement in the science of his profession. He afterwards spent a brief period, for the same purpose, in the Royal Military College of Sandhurst; and erelong he obtained a commission as lieutenant in the 15th or King's Hussars, in which distinguished corps his father lived to see him Major.

It will also be seen, that during this visit to London Sir Walter was released from considerable anxiety on account of his daughter Sophia, whom he had left in a weak state of health at Edinburgh, by the intelligence of her safe accouchement of a boy, — John Hugh Lockhart, the "Hugh Littlejohn" of the Tales of a Grandfather. The approaching marriage of Captain, now Sir Adam Ferguson, to which some jocular allusions occur, may be classed with these objects of family interest; and that event was the source of unmixed satisfaction to Scott, as it did not interrupt his enjoyment of his old friend's society in the country; for the Captain, though he then pitched a tent for himself, did so at a very short distance from Huntly Burn. I believe the ensuing extracts will need no further commentary.

TO MRS. LOCKHART, GREAT KING STREET, EDINBURGH.

DITTON PARK, February 18, 1821.

MY DEAREST SOPHIA, — I received as much pleasure, and was relieved from as much anxiety, as ever I felt in my life, by Lockhart's kind note, which acquainted me with the happy period that has been put to your suffering, and, as I hope and trust, to the complaints which occasioned it. You are now, my dearest girl, beginning a new course of pleasures, anxieties, and duties, and the best I can wish for you is, that your little boy may prove the same dutiful and affectionate child which you have always been to me, and that God may give him a sound and healthy mind, with a good constitution of body — the greatest blessings which this earth can bestow. Pray be extremely careful of yourself for some time. Young women are apt to injure their health by thinking themselves well too soon. I beg you to be cautious in this respect.

The news of the young stranger's arrival was most joyfully received here, and his health and yours toasted in a bumper. Lady Anne is quite well, and Isabella also; and Lady Charlotte, who has rejoined them, is a most beautiful creature indeed. This place is all light and splendor, compared to London, where I was forced to use candles till ten o'clock at least. I have a gay time of it. To-morrow I return to town, and dine with old Sotheby; on Tuesday with the Duke of Wellington; Wednesday with Croker, and so on. Love to L., the Captain, and the Violet, and give your bantling a kiss extraordinary for Grandpapa. I hope Mungo [1] approves of the child, for that is a serious point. There are no dogs in the hotel where I lodge, but a tolerably conversible cat, who eats a mess of cream with me in the morning. The little chief and his brother have come over from Eton to see me, so I must break off. — I am, my dear love, most affectionately yours,

WALTER SCOTT.

TO WALTER SCOTT, ESQ., PORTOBELLO BARRACKS, DUBLIN.

WATERLOO HOTEL, Jermyn Street,
February 19, 1821.

MY DEAR WALTER, — I have just received your letter. I send you a draft for £50, which you must make go as far as you can.

There is what I have no doubt is a very idle report here, of your paying rather marked attention to one young lady in particular. I beg you would do nothing that can justify such a rumor, as it would excite my *highest displeasure* should you either entangle yourself or any other person. I am, and have always been, quite

---

[1] Mungo was a favorite Newfoundland dog.

frank with you, and beg you will be equally so with me. One should, in justice to the young women they live with, be very cautious not to give the least countenance to such rumors. They are not easily avoided, but are always highly prejudicial to the parties concerned; and what begins in folly ends in serious misery — *avis au lecteur*.

Believe me, dear Cornet, your affectionate father,

WALTER SCOTT.

P. S. — I wish you could pick me up the Irish lilt of a tune to "Patrick Fleming." The song begins, —

> " Patrick Fleming was a gallant soldier,
> He carried his musket over his shoulder.
> When I cock my pistol, when I draw my raper,
> I make them stand in awe of me, for I am a taker.
> Falala," etc.

From another verse in the same song, it seems the hero was in such a predicament as your own: —

> " If you be Peter Fleming, as I suppose you be, sir,
> We are three pedlars walking on so free, sir.
> We are three pedlars a-walking on to Dublin,
> With nothing in our pockets to pay for our lodging.
> Falala," etc.

TO WALTER SCOTT, ESQ., 18TH HUSSARS, CAPPOQUIN.

LONDON, 17th March, 1821.

MY DEAR COMMANDANT OF CAPPOQUIN, — Wishing you joy of your new government, these are to inform you that I am still in London. The late aspersion on your regiment induced me to protract my stay here, with a view to see the Duke of York on your behalf, which I did yesterday. His Royal Highness expressed himself most obligingly disposed, and promised to consider what could best be done to forward your military education. I told him frankly, that in giving you to the King's service I had done all that was in my power to show our attachment to his Majesty and the country which had been so kind to me, and that it was my utmost ambition that you should render yourself capable of serving them both well. He said he would give the affair his particular consideration, and see whether he could put you on the establishment at Sandhurst, without any violent infringement on the rules; and hinted that he would make an exception to the rule of seniority of standing and priority of application in your favor when an opportunity occurs.

From H. R. H.'s very kind expressions, I have little doubt you will have more than justice done you in the patronage necessary to facilitate your course through life; but it must be by your own exertions, my dearest boy, that you must render yourself qualified to avail yourself of the opportunities which you may have offered to you. Work, therefore, as hard as you can, and do not be discontented for want of assistance of masters, etc., because the knowledge which we acquire by our own unaided efforts, is much more tenaciously retained by the memory, while the exertion necessary to gain it strengthens the understanding. At the same time, I would inquire whether there may not be some Catholic priest, or Protestant clergyman, or scholar of any description, who, for love or money, would give you a little assistance occasionally. Such persons are to be found almost everywhere; not professed teachers, but capable of smoothing the road to a willing student. Let me earnestly recommend in your reading to keep fast to particular hours, and suffer no one thing to encroach on the other.

Charles's last letter was uncommonly steady, and prepared me for one from Mr. Williams, in which he expresses satisfaction with his attention, and with his progress in learning, in a much stronger degree than formerly. This is truly comfortable, and may relieve me from the necessity of sending the poor boy to India.

All in Edinburgh are quite well, and no fears exist, saving those of little Catherine[1] for the baby, lest the

[1] Mrs. Lockhart's maid.

fairies take it away before the christening. I will send some books to you from hence, if I can find means to transmit them. I should like you to read with care the campaigns of Buonaparte, which have been written in French with much science.[1]

I hope, indeed I am sure, I need not remind you to be very attentive to your duty. You have but a small charge, but it is a charge, and rashness or carelessness may lead to discredit in the commandant of Cappoquin, as well as in a field-marshal. In the exercise of your duty, be tender of the lower classes; and as you are strong, be merciful. In this you will do your master good service, for show me the manners of the man, and I will judge those of the master.

In your present situation, it may be interesting to you to know that the bill for Catholic Emancipation will pass the Commons without doubt, and very probably the Peers also, unless the Spiritual Lords make a great rally. Nobody here cares much about it, and if it does not pass this year, it will the next, without doubt.

Among other improvements, I wish you would amend your hand. It is a deplorable scratch, and far the worst of the family. Charles writes a firm good hand in comparison.

You may address your next to Abbotsford, where I long to be, being heartily tired of fine company and fine living, from dukes and duchesses, down to turbot and plovers' eggs. It is very well for a while, but to be kept at it makes one feel like a poodle dog compelled to stand forever on his hind legs. — Most affectionately yours,   WALTER SCOTT.

———

During this visit to London, Sir Walter appears to have been consulted by several persons in authority as to the project of a Society of Literature, for which the

[1] This letter was followed by a copy of General Jomini's celebrated work.

King's patronage had been solicited, and which was established soon afterwards — though on a scale less extensive than had been proposed at the outset. He expressed his views on this subject in writing at considerable length to his friend the Hon. John Villiers (afterwards Earl of Clarendon); [1] but of that letter, described to me as a most admirable one, I have as yet failed to recover a copy. I have little doubt that both the letter in question, and the following, addressed, soon after his arrival at Abbotsford, to the then Secretary of State for the Home Department, were placed in the hands of the King; but it seems probable, that whatever his Majesty may have thought of Scott's representations, he considered himself as already, in some measure, pledged to countenance the projected academy.

TO THE RIGHT HON. THE LORD VISCOUNT SIDMOUTH, ETC., ETC., ETC., WHITEHALL.

ABBOTSFORD, April 20, 1821.

MY DEAR LORD, — Owing to my retreat to this place, I was only honored with your Lordship's letter yesterday. Whatever use can be made of my letter to stop the very ill-contrived project to which it relates, will answer the purpose for which it was written. I do not well remember the terms in which my remonstrance to Mr. Villiers was couched, for it was positively written betwixt sleeping and waking; but your Lordship will best judge how far the contents may be proper for his Majesty's eye; and if the sentiments appear a little in dishabille, there is the true apology that they were never intended to go to Court. From more than twenty years' intercourse with the literary world, during which I have been more or less acquainted with every distinguished writer of my day, and, at the same time, an accurate student of the habits and tastes of the reading public, I am enabled to say, with a feeling next to certainty, that

[1] The third Earl (of the Villierses) died in 1838.

the plan can only end in something very unpleasant. At all events, his Majesty should get out of it; it is nonsense to say or suppose that any steps have been taken which, in such a matter, can or ought to be considered as irrevocable. The fact is, that nobody knows as yet how far the matter has gone beyond the *projet* of some well-meaning but misjudging persons, and the whole thing is asleep and forgotten so far as the public is concerned. The Spanish proverb says, "God help me from my friends, and I will keep myself from my enemies;" and there is much sense in it; for the zeal of misjudging adherents often contrives, as in the present case, to turn to matter of reproach the noblest feelings on the part of a sovereign.

Let men of letters fight their own way with the public, and let his Majesty, according as his own excellent taste and liberality dictate, honor with his patronage, expressed in the manner fitted to their studies and habits, those who are able to distinguish themselves, and alleviate by his bounty the distresses of such as, with acknowledged merit, may yet have been unfortunate in procuring independence. The immediate and direct favor of the Sovereign is worth the patronage of ten thousand societies. But your Lordship knows how to set all this in a better light than I can, and I would not wish the cause of letters in better hands.

I am now in a scene changed as completely as possible from those in which I had the great pleasure of meeting your Lordship lately, riding through the moors on a pony, instead of traversing the streets in a carriage, and drinking whiskey-toddy with mine honest neighbors, instead of Champagne and Burgundy. I have gained, however, in point of exact political information; for I find we know upon Tweedside with much greater accuracy what is done and intended in the Cabinet, than ever I could learn when living with the Ministers five days in the week. Mine honest Teviotdale friends, whom I left

in a high Queen-fever, are now beginning to be somewhat ashamed of themselves, and to make as great advances towards retracting their opinion as they are ever
known to do, which amounts to this: "God judge me,
Sir W——, the King's no been so dooms far wrong
after a' in yon Queen's job like;" which, being inter-
preted, signifies, "We will fight for the King to the
death." I do not know how it was in other places; but
I never saw so sudden and violent a delusion possess the
minds of men in my life, even those of sensible, steady,
well-intentioned fellows, that would fight knee-deep
against the Radicals. It is well over, thank God.

My best compliments attend the ladies. I ever am,
my dear Lord, your truly obliged and faithful humble
servant,   WALTER SCOTT.

I have thought it right to insert the preceding letter,
because it indicates with sufficient distinctness what
Scott's opinions always were as to a subject on which,
from his experience and position, he must have reflected
very seriously. In how far the results of the establishment of the Royal Society of Literature have tended to
confirm or to weaken the weight of his authority on these
matters, I do not presume to have formed any judgment.
He received, about the same time, a volume of poetry
by Allan Cunningham, which included the drama of Sir
Marmaduke Maxwell; and I am happy to quote his letter of acknowledgment to that high-spirited and independent author in the same page with the foregoing
monition to the dispensers of patronage.

TO MR. ALLAN CUNNINGHAM, ECCLESTONE STREET, PIMLICO.

ABBOTSFORD, 27th April.

DEAR ALLAN,—Accept my kind thanks for your
little modest volume, received two days since. I was
acquainted with most of the pieces, and yet I perused
them all with renewed pleasure, and especially my old

friend Sir Marmaduke with his new face, and by the assistance of an April sun, which is at length, after many a rough blast, beginning to smile on us. The drama has, in my conception, more poetical conception and poetical expression in it, than most of our modern compositions. Perhaps, indeed, it occasionally sins even in the richness of poetical expression; for the language of passion, though bold and figurative, is brief and concise at the same time. But what would, in acting, be a more serious objection, is the complicated nature of the plot, which is very obscure. I hope you will make another dramatic attempt; and, in that case, I would strongly recommend that you should previously make a model or skeleton of your incidents, dividing them regularly into scenes and acts, so as to insure the dependence of one circumstance upon another, and the simplicity and union of your whole story. The common class of readers, and more especially of spectators, are thick-skulled enough, and can hardly comprehend what they see and hear, unless they are hemmed in, and guided to the sense at every turn.

The unities of time and place have always appeared to me fopperies, as far as they require close observance of the French rules. Still, the nearer you can come to them, it is always, no doubt, the better, because your action will be more probable. But the unity of action — I mean that continuity which unites every scene with the other, and makes the catastrophe the natural and probable result of all that has gone before — seems to me a critical rule which cannot safely be dispensed with. Without such a regular deduction of incidents, men's attention becomes distracted, and the most beautiful language, if at all listened to, creates no interest, and is out of place. I would give, as an example, the suddenly entertained and as suddenly abandoned jealousy of Sir Marmaduke (p. 85), as a useless excrescence in the action of the drama.

I am very much unaccustomed to offer criticism, and when I do so, it is because I believe in my soul that I am endeavoring to pluck away the weeds which hide flowers well worthy of cultivation. In your case, the richness of your language, and fertility of your imagination, are the snares against which I would warn you. If the one had been poor, and the other costive, I would never have made remarks which could never do good, while they only gave pain. Did you ever read Savage's beautiful poem of The Wanderer? If not, do so, and you will see the fault which, I think, attaches to Lord Maxwell — a want of distinct precision and intelligibility about the story, which counteracts, especially with ordinary readers, the effect of beautiful and forcible diction, poetical imagery, and animated description.

All this freedom you will excuse, I know, on the part of one who has the truest respect for the manly independence of character which rests for its support on honest industry, instead of indulging the foolish fastidiousness formerly supposed to be essential to the poetical temperament, and which has induced some men of real talents to become coxcombs — some to become sots — some to plunge themselves into want — others into the equal miseries of dependence, merely because, forsooth, they were men of genius, and wise above the ordinary, and, I say, the manly duties of human life.

> " I 'd rather be a kitten, and cry, Mew ! " [1]

than write the best poetry in the world on condition of laying aside common sense in the ordinary transactions and business of the world; and therefore, dear Allan, I wish much the better to the Muse whom you meet by the fireside in your hours of leisure when you have played your part manfully through a day of labor. I should like to see her making those hours also a little profitable. Perhaps something of the dramatic romance, if you could

[1] *1st King Henry IV*. Act III. Scene 1.

hit on a good subject, and combine the scenes well, might answer. A beautiful thing with appropriate music, scenes, etc., might be woven out of the Mermaid of Galloway.

When there is any chance of Mr. Chantrey coming this way, I hope you will let me know; and if you come with him, so much the better. I like him as much for his manners as for his genius.

> " He is a man without a clagg ;
> His heart is frank without a flaw."

This is a horrible long letter for so vile a correspondent as I am. Once more, my best thanks for the little volume, and believe me yours truly,

WALTER SCOTT.

I now return to Sir Walter's correspondence with the Cornet at Cappoquin.

TO WALTER SCOTT, ESQ., 18TH HUSSARS.

ABBOTSFORD, April 21, 1821.

MY DEAR WALTER, — . . . A democrat in any situation is but a silly sort of fellow, but a democratical soldier is worse than an ordinary traitor by ten thousand degrees, as he forgets his military honor, and is faithless to the master whose bread he eats. Three distinguished heroes of this class have arisen in my time — Lord Edward Fitzgerald, Colonel Despard, and Captain Thistlewood — and, with the contempt and abhorrence of all men, they died the death of infamy and guilt. If a man of honor is unhappy enough to entertain opinions inconsistent with the service in which he finds himself, it is his duty at once to resign his commission; in acting otherwise, he disgraces himself forever. . . . The reports are very strange, also, with respect to the private conduct of certain officers. . . . Gentlemen maintain their characters even in following their most licentious pleasures, otherwise they resemble the very scavengers in the streets. . . . I had written you a long letter on other subjects, but these circumstances have altered my plans, as well as given me great uneasiness on account of the effects which the society you have been keeping may have had on your principles, both political and moral. Be very frank with me on this subject. I have a title to expect perfect sincerity, having always treated you with openness on my part.

Pray write immediately, and at length. — I remain your affectionate father,   WALTER SCOTT.

TO THE SAME.

ABBOTSFORD, April 28, 1821.

DEAR WALTER, — . . . The great point in the mean while is to acquire such preliminary information as may render you qualified to profit by Sandhurst when you get thither. Amongst my acquaintance, the men of greatest information have been those who seemed but indifferently situated for the acquisition of it, but who exerted themselves in proportion to the infrequency of their opportunities.

The noble Captain Ferguson was married on Monday last. I was present at the bridal, and I assure you the like hath not been seen since the days of Lesmahago. Like his prototype, the Captain advanced in a jaunty military step, with a kind of leer on his face that seemed to quiz the whole affair. You should write to your brother sportsman and soldier, and wish the veteran joy of his entrance into the band of Benedicts. Odd enough that I should christen a grandchild and attend the wedding of a contemporary within two days of each other. I have sent John of Skye with Tom, and all the rabblement which they can collect, to play the pipes, shout, and fire guns below the Captain's windows this morning; and I am just going over to hover about on my pony, and witness their reception. The happy pair returned to Huntly Burn on Saturday; but yesterday being Sunday, we permitted them to enjoy their pillows in quiet. This morning they must not expect to get off so well. Pray write soon, and give me the history of your still-huntings, etc. — Ever yours affectionately,

W. SCOTT.

TO CHARLES SCOTT, ESQ.

Care of the Rev. Mr. Williams, Lampeter.

ABBOTSFORD, 9th May, 1821.

MY DEAR CHARLES, — I am glad to find, by your letter just received, that you are reading Tacitus with some relish. His style is rather quaint and enigmatical, which makes it difficult to the student; but then his pages are filled with such admirable apothegms and maxims of political wisdom, as infer the deepest knowledge of human nature; and it is particularly necessary that any one who may have views as a public speaker should be master of his works, as there is neither ancient nor modern who affords such a selection of admirable quotations. You should exercise yourself frequently in trying to make translations of the passages which most strike you, trying to invest the sense of Tacitus in as good English as you can. This will answer the double purpose of making yourself familiar with the Latin author, and giving you the command of your own language, which no person will ever have who does not study English composition in early life. . . . I conclude somewhat abruptly, having trees to cut, and saucy Tom watching me like a Calmuck with the axe in his hand.

Yours affectionately,

W. SCOTT.

TO WALTER SCOTT, ESQ., 18TH HUSSARS, CAPPOQUIN.

ABBOTSFORD, 10th May, 1821.

DEAR WALTER, — I wrote yesterday, but I am induced immediately to answer your letter, because I think you expect from it an effect upon my mind different from what it produces. A man may be violent and outrageous in his liquor, but wine seldom makes a gentleman a blackguard, or instigates a loyal man to utter sedition. Wine unveils the passions and throws away restraint, but it does not create habits or opinions which did not previously exist in the mind. Besides, what sort of defence is this of intemperance? I suppose if a private commits riot, or is disobedient in his cups, his officers do not admit whiskey to be an excuse. I have seen enough of that sort of society where habitual indulgence drowned at last every distinction between what is worthy and unworthy, — and I have seen young men with the fairest prospects, turn out degraded miserable outcasts before their life was half spent, merely from soaking and sotting, and the bad habits these naturally lead to. You tell me * * * and * * * frequent good society, and are well received in it; and I am very glad to hear this is the case. But such stories as these will soon occasion their seclusion from the *best* company. There may remain, indeed, a large enough circle, where ladies, who are either desirous to fill their rooms or to marry their daughters, will continue to receive any young man in a showy uniform, however irregular in private life; but if these cannot be called *bad* company, they are certainly anything but *very good*, and the facility of access makes the *entrée* of little consequence.

I mentioned in my last that you were to continue in the 18th until the regiment went to India, and that I trusted you would get the step within the twelve months that the corps yet remains in Europe, which will make your exchange easier. But it is of far more importance that you learn to command yourself, than that you should be raised higher in commanding others. It gives me pain to write to you in terms of censure, but *my duty* must be done, else I cannot expect you to do *yours*. All here are well, and send love. — I am your affectionate father,   WALTER SCOTT.

EDINBURGH, 15th May, 1821.

DEAR WALTER, — I have your letter of May 6th, to which it is unnecessary to reply very particularly. I would only insinuate to you that the *lawyers* and *gossips* of Edinburgh, whom your military politeness handsomely classes together in writing to a lawyer, know and care as little about the 18th as they do about the 19th, 20th, or 21st, or any other regimental number which does not happen for the time to be at Piershill, or in the Castle. Do not fall into the error and pedantry of young military men, who, living much together, are apt to think themselves and their actions the subject of much talk and rumor among the public at large. — I will transcribe Fielding's account of such a person, whom he met with on his voyage to Lisbon, which will give two or three hours' excellent amusement when you choose to peruse it : —

" In his conversation it is true there was something military enough, as it consisted chiefly of oaths, and of the great actions and wise sayings of Jack, Will, and Tom of *ours*, a phrase eternally in his mouth, and he seemed to conclude that it conveyed to all the officers such a degree of public notoriety and importance that it entitled him, like the head of a profession, or a first minister, to be the subject of conversation amongst those who had not the least personal acquaintance with him."

Avoid this silly narrowness of mind, my dear boy, which only makes men be looked on in the world with ridicule and contempt. Lawyer and gossip as I may be, I suppose you will allow I have seen something of life in most of its varieties; as much at least as if I had been, like you, eighteen months in a cavalry regiment, or, like Beau Jackson in Roderick Random, had cruised for half a year in the chops of the Channel. Now, I have never remarked any one, be he soldier, or divine, or lawyer, that was exclusively attached to the narrow habits of his own profession, but what such person became a great twaddle in good society, besides, what is of much more importance, becoming narrow-minded, and ignorant of all general information.

That this letter may not be unacceptable in all its parts, I enclose your allowance without stopping anything for the hackney. Take notice, however, my dear Walter, that this is to last you till midsummer. — We came from Abbotsford yesterday, and left all well, excepting that Mr. Laidlaw lost his youngest child, an infant, very unexpectedly. We found Sophia, Lockhart, and their child in good health, and all send love.

I remain your affectionate father,
WALTER SCOTT.

TO WALTER SCOTT, ESQ., 18TH HUSSARS.

EDINBURGH, 26th May, 1821.

MY DEAR WALTER, — I see you are of the mind of the irritable prophet Jonah, who persisted in maintaining "he did well to be angry," even when disputing with Omnipotence. I am aware that Sir David is considered as a severe and ill-tempered man; and I remember a story that, when report came to Europe that Tippoo's prisoners (of whom Baird was one) were chained together two and two, his mother said, "God pity the poor lad that's chained to *our Davie.*" But though it may be very true that he may have acted towards you with caprice and severity, yet you are always to remember, — 1*st*, That in becoming a soldier you have subjected yourself to the caprice and severity of superior officers, and have no comfort except in contemplating the prospect of commanding others in your turn. In the mean while, you have in most cases no remedy so useful as patience and submission. But, 2*dly*, As you seem disposed to admit that you yourselves have been partly to blame, I submit to you, that in turning the magnifying end of the telescope on Sir D.'s faults, and the diminishing one on your own, you take the least useful mode of considering the matter. By studying *his* errors, you can acquire no knowledge that will be useful to you till you become Commander-in-Chief in Ireland, — whereas, by reflecting on *your own*, Cornet Scott and his companions may reap some immediate moral advantage. Your fine of a dozen of claret, upon any one who shall introduce females into your mess in future, reminds me of the rule of a country club, that whoever "behaved ungenteel" should be fined in a pot of porter. Seriously, I think there was bad taste in the style of the forfeiture.

I am well pleased with your map, which is very businesslike. There was a great battle fought between the English and native Irish near the Blackwater, in which the former were defeated, and Bagenal the Knight-Marshal killed. Is there any remembrance of this upon the spot? There is a clergyman in Lismore, Mr. John Graham — originally, that is by descent, a Borderer. He lately sent me a manuscript which I intend to publish, and I wrote to him enclosing a cheque on Coutts. I wish you could ascertain if he received my letter safe. You can call upon him with my compliments. You need only say I was desirous to know if he had received a letter from me lately. The manuscript was written by a certain Mr. Gwynne, a Welsh loyalist in the great Civil War, and afterwards an officer in the guards of Charles II. This will be an object for a ride to you.[1]

I presided last night at the dinner of the Celtic Society, "all plaided and plumed in their tartan array," and such jumping, skipping, and screaming you never saw. Chief-Baron Shepherd dined with us, and was very much pleased with the extreme enthusiasm of the

---

[1] The Rev. John Graham is known as the author of a *History of the Siege of Londonderry, Annals of Ireland*, and various political tracts. Sir Walter Scott published *Gwynne's Memoirs*, with a Preface, etc., in 1822.

Gael when liberated from the thraldom of breeches. You were voted a member by acclamation, which will cost me a tartan dress for your long limbs when you come here. If the King takes Scotland in coming or going to Ireland (as has been talked of), I expect to get you leave to come over. — I remain your affectionate father,

WALTER SCOTT.

P. S. — I beg you will not take it into your wise noddle that I will act either hastily or unadvisedly in your matters. I have been more successful in life than most people, and know well how much success depends, first upon desert, and then on knowledge of the *carte de pays.*

The following letter begins with an allusion to a visit which Captain Ferguson, his bride, and his youngest sister, Miss Margaret Ferguson, had been paying at Ditton Park: —

TO THE LORD MONTAGU, ETC., ETC.

EDINBURGH, 21st May, 1821.

MY DEAR LORD, — I was much diverted with the account of Adam and Eve's visit to Ditton, which, with its surrounding moat, might make no bad emblem of Eden, but for the absence of snakes and fiends. He is a very singular fellow; for, with all his humor and knowledge of the world, he by nature is a remarkably shy and modest man, and more afraid of the possibility of intrusion than would occur to any one who only sees him in the full stream of society. His sister Margaret is extremely like him in the turn of thought and of humor, and he has two others who are as great curiosities in their way. The eldest is a complete old maid, with all the gravity and shyness of the character, but not a grain of its bad humor or spleen; on the contrary, she is one of the kindest and most motherly creatures in the world. The second, Mary, was in her day a very pretty girl;

but her person became deformed, and she has the sharpness of features with which that circumstance is sometimes attended. She rises very early in the morning, and roams over all my wild land in the neighborhood, wearing the most complicated pile of handkerchiefs of different colors on her head, and a stick double her own height in her hand, attended by two dogs, whose powers of yelping are truly terrific. With such garb and accompaniments, she has very nearly established the character in the neighborhood of being *something no canny* — and the urchins of Melrose and Darnick are frightened from gathering hazel-nuts and cutting wands in my cleugh, by the fear of meeting *the daft lady*. With all this quizzicality, I do not believe there ever existed a family with so much mutual affection and such an overflow of benevolence to all around them, from men and women down to hedge-sparrows and lame ass-colts, more than one of which they have taken under their direct and special protection.

I am sorry there should be occasion for caution in the case of little Duke Walter, but it is most lucky that the necessity is early and closely attended to. How many actual valetudinarians have outlived all their robust contemporaries, and attained the utmost verge of human life, without ever having enjoyed what is usually called high health. This is taking the very worst view of the case, and supposing the constitution habitually delicate. But how often has the strongest and best confirmed health succeeded to a delicate childhood — and such, I trust, will be the Duke's case. I cannot help thinking that this temporary recess from Eton may be made subservient to Walter's improvement in general literature, and particularly in historical knowledge. The habit of reading useful, and at the same time entertaining books of history, is often acquired during the retirement which delicate health in convalescence imposes on us. I remember we touched on this point at Ditton; and I think again, that though classical learning be the *Shibboleth* by which we judge, generally speaking, of the proficiency of the youthful scholar, yet, when this has been too exclusively and pedantically impressed on his mind as the one thing needful, he very often finds he has entirely a new course of study to commence, just at the time when life is opening all its busy or gay scenes before him, and when study of any kind becomes irksome.

For this species of instruction I do not so much approve of tasks and set hours for serious reading, as of the plan of endeavoring to give a taste for history to the youths themselves, and suffering them to gratify it in their own way, and at their own time. For this reason I would not be very scrupulous what books they began with, or whether they began at the middle or end. The knowledge which we acquire of free will and by spontaneous exertion, is like food eaten with appetite — it digests well, and benefits the system ten times more than the double cramming of an alderman. If a boy's attention can be drawn in conversation to any interesting point of history, and the book is pointed out to him where he will find the particulars conveyed in a lively manner, he reads the passage with so much pleasure that he very naturally recurs to the book at the first unoccupied moment, to try if he cannot pick more amusement out of it; and when once a lad gets the spirit of information, he goes on himself with little trouble but that of selecting for him the best and most agreeable books. I think Walter has naturally some turn for history and historical anecdote, and would be disposed to read as much as could be wished in that most useful line of knowledge; — for in the eminent situation he is destined to by his birth, acquaintance with the history and institutions of his country, and her relative position with respect to others, is a *sine qua non* to his discharging its duties with propriety. All this is extremely like prosing, so I will harp on that string no longer.

Kind compliments to all at Ditton; you say nothing of your own rheumatism. I am here for the session, unless the wind should blow me south to see the coronation, and I think 800 miles rather a long journey to see a show.

I am always, my dear Lord,

Yours very affectionately,

WALTER SCOTT.

CHAPTER LII

1821

ON the 4th of June, Scott, being then on one of his
short Sessional visits to Abbotsford, received the painful
intelligence that his friend John Ballantyne's maladies
had begun to assume an aspect of serious and even immediate danger. The elder brother made the communication in these terms: —

TO SIR WALTER SCOTT, BART., OF ABBOTSFORD, MELROSE.

EDINBURGH, Sunday, 3d June, 1821.

DEAR SIR, — I have this morning had a most heart-break-
ing letter from poor John, from which the following is an extract. You will judge how it has affected me, who, with all
his peculiarities of temper, love him very much. He says, —

"A spitting of blood has commenced, and you may guess the
situation into which I am plunged. We are all accustomed to
consider death as certainly inevitable; but his obvious approach
is assuredly the most detestable and abhorrent feeling to which
human nature can be subject."

This is truly doleful. There is something in it more absolutely bitter to my heart than what I have otherwise suffered.
I look back to my mother's peaceful rest, and to my infant's

blessedness — if life be not the extinguishable worthless spark which I cannot think it — but here, cut off in the very middle of life, with good means and strong powers of enjoying it, and nothing but reluctance and repining at the close — I say the truth when I say that I would joyfully part with my right arm to avert the approaching result. Pardon this, dear sir; my heart and soul are heavy within me.

. . . .

With the deepest respect and gratitude,
J. B.

At the date of this letter, the invalid was in Roxburgh-shire; but he came to Edinburgh a day or two after-wards, and died there on the 16th of the same month. I accompanied Sir Walter when one of their last interviews took place, and John's deathbed was a thing not to be forgotten. We sat by him for perhaps an hour, and I think half that space was occupied with his predictions of a speedy end, and details of his last will, which he had just been executing, and which lay on his coverlid; the other half being given, five minutes or so at a time, to questions and remarks, which intimated that the hope of life was still flickering before him — nay, that his interest in all its concerns remained eager. The proof sheets of a volume of his Novelists' Library lay also by his pillow; and he passed from them to his will, and then back to them, as by jerks and starts the unwonted veil of gloom closed upon his imagination, or was withdrawn again. He had, as he said, left his great friend and patron £2000 towards the completion of the new library at Abbotsford, — and the spirit of the auctioneer virtuoso flashed up as he began to describe what would, he thought, be the best style and arrangement of the book-shelves. He was interrupted by an agony of asthma, which left him with hardly any signs of life; and ulti-mately he did expire in a fit of the same kind. Scott was visibly and profoundly shaken by this scene and its sequel. As we stood together a few days afterwards, while they were smoothing the turf over John's remains in the Canongate Churchyard, the heavens, which had been dark and slaty, cleared up suddenly, and the mid-summer sun shone forth in his strength. Scott, ever awake to the "skiey influences," cast his eye along the overhanging line of the Calton Hill, with its gleaming walls and towers, and then turning to the grave again, "I feel," he whispered in my ear, "I feel as if there would be less sunshine for me from this day forth."

As we walked homewards, Scott told me, among other favorable traits of his friend, one little story which I must not omit. He remarked one day to a poor student of divinity attending his auction, that he looked as if he were in bad health. The young man assented with a sigh. "Come," said Ballantyne, "I think I ken the secret of a sort of draft that would relieve you — particularly," he added, handing him a cheque for £5 or £10 — "particularly, my dear, if taken upon an empty stomach."

John died in his elder brother's house in St. John Street; a circumstance which it gives me pleasure to re-cord, as it confirms the impression of their affectionate feelings towards each other at this time, which the reader must have derived from James's letter to Scott last quoted. Their confidence and cordiality had undergone considerable interruption in the latter part of John's life; but the close was in all respects fraternal.

A year and a half before John's exit, — namely, on the last day of 1819, — he happened to lay his hand on an old pocketbook, which roused his reflections, and he filled two or three of its pages with a brief summary of the most active part of his life, which I think it due to his character, as well as Sir Walter Scott's, to transcribe in this place.

"31st Dec., 1819. In moving a bed from the fireplace to-day upstairs, I found an old memorandum-book, which enables

me to trace the following recollections of *this day*, the last of
the year.

"1801. A shopkeeper in Kelso; at this period my difficulties had not begun in business; was well, happy, and 27 years
old; new then in a connection which afterwards gave me great
pain, but can never be forgotten.

"1802. 28 old: In Kelso as before — could scarcely be
happier — hunted, shot, kept * * * *'s company, and neglected
business, the fruits whereof I soon found.

"1803. 29: Still fortunate, and happy from same cause.
James in Edinburgh thriving as a printer. When I was
ennuied at home, visited him. Business neglected every way.

"1804. 30: Material change; getting into difficulties; all
wrong, and changes in every way approaching.

"1805. 31: All consummated; health miserable all summer and * * * * designated in an erased mem, *the scoundrel.* I
yet recollect the cause — can I ever forget it? My furniture,
goods, etc., sold at Kelso, previous to my going to Edinburgh to
become my brother's clerk; whither I *did* go, for which God
be praised eternally, on Friday, 3d January, 1806, on £200
a year. My effects at Kelso, with labor, paid my debts, and
left me penniless.

"From this period till 1808. 34: I continued in this situation — then the scheme of a bookselling concern in Hanover
Street was adopted, which I was to manage; it was £300
a year, and one fourth of the profits besides.

"1809. 35: Already the business in Hanover Street getting
into difficulty, from our ignorance of its nature, and most extravagant and foolish advances from its funds to the printing
concern. I ought to have resisted this, but I was thoughtless,
although not young, or rather reckless, and lived on as long as
I could make ends meet.

"1810. 36: Bills increasing — the destructive system of
accommodations adopted.

"1811. 37: Bills increased to a most fearful degree. Sir
Wm. Forbes and Co. shut their account. No bank would discount with us, and everything leading to irretrievable failure.

"1812. 38: The first partner stepped in, at a crisis so tremendous, that it shakes my soul to think of it. By the most
consummate wisdom, and resolution, and unheard-of exertions,

he put things in a train that finally (so early as 1817) paid even himself (who ultimately became the sole creditor of the house) *in full*, with a balance of a thousand pounds.

"1813. 39: In business as a literary auctioneer in Prince's Street; from which period to the present I have got gradually forward, both in that line and as third of a partner of the works of the Author of Waverley, so that I am now, at 45, worth about (I owe £2000) £5000, with, however, alas, many changes — my strong constitution much broken; my father and mother dead, and James estranged — the chief enjoyment and glory of my life being the possession of the friendship and confidence of the greatest of men."

In communicating John's death to the Cornet, Sir Walter says: "I have had a very great loss in poor John Ballantyne, who is gone, after a long illness. He persisted to the very last in endeavoring to take exercise, in which he was often imprudent, and was up and dressed the very morning before his death. In his will the grateful creature has left me a legacy of £2000, life-rented, however, by his wife; and the rest of his little fortune goes betwixt his two brothers. I shall miss him very much, both in business, and as an easy and lively companion, who was eternally active and obliging in whatever I had to do."

I am sorry to take leave of John Ballantyne with the remark, that his last will was a document of the same class with too many of his *states* and *calendars*. So far from having £2000 to bequeath to Sir Walter, he died as he had lived, ignorant of the situation of his affairs, and deep in debt.[1]

The two following letters, written at Blair-Adam,

[1] No specimen of John's inaccuracy as to business-statements could be pointed out more extraordinary than his assertion in the above sketch of his career, that the bookselling concern, of which he had had the management, was finally wound up with a balance of £1000 in favor of the first partner. At the time he refers to (1817), John's name was on floating bills to the extent of at least £10,000, representing *part* of the debt which had been accumulated on the bookselling house, and which, on its dissolution, was assumed by the printing company in the Canongate. — (1839.)

where the Club were as usual, assembled for the dog-
days, have been selected from among several which Scott
at this time addressed to his friends in the South, with
the view of promoting Mr. Mackay's success in his *début*
on the London boards as Bailie Jarvie.

TO MISS JOANNA BAILLIE, HAMPSTEAD.

The immediate motive of my writing to you, my dearest friend, is to make Mrs. Agnes and you aware that
a Scots performer, called Mackay, is going up to London
to play Bailie Nicol Jarvie for a single night at Covent
Garden, and to beg you of all dear loves to go and see
him; for, taking him in that single character, I am not
sure I ever saw anything in my life possessing so much
truth and comic effect at the same time: he is completely
the personage of the drama, the purse-proud consequen-
tial magistrate, humane and irritable in the same moment,
and the true Scotsman in every turn of thought and
action; his variety of feelings towards Rob Roy, whom
he likes, and fears, and despises, and admires, and pities
all at once, is exceedingly well expressed. In short, I
never saw a part better sustained, certainly; I pray you
to collect a party of Scotch friends to see it. I have
written to Sotheby to the same purpose, but I doubt
whether the exhibition will prove as satisfactory to those
who do not know the original from which the resemblance is taken. I observe the English demand (as is
natural) broad caricature in the depicting of national
peculiarities: they did so as to the Irish till Jack Johnstone taught them better, and at first I should fear
Mackay's reality will seem less ludicrous than Liston's
humorous extravagances. So let it not be said that a
dramatic genius of Scotland wanted the countenance and
protection of Joanna Baillie: the Doctor and Mrs. Baillie
will be much diverted if they go also, but somebody said
to me that they were out of town. The man, I am told,
is perfectly respectable in his life and habits, and conse-

quently deserves encouragement every way. There is a great difference betwixt his *bailie* and all his other performances: one would think the part made for him, and him for the part — and yet I may do the poor fellow injustice, and what we here consider as a falling off may arise from our identifying Mackay so completely with the worthy Glasgow magistrate, that recollections of Nicol Jarvie intrude upon us at every corner, and mar the personification of any other part which he may represent for the time.

I am here for a couple of days with our Chief-Commissioner, late Willie Adam, and we had yesterday a delightful stroll to Castle-Campbell, the Rumbling Brig, Cauldron Linns, etc. The scenes are most romantic, and I know not by what fatality it has been, that living within a step of them, I never visited any of them before. We had Sir Samuel Shepherd with us, a most delightful person, but with too much English fidgetiness about him for crags and precipices, — perpetually afraid that rocks would give way under his weight which had over-brow'd the torrent for ages, and that good well-rooted trees, moored so as to resist ten thousand tempests, would fall because he grasped one of their branches; he must certainly be a firm believer in the simile of the lover of your native land, who complains, —

> " I leant my back unto an aik,
> I thought it was a trusty tree,
> But first it bow'd and then it brake," etc., etc., etc. [1]

Certes these Southrons lack much the habits of the wood and wilderness, — for here is a man of taste and genius, a fine scholar and a most interesting companion, haunted with fears that would be entertained by no shopkeeper from the Luckenbooths or the Saut Market. A sort of *Cockneyism* of one kind or another pervades their men of professional habits, whereas every Scotchman,

[1] Ballad of the Marchioness of Douglas, " O waly, waly, up yon bank ! " etc.

with very few exceptions, holds country exercises of all kinds to be part of his nature, and is ready to become a traveller, or even a soldier on the slightest possible notice. The habits of the moorfowl shooting, salmon-fishing, and so forth, may keep this much up among the gentry, a name which our pride and pedigree extend so much wider than in England; and it is worth notice that these amusements, being cheap and tolerably easy come at by all the petty dunniewassals, have a more general influence on the national character than fox-hunting, which is confined to those who can mount and keep a horse worth at least 100 guineas. But still this hardly explains the general and wide difference betwixt the countries in this particular. Happen how it will, the advantage is much in favor of Scotland: it is true that it contributes to prevent our producing such very accomplished lawyers, divines, or artisans [1] as when the whole mind is bent with undivided attention upon attaining one branch of knowledge, — but it gives a strong and muscular character to the people in general, and saves men from all sorts of causeless fears and flutterings of the heart, which give quite as much misery as if there were real cause for entertaining apprehension. This is not furiously to the purpose of my letter, which, after recommending Monsieur Mackay, was to tell you that we are all well and happy. Sophia is getting stout and pretty, and is one of the wisest and most important little mammas that can be seen anywhere. Her bower is *bigged in gude green wood*, and we went last Saturday

[1] The great engineer, James Watt, of Birmingham — in whose talk Scott took much delight — told him, that though hundreds probably of his northern countrymen had sought employment at his establishment, he never could get one of them to become a first-rate artisan. "Many of them," said he, "were too good for that, and rose to be valuable clerks and book-keepers; but those incapable of this sort of advancement had always the same insuperable aversion to toiling so long at any one point of mechanism as to gain the highest wages among the workmen." I have no doubt Sir Walter was thinking of Mr. Watt's remark when he wrote the sentence in the text.

in a body to enjoy it, and to consult about furniture; and we have got the road stopt which led up the hill, so it is now quite solitary and approached through a grove of trees, actual well-grown trees, not Lilliputian forests like those of Abbotsford. The season is dreadfully backward. Our ashes and oaks are not yet in leaf, and will not be, I think, in anything like full foliage this year, such is the rigor of the east winds. — Always, my dear and much respected friend, most affectionately yours,   W. SCOTT.

BLAIR-ADAM, 11 June, 1821,
   In full sight of Lochleven.

P. S. — Pray read, or have read to you by Mrs. Agnes, The Annals of the Parish. Mr. Galt wrote the worst tragedies ever seen, and has now written a most excellent novel, if it can be called so.

TO THE LORD MONTAGU, ETC., ETC., LONDON.

BLAIR-ADAM, June 11, 1821.

MY DEAR LORD, — There is a man going up from Edinburgh to play one night at Covent Garden, whom, as having the very unusual power of presenting on the stage a complete Scotsman, I am very desirous you should see. He plays Bailie Nicol Jarvie in Rob Roy, but with a degree of national truth and understanding, which makes the part equal to anything I have ever seen on the stage, and I have seen all the best comedians for these forty years. I wish much, if you continue in town till he comes up, that you would get into some private box and take a look of him. Sincerely, it is a real treat — the English will not enjoy it, for it is not broad enough, or sufficiently caricatured for their apprehensions, but to a Scotsman it is inimitable, and you have the Glasgow Bailie before you, with all his bustling conceit and importance, his real benevolence, and his irritable habits. He will want in London a fellow who, in the character of the Highland turnkey, held the back-

hand to him admirably well. I know how difficult it is
for folks of condition to get to the theatre, but this is
worth an exertion, — and, besides, the poor man (who I
understand is very respectable in private life) will be, to
use an admirable simile (by which one of your father's
farmers persuaded the Duke to go to hear his son, a pro-
bationer in divinity, preach his first sermon in the town
of Ayr), *like a cow in a fremd loaning*, and glad of
Scots countenance.

I am glad the Duke's cold is better — his stomach will
not be put to those trials which ours underwent in our
youth, when deep drinking was the fashion. I hope he
will always be aware, however, that his is not a strong
one.

Campbell's Lives of the Admirals is an admirable
book, and I would advise your Lordship e'en to redeem
your pledge to the Duke on some rainy day. You do
not run the risk from the perusal which my poor mother
apprehended. She always alleged it sent her eldest son
to the navy, and did not see with indifference any of her
younger olive branches engaged with Campbell except
myself, who stood in no danger of the cockpit or quarter-
deck. I would not swear for Lord John though. Your
Lordship's tutor was just such a well-meaning person as
mine, who used to take from me old Lindsay of Pitscot-
tie, and set me down to get by heart Rollin's infernal
list of the Shepherd Kings, whose hard names could have
done no good to any one on earth, unless he had wished
to raise the devil, and lacked language to conjure with.
— Always, my dear Lord, most truly yours,

WALTER SCOTT.

The coronation of George IV., preparations for which
were (as has been seen) in active progress by March,
1820, had been deferred, in consequence of the unhappy
affair of the Queen's Trial. The 19th of July, 1821,
was now announced for this solemnity, and Sir Walter

resolved to be among the spectators. It occurred to him that if the Ettrick Shepherd were to accompany him, and produce some memorial of the scene likely to catch the popular ear in Scotland, good service might thus be done to the cause of loyalty. But this was not his only consideration. Hogg had married a handsome and most estimable young woman, a good deal above his own original rank in life, the year before; and expecting with her a dowry of £1000, he had forthwith revived the grand ambition of an earlier day, and become a candidate for an extensive farm on the Buccleuch estate, at a short distance from Altrive Lake. Various friends, supposing his worldly circumstances to be much improved, had supported his application, and Lord Montagu had received it in a manner for which the Shepherd's letters to Scott express much gratitude. Misfortune pursued the Shepherd — the unforeseen bankruptcy of his wife's father interrupted the stocking of the sheep-walk; and the arable part of the new possession was sadly mismanaged by himself. Scott hoped that a visit to London, and a coronation poem, or pamphlet, might end in some pension or post that would relieve these difficulties, and he wrote to Hogg, urging him to come to Edinburgh, and embark with him for the great city. Not doubting that this proposal would be eagerly accepted, he, when writing to Lord Sidmouth, to ask a place for himself in the Hall and Abbey of Westminster, mentioned that Hogg was to be his companion, and begged suitable accommodation for him also. Lord Sidmouth, being overwhelmed with business connected with the approaching pageant, answered by the pen of the Under-Secretary of State, Mr. Hobhouse, that Sir Walter's wishes, both as to himself and the Shepherd, should be gratified, *provided* they would both dine with him the day after the coronation, in Richmond Park, "where," says the letter before me, "his Lordship will invite the Duke of York and a few other Jacobites to meet you." All this being made known to the tenant of Mount-Benger, he wrote to Scott, as he says, "with the tear in his eye," to signify, that if he went to London he must miss attending the great annual Border fair, held on St. Boswell's Green, in Roxburghshire, on the 18th of every July; and that his absence from that meeting so soon after entering upon business as a store-farmer, would be considered by his new compeers as highly imprudent and discreditable. "In short," James concludes, "the thing is impossible. But as there is no man in his Majesty's dominions admires his great talents for government, and the energy and dignity of his administration, so much as I do, I will write something at home, and endeavor to give it you before you start." The Shepherd probably expected that these pretty compliments would reach the royal ear; but however that may have been, his own Muse turned a deaf ear to him — at least I never heard of anything that he wrote on this occasion.

Scott embarked without him, on board a new steamship called The City of Edinburgh, which, as he suggested to the master, ought rather to have been christened The New Reekie. This vessel was that described and lauded in the following letter: —

TO THE LORD MONTAGU, ETC., ETC.

EDINBURGH, July 1, 1821.

MY DEAR LORD, — I write just now to thank you for your letter. I have been on board the steamship, and am so delighted with it, that I think I shall put myself aboard for the coronation. It runs at nine knots an hour (*me ipso teste*) against wind and tide, with a deck as long as a frigate's to walk upon, and to sleep on also, if you like, as I have always preferred a cloak and a mattress to these crowded cabins. This reconciles the speed and certainty of the mail-coach with the ease and convenience of being on shipboard. So I really think I will run up to see the grandee show, and run down again. I scorn to mention economy, though the expense is not one fifth, and that is something in hard times, especially to me, who, to choose, would always rather travel in a public conveyance, than with my domestic's good company in a po-chay.

But now comes the news of news. I have been instigating the great Caledonian Boar, James Hogg, to undertake a similar trip — with the view of turning an honest penny, to help out his stocking, by writing some sort of Shepherd's Letters, or the like, to put the honest Scots bodies up to this whole affair. I am trying with Lord Sidmouth to get him a place among the newspaper gentry to see the ceremony. It is seriously worth while to get such a popular view of the whole as he will probably hit off.

I have another view for this poor fellow. You have heard of the Royal Literary Society, and how they propose to distribute solid pudding, *alias* pensions, to men of genius. It is, I think, a very problematical matter, whether it will do the good which is intended; but if they do mean to select worthy objects of encouragement, I really know nobody that has a better or an equal claim to poor Hogg. Our friend Villiers takes a great charge of this matter, and good-naturedly forgave my stating to him a number of objections to the first concoction, which was to have been something resembling the French Academy. It has now been much modified. Perhaps there may be some means fallen upon, with your Lordship's assistance, of placing Hogg under Mr. Villiers's view. I would have done so myself, but only I have battled the point against the whole establishment so keenly, that it would be too bad to bring forward a protégé of my own to take advantage of it. They intended at one time to give pensions of about £100 a year to thirty persons. I know not where they could find half a dozen with such pretensions as the Shepherd's.

There will be risk of his being lost in London, or kidnapped by some of those ladies who open literary *mena-geries* for the reception of *lions*. I should like to see him at a rout of blue-stockings. I intend to recommend him to the protection of John Murray the bookseller; and I hope he will come equipped with plaid, kent, and colley.[1]

I wish to heaven Lord Melville would either keep the Admiralty, or in Hogg's phrase, —

> " O I would eagerly press him
> The keys of the *east* to require," —

for truly the Board of Control is the Corn Chest for Scotland, where we poor gentry must send our younger sons, as we send our black cattle to the south. — Ever most truly yours,   WALTER SCOTT.

From London, on the day after the coronation, Sir Walter addressed a letter descriptive of the ceremonial to his friend James Ballantyne, who published it in his newspaper. It has been since reprinted — but not in any collection of Scott's own writings; and I therefore insert it here. It will probably possess considerable interest for the student of English history and manners in future times; for the coronation of George the Fourth's successor was conducted on a vastly inferior scale of splendor and expense — and the precedent of curtailment in any such matters is now seldom neglected.

TO THE EDITOR OF THE EDINBURGH WEEKLY JOURNAL.

LONDON, July 20, 1821.

SIR, — I refer you to the daily papers for the details of the great National Solemnity which we witnessed yesterday, and will hold my promise absolved by sending a few general remarks upon what I saw with surprise amounting to astonishment, and which I shall never forget. It is, indeed, impossible

---

[1] *Kent* is the shepherd's staff — *Colley* his dog. Scott alludes to the old song of the *Lea Rig*, —

> " Nae herds wi' kent and colley there," etc.

to conceive a ceremony more august and imposing in all its parts, and more calculated to make the deepest impression both on the eye and on the feelings. The most minute attention must have been bestowed to arrange all the subordinate parts in harmony with the rest; so that, amongst so much antiquated ceremonial, imposing singular dresses, duties, and characters, upon persons accustomed to move in the ordinary routine of society, nothing occurred either awkward or ludicrous which could mar the general effect of the solemnity. Considering that it is but one step from the sublime to the ridiculous, I own I consider it as surprising that the whole ceremonial of the day should have passed away without the slightest circumstance which could derange the general tone of solemn feeling which was suited to the occasion.

You must have heard a full account of the only disagreeable event of the day. I mean the attempt of the misguided lady, who has lately furnished so many topics of discussion, to intrude herself upon a ceremonial, where, not being in her proper place, to be present in any other must have been voluntary degradation. That matter is a fire of straw which has now burnt to the very embers, and those who try to blow it into life again will only blacken their hands and noses, like mischievous children dabbling among the ashes of a bonfire. It seems singular, that being determined to be present at all hazards, this unfortunate personage should not have procured a Peer's ticket, which, I presume, would have insured her admittance. I willingly pass to pleasanter matters.

The effect of the scene in the Abbey was beyond measure magnificent. Imagine long galleries stretched among the aisles of that venerable and august pile — those which rise above the altar pealing back their echoes to a full and magnificent choir of music — those which occupied the sides filled even to crowding with all that Britain has of beautiful and distinguished, and the cross-gallery most appropriately occupied by the Westminster schoolboys, in their white surplices, many of whom might on that day receive impressions never to be lost during the rest of their lives. Imagine this, I say, and then add the spectacle upon the floor, — the altar surrounded by the Fathers of the Church, the King encircled by the Nobility of the land and the Counsellors of his throne, and by warriors wearing the

honored marks of distinction bought by many a glorious danger ; — add to this the rich spectacle of the aisles crowded with
waving plumage, and coronets, and caps of honor, and the sun,
which brightened and saddened as if on purpose, now beaming
in full lustre on the rich and varied assemblage, and now dart-
ing a solitary ray, which catched, as it passed, the glittering
folds of a banner, or the edge of a group of battle-axes or par-
tizans, and then rested full on some fair form, "the cynosure of
neighboring eyes," whose circlet of diamonds glistened under
its influence. Imagine all this, and then tell me if I have
made my journey of four hundred miles to little purpose. I
do not love your *cui bono* men, and therefore I will not be
pleased if you ask me in the damping tone of sullen philosophy,
what good all this has done the spectators. If we restrict life
to its real animal wants and necessities, we shall indeed be satisfied with "food, clothes, and fire;" but Divine Providence,
who widened our sources of enjoyment beyond those of the
animal creation, never meant that we should bound our wishes
within such narrow limits; and I shrewdly suspect that those
non est tanti gentlefolks only depreciate the natural and unaffected pleasure which men like me receive from sights of splendor and sounds of harmony, either because they would seem
wiser than their simple neighbors at the expense of being less
happy, or because the mere pleasure of the sight and sound is
connected with associations of a deeper kind, to which they are
unwilling to yield themselves.

Leaving these gentlemen to enjoy their own wisdom, I still
more pity those, if there be any, who (being unable to detect a
peg on which to hang a laugh) sneer coldly at this solemn festival, and are rather disposed to dwell on the expense which
attends it, than on the generous feelings which it ought to
awaken. The expense, so far as it is national, has gone directly and instantly to the encouragement of the British manufacturer and mechanic ; and so far as it is personal to the persons of rank attendant upon the Coronation, it operates as a
tax upon wealth and consideration for the benefit of poverty
and industry ; a tax willingly paid by the one class, and not
the less acceptable to the other because it adds a happy holiday
to the monotony of a life of labor.

But there were better things to reward my pilgrimage than

the mere pleasures of the eye and ear; for it was impossible, without the deepest veneration, to behold the voluntary and solemn interchange of vows betwixt the King and his assembled People, whilst he, on the one hand, called God Almighty to witness his resolution to maintain their laws and privileges, whilst they called, at the same moment, on the Divine Being, to bear witness that they accepted him for their liege Sovereign, and pledged to him their love and their duty. I cannot describe to you the effect produced by the solemn, yet strange mixture of the words of Scripture, with the shouts and acclamations of the assembled multitude, as they answered to the voice of the Prelate, who demanded of them whether they acknowledged as their Monarch the Prince who claimed the sovereignty in their presence. It was peculiarly delightful to see the King receive from the royal brethren, but in particular from the Duke of York, the fraternal kiss in which they acknowledged their sovereign. There was an honest tenderness, an affectionate and sincere reverence in the embrace interchanged betwixt the Duke of York and his Majesty, that approached almost to a caress, and impressed all present with the electrical conviction, that the nearest to the throne in blood was the nearest also in affection. I never heard plaudits given more from the heart than those that were thundered upon the royal brethren when they were thus pressed to each other's bosoms, — it was an emotion of natural kindness, which, bursting out amidst ceremonial grandeur, found an answer in every British bosom. The King seemed much affected at this and one or two other parts of the ceremonial, even so much so as to excite some alarm among those who saw him as nearly as I did. He completely recovered himself, however, and bore (generally speaking) the fatigue of the day very well. I learn from one near his person, that he roused himself with great energy, even when most oppressed with heat and fatigue, when any of the more interesting parts of the ceremony were to be performed, or when anything occurred which excited his personal and immediate attention. When presiding at the banquet, amid the long line of his Nobles, he looked " every inch a King; " and nothing could exceed the grace with which he accepted and returned the various acts of homage rendered to him in the course of that long day.

It was also a very gratifying spectacle to those who think like me, to behold the Duke of Devonshire and most of the distinguished Whig nobility assembled round the throne on this occasion; giving an open testimony that the differences of political opinions are only skin-deep wounds, which assume at times an angry appearance, but have no real effect on the wholesome constitution of the country.

If you ask me to distinguish who bore him best, and appeared most to sustain the character we annex to the assistants in such a solemnity, I have no hesitation to name Lord Londonderry, who, in the magnificent robes of the Garter, with the cap and high plume of the order, walked alone, and by his fine face and majestic person formed an adequate representative of the order of Edward III., the costume of which was worn by his Lordship only. The Duke of Wellington, with all his laurels, moved and looked deserving the baton, which was never grasped by so worthy a hand. The Marquis of Anglesea showed the most exquisite grace in managing his horse, notwithstanding the want of his limb, which he left at Waterloo. I never saw so fine a bridle-hand in my life, and I am rather a judge of "noble horsemanship." Lord Howard's horse was worse bitted than those of the two former noblemen, but not so much so as to derange the ceremony of retiring back out of the Hall.

The Champion was performed (as of right) by young Dymocke, a fine-looking youth, but bearing, perhaps, a little too much the appearance of a maiden-knight to be the challenger of the world in a King's behalf. He threw down his gauntlet, however, with becoming manhood, and showed as much horsemanship as the crowd of knights and squires around him would permit to be exhibited. His armor was in good taste, but his shield was out of all propriety, being a round *rondache*, or Highland target, a defensive weapon which it would have been impossible to use on horseback, instead of being a three-corner'd, or *heater-shield*, which in time of the tilt was suspended round the neck. Pardon this antiquarian scruple, which, you may believe, occurred to few but myself. On the whole, this striking part of the exhibition somewhat disappointed me, for I would have had the Champion less embarrassed by his assistants, and at liberty to put his horse on the *grand pas*. And yet the young Lord of Scrivelsbaye looked and behaved extremely well.

Returning to the subject of costume, I could not but admire what I had previously been disposed much to criticise, — I mean the fancy dress of the Privy-Councillors, which was of white and blue satin, with trunk-hose and mantles, after the fashion of Queen Elizabeth's time. Separately, so gay a garb had an odd effect on the persons of elderly or ill-made men ; but when the whole was thrown into one general body, all these discrepancies disappeared, and you no more observed the particular manner or appearance of an individual, than you do that of a soldier in the battalion which marches past you. The whole was so completely harmonized in actual coloring, as well as in association, with the general mass of gay and gorgeous and antique dress which floated before the eye, that it was next to impossible to attend to the effect of individual figures. Yet a Scotsman will detect a Scotsman amongst the most crowded assemblage, and I must say that the Lord Justice-Clerk of Scotland[1] showed to as great advantage in his robes of Privy-Councillor, as any by whom that splendid dress was worn on this great occasion. The common Court-dress used by the Privy-Councillors at the last coronation must have had a poor effect in comparison of the present, which formed a gradation in the scale of gorgeous ornament, from the unwieldy splendor of the heralds, who glowed like huge masses of cloth of gold and silver, to the more chastened robes and ermine of the Peers. I must not forget the effect produced by the Peers placing their coronets on their heads, which was really august.

The box assigned to the foreign Ambassadors presented a most brilliant effect, and was perfectly in a blaze with diamonds. When the sunshine lighted on Prince Esterhazy, in particular, he glimmered like a galaxy. I cannot learn positively if he had on that renowned coat which has visited all the courts of Europe save ours, and is said to be worth £100,000, or some such trifle, and which costs the Prince £100 or two every time he puts it on, as he is sure to lose pearls to that amount. This was a hussar dress, but splendid in the last degree ; perhaps too fine for good taste — at least it would have appeared so anywhere else. Beside the Prince sat a

---

[1] Scott's schoolfellow, the Right Hon. D. Boyle.

good-humored lass, who seemed all eyes and ears (his daughter-in-law, I believe), who wore as many diamonds as if they had been Bristol stones. An honest Persian was also a remarkable figure, from the dogged and imperturbable gravity with which he looked on the whole scene, without ever moving a limb or a muscle during the space of four hours. Like Sir Wilful Witwoud, I cannot find that your Persian is orthodox ; for if he scorned everything else, there was a Mahometan paradise extended on his right hand along the seats which were occupied by the peeresses and their daughters, which the Prophet himself might have looked on with emotion. I have seldom seen so many elegant and beautiful girls as sat mingled among the noble matronage of the land ; and the waving plumage of feathers, which made the universal head-dress, had the most appropriate effect in setting off their charms.

I must not omit that the foreigners, who are apt to consider us as a nation *en frac*, and without the usual ceremonials of dress and distinction, were utterly astonished and delighted to see the revival of feudal dresses and feudal grandeur when the occasion demanded it, and that in a degree of splendor which they averred they had never seen paralleled in Europe.

The duties of service at the Banquet, and of attendance in general, were performed by pages drest very elegantly in Henri Quatre coats of scarlet, with gold lace, blue sashes, white silk hose, and white rosettes. There were also marshal's-men for keeping order, who wore a similar dress, but of blue, and having white sashes. Both departments were filled up almost entirely by young gentlemen, many of them of the very first condition, who took these menial characters to gain admission to the show. When I saw many of my young acquaintance thus attending upon their fathers and kinsmen, the Peers, Knights, and so forth, I could not help thinking of Crabbe's lines, with a little alteration : —

> 'T was schooling pride to see the menial wait,
> Smile on his father, and receive his plate.

It must be owned, however, that they proved but indifferent valets, and were very apt, like the clown in the pantomime, to eat the cheer they should have handed to their masters, and to play other *tours de page*, which reminded me of the caution of our proverb " not to man yourself with your kin." The Peers, for example, had only a cold collation, while the Aldermen of London feasted on venison and turtle; and similar errors necessarily befell others in the confusion of the evening. But these slight mistakes, which indeed were not known till afterwards, had not the slightest effect on the general grandeur of the scene.

I did not see the procession between the Abbey and Hall. In the morning a few voices called *Queen! Queen!* as Lord Londonderry passed, and even when the Sovereign appeared. But these were only signals for the loud and reiterated acclamations in which these tones of discontent were completely drowned. In the return, no one dissonant voice intimated the least dissent from the shouts of gratulation which poured from every quarter; and certainly never Monarch received a more general welcome from his assembled subjects.

You will have from others full accounts of the variety of entertainments provided for John Bull in the Parks, the River, in the Theatres, and elsewhere. Nothing was to be seen or heard but sounds of pleasure and festivity; and whoever saw the scene at any one spot, was convinced that the whole population was assembled there, while others found a similar concourse of revellers in every different point. It is computed that about *five hundred thousand people* shared in the Festival in one way or another; and you may imagine the excellent disposition by which the people were animated, when I tell you, that, excepting a few windows broken by a small bodyguard of ragamuffins, who were in immediate attendance on the Great Lady in the morning, not the slightest political violence occurred to disturb the general harmony — and that the assembled populace seemed to be universally actuated by the spirit of the day — loyalty, namely, and good-humor. Nothing occurred to damp those happy dispositions; the weather was most propitious, and the arrangements so perfect, that no accident of any kind is reported as having taken place. — And so concluded the coronation of GEORGE IV., whom GOD long preserve. Those who witnessed it have seen a scene calculated to raise the country in their opinion, and to throw into the shade all scenes of similar magnificence, from the Field of the Cloth of Gold down to the present day. I remain, your obedient servant, AN EYE-WITNESS.

At the close of this brilliant scene, Scott received a mark of homage to his genius which delighted him not less than Laird Nippy's reverence for the *Sheriff's Knoll*, and the Sheffield cutler's dear acquisition of his signature on a visiting ticket. Missing his carriage, he had to return home on foot from Westminster, after the banquet — that is to say, between two or three o'clock in the morning; — when he and a young gentleman his companion found themselves locked in the crowd, somewhere near Whitehall, and the bustle and tumult were such that his friend was afraid some accident might happen to the lame limb. A space for the dignitaries was kept clear at that point by the Scots Greys. Sir Walter addressed a sergeant of this celebrated regiment, begging to be allowed to pass by him into the open ground in the middle of the street. The man answered shortly, that his orders were strict — that the thing was impossible. While he was endeavoring to persuade the sergeant to relent, some new wave of turbulence approached from behind, and his young companion exclaimed in a loud voice, "Take care, Sir Walter Scott, take care!" The stalwart dragoon, on hearing the name, said, "What! Sir Walter Scott? He shall get through anyhow!" He then addressed the soldiers near him: "Make room, men, for Sir Walter Scott, our illustrious countryman!" The men answered, "Sir Walter Scott! — God bless him!" — and he was in a moment within the guarded line of safety.

I shall now take another extract from the *memoranda* with which I have been favored by my friend Allan Cunningham. After the particulars formerly quoted about Scott's sitting to Chantrey in the spring of 1820, he proceeds as follows: —

" I saw Sir Walter again, when he attended the coronation, in 1821. In the mean time his bust had been wrought in marble, and the sculptor desired to take the advantage of his visit to communicate such touches of expression or lineament as the new material rendered necessary. This was done with a happiness of eye and hand almost magical : for five hours did the poet sit, or stand, or walk, while Chantrey's chisel was passed again and again over the marble, adding something at every touch.

" ' Well, Allan,' he said, when he saw me at this last sitting, ' were you at the coronation ? it was a splendid sight.' — ' No, Sir Walter,' I answered, ' places were dear and ill to get : I am told it was a magnificent scene : but having seen the procession of King Crispin at Dumfries, I was satisfied.' I said this with a smile : Scott took it as I meant it, and laughed heartily. ' That 's not a bit better than Hogg,' he said. ' He stood balancing the matter whether to go to the coronation or the fair of Saint Boswell — and the fair carried it.'

" During this conversation, Mr. Bolton the engineer came in. Something like a cold acknowledgment passed between the poet and him. On his passing into an inner room, Scott said, ' I am afraid Mr. Bolton has not forgot a little passage that once took place between us. We met in a public company, and in reply to the remark of some one, he said, " That 's like the old saying, — in every quarter of the world you will find a Scot, a rat, and a Newcastle grindstone." This touched my Scotch spirit, and I said, " Mr. Bolton, you should have added — *and a Brummagem button.*" There was a laugh at this, and Mr. Bolton replied, "We make something better in Birmingham than buttons — we make steam-engines, sir."

" ' I like Bolton,' thus continued Sir Walter ; ' he is a brave man, — and who can dislike the brave ? He showed this on a remarkable occasion. He had engaged to coin for some foreign prince a large quantity of gold. This was found out by some desperadoes, who resolved to rob the premises, and as a preliminary step tried to bribe the porter. The porter was an honest fellow, — he told Bolton that he was offered a hundred pounds to be blind and deaf next night. "Take the money," was the answer, " and I shall protect the place." Midnight came — the gates opened as if by magic — the interior doors, secured with patent locks, opened as of their own accord — and three men with dark lanterns entered and went straight to the gold. Bolton had prepared some flax steeped in turpentine — he dropt fire upon it, a sudden light filled all the place, and with his assistants, he rushed forward on the robbers, — the leader saw in a moment he was betrayed, turned on the porter, and shooting him dead, burst through all obstruction, and with an ingot of gold in his hand, scaled the wall and escaped.'

"'That is quite a romance in robbing,' I said; — and I had nearly said more, for the cavern scene and death of Meg Merrilies rose in my mind; — perhaps the mind of Sir Walter was taking the direction of the Solway too, for he said, 'How long have you been from Nithsdale?' — 'A dozen years.' 'Then you will remember it well. I was a visitor there in my youth; my brother was at Closeburn school, and there I found Creehope Linn, a scene ever present to my fancy. It is at once fearful and beautiful. The stream jumps down from the moorlands, saws its way into the freestone rock of a hundred feet deep, and, in escaping to the plain, performs a thousand vagaries. In one part it has actually shaped out a little chapel, — the peasants call it the Sutors' Chair. There are sculptures on the sides of the linn too, not such as Mr. Chantrey casts, but etchings scraped in with a knife perhaps, or a harrow-tooth. — Did you ever hear,' said Sir Walter, 'of Patrick Maxwell, who, taken prisoner by the King's troops, escaped from them on his way to Edinburgh, by flinging himself into that dreadful linn on Moffat water, called the Douglasses' Beef-tub?' — 'Frequently,' I answered; 'the country abounds with anecdotes of those days: the popular feeling sympathizes with the poor Jacobites, and has recorded its sentiments in many a tale and many a verse.' — 'The Ettrick Shepherd has collected not a few of those things,' said Scott, 'and I suppose many snatches of song may yet be found.' — C. 'I have gathered many such things myself, Sir Walter, and as I still propose to make a collection of all Scottish songs of poetic merit, I shall work up many of my stray verses and curious anecdotes in the notes.' — S. 'I am glad that you are about such a thing; any help which I can give you, you may command; ask me any questions, no matter how many, I shall answer them if I can. Don't be timid in your selection; our ancestors fought boldly, spoke boldly, and sang boldly too. I can help you to an old characteristic ditty not yet in print: —

" There dwalt a man into the wast
    And O gin he was cruel,

> For on his bridal night at e'en
> He gat up and grat for gruel.
>
> " They brought to him a gude sheep's head,
> A bason, and a towel;
> Gar take thae whim-whams far frae me,
> I winna want my gruel." '

" C. — ' I never heard that verse before: the hero seems related to the bridegroom of Nithsdale, —

> " The bridegroom grat as the sun gade down,
> The bridegroom grat as the sun gade down;
> To ony man I'll gie a hunder marks sae free,
> This night that will bed wi' a bride for me." '

" S. — ' A cowardly loon enough. I know of many crumbs and fragments of verse which will be useful to your work; the Border was once peopled with poets, for every one that could fight could make ballads, some of them of great power and pathos. Some such people as the minstrels were living less than a century ago.' — C. 'I knew a man, the last of a race of district tale-tellers, who used to boast of the golden days of his youth, and say, that the world, with all its knowledge, was grown sixpence a day worse for him.' — S. 'How was that? how did he make his living? — by telling tales, or singing ballads?' — C. 'By both: he had a devout tale for the old, and a merry song for the young; he was a sort of beggar.' — S. 'Out upon thee, Allan — dost thou call that begging? Why, man, we make our bread by story-telling, and honest bread it is.' "

I ought not to close this extract without observing that Sir F. Chantrey presented the original bust, of which Mr. Cunningham speaks, to Sir Walter himself; by whose remotest descendants it will undoubtedly be held in additional honor on that account. The poet had the further gratification of learning that three copies were executed in marble before the original quitted the studio: One for Windsor Castle — a second for Apsley House — and a third for the friendly sculptor's own private collection. The casts of this bust have since been multiplied beyond perhaps any example whatever.

Sir Walter returned to Scotland in company with his friend William Stewart Rose; and they took the way by Stratford-upon-Avon, where, on the wall of the room in which Shakespeare is supposed to have been born, the autograph of these pilgrims may still, I believe, be traced.

CHAPTER LIII

PUBLICATION OF MR. ADOLPHUS'S LETTERS ON THE AUTHORSHIP OF WAVERLEY

1821

DURING Scott's visit to London in July, 1821, there appeared a work which was read with eager curiosity and delight by the public — with much private diversion besides by his friends — and which he himself must have gone through with a very odd mixture of emotions. I allude to the volume entitled "Letters to Richard Heber, Esq., containing critical remarks on the series of novels beginning with Waverley, and an attempt to ascertain their author;" which was soon known to have been penned by Mr. John Leycester Adolphus, a distinguished alumnus of the University then represented in Parliament by Sir Walter's early friend Heber.[1] Previously to the publication of these letters, the opinion that Scott was the author of Waverley had indeed become well settled in the English, to say nothing of the Scottish mind; a great variety of circumstances, external as well as internal, had by degrees coöperated to its general establishment: yet there were not wanting persons who still

---

[1] [John Leycester Adolphus, son of John Adolphus, eminent as a barrister and the author of various historical works, was born in 1795, and was educated at Merchant Taylors', and St. John's College, Oxford, where in 1814 he gained the Newdigate prize for English verse. He held a reputable position in his father's profession, and, beside the work described in the text, published *Letters from Spain in 1856 and 1857*. He also wrote a number of clever metrical *jeux d'esprit*. He was engaged in completing his father's *History of England under George III.* at the time of his death in 1862.]

dissented, or at least affected to dissent from it. It was
reserved for the enthusiastic industry, and admirable ingenuity of this juvenile academic, to set the question at
rest by an accumulation of critical evidence which no
sophistry could evade, and yet produced in a style of
such high-bred delicacy, that it was impossible for the
hitherto "veiled prophet" to take the slightest offence
with the hand that had forever abolished his disguise.
The only sceptical scruple that survived this exposition
was extinguished in due time by Scott's avowal of the
sole and unassisted authorship of his novels; and now
Mr. Adolphus's Letters have shared the fate of other
elaborate arguments, the thesis of which has ceased to be
controverted. Hereafter, I am persuaded, his volume
will be revived for its own sake; — but, in the mean time,
regarding it merely as forming, by its original effect, an
epoch in Scott's history, I think it my duty to mark my
sense of its importance in that point of view, by transcribing the writer's own summary of its

CONTENTS.

" LETTER I. — Introduction — General reasons for believing
the novels to have been written by the author of Marmion.

" LETTER II. — Resemblance between the novelist and poet
in their tastes, studies, and habits of life, as illustrated by their
works — Both Scotchmen — Habitual residents in Edinburgh —
Poets — Antiquaries — German and Spanish scholars — Equal
in classical attainment — Deeply read in British history —
Lawyers — Fond of field sports — Of dogs — Acquainted with
most manly exercises — Lovers of military subjects — The
novelist apparently not a soldier.

" LETTER III. — The novelist is, like the poet, a man of
good society — His stories never betray forgetfulness of honorable principles, or ignorance of good manners — Spirited pictures of gentlemanly character — Colonel Mannering — Judicious treatment of elevated historical personages — The novelist
quotes and praises most contemporary poets, except the author
of Marmion — Instances in which the poet has appeared to

slight his own unacknowledged, but afterwards avowed productions.

" LETTER IV. — Comparison of the works themselves — All distinguished by good morals and good sense — The latter particularly shown in the management of character — Prose style — its general features — Plainness and facility — Grave banter — Manner of telling a short story — Negligence — Scotticisms — Great propriety and correctness occasionally, and sometimes unusual sweetness.

" LETTER V. — Dialogue in the novels and poems — Neat colloquial turns in the former, such as cannot be expected in romantic poetry — Happy adaptation of dialogue to character, whether merely natural, or artificially modified, as by profession, local habits, etc. — Faults of dialogue, as connected with character of speakers — Quaintness of language and thought — Bookish air in conversation — Historical personages alluding to their own celebrated acts and sayings — Unsuccessful attempts at broad vulgarity — Beauties of composition peculiar to the dialogue — Terseness and spirit — These qualities well displayed in quarrels ; but not in scenes of polished raillery — Eloquence.

" LETTER VI. — The poetry of the author of Marmion generally characterized — His habits of composition and turn of mind as a poet, compared with those of the novelist — Their descriptions simply conceived and composed, without abstruse and far-fetched circumstances or refined comments — Great advantage derived by both from accidental combinations of images, and the association of objects in the mind with persons, events, etc. — Distinctness and liveliness of effect in narrative and description — Narrative usually picturesque or dramatic, or both — Distinctness, etc., of effect, produced in various ways — Striking pictures of individuals — Their persons, dress, etc. — Descriptions sometimes too obviously picturesque — Subjects for painters — Effects of light frequently noticed and finely described — Both writers excel in grand and complicated scenes — Among detached and occasional ornaments, the similes particularly noticed — Their frequency and beauty — Similes and metaphors sometimes quaint, and pursued too far.

" LETTER VII. — Stories of the two writers compared — These are generally connected with true history, and have their

scene laid in a real place — Local peculiarities diligently attended to — Instances in which the novelist and poet have celebrated the same places — they frequently describe these as seen
by a traveller (the hero or some other principal personage) for
the first time — Dramatic mode of relating story — Soliloquies
— Some scenes degenerate into melodrame — Lyrical pieces
introduced sometimes too theatrically — Comparative unimpor-
tance of heroes — Various causes of this fault — Heroes re-
jected by ladies, and marrying others whom they had before
slighted — Personal struggle between a civilized and a barba-
rous hero — Characters resembling each other — Female portraits in general — Fathers and daughters — Characters in
Paul's Letters — Wycliffe and Risingham — Glossin and Hat-
teraick — Other characters compared — Long periods of time
abruptly passed over — Surprises, unexpected discoveries, etc.
— These sometimes too forced and artificial — Frequent recourse to the marvellous — Dreams well described — Living
persons mistaken for spectres — Deaths of Burley, Risingham,
and Rashleigh.

"LETTER VIII. — Comparison of particular passages —
Descriptions — Miscellaneous thoughts — Instances in which
the two writers have resorted to the same sources of information, and borrowed the same incidents, etc. — Same authors
quoted by both — the poet, like the novelist, fond of mentioning
his contemporaries, whether as private friends or as men pub-
licly distinguished — Author of Marmion never notices the
Author of Waverley (see Letter III.) — Both delight in frequently introducing an antiquated or fantastic dialect — Peculiarities of expression common to both writers — Conclusion."

I wish I had space for extracting copious specimens of
the felicity with which Mr. Adolphus works out these
various points of his problem. As it is, I must be contented with a narrow selection — and I shall take two or
three of the passages which seem to me to connect themselves most naturally with the main purpose of my own
compilation.

"A thorough knowledge and statesmanlike understanding of
the domestic history and politics of Britain at various and dis-

tant periods ; a familiar acquaintance with the manners and prevailing spirit of former generations, and with the characters and habits of their most distinguished men, are of themselves no cheap or common attainments ; and it is rare indeed to find them united with a strong original genius, and great brilliancy of imagination. We know, however, that the towering poet of Flodden Field is also the diligent editor of Swift and Dryden, of Lord Somers's Tracts, and of Sir Ralph Sadler's State Papers ; that in these and other parts of his literary career he has necessarily plunged deep into the study of British history, biography, and antiquities, and that the talent and activity which he brought to these researches have been warmly seconded by the zeal and liberality of those who possessed the amplest and rarest sources of information. ' The Muse found him,' as he himself said long ago, ' engaged in the pursuit of historical and traditional antiquities, and the excursions which he has made in her company have been of a nature which increases his attachment to his original study.' Are we then to suppose that another writer has combined the same powers of fancy with the same spirit of investigation, the same perseverance, and the same good fortune ? and shall we not rather believe, that the labor employed in the illustration of Dryden has helped to fertilize the invention which produced Montrose and Old Mortality ? . . .

" However it may militate against the supposition of his being a poet, I cannot suppress my opinion, that our novelist is a ' man of law.' He deals out the peculiar terms and phrases of that science (as practised in Scotland) with a freedom and confidence beyond the reach of any uninitiated person. If ever, in the progress of his narrative, a legal topic presents itself (which very frequently happens), he neither declines the subject, nor timidly slurs it over, but enters as largely and formally into all its technicalities, as if the case were actually ' before the fifteen.' The manners, humors, and professional *bavardage* of lawyers, are sketched with all the ease and familiarity which result from habitual observation. In fact, the subject of law, which is a stumbling-block to others, is to the present writer a spot of repose ; upon this theme he lounges and gossips, he is *discinctus et soleatus*, and, at times, almost forgets that when an author finds himself at home and perfectly at ease, he is in great danger of falling asleep. — If, then, my inferences are correct, the unknown writer who was just now proved to be an excellent poet, must also be pronounced a follower of the law : the combination is so unusual, at least on this side of the Tweed, that, as Juvenal says on a different occasion —

>   . . . 'bimembri
> Hoc monstrum puero, vel mirandis sub aratro
> Piscibus inventis, et fœtæ comparo mulsæ.'

Nature has indeed presented us with one such prodigy in the author of Marmion ; and it is probable, that in the author of Waverley, we only see the same specimen under a different aspect ; for, however sportive the goddess may be, she has too much wit and invention to wear out a frolic by many repetitions. . . .

"A striking characteristic of both writers is their ardent love of rural sports, and all manly and robust exercises. — But the importance given to the canine race in these works ought to be noted as a characteristic feature by itself. I have seen some drawings by a Swiss artist, who was called the Raphael of cats ; and either of the writers before us might, by a similar phrase, be called the Wilkie of dogs. Is it necessary to justify such a compliment by examples ? Call Yarrow, or Lufra, or poor Fangs, Colonel Mannering's Plato, Henry Morton's Elphin, or Hobbie Elliot's Kilbuck, or Wolfe of Avenel Castle : — see Fitz-James's hounds returning from the pursuit of the lost stag —

> 'Back limped with slow and crippled pace
> The sulky leaders of the chase ' —

or swimming after the boat which carries their Master —

> 'With heads erect and whimpering cry
> The hounds behind their passage ply.'

See Captain Clutterbuck's dog *quizzing* him when he missed a bird, or the scene of 'mutual explanation and remonstrance' between 'the venerable patriarchs old Pepper and Mustard,' and Henry Bertram's rough terrier Wasp. If these instances are not sufficient, turn to the English bloodhound assailing the young Buccleuch, —

> 'And hark ! and hark ! the deep-mouthed bark
> Comes nigher still and nigher ;

> Bursts on the path a dark blood-hound,
> His tawny muzzle tracked the ground,
>   And his red eye shot fire.
> Soon as the wildered child saw he,
> He flew at him right furiouslie. . . .
> I ween you would have seen with joy
> The bearing of the gallant boy. . . .
> So fierce he struck, the dog, afraid,
> At cautious distance hoarsely bayed,
>   But still in act to spring.'

Or Lord Ronald's deerhounds, in the haunted forest of Glenfinlas, —

> ' Within an hour return'd each hound ;
>   In rush'd the rousers of the deer ;
> They howl'd in melancholy sound,
>   Then closely couch beside the seer. . . .
> Sudden the hounds erect their ears,
>   And sudden cease their moaning howl ;
> Close press'd to Moy, they mark their fears
>   By shivering limbs and stifled growl.
> Untouch'd the harp began to ring,
>   As softly, slowly, oped the door,' etc.

Or look at Cedric the Saxon, in his antique hall, attended by his greyhounds and slowhounds, and the terriers which ' waited with impatience the arrival of the supper ; but, with the sagacious knowledge of physiognomy peculiar to their race, forbore to intrude upon the moody silence of their master.' To complete the picture, ' One grisly old wolf-dog alone, with the liberty of an indulged favorite, had planted himself close by the chair of state, and occasionally ventured to solicit notice by putting his large hairy head upon his master's knee, or pushing his nose into his hand. Even he was repelled by the stern command, " Down, Balder, down ! I am not in the humor for foolery." '

" Another animated sketch occurs in the way of simile : — ' The interview between Ratcliffe and Sharpitlaw had an aspect different from all these. They sate for five minutes silent, on opposite sides of a small table, and looked fixedly at each other, with a sharp, knowing, and alert cast of countenance, not unmingled with an inclination to laugh, and resembled, more than anything else, two dogs, who, preparing for a game at romps, are seen to couch down, and remain in that posture for a little time, watching each other's movements, and waiting which shall begin the game.'

"Let me point out a still more amusing study of canine life: 'While the Antiquary was in full declamation, Juno, who held him in awe, according to the remarkable instinct by which dogs instantly discover those who like or dislike them, had peeped several times into the room, and, encountering nothing very forbidding in his aspect, had at length presumed to introduce her full person, and finally, becoming bold by impunity, she actually ate up Mr. Oldbuck's toast, as, looking first at one, then at another of his audience, he repeated with self-complacence, —

> "'Weave the warp, and weave the woof.' —

You remember the passage in the Fatal Sisters, which, by the way, is not so fine as in the original — But, hey-day! my toast has vanished! I see which way — Ah, thou type of womankind, no wonder they take offence at thy generic appellation!" — (So saying, he shook his fist at Juno, who scoured out of the parlor.) '

"In short, throughout these works, wherever it is possible for a dog to contribute in any way to the effect of a scene, we find there the very dog that was required, in his proper place and attitude. In Branksome Hall, when the feast was over, —

> 'The stag-hounds, weary with the chase,
> Lay stretched upon the rushy floor,
> And urged, in dreams, the forest race
> From Teviot-stone to Eskdale-moor.'

The gentle Margaret, when she steals secretly from the castle,

> 'Pats the shaggy blood-hound
> As he rouses him up from his lair.'

When Waverley visits the Baron of Bradwardine, in his concealment at Janet Gellatley's, Ban and Buscar play their parts in every point with perfect discretion; and in the joyous company that assembles at Little Veolan, on the Baron's enlargement, these honest animals are found 'stuffed to the throat with food, in the liberality of Macwheeble's joy,' and 'snoring on the floor.' In the perilous adventure of Henry Bertram, at Portanferry gaol, the action would lose half its interest, without the by-play of little Wasp. At the funeral ceremony of Duncraggan (in The Lady of the Lake), a principal mourner is

> —— 'Stumah, who, the bier beside,
> His master's corpse with wonder eyed;
> Poor Stumah! whom his least halloo
> Could send like lightning o'er the dew.'

Ellen Douglas smiled (or did not smile)

> —— ' to see the stately drake,
> Lead forth his fleet upon the lake,
> While her vexed spaniel from the beach,
> Bayed at the prize beyond his reach.'

"I will close this growing catalogue of examples with one of the most elegant descriptions that ever sprang from a poet's fancy : —

> 'Delightful praise! like summer rose,
> That brighter in the dew-drop glows,
> The bashful maiden's cheek appeared,
> For Douglas spoke, and Malcolm heard.
> The flush of shame-faced joy to hide,
> The hounds, the hawk, her cares divide;
> The loved caresses of the maid
> The dogs with crouch and whimper paid;
> And, at her whistle, on her hand,
> The falcon took his favorite stand,
> Closed his dark wing, relaxed his eye,
> Nor, though unhooded, sought to fly.'

.   .   .   .

"Their passion for martial subjects, and their success in treating them, form a conspicuous point of resemblance between the novelist and poet. No writer has appeared in our age (and few have ever existed) who could vie with the author of Marmion in describing battles and marches, and all the terrible grandeur of war, except the author of Waverley. Nor is there any man of original genius and powerful inventive talent as conversant with the military character, and as well schooled in tactics, as the author of Waverley, except the author of Marmion. Both seem to exult in camps, and to warm at the approach of a soldier. In every warlike scene that awes and agitates, or dazzles and inspires, the poet triumphs; but where any effect is to be produced by dwelling on the minutiæ of military habits and discipline, or exhibiting the blended hues of individual humor and professional peculiarity, as they present themselves in the mess-room or the guard-room, every advantage is on the side of the novelist. I might illustrate this position by tracing all the gradations of character marked out in the novels, from the Baron of Bradwardine to Tom Halliday : but the examples are too well known to require enumeration, and too generally admired to stand in need of panegyric. Both writers, then, must have bestowed a greater attention on military subjects, and have mixed more frequently in the society of soldiers, than is usual with persons not educated to the profession of arms.

" It may be asked, why we should take for granted that the writer of these novels is not himself a member of the military profession ? The conjecture is a little improbable if we have been right in concluding that the minuteness and multiplicity of our author's legal details are the fruit of his own study and practice, although the same person may certainly, at different periods of life, put on the helmet and the wig, the gorget and the band ; attend courts and lie in trenches ; head a charge and lead a cause. I cannot help suspecting, however (it is with the greatest diffidence I venture the remark), that in those warlike recitals which so strongly interest the great body of readers, an army critic would discover several particulars that savor more of the amateur than of the practised campaigner. It is not from any technical improprieties (if such exist) that I derive this observation, but, on the contrary, from a too great minuteness and over-curious diligence, at times perceptible in the military details ; which, amidst a seeming fluency and familiarity, betray, I think, here and there, the lurking vestiges of labor and contrivance, like the marks of pickaxes in an artificial grotto. The accounts of operations in the field, if not more circumstantial than a professional author would have made them, are occasionally circumstantial on points which such an author would have thought it idle to dwell upon. A writer who derived his knowledge of war from experience would, no doubt, like the Author of Waverley, delight in shaping out imaginary manœuvres, or in filling up the traditional outline of those martial enterprises and conflicts, which have found a place in history ; perhaps, too, he would dwell on these parts of his narrative a little longer than was strictly necessary ; but in describing (for example) the advance of a party of soldiers,

threatened by an ambuscade, he would scarcely think it worth
while to relate at large that the captain ' re-formed his line of
march, commanded his soldiers to unsling their firelocks and
fix their bayonets, and formed an advanced and rear-guard,
each consisting of a non-commissioned officer and two privates,
who received strict orders to keep an alert look-out: ' or that
when the enemy appeared, ' he ordered the rear-guard to join
the centre, and both to close up to the advance, doubling his
files, so as to occupy with his column the whole practicable part
of the road,' etc. Again, in representing a defeated corps retiring and pressed by the enemy, he would probably never
think of recording (as our novelist does in his incomparable
narrative of the engagement at Drumclog) that the commanding officer gave such directions as these : · Let Allan form the
regiment, and do you two retreat up the hill in two bodies,
each halting alternately as the other falls back. I 'll keep the
rogues in check with the rear-guard, making a stand and facing
from time to time.' I do not offer these observations for the
purpose of depreciating a series of military pictures, which
have never been surpassed in richness, animation, and distinctness ; I will own, too, that such details as I have pointed out
are the fittest that could be selected for the generality of novel-
readers ; I merely contend, that a writer practically acquainted
with war would either have passed over these circumstances as
too common to require particular mention, or if he had thought
it necessary to enlarge upon these, would have dwelt with pro-
portionate minuteness on incidents of a less ordinary kind,
which the recollections of a soldier would have readily supplied,
and his imagination would have rested on with complacency.
He would, in short, have left as little undone for the military,
as the present author has for the legal part of his narratives.
But the most ingenious writer who attempts to discourse with
technical familiarity on arts or pursuits with which he is not
habitually conversant, will too surely fall into a superfluous
particularity on common and trivial points, proportioned to his
deficiency in those nicer details which imply practical knowledge. . . .

> " ' The prince of darkness is a gentleman.' [1]

" Another point of resemblance between the author of Wa-

[1] *King Lear*, Act III. Scene 4.

verley and him of Flodden Field is, that both are unquestionably men of good society. Of the anonymous writer I infer
this from his works ; of the poet it is unnecessary to deduce
such a character from his writings, because they are not anonymous. I am the more inclined to dwell upon this merit in the
novelist, on account of its rarity ; for among the whole multitude of authors, well or ill educated, who devote themselves to
poetry or to narrative or dramatic fiction, how few there are
who give any proof in their works, of the refined taste, the instinctive sense of propriety, the clear spirit of honor, nay, of
the familiar acquaintance with conventional forms of good-
breeding, which are essential to the character of a gentleman !
Even of the small number who, in a certain degree, possess
these qualifications, how rarely do we find one who can so conduct his fable, and so order his dialogue throughout, that nothing shall be found either repugnant to honorable feelings, or
inconsistent with polished manners ! How constantly, even in
the best works of fiction, are we disgusted with such offences
against all generous principle, as the reading of letters by those
for whom they were not intended ; taking advantage of acci-
dents to overhear private conversation ; revealing what in honor
should have remained secret ; plotting against men as enemies,
and at the same time making use of their services ; dishonest
practices on the passions or sensibilities of women by their admirers ; falsehoods, not always indirect ; and an endless variety of low artifices, which appear to be thought quite legitimate
if carried on through subordinate agents. And all these knav-
eries are assigned to characters which the reader is expected to
honor with his sympathy, or at least to receive into favor before
the story concludes.

  "The sins against propriety in manners are as frequent and
as glaring. I do not speak of the hoyden vivacity, harlot tenderness, and dancing-school affability, with which vulgar novel-
writers always deck out their countesses and *principessas*,
chevaliers, dukes, and marquises ; but it would be easy to produce, from authors of a better class, abundant instances of
bookish and laborious pleasantry, of pert and insipid gossip or
mere slang, the wrecks, perhaps, of an obsolete fashionable
dialect, set down as the brilliant conversation of a witty and
elegant society ; incredible outrages on the common decorum

of life, represented as traits of eccentric humor; familiar raillery pushed to downright rudeness; affectation or ill-breeding
over-colored so as to become insupportable insolence; extravagant rants on the most delicate topics indulged in before all
the world; expressions freely interchanged between gentlemen,
which, by the customs of that class, are neither used nor toler-
ated; and quarrels carried on most bombastically and abu-
sively, even to mortal defiance, without a thought bestowed
upon the numbers, sex, nerves, or discretion of the bystanders.

"You will perceive, that in recapitulating the offences of
other writers, I have pronounced an indirect eulogium on the
Author of Waverley. No man, I think, has a clearer view of
what is just and honorable in principle and conduct, or possesses in a higher degree that elegant taste, and that chivalrous
generosity of feeling, which, united with exact judgment, give
an author the power of comprehending and expressing, not
merely the right and fit, but the graceful and exalted in human
action. As an illustration of these remarks, a somewhat
homely one perhaps, let me call to your recollection the incident, so wild and extravagant in itself, of Sir Piercie Shafton's
elopement with the miller's daughter. In the address and
feeling with which the author has displayed the high-minded
delicacy of Queen Elizabeth's courtier to the unguarded village
nymph, in his brief reflections arising out of this part of the
narrative, and indeed in his whole conception and management
of the adventure, I do not know whether the moralist or the
gentleman is most to be admired: it is impossible to praise too
warmly either the sound taste, or the virtuous sentiment which
have imparted so much grace and interest to such a hazardous
episode.

"It may, I think, be generally affirmed, on a review of all
the six-and-thirty volumes, in which this author has related the
adventures of some twenty or more heroes and heroines (without counting second-rate personages), that there is not an unhandsome action or degrading sentiment recorded of any person who is recommended to the full esteem of the reader. To
be blameless on this head is one of the strongest proofs a writer
can give of honorable principles implanted by education and
refreshed by good society.

"The correctness in morals is scarcely more remarkable

than the refinement and propriety in manners, by which these novels are distinguished. Where the character of a gentleman is introduced, we generally find it supported without affectation or constraint, and often with so much truth, animation, and dignity, that we forget ourselves into a longing to behold and converse with the accomplished creature of imagination. It is true that the volatile and elegant man of wit and pleasure, and the gracefully fantastic *petite-maîtresse*, are a species of character scarcely ever attempted, and even the few sketches we meet with in this style are not worthy of so great a master. But the aristocratic country gentleman, the ancient lady of quality, the gallant cavalier, the punctilious young soldier, and the jocund veteran, whose high mind is mellowed, not subdued by years, are drawn with matchless vigor, grace, and refinement. There is, in all these creations, a spirit of gentility, not merely of that negative kind which avoids giving offence, but of a strong, commanding, and pervading quality, blending unimpaired with the richest humor and wildest eccentricity, and communicating an interest and an air of originality to characters which, without it, would be wearisome and insipid, or would fade into commonplace. In Waverley, for example, if it were not for this powerful charm, the severe but warmhearted Major Melville and the generous Colonel Talbot would become mere ordinary machines for carrying on the plot, and Sir Everard, the hero of an episode that might be coveted by Mackenzie, would encounter the frowns of every impatient reader, for unprofitably retarding the story at its outset.

" But without dwelling on minor instances, I will refer you at once to the character of Colonel Mannering, as one of the most striking representations I am acquainted with, of a gentleman in feelings and in manners, in habits, taste, predilections; nay, if the expression may be ventured, a gentleman even in prejudices, passions, and caprices. Had it been less than all I have described; had any refinement, any nicety of touch, been wanting, the whole portrait must have been coarse, common, and repulsive, hardly distinguishable from the moody father and domineering chieftain of every hackneyed romance-writer. But it was no vulgar hand that drew the lineaments of Colonel Mannering : no ordinary mind could have conceived that exquisite combination of sternness and sensibility, injurious haughtiness and chivalrous courtesy; the promptitude, decision, and imperious spirit of a military disciplinarian; the romantic caprices of an untamable enthusiast; generosity impatient of limit or impediment; pride scourged but not subdued by remorse; and a cherished philosophical severity, maintaining ineffectual conflicts with native tenderness and constitutional irritability. Supposing that it had entered into the thoughts of an inferior writer to describe a temper of mind at once impetuous, kind, arrogant, affectionate, stern, sensitive, deliberate, fanciful; supposing even that he had had the skill to combine these different qualities harmoniously and naturally, — yet how could he have attained the Shakespearean felicity of those delicate and unambitious touches, by which this author shapes and chisels out individual character from general nature, and imparts a distinct personality to the creature of his invention? Such are (for example) the slight tinge of superstition, contracted by the romantic young Astrologer in his adventure at Ellangowan, not wholly effaced in maturer life, and extending itself by contagion to the mind of his daughter," etc., etc.

It would have gratified Mr. Adolphus could he have known when he penned these pages a circumstance which the reperusal of them brings to my memory. When Guy Mannering was first published, the Ettrick Shepherd said to Professor Wilson, "I have done wi' doubts now. Colonel Mannering is just Walter Scott, painted by himself." This was repeated to James Ballantyne, and he again mentioned it to Scott — who smiled in approbation of the Shepherd's shrewdness, and often afterwards, when the printer expressed an opinion in which he could not concur, would cut him short with, "James — James — you 'll find that Colonel Mannering has laid down the law on this point." — I resume my extract: —

"All the productions I am acquainted with, both of the poet and of the prose writer, recommend themselves by a native piety and goodness, not generally predominant in modern works of imagination; and which, where they do appear, are too often disfigured by eccentricity, pretension, or bad taste. In the works before us there is a constant tendency to promote the desire of excellence in ourselves, and the love of it in our neighbors, by making us think honorably of our general nature. Whatever kindly or charitable affection, whatever principle of manly and honest ambition exists within us, is roused and stimulated by the perusal of these writings ; our passions are won to the cause of justice, purity, and self-denial ; and the old, indissoluble ties that bind us to country, kindred, and birthplace, appear to strengthen as we read, and brace themselves more firmly about the heart and imagination. Both writers, although peculiarly happy in their conception of all chivalrous and romantic excellencies, are still more distinguished by their deep and true feeling and expressive delineation of the graces and virtues proper to domestic life. The gallant, elevated, and punctilious character which a Frenchman contemplates in speaking of ' *un honnête homme*,' is singularly combined, in these authors, with the genial, homely good qualities that win from a Caledonian the exclamation of ' honest man !' But the crown of their merits, as virtuous and moral writers, is the manly and exemplary spirit with which, upon all seasonable occasions, they pay honor and homage to religion, ascribing to it its just preëminence among the causes of human happiness, and dwelling on it as the only certain source of pure and elevated thoughts, and upright, benevolent, and magnanimous actions.

" This, then, is common to the books of both writers, — that they furnish a direct and distinguished contrast to the atrabilious gloom of some modern works of genius, and the wanton, but not artless levity of others. They yield a memorable, I trust an immortal, accession to the evidences of a truth not always fashionable in literature, that the mind of man may put forth all its bold luxuriance of original thought, strong feeling, and vivid imagination, without being loosed from any sacred and social bond, or pruned of any legitimate affection ; and that the Muse is indeed a ' heavenly goddess,' and not a graceless, lawless runagate,

' ἀφρήτωρ, ἀθέμιστος, ἀνέστιος.'

" Good sense, the sure foundation of excellence in all the arts, is another leading characteristic of these productions.

Assuming the author of Waverley and the author of Marmion to be the same person, it would be difficult in our times to find a second equally free from affectation, prejudice, and every other distortion or depravity of judgment, whether arising from ignorance, weakness, or corruption of morals. It is astonishing that so voluminous and successful a writer should so seldom be betrayed into any of those 'fantastic tricks' which, in such a man, make 'the angels weep,' and (è converso) the critics laugh. He adopts no fashionable cant, colloquial, philosophical, or literary ; he takes no delight in being unintelligible ; he does not amuse himself by throwing out those fine sentimental and metaphysical threads which float upon the air, and tease and tickle the passengers, but present no palpable substance to their grasp ; he aims at no beauties that 'scorn the eye of vulgar light ; ' he is no dealer in paradoxes ; no affecter of new doctrines in taste or morals ; he has no eccentric sympathies or antipathies ; no maudlin philanthropy, or impertinent cynicism ; no nondescript hobby-horse ; and with all his matchless energy and originality of mind, he is content to admire popular books, and enjoy popular pleasures ; to cherish those opinions which experience has sanctioned ; to reverence those institutions which antiquity has hallowed ; and to enjoy, admire, cherish, and reverence all these with the same plainness, simplicity, and sincerity as our ancestors did of old.

. . . .

" I cannot help dwelling for a moment on the great similarity of manner apparent in the female portraits of the two writers. The pictures of their heroines are executed with a peculiar fineness, delicacy, and minuteness of touch, and with a care at times almost amounting to timidity, so that they generally appear more highly finished, but less boldly and strikingly thrown out, than the figures with which they are surrounded. Their elegance and purity are always admirable, and are happily combined, in most instances, with unaffected ease and natural spirit. Strong practical sense is their most prevailing characteristic, unaccompanied by any repulsive air of selfishness, pedantry, or unfeminine harshness. Few writers have ever evinced, in so strong a degree as the authors of Marmion and Waverley, that manly regard, and dignified but enthusiastic devotion, which may be expressed by the term loyalty

to the fair sex, the honorable attribute of chivalrous and romantic ages. If they touch on the faults of womankind, their
satire is playful, not contemptuous; and their acquaintance
with female manners, graces, and foibles, is apparently drawn,
not from libertine experience, but from the guileless familiarity
of domestic life.

" Of all human ties and connections there is none so frequently brought in view, or adorned with so many touches of
the most affecting eloquence by both these writers, as the pure
and tender relation of father and daughter. Douglas and
Ellen in The Lady of the Lake will immediately occur to you
as a distinguished example. Their mutual affection and solicitude; their pride in each other's excellencies; the parent's
regret of the obscurity to which fate has doomed his child;
and the daughter's self-devotion to her father's welfare and
safety, constitute the highest interest of the poem, and that
which is most uniformly sustained; nor does this or any other
romance of the same author contain a finer stroke of passion
than the overboiling of Douglas's wrath, when, mixed as a
stranger with the crowd at Stirling, he sees his daughter's
favorite Lufra chastised by the royal huntsman.

" In Rokeby, the filial attachment and duteous anxieties of
Matilda form the leading feature of her character, and the
chief source of her distresses. The intercourse between King
Arthur and his daughter Gyneth, in The Bridal of Triermain,
is neither long, nor altogether amicable; but the monarch's
feelings on first beholding that beautiful ' slip of wilderness,'
and his manner of receiving her before the queen and court,
are too forcibly and naturally described to be omitted in this
enumeration.

" Of all the novels, there are at most but two or three in
which a fond father and affectionate daughter may not be
pointed out among the principal characters, and in which the
main interest of many scenes does not arise out of that paternal and filial relation. What a beautiful display of natural
feeling, under every turn of circumstances that can render the
situations of child and parent agonizing or delightful, runs
through the history of David Deans and his two daughters!
How affecting is the tale of Leicester's unhappy Countess,
after we have seen her forsaken father consuming away with

moody sorrow in his joyless manor-house! How exquisite are the grouping and contrast of Isaac, the kind but sordid Jew, and his heroic Rebecca, of the buckram Baron of Bradwardine and the sensitive Rose, the reserved but ardent Mannering, and the flighty coquette Julia! In The Antiquary, and Bride of Lammermoor, anxiety is raised to the most painful height by the spectacle of father and daughter exposed together to imminent and frightful peril. The heroines in Rob Roy and The Black Dwarf are duteous and devoted daughters, the one of an unfortunate, the other of an unworthy parent. In the whole story of Kenilworth there is nothing that more strongly indicates a master-hand than the paternal carefulness and apprehensions of the churl Foster; and among the most striking scenes in A Legend of Montrose is that in which Sir Duncan Campbell is attracted by an obscure yearning of the heart toward his unknown child, the supposed orphan of Darlinvarach."

I must not attempt to follow out Mr. Adolphus in his most ingenious tracings of petty coincidences in thought, and, above all, in expression, between the poet of Marmion and the novelist of Waverley. His apology for the minuteness of his detail in that part of his work is, however, too graceful to be omitted: "It cannot, I think, appear frivolous or irrelevant, in the inquiry we are pursuing, to dwell on these minute coincidences. Unimportant indeed they are if looked upon as subjects of direct criticism; but considered with reference to our present purpose, they resemble those light substances which, floating on the trackless sea, discover the true setting of some mighty current: they are the buoyant driftwood which betrays the hidden communication of two great poetic oceans."

I conclude with re-quoting a fragment from one of the quaint tracts of Sir Thomas Urquhart. The following is the epigraph of Mr. Adolphus's 5th Letter:—

"O with how great liveliness did he represent the conditions of all manner of men! From the overweening monarch to the

peevish swaine, through all intermediate degrees of the superficial courtier or proud warrior, dissembling churchman, doting
old man, cozening lawyer, lying traveler, covetous merchant,
rude seaman, pedantick scolar, the amorous shepheard, envious
artisan, vain-glorious master, and tricky servant; —— He had
all the jeers, squibs, flouts, buls, quips, taunts, whims, jests,
clinches, gybes, mokes, jerks, with all the several kinds of
equivocations and other sophistical captions, that could properly
be adapted to the person by whose representation he intended
to inveagle the company into a fit of mirth!"

I have it not in my power to produce the letter in
which Scott conveyed to Heber his opinion of this work.
I know, however, that it ended with a request that he
should present Mr. Adolphus with his thanks for the
handsome terms in which his poetical efforts had been
spoken of throughout, and request him, in the name of
the *author of Marmion*, not to revisit Scotland without
reserving a day for Abbotsford; and the *Eidolon* of the
author of *Waverley* was made, a few months afterwards,
to speak as follows in the Introduction to The Fortunes
of Nigel: "These letters to the member for the University of Oxford show the wit, genius, and delicacy of
the author, which I heartily wish to see engaged on a
subject of more importance; and show, besides, that the
preservation of my character of *incognito* has engaged
early talent in the discussion of a curious question of
evidence. But a cause, however ingeniously pleaded, is
not therefore gained. You may remember the neatly
wrought chain of circumstantial evidence, so artificially
brought forward to prove Sir Philip Francis's title to the
Letters of Junius, seemed at first irrefragable; yet the
influence of the reasoning has passed away, and Junius,
in the general opinion, is as much unknown as ever.
But on this subject I will not be soothed or provoked
into saying one word more. To say who I am not, would
be one step towards saying who I am; and as I desire
not, any more than a certain Justice of Peace mentioned

by Shenstone, the noise or report such things make in the world, I shall continue to be silent on a subject which, in my opinion, is very undeserving the noise that has been made about it, and still more unworthy of the serious employment of such ingenuity as has been displayed by the young letter-writer."

CHAPTER LIV

1821

WHEN Sir Walter returned from London, he brought
with him the detailed plans of Mr. Atkinson for the
completion of his house at Abbotsford; which, however,
did not extend to the gateway or the beautiful screen
between the court and the garden — for these graceful
parts of the general design were conceptions of his own,
reduced to shape by the skill of the Messrs. Smith of
Darnick. It would not, indeed, be easy for me to appor-
tion rightly the constituent members of the whole edifice;
— throughout there were numberless consultations with
Mr. Blore, Mr. Terry, and Mr. Skene, as well as with
Mr. Atkinson — and the actual builders placed considerable inventive talents, as well as admirable workmanship,
at the service of their friendly employer. Every preparation was now made by them, and the foundations might
have been set about without farther delay; but he was

very reluctant to authorize the demolition of the rustic porch of the old cottage, with its luxuriant overgrowth of roses and jessamines; and, in short, could not make up his mind to sign the death-warrant of this favorite bower until winter had robbed it of its beauties. He then made an excursion from Edinburgh, on purpose to be present at its downfall — saved as many of the creepers as seemed likely to survive removal, and planted them with his own hands about a somewhat similar porch, erected expressly for their reception, at his daughter Sophia's little cottage of Chiefswood.

There my wife and I spent this summer and autumn of 1821 — the first of several seasons, which will ever dwell on my memory as the happiest of my life. We were near enough Abbotsford to partake as often as we liked of its brilliant society; yet could do so without being exposed to the worry and exhaustion of spirit which the daily reception of newcomers entailed upon all the family except Sir Walter himself. But, in truth, even he was not always proof against the annoyances connected with such a style of open-house-keeping. Even his temper sunk sometimes under the solemn applauses of learned dulness, the vapid raptures of painted and periwigged dowagers, the horse-leech avidity with which underbred foreigners urged their questions, and the pompous simpers of condescending magnates. When sore beset at home in this way, he would every now and then discover that he had some very particular business to attend to on an outlying part of his estate, and craving the indulgence of his guests overnight, appear at the cabin in the glen before its inhabitants were astir in the morning. The clatter of Sibyl Grey's hoofs, the yelping of Mustard and Spice, and his own joyous shout of *reveillée* under our windows, were the signal that he had burst his toils, and meant for that day to "take his ease in his inn." On descending, he was to be found seated with all his dogs and ours about him, under a spreading

ash that overshadowed half the bank between the cottage
and the brook, pointing the edge of his woodman's axe
for himself, and listening to Tom Purdie's lecture touching the plantation that most needed thinning. After
breakfast, he would take possession of a dressing-room
upstairs, and write a chapter of The Pirate; and then,
having made up and despatched his packet for Mr. Ballantyne, away to join Purdie wherever the foresters were
at work — and sometimes to labor among them as strenuously as John Swanston himself — until it was time
either to rejoin his own party at Abbotsford, or the quiet
circle of the cottage. — When his guests were few and
friendly, he often made them come over and meet him
at Chiefswood in a body towards evening; [1] and surely
he never appeared to more amiable advantage than when
helping his young people with their little arrangements
upon such occasions. He was ready with all sorts of
devices to supply the wants of a narrow establishment;
he used to delight particularly in sinking the wine in
a well under the *brae* ere he went out, and hauling up
the basket just before dinner was announced — this primitive process being, he said, what he had always practised when a young housekeeper; and in his opinion far
superior in its results to any application of ice; and, in
the same spirit, whenever the weather was sufficiently
genial, he voted for dining out of doors altogether, which
at once got rid of the inconvenience of very small

[1] [Among the friendly visitors at this time was Mr. Charles Young, who
brought with him his son. The latter in his diary sketches, not without
some vivid touches, the days spent at Abbotsford. One slight incident
connected with Scott's greeting of his guests may be noted. On hearing
the lad's Christian name, he exclaimed with emphasis, " Why, whom is he
called after ? " On being told that the name was in memory of the boy's
mother, Julia Anne, he replied, " Well, it is a capital name for a novel, I
must say ; " a remark which Julian Young naturally recalled when *Peveril*
was published. The Youngs also visited Chiefswood, and the youthful
diarist was much impressed by Lockhart's strikingly handsome face, while
" his deference and attention to his father-in-law were delightful to witness." — See *Memoir of Charles Mayne Young*, pp. 88–96.]

rooms, and made it natural and easy for the gentlemen to help the ladies, so that the paucity of servants went for nothing. Mr. Rose used to amuse himself with likening the scene and the party to the closing act of one of those little French dramas, where "Monsieur le Comte" and "Madame la Comtesse" appear feasting at a village bridal under the trees; but in truth, our "M. le Comte" was only trying to live over again for a few simple hours his own old life of Lasswade.

When circumstances permitted, he usually spent one evening at least in the week at our little cottage; and almost as frequently he did the like with the Fergusons, to whose table he could bring chance visitors, when he pleased, with equal freedom as to his daughter's. Indeed it seemed to be much a matter of chance, any fine day when there had been no alarming invasion of the Southron, whether the three families (which, in fact, made but one) should dine at Abbotsford, Huntly Burn, or at Chiefswood; and at none of them was the party considered quite complete, unless it included also Mr. Laidlaw. Death has laid a heavy hand upon that circle — as happy a circle I believe as ever met. Bright eyes now closed in dust, gay voices forever silenced, seem to haunt me as I write. With three exceptions, they are all gone. Even since the last of these volumes [1] was finished, she whom I may now sadly record as, next to Sir Walter himself, the chief ornament and delight at all those simple meetings — she to whose love I owed my own place in them — Scott's eldest daughter, the one of all his children who in countenance, mind, and manners, most resembled himself, and who indeed was as like him in all things as a gentle innocent woman can ever be to a great man deeply tried and skilled in the struggles and perplexities of active life — she, too, is no more. And in the very hour that saw her laid in her grave, the only

[1] The 4th vol. of the original edition was published in July — the 5th (of which this was the sixth chapter) in October, 1837.

other female survivor, her dearest friend Margaret Ferguson, breathed her last also. — But enough — and more than I intended — I must resume the story of Abbotsford.

During several weeks of that delightful summer, Scott had under his roof Mr. William Erskine and two of his daughters; this being, I believe, their first visit to Tweedside since the death of Mrs. Erskine in September, 1819. He had probably made a point of having his friend with him at this particular time, because he was desirous of having the benefit of his advice and corrections from day to day as he advanced in the composition of The Pirate — with the localities of which romance the Sheriff of Orkney and Zetland was of course thoroughly familiar. At all events, the constant and eager delight with which Erskine watched the progress of the tale has left a deep impression on my memory; and indeed I heard so many of its chapters first read from the MS. by him, that I can never open the book now without thinking I hear his voice. Sir Walter used to give him at breakfast the pages he had written that morning; and very commonly, while he was again at work in his study, Erskine would walk over to Chiefswood, that he might have the pleasure of reading them aloud to my wife and me under our favorite tree, before the packet had to be sealed up for the printer, or rather for the transcriber in Edinburgh. I cannot paint the delight and the pride with which he acquitted himself on such occasions. The little artifice of his manner was merely superficial, and was wholly forgotten as tender affection and admiration, fresh as the impulses of childhood, glistened in his eye, and trembled in his voice.

This reminds me that I have not yet attempted any sketch of the person and manners of Scott's most intimate friend. Their case was no contradiction to the old saying, that the most attached comrades are often very unlike each other in character and temperament. The mere physical contrast was as strong as could well be, and this is not unworthy of notice here; for Erskine was, I think, the only man in whose society Scott took great pleasure, during the more vigorous part of his life, that had neither constitution nor inclination for any of the rough bodily exercises in which he himself delighted. The Counsellor (as Scott always called him) was a little man of feeble make, who seemed unhappy when his pony got beyond a foot-pace, and had never, I should suppose, addicted himself to any out-of-doors sport whatever. He would, I fancy, have as soon thought of slaying his own mutton as of handling a fowling-piece: he used to shudder when he saw a party equipped for coursing, as if murder were in the wind; but the cool meditative angler was in his eyes the abomination of abominations. His small elegant features, hectic cheek, and soft hazel eyes, were the index of the quick sensitive gentle spirit within. He had the warm heart of a woman, her generous enthusiasm, and some of her weaknesses. A beautiful landscape, or a fine strain of music, would send the tears rolling down his cheek; and though capable, I have no doubt, of exhibiting, had his duty called him to do so, the highest spirit of a hero or a martyr, he had very little command over his nerves amidst circumstances such as men of ordinary mould (to say nothing of iron fabrics like Scott's) regard with indifference. He would dismount to lead his horse down what his friend hardly perceived to be a descent at all; grew pale at a precipice; and, unlike the White Lady of Avenel, would go a long way round for a bridge.

Erskine had as yet been rather unfortunate in his professional career, and thought a sheriffship by no means the kind of advancement due to his merits, and which his connections might naturally have secured for him. These circumstances had at the time when I first observed him tinged his demeanor; he had come to intermingle a certain wayward snappishness now and then

with his forensic exhibitions, and in private seemed inclined (though altogether incapable of abandoning the
Tory party) to say bitter things of people in high places;
but with these exceptions, never was benevolence towards
all the human race more lively and overflowing than his
evidently was, even when he considered himself as one
who had reason to complain of his luck in the world.
Now, however, these little asperities had disappeared;
one great real grief had cast its shadow over him, and
submissive to the chastisement of heaven, he had no
longer any thoughts for the petty misusage of mankind.
Scott's apprehension was, that his ambition was extinguished with his resentment; and he was now using every
endeavor, in connection with their common friend the
Lord Advocate Rae, to procure for Erskine that long-
coveted seat on the bench, about which the subdued
widower himself had ceased to occupy his mind. By and
by these views were realized to Scott's high satisfaction,
and for a brief season with the happiest effect on Erskine's own spirits; — but I shall not anticipate the
sequel.

Meanwhile he shrunk from the collisions of general
society in Edinburgh, and lived almost exclusively in his
own little circle of intimates. His conversation, though
somewhat precise and finical on the first impression, was
rich in knowledge. His literary ambition, active and
aspiring at the outset, had long before this time merged
in his profound veneration for Scott; but he still read
a great deal, and did so as much I believe with a view
to assisting Scott by hints and suggestions, as for his
own amusement. He had much of his friend's tact in
extracting the picturesque from old, and, generally
speaking, dull books; and in bringing out his stores he
often showed a great deal of quaint humor and sly wit.

Scott, on his side, respected, trusted, and loved him,
much as an affectionate husband does the wife who gave
him her heart in youth, and thinks his thoughts rather

than her own in the evening of life; he soothed, cheered, and sustained Erskine habitually. I do not believe a more entire and perfect confidence ever subsisted than theirs was and always had been in each other; and to one who had duly observed the creeping jealousies of human nature, it might perhaps seem doubtful on which side the balance of real nobility of heart and character, as displayed in their connection at the time of which I am speaking, ought to be cast.

Among the common friends of their young days, of whom they both delighted to speak — and always spoke with warm and equal affection — was the sister of their friend Cranstoun, the confidant of Scott's first unfortunate love, whom neither had now seen for a period of more than twenty years. This lady had undergone domestic afflictions more than sufficient to have crushed almost any spirit but her own. Her husband, the Count Purgstall, had died some years before this time, leaving her an only son, a youth of the most amiable disposition, and possessing abilities which, had he lived to develop them, must have secured for him a high station in the annals of genius. This hope of her eyes, the last heir of an illustrious lineage, followed his father to the tomb in the nineteenth year of his age. The desolate Countess was urged by her family in Scotland to return, after this bereavement, to her native country; but she had vowed to her son on his deathbed, that one day her dust should be mingled with his; and no argument could induce her to depart from the resolution of remaining in solitary Styria. By her desire, a valued friend of the house of Purgstall, who had been born and bred up on their estates, the celebrated Orientalist, Joseph von Hammer, compiled a little memoir of The Two Last Counts of Purgstall, which he put forth, in January, 1821, under the title of Denkmahl, or Monument; and of this work the Countess sent a copy to Sir Walter (with whom her correspondence had been during several years suspended), by the hands of her eldest brother, Mr. Henry Cranstoun, who had been visiting her in Styria, and who at this time occupied a villa within a few miles of Abbotsford. Scott's letter of acknowledgment never reached her; and indeed I doubt if it was ever despatched. He appears to have meditated a set of consolatory verses for its conclusion, and the Muse not answering his call at the moment, I suspect he had allowed the sheet, which I now transcribe, to fall aside and be lost sight of among his multifarious masses of MS.

TO THE COUNTESS PURGSTALL, ETC., ETC.

MY DEAR AND MUCH-VALUED FRIEND, — You cannot imagine how much I was interested and affected by receiving your token of your kind recollection, after the interval of so many years. Your brother Henry breakfasted with me yesterday, and gave me the letter and the book, which served me as a matter of much melancholy reflection for many hours.

Hardly anything makes the mind recoil so much upon itself, as the being suddenly and strongly recalled to times long past, and that by the voice of one whom we have so much loved and respected. Do not think I have ever forgotten you, or the many happy days I passed in Frederick Street, in society which fate has separated so far, and for so many years.

The little volume was particularly acceptable to me, as it acquainted me with many circumstances, of which distance and imperfect communication had either left me entirely ignorant, or had transmitted only inaccurate information.

Alas, my dear friend, what can the utmost efforts of friendship offer you, beyond the sympathy which, however sincere, must sound like an empty compliment in the ear of affliction? God knows with what willingness I would undertake anything which might afford you the melancholy consolation of knowing how much your old and early friend interests himself in the sad event which has so deeply wounded your peace of mind. The verses, therefore, which conclude this letter, must not be weighed according to their intrinsic value, for the more inadequate they are to express the feelings they would fain convey, the more they show the author's anxious wish to do what may be grateful to you.

In truth, I have long given up poetry. I have had my day with the public; and being no great believer in poetical immortality, I was very well pleased to rise a winner, without continuing the game till I was beggared of any credit I had acquired. Besides, I felt the prudence of giving way before the more forcible and powerful genius of Byron. If I were either greedy, or jealous of poetical fame — and both are strangers to my nature — I might comfort myself with the thought, that I would hesitate to strip myself to the contest so fearlessly as Byron does; or to command the wonder and terror of the public, by exhibiting, in my own person, the sublime attitude of the dying gladiator. But with the old frankness of twenty years since, I will fairly own, that this same delicacy of mine may arise more from conscious want of vigor and inferiority, than from a delicate dislike to the nature of the conflict. At any rate, there is a time for everything, and without swearing oaths to it, I think my time for poetry has gone by.

My health suffered horridly last year, I think from over-labor and excitation; and though it is now apparently restored to its usual tone, yet during the long and painful disorder (spasms in the stomach) and the frightful process of cure, by a prolonged use of calomel, I learned that my frame was made of flesh, and not of iron — a conviction which I will long keep in remembrance, and avoid any occupation so laborious and agitating as poetry must be, to be worth anything.

In this humor I often think of passing a few weeks on the Continent — a summer vacation if I can — and of

course my attraction to Gratz would be very strong. I
fear this is the only chance of our meeting in this world
— we, who once saw each other daily! for I understand
from George and Henry that there is little chance of
your coming here. And when I look around me, and
consider how many changes you would see in feature,
form, and fashion, amongst all you knew and loved; and
how much, no sudden squall, or violent tempest, but the
slow and gradual progress of life's long voyage, has sev-
ered all the gallant fellowships whom you left spreading
their sails to the morning breeze, I really am not sure
that you would have much pleasure.

The gay and wild romance of life is over with all of us.
The real, dull, and stern history of humanity has made a
far greater progress over our heads; and age, dark and
unlovely, has laid his crutch over the stoutest fellow's
shoulders. One thing your old society may boast, that
they have all run their course with honor, and almost all
with distinction; and the brother suppers of Frederick
Street have certainly made a very considerable figure in
the world, as was to be expected from her talents under
whose auspices they were assembled.

One of the most pleasant sights which you would see
in Scotland, as it now stands, would be your brother
George in possession of the most beautiful and romantic
place in Clydesdale — Corehouse. I have promised often
to go out with him, and assist him with my deep experience as a planter and landscape gardener. I promise you
my oaks will outlast my laurels; and I pique myself more
upon my compositions for manure than on any other compositions whatsoever to which I was ever accessary. But
so much does business of one sort or other engage us
both, that we never have been able to fix a time which
suited us both; and with the utmost wish to make out the
party, perhaps we never may.

This is a melancholy letter, but it is chiefly so from
the sad tone of yours — who have had such real disasters

to lament — while mine is only the humorous sadness, which a retrospect on human life is sure to produce on the most prosperous. For my own course of life, I have only to be ashamed of its prosperity, and afraid of its termination; for I have little reason, arguing on the doctrine of chances, to hope that the same good fortune will attend me forever. I have had an affectionate and promising family, many friends, few unfriends, and, I think, no enemies — and more of fame and fortune than mere literature ever procured for a man before.

I dwell among my own people, and have many whose happiness is dependent on me, and which I study to the best of my power. I trust my temper, which you know is by nature good and easy, has not been spoiled by flattery or prosperity; and therefore I have escaped entirely that irritability of disposition which I think is planted, like the slave in the poet's chariot, to prevent his enjoying his triumph.

Should things, therefore, change with me — and in these times, or indeed in any times, such change is to be apprehended — I trust I shall be able to surrender these adventitious advantages, as I would my upper dress, as something extremely comfortable, but which I can make shift to do without.[1] . . .

As I may have no occasion hereafter to allude to the early friend with whose sorrows Scott thus sympathized amidst the meridian splendors of his own worldly career, I may take this opportunity of mentioning, that Captain Basil Hall's conjecture, of her having been the original of Diana Vernon, appeared to myself from the first chimerical; and that I have since heard those who knew her

[1] In communicating this letter to my friend Captain Hall, when he was engaged in his Account of a Visit to Madame de Purgstall during the last months of her life, I suggested to him, in consequence of an expression about Scott's health, that it must have been written in 1820. The date of the *Denkmahl*, to which it refers, is, however, sufficient evidence that I ought to have said 1821.

best in the days of her intercourse with Sir Walter, express the same opinion in the most decided manner. But to return.

While The Pirate was advancing under Mr. Erskine's eye, Scott had even more than the usual allowance of minor literary operations on hand. He edited a reprint of a curious old book, called Franck's Northern Memoir, and the Contemplative Angler; and he also prepared for the press a volume published soon after, under the title of "Chronological Notes on Scottish Affairs, 1680 to 1701, from the Diary of Lord Fountainhall." The professional writings of that celebrated old lawyer had been much in his hands from his early years, on account of the incidental light which they throw on the events of a most memorable period in Scottish history: and he seems to have contemplated some more considerable selection from his remains, but to have dropped these intentions, on being given to understand that they might interfere with those of Lord Fountainhall's accomplished representative, the present Sir Thomas Dick Lauder, Baronet. It is, however, to be regretted that Sir Thomas's promise of a Life of his eminent ancestor has not yet been redeemed.

In August appeared the volume of the Novelists' Library containing Scott's Life of Smollett; and it being now ascertained that John Ballantyne had died a debtor, the editor offered to proceed with this series of prefaces, on the footing that the whole profits of the work should go to his widow. Mr. Constable, whose health was now beginning to break, had gone southwards in quest of more genial air, and was at Hastings when he heard of this proposition. He immediately wrote to me, entreating me to represent to Sir Walter that the undertaking, having been coldly received at first, was unlikely to grow in favor if continued on the same plan — that in his opinion the bulk of the volumes, and the small type of their text, had been unwisely chosen, for a work of mere entertainment, and could only be suitable for one of reference; that Ballantyne's Novelists' Library, therefore, ought to be stopped at once, and another in a lighter shape, to range with the late collected edition of the first series of the Waverley Romances, announced with his own name as publisher, and Scott's as editor. He proposed at the same time to commence the issue of a Select Library of English Poetry, with prefaces and a few notes by the same hand; and calculating that each of these collections should extend to twenty-five volumes, and that the publication of both might be concluded within two years — "the writing of the prefaces, etc., forming perhaps an occasional relief from more important labors "! — the bookseller offered to pay their editor in all the sum of £6000: a small portion of which sum, as he hinted, would undoubtedly be more than Mrs. John Ballantyne could ever hope to derive from the prosecution of her husband's last publishing adventure. Various causes combined to prevent the realization of these magnificent projects. Scott now, as at the beginning of his career of speculation, had views about what a collection of English Poetry should be, in which even Constable could not, on consideration, be made to concur; and I have already explained the coldness with which he regarded further attempts upon our Elder Novelists. The Ballantyne Library crept on to the tenth volume, and was then dropped abruptly; and the double negotiation with Constable was never renewed.

Lady Louisa Stuart had not, I fancy, read Scott's Lives of the Novelists until, some years after this time, they were collected into two little piratical duodecimos by a Parisian bookseller; and on her then expressing her admiration of them, together with her astonishment that the speculation of which they formed a part should have attracted little notice of any sort, he answered as follows: "I am delighted they afford any entertainment, for they are rather flimsily written, being done merely

to oblige a friend: they were yoked to a great, ill-condi-
tioned, lubberly, double-columned book, which they were
as useful to tug along as a set of fleas would be to draw
a mail-coach. It is very difficult to answer your Ladyship's curious question concerning change of taste; but
whether in young or old, it takes place insensibly without the parties being aware of it.[1] A grand-aunt of my
own, Mrs. Keith of Ravelston, — who was a person of
some condition, being a daughter of Sir John Swinton
of Swinton, — lived with unabated vigor of intellect to
a very advanced age. She was very fond of reading,
and enjoyed it to the last of her long life. One day
she asked me, when we happened to be alone together,
whether I had ever seen Mrs. Behn's novels? — I confessed the charge. — Whether I could get her a sight of
them? — I said, with some hesitation, I believed I could;
but that I did not think she would like either the manners, or the language, which approached too near that
of Charles II.'s time to be quite proper reading. 'Nevertheless,' said the good old lady, 'I remember them
being so much admired, and being so much interested in
them myself, that I wish to look at them again.' To
hear was to obey. So I sent Mrs. Aphra Behn, curiously
sealed up, with 'private and confidential' on the packet,
to my gay old grand-aunt. The next time I saw her
afterwards, she gave me back Aphra, properly wrapped
up, with nearly these words: 'Take back your bonny
Mrs. Behn; and, if you will take my advice, put her in
the fire, for I found it impossible to get through the very

---

[1] [Lady Louisa in her letter, written in 1826, after speaking of the delight which the *Lives* had given to some of her friends, tells of their being
induced, by something said of Mackenzie, to read aloud *The Man of Feeling*. The experiment failed sadly, the (supposedly) finest touches only
causing laughter. And yet the writer could remember when the book
had been read with rapture and many tears. In her girlhood the *Nouvel'e
Héloïse* was the prohibited book which all young persons longed to read.
Now she finds that if it falls in their way, it interests them not at all. So
she propounds the question which Sir Walter tries to answer. — See *Selections from the Manuscripts of Lady Louisa Stuart*, pp. 233-236.]

first novel. But is it not,' she said, ' a very odd thing that I, an old woman of eighty and upwards, sitting alone, feel myself ashamed to read a book which, sixty years ago, I have heard read aloud for the amusement of large circles, consisting of the first and most creditable society in London?' This, of course, was owing to the gradual improvement of the national taste and delicacy. The change that brings into and throws out of fashion particular styles of composition, is something of the same kind. It does not signify what the greater or less merit of the book is; — the reader, as Tony Lumpkin says, must be in a concatenation accordingly — the fashion, or the general taste, must have prepared him to be pleased, or put him on his guard against it. It is much like *dress*. If Clarissa should appear before a modern party in her lace ruffles and head-dress, or Lovelace in his wig, however genteelly powdered, I am afraid they would make no conquests; the fashion which makes conquests of us in other respects, is very powerful in literary composition, and adds to the effect of some works, while in others it forms their sole merit."

Among other miscellaneous work of this autumn, Scott amused some leisure hours with writing a series of Private Letters, supposed to have been discovered in the repositories of a Noble English Family, and giving a picture of manners in town and country during the early part of the reign of James I. These letters were printed as fast as he penned them, in a handsome quarto form, and he furnished the margin with a running commentary of notes, drawn up in the character of a disappointed chaplain, a keen Whig, or rather Radical, overflowing on all occasions with spleen against Monarchy and Aristocracy. When the printing had reached the 72d page, however, he was told candidly by Erskine, by James Ballantyne, and also by myself, that, however clever his imitation of the epistolary style of the period in question, he was throwing away in these letters the materials of as

good a romance as he had ever penned; and a few days
afterwards he said to me — patting Sibyl's neck till she
danced under him, — "You were all quite right: if the
letters had passed for genuine they would have found
favor only with a few musty antiquaries, and if the joke
were detected, there was not story enough to carry it off.
I shall burn the sheets, and give you Bonny King Jamie
and all his tail in the old shape, as soon as I can get
Captain Goffe within view of the gallows."

Such was the origin of The Fortunes of Nigel. As
one set of the uncompleted Letters has been preserved,
I shall here insert a specimen of them, in which the
reader will easily recognize the germ of more than one
scene of the novel.[1]

JENKIN HARMAN TO THE LORD ——.

MY LORD, — Towching this new mishappe of Sir Thomas,
whereof your Lordshippe makes querie of me, I wolde hartilie
that I could, truth and my bounden dutie alweys firste satisfied, make suche answer as were fullie pleasaunte to me to
write, or unto your Lordshippe to reade. But what remedy?
young men will have stirring bloodes; and the courtier-like
gallants of the time will be gamesome and dangerous, as they
have beene in dayes past. I think your Lordshippe is so wise
as to caste one eye backe to your own more juvenile time,
whilest you looke forward with the other upon this mischaunce,
which, upon my lyfe, will be founde to be no otherwise harmful

---

[1] [Two of Sir Walter's friends were to assist him in these *Private Letters*. On June 16 he writes to Mr. Morritt: "Pray, my good Lord of
Rokeby, be my very gracious good lord, and think of our pirated letters.
It will be an admirable amusement for you, and I hold you accountable
for two or three academical epistles of the period, full of thumping quotations of Greek and Latin in order to explain what needs no explanation,
and fortify sentiments which are indisputable." In another letter, one of
his last, written to Lockhart from Naples in the spring of 1832, Scott
says: "You may remember a work in which our dear and accomplished
friend, Lady Louisa, condescended to take an oar, and which she handled
most admirably. It is a supposed set of extracts . . . from a collection in
James VI.'s time, the costume admirably preserved, and like the fashionable wigs more natural than one's own hair." — *Familiar Letters*, vol. ii.
p. 120, and *Journal*, vol. ii. p. 473.]

to Sir Thomas than as it shews him an hastie Hotspur of the
day, suddenlie checking at whatsoever may seem to smirche
his honour. As I am a trew man, and your Lordship's poore
kinsman and bounden servant, I think ther lives not a gentleman more trew to his friende than Sir Thomas ; and although
ye be but brothers uterine, yet so dearly doth he holde your
favour, that his father, were the gode knight alyve, should not
have more swaye with him than shalle your Lordship ; and,
also, it is no kindly part to sow discord betwene brethrene ;
for, as the holy Psalmist saythe, " *Ecce quam bonum et quam
jucundum habitare fratres,*" etc.   And moreover, it needes not
to tell your Lordshippe that Sir Thomas is suddene in his
anger ; and it was but on Wednesday last that he said to me,
with moche distemperature, — Master Jenkin, I be tolde that
ye meddle and make betwene me and my Lorde my brother ;
wherfore, take this for feyr warninge, that when I shall fynde
you so dooyng, I will incontinent put my dager to the hilte in
you : — and this was spoken with all earnestness of visage and
actioun, grasping of his poinard's handle, as one who wolde
presentlie make his words good. Surely, my Lord, it is not
fair carriage toward you pore kinsman if anie out of your
house make such reports of me, and of that which I have written to you in sympleness of herte, and in obedience to your
commandemente, which is my law on this matter. Truely,
my Lord, I wolde this was well looked to, otherweys my re-
warde for trew service might be to handsell with my herte's
blode the steel of a Milan poignado. Natheless, I will procede
with my mater, fal back fal edge, trustyng all utterly in the
singleness of my integretie, and in your Lordshippe's discretioun.

My Lorde, the braule which hath befallen chaunced this
waye, and not otherwise. It hap'd that one Raines, the master
of the ordinarie where his honour Sir Thomas eteth well nie
dailie (when he is not in attendance at courte, wherein he is
perchance more slacke than were wise), shoulde assemble some
of the beste who haunte his house, havyng diet ther for money.
The purpose, as shewn forthe, was to tast a new piece of choice
wyne, and ther Sir Thomas must nedes be, or the purpos holdes
not, and the Alicant becometh Bastard. Wel, my Lord, dice
ther wer and music, lustie helthes and dizzie braines, — some
saye fair ladyes also, of which I know nought, save that suche

the courtiers and Graie's-Inn men ; so that yf close hede be not given, I doubt me we shall here of more *Gesto Graiorum*. Thei will not be persuaded but that the quarrel betwixt Sir Thomas and young Darcie was simulate ; and that Master Dutton's hurte wes wilful ; whereas, on my lyfe, it will not be founde so.

The counseyl hath taen the matter up, and I here H. M. spoke many things gravely and solidly, and as one who taketh to hert such unhappie chaunces, both against brauling and drinking. Sir Thomas, with others, hath put in plegge to be forthcoming ; and so strictly taken up was the unhappie mater of the Scots Lord,[1] that if Booth shulde die, which God forefend, there might be a fereful reckoning : For one cityzen sayeth, I trust falslie, he saw Sir Thomas draw back his hand, having in it a drawn sword, just as the constabel felle. It seems but too constant, that thei were within but short space of ech other when his unhappy chaunce befel. My Lord, it is not for me to saie what course your Lordshippe should steer in this storm, onlie that the Lord Chansellour's gode worde wil, as resen is, do yeoman's service. Schulde it come to fine or imprisonment, as is to be fered, why should not your Lordshippe cast the weyght into the balance for that restraint which goode Sir Thomas must nedes bear himself, rather than for such penalty as must nedes pinche the purses of his frendes. Your Lordship always knoweth best ; but surely the yonge knyght hath but litel reson to expect that you shulde further engage yourself in such bondes as might be necessary to bring this fine unto the Chequer. Nether have wise men helde it unfit that heated bloode be coold by sequestration for a space from temptation. There is dout, moreover, whether he may not hold himself bounden, according to the forme of faythe which such gallants and stirring spirits profess, to have further meeting with Master Philip Darcie, or this same Dutton, or with bothe, on this rare dependence of an woodcocke's hede, and a quart-pot ; certeynly, methoughte, the last tym we met, and when he bare himself towards me, as I have premonish'd your Lordshippe, that he was fitter for quiet residence under safe keeping, than for a free walk amongst peceful men.

---

[1] " Perhaps the case of Lord Sanquhar. His Lordship had the misfortune to be hanged, for causing a poor fencing-master to be assassinated, which seems the unhappy matter alluded to."

And thus, my Lord, ye have the whole mater before you; trew ye shall find it, — my dutie demands it, — unpleasing, I cannot amende it: But I truste neither more evil *in esse* nor *in posse*, than I have set forth as above. From one who is ever your Lordshippe's most bounden to command, etc. — J. H.

I think it must have been about the middle of October that he dropped the scheme of this fictitious correspondence. I well remember the morning that he began The Fortunes of Nigel. The day being destined for Newark Hill, I went over to Abbotsford before breakfast, and found Mr. Terry (who had been staying there for some time) walking about with his friend's master-mason (John Smith), of whose proceedings he took a fatherly charge, as he might well do, since the plan of the building had been in a considerable measure the work of his own taste. While Terry and I were chatting, Scott came out, bare-headed, with a bunch of MS. in his hand, and said, "Well, lads, I 've laid the keel of a new lugger this morning — here it is — be off to the waterside, and let me hear how you like it." Terry took the papers, and walking up and down by the river, read to me the first chapter of Nigel. He expressed great delight with the animated opening, and especially with the contrast between its thorough stir of London life, and a chapter about Norna of the Fitful-head, in the third volume of The Pirate, which had been given to him in a similar manner the morning before. I could see that (according to the Sheriff's phrase) *he smelt roast meat;* here there was every prospect of a fine field for the art of *Terryfication*. The actor, when our host met us returning from the haugh, did not fail to express his opinion that the new novel would be of this quality. Sir Walter, as he took the MS. from his hand, eyed him with a gay smile, in which genuine benevolence mingled with mock exultation, and then throwing himself into an attitude of comical dignity, he rolled out, in the tones of John Kemble, one of the loftiest bursts of Ben Jonson's Mammon: —

> " Come on, sir. Now you set your foot on shore
> In *Novo orbe* —
> ——————— Pertinax, my Surly,[1]
> Again I say to thee aloud, Be rich,
> This day thou shalt have ingots."

This was another period of "refreshing the machine."
Early in November, I find Sir Walter writing thus to
Constable's partner, Mr. Cadell: "I want two books,
Malcolm's London Redivivus, or some such name, and
Derham's Artificial Clock-maker." [The reader of Nigel
will understand these requests.] "All good luck to you,
commercially and otherwise. I am grown a shabby
letter-writer, for my eyes are not so young as they were,
and I grudge everything that does not go to press."
Such a feeling must often have been present with him;
yet I can find no period when he grudged writing a letter
that might by possibility be of use to any of his family
or friends, and I must quote one of the many which
about this very time reached his second son.

TO MR. CHARLES SCOTT.

Care of the Rev. Mr. Williams, Lampeter.

21st November, 1821.

MY DEAR CHARLES, — I had the pleasure of your letter two days since, being the first symptom of your being
alive and well which I have had *directly* since you left
Abbotsford. I beg you will be more frequent in your
communications, which must always be desirable when
you are at such a distance. I am very glad to hear you
are attending closely to make up lost time. Sport is a
good thing both for health and pastime; but you must
never allow it to interfere with serious study. You have,
my dear boy, your own fortune to make, with better assistance of every kind than I had when the world first

---

[1] The fun of this application of " my Surly" will not escape any one
who remembers the kind and good-humored Terry's power of assuming a
peculiarly saturnine aspect. This queer grimness of look was invaluable
to the comedian in several of his best parts; and in private he often
called it up when his heart was most cheerful.

opened on me; and I assure you that had I not given some attention to learning (I have often regretted that, from want of opportunity, indifferent health, and some indolence, I did not do all I might have done), my own situation, and the advantages which I may be able to procure for you, would have been very much bounded. Consider, therefore, study as the principal object. Many men have read and written their way to independence and fame; but no man ever gained it by exclusive attention to exercises or to pleasures of any sort. You do not say anything of your friend Mr. Surtees,[1] who I hope is well. We all remember him with much affection, and should be sorry to think we were forgotten.

Our Abbotsford Hunt went off extremely well. We killed seven hares, I think, and our dogs behaved very well. A large party dined, and we sat down about twenty-five at table. Every gentleman present sung a song, *tant bien que mal*, excepting Walter, Lockhart, and I myself. I believe I should add the melancholy Jaques, Mr. Waugh, who, on this occasion, however, was not melancholy.[2] In short, we had a very merry and sociable party.

There is, I think, no news here. The hedger, Captain Davidson,[3] has had a bad accident, and injured his leg much by the fall of a large stone. I am very anxious about him as a faithful and honest servant. Every one else at Abbotsford, horses and dogs included, are in great preservation.

[1] Mr. Villiers Surtees, a schoolfellow of Charles Scott's at Lampeter, had spent the vacation of this year at Abbotsford. He is now one of the Supreme Judges at the Mauritius.

[2] Mr. Waugh was a retired West Indian, of very dolorous aspect, who had settled at Melrose, built a large house there, surrounded it and his garden with a huge wall, and seldom emerged from his own precincts except upon the grand occasion of the Abbotsford Hunt. The villagers called him " the Melancholy Man " — and considered him as already " dreein' his dole for doings amang the poor niggers."

[3] This hedger had got the title of Captain, in memory of his gallantry at some *row*.

You ask me about reading history. You are quite right to read Clarendon — his style is a little long-winded; but, on the other hand, his characters may match those of the ancient historians, and one thinks they would know the very men if you were to meet them in society. Few English writers have the same precision, either in describing the actors in great scenes, or the deeds which they performed. He was, you are aware, himself deeply engaged in the scenes which he depicts, and therefore colors them with the individual feeling, and sometimes, doubtless, with the partiality of a partisan. Yet I think he is, on the whole, a fair writer; for though he always endeavors to excuse King Charles, yet he points out his mistakes and errors, which certainly are neither few nor of slight consequence. Some of his history regards the country in which you are now a resident; and you will find that much of the fate of that Great Civil War turned on the successful resistance made by the city of Gloucester, and the relief of that place by the Earl of Essex, by means of the trained bands of London, — a sort of force resembling our local militia or volunteers. They are the subject of ridicule in all the plays and poems of the time; yet the sort of practice of arms which they had acquired, enabled them to withstand the charge of Prince Rupert and his gallant cavalry, who were then foiled for the first time. Read, my dear Charles, read, and read that which is useful. Man only differs from birds and beasts, because he has the means of availing himself of the knowledge acquired by his predecessors. The swallow builds the same nest which its father and mother built; and the sparrow does not improve by the experience of its parents. The son of the learned pig, if it had one, would be a mere brute, fit only to make bacon of. It is not so with the human race. Our ancestors lodged in caves and wigwams, where we construct palaces for the rich, and comfortable dwellings for the poor; and why is this — but because our eye is enabled to look back upon the past, to improve upon our ancestors' improvements, and to avoid their errors? This can only be done by studying history, and comparing it with passing events. God has given you a strong memory, and the power of understanding that which you give your mind to with attention — but all the advantage to be derived from these qualities must depend on your own determination to avail yourself of them, and improve them to the uttermost. That you should do so, will be the greatest satisfaction I can receive in my advanced life, and when my thoughts must be entirely turned on the success of my children. Write to me more frequently, and mention your studies particularly, and I will on my side be a good correspondent.

I beg my compliments to Mr. and Mrs. Williams. I have left no room to sign myself your affectionate father,

W. S.

To return to business and Messrs. Constable. — Sir Walter concluded, before he went to town in November, another negotiation of importance with this house. They agreed to give for the remaining copyright of the four novels published between December, 1819, and January, 1821 — to wit, Ivanhoe, The Monastery, The Abbot, and Kenilworth — the sum of five thousand guineas. The stipulation about not revealing the author's name, under a penalty of £2000, was repeated. By these four novels, the fruits of scarcely more than twelve months' labor, he had already cleared at least £10,000 before this bargain was completed. They, like their predecessors, were now issued in a collective shape, under the title of "Historical Romances, by the Author of Waverley."

I cannot pretend to guess what the actual state of Scott's pecuniary affairs was at the time when John Ballantyne's death relieved them from one great source of complication and difficulty. But I have said enough to satisfy every reader, that when he began the second,

and far the larger division of his building at Abbotsford,
he must have contemplated the utmost sum it could cost
him as a mere trifle in relation to the resources at his
command.   He must have reckoned on clearing £30,000
at least in the course of a couple of years by the novels
written within such a period.   The publisher of his
Tales, who best knew how they were produced, and what
they brought of gross profit, and who must have had the
strongest interest in keeping the author's name untar-
nished by any risk or reputation of failure, would willingly, as we have seen, have given him £6000 more
within a space of two years for works of a less serious
sort, likely to be despatched at leisure hours, without at
all interfering with the main manufacture.   But alas,
even this was not all.   Messrs. Constable had such faith
in the prospective fertility of his imagination, that they
were by this time quite ready to sign bargains and grant
bills for novels and romances to be produced hereafter,
but of which the subjects and the names were alike unknown to them and to the man from whose pen they
were to proceed.[1]   A forgotten satirist well says, —

> " The active principle within
>   Works on some brains the effect of gin ; "

but in his case, every external influence combined to stir
the flame, and swell the intoxication of restless exuberant
energy.   His allies knew, indeed, what he did not, that
the sale of his novels was rather less than it had been in
the days of Ivanhoe; and hints had sometimes been
dropped to him that it might be well to try the effect of
a pause.   But he always thought — and James Ballantyne had decidedly the same opinion — that his best
things were those which he threw off the most easily and
swiftly; and it was no wonder that his booksellers, seeing

---

[1] Mr. Cadell says : " This device for raising the wind was the only real
legacy left by John Ballantyne to his generous friend ; it was invented
to make up for the bad book stock of the Hanover Street concern, which
supplied so much good money for the passing hour." — (1848.)

how immeasurably even his worst excelled in popularity, as in merit, any other person's best, should have shrunk from the experiment of a decisive damper. On the contrary, they might be excused for from time to time flattering themselves that if the books sold at a less rate, this might be counterpoised by still greater rapidity of production. They could not make up their minds to cast the peerless vessel adrift; and, in short, after every little whisper of prudential misgiving, echoed the unfailing burden of Ballantyne's song — to push on, hoisting more and more sail as the wind lulled.

He was as eager to do as they could be to suggest — and this I well knew at the time. I had, however, no notion, until all his correspondence lay before me, of the extent to which he had permitted himself thus early to build on the chances of life, health, and continued popularity. Before The Fortunes of Nigel issued from the press, Scott had exchanged instruments, and received his bookseller's bills, for no less than four "works of fiction" — not one of them otherwise described in the deeds of agreement — to be produced in unbroken succession, each of them to fill at least three volumes, but with proper saving clauses as to increase of copy-money, in case any of them should run to four. And within two years all this anticipation had been wiped off by Peveril of the Peak, Quentin Durward, St. Ronan's Well, and Redgauntlet; and the new castle was by that time complete, and overflowing with all its splendor; but by that time the end also was approaching!

The splendid romance of The Pirate was published in the beginning of December, 1821; and the wild freshness of its atmosphere, the beautiful contrast of Minna and Brenda, and the exquisitely drawn character of Captain Cleveland, found the reception which they deserved. The work was analyzed with remarkable care in the Quarterly Review, by a critic second to few, either in the manly heartiness of his sympathy with the felicities of genius, or in the honest acuteness of his censure in cases of negligence and confusion. This was the second of a series of articles in that Journal, conceived and executed in a tone widely different from those given to Waverley, Guy Mannering, and The Antiquary. I fancy Mr. Gifford had become convinced that he had made a grievous mistake in this matter, before he acquiesced in Scott's proposal about "quartering the child" in January, 1816; and if he was fortunate in finding a contributor able and willing to treat the rest of Father Jedediah's progeny with excellent skill, and in a spirit more accordant with the just and general sentiments of the public, we must also recognize a pleasing and honorable trait of character in the frankness with which the recluse and often despotic editor now delegated the pen to Mr. Senior.

On the 13th December, Sir Walter received a copy of Cain, as yet unpublished, from Lord Byron's bookseller, who had been instructed to ask whether he had any objection to having the "Mystery" dedicated to him. He replied in these words: —

TO JOHN MURRAY, ESQ., ALBEMARLE STREET, LONDON.

EDINBURGH, 17th December, 1821.

MY DEAR SIR, — I accept with feelings of great obligation the flattering proposal of Lord Byron to prefix my name to the very grand and tremendous drama of Cain. I may be partial to it, and you will allow I have cause; but I do not know that his Muse has ever taken so lofty a flight amid her former soarings. He has certainly matched Milton on his own ground. Some part of the language is bold, and may shock one class of readers, whose tone will be adopted by others out of affectation or envy. But then they must condemn the Paradise Lost, if they have a mind to be consistent. The fiendlike reasoning and bold blasphemy of the fiend and of his pupil lead exactly to the point which was to be expected — the commission of the first murder, and the ruin and despair of the perpetrator.

I do not see how any one can accuse the author himself of Manichæism. The devil takes the language of that sect, doubtless; because, not being able tŏ deny the existence of the Good Principle, he endeavors to exalt himself — the Evil Principle — to a seeming equality with the Good; but such arguments, in the mouth of such a being, can only be used to deceive and to betray. Lord Byron might have made this more evident, by placing in the mouth of Adam, or of some good and pro-tecting spirit, the reasons which render the existence of moral evil consistent with the general benevolence of the Deity. The great key to the mystery is, perhaps, the imperfection of our own faculties, which see and feel strongly the partial evils which press upon us, but know too little of the general system of the universe, to be aware how the existence of these is to be reconciled with the benevolence of the great Creator. — Ever yours truly,   WALTER SCOTT.

In some preceding narratives of Sir Walter Scott's Life, I find the principal feature for 1821 to be an affair of which I have as yet said nothing; and which, notwith-standing the examples I have before me, I must be excused for treating on a scale commensurate with his real share and interest therein. I allude to an unfortunate newspaper, by name The Beacon, which began to be published in Edinburgh in January, 1821, and was abruptly discontinued in the August of the same year. It originated in the alarm with which the Edinburgh Tories contemplated the progress of Radical doctrines during the agitation of the Queen's business in 1820 — and the want of any adequate counteraction on the part of the Ministerial newspapers in the north. James Bal-lantyne had on that occasion swerved from his banner — and by so doing given not a little offence to Scott. He

approved, therefore, of the project of a new Weekly
Journal, to be conducted by some steadier hand;[1] and
when it was proposed to raise the requisite capital for
the speculation by private subscription, expressed his
willingness to contribute whatever sum should be named
by other gentlemen of his standing. This was accepted
of course; but every part of the advice with which the
only man in the whole conclave that understood a jot
about such things coupled his tender of alliance, was
departed from in practice. No experienced and responsible editor of the sort he pointed out as indispensable
was secured; the violence of disaffected spleen was encountered by a vein of satire which seemed more fierce
than frolicsome; the Law Officers of the Crown, whom
he had most strenuously cautioned against any participation in the concern, were rash enough to commit themselves in it; the subscribers, like true Scotchmen, in
place of paying down their money, and thinking no more
of that part of the matter, chose to put their names to
a bond of security on which the sum-total was to be
advanced by bankers; and thus, by their own over-cau-
tion as to a few pounds, laid the foundation for a long
train of humiliating distresses and disgraces; and finally,
when the rude drollery of the young hot bloods to whom
they had entrusted the editorship of their paper, produced its natural consequences, and the ferment of Whig
indignation began to boil over upon the dignified patrons
of what was denounced as a systematic scheme of calumny
and defamation — these seniors shrunk from the dilemma
as rashly as they had plunged into it, and instead of com-
pelling the juvenile allies to adopt a more prudent course,
and gradually give the journal a tone worthy of open approbation, they, at the first blush of personal difficulty,

[1] It has been asserted, since this work first appeared, that the editorship of the proposed journal was offered to Ballantyne, and declined by
him. If so, he had no doubt found the offer accompanied with a requisition of political pledges, which he could not grant — (1839.)

left their instruments in the lurch, and, without even consulting Scott, ordered the Beacon to be extinguished at an hour's notice.

A more pitiable mass of blunder and imbecility was never heaped together than the whole of this affair exhibited; and from a very early period Scott was so disgusted with it, that he never even saw the newspaper, of which Whigs and Radicals believed, or affected to believe, that the conduct and management were in some degree at least under his dictation. The results were lamentable: the Beacon was made the subject of Parliamentary discussion, from which the then heads of Scotch Toryism did not escape in any very consolatory plight; but above all, the Beacon bequeathed its rancor and rashness, though not its ability, to a Glasgow paper of similar form and pretensions, entitled The Sentinel. By that organ the personal quarrels of the Beacon were taken up and pursued with relentless industry; and finally, the Glasgow editors disagreeing, some moment of angry confusion betrayed a box of MSS., by which the late Sir Alexander Boswell of Auchinleck was revealed as the writer of certain truculent enough pasquinades. A leading Edinburgh Whig, who had been pilloried in one or more of these, challenged Boswell — and the Baronet fell in as miserable a quarrel as ever cost the blood of a high-spirited gentleman.[1]

This tragedy occurred in the early part of 1822; and

---

[1] [James Stuart of Dunearn was Boswell's opponent. Lockhart in writing to Scott of Sir Alexander's death [March 27] adds: " I hope I need not say how cordially I enter into the hope you express, that this bloody lesson may be a sufficient and lasting one. I can never be sufficiently grateful for the advice which kept *me* from having any hand in all these newspaper skirmishes. Wilson also is totally free from any concern in any of them, and for this I am sure he also feels himself chiefly indebted to your counsel." — *Familiar Letters*, vol. ii. p. 137. Stuart's trial took place on June 10, and his acquittal was hailed as a triumph by the Whigs. Lord Cockburn was one of Stuart's counsel, and in his *Memorials*, pp. 392-399, will be found an account of the affair, as viewed by a distinguished member of that party.]

soon afterwards followed those debates on the whole business in the House of Commons, for which, if any reader
feels curiosity about them, I refer him to the Parliamentary Histories of the time.   A single extract from one
of Scott's letters to a member of the then Government
in London will be sufficient for my purpose; and abun-
dantly confirm what I have said as to his personal part
in the affairs of the Beacon: —

TO J. W. CROKER, ESQ., ADMIRALTY.

My DEAR CROKER, — . . . I had the fate of Cassan-
dra in the Beacon matter from beginning to end.   I endeavored in vain to impress on them the necessity of
having an editor who was really up to the business, and
could mix spirit with discretion — one of those "gentlemen of the press," who understand the exact lengths to
which they can go in their vocation.   Then I wished
them, in place of that *Bond*, to have each thrown down
his hundred pounds, and never inquired more about it —
and lastly, I exclaimed against the Crown Counsel being
at all concerned.   In the two first remonstrances I was
not listened to — in the last I thought myself successful,
and it was not till long afterwards that I heard they had
actually subscribed the Bond.   Then the hasty renuncia-
tion of the thing, as if we had been doing something
very atrocious, put me mad altogether.   The younger
brethren, too, allege that they are put into the front of
the fight, and deserted on the first pinch; and on my
word I cannot say the accusation is altogether false,
though I have been doing my best to mediate betwixt the
parties, and keep the peace if possible.   The fact is, it
is a blasted business, and will continue long to have bad
consequences. — Yours in all love and kindness,

WALTER SCOTT.

APPENDIX

THE DURHAM GARLAND

IN THREE PARTS

[The following is the *Garland* referred to at pages 4 and 26, in connection with the novel of Guy Mannering. The ballad was taken down from the recitation of Mrs. Young of Castle-Douglas, who, as her family informed Mr. Train, had long been in the habit of repeating it over to them once in the year, in order that it might not escape from her memory.]

PART I

1

A WORTHY Lord of birth and state,
Who did in Durham live of late —
But I will not declare his name,
By reason of his birth and fame.

2

This Lord he did a-hunting go ;
If you the truth of all would know,
He had indeed a noble train,
Of Lords and Knights and Gentlemen.

3

This noble Lord he left the train
Of Lords and Knights and Gentlemen ;
And hearing not the horn to blow,
He could not tell which way to go.

4

But he did wander to and fro,
Being weary, likewise full of woe :
At last Dame Fortune was so kind
That he the Keeper's house did find.

5

He went and knocked at the door,
He thought it was so late an hour.
The Forester did let him in,
And kindly entertained him.

6

About the middle of the night,
When-as the stars did shine most bright,
This Lord was in a sad surprise,
Being wakened by a fearful noise.

7

Then he did rise and call with speed,
To know the reason then indeed,
Of all that shrieking and those cries
Which did disturb his weary eyes.

8

" I 'm sorry, Sir," the Keeper said,
" That you should be so much afraid ;
But I do hope all will be well,
For my wife she is in travail."

9

The noble Lord was learned and wise,
To know the Planets in the skies.
He saw one evil Planet reign,
He called the Forester again.

10

He gave him then to understand,
He 'd have the Midwife hold her hand ;
But he was answered by the maid,
" My Mistress is delivered."

11

At one o'clock that very morn,
A lovely infant there was born ;
It was indeed a charming boy,
Which brought the man and wife much joy.

12

The Lord was generous, kind, and free,
And proffered Godfather to be ;
The Goodman thanked him heartily
For his goodwill and courtesy.

13

A parson was sent for with speed,
For to baptize the child indeed ;
And after that, as I heard say,
In mirth and joy they spent the day.

14

This Lord did noble presents give,
Which all the servants did receive.
They prayed God to enrich his store,
For they never had so much before.

15

And likewise to the child he gave
A present noble, rich, and brave ;
It was a charming cabinet,
That was with pearls and jewels set.

16

And within it was a chain of gold,
Would dazzle eyes for to behold ;
A richer gift, as I may say,
Was not beheld this many a day.

17

He charged his father faithfully,
That he himself would keep the key,
Until the child could write and read —
And then to give him it indeed ; —

18

" Pray do not open it at all
Whatever should on you befall ;
For it may do my godson good,
If it be rightly understood."

19

This Lord did not declare his name,
Nor yet the place from whence he came,
But secretly he did depart,
And left them grieved to the heart.

PART II

1

The second part I now unfold,
As true a story as e'er was told,

Concerning of a lovely child,
Who was obedient, sweet, and mild.

2

This child did take his learning so,
If you the truth of all would know,
At eleven years of age indeed,
Both Greek and Latin he could read.

3

Then thinking of his cabinet,
That was with pearls and jewels set,
He asked his father for the key,
Which he gave him right speedily;

4

And when he did the same unlock,
He was with great amazement struck
When he the riches did behold.
And likewise saw the chain of gold.

5

But searching farther he did find
A paper which disturbed his mind,
That was within the cabinet,
In Greek and Latin it was writ.

6

My child, serve God that is on high,
And pray to him incessantly;
Obey your parents, love your king,
That nothing may your conscience sting.

7

At seven years hence your fate will be,
You must be hanged upon a tree;
Then pray to God both night and day,
To let that hour pass away.

8

When he these woeful lines did read,
He with a sigh did say indeed,
" If hanging be my destiny,
My parents shall not see me die;

9

" For I will wander to and fro,
I 'll go where I no one do know;
But first I 'll ask my parents' leave,
In hopes their blessing to receive."

10

Then locking up his cabinet,
He went from his own chamber straight
Unto his only parents dear,
Beseeching them with many a tear

11

That they would grant what he would have —
" But first your blessing I do crave,
And beg you 'll let me go away,
'T will do me good another day."

12

* * * * *
* * * * *

" And if I live I will return,
When seven years are past and gone."

13

Both man and wife did then reply,
" I fear, my son, that we shall die ;
If we should yield to let you go,
Our aged hearts would break with woe."

14

But he entreated eagerly,
While they were forced to comply,
And give consent to let him go,
But where, alas! they did not know.

15

In the third part you soon shall find,
That fortune was to him most kind,
And after many dangers past,
He came to Durham at the last.

PART III

1

He went by chance, as I heard say,
To that same house that very day
In which his Godfather did dwell ;
But mind what luck to him befell —

2

This child did crave a service there,
On which came out his Godfather,

And seeing him a pretty youth,
He took him for his Page in truth.

3

Then in this place he pleased so well,
That 'bove the rest he bore the bell;
This child so well the Lord did please,
He raised him higher by degrees.

4

He made him Butler sure indeed,
And then his Steward with all speed,
Which made the other servants spite,
And envy him both day and night.

5

He was never false unto his trust,
But proved ever true and just;
And to the Lord did hourly pray
To guide him still both night and day.

6

In this place, plainly it appears,
He lived the space of seven years;
His parents then he thought upon,
And of his promise to return.

7

Then humbly of his Lord did crave,
That he his free consent might have
To go and see his parents dear,
He had not seen this many a year.

8

Then having leave, away he went,
Not dreaming of the false intent
That was contrived against him then
By wicked, false, deceitful men.

9

They had in his portmanteau put
This noble Lord's fine golden cup;
That when the Lord at dinner was,
The cup was missed as come to pass.

10

" Where can it be ? " this Lord did say,
" We had it here but yesterday."

The Butler then replied with speed,
" If you will hear the truth indeed,

11

" Your darling Steward which is gone,
With feathered nest away is flown ;
I 'll warrant you he has that, and more
That doth belong unto your store."

12

" No," says this Lord, " that cannot be,
For I have tried his honesty ; "
" Then," said the Cook, " my Lord, I die
Upon a tree full ten feet high."

13

Then hearing what these men did say,
He sent a messenger that day,
To take him with a hue and cry,
And bring him back immediately.

14

They searched his portmanteau with speed,
In which they found the cup indeed ;
Then was he struck with sad surprise,
He could not well believe his eyes.

15

The assizes then were drawing nigh,
And he was tried and doomed to die ;
And his injured innocence
Could nothing say in his defence.

16

But going to the Gallows tree,
On which he thought to hanged be,
He clapped his hands upon his breast,
And thus in tears these words exprest : —

17

" Blind Fortune will be Fortune still,
I see, let man do what he will ;
For though this day I needs must die,
I am not guilty — no, not I."

18

This noble Lord was in amaze,
He stood and did with wonder gaze ;

Then he spoke out with words so mild, —
" What mean you by that saying, Child ? "

19

" Will that your Lordship," then said he,
" Grant one day's full reprieve for me,
A dismal story I 'll relate,
Concerning of my wretched fate."

20

" Speak up, my Child," this Lord did say,
" I say you shall not die this day —
And if I find you innocent,
I 'll crown your days with sweet content."

21

He told him all his dangers past,
He had gone through from first to last,
He fetched the chain and cabinet,
Likewise the paper that was writ.

22

When that this noble Lord did see,
He ran to him most eagerly,
And in his arms did him embrace,
Repeating of those words in haste. —

23

" My Child, my Child, how blessed am I
Thou art innocent, and shalt not die ;
For I 'm indeed thy Godfather,
And thou wast born in fair Yorkshire.

24

" I have indeed one daughter dear,
Which is indeed my only heir ;
And I will give her unto thee,
And crown you with felicity."

25

So then the Butler and the Cook
('T was them that stole the golden cup)
Confessed their faults immediately,
And for it died deservedly.

26

This goodly youth, as I do hear,
Thus raised, sent for his parents dear,
Who did rejoice their Child to see —
And so I end my Tragedy.

NARRATIVE OF THE LIFE OF JAMES ANNESLEY.

(See Note, p. 26.)

"Lord and Lady Altham, of Dunmain, in the county of
Wexford, had been for many years married and childless, when,
in the year 1715, their warmest hopes and wishes were realized
by the birth of an heir to their estates and title. On that joyful evening the hospitality of the house of Dunmain was claimed
by a young gentleman travelling from Dublin, named ' Master
Richard Fitzgerald,' who joined Lord Altham and his household in drinking the healths of the ' lady in the straw,' and the
long expected heir, in the customary groaning drink. It does
not appear that Master Fitzgerald was learned in astrology, or
practised any branch of the ' Black art,' or that he used any
spell with reference to the infant more potent than these hearty
libations and sincere good wishes for his future prosperity.
Next day, before leaving the hospitable mansion, the little hero
of this tale was presented to the stranger, who ' kissed him, and
gave the nurse half-a-guinea.'

" Of Fitzgerald we have only to add, that he entered the
army and became a distinguished officer in the service of the
queen of Hungary, and that twenty-eight years afterwards he
returned to Ireland to assist in recovering for his former infan-
tile friend the estates and titles of his ancestors, which had been
for many years iniquitously withheld from him.

" Lord and Lady Altham lived unhappily together, and a
separation took place soon after the birth of their son. Her
Ladyship, shamefully neglected by her husband, resided in England during the remainder of her life, and from disease and
poverty was reduced to a state of extreme imbecility both of
body and mind.

" James Annesley, the infant son of this unhappy mother,
was entrusted, by Lord Altham, to the charge of a woman of
indifferent character, named Joan or Juggy Landy. Juggy
was a dependent of the family, and lived in a cabin on the
estate, about a quarter of a mile from the house of Dunmain.
This hut is described as a ' despicable place, without any furniture except a pot, two or three trenchers, a couple of straw

beds on the floor,' and ' with only a bush to draw in and out
for a door.' Thus humbly and inauspiciously was the boy
reared under the care of a nurse, who, however unfortunate or
guilty, appears to have lavished upon her young charge the
most affectionate attention. From some unexplained cause,
however. Juggy Landy incurred the displeasure of Lord Altham, who took the boy from her, and ordered his groom to
' horsewhip her,' and ' to set the dogs upon her,' when she persisted in hovering about the premises to obtain a sight of her
former charge.

" Lord Altham now removed with his son to Dublin where he
appears to have entered upon a career of the most dissipated
and profligate conduct. We find him reduced to extreme pecuniary embarrassment, and his property became a prey to low
and abandoned associates ; one of whom, a Miss Kennedy, he
ultimately endeavored to introduce to society as his wife. This
worthless woman must have obtained great ascendancy over his
Lordship, as she was enabled to drive James Annesley from his
father's protection, and the poor boy became a houseless vaga-
bond, wandering about the streets of Dublin, and procuring a
scanty and precarious subsistence ' by running of errands and
holding gentlemen's horses.'

" Meantime Lord Altham's pecuniary difficulties had so increased as to induce him to endeavor to borrow money on his
reversionary interest in the estates of the Earl of Anglesey, to
whom he was heir-at-law. In this scheme he was joined by
his brother Captain Annesley, and they jointly succeeded in
procuring several small sums of money. But as James Annesley would have proved an important legal impediment to
these transactions, he was represented to some parties to be
dead ; and where his existence could not be denied, he was
asserted to be the natural son of his Lordship and of Juggy
Landy.

" Lord Altham died in the year 1727, ' so miserably poor
that he was actually buried at the public expense.' His brother
Captain Annesley attended the funeral as chief mourner, and
assumed the title of Baron Altham, but when he claimed to
have this title registered he was refused by the king-at-arms,
' on account of his nephew being reported still alive, and for
want of the honorary fees.' Ultimately, however, by means

which are stated to have been 'well known and obvious,' he succeeded in procuring his registration.

"But there was another and a more sincere mourner at the funeral of Lord Altham than the successful inheritor of his title: a poor boy of twelve years of age, half naked, bareheaded and barefooted, and wearing, as the most important part of his dress, an old yellow livery waistcoat,[1] followed at a humble distance, and wept over his father's grave. Young Annesley was speedily recognized by his uncle, who forcibly drove him from the place, but not before the boy had made himself known to several old servants of his father, who were attending the corpse of their late lord to the tomb.

"The usurper now commenced a series of attempts to obtain possession of his nephew's person, for the purpose of transporting him beyond seas, or otherwise ridding himself of so formidable a rival. For some time, however, these endeavors were frustrated, principally through the gallantry of a brave and kind-hearted butcher, named Purcel, who, having compassion upon the boy's destitute state, took him into his house and hospitably maintained him for a considerable time; and on one occasion, when he was assailed by a numerous party of his uncle's emissaries, Purcel placed the boy between his legs, and stoutly defending him with his cudgel, resisted their utmost efforts, and succeeded in rescuing his young charge.

"After having escaped from many attempts of the same kind, Annesley was at length kidnapped in the streets of Dublin, dragged by his uncle and a party of hired ruffians to a boat, and carried on board a vessel in the river, which immediately sailed with our hero for America, where, on his arrival, he was apprenticed as a plantation slave, and in this condition he remained for the succeeding thirteen years.

"During his absence his uncle, on the demise of the Earl of Anglesey, quietly succeeded to that title and immense wealth.

"While forcibly detained in the plantations, Annesley suffered many severe hardships and privations, particularly in his frequent unsuccessful attempts to escape. Among other incidents which befell him, he incurred the deadly hatred of one master, in consequence of a suspected intrigue with his wife —

---

[1] *Vide* "Green-breeks" in the General Introduction to the *Waverley Novels*. Surely *Yellow Waistcoat* was his prototype.

a charge from which he was afterwards honorably acquitted. The daughter of a second master became affectionately attached to him ; but it does not appear that this regard was reciprocal. And finally, in effecting his escape, he fell into the hands of some hostile negroes, who stabbed him severely in various places ; from the effects of which cruelty he did not recover for several months.

" At the end of thirteen years, Annesley, who had now attained the age of twenty-five, succeeded in reaching Jamaica in a merchant vessel, and he immediately volunteered himself as a private sailor on board a man-of-war. Here he was at once identified by several officers ; and Admiral Vernon, who was then in command of the British West India fleet, wrote home an account of the case to the Duke of Newcastle (the Premier), and, ' in the mean time, supplied him with clothes and money, and treated him with the respect and attention which his rank demanded.'

" The Earl of Anglesey no sooner heard of these transactions on board the fleet, than he used every effort to keep possession of his usurped title and property, and ' the most eminent lawyers within the English and Irish bars were retained to defend a cause, the prosecution of which was not as yet even threatened.'

" On Annesley's arrival in Dublin, ' several servants who had lived with his father came from the country to see him. They knew him at first sight, and some of them fell on their knees to thank heaven for his preservation, — embraced his legs, and shed tears of joy for his return.'

" Lord Anglesey became so much alarmed at the probable result of the now threatened trial, that he expressed his intention to make a compromise with the claimant, renounce the title, and retire into France ; and with this view he commenced learning the French language. But this resolution was given up, in consequence of an occurrence which encouraged the flattering hope that his opponent would be speedily and most effectually disposed of.

" After his arrival in England, Annesley unfortunately occasioned the death of a man by the accidental discharge of a fowling-piece which he was in the act of carrying. Though there could not exist a doubt of his innocence from all intention of such a deed, the circumstance offered too good a chance to be lost sight of by his uncle, who employed an attorney named Gifford, and with his assistance used every effort at the coroner's inquest, and the subsequent trial, to bring about a verdict of murder. In this, however, he did not succeed, although 'he practised all the unfair means that could be invented to procure the removal of the prisoner to Newgate from the healthy gaol to which he had been at first committed;' and 'the Earl even appeared in person on the bench, endeavoring to intimidate and browbeat the witnesses, and to inveigle the prisoner into destructive confessions.' Annesley was honorably acquitted, after his uncle had expended nearly one thousand pounds on the prosecution.

"The trial between James Annesley, Esq., and Richard, Earl of Anglesey, before the Right Honorable the Lord Chief Justice and other Barons of the Exchequer, commenced on the 11th November, 1743, and was continued for thirteen days. The defendant's counsel examined an immense number of witnesses in an attempt to prove that Annesley was the illegitimate son of the late Baron Altham. The Jury found for the plaintiff; but it did not prove sufficient to recover his title and estates: for his uncle 'had recourse to every device the law allowed, and his powerful interest procured a writ of error which set aside the verdict.' Before another trial could be brought about, Annesley died without male issue, and Lord Anglesey consequently remained in undisturbed possession.

"It is presumed that the points of resemblance between the leading incidents in the life of this unfortunate young nobleman and the adventures of Henry Bertram in Guy Mannering, are so evident as to require neither comment nor enumeration to make them apparent to the most cursory reader of the Novel. The addition of a very few other circumstances will, it is believed, amount to a proof of the identity of the two stories.

"The names of many of the witnesses examined at the trial have been appropriated — generally with some slight alteration — to characters in the novel. Among others, one of them is named *Henry Brown*, while *Henry* Bertram, alias Vanbeest

Brown, is the hero of the story. An Irish priest was examined, named *Abel Butler ;* while we find ABEL *Samson* in Guy Mannering, and *Reuben* BUTLER in The Heart of Mid-Lothian, — all three corresponding in profession as in name. Gifford and Glossin, although somewhat alike in patronymic, resemble each other still more in character and the abuse of their common profession. Gifford had an associate in iniquity named ' Jans,' while ' Jans Jansen ' is the *alias* assumed by Glossin's accomplice Dirk Hatterick. Again, we find *Arthur* Lord Altham and Mr. MacMullan in the history, and *Arthur* Melville, Esquire, and *Mr. MacMorlan* in the fiction. *Kennedy* and *Barnes* appear *unaltered* in each.

"A remarkable expression used by one of the witnesses in reference to Annesley — ' *he is the right heir if right might take place* ' — has probably served as a hint for the motto of the Bertram family, — '*Our right makes our might.*' "

Gentleman's Magazine, July, 1840.

END OF VOLUME III